DATE DUE

S0-BBM-611

Notes on

THE NEW WORLD GUIDES TO THE
LATIN AMERICAN REPUBLICS

By Earl Parker Hanson
Editor in Chief

T HE NEW WORLD GUIDES TO THE LATIN AMERICAN REPUBLICS
were designed to present reliable travel information and background material on each of the Latin American republics. They
were planned to contain more authoritative guidebook data on
the whole vast area of Latin America than had ever before been
gathered together in convenient and usable form. They represent,
in these two volumes of approximately 800,000 words, the equivalent of 21 condensed Baedekers or Blue Guides. Much detailed
information is for the first time being made available here. In
dealing with each of the republics, our aim was to furnish a
rounded and interesting historical and cultural background for
the more detailed data. Thus, the introductory pages to each of
the guides present the history and the general picture of a particular country. These pages are followed by the "Practical
Information" and the "Regional Guide," together with Index
and Maps. Necessarily, the guides vary greatly in length. In
Volume I, for example, the guide to Mexico occupies more than
160 pages while the guide to Costa Rica is contained in about

30 pages. In the front section of each volume of the guides, a variety of valuable information is presented, including bibliography, a list of holidays, conversion table of weights and measures, etc.

The complexity, the richness, and the variety of the subject matter made it difficult to keep within the prescribed two-volume limit; from the beginning, the selection, treatment, and arrangement of the material was a challenging task but, at the same time, a fascinating one. Our problems were intensified by the extraordinary scarcity of entirely reliable basic sources on a number of countries dealt with. Authorities contradicted each other; reference books were at variance; original materials had great information gaps in them. These conditions make it inevitable that the first edition of the guides will contain errors, most of which, we trust, will be of the trivial sort. Nevertheless, having just completed a reading of the proofs and attempting to form a judgment of the work as a whole, I am gratified to see that we succeeded in producing something that is much better and far more complete than we had at first anticipated. After spending over a year combing through all the guidebook material available on Latin America, there is today no doubt in my mind that what has grown out of our pioneer efforts is the best thing of its kind ever produced in any language. But—and this is important—we realize that a guide of this nature is a living and growing thing, and that it may take years of further research, checking, and careful editing to create the definitive NEW WORLD GUIDES TO THE LATIN AMERICAN REPUBLICS.

ORIGIN OF THE IDEA

The idea for the guides originated in the Office of the Coordinator of Inter-American Affairs — popularly known as the Rockefeller Committee — late in 1940. It was clear (and I speak as an outside observer and not for the Office of the Coordinator) that tourist traffic between the American republics would continue to increase and that something like a Baedeker, or a series of them, was going to be needed to stimulate and direct that traffic, in addition to furthering the good will and mutual understanding of the republics south of us. I was privileged early to act as adviser to the Office of the Coordinator on

acterize the entire work. The libraries of the United States are full of books on Latin America; there are many men in the United States who know Latin America well; but when it came to that wealth of detailed and wholly authentic information that is needed for a guide, we found the usual sources slim indeed. We turned to consulates, other agencies of the various nations treated, and especially to the various travel and transportation companies. Many of the latter had, quite rightly, regarded their files of information as trade secrets, to be zealously guarded from competing firms; now they literally opened their files to us. We called meetings of representatives of the various air and steamship lines, asking their help. They all agreed to give it, fully, and without hesitation. With their cooperation and with that of the various tourist bureaus, banks, United States Government agencies, and the Latin American governments, we soon found that we had access to what was undoubtedly the greatest body of source materials ever available for a purpose such as ours. It would be quite impossible for me to list all the individuals and organizations that gave so generously of their time and help to the NEW WORLD GUIDES. Mr. Raye Platt of the American Geographical Society of New York has declared: "As editor for many years of this Society's Millionth Map of Hispanic America, I have had considerable experience of the extent to which it is possible to secure collaboration from the governments of the Latin American republics and from individuals and scientific and commercial organizations for a worthwhile international project, but I was astonished at the collaboration that the editors of the NEW WORLD GUIDES were able to secure even when the project was in its first formative stages. . . . Quickly and thoroughly the preparation of the guides took on the proportions of a task of international cooperation.

PREPARING THE TEXT

Preparing the text with all available information at hand, the editor and his staff proceeded to prepare first drafts of each of the guides. But their activity soon had to be supplemented by the work of free-lance writers, who knew the countries and had written authoritatively on them. Source materials were turned over to these writers, who were asked to prepare their contributions along the lines indicated by the editor. As soon as a first draft of a guide was ready, a number of mimeographed copies of it were prepared. These were sent, with requests for criticism, correction, and advice to representatives of the United States Government and of the country treated, to experts employed by business firms having dealings with the country, to scholars who had special knowledge of the country, and many others. Again literally hundreds of individuals, organizations, and governments gave freely of their help. The preparation of the guides had become a cooperative venture in the truest sense of the word and on an international scale. Again, as in the collection of the source materials, every Latin American government as well as many departments of the United States Government cooperated wholeheartedly, as did the many individuals and business firms and learned societies with whom we had established relations.

Moreover, we sent many first drafts to Latin America, and a steady stream of travelers, just returned from those regions, called at our office, with the gratifying information that they had heard of the project through government employees, hotel keepers, and travel agents who were discussing the work. In every case we got what information we could from the travelers. People about to go to Latin America had also heard of us and often called on us for help. This help we gave as freely as we could. In return we asked that the travelers take copies of our first drafts south with them, check them for us as completely as possible, and send us detailed criticisms.

By such numerous ways we obtained the material for second drafts. Often we could not possibly avail ourselves of all the advice and information put at our disposal, particularly when two sources were completely at odds. Inevitably we found individuals who criticized the guides for failing to include some personal political—or geographical—preference. In one typical case, for instance, a highlander from one of the West Coast nations was deeply hurt because we hadn't done justice to one of his favorite beauty spots in the Andes, while a lowlander from the same country complained that the place in mention was bleak, desolate, and uninteresting, that it would give visitors a wrong impression of his country, that we had given it much too much prominence, and that it should be glossed over with a mere passing reference. So it went. But the work of rewriting and editing, of tearing down and building up again, also went steadily on.

DECEMBER 7, 1941

In the midst of all this activity, the United States was plunged into war. For a time there was no way of knowing what would, or should, happen to the project. Was this the time to publish travel guides? Should the finished and unfinished materials be set aside for the duration? Or should the drafts themselves be put into final shape first? Would we be able to finish the work, with our staff being dispersed for more direct participation in the war effort, and with many sources of information being closed off? A canvass of opinion was made among those who had worked with us, had seen the results of our activity, and were able to judge the work's value in wartime. Gratifyingly enough, the response was almost unanimous: the guides would have decided value—especially in wartime—for the information they contained. The project had by this time run into unavoidable delays and added expenses, but the editor and his staff were heartened and the work was pushed along.

PUBLICATION

Now the NEW WORLD GUIDES are ready for publication. Hundreds of people will share with me the pride of authorship and the inevitable "first night" author's worry. The reader of the guides will soon discover as we did that, while old Dr. Baedeker wrote his books in a relatively stable world, we have had to deal with a New World that is decidedly alive and in a state of constant change. Nevertheless, it is our hope that, while the work may now draw down upon itself much criticism and wise counsel, it will stand up reasonably well under the

the scope, nature, and final form of the guides. Naturally I, and all members of the Council who have had the good fortune of residence in the Latin American republics, were happy to have this opportunity to express, through the guides, the gratitude and high respect we feel toward them. Hence the principal feature of the editorial policy was that the various nations must not be dealt with, as they too often have been by United States journalists, travelers, and superficial observers, as mere picturesque panoramas, exotic playgrounds, and colorful though backward vacation lands; on the contrary, it was emphasized that Hispanic America is a group of varied nations that cannot be described in generalities—nations with an older culture than that of the United States, with well-developed political institutions, with vast and varied natural resources—a complex land, with a large and dramatic range of setting and climate. The stress on history in these guides is due to a fundamental editorial attitude, that nothing serves so well as history to present a populated geographical area as a national entity and as a political, economic, and cultural unit.

STAFF WORK

Many ideas and plans for procedure were carefully considered, all of them dominated by the need for producing the guides as swiftly as possible. First, it was thought wise to send men to the various parts of Latin America to gather material, but this seemed impractical on grounds of cost, delays involved, and the realization that more material on the Latin American republics already existed, in one form or another, in the United States than a dozen men could gather in a year. Second, there was the idea of writing a first draft of the guides and then sending men to the various countries to check, edit, rewrite, and prepare a finished text. But almost immediately it was recognized that this too was highly impractical procedure. Instead, it was decided to set up headquarters in a subsidiary office of Duell, Sloan and Pearce, to form a compact and versatile staff for basic office work, and to rely upon widespread cooperation from the various sources of information.

COLLECTING MATERIALS

In collecting source material, we had the first indication of that spirit of wholehearted cooperation that has come to char-

methods of procedure, and was selected as editor in chief of the project while preliminary details were being worked out and publishing arrangements were being made with the firm of Duell, Sloan and Pearce.

ADVISORY COUNCIL

For purposes of general guidance, control, criticism, an Advisory Council was set up, composed of some of the most eminent United States authorities in the Hispanic American field. This Advisory Council included:

Robert Spiers Benjamin, Former Executive Secretary, Publications Section, Coordinator of Inter-American Affairs.

John Peale Bishop, Former Chief, Publications Section, Coordinator of Inter-American Affairs.

Lewis Hanke, Director, Hispanic Foundation, Library of Congress.

Earl Parker Hanson, Geographer, Editor in Chief.

Francisco J. Hernandez, Chief, Travel Division, Pan American Union.

Waldo G. Leland, Director, American Council of Learned Societies.

Philip Ainsworth Means, Historian, Authority on Andean Archeology.

Raye Platt, Research Associate, Department of Hispanic-American Research, American Geographical Society.

L. S. Rowe, Director General, Pan American Union.

Robert C. Smith, Assistant Director, Hispanic Foundation, Library of Congress.

Monroe Wheeler, Chairman, Publications Committee, Coordinator of Inter-American Affairs.

It was this council that established the editorial policy, decided upon general questions of procedure, and helped to plan

3

acid test of the realities in the nations covered. We feel that we are well on the way to establishing an institution that will become as solid in its field as the Baedekers and the Blue Guides are in theirs, and as truly American as the other two are European.

In Two Volumes

Volume I—Mexico and Central America

Volume II—South America

Each Volume..$2.50

The Set..$5.00

Duell, Sloan and Pearce, New York

THE NEW WORLD GUIDES TO THE

LATIN AMERICAN

REPUBLICS

SPONSORED BY THE OFFICE OF THE U. S. COORDINATOR

OF INTER-AMERICAN AFFAIRS   VOLUME ONE

EARL PARKER HANSON, EDITOR-IN-CHIEF

ASSOCIATES: ANTONIO COLORADO, NATALIE RAYMOND
DOROTHY TEALL

DUELL, SLOAN AND PEARCE   NEW YORK

ADVISORY COUNCIL

NOTE ON FIRST EDITION

These guides were prepared for normal travel use in normal times. The present edition is published in wartime, when all travel is seriously curtailed. However, the publishers feel that by presenting the guides now they are performing a dual service, not only to the cause of inter-American understanding, but also to THE NEW WORLD GUIDES and to the traveling public for whom they were written. A guidebook grows and becomes perfected gradually through the uses to which it is put and as it is checked against conditions in the countries covered. The effort has been to make these guides as complete and as accurate as possible, but the present is in a sense a provisional edition, the publication of which should help to eliminate errors of fact, omission, and interpretation. The publishers will be grateful for critical comments on the basis of which improvements may be made in the next edition.

DUELL, SLOAN AND PEARCE
270 Madison Ave., New York

CONTENTS

HOW THE GUIDES WERE PREPARED

The surge of travel between the American republics, which has grown tremendously in recent years and will continue to grow after the war, as the Western Hemisphere becomes more closely knit, has long needed some such comprehensive guides as the Baedeker and Blue Guides that have for years played an important part in European travel. It was in recognition of that need that the Coordinator of Inter-American Affairs undertook, early in 1941, to sponsor the preparation of guides to all the Latin American republics for publication in two volumes.

General questions of policy and format were determined by the advisory council, representing the Coordinator of Inter-American Affairs and various private and public institutions having to do directly with Latin America. In order, for instance, to present the various republics as nations rather than as collections of sights and points of interest, it was decided to precede the guide to each country by a short resumé of that country's history. Since limitations of space demanded that the work be highly condensed, it has been written primarily for the general traveler; the specialist will find only indications of where to look for information in his particular field. In cultural matters the emphasis was placed on art, architecture, and, in some cases, archeology, since they involve visual matters that every visitor sees everywhere. In the regional guides it was decided to make every effort to go beyond the beaten path of conducted tourist travel and to indicate worthwhile trips to the more venturesome who do not always insist on the highest cosmopolitan standards in hotel and transportation facilities.

Necessarily, these guides are compilations of existing materials, prepared by writers and research workers. In a very real sense of the word, however, they are also the results of co-operative efforts on the part of literally hundreds of individuals, institutions, and agencies of the various governments concerned. The task of assembling the source materials involved combing libraries, the files of a large number of transportation companies, consulates, government tourist bureaus, and so on for existing guidebooks in various languages, official reports, maps, timetables, steamship circulars, and other descriptive literature. Thousands of items were collected, and from these materials the first drafts were prepared, sometimes by the staff and sometimes by outside writers. The signatures appearing with the various guides cover only individual sections such as those on history and art over which they appear. The sections on practical information and the regional guides were in all cases revised, rewritten, and amplified so drastically by the staff that they are really collaborative. Some 50 copies were made of each of the first drafts and distributed widely with requests for comments and criticisms. On the basis of such comments the work of final editing prior to publication was done.

The people who contributed freely, especially with criticisms, are too numerous to be mentioned here. They include a number of specialists, educators, consuls, ambassadors, ministers, and other officials of all the American republics, travel agents, officials of transportation companies, and others. Especially valuable criticisms were also received from Lillian Schoedler, Albert Franklin, and Robert H. Evans as interested and extremely helpful private individuals. The Hispanic Foundation of the Library of Congress, the Pan American Union, and the American Geographical Society of New York gave constant invaluable help. Similar unfailing help was given by Ivan Bullot of Exprinter Travel Service, Charles Larrabee of Pan American Airways, J. Stanton Robbins of the Grace Line, L. E. Archer of the Moore-McCormack Lines, and Edmund S. Whitman of the United Fruit Company line. Acknowledgments are also due to the writers whose names appear with parts of these guides and especially to the staff which bore the brunt of the work.

The latter, besides the assistant editors listed on the title page, consisted of Elisa Montes Díaz, Lillian Hess, Carol Jackson, and Dorothy Upjohn. Dale Kramer did valuable work in editing and rewriting. Dorothy Teall, besides preparing the manuscripts for publication, played a large part in preparing the second drafts. All the maps were drawn by Rafael Palacios.

While constant efforts were made to achieve a uniformly high standard of accuracy and completeness, the present edition doubtless contains errors of fact, interpretation, and omission. Both the publishers and the advisory council will be grateful for critical suggestions, on the basis of which future editions may be improved.

Advisory Council:

ROBERT SPIERS BENJAMIN
JOHN PEALE BISHOP
LEWIS HANKE
EARL P. HANSON (editor)
FRANCISCO HERNANDEZ
WALDO G. LELAND

PHILIP AINSWORTH MEANS
RAYE R. PLATT
L. S. ROWE
ROBERT C. SMITH
MONROE WHEELER

New York, December 1, 1942

HOW TO USE THE GUIDES

These guides were prepared as condensed reference works on travel in Latin America for use by the average traveler. Since no guide can be a complete manual of travel in any one country, partly because of limitations of space, partly because of constant changes in local conditions, and partly because of the widely varying needs and demands of individual travelers, THE NEW WORLD GUIDES are designed to supplement rather than supplant the functions of travel agents and other sources of detailed information. For further information the prospective traveler is referred to the Travel Division of the Pan American Union and to his travel agent.

The introductory material in this volume deals both with matters that are common to all Latin American countries and with matters that are of interest primarily to specialists in various fields. For instance, the conversion tables of weights and measures will be found useful everywhere, since all Latin American countries use the metric system, sometimes side by side with old Spanish systems, and since the guides themselves use the units familiar in the United States. The introductory sections on bibliography, educational facilities, and mountaineering are designed for those with special interests and are necessarily brief, indicating largely sources of additional information.

The maps of cities and countries were made up in accordance with the latest information available. However, they had to be fitted into a situation that is constantly in a state of flux. The best available information was doubtless incorrect in spots, and better information may come to light even before these guides are published. Moreover, many of the cities described are constantly changing the names of streets, adding new streets, etc. Then, too, there is at present an intense activity in road-building throughout Latin America, which will make some of these maps out of date shortly after publication or even before publication. With those conditions in mind, all the maps were made more or less schematic, showing general layout and avoiding too much detail. For use in the field, the traveler should provide himself with the latest detailed maps, as described on page 30. Up-to-date maps of most of the large cities can usually be obtained in the cities themselves.

The various sections of practical information are designed to give general overall information on the countries in question. Such things as steamship schedules and passport regulations, however, have had to be omitted because of rapidly changing conditions. As indicated in the text, all information on how to reach the various countries, on fares, and on transportation services is as of 1941. In many cases that information has no relation to the present wartime realities, which change constantly. Up-to-the-minute information on those matters is easily obtainable from steamship companies and consulates whose addresses are given in the guides. The locations of the consulates are here given as published in the latest edition of the United States Congressional Directory, arranged in alphabetical order by states. No distinction was made between honorary consuls, consuls general, vice-consuls, and so on, since their functions in giving information and visaing passports are the same.

Many Latin American nations maintain national tourist bureaus, organized to give information and to help travelers in every way possible. The sections on local sources of information refer to official tourist bureaus and other sources in the various countries where pertinent information may be obtained. Travelers are urged to avail themselves of the facilities listed, since local sources can be invaluable for making detailed arrangements, advising on road conditions, helping to organize excursions for fishing and other sports, advising on legal matters, and so forth. Also, local offices often have maps and items of descriptive literature whose completeness in some cases far exceeds that permitted by the space limitations of these guides.

The information here given on roads is necessarily also brief and superficial. While an increasing number of travelers have in late years transported their own cars to the Latin American countries, these guides have on the whole been prepared primarily for travelers using established means of transportation. Those who plan to use their own cars should consult such organizations as the American Automobile Association for detailed information.

The sections on costs of living and travel too are only brief hints. Such matters are subject to rapid change with economic and exchange variations in any one country. However, there are few exceptions to the general rule that the traveler who does not demand the most expensive and luxurious accommodations can get along well on $5 a day. Exceptions are indicated in individual guides.

The notes on local foods should be read in the knowledge that international cooking is found in all the larger Latin American centers but that each of the countries also has its own national dishes, available to those who know what to ask for.

The organization of the regional guides represents a compromise between two guidebook styles, the one that takes the traveler on predetermined tours, with every stop and every sight arranged to the last detail, and the one that lists points of interest in alphabetical order, letting the reader arrange them for himself. Here the regional guides begin with the principal port of entry and then cover the country region by region, with the various points arranged in the same general order in which they are encountered on following the main methods and routes of transportation.

The arrangement of the city guides follows the same general pattern in nearly all cases. The first parts of the city guides, together with the accompanying maps, should give the reader a general orientation with respect to city plan and location of the city's most interesting features. Throughout the city guides an effort has been made to give street names as they are used locally rather than in translation. Variations in the style of street names in these guides reflect variations in local usage between countries and cities. So, for instance, West Second Street may be Calle 2 Oeste in one city, Calle 2ª Oeste, 2ª Calle Oeste, Calle 2 Poniente, or 2 Calle Poniente in others. C. 2ª O. may mean West Second Street in one city but East Second Street in another—Calle 2ª Oriente as against the more usual C. 2ª Este. Such variations in nomenclature are made clear in the individual city guides.

Wherever possible, precise street addresses are given for points of interest in the cities covered. The fact that such addresses are sometimes lacking for want of information should not inconvenience the traveler. In most Latin American cities residents are far less conscious of street names and numbers than in the United States. Taxi service is usually excellent, and the general rule is that a taxi driver can take the visitor to any point much more easily if the point is merely named than if its street address is given.

Specific points of interest in the cities are usually listed under such general headings as public buildings, churches, and museums, rather than arranged by location. City sight-seeing is a complicated matter, with many varying itineraries. The maps will help the traveler to find his way around in the major cities; in smaller places orientation is usually automatic once the city is reached.

For convenience the last item in each city guide is always that of hotels. In these guides hotels are rated according to local prices. Those in the upper rate brackets for the country in question are indicated by two stars, those in the middle brackets by one star, and those in the lower brackets, as well as those on which information was not available, are listed without being starred. Within any one price range, no differentiation is made here between hotels on the basis of quality, since quality is usually an intangible that depends on the taste of the traveler. Where hotels are mentioned in the smaller and more out-of-the-way places, however, their listing must often be accepted with care by those whose travel experiences have been confined to the United States and Europe. While hotel accommodations in the larger Latin American centers are on the whole equal in quality to those found anywhere else and while many of the smaller towns of the more advanced countries have very good hotels and inns, many such establishments in the smaller centers are definitely deficient in accommodations and service. Preliminary inquiry of the local sources listed in these guides will usually yield information on hotel quality that will save much discomfort en route.

The population figures given with various cities and towns are indicative only and are in many cases not to be taken too literally. Official Latin American population statistics are sometimes rather vague. Sometimes, too, they are poorly defined. So, for instance, the population figures given for a number of towns in this volume may well be meant to apply, not to the towns themselves, but to the entire townships or other political divisions in which those towns are found. In other cases, especially in some of the smaller countries, the figures given may well reflect more patriotic guessing than actual counts. That difficulty, however, is common to a great many Latin American census figures.

In general the regional guides are organized around existing established travel facilities such as railroads and bus lines. In a few places, however, indications are given of trips that should be made only by the hardier travelers and that require such special transport facilities as packtrains or chartered small boats. Such trips are rewarding to the more adaptable, though they cannot be outlined in detail in a work of this kind. The adventurous traveler who is interested in such trips need remember little more than two general rules. In the capital cities, far removed geographically and in spirit from the pioneer regions in question, nearly everybody will try to discourage the visitor from attempting such journeys; in the cities and towns whence such adventurous journeys must begin and where they are normal to daily life, nearly everybody will not only encourage them but will also be eager to give full and complete help and information.

The problem of pro-Axis establishments gave rise to difficulties, in part because the blacklist of such establishments changes constantly. Travelers using this wartime edition are requested to apply to the U. S. consul immediately upon arrival in any country for the latest copy of the blacklist for that country.

E. P. H.

NEW WORLD GUIDE TO
LATIN AMERICA

LATIN AMERICA'S CULTURAL AND HISTORIC FOUNDATIONS

BY PHILIP AINSWORTH MEANS

The territory included in these volumes is so vast that many find it difficult to conceive of it as an integrated whole. The difficulty is reasonable since the area described in these two volumes includes 20 independent republics, each with its own national individuality and each with its stirring history and its distinctive culture.

Nevertheless, certain historical, cultural, and psychological facts are basically common to all of the Latin American republics, which makes it altogether logical to group them together in one work. To begin with, they all speak some language directly derived from the Latin: Portuguese in Brazil; Spanish, with many national variations, in 18 of the republics, and French in Haiti. Moreover, the prevailing religion of Latin America is the Catholic faith. Finally, in all the republics except Haiti, the cultural character—including art and architecture, ways of thought, and modes of life—is largely derived from either Spain or Portugal. This last fact alone serves to bind Latin America into a coherent whole. Nor is it contradicted by the fact that in Mexico, Central America, and western South America the Spanish civilization first overcame and later largely blended with highly developed native civilizations, with the result that modern culture in those regions is deeply colored by Indian influences, apparent not only in the composition of the population but also in folkways and in innumerable such tangible forms as art and architecture.

The impressive and dramatic story of the Spanish discoveries and conquests between 1492 and the end of the 16th century throughout Spanish America is here related separately for each country in turn. In like manner is related the equally dramatic tale of the Portuguese discovery and settlement of Brazil. The manner in which the two Latin and Catholic powers of the Iberian peninsula came to divide the New World between them stresses sufficiently the Catholic and the Latin character of both the nations concerned. Pope Alexander VI, by a series of bulls in 1493, supplemented by the Treaty of Tordesillas in 1494, set up a north-to-south line of demarcation 370 leagues west of the Cape Verde Islands which effectively set apart from one another the Spanish colonies west of the line and the Portuguese sphere to the east. By this combination of papal authority with diplomacy Portuguese and Spanish American realms were created, and both continue today to comprise what we call Latin America.

Almost from the very moment of the discovery by Columbus in 1492 a powerful stream of political, ecclesiastical, and cultural influences began to pour westward from Spain and Portugal into America. Governmental machinery, including viceregal rule by the king of Castile's personal representatives, the viceroys of New Spain or Mexico and of Peru, was established, as were also many other governmental institutions, mainly of Spanish or Portuguese origin. In regions where before the discovery the native peoples had already arrived at admirable social and political control, notably in Peru, some of their native institutions were woven into the fabric of colonial rule. Unfortunately, however, this was too often done in perverted form and

17

chiefly for the sake of getting a maximum of work out of the natives. Nevertheless, the intention and the theory of both the crown and the Church was to Christianize and otherwise to benefit the native peoples. It was the uncontrolled avarice of individuals, often both lay and clerical, inside as well as outside the administration, which all too frequently made colonial rule oppressive. However, Latin America to this day contains millions of Indians and of Indian-descended people. As a result a vast amount of Latin American culture, customs, institutions, art, and architecture, while predominantly of Iberian origin, is still strongly and picturesquely colored by Indian influences.

LATIN AMERICAN ART

BY ROBERT C. SMITH

The pre-conquest art of the Indians is pure American art. In many regions it never went beyond the simplest techniques and the crudest objects, but in some places and at certain periods things were produced whose beauty is reminiscent of the finest achievements of the Greek and Chinese civilizations. The so-called Latin American art arose since the conquest. It has developed within a European framework, and its models, with few exceptions, have been European. But it has never been entirely imitative, and seldom has it entirely lost contact with the older art of the Indian.

During the colonial period each successive architectural style of Spain was brought to Latin America. At the beginning of the 16th century when the Spaniards built their first cities on the Caribbean islands the old Gothic style in Spain was fighting a losing battle with the new Renaissance style based on the ancient architecture of Greece and Rome. In Madrid, Seville, and Valladolid churches and palaces were begun with Gothic pointed piers and vaults and finished with pseudo-Doric and Ionic portals. This style, half Gothic and half Renaissance, half old and half new, was the style of the conquest itself and of the first cathedral in America. The latter, the cathedral of Santo Domingo, built in the first half of the 16th century, is the masterpiece of the Spanish architect Rodrigo Gil de Liendo; it may be considered the fountainhead of all subsequent Renaissance architecture in America.

As the Spanish conquest moved westward in the 16th century the Yucatán coast of Mexico became the next area to receive European methods of building and styles of decoration. In Mérida, its capital, a fine town house was erected for the Montejo family whose portal recalls the contemporary palace architecture of the Castilian cities of Salamanca, Guadalajara, or Toledo. But here, especially in the naturalistic supporting figures, are reminiscences of the Indian technique of carving, a direct link with the old Maya art of the region. Indian craftsmen soon began to be employed in construction throughout Latin America, and a new Hispano-Indian art began to flourish, especially in those places where the Indian art had reached its highest development. This fact, together with the presence of mines of gold and silver, contributed most to the splendid colonial artistic achievements of Mexico, land of the Aztecs and Mayas, the Maya Guatemala, and the highlands of Bolivia and Peru.

The greatest builders of the 16th century in Mexico were the religious orders who invaded the countryside to convert the Indians. Before the close of the century the country was dotted with monasteries and churches that were generally of simple, solid masonry, with their decoration concentrated on sculptured entrance doors. One of the most splendid of these structures is the Augustinian foundation of Actopán, projected by Friar Andrés de Mata in 1548.

Another important element in Hispanic American architecture of the time was the so-called mudéjar influence. The word refers to the Moorish culture and art which lived on in Spain after the final defeat of the Moors at the end of the 15th century. The spirit and techniques which had produced the Alhambra and the Generalife palaces continued for several centuries to make themselves felt in Spanish art. The prime example of the mudéjar style in Latin America is the celebrated Capilla Real at Cholula in Mexico. It is essentially the system of the mosque at Cordova in Spain, a vast honeycomb of small interrelated parts, seemingly without beginning or end, typical of Islamic building. The main force of mudéjar influence was felt in the minor arts and in decorative details of architecture, in countless screens, tiles, wooden ceilings, balconies, and in such brick and plaster friezes of complicated and beautiful Islamic designs as those in the Jesuit church at Quito, from the 17th century.

The Baroque style was born in Europe in the 17th century. This style, a reaction against the pseudo-classicism of the Renaissance, substituted the curved line for the straight line, filled surfaces with rich decoration, and used sculpture and painting lavishly. The Baroque style flourished in Latin America from the middle of the 17th century almost to the end of the colonial period. Practiced from California to Argentina, it developed as many local variations as the dialects of a language. Again, it was in the regions where the former Indian cultures had progressed farthest that most indigenous influence was felt and the widest departures were made from the forms established by the architects of Spain.

In the colonial buildings of Central America gleaming white plaster replaced the multicolored tiles prevalent in Mexico. The church of La Merced which resisted the earthquake that in 1773 destroyed Guatemala's old capital of Antigua has the sturdy towers and generally low proportions that distinguish most Baroque buildings erected far from the great colonial centers of Latin America. The 18th-century cathedral of Tegucigalpa in Honduras shows a related tendency toward simplicity that sometimes distinguished these provincial buildings, especially in the earthquake country of the south, where the possibility of destruction influenced construction.

At Lima, where there was a viceregal court second only to that of Mexico, a great deal of colonial building has survived. But there, as in Colombia, Chile, and to a large extent Ecuador, little indigenous influence is felt. Lima was far from the centers of Inca culture.

In the Indian towns of the Peruvian and Bolivian highlands American Baroque architecture took its most native and original form. In many ways Christian churches were paganized by native craftsmen. No less interesting, though less striking, is the influence of the Guaraní Indians upon the architecture of the Jesuit churches in Paraguay. For the most splendid of these buildings, the church of Trinidad, now in ruins, designed by J. B. Prímoli in 1745, Indian sculptors produced decorative sculptures of heroic proportions that vaguely imitate the exotic and flamboyant vegetation of their native jungles. Dry-laid cut stone and other technical procedures connect this style with the art of the Incas.

In colonial Brazil the native Baroque was imported from Portugal, where it had had a development independent of that of Spain. Churches here were smaller than in Spanish America and less massively constructed. Cupolas and vaults were as rare in Brazil as they were common in the rest of Latin America. Brazilian colonial churches therefore lacked the solemnity and grandeur of those derived from Spain. But they have a distinct personality based on an elegant informality of design. At Ouro Preto, the center of a rich gold-mining region, a distinguished school of architects, sculptors, and painters matured in the mid-18th century. Antonio Francisco Lisbôa, called Aleijadinho, overshadowed all his contemporaries in sculpture and architecture. Typical of his work is the church of San Francisco at Ouro Preto, whose elaborate doorway he carved with such delicate grace that he reveals himself there, as in a series of other brilliant works, to be one of the greatest Latin American artists.

After persisting for a century the Baroque was itself displaced by a new reaction to the simplicity and correctness of the classic. The resulting neo-classic movement, originating in Italy in the middle of the 18th century, swept the world for the next hundred years. It was the movement that brought temple fronts to the churches and public buildings of New England villages and Greek and Roman porticoes to mansions in the southern United States.

In Latin America this strict imitation of classical proportions put an end to indigenous influences for a long time. It struck a lasting blow at the crafts themselves and in some places choked folk art effectively for a century. The neo-classic revival did, however, bring a series of well-designed, distinguished buildings to Latin America. One of the earliest of these is the government building on the Plaza de Armas in Havana, completed in the late 18th century on plans from Spain. Santiago de Chile's palace of La Moneda, an early 19th-century work of the Spanish architect Toesca, is a typical example of the full-fledged neo-classic style in Latin America. It is a monument of large, impressive simplicity, its entrance imitating a Roman arch of triumph. A typical Spanish American neo-classic cathedral is that of Guatemala City, completed in 1815 by the Spanish architect Santiago Marqui. In comparison with a Baroque church it is severe, restrained, and static. But the imitation of classic buildings seldom went so far as to reproduce the actual form of an ancient Greek or Roman temple. That the Latin American lovers of the antique restrained their enthusiasm is proved by the splendid buildings of Manuel Tolsa in Mexico City, by Francisco Tresguerras in Celaya and Querétaro, and by a host of neo-classic buildings in Argentina, Uruguay, Brazil, and Venezuela, where architectural flowering came later than in other parts of Latin America.

Latin American sculpture at this period was almost entirely religious —devoted to fabricating altarpieces and devotional figures and to an immense amount of decorative relief carving for the interiors and exteriors of churches. Early in the 17th century Quito had become a center for the production of wood sculpture; as the period wore on it became one of the principal centers of exportation for all of Latin America. The 17th-century high altar of the Franciscan church in Quito is one of the best examples of the magnificent use made by the local school of carved and gilded wood on the Baroque principles of contemporary architecture. The most famous Quito sculptor was unquestionably Manuel Caspicara, an Indian of Ecuador, who has left one surpassing masterpiece in the Stigmata of St. Francis, a wood-carving in the Cantuña church. The cities of the highlands are famous for their richly carved Baroque pulpits, in some of which indigenous elements occur. A final reflection of the sculpture of the period is found in the splendid silver made in Mexico, Peru, and Buenos Aires.

The first landscapes painted by Europeans in America were made in Brazil. In the northern city of Pernambuco, which was a Dutch colony 1630-45, Frans Post of Haarlem painted the surrounding country with Netherlandish care. His canvases are an invaluable record of 17th-century life in the towns and on the plantations of Pernambuco. His companion Albert Eckhout painted Negro slaves whom the Portuguese had brought to Brazil. Not only are his paintings splendid portraits, but they are also important documents of social history. The work of these Dutchmen, careful observers of the details of early life, was unfortunately not taken up in Spanish America. If it had been we should now know a great deal more than we do about the social history of the colonial period. Instead the demand was for altarpieces and portraits, paintings in the style of the popular school of Seville, and artists almost without exception conformed to these patterns.

Outstanding among the early self-taught Creole craftsmen was Gregorio Vásquez de Arce y Ceballos, born at Bogotá in 1638, the greatest artist Colombia has yet produced. He decorated most of the churches of Bogotá with religious paintings of distinguished coloring, well-articulated figures, and striking portraits. Typical of the latter is his 1698 portrait of the Knight of Calatrava, which, though technically far different, has something of El Greco's overwhelming dignity. Vásquez, together with Manuel Santiago in Quito and Miguel Cabrera and others in Mexico, was a kind of court painter, wealthy and honored. Far more numerous were the anonymous craftsmen who produced the devotional paintings, usually representing Our Lady in some special invocation with portraits of the persons who commissioned the painting kneeling below. This picturesque art flourished at Quito and Cuzco and from the latter place spilled over into the high country in the north of Argentina.

At the close of the 18th century the imitation of Goya united all of Latin America in painting, just as neo-classicism was bringing it together in architecture. Within a brief period everyone insisted on being painted with some of the mannerisms of the well-known Spanish master. In 1830 the wars of independence had made republics of the former Spanish and Portuguese colonies, but artistically they were as dependent on Europe as before. Academies of painting and schools of architecture that had been set up at the end of the 18th and beginning of the 19th centuries continued to import their professors from France and Spain. Pupils of Napoleon's painter David had schools in Mexico, Cuba, and Brazil. Other Frenchmen were in Argentina, Chile, and Ecuador. Their best pupils won grants to study in Europe, whence they returned home to teach what they had learned. Yet in spite of acres of dull historical canvases, in spite of pompous portraits, Latin American 19th-century painting produced one category that has universal appeal today. It is the so-called costumbrista painting.

Probably no part of the world excited the curiosity of educated Europeans more than Latin America in the last century. Merchants, scientists, explorers, and diplomats of all nations journeyed from Tierra del Fuego to the Río Grande. With them also came artists to illustrate their numerous books of travels. Their lithographs, engravings, and aquatints are usually as picturesque as the titles and the descriptions of the volumes themselves. Because they represent views of the cities, scenes in the streets and countryside, daily life in all its aspects, these illustrations are called costumbrista pictures, or scenes of local customs. Essentially these costumbrista pictures are the continuation of that tradition of sincere and careful social documentation begun by Frans Post and the other Dutchmen of 17th-century Pernambuco. By the end of the 19th century they had been universally replaced by the ubiquitous photograph. Costumbrista painting was an art of Europeans for Europeans. It was a skillful recording of the native scene but not an interpretation of it. The Indian, that hitherto basic element in Latin American art, sat for it as a passive and picturesque subject; he did not produce it. Through it in most instances the mystery and the dignity of the Indian were travestied because of a lack of understanding. A tradition had been broken, and a cultural as well as political revolution was necessary to re-establish it.

It was fitting that this revolution should begin in Mexico. Here the American tradition reappeared and slowly spread to other parts of Latin America to replace the sterility of the academic style. The story of how a Mexican generation rediscovered this heritage and used it to create a new American art is now well known. Orozco, Rivera, Charlot, and a host of well-trained artists created in their first frescoes of the early 1920's a solid, vigorous, and indigenous style, vitalized it with a social and didactic message, and with it broke a long foreign pictorial tradition. The Indian is the soul of this new art, and the art has succeeded wherever the Indian tradition has existed and survived. In Peru a great national school has grown up, inspired by the Mexican José Sabogal; his pupils Camilo Blas, Jorge Reinoso, Julia Codesido, and Francisco González Gamarra have painted the Peruvian Indians in a style of simple heroic forms, vigorous patterns, and splendid color that replaces the awkward naturalism of their predecessors. In Ecuador, Camilo Egas has painted the Indian festivals of his country in a similar style, based on indigenous traditions, and Eduardo Kingman has shown their faces in his powerful woodcuts. In Bolivia, Cecilio Guzmán de Rojas; in Costa Rica, Max Jiménez; in El Salvador, Mejía Vides, all have created the same powerful and picturesque forms. In Guatemala, Carlos Mérida; in Nicaragua, Carmen Sequeira, have evolved the same exquisite patterns from the Indian art of their countries. The Colombian painter Luis Alberto Acuña has combined the sturdy forms of mestizos and Indians with the landscapes of his country to produce powerful original compositions. Nor has sculpture been excluded from the range of the new movement. Marina Núñez del Prado, a gifted young Bolivian sculptress, has interpreted in her simplified reliefs and statues the strength of the Indian and the grace of his dances. The animals of the Argentine Carlos Máximo Maldonado derive from the plastic abstractions of indigenous Peruvian sculpture.

Certain of the Latin American republics such as Brazil and Cuba, where strong traditions of Indian art have not survived or never have existed, have lately turned to the Negro. In São Paulo, when emigrants from Europe brought news of the European artistic revolution at the very time that the new Mexican school was born, Tarsila do Amaral, Calvalcanti, and Lasar Segall laid the basis for a regional style which has culminated in the monumental art of Cândido Portinari. In place of the European tradition these artists employed the solid forms and persistent rhythms of the African Negro slaves. The results have been as successful and as characteristic as those achieved in the Indian lands, and their art has had as profound a social significance for their country. In Cuba, where the same elements of African culture were at hand, a related style has been developed, not only in the frescoes of the mulatto Alberto Peña, but in the tender painting of Negroes and the poor white guajiros of Antonio Gattorno and in Rita Longa's warm and intimate sculpture.

But in Chile, Argentina, Uruguay, and Venezuela neither the Indian nor the Negro was a factor in the national culture. The art of these countries has remained at heart European, as untouched by the American or African tradition as our own contemporary painting. Keenly sensitive to their problems, yet rightly unwilling to imitate the Indianism of their neighbors, the Chilean Roberto Humeres and the Uruguayan C. W. Aliseris have painted Impressionist landscapes which might have been produced in French gardens on the banks of the Seine; Armando Lira and Camilo Mori look upon their native Chile through the eyes of a follower of Cézanne and a local Salvador Dali respectively. Lino Spilimbergo in Buenos Aires and Ricardo Aguerre in Montevideo experiment with recent European structural styles. The distinguished Argentine, Emilio Pettoruti, and many others are still wedded to abstract art. Many Chileans believe that these moderns are building a new American art which will somehow create a new fusion, uniting American elements with European influences.

Nowhere in Latin America has Indian influence seriously affected modern architecture. On the other hand the Baroque influence had a revival which is not yet dead. Legion in South America and in Mexico are the ornate domed expansive structures of glistening marble in which senates meet, works of art and books are housed, international conferences convene. Prime examples are the Palace of Fine Arts in Mexico City, the Monroe Palace in Rio de Janeiro, and the more sober but no less monumental Capitol in Havana, all built since the turn of the century. But throughout Latin America, perhaps more than in the United States, a new reaction to severity has now set in. There are already many distinguished examples of strictly functional building according to international formulas, like the beautiful building of the Brazilian press in Rio de Janeiro, completed lately by the architects Milton and Marcelo Roberto.

Such, then, has been the general development of Latin American art. Since the beginning of the colonial period two elements have been at work—one Indian, the other European. A third element, that of place, has had its influence. In general, where a great Indian tradition existed before the conquest it has been reflected in the colonial and modern art of the region. To that extent the Indian element has dominated the European in Latin American art. Where no important pre-conquest tradition existed the European elements have often remained supreme.

BIBLIOGRAPHIC NOTES

BY RAYE R. PLATT

A brief supplementary reading list is presented here for those who want further opportunities than are provided in the introductory notes to the various regional guides to acquaint themselves with the countries in question. For obvious reasons it is restricted to books written for the general reading public and to books of recent publication. It is to be noted also that only books in English are listed, since they are more accessible to the English-speaking people of the Americas for whom the guides are designed and also because the percentage of readers who know Spanish and Portuguese well enough to read books in those languages easily and pleasurably is still very small.

The present list is compiled from items in the library of the American Geographical Society of New York and only from those items with which the compiler is personally familiar. It therefore reflects a personal taste. Any bibliographic list that even approached completeness and came anywhere near meeting all tastes would be far too long and cumbersome for the rather rigid space requirements of these guides. Space requirements also preclude the inclusion of a guide to the extensive literature in the form of articles in scientific and cultural periodicals and in popular magazines. Attention is called, however, to the numerous articles on the Latin American countries published in the Geographical Review, the quarterly publication of the American Geographical Society of New York; the National Geographic Magazine, the monthly publication of the National Geographic Society, Washington, D. C.; and the bulletin of the Pan American Union, the monthly publication of the Pan American Union, Washington, D. C.

For an annotated bibliography of all recent publications in the principal fields of the humanities and the social sciences—anthropology, art, economics, education, folklore, geography, government, history, international relations, languages and literature, law, music, philosophy—the highest recommendation should be given the Handbook of Latin American Studies, prepared by a group of specialists and published by the Committee on Latin American Studies of the American Council of Learned Societies. This has appeared annually since 1935. The Pan American Union issues frequent classified bibliographies, usually in mimeograph form, of current periodical literature as well as books.

HISTORY: PRE-CONQUEST

MEXICO

Bernardino de Sahagún: A History of Ancient Mexico by Fray Bernardino de Sahagún, translated by Fanny R. Bandelier from the Spanish of Carlos María de Bustamente. Fiske University Press, Nashville, Ky., 1932.

Lewis Spence: The Civilization of Ancient Mexico. Putnam, New York, 1912.

George Clapp Vaillant: Aztecs of Mexico; Origin, Rise and Fall of the Aztec Nation. Doubleday, Doran, Garden City, N. Y., 1941.

CENTRAL AMERICA

The Mayas and their Neighbors. Appleton-Century, New York, 1940.

A series of articles on a wide range of studies of the Middle American Indians, dedicated to Alfred Marston Tozzer by his students and colleagues in recognition of his services in Middle American research.

Thomas Gann: Ancient Cities and Modern Tribes; Exploration and Adventure in Mayaland. Scribner, New York, 1926.

Herbert J. Spinden: Ancient Civilizations of Mexico and Central America. American Museum of Natural History, Handbook Series No. 3. New York, 1928.

GUATEMALA

Louis Adamic: The House at Antigua; a Restoration. Harper, New York, 1937.

HISTORY: POST-CONQUEST

MEXICO

Herbert Ingram Priestley: The Mexican Nation, a History. Macmillan, New York, 1923.

J. Fred Rippey: The United States and Mexico. Knopf, New York, 1927.

Henry B. Parkes: A History of Mexico. Houghton Mifflin, Boston, 1938.

CENTRAL AMERICA

Samuel Crowther: The Romance and Rise of the American Tropics. Doubleday, Doran, Garden City, N. Y., 1929.

GUATEMALA

Chester Lloyd Jones: Guatemala, Past and Present. University of Minnesota Press, Minneapolis, 1940.

PANAMA

William D. McCain: The United States and the Republic of Panama. Duke University Press, 1937.

Miles P. Du Val: Cadiz to Cathay; the Story of the Long Struggle for a Waterway across the American Isthmus. Stanford University Press, 1940.

Darrell H. Smith: The Panama Canal; Its History, Activities, and Organizations. Johns Hopkins Press, Baltimore, Md., 1927.

William D. McCann: The United States and the Republic of Panama; with a foreword by J. Fred Rippey. Duke University Press, 1937.

CUBA

Charles E. Chapman: History of the Cuban Republic. Macmillan, New York, 1927.

HAITI

J. N. Léger: Haiti; Her History and Her Detractors. New York, 1928.

Sumner Welles: Naboth's Vineyard; the Dominican Republic, 1844-1924, with a foreword by the Hon. L. S. Rowe. Payson & Clark, New York, 1929.

PUERTO RICO
Knowlton Mixer: Puerto Rico; History and Conditions, Social, Economic and Political. Macmillan, New York, 1929.

ECONOMIC AND SOCIAL CONDITIONS

MEXICO
Frank Tannenbaum: The Mexican Agrarian Revolution. Macmillan, New York, 1929.

Nathaniel Weyl: The Reconquest of Mexico; the Years of Lázaro Cárdenas. Oxford University Press, New York, 1939.

Stuart Chase and Marion Tyler: Mexico: a Study of Two Americans. Illustrated by Diego Rivera. Macmillan, New York, 1931.

Ernest H. Gruening: Mexico and Its Heritage. Century, New York, 1928.

Hubert C. Herring and Herbert Weinstock, eds.: Renascent Mexico. Introduction by Ernest Gruening. Covici, Friede, New York, 1935. Papers from the annual seminar conducted in Mexico by the Committee on Cultural Relations with Latin America.

José Vasconcelos and Manuel Gomio: Aspects of Mexican Civilization. Norman Wait Harris Foundation Lectures, 1926. University of Chicago Press, 1926.

Eyler N. Simpson: The Ejido, Mexico's Way Out. University of North Carolina Press, 1937.

George M. McBride: The Land Systems of Mexico. American Geographical Society, New York, 1923.

CENTRAL AMERICA
D. G. Munro: The Five Republics of Central America. Oxford University Press, 1918.

A. Curtis Wilgus, ed.: The Caribbean Area. George Washington University Press, 1934. Seminar conference lectures delivered at George Washington University, July 2-August 11, 1935.

Chester Lloyd Jones: Caribbean Backgrounds and Prospects. Appleton, New York, 1931.

Chester Lloyd Jones: The Caribbean Area Since 1900. Prentice-Hall, New York, 1936.

Charles D. Kepner: Social Aspects of the Banana Industry. Columbia University Press, 1936.

Clarence F. Jones: Caribbean America, Its Problems and Advances. In Modern Hispanic America. George Washington University Press, 1933. Series of 22 papers from the George Washington University Seminar Conference of Hispanic American Affairs.

GUATEMALA
Chester Lloyd Jones: Guatemala, Past and Present. University of Minnesota Press, 1940.

COSTA RICA
Chester Lloyd Jones: Costa Rica and Civilization in the Caribbean. University of Wisconsin Press, 1935.

PANAMA
Arthur Bullard: Panama; the Canal, the Country and the People. Macmillan, New York, 1914.

Hugh Gordon Miller: The Isthmian Highway; a Review of the Problems of the Caribbean. Macmillan, New York, 1929.

CUBA

Leland H. Jenks: One Cuban Colony. New York, 1926.

DOMINICAN REPUBLIC

M. M. Knight: The Americans in Santo Domingo. New York, 1928.
Lawrence de Besault: President Trujillo, His Work and the Dominican Republic. Washington Publishing Co., Washington, D. C., 1936.

PUERTO RICO

Victor S. Clark, ed.: Porto Rico and Its Problems. Brookings Institution, Washington, D. C., 1930.
José Enamorado-Cuesta: Porto Rico, Past and Present; the Island after Thirty Years of American Rule. Eureka Printing Co., New York, 1929.
Arthur D. Gayer, Paul T. Homan, and Earle K. James: The Sugar Economy of Puerto Rico. Columbia University Press, 1935.

DESCRIPTION AND LIFE OF THE PEOPLE

MEXICO

D. H. Lawrence: Mornings in Mexico. Knopf, New York, 1927.
Erna Fergusson: Fiesta in Mexico. With illustrations by Valentín Vidaurreta. Knopf, New York, 1934.
Harry A. Franck: Trailing Cortez through Mexico. With 67 reproductions of photographs by the author. Stokes, New York, 1935.
Rodney Gallop: Mexican Mosaic. Illustrated with photographs by the author and with drawings by his wife. Faber and Faber, London, 1939.
R. H. K. Marett: An Eye-Witness of Mexico. Oxford University Press, New York, 1939.
Harry A. Franck and Herbert C. Lanks: The Pan American Highway from Río Grande to the Canal Zone. Appleton-Century, New York, 1940.
Lesley Byrd Simpson: Many Mexicos. Putnam, New York, 1941.

CENTRAL AMERICA

Wallace Thompson: Rainbow Countries of Central America. Dutton, New York, 1926.

GUATEMALA

Aldous Huxley: Beyond the Mexique Bay. Harper, New York, 1934.
Erna Fergusson: Guatemala. New York, 1937.
Joseph H. Jackson: Notes on a Drum; Travel Sketches in Guatemala. Macmillan, New York, 1937.
Vera Kelsey and Lilly de Jongh Osborne: Four Keys to Guatemala. Funk and Wagnalls, New York, 1939.
Joaquin Muñoz and Anna Bell Ward: Guatemala, Ancient and Modern. Pyramid Press, New York, 1940.

PANAMA

Alpheus Hyatt Verrill: Panama, Past and Present. Illustrated with photographs by the author. Dodd, Mead, New York, 1921.

Jean Sadler Heald: Picturesque Panama, the Panama Railroad, the Panama Canal. C. Teich and Co., Chicago, 1928.

HAITI

Melville J. Herskovitz: Life in a Haitian Valley. Knopf, New York, 1937.

PUERTO RICO

Trumbull White: Puerto Rico and Its People. With 47 reproductions of photographs and a map. Stokes, New York, 1938.

Daisy Reck: Puerto Rico and the Virgin Islands. Farrar and Rinehart, New York, 1939.

Merle E. Colby: Puerto Rico; a Profile in Pictures. Duell, Sloan and Pearce, New York, 1940.

Cynthia P. Maus: Puerto Rico in Pictures and Poetry; an Anthology of Beauty on America's "Paradise of the Atlantic." Caxton Printers, Caldwell, Idaho, 1941.

BY RAYE R. PLATT

In these guides detailed maps have been supplied only for the central zones of some of the more important cities. To supply complete regional maps even for the sections about which full information is available would be a monumental task. Except for small areas there are no maps of the countries covered by Volume I that are comparable even to the road maps familiar to motorists in the United States. However, since good maps are an important item in the traveler's equipment and a necessary item if he is to get any real understanding of the country he is visiting, the traveler is urged to provide himself with the best available maps of the countries visited. Only small sections of the territory embraced by this volume are covered by maps corresponding to the inch-to-the-mile topographic sheets produced by the United States Geological Survey. The maps recommended below come from a number of different sources of varying degrees of accuracy. Despite their possible numerous errors, they represent the best obtainable at present.

PUBLICATIONS OF THE AMERICAN GEOGRAPHICAL SOCIETY

The American Geographical Society of New York has compiled and published two sets of maps of Latin America. Both of these are topographical-political maps; that is, they indicate elevations and the character of the topography by contours and colorings and show international and internal administrative boundaries. The first of these is a map of Latin America on the scale of 1:1,000,000, or about 16 miles to the inch, in 107 sheets, each measuring 6 degrees of longitude by 4 degrees of latitude. The size and administrative importance of cities and towns are indicated; character of roads and gauge of railroads are shown by symbol; and the status of the surveying of rivers, coastline, and contours is indicated by solid or broken lines. Twenty-one sheets of this map are required to cover the countries included in Volume I. Sheets pertaining to a given section can be purchased separately. An index map showing the areas covered by the sheets can be secured by addressing the American Geographical Society, Broadway at 156th St., New York.

For those who do not require a map of such large scale and detail the Society has produced another set of maps in three sheets covering Mexico, the West Indies, and Central and South America on a scale of 1:5,000,000, or about 79 miles to the inch. In general the style of reproduction of the 1:1,000,000 map is followed. The three sheets may be purchased separately; one sheet covers the countries considered in Volume I. Topography is indicated by contour and colorings, and settlements are classified according to size and administrative importance. Railroads and all-weather roads are indicated; the progress of the Pan American Highway in its various sections is shown by special symbols.

A SELECTION OF OTHER MAPS PUBLISHED IN THE UNITED STATES

MEXICO, CENTRAL AMERICA AND THE WEST INDIES. Compiled and drawn by the cartographic section of the National Geographic Society for the National Geographic Magazine. Boundaries, capitals of countries and administrative subdivisions, railroads, and selection of roads. Scale 1:5,702,400 or 90 miles to the inch. 1939.

REPUBLIC OF MEXICO. Compiled and drawn by the cartographic section of the War Department Map Collection, Office of the Chief of Engineers, U. S. Army. Cities and towns classified, railroads, characters of roads, and air navigation information. Topography shown by contours. Scale 1:2,500,000. 1939.

CENTRAL AMERICA. Compiled and published by the Geographic Board, Military Intelligence Division, General Staff, U. S. Army. Scale 1:250,000; 34 sheets. 1929-35.

ARCHEOLOGICAL SITES IN THE MAYA AREA. Put out by the Middle America Research Institute, Tulane University, New Orleans, for use with their Index of Maya Sites. Based on sheets of the American Geographical Society Map of Hispanic America, 1:1,000,000, and used with special permission of the Society. Scale 1:500,000. 1940.

TOPOGRAPHIC MAP OF PUERTO RICO. Scale 1:25,000 and 1:20,000; 12 sheets. U. S. Geological Survey, 1935-41.

MAPS PUBLISHED IN THE LATIN AMERICAN COUNTRIES

MEXICO. State map of Mexico, published 1910-27, on scales varying from 1:100,000 to 1:500,000. Dirección de Estudios Geográficos y Climatológicos, Tacubaya, México. Some of these maps show topography by contour, but most of them have only line shadings.
—Nueva Carta de la República Mexicana. Dirección de Geografía, Meteorología e Hidrología, Secretaría de Agricultura y Fomento, Tacubaya, México. Scale 1:500,000. In course of publication; 31 sheets published 1929-37.—Carta General de la República Mexicana. Dirección de Geografía, Meteorología e Hidrología, Secretaría de Agricultura y Fomento, México, D. F. Scale 1:2,000,000.

GUATEMALA. Mapa del Estado de Guatemala, República de Centro América. Compilado por Disposición del Supremo Gobierno por Claudio Urrutía, Ingeniero. Topography shown by contours. Scale 1:400,000. 1923.

HONDURAS. Carta General de la República de Honduras, América Central. Instituto Pan-Americano de Geografía e Historia, Tacubaya, México. Scale 1:500,000; 4 sheets. 1932-33.—Mapa General de la República de Honduras, Levantado por el Prof. Jesús Aguilar Paz. Tipo-Lito Aristón, Tegucigalpa, Honduras. Scale 1:500,000. 1933.

EL SALVADOR. El Salvador, Físico, Económico, Minero, Político, Industrial, Commercial, 1525-1925. Liceo Salvadoreño, San Salvador, El Salvador. Scale 1:625,000. 1926.

NICARAGUA. Mapa de la República de Nicaragua y Parte de las de Honduras y Costa Rica, por Clifford D. Hamp, Recaudor General de Aduanas de Nicaragua, Aprobado por el Gobierno de Nicaragua. Engraved and printed by Rand McNally and Co., New York and Chicago. Scale 1:500,000. 1924.

COSTA RICA. Mapa de Costa Rica, por los Ingenieros Ricardo Fernández Peralta y José Fabio Gongora. Editado por el Instituto Panamericano de Geografía e Historia, Tacubaya, México, D. F. Topography shown by contours and coloration. Scale 1:400,000. January 1941.

PANAMA. Mapa de la República de Panama, Arreglado por William A. Buesemeister, Francisco Leyton Uribe, y Max Lemm, bajo la Dirección de Sabas A. Villegas, Ordenado y Aprobado por el Gobierno de Panamá en 1924 y Compilado en Cooperación con la American Geographical Society of New York. Reproduced from drawings made from the Panama sheet of the American Geographical Society's 1:1,000,000 Map of Hispanic America. Scale 1:500,000. 1925.

CUBA. Carta Militar de la República de Cuba, Corregida en la Sección de Ingeniería de la Ayudantia General del Cuartel General del Ejército Constitucional. Contoured map in process of production. Scale 1:100,000. 1933-34.

HAITI AND THE DOMINICAN REPUBLIC. Mapa de la Isla de Santo Domingo, Compilado por el Ingeniero Casimiro Gómez. Lithographed by Rand McNally and Co., New York and Chicago. Scale 1:400,000. 1938.

PUERTO RICO. Map of the Island of Puerto Rico showing roads and railroads, to accompany annual report, 1939-1940. Department of the Interior, Bureau of Public Works, San Juan, P. R. Scale 1:500,000.

THE PAN AMERICAN UNION

BY L. S. ROWE

Director General

The Pan American Union is an international organization created and maintained by the 21 American republics. Originally known as the International Bureau of the American Republics, it was established in 1890 in accordance with a resolution passed on April 14 of that year at the First International Conference of American States, held at Washington in 1889-90 and presided over by James G. Blaine, then Secretary of State for the United States. Its work was greatly expanded by resolutions of subsequent conferences, the eighth of which was held at Lima, Peru, in 1938. April 14 is now celebrated annually in the Americas as Pan American Day.

The Pan American Union is under the direction of a governing board composed of the Secretary of State of the United States and the ambassadors, ministers, and chargés d'affaires of the other American republics accredited to the government of the United States. The chairman of the board, under the terms of a resolution adopted at the Fifth International Conference of American States, is elected each year. The board meets on the first Wednesday of each month to consider matters of common interest to the republics of the American continent. The executive officers of the Union are a director general and an assistant director, appointed by and responsible to the governing board.

The activities of the Pan American Union may be considered from the official and the unofficial point of view. Officially the Pan American Union serves as the permanent organ of the International Conferences of American States. In this capacity the Union prepares the program and regulations of each conference, compiles documentary material on the topics included in the agenda for the information of the delegates, and, following each conference, assists in obtaining ratification of the treaties and conventions that may have been signed and in securing action on the resolutions adopted at the conferences. From an international standpoint this is a most important function, since one of the great dangers confronting all international conferences is the absence of a permanent organization to give effect to the conclusions reached by such assemblies.

The purpose of the Pan American Union is to promote peace, commerce, and friendship between the republics of the American continent by fostering economic, juridical, social, and cultural relations. The administrative divisions of the Pan American Union are organized to give effect to these purposes. Special divisions have been created on foreign trade, statistics, economics, intellectual co-operation, juridical matters, agricultural co-operation, and labor and social information. All these divisions maintain close relations with official and unofficial bodies in the countries that are members of the Union, and their facilities are available to everyone interested in the American republics or in inter-American relations.

In the economic field the Pan American Union is equipped with a well-organized foreign trade division, statistical division, and division of commercial and economic information. Annual reports are published on the export and import trade of each country, and the Union also issues reports on the principal commodities of the American republics as well as a monthly review entitled Commercial Pan America in which economic subjects of current interest are discussed.

One of the principal functions of the Pan American Union during recent years has been the promotion of closer cultural ties between the American republics. The Division of Intellectual Co-operation aims to encourage the interchange of professors and students and furnishes students with accurate information relative to conditions of admission, courses of study, and cost of living in the countries in which they wish to pursue their work.

The Pan American Union is the depository of the instruments of ratification of Pan American treaties and conventions and through its Juridical Division co-operates in the work of codifying international law in the Western Hemisphere. Since agriculture is the basic industry of all the republics of America and especially those of Latin America, a separate Division of Agricultural Co-operation was established several years ago, and more recently a Division of Labor and Social Information was organized to meet the increasing number of inquiries on these subjects received from every section of the continent.

One of the most recent activities undertaken by the Pan American Union is that of promoting tourist travel in the American republics, and to this end a Travel Division has been established. This division is in close touch with official agencies from which it constantly receives information and data on travel conditions and tourist attractions in the several republics, and it also maintains contact with transportation companies, hotel associations, and other organizations interested in travel throughout the continent. The information received from these sources is compiled and published and is available to anyone interested in travel in the Americas. The republics of Latin America offer every variety of attraction to the tourist, and travelers who visit these countries return enthusiastic about their many beauties and attractions. The republics of Latin America offer a natural field of travel which is certain to attract an increasing number of visitors from the United States.

In addition to its many specialized activities the Pan American Union publishes monographs and pamphlets intended to make the republics of the American continent better known. A monthly bulletin is published in English, Spanish, and Portuguese which contains detailed information relating to the cultural, economic, and social development of the republics of America. By this bulletin and through other publications of the Union closer acquaintance, closer cultural ties, and closer commercial relations are fostered.

THE TRAVEL AGENT

BY FRED H. DIETZ

Executive Secretary, A.S.T.A.

"Consult your travel agent" has become a familiar slogan of transportation companies in their publicity and advertising because from long experience they have found that the extensive chain of travel bureaus throughout the country is their best sales outlet. A travel agent can render prospective travelers invaluable services free of charge, because he is remunerated on a commission basis by the travel organizations he represents. His advice is unbiased, since he has no particular advantage in recommending one service rather than another. It is his business to have always on hand the very latest information on passport regulations, travel facilities, hotel accommodations, costs, and so on.

As official representatives of all leading steamship lines, air carriers, hotels, resorts, and sightseeing companies, travel agents base their recommendations on the time at the traveler's disposal, with due regard to the traveler's desires in the matter of expenditures. Furthermore, travel agents relieve their clients of much work in attending to a number of formalities in connection with passports and other essential documents, assisting with baggage, and, in the case of steamship travel, reserving dining-room tables and choice location for deck chairs. The agents' representatives in foreign countries are helpful in solving foreign-language problems, reserving hotel rooms, arranging local transportation, facilitating social and business contacts, advising on currency problems, and making shopping suggestions. For those who desire such advice travel agents arrange day-by-day itineraries covering the points that interest their clients. These itineraries are fully budgeted and are laid out with precision, giving ample time at the stopovers.

The reader is cordially invited to make full use of the facilities of travel agents, many of whom belong to the American Steamship and Tourist Agents Association, known throughout the world as the A. S. T. A., with members in 174 cities in 34 states of the United States as well as in the eastern cities of Canada.

PRINCIPAL CATHOLIC HOLIDAYS

Feasts of the Roman Catholic Church are classified as movable and immovable.

The movable feasts are dated with reference to the Feast of the Resurrection, or Easter, which is the central Christian feast. Easter falls on the first Sunday following the first full moon on or after March 21. It can therefore occur on any date between March 22 and April 25.

CARNIVAL is usually celebrated during the three days preceding Ash Wednesday, a last round of gaiety before the fasting of Lent. A familiar festivity of this period is the Mardi Gras or Shrove Tuesday in New Orleans. In Latin American countries these three days are usually very gay and may be the occasion for a great mummers' parade as in Rio de Janeiro.

LENT, known as Cuaresma in Spanish America, is a period of 40 days of fasting, not including Sundays. Lent begins on Ash Wednesday, anywhere from February 4 to March 10, and ends at noon on Holy Saturday, the day before Easter. Ash Wednesday (Miércoles de Ceniza) takes its name from the ceremony of blessing and imposition of ashes peculiar to this day. The last two weeks of Lent, the most important, are Passiontide. This period starts with Passion Sunday (Domingo de la Pasión), the second Sunday before Easter, marked by the veiling of all the images in churches and certain variations in the prayers of the Mass.

HOLY WEEK (Semana Santa) is the last week of Lent. It starts with Palm Sunday (Domingo de Ramos), which commemorates Christ's entry into Jerusalem. On this day palms are blessed and a procession with palms takes place. The Thursday of Holy Week is Holy Thursday or Maundy Thursday (Jueves Santo). Good Friday (Viernes Santo) commemorates the passion and death of Jesus. It is a day of fasting, abstinence, and penitence. Holy Saturday (Sábado Santo) is an anticipation of Easter, and its Mass is known as Misa de Gloria in Spanish. Easter (Día de la Resurrección, also often called Pascua) is a day of great rejoicing and feasting.

ASCENSION DAY (Día de la Ascensión) occurs 40 days after Easter, always on a Thursday. The date may fall from April 30 to June 3. It is a universal holy day of obligation, commemorating Christ's ascension to heaven. During the principal Mass the paschal candle, lighted on Holy Saturday, is extinguished.

PENTECOST (Pentecostés) commemorates the visible descent of the Holy Ghost upon the apostles and the establishment of the Church. It ranks with Easter in importance. The feast always falls on a Sunday, between May 10 and June 13.

TRINITY SUNDAY, the first Sunday after Pentecost, is the feast of the Most Holy Trinity (La Santísima Trinidad).

CORPUS CHRISTI, meaning literally Body of Christ, is the Thursday after Trinity Sunday. It celebrates the institution of the Blessed Sacrament.

The immovable feasts occur on fixed dates. Only the most important are listed here.

JANUARY 1. Feast of the Circumcision of the Child Jesus.

JANUARY 6. Epiphany, from the Greek word meaning manifestation, referring in this connection to the manifestation of Christ's divinity to the Magi. The popular name of the feast in Spanish America is Día de los Reyes (Day of the Kings), and it is celebrated as a day of gift-giving, similar to Christmas in the United States. It is preeminently a children's day.

FEBRUARY 2. Feast of the Purification of the Blessed Virgin Mary, sometimes called Candlemas (La Candelaria), commemorating the ritual purification of the Virgin in the temple after childbirth. Candles are blessed and a procession held, climaxed by church services. The origin of the candle blessing on this day lies in the words of Simeon, "a light to enlighten the gentiles," spoken when the Virgin came to the temple.

MARCH 19. Feast of St. Joseph (San José), foster father of Christ.

MARCH 25. Feast of the Annunciation (La Anunciación), commemorating the actual moment of the Incarnation, when the angel announced to the Virgin Mary that God the Son was to be born of her.

JUNE 29. Feast of St. Peter and St. Paul (San Pedro y San Pablo).

AUGUST 15. Feast of the Assumption (La Asunción). The Church teaches that at the death of the Blessed Virgin Mary her body was preserved from corruption and was shortly afterward assumed into heaven and reunited to her soul.

SEPTEMBER 8. Nativity or birth of the Blessed Virgin Mary (La Natividad).

NOVEMBER 1. All Saints' Day (Día de Todos los Santos), commemorating all the saints of God, canonized and uncanonized, known and unknown.

NOVEMBER 2. All Souls' Day (Día de los Muertos), a day of solemn commemoration of all the faithful departed, when the Church prays especially for them.

DECEMBER 8. Feast of the Immaculate Conception (Día de la Inmaculada Concepción), commemorating the extraordinary privilege by which the Virgin Mary at the first instant of her conception was preserved exempt from all stain of original sin.

DECEMBER 25. Christmas (La Navidad or Pascua de Navidad).

DECEMBER 28. Feast of the Holy Innocents (Día de los Santos Inocentes), in memory of the children massacred by order of Herod three days after the birth of Christ. This is celebrated as a holiday resembling April Fool's Day in the United States.

EDUCATIONAL OPPORTUNITIES IN LATIN AMERICA

BY DOROTHY M. FIELD

STUDY IN LATIN AMERICAN UNIVERSITIES

During the last few years North Americans have become increasingly interested in the history, culture, and social and economic problems of the republics to the south of us. This interest has been reflected not only in the rapid development of courses in Latin American subjects in our own universities but also in the number of North Americans who have begun to go to Latin American universities for one or more years of study.

Since Latin American universities do not always print catalogues, many students from the United States go down there expecting either to take undergraduate courses in a liberal arts college or to do graduate work in their special field of research. Before making definite plans to study in Latin America the student should realize that the academic system is different from ours and should find out whether the university to which he proposes to go offers courses in his field of interest.

The student should understand that the liberal arts college as a part of the system of higher education is unique in the United States. In Latin America, as in other parts of the world, after completing his elementary and secondary education the student enters his field of professional specialization in the university. He follows a prescribed curriculum over a period usually ranging from five to seven years, at the end of which time a thesis must be presented and a degree is given. This degree, though sometimes called the doctorado, is not equivalent to a Ph.D. in this country. No graduate work, as the term is understood in the United States (i.e., a series of advanced elective courses), is offered in the university, though it is, of course, possible to do independent research outside of the university or in institutes connected with some universities.

Courses are offered in different faculties or departments of the university. Some of the most common faculties are listed below as a guide to students:

Faculty of Law and Political Science (sometimes known as the Faculty of Juridical and Social Sciences), whose courses stress political science, legal theory, international law, and the laws of the country;

Faculty of Medicine, which sometimes includes courses in pharmacy, dentistry, and so on (there are Faculties of Pharmacy and Dentistry, independent of the Faculty of Medicine, in some universities);

Faculty of Engineering, which often includes courses in architecture and chemistry;

Faculty of Physical and Natural Sciences, where courses in engineering and architecture may also be given;

Faculty of Agronomy and Veterinary Science;

Faculty of Commerce and Economic Sciences;

NOTE. Study in Latin American Universities is reprinted by permission from the News Bulletin of the Institute of International Education, December, 1941.

Faculty of Philosophy and Letters, which offers courses in history, literature, philosophy, and sometimes education.

Since Latin American legal systems are derived from Roman rather than Anglo-Saxon law, work in the Faculty of Law probably would not count toward a law degree in the United States. In the Faculties of Medicine, Engineering, and Sciences there are usually not as many laboratory facilities as in North American universities and therefore full credit for those courses is not always given in the United States. The Faculty of Agronomy and Veterinary Science offers more comprehensive and specialized courses than are usually found in the United States. The Faculty of Commerce has courses in international trade and economics similar to those offered in the United States. The closest approach to our own liberal arts college is the Faculty of Philosophy and Letters, and this is the faculty which North American students usually attend.

A student from the United States should realize that campus life as we know it here does not exist in Latin American countries. In very few countries do they have dormitories. Except in the case of Mexico and Cuba, which have received a large number of students from this country over a period of years, it is very hard to find a private home where the student can stay and enjoy family life. Therefore the student should plan to live in a boarding house or apartment and should count on at least $40 a month to cover room, board, and necessary incidentals. As the universities do not charge tuition, this should be the only expense aside from travel and a nominal matriculation fee at the university, which probably would not exceed $35.

A student who is granted a passport under the present war condition and wishes to secure credit at a United States college or university for studies in Latin America should make arrangements with his dean before his departure.

The following list should help students in selecting the university best suited to their needs. It is based on Latin American Universities, published by the Division of Intellectual Co-operation, Pan American Union, Washington, D. C. (1940), and is a selective list of the universities in the capitals of South America, Mexico, and Cuba. In nearly all cases the attendance is over 1000. Asterisks indicate the largest universities, with an enrolment of 5000 or more students.

UNIVERSITIES	ACADEMIC YEAR
1. Universidad Nacional de Buenos Aires,* Buenos Aires, Argentina	March-November
2. Universidad Nacional del Litoral,* Corrientes, Rosario, and Santa Fe, Argentina.	March-November
3. Universidad Nacional de La Plata,* La Plata, Argentina	March-November
4. Universidad Mayor de San Andrés, La Paz, Bolivia	March-December
5. Universidade do Brasil,* Rio de Janeiro, Brazil.	March-December
6. Universidade de São Paulo, São Paulo, Brazil.	March-November
7. Universidad de Chile,* Santiago, Chile . .	April-January
8. Universidad Católica de Chile,* Santiago, Chile.	April-December
9. Universidad Nacional de Colombia, Bogotá, Colombia	February-November
10. Universidad de la Habana,* Havana, Cuba . .	October-May

11. Universidad Central del Ecuador, Quito, Ecuador.   October-July
12. Universidad Nacional Autónoma de México,*
    Mexico City, Mexico . . . . February-November
13. Universidad Nacional del Paraguay, Asunción, Paraguay
    March-November
14. Universidad Católica del Perú, Lima, Peru . . April-January
15. Universidad Mayor de San Marcos,* Lima, Peru. April-January
16. Universidad de la República, Montevideo, Uruguay
    March-October
17. Universidad Central de Venezuela, Caracas, Venezuela
    September-June

SUBJECTS OFFERED

Agronomy: 1, 2, 3, 5, 6, 7, 8, 9, 10, 11, 16

Architecture: 1, 4, 5, 7, 8, 9, 10, 11, 12, 16

Art: 3, 4, 5, 7, 8, 9, 12

Commerce: 1, 2, 7, 8, 10, 12, 14, 15

Education: 3, 5, 6, 7, 10, 11, 14, 15

Engineering: all except 2, 3, 15

History and literature: all except 2, 4, 9, 16, 17

Law: all

Medicine: all except 14

Music: 5, 7, 9, 12

Natural sciences: all except 4, 14, 16, 17

Social problems: 2, 5, 12

Veterinary science: 1, 3, 5, 6, 7, 9, 10, 11, 12, 16

SUMMER SCHOOLS IN LATIN AMERICA

Summer schools in Latin America are of comparatively recent origin, largely in response to the growing desire in the United States to get more first-hand knowledge of Latin Americans and their culture. So far there have been three summer schools for North Americans only and three others established primarily for the natives of the country but with special courses for North Americans and other foreigners.

In the first category is the National University of Mexico, which led all the others by inaugurating a summer school for North Americans in 1920. By 1941 it had a record attendance of 1022 students, representing 41 different states and Alaska. Next came the university of Brazil in Rio de Janeiro, which established a summer session in 1931, repeated it in 1932, and had preparations under way for a 1942 session before the entrance of the United States into war made the realization of these plans impossible. The university of San Marcos, in Lima, Peru, organized its summer school in 1940 and had a total attendance of 54 students. The number was raised to 93 for the second session in 1941.

The university of Chile was the first to have a national summer school to which North Americans and other foreigners were also admitted. Every year since 1936 it has held a January summer school (during summer vacation in Chile) and a July-August summer school (during winter vacation). In January 1941 attendance reached its peak —1300 students, of whom 1222 were Chilean, 15 North American, 34 from the other American republics, and 29 from Europe. The July-August session had a total of 410 students—316 Chileans, 59 North Americans, 22 from the other American republics, and 13 Europeans.

The other summer schools created especially for nationals but also including foreigners are the Inter-American Summer University in San José, C. R., and the university of Havana's summer school in Havana, Cuba. Both these schools were set up in 1941 and were to be open again in 1942. A total of 242 students attended the Inter-American Summer University, of whom 221 were Costa Ricans and 21 North Americans. At the summer school in Havana there were 238 students, 143 of whom were Cubans, 89 North Americans, 3 from other American countries, and 3 from Europe.

The majority of these summer sessions have only 20 hours of classes or less, and therefore credit is seldom granted in colleges and universities of the United States for work done at them. However, at the present time the university of Havana and the National University of Mexico offer 30-hour courses which are generally recognized in the United States. To make sure of securing credit, students should check with their dean or department head before attending the summer school.

No scholarships have ever been granted for summer schools in Latin America, with the exception of the January session in Chile. Since 1936 the university of Chile has granted two scholarships annually to United States students. These have been administered by the Institute of International Education and until 1941 were supplemented by a $500 travel and study fellowship granted by the Carnegie Endowment for International Peace.

The entrance of the United States into war on December 8, 1941, will put off the development of further summer schools in Latin America. We must expect that for the duration few North Americans will be able to study in South America, although they may continue to go in limited numbers to such near-by countries as Costa Rica, Cuba, and Mexico.

Further information on summer sessions may be secured direct from the Latin American universities or from the following organizations in the United States:

Institute of International Education, 2 W. 45th St., New York.

Pan American Union, Washington, D. C.

United States Office of Education, Washington, D. C.

THE PAN AMERICAN HIGHWAY

BY J. S. GAVIGAN

Foreign Travel Division
American Automobile Association

After many years of comparative neglect the Pan American Highway, linking the United States with the Central American countries and the Panama Canal, has at last been recognized as one of the principal bulwarks of hemispheral defense and solidarity and is receiving the attention that the project so richly deserves. Funds have been allocated, and work is progressing on the construction of two sections of the highway which are now considered impassable and the general improvement of those sections which have already been completed.

Mexico has constructed a beautiful highway from Nuevo Laredo, at the Texas border, to Mexico City. This spectacular road has already proved its popularity with travelers and will undoubtedly bear an increasingly heavy traffic in future years. The road south from Mexico City to the Guatemalan border is one of the two uncompleted sections mentioned above and is not to be attempted by the ordinary tourist. The road as far south of Mexico City as Mitla is passable during the dry season, but beyond that point it would require a fully equipped expedition to make its way over the rough terrain to Tapachula near the Guatemalan border.

The Pan American Highway through Guatemala from Mexico to El Salvador is 300 miles in length. It is now completed and is open to traffic throughout the year. The road is extremely mountain-cut, at two places rising to a height of about 10,000 feet, the highest altitude reached by the highway north of the Panama Canal.

El Salvador has constructed its section of the through highway, from border to border, and has surfaced all but a short section near the Honduran frontier.

The distance across Honduras, following the route of the highway, is only 87 miles. Sufficient work has been done on this road to permit the passage of automobiles during the dry season, although from Choluteca to the Nicaraguan frontier it is little more than a trail.

The Pan American Highway is nonexistent in Costa Rica. There are a few roads in and around San José. In the dry season the road from the Honduran border to San José may be traveled with great difficulty over a deeply rutted trail, but from that city south to the Panamanian border it cannot be negotiated by any type of wheeled vehicle. Efforts are being made to complete the road through this section in the shortest possible time, which is expected to be 1945.

From David, Panama, there is an adequate road to the Canal Zone. The road to the Colombian border has not yet been surveyed, and it probably will be many years before it will be possible to motor between the two continents. To bridge this gap in the Pan American Highway system at the present time a car must be shipped from Panama to either a Venezuelan or Colombian port.

Special bonds, driving permits, and license plates are usually required for motoring in foreign countries. Arrangements need not be made in advance to enter a car into Mexico, but they should be made for Central American countries. The procedure, because of the different regulations in each country, is rather complicated at the present time. The Federation of Inter-American Automobile Clubs has been organized for the purpose of simplifying motoring in this hemisphere. Efforts are being made to insure the recognition of one set of international driving permits, license plates, and customs documents in all of the American republics, and there is no doubt that by the time the Pan American Highway is completed, crossing the borders of these countries in a car will be almost as simple as traveling from one state to another in the United States.

Motoring is, without doubt, the most practical and enjoyable way to see and appreciate the many attractions of a foreign country, but until the Pan American Highway is fully completed and improved, the American Automobile Association advises against any attempt to travel by automobile south of Mexico City and through Central America.

Further information concerning local regulations for motoring in Mexico or the Central American republics may be obtained by applying to the Foreign Travel Division of the American Automobile Association, 530 Fifth Ave., New York.

MOUNTAINEERING

BY ANDREW BAKEWELL

American Geographical Society of New York

The vast extent of the Western Hemisphere known as Hispanic America, stretching from the Río Grande to Tierra del Fuego, offers an almost unlimited field for mountaineering. The scope is so broad and the mountains so varied that the possibilities can only be briefly sketched here and the matter of choice left to individual taste. American mountaineers have to a large extent neglected this field, and much yet remains to be done, both in serious mountaineering exploration and in casual climbing.

Local Alpine clubs exist in various parts of Latin America through which help may be obtained for arranging mountaineering expeditions and excursions. For information on these and on such questions as outfitting, the reader is referred to the American Alpine Club, 140 E. 46th St., New York, or to the American Geographical Society, Broadway at 156th St., New York.

MEXICO, CENTRAL AMERICA, AND THE CARIBBEAN

Rising almost in the environs of the city of Mexico are two of the most famous mountains below the Río Grande—Popocatépetl (17,883 feet) and Ixtaccíhuatl (17,338 feet). Both are easily reached from the town of Amecameca and may be climbed with local guides. A road has been constructed up to the pass between the two mountains. It is also possible to drive up to 13,500 feet on the Nevado de Toluca (15,016 feet). Orizaba, the third highest elevation on the North American continent, rises to 18,696 feet on the edge of the Mexican tableland between Veracruz and Mexico City. Malintzin (14,648 feet) is an isolated cone lying between Orizaba and Popocatépetl. On the border of the states of Colima and Jalisco are the Nevado de Colima (14,235 feet) and the volcano Colima (12,628 feet); both have been ascended.

Central America, in the area of Guatemala, is a land of volcanoes. None are snow-capped, and some are active. They present no difficulties of an Alpine nature, and the majority have been ascended. Tajumulco (13,812 feet) is the highest peak in Central America. Agua (12,307 feet), Fuego (12,851 feet), and Acatenango (12,986 feet) are within sight of Guatemala City. In Costa Rica the highest peaks are in the Cordillera de Talamanca. Among them are Cerro Chiripo Grande (12,585 feet), Cerro Buena Vista (11,611 feet), and Pico Blanco (11,693 feet).

The Caribbean area contains many mountainous islands. Nearly all the summits are covered with vegetation and offer little to attract the climber. Ascending the less accessible peaks reduces itself to cutting a way through jungle and requires the use of a machete rather than an ice ax. Nevertheless the mountains have a verdant beauty of their own and have not yet divulged all their mysteries. In Cuba the Sierra Maestra culminates in the Pico Turquino (6560 feet). Rucilla or Pico del Yaque (9692 feet) in the central cordillera of the island of Santo Domingo is the highest point in the West Indies.

REFERENCE MATERIALS

BIBLIOGRAPHY. The best sources in English on mountaineering in Latin America are the following: Mountaineering, The Lonsdale Library, Vol. XVIII, Lippincott, Philadelphia; High Conquest, by James Ramsey Ullman, Lippincott, Philadelphia, 1941; American Alpine Journal, published by the American Alpine Club; Alpine Journal (British), published by the Alpine Club, 74 S. Audley, London, S. W. 1, England.

MAPS. Adequate maps of specific areas are locally available in a few of the Latin American countries. Only one general map of the entire area exists that is detailed enough to serve the needs of mountaineers. That is the Millionth Map of Hispanic America, published by the American Geographical Society, Broadway at 156th St., New York. On the scale of 1:1,000,000, a little less than 16 miles to the inch, it is published in a large number of sheets, each small enough to be handled easily in the field.

WEIGHTS AND MEASURES

The metric system is officially in use in all the Latin American republics. In some, however, old Spanish units are still in wide popular use side by side with the metric units. These units should be known by all who travel outside of the largest and most developed centers.

METRIC SYSTEM

Length

METRIC TO U. S.

1 meter (m.)	39.37 in.
1 kilometer (km.—1000 meters)	0.62 miles

U. S. TO METRIC

1 foot	0.30 m.
1 yard	0.91 m.
1 mile	1.61 km.

Area

METRIC TO U. S.

1 sq. m.	10.76 sq. ft.
1 sq. km.	0.39 sq. miles
1 hectare (10,000 sq. m.)	2.47 acres

U. S. TO METRIC

1 sq. ft.	0.09 sq. m.
1 sq. mile	2.59 sq. km.
1 acre	0.40 hectares

Volume

METRIC TO U. S.

1 liter	1.06 qt.
1 hectoliter (100 liters)	2.84 bu.

U. S. TO METRIC

1 qt.	0.95 liters
1 gal.	3.79 liters

Weight

METRIC TO U. S.

1 gram	0.04 oz. av.
1 kilogram (1000 grams)	2.20 lb. av.

U. S. TO METRIC

1 oz.	28.35 grams
1 lb.	0.45 kilograms

Temperature

CENTIGRADE TO FAHRENHEIT

Degrees Centigrade times 1.8, plus 32, gives equivalent degrees Fahrenheit. (For instance, 20° C. times 1.8 is 36, plus 32 is 68° F.)

FAHRENHEIT TO CENTIGRADE

Degrees Fahrenheit minus 32, divided by 1.8, gives equivalent degrees Centigrade. (For instance, 86° F. minus 32 is 54, divided by 1.8 is 30° C.)

SPANISH UNITS

1 arroba	25 lb.
1 quintal	101 lb.
1 vara	33 in.
1 legua (league)	3 miles

THE UNITED STATES OF MEXICO

MEXICO

BY JESSE J. DOSSICK

Mexico is a country of sharp and dramatic contrasts: grandiose monuments of a mysterious prehistoric past against a 20th-century background, stately medieval palaces and ancient cathedrals flanked by modernistically designed office buildings, oxcarts and aeroplanes, tractors and forked-stick plows, automobiles and pack burros, primitive handicrafts and progressive industry. These contrasts extend to the landscape, warm valleys and rocky pine-clad mountains, hot desert lands and swamps, rugged snow-capped peaks and jungles. The successful experiments of the United States of Mexico (Estados Unidos Mexicanos) in social reform and great natural resources make it an important nation, especially to the United States of America, its neighbor on the north. The country's culture, its people, and its history make it a fascinating playground and field of exploration for all travelers.

HISTORY

The name of Mexico, written México in Spanish usage, is closely associated with a group of aboriginal tribes who called themselves the Mexica or Aztecs. The name is derived from their tribal war god Mexitl, also known as Huitzilopochtli. The Spanish invaders applied the name of Mexico to all the lands dominated by the Aztecs at the time of the conquest. Mexican historians divide their country's history into four fundamental periods. The first is that preceding the conquest, extending from the remotest times to 1521. The second is that of New Spain or colonial Mexico, including the period of transplantation of Spanish culture and the work of exploration, discovery, and colonization during the three centuries that followed 1521. The third period follows the winning of independence, marked by the establishment of the republic and its development during the 19th century up to the revolution which began in 1910. The fourth, an era of social and national renovation, extends to the present day.

ANCIENT CIVILIZATIONS. As a result of archeological studies it is safe to say that from prehistoric times to the coming of the Spaniards the Mexican earth was trod by a succession of nomadic races with differing languages, customs, and degrees of culture. For the purpose of this brief historical outline they may be narrowed to four principal groups: archaic, Maya, Toltec, and Aztec. Students of Mexican antiquities declare that these various races were created by the amalgamation and interbreeding of disparate tribes, the experience and achievements of each contributing to a progressive development. Each succeeding combination built a civilization, waged wars, and engaged in commerce and exploration. In the process they usually absorbed some of the language, religion, science, and art of their predecessors. Reconstructions of Mexican history before the Spanish conquest are largely speculative, and statements about the early periods are provisional.

The most widely accepted theory concerning the origins of the first inhabitants of the Americas is that they came across the islands of the Bering Sea from Asia into Alaska. Cuicuilco, a temple pyramid in the valley of Mexico, which belongs to this period and is thought by some scholars to be the oldest structure built by human hands on the Amer-

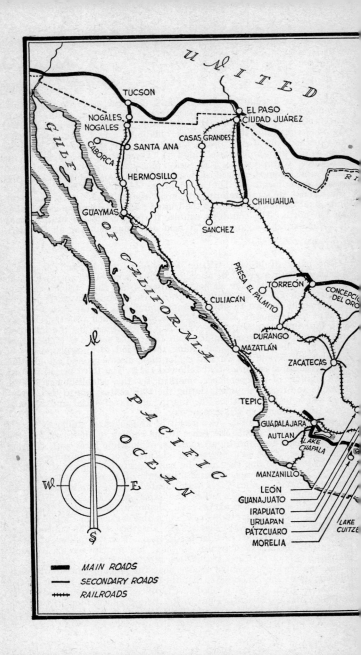

ican continent, may have been ancient when the Pharaohs began their building operations on the banks of the Nile. The earliest pyramids, the relatively advanced stage of architecture and sculpture, the pottery and other products of human workmanship which have been unearthed by archeologists, indicate a civilization of some sophistication.

Later, but hundreds of years before Christ, the Mayas appeared. They discovered the lunar month and the length of the year, devised a calendar, and developed a chronology and writing. At the time Christ was born, a Maya empire of great cities was flourishing in what is now Guatemala. For more than a century before the year 600 its civilization was perhaps second to none of the period. During the 7th to 10th centuries the Mayas abandoned their remarkable cities with their magnificent temples and monuments and migrated to the peninsula of Yucatán, where during the 10th to 12th centuries their culture reappeared in an even more elaborate form in the cities of Chichén-Itzá, Uxmal, and scores of others. Wars occupied the Maya tribes until the 13th century, when a powerful personage, Kukul Can or Quetzalcoatl, seems to have combined them into a single empire. A great revival of the arts occurred during the peace that prevailed during the next two centuries. The empire broke up in the 15th century, and perhaps as a result of tribal wars and pestilence the race disintegrated rapidly. Other groups meanwhile had made their appearance on the Mexican plateau, the Olmecs, Toltecs, Chichimecs, and Acolhuas. In southern Oaxaca the Zapotecs evolved a culture almost as advanced as that of the Mayas; remains of their civilization are to be found at Mitla and Monte Albán. The Mixtecs and Olmecs developed their own cultures in the mountains of northern Oaxaca and Puebla, the Tarascans in Michoacán, and the Toltecs dominated the valley of Mexico.

The Toltecs, a warlike race of unknown origin, moving southward from their original home on the Pacific coast hundreds of miles to the north, colonized the valley of Mexico about the 6th century B.C. and built their chief city at Teotihuacán, northeast of Lake Texcoco, settling also at Tollán, Cholula, Xochicalco, and Atzcapotzalco. Apparently the advanceguard of the Nahuas—the linguistic family to which all the late arrivals in the valley of Mexico belonged—this race by the 9th or 10th century after Christ seem to have extended their power over most of southern Mexico. The Toltecs achieved a high degree of civilization; they were master craftsmen and builders of vast and handsome cities, and their trade reached hundreds of miles beyond their borders. They had a fixed form of government with complicated laws of a military, political, social, and religious nature. But civil wars, pestilence, and famine disrupted the empire, and apparently at some time before the 13th century Teotihuacán was abandoned. The Toltecs were driven southward by new and barbaric Nahua invaders from the mountains of the north. Many of the Toltecs remained behind, however, and were absorbed by the new wave of invaders, known as the Chichimecs, a group of kindred tribes who made their homes beside the lakes in the valley of Mexico or Anáhuac, as it was called at the time. Much as the Romans after their conquest of Greece fell under the influence of Hellenic civilization, so these new Nahua nomads from the north, in conquering the Toltecs, were influenced by the superior civilization of the defeated people. The early history of the migratory Chichimecs is not easy to ascertain from the tangled migration myths, which relate that the invaders were practically a barbarous people, while modern archeologists credit them with a fair degree of culture. At any rate, devoting themselves to agriculture and the arts and crafts, they adopted the ideas and customs of the Toltecs and then improved upon them.

The Aztecs, who were similarly to borrow from the Toltecs, were the last of the invading Nahua tribes to reach the valley of Mexico. According to their legends they left a land called Aztlán somewhere in the north between the 9th and 13th centuries of the Christian era and after much wandering arrived on the Mexican plateau. After some fighting with the tribes of the valley for the right to remain, they laid the foundations of their new and permanent home on some unwanted patches of dry land surrounded by swamps and marshes near the Lake of Texcoco. From this date, A.D. 1325, their historical period may be said to begin, since their record from that time to the conquest appears fairly definite and reliable. For a number of years the Aztecs were comparatively unimportant, exercising little influence in the vicinity. Their city Tenochtitlán, built partly on small islands in the middle of the salt-water lake and partly on new land held in place by piles driven into the lake bottom, was to prove an ideal defensive site. During the early years of the occupation the central part of the city was on dry land, laboriously reclaimed, while the outlying dwellings stood on piles in the water. Canals traversing the city and crossed by bridges ran into causeways at various points. This system of causeways connecting the city with the mainland and protected by drawbridges, together with the reclamation of the land, was their first major achievement.

Early in the 15th century, nearly a century after the founding of Tenochtitlán, the Aztecs threw off the yoke of surrounding tribes and formed an offensive and defensive alliance with two neighboring kindred groups, at Tezcuco—the Acolhua branch of the Nahua stock—and Tlacopán. Of the spoils and tribute that they took, the Tezcucans and Aztecs each received two-fifths and the people of Tlacopán the remaining fifth. Within a comparatively short time the Aztecs made their city the most powerful defensive stronghold ever held by Indians up to the 16th century. The impregnability of Tenochtitlán was an important factor in their rise to power. As the numbers of the Aztecs gradually increased they built highways and other well-planned cities. Their influence came to be felt throughout the greater part of Mexico. The first major Aztec war chieftain, Acamapichtli, was elected 50 years after the founding of Tenochtitlán and ruled till near the end of the 14th century. After his time, under Huitzilihuitl, the second ruler, the wars were fought which won the Aztecs decisive leadership among the peoples of Mexico. By clever political tactics, executive ability, and prowess in war they gradually assumed the paramount position in the confederacy. Tezcuco, under the encouragement and sagacious rule of Netzahualcoyotl in the 15th century, became the intellectual and artistic center of the valley and maintained its position as such until the Spanish conquest. The third member of the tripartite confederacy, Tlacopán, declined in importance.

The empire of the Aztecs, outrivaling that of the Toltecs, did not cover the extensive territories which make up the Mexico of today. Its boundaries cannot be determined with certainty, although it is believed that at the height of their supremacy the area controlled or effectively influenced extended north through the highlands of northern Mexico, east to Veracruz and Tampico, south to the distant regions of Chiapas and Yucatán, even to Tehuantepec and far-off Guatemala and Nicaragua, and west to the Pacific. No efforts were made by the Aztecs to weld the neighboring tribes, who gave momentary and reluctant fealty, into a solid commonwealth; they were permitted to retain their customs and social and religious organization, provided the payment of tribute was punctual. More is known concerning the social and political organization of the Aztecs, especially of Tenochtitlán with its possible 100,000 inhabitants and its magnificent palaces, than about the civilization of any other Indians of Mexico, for the early Spanish friars and historians studied them well. The Aztecs are, then, says Herbert I. Priestly in his book The Mexican Nation, "if not typical, the best representatives of early Mexican culture, and while our knowledge of the other peoples is often indirect or even allusive, we are safe in assuming that in few essentials did they differ materially from, and certainly not in complexity of or height of development, the dominant element of the Nahua group." At the time of the Spanish conquest the Aztec government was approximating an elective monarchy, with the tribal chieftain at the head of an executive council made up of all the chieftains of some 20 clans.

The peoples described were highly proficient in the manufacture of pottery and woven fabrics; some were skilled metal workers. By means of complicated hieroglyphic writings some of them were able to record their history, traditions, religious festivals and formulas, tribute rolls, arts and sciences, and the like. These ancient Mexicans were good agriculturists and admirable builders and organizers, and besides large and well-equipped armies they supported a vast hierarchy of priests. All formal education was intrusted to the priests and usually administered from the temples, thousands of which, truly magnificent and imposing in their grandeur, dotted the land.

THE CONQUEST. From the beginning of the reign of Moctezuma or Montezuma II in 1502 Spanish navigators had been exploring the neighborhood of the Mexican coast in an effort to find and conquer the great Indian kingdoms mentioned in the tales which had reached them in Cuba. In a simple slave-hunting expedition from Cuba, Francisco Hernández de Córdoba discovered Yucatán and Campeche in 1517. A year later Juan de Grijalva, on a similar venture, landed on the island of Cozumel off the northeast coast of Yucatán. He was the first to use the name New Spain for Mexican territory. The governor of Cuba, Diego Velázquez de León, toward the end of that year, commissioned 34-year-old Hernán Cortés to head another expedition of exploration and conquest. In spite of Velázquez' jealous last-minute attempt to replace him, Cortés sailed and, after harrowing adventures, on April 21, 1519, audaciously entered the empire of Moctezuma, disembarking at San Juan de Ulúa near the present Veracruz with more than 500 soldiers, some horses, and some cannon.

A cordial reception by Moctezuma's messengers and ambassadors was followed by hostility which mounted as Cortés proceeded to the interior, accompanied by the Totonacs, Tlaxcaltecs, and other Indian tribes who hoped to throw off the hateful yoke of the Aztecs. Moctezuma made efforts through diplomatic promises and rich gifts to prevent the entrance of the Spaniards into the environs of Tenochtitlán but to no avail. When they finally reached the Mexican capital in November 1519 no resistance was offered; instead the Aztecs, though uneasy, greeted the invaders with more presents. Here the adventurers remained until June 1520, when during Cortés' absence Pedro de Alvarado, one of his lieutenants, fearing an Aztec uprising, caused the slaughter of several hundred unsuspecting Indians. The enraged populace turned against the Spaniards, and Moctezuma, held as a hostage, died either from wounds at the hands of his own people when he was exposed during the battle or at the hands of the Spaniards. The Spaniards managed to fight their way out of Tenochtitlán with great losses during the night of June 30, which became known as the Sorrowful Night (Noche Triste). The next year Cortés returned with reinforcements and began a siege of the capital, which, despite the valiant defense by Cuauhtémoc, the new tribal chieftain, fell on Aug. 13, 1521.

The Venice-like Tenochtitlán had been ruthlessly demolished. The great temples were razed to the ground, the canals drained, the causeways destroyed. Over the ruins of the ancient Aztec capital a new city was built. The destruction of the Aztec civilization resulted in the loss of its art, its religion, its social structure, and its language. The development of the arts and sciences and the growth of the communities of the ancient Mexican empire came to an abrupt halt. The gradual four-centuries-long disintegration of a great people was begun.

COLONIAL PERIOD. Immediately after the conquest and the reconstruction of Tenochtitlán, Cortés, with the aid of such able lieutenants as Alvarado, Olid, Sandoval, and Orozco, extended the Spanish conquest over the rest of Mexico and Central America. In 1535 the viceroyalty of New Spain was established with its seat in Mexico City, which the Spaniards had erected over the ruins of Tenochtitlán. The first viceroy, Antonio de Mendoza, who served for 15 years until 1550, was a sincere, energetic, and capable man who without delay established an orderly form of government in place of the haphazard administration of military leaders. He fostered agriculture and attempted to educate and to improve the condition of the natives. In 1536 the Colegio de Santa Cruz de Tlaltelalco was founded by the Franciscans for the purpose of educating Indian boys. Mendoza tried also to build up Spanish culture in Mexico. In 1534 the first printing press was set up in Mexico City and soon the first book was issued in the Americas.

Mendoza promoted the exploring expeditions of Francisco de Coronado and others, and gradually in the ensuing years the influence of Spain was extended and consolidated, not only by soldiers and colonists such as Francisco de Ibarra and Luis de Carbajal, but also by missionaries imbued with the spiritual zeal of Juan de Zumárraga, the first bishop. The Franciscans, Augustinians, Dominicans, and Jesuits built churches, monasteries, and schools, frequently on the sites of pagan temples and edifices and using materials of the razed structures. The university of Mexico was founded in 1553. The tribunal of the Inquisition was established in 1571, and the Jesuits arrived the next year. Church and state went hand in hand; faithfulness to the Church signified acceptance of Spanish rule. The methods and character of Old World Spanish life, with all its good and bad features, were easily transplanted in Mexico. Intermarriage of Indians and Spaniards began with the conquest, and the greatest number and some of the most vigorous of the Mexican population are of mixed blood.

Antonio de Mendoza was followed by threescore other viceroys in the 271 years after 1550; of these, the two Velascos and Antonio María Bucareli contributed most to the development of the country. The refinements of colonial life grew apace, visible in education, literature, painting, sculpture, music, drama, architecture, and social amenities. The Franciscans opened a great number of schools for Indian boys. Prominent as teachers were the friars Andrés de Olmos, a great linguist; Bernardino de Sahagún, the distinguished historian and writer on Mexican ethnology; and Pedro de Gante, whose school—the first—had facilities for instructing a thousand children. The Jesuits accomplished their great work in education in the provinces. By 1767, the year of their expulsion, they had 23 colleges and several seminaries in Mexico.

At the end of the 16th century a new Mexico was emerging. Mining, farming, stock-raising, and sugar-refining were the chief industries. All civil and military authority, with few exceptions, was in the hands of royal officials over whom stood the viceroy, literally a substitute king, and the audiencia, a body which acted both as a council of state and as the supreme court within the colonies. Spanish rule extended many leagues beyond the limits of the old Aztec empire. As a result of mining booms, settlements existed in what is now the states of Zacatecas, Nuevo León, San Luis Potosí, Durango, Chihuahua, Sonora, and Sinaloa. The far distant regions of Texas, Arizona, and New Mexico had been reached by exploring expeditions. In 1609 Santa Fe, now in New Mexico, was founded. The 16th century also witnessed the establishment of cities and large towns that are important today—Veracruz on the Gulf, Acapulco on the Pacific, Guanajuato, Guadalajara, Zacatecas, Aguascalientes, Durango, Sombrerete, Saltillo, Monterrey, Culiacán, Puebla, Valladolid, Oaxaca, and a score of others.

The 17th century saw the growth of the Inquisition; exploitation of mineral deposits; the establishment of Franciscan and Jesuit missions along an ever-widening frontier from Louisiana to Lower California; the permanent occupation of Coahuila, northern Chihuahua, and Sonora; and penetration into Lower California and eastern Texas. Most famous in the field of literature was the amazing Juana Inés de la Cruz (1651-95), a nun in the convent of San Jerónimo. Her poems have been called "the softest and most delicate that ever came from a woman's pen." Another individual born in the 17th century whose fame spread throughout Latin America because of his literary accomplishments and encyclopedic knowledge was Carlos de Sigüenza y Góngora (1645-1700). A journalist and critic, who probably established the first publication on the order of a newspaper in New Spain, El Mercurio Volante (The Flying Mercury), Sigüenza was also poet, philosopher, mathematician, engineer, cartographer, geographer, astronomer, philologist, ethnologist, anthropologist, and historian; and he established a museum of Mexican antiquities. In the second half of the 18th century missions were established in California. Just prior to the close of that century there was a spurt of interest in the teaching of the theoretical and the exact sciences, and in 1792 a school of mines was established by José Fausto Elhuyar, the great metallurgist, which gave a remarkably practical course of studies. At this time also Antonio Alzate, the distinguished scientist, was producing encyclopedic essays on a wide range of scientific and philosophical subjects.

Essentially, however, the Spanish colonial system in the 17th and 18th centuries, as in the 16th, was complex, sluggish, expensive, and showy—accompanied by high taxes, bribery, sale of offices, and many other evil practices. Most of the inhabitants of New Spain were denied any share in the government, since only Spaniards born in Spain could hold office. Officials were not responsible to the people.

The strong demand for labor on the plantations, in sugar mills, in household service, for construction work, navigation, drainage of canals, and erection of churches, dwellings, and public buildings, but especially in the mines, resulted in the exploitation and abuse of the repartimientos and the encomienda system, which consisted essentially of grants of large tracts of land with the right to make use of the labor of the natives and which had originally been intended as a means of distributing the Indians so that their services could be utilized in the development of the country's resources while they were instructed in the Christian religion. Cruelty resulted in great loss of life among the native population in spite of the protective Laws of the Indies. The policy of Spain was primarily designed to keep her colonies in a continual state of dependency and to get all possible profit for Spain. Efforts to establish industries in Mexico that might compete with those of Spain were discouraged or prohibited. Commerce to and from New Spain was carried on by Spanish ships only. No agricultural product was allowed to be raised in Mexico that might in any way come into competition with a similar product of Spain. Heavy taxes were another cause for grievance.

On the other hand Spain from time to time made attempts to curb the exploitation of the Indians by Spanish landowners and mining operators. Bartolomé de las Casas, known as the Protector of the Indians, worked for this cause in Mexico as well as in other countries. Vasco de Quiroga in Michoacán also labored devotedly for the welfare of the native population and even today is recalled by the Indians as Tata Vasco—"our father Vasco." Spain also made numerous improvements in colonial living conditions, beautified cities and towns, built highways for commerce, improved harbors, and encouraged literature, art, and education. But the evils of the Spanish administration far outweighed the good. The existence of peonage and the herding of the Indians in towns, mining camps, and ranches under the pretense of civilizing and Christianizing them stripped them of the means of sustaining their native civilization and culture. Corruption and inefficiency characterized the colonial system of government. The abuses stirred the brewing pot to a point where it boiled over into strong protests and uprisings against Spanish authority.

The surge of revolutionary feeling which spread over the world following the success of the 13 North American colonies against England, the publication of the philosophical tracts of the precursors of the French revolution, and that revolution itself affected Mexico strongly. Discontent was rife among the masses of Indian and mestizo or mixed blood, and they were easily persuaded to follow the leadership of the Creoles, of Spanish blood but born on American soil, to whom all political leadership and economic advantage had been denied.

WARS OF INDEPENDENCE. The Napoleonic invasion of Spain and the overthrow of Charles IV of Spain was the final spark that set off the revolution in Mexico as elsewhere in Spanish America. A group of revolutionary patriots gathered around Miguel Hidalgo y Costilla, curate of Dolores, who raised the standard of revolt in 1810 with the slogan, "Long live Our Lady of Guadalupe! Perish the Spaniards!" This Cry of Dolores (Grito de Dolores) became the rallying slogan of the revolution in New Spain. In mustering immense numbers of armed natives Hidalgo aimed at the establishment of political independence and free land in Mexico. After several astonishingly successful encounters, during which town after town attached itself to the patriot cause, he arrived with a force of about 80,000 poorly armed men at Monte de las Cruces, where he clashed with the best troops at the government's disposal. Victorious, he could have taken the capital, but instead withdrew cautiously, whereupon success left him. He was completely routed by Félix María Calleja at the battle of Puente de Calderón in January 1811. Fleeing north with a few followers, Hidalgo was captured in an ambuscade and executed the following year.

The priest José María y Pavón, able lieutenant, friend, and disciple of Hidalgo, kept the flame of independence alive. He assembled a supreme revolutionary junta or council at Chilpancingo in September 1813, and two months later a representative congress issued a declaration of independence from Spain and put forth a program which included the abolition of slavery, eradication of class distinctions, correction of tax abuses, and other important and even more radical reforms. In the latter part of 1815 Morelos was overtaken and defeated by a large force of royalists at Texmaluca. He was captured, taken to Mexico City for trial by the Inquisition, convicted, and executed on Dec. 22, 1815, at San Cristóbal Ecatépec.

The movement for independence seemed to have been defeated. The dramatic campaign of the young Spanish adventurer Francisco Javier Mina, whose revolutionary ideals, like those of Lafayette, impelled him to leave Europe for the New World, met with disaster in 1817, when he was executed. The ex-mule driver Vicente Guerrero, one of the stubbornest leaders of the movement for independence and for a long time the sole active supporter of the cause, was driven into the wilds, where he carried on guerrilla warfare. But somehow the revolution continued. The war took a new turn when the loyalist general Agustín de Iturbide made common cause with the patriots, joined forces with Vicente Guerrero, and proclaimed an independent Mexico in 1821, establishing a conservative government on the Plan of Iguala. Embodied in this plan were three guarantees, those of unity, religion, and independence. The Mexican flag today still symbolizes these guarantees with green for unity, white for religion, and red for independence. But the plan proposed an independent monarchy with a ruler from the Spanish royal family, and it failed. Iturbide, by an adroit coup in 1822, made himself emperor of Mexico as Agustín I. He was aided by the strong conservative minority composed of the higher clergy and large landowners. His reign was not peaceful. Almost exactly a year later he was deposed through the connivance of Gen. Antonio López de Santa Ana, an erstwhile ally, who led a successful uprising of the army against him. Iturbide wrote out his abdication, was exiled, and finally was executed when he unwisely returned to Mexico the following year.

On Oct. 4, 1824, a constitution establishing a federal regime and modeled on the Spanish constitution of 1812 as well as on that of the United States was adopted, and Gen. Guadalupe Victoria, revolutionary leader, was chosen president of the new Mexican republic. Embracing an enormous area, handicapped by ponderous natural barriers, and lacking adequate communications, the new republic was beset by grave problems. Its heterogeneous population, with no sense of civic consciousness and national unity, was not prepared for the institutions of democracy; the republican form of government was a premature attempt. A struggle of great significance followed. The conservative party was resolved to maintain a highly centralized colonial form of government. The liberal party wanted federated sovereign states and independence for the oppressed masses. When Gen. Vicente Guerrero was installed as president in 1829 he in turn was buffeted about by a number of insurrections and finally was captured and put to death by his enemies. His vice-president Anastasio Bustamente rose and fell, and Santa Ana was declared dictator in the middle of 1833. Santa Ana nullified all reform measures. Texas, which was under Mexican jurisdiction, was angered by his determination to centralize the government; it had already been disaffected by Guerrero's abolition of slavery in 1829, for cattle ranchers and cotton growers who had come into Texas from the United States believed slavery essential to their welfare. In 1836 Texas rebelled and declared her independence after Santa Ana's disastrous defeat by Sam Houston at San Jacinto.

Texas was annexed to the United States on March 1, 1845. War between Mexico and the United States broke out in 1846. There was outspoken criticism of the conflict in the United States, but the administration in Washington forced the issue and explicitly ordered Gen. Zachary Taylor into Mexico with a U. S. army. In 1847 Gen. Winfield Scott occupied the capital, and under the terms of the treaty of Guadalupe Hidalgo in 1848 all the territory from Texas to California and from the Río Grande to Oregon was ceded to the United States in return for $15,000,000. The Gadsden Purchase in 1853, at a price of $10,000,000, added a small strip in southern Arizona for a railroad right-of-way. After the war Mexico was confronted not only with the problem of reconstruction but also with an active revolution. The revolution was soon crushed, but the country's poor financial condition hampered the government's peaceful progress, and finally in 1853 Santa Ana once again proclaimed himself dictator with the title of Most Serene Highness. His autocratic and corrupt rule and persecution of freedom of thought wearied Mexico and resulted in a number of revolutions. The liberal groups and the Indians embraced the Plan of Ayutla, framed in 1854, and finally succeeded in deposing Santa Ana.

The triumph of the Ayutla revolution brought to the fore the leaders of the reform movement: Juan Alvarez, Ignacio Comonfort, Melchor Ocampo, Miguel Lerdo de Tejada, Ignacio Ramírez, Guillermo Prieto, Ignacio Altamirano, and Riva Palacio. Standing above them all was Benito Juárez. A modern Mexican historian, Alfonso Teja Zabre, writes in his Guide to Mexican History: "Just as Hidalgo and Morelos, being the first and greatest, represented the liberating movement of 1810, and Guerrero stood for consummation of independence; just as Iturbide stands for the transition between the colonial period and that of independence; just as Santa Ana is the outstanding figure of the alternating periods of military dictatorship and anarchy that went on until the middle of the 19th century, so Juárez is Mexico's representative personality during the period of Reform, the Intervention and the Empire." A full-blooded Zapotec Indian of humble origin, sometimes compared to Abraham Lincoln because of similarities of career and character, Juárez had made his mark as the efficient, honest, and progressive governor of the state of Oaxaca. Even his worst enemies acknowledged his unswerving loyalty to the cause of democracy and respected his integrity. In his capacity as minister of justice in President Comonfort's new liberal cabinet, Juárez, with the aid of Lerdo de Tejada and Ocampo, took the first decisive steps toward a genuinely liberal economic and social transformation of Mexico through the passage of the reform laws. Under these decrees the jurisdiction of the privileged military and church courts was curtailed and class legislation abolished. These and the other important liberal ideas of federalism were confirmed in the constitution of 1857, which provided for popular education, freedom of the press and speech, practical separation of Church and state, the suppression of religious orders, civil marriage, and the secularization of those portions of the estates of the religious orders not used for purposes of worship.

The church hierarchy, outraged, supported the conservative party's reactionary uprising which was immediately set in operation by the generals Miguel Miramón and Félix Zuloaga. There ensued three years of civil war, known as the war of reform, in which crops were ruined, industries paralyzed, and the land desolated. When Comonfort saw that his appeasement policy in the beginning of the struggle met with no success he resigned, and Juárez, as a consequence of being chief justice of the nation, was raised to the presidency. By January 1861 the Juaristas had retaken the capital city and claimed complete victory. In June 1861, Juárez was formally proclaimed constitutional president of Mexico. On October 31 of the same year France, England, and Spain signed a compact in London for joint intervention in Mexico for the protection of their interests. It is probable that no government ever faced a more stupendous task than that which confronted Juárez after the three years of bloody internecine strife. Mexico lay in ruin and poverty. Juárez was forced to suspend payments on the national debt. A joint force of British, French, and Spaniards landed at Veracruz for the purpose of taking over the customs until their demands should be satisfied. England and Spain withdrew shortly, but Napoleon III ordered aggressive action against Mexico, for he desired to re-establish a French colonial empire in the New World. Even the famous May 5 (Cinco de Mayo) victory of the Juarista forces at Puebla in 1862 could not prevent the occupation of the capital by the French troops. A new government was organized by the French with elements unfavorable to Juárez. Archduke Maximilian of Austria was invited to leave Europe with his wife Carlotta to become emperor. But Juárez was not disposed to abandon his cause. His guerrilla bands harassed the French invaders incessantly.

Maximilian's regime lasted only as long as foreign imperialist troops remained. As a result of his sincere but misguided efforts at reform, his religious tolerance, and his administrative mistakes he failed to reconcile the republican, liberal, and clerical parties. The pressing demands of its Civil War had prevented the United States from taking a firm stand against the French, but after the establishment of peace the Johnson administration issued an ultimatum to Napoleon III to withdraw his French armies. Gen. Phil Sheridan was sent to the Río Grande with 52,000 picked men. When Napoleon acceded, withdrawing the French forces in 1867, Maximilian found himself hopelessly alone. He was captured by the Juaristas at Querétaro and executed by a firing squad on the morning of June 19, on the Cerro de las Campanas. Juárez returned to the capital and resumed the slow task of reorganization, again facing national economic destitution and political disturbance caused by the tenacious remnants of the reactionary elements. Death interrupted his efforts at reconstruction on July 18, 1872. Sebastián Lerdo de Tejada, a scholar of distinguished attainments, followed him in office, only to be overthrown after four years through the political trickery of Porfirio Díaz.

From 1876 until 1911 General Díaz ruled the country. His only chance, he said, was "to establish a dictatorial system of absolutely personal control." Under the guise of an enlightened liberal democracy and through his policy of conciliation he brought an era of unprecedented peace and prosperity to the Mexican nation. He slowly organized a powerful political machine and established a ruthless mounted rural police who eliminated the widespread banditry. He established friendly relations with the rulers of the world and forwarded the exploitation of his nation's natural resources by inviting and protecting the foreign capital that came in for that purpose. In fact he deeded away thousands of acres of land for a song. But debts were paid, the national credit bettered, and foreign trade stimulated. Díaz secured passage of the necessary tariff laws to protect Mexican industries and encouraged the development of a network of railroads. The population increased rapidly, and Mexico became one of the respected nations of the world. Palatial buildings were erected. The valley of Mexico was drained, bringing to an end the recurrent floods and consequent fevers that had taken a gigantic toll in deaths each year. The basic social and economic problems that had brought disorder to Mexico for the last four centuries remained, however. Not more than 3 per cent of Mexico's heads of families possessed any land. Peons on the large estates and in the mines were economically enslaved. Communal villages were deprived of their lands; hundreds of thousands of peasants, uprooted from the soil, were forced to incur debts which led them into peonage. The fertile valley lands of the Yaquis of Sonora were illegally transferred to wealthy Creoles, and the Indians were sold into forced labor and shipped by carloads to the tobacco and henequen plantations of the Quintana Roo territory and Yucatán, where they died by the hundreds. More than 80 per cent of the people were illiterate, and the value of the few schools was limited because of the miserable pay of the teachers and the wretched half-starved condition of the children.

Díaz, supremely confident, up to his last moment of power remained blind to the spirit of revolt among the people. Finally opposition to the evils of the political system precipitated the revolution of 1910, led by Francisco I. Madero, an idealistic, humanitarian member of a rich landowning family of Coahuila. Díaz resigned and departed for Paris. In the election held on Oct. 15, 1911, Madero won on a platform which held out promises of restoring to the Indian villages the land that had been taken from them, reforming the suffrage, improving local and national government, guarding the freedom of the press, and limiting the president to a single term. But Madero, while truly inspired by ideals of democracy and popular suffrage, lacked a definite program which would have enabled his administration to achieve economic alleviation of the exploited Indian masses. He never had a real comprehension of the grievances inherent in the national situation, and he proved incapable of coping with it. Exactly a year after Madero assumed the presidency, Gen. Félix Díaz, a nephew of Porfirio Díaz, headed an insurrection with the support of corrupt politicians and army officers. This, like lesser movements before it, was crushed with ease, but Madero refused to execute the leaders. Then Gen. Victoriano Huerta, placed in command of the troops in the Federal District, joined the traitors. The coup succeeded, and Madero, with the vice-president Piño Suárez, was seized and was brutally murdered in February 1913.

When Huerta made himself provisional president the Maderista governor of Coahuila, Venustiano Carranza, began a counter-revolution with the aid of loyal elements from the northern states of Chihuahua and Sonora. The shocking news of the manner of Madero's death provoked great hostility to Huerta in the United States. President Woodrow Wilson created difficulties for Huerta and was open in his friendliness to Carranza's forces, the so-called constitutionalists. Under the military leadership of the generals Alvaro Obregón of Sonora, Pablo González of Coahuila, and Pancho Villa of Durango decisive victories were registered against the government troops, and Mexico City was taken. Huerta fled the country in July 1914. Carranza and Villa quarreled and separated, and henceforth Villa was regarded as a rebel chieftain. There followed a series of clashes between the armies of Carranza, Villa, and Emiliano Zapata, the last the outstanding representative of agrarian reform, whose battle cry of land and liberty (Tierra y Libertad) for the peasants made him the most beloved revolutionary in southern Mexico. By 1915 Carranza's constitutionalist government had won foreign recognition. A new constitution was forced upon him by his party in 1917. Restating more vigorously the principles outlined in the old Juárez constitution of 1857, it provided for freedom of worship and division of large landed estates, declared that the nation was the original owner of all natural resources, confiscated all Church property, placed many restrictions on religious activities, and provided for the protection of labor against exploitation.

In 1920, when it was evident that Carranza intended to swing the election of his successor to a figurehead, Gen. Alvaro Obregón engineered a successful revolt. Carranza was killed while attempting to escape. Obregón, the strongest political figure Mexico had produced since Díaz, took office on Dec. 1, 1920, after an ad-interim rule by Adolfo de la Huerta. During Obregón's administration there was great educational activity. Trade unions and peasants' organizations were encouraged. A program of land reallotment was started, and a more friendly face was presented to foreign powers. Gen. Plutarco Elías Calles followed Obregón in the presidency in 1924 and pushed the reforms initiated by the previous government. Shortly thereafter Calles began to enforce rigidly the religious provisions and the oil and land laws of the 1917 constitution. The anti-Church laws provoked a strike on the part of the clergy, and no religious services were held. The Cristero rebellion of Church supporters, which was dealt with vigorously, caused many deaths and resulted in banditry. The land and oil disputes with the United States were, however, ironed out with the aid of Ambassador Dwight Morrow, who had won the confidence of the Mexicans. In the presidential election of June 1, 1928, Obregón was re-elected, but 16 days later he was assassinated by a young religious fanatic. It became necessary to choose a provisional president for a two-year period, and Emilio Portes Gil, a lawyer and former governor of the state of Tamaulipas, was named. In 1930 Pascual Ortiz Rubio, an engineer from Michoacán and formerly ambassador to Brazil, was elected with the aid of Calles and his ruling clique. In 1932, however, as a result of political differences with Calles and in spite of a peaceful and seemingly progressive administration, Ortiz Rubio was forced to resign. Gen.

Abelardo Rodríguez, supported by Calles, was named by Congress to succeed to the office.

CONTEMPORARY MEXICO. On March 20, 1933, an amendment was added to the constitution which limited the presidential term to six years, with re-election prohibited, and the terms of senators and deputies to six and three years respectively with no consecutive re-election. In 1934 Gen. Lázaro Cárdenas, as the candidate of the National Revolutionary Party, only semiofficial in status but the strongest political group in the country, was elected president in one of the most orderly of Mexico's elections. Immediately upon taking office Cárdenas took vigorous measures to insure the successful administration of a six-year plan for economic, social, and intellectual reform which had been formulated by the National Revolutionary Party. During 1935 Calles attempted to act in his capacity of unofficial president, expecting to pull strings as heretofore. He discovered that Cárdenas was no puppet. Feeling that Calles' presence was a disturbing influence, Cárdenas swiftly deported him by airplane to Texas; Calles went on to California to reside with his daughter.

The keynote of the Cárdenas program, it has been declared by Howard S. Phillips, editor of the publication Mexican Life, "has been the fundamental reorganization of national agriculture through redistribution of land to the peasantry. The total area of land redistributed during the foregoing six years, amounting to 18,352,275 hectares, exceeds by more than double the area parceled out in all the preceding 17 years, or since the initiation of the agrarian reform. Approximately one-third of Mexico's population of 20,000,000 obtains its livelihood upon such redistributed lands."

The government invested 160,000,000 pesos in 57 irrigation projects to reclaim extensive arid lands, including the three great dams of Río Yaqui-Angostura in Sonora, the Palmito in Durango and Río San Juan, and El Azúcar in Tamaulipas. More than 300,000,000 pesos were invested in road-building and railroad construction to unify the country through a modern system of communications. The Pan American Highway was opened from Laredo, Tex., to Mexico City in 1936. Another 100,000,000 pesos were laid out for hydraulic power plants, the establishment of agricultural training stations, and the deepening of harbors. Great progress was made in education and health. The country enjoyed peace and stability. Early in 1938 the National Revolutionary Party was reorganized to include all workers, peasants, soldiers, and professional and white-collar workers under the new name of the Party of the Mexican Revolution. It is the dominant political group of the nation, and nomination by it is tantamount to election. The P.R.M. is not, in the words of recent biographers of Cárdenas, "an organization of the elite, such as the Communist Party of the Soviet Union, the Italian Fascist Party, and the German N.S.D.A.P." Mexico has more than a dozen other legal political parties, ranging from the extreme right to the extreme left.

Highlight of 1940 was the campaign for the presidency between Gen. Manuel Avila Camacho, former minister of national defense, candidate of the P.R.M., and Gen. Juan Andreu Almazán of Monterrey, one of the best generals in the Mexican army and one of the richest men in Mexico. On September 1, two months after the election, the Mexican Congress announced the official count and confirmed the election of Avila Camacho by an overwhelming majority. Since his inauguration on Dec. 1, 1940, Avila Camacho has on several occasions displayed his friendship for the United States and has taken notable steps to co-operate with all the American nations in hemisphere defense. He effected a friendly settlement between the United States and Mexico of major questions which had been open for many years. On Nov. 19, 1941, agreements were signed by Francisco Castillo Nájera, the Mexican ambassador, and U. S. Secretary of State Cordell Hull. These agreements called for a settlement of the long-pending dispute over the expropriation of U. S. oil properties in Mexico and for the payment by Mexico of $40,000,000 in full settlement of general and agrarian claims, aside from oil, by U. S. citizens against Mexico; they also announced the intention to negotiate a reciprocal trade agreement, an agreement for financial assistance to Mexico to stabilize the peso, an agreement to purchase newly mined Mexican silver, and a $30,000,000 loan to assist in the financing of Mexico's highway construction program.

As a result of improved communications and a favorable rate of exchange, travel from the United States has increased considerably. Railroads have improved their schedules, airways have shortened the distance from U. S. cities, boat excursions have become increasingly popular, and the Pan American Highway into Mexico is admittedly one of the most fascinating routes of the continent.

THE PEOPLE

For all of its 767,000 square miles Mexico has only 20,000,000 inhabitants, a little less than the population of New York and Pennsylvania combined. Yet Mexico is by far the most densely populated of the larger Latin American countries. The great plateau of south central Mexico, comprising only one-sixth of the country's area, contains two-thirds of the cities and nearly two-thirds of the population. Mexico City, on this plateau, has a population five times that of the second largest city, Guadalajara, and is the national capital. In Mexico City reside many intellectuals, artists, scientists, and scholars, who are largely responsible for giving it the character of a cosmopolitan city. The tropical plains in the south and the arid land in the north are very thinly populated.

The Mexican nation may be divided roughly into three racial groups: 10 per cent white, mostly of pure European, largely Spanish, descent with a sprinkling of U. S. nationals; 30 per cent pure Indian, of 50-odd tribes and dialects, the descendants of the indigenous population of inhabited Mexico before the Spanish conquest; and 60 per cent mixed or mestizo, a blend of white and Indian. There are also tiny minorities of Chinese, Japanese, Arabs, and Negroes. The sophisticated minority is urban in character and European in origin, while the aboriginal tribes —such as the Tarahumare, the Tepehuane, the Cora, and the Huichol of the northwest and the Lacandones of the south—remain largely primitive. Between is the vast majority, whose culture, according to Mexican anthropologists, is neither tribal nor cosmopolitan. From the upper classes to the poorest field workers Mexicans are invariably courteous and kindly. They are eloquent, with a natural tendency toward exaggeration, somewhat prone to flattery, and fond of outward display and ceremony. A marked politeness of manner is something that the foreigner should cultivate; the slightest indication of brusqueness or discourtesy is looked upon as ill-bred in Mexico. Mexicans are very hospitable; they enjoy dining with genial friends, discussing the news of the day volubly and with good humor. T. Philip Terry, in his Guide to Mexico, remarks that the best-liked visitors are those who are amiable, tolerant, and polite; that is, simpático or appreciative. A temporary adoption of the Mexican's ways and customs aids the traveler immensely.

The white Mexicans are mostly Spanish in appearance, slender and with dark hair and eyes. In the tropical areas their skin is usually sallow, but in the colder regions rosy cheeks and even fair hair are seen. Aquiline noses and thin lips are common. These people are lively and intelligent, active, and generally expert riders and dancers. Though passionate and sometimes vain, they invariably maintain a dignified and polite bearing. Mexican society of the upper class is far more exclusive and old-fashioned than Spanish society in Madrid, though the strict system of supervision of children is slowly breaking down under the pressure of foreign example and education. Family ties are close, and children display love and respect for their parents.

The mestizos or people of mixed blood are a homogeneous race in so far as they speak Spanish, the language of the Creoles, with only slight differences of pronunciation, have the same customs, and usually have the same religion. They show the same general characteristics as other Spanish American peoples whose Spanish manners and customs have been modified by native blood and traditions and the influence of a tropical climate. The dissimilar races from whom the Mexicans have sprung, however, are not as yet sufficiently fused to form a representative type. Every degree between European and Indian is represented, and there are Negro and other strains. In consequence of the extremely mixed physical heritage of the people, practically no color prejudice exists in Mexico; the varied mestizo population is classified rather according to education and position. The mestizos are seldom above middle stature. They usually have thick dark hair, brown or black eyes, and light brown skin. The small hands and feet and the flashing white teeth of the Indian along with the high forehead and aquiline nose of the Spaniard are often seen.

It is difficult to ascertain the exact number of Indians, because no distinct line is drawn between Indian and mestizo. Names, invariably Spanish, furnish no clue. As a result of living for centuries in localities of widely differing elevation, atmospheric pressure, temperature, humidity, foods, and diseases the Indians differ among themselves in color, physique, and temperament. Most, however, are rather short, with reddish brown skin, slightly prominent cheekbones, low forehead, wide nose, and fairly thick lips; eyes are large and black, the hair black, straight, and coarse; hands and feet are finely made. Though slender, the Indians are strong. They strike foreigners as sad-looking, but they are really a cheerful people. Brave and capable of great endurance, making good soldiers if necessary, the Indians are nevertheless by nature quiet, serious, amiable, and peaceful. They are agriculturists, not hunters. Their standard of life, though low, is comparable with that of southeastern Europe rather than with that of aborigines. The Indian diet consists of tortillas or flat corn cakes, frijoles or beans, chile, potatoes, and sometimes meat. Indian houses are generally one-room huts of adobe or, on the high plateau, wooden shingles. The Indian man wears simple cotton trousers and shirt with a sarape or colored blanket for warmth and a large wide-brimmed hat. The woman's usual garments are a sleeveless blouse, a skirt, and a rebozo or shawl. In some areas, especially Tehuantepec, elaborate costumes are worn on holidays.

The outstanding Indian linguistic families in Mexico, each with its own customs and racial characteristics as well as dialect, according to the 1930 census, are as follows: Nahuatl (685,389), of which the Aztec tribes were the most conspicuous and prominent before the conquest; Pima (68,210), in the western and northern states as far south as Guadalajara; Yuma (125), the remnants of a once great tribe occupying the peninsula of Lower California; Seri (160), in dwindling numbers in the state of Sonora and on Tiburón Island off the coast; Tarasca (44,371), in Michoacán, Guerrero, and Jalisco; Zoque-Mixe (96,607), mostly in Oaxaca, though also in Guerrero and Puebla; Totonac (94,211), in the northern part of Puebla and Veracruz; Mixtec-Zapotec (501,131), mostly in Oaxaca; Otomí (299,742), spread over Guanajuato, Hidalgo, Querétaro, San Luis Potosí, and Michoacán; Maya-Quiché (457,628), in Yucatán, Chiapas, and Veracruz (41,271 Huastecas); Matlatzinca (1167), dwelling under various tribal names in Oaxaca; and Algonquin (495), in Coahuila.

The Indian heritage is of paramount importance in any comparison of Mexico with the United States. Robert Redfield, dean of social sciences at the university of Chicago and an authority on Mexican folk culture, has written that "it is probably safe to say that biologically speaking Mexico is 300 times as Indian as the United States." If the Indian traditions were to be raveled out of present-day Mexican life the pattern would disintegrate. The Indian's influence is present in food, clothing, and the market system. It is found in the churches, in the general Mexican philosophy of life, in social organization. This does not imply that Mexico is an Indian nation. But whatever has been adopted from the white man's culture the Indians have managed to stamp with their own mark. The ultimate aim of the Mexican revolution is to fuse the Indian way of life with whatever is valuable in contemporary civilization, integrating Indian qualities into modern society without at the same time destroying them.

Over 90 per cent of the Mexican people are of the Roman Catholic faith. The attempts of the Mexican government to enforce constitutional provisions affecting religion—attempts which resulted in friction with the Catholic Church—were softened during the latter part of President Cárdenas' administration (1934-40). His successor, President Avila Camacho, has displayed an even more sympathetic attitude toward the Church.

While Spanish is the official language, a large percentage of the Indians speak their various tribal tongues only. Because of environment and Indian influence, Mexican Spanish differs somewhat from the mother tongue in pronunciation, vocabulary, and idiomatic expression. It is pronounced more softly, but is at the same time virile and rich. English is spoken, especially in regions popular with travelers. Nevertheless the traveler will benefit by acquiring a simple Spanish vocabulary. Two books that are helpful for this purpose are T. Philip Terry's Short Cut to Spanish and Frances Toor's Spanish for Your Mexican and Cuban Visits.

Mexicans have definite opinions regarding their neighbors to the north. For example, they are opposed to standardization, which seems to them to indicate a lack of personality. As Rafael Heliodoro Valle, Mexican journalist and eminent bibliographer, has explained: "When we [Mexicans] order ham and eggs or hot dogs, whether in San Francisco, Boston, New Orleans, or Chicago, we are exasperated to find that each dish seems to have been prepared by the same cook, all being identical in flavor, size, and price. This is not the case in Mexico, where everything—the songs, the liquors, the meals, the likes and dislikes of the people—is very diverse. For Mexico is a country of contrasts, not of similarities." Yet Mexicans admit that there is a strong tendency to imitate the United States not only in that which is worthy of imitation but in much that is not. Señor Valle, writing before the United States went to war, continued: "When it concerns our better-class journalism, no one can deny that the Mexican press follows the principal outlines of that of the United States, especially in the matter of format and in the scandalous, or yellow, note. . . .

"Anything that happens in the United States is news in Mexico. This is shown by our daily press, which interested itself to an extraordinary degree in the result of the last presidential election in the United States. Besides, the public is always interested in the smallest details of the cable news of the international policies of the United States. This is particularly true when there is news of a difference of opinion with Japan—a country which, we think, the United States will sooner or later have to fight. . . . On less serious topics, I might add that the Mexican sporting public gets very much exercised over reports of the baseball and boxing world championship contests, while the public is avid for news of your moving picture stars."

THE LAND

The republic of Mexico is divided into 28 states, two territories, and a Federal District. Its boundaries are the United States on the north, the long curve of the Gulf of Mexico and the Caribbean Sea on the east, Guatemala and British Honduras on the southeast, and the Pacific Ocean on the south and west. With an area of over 767,000 square miles, Mexico is 19 times the size of Ohio, four times the size of Spain, and nearly six and a half times as large as Italy.

States and territories may be conveniently classified in geographical groupings. The central states, including the Federal District, consist of Aguascalientes, Durango, Guanajuato, Hidalgo, México, Morelos, Puebla, Querétaro, San Luis Potosí, Tlaxcala, and Zacatecas; Gulf states: Campeche, Tabasco, Tamaulipas, Veracruz, Yucatán, and the neighboring territory of Quintana Roo; N states: Chihuahua, Coahuila, Nuevo León, and Sonora; Pacific states: Colima, Chiapas, Guerrero, Jalisco, Michoacán, Nayarit, Oaxaca, Sinaloa, and the territory of Baja (Lower) California.

The area of Mexico may be divided physically into the central plateau, the mountains of the Sierra Madre, the coastal plains (Atlantic, Gulf, and Pacific), the peninsulas of Lower California and Yucatán, the isthmus of Tehuantepec, and the Chiapas highlands. The central plateau, comprising central and N portions of the republic, is for the most part fairly level, gradually rising in altitude from about 3600 feet in the vicinity of El Paso, Tex., at the United States border, to a range of mountains of 8000-9000 feet. E and W of the plateau are the Sierra Madre Oriental, which follows the coast of the Gulf of Mexico, and the

Sierra Madre Occidental, bordering the Pacific coastal area. S and SE of Mexico City lie the broken plateau of the Mesa del Sur and the Chiapas highlands. On the central plateau, with some few exceptions, are the principal cities of the republic. Chief of a number of large valleys and canyons formed by transverse mountain ranges is the valley of Mexico.

Rivers are numerous in Mexico, but few are navigable. Exceptions are the Río Grijalva and the Río Usumacinta in the tropical SE states, emptying into the Gulf of Mexico. These rivers were the only means of transportation in the region until the advent of aviation. The latter river, 450 miles long, suggests the Mississippi in its majestic volume. The Río Grande del Norte flows for over 1000 miles between the United States and Mexico but is useless for navigation during most of the year. The Río Yaqui in Sonora, navigable for small boats, is 391 miles long and empties into the Gulf of California. The Río Balsas, 428 miles long, in the states of Oaxaca and Guerrero, empties into the Pacific. The Río Pánuco in the east, 360 miles long, empties into the Gulf of Mexico. The Río Grande de Santiago, 624 miles long, flows into the Pacific and is called the Lerma before reaching Lake Chapala. Many of the rivers are used as sources of waterpower and for purposes of irrigation.

Aside from coastal lagoons Mexico has few large lakes. Lake Chapala, SE of the city of Guadalajara, 70 miles long and 20 miles wide, is the largest. Lake Pátzcuaro and Lake Cuitzeo in Michoacán and Lake Tamiahua in Veracruz are known for their beauty and attractive surroundings. The lakes of Texcoco, Xochimilco, and Chalco in the valley of Mexico are of historical interest. Many small lakes scattered throughout the mountain area, justly famous for their beauty, have been developed as summer resorts.

Mexico possesses no great natural and well-placed harbors, though 55 ports exist. The chief of them, Veracruz and Tampico on the E coast, have been greatly improved by the government. Puerto México or Coatzacoalcos and Frontera are also on the E coast. On the Pacific side is Acapulco, one of the ideal harbors of the world in spite of its smallness. Manzanillo, next in importance on the W coast, is the terminus of the only direct railroad line from Mexico City to the Pacific. Salina Cruz in Oaxaca, the Pacific terminus of the Tehuantepec National Railway; Mazatlán in Sinaloa, chief port of the Southern Pacific Railway of Mexico, and Guaymas in Sonora are also on the W coast.

Mexico's climate ranges from tropical to cold according to altitude. Tierra caliente or hot lowland, steamy, swampy, and jungle-bound, extends from sea level up to about 3000 feet and includes the seacoast regions, the Yucatán peninsula, the isthmus of Tehuantepec, much of Chiapas, Oaxaca, and Guerrero, and part of the E plateau. In tierra templada or the temperate zone, the region between the altitudes of 3000 and 6500 feet, summers do not have the humidity of the lowland, and winters are spared the cold winds of the highland. From 6500 feet elevation up to the snow line is tierra fría or the cold zone. In the lower regions of this climatic zone are many of the principal cities, including Mexico City. The days are comfortably warm and the nights cool. A fourth zone, tierra helada or frozen land, includes the mountain peaks above the snow line. Indian villages are found even at the tree line, at 10,000 feet altitude or more. Mexico has two seasons, the rainy, June-September inclusive, and the dry, which is all the rest of the year. These seasons vary somewhat with altitude and latitude.

The seacoast regions, the isthmus of Tehuantepec, the Yucatán peninsula, the S states of Oaxaca and Guerrero, and the slopes of the sierras are thickly covered with forests. Tree varieties range from pine and oak to valuable hardwoods and dyewoods. Desert virtually dominates N Mexico and Lower California, with numerous species of cacti as the characteristic flora. The regions of tierra caliente are the richest; there the vegetation is amazing in its luxuriant growth. The central plateau, which has been the most thickly settled part of the country from remotest antiquity, is very fertile but somewhat dry. The most important plants are wheat, corn, sugar cane, tobacco, cotton, rubber, henequen, maguey, vanilla, ginger, chicle, castor oil, and cacao; woods and fruits of the temperate and tropical zones are also grown.

In spite of somewhat unfavorable topography Mexico is essentially an agricultural country, and approximately 77 per cent of the employed population makes its living in rural industries. Corn, the basic food of the people from antiquity, remains the chief crop. Other important crops are beans, cereals, rice, potatoes, henequen, cotton, coffee, sugar, tobacco, and innumerable varieties of fruit and vegetables— bananas, tomatoes, chickpeas, etc. Cattle raising is also very important. The most important and highly developed industries are mining and oil production. Mexico ranks high among the nations of the world in production of silver, gold, lead, zinc, copper, antimony, iron, mercury, and tin. The chief mineral zone comprises an area 50 miles wide extending from the state of Chihuahua, N, to a S point in the isthmus of Tehuantepec, then NE to Chiapas. Manufacturing is developing with great strides. The principal manufactures are textiles, foodstuffs, foundry products, leather goods, paper, pottery, cement, cigars and cigarettes, clothing, toilet goods, lumber and forest products, soft drinks, glassware, candles, matches, furniture, paints and varnishes, bricks and tiles, printing, photography, brewing, distilling, and meat products. The traveler is likely to be more interested in such handicrafts as wrought silver, hammered jewelry, carved wood, glassware, tiles, tooled leather, sarapes or blankets, embroidery, and lacquered ware.

ART AND ARCHITECTURE

BY GEORGE KUBLER

During the colonial era Mexico was both a province and a metropolitan area. It was provincial as regards Spain, metropolitan with respect to the remainder of America—metropolitan because the fundamental problems of colonial life were first solved in Mexico and because these solutions were widely adopted elsewhere in the Spanish colonial world. The great task at all times was to bring the dense Indian populations of high but alien culture into the Christian family. The means selected to achieve that end depended heavily on art and architecture. For proper indoctrination the Indians had to be kept together; hence their living in towns of European style became necessary. If they were to be Christians it was essential that they worship in Christian churches and chapels and that their entire communal life be centered in the Church. If their economic activity was to become highly productive an ample water supply, adequate communications, and a central government were indispensable. In such a framework architecture, painting, and sculpture all served one and the same purpose, not to provide esthetic gratification alone, but to equip the Christian community. The architects planned and built towns whose edifices were to house a Christian state rather than an Indian tribe (e.g. Tula in Hidalgo, 1529; Uruapan in Michoacán, 1533; or Huaquechula in Puebla, 1533). The sculptors and the painters had as their task the illustration of Christian life by means of symbol and figure.

In this work the colonists met with prolonged resistance. The Indian civilizations of Mexico were too firmly rooted to vanish overnight, and their survival within the new culture is obvious everywhere. The architects, for instance, rarely were able to experiment with novel building forms, because the available laboring population held to its own traditional techniques. In sculpture and painting as well, Indian resistance to Christian teachings made it difficult for craftsmen to experiment with new kinds of form. The ecclesiastical market for their work demanded stereotyped, unequivocal illustrations of Christian doctrine. Nevertheless one outlet was always available to creative energies, for simplicity of structure and lucidity of doctrine were known to have more effect upon the Indians if presented in sumptuous dress. Indeed colonial art, however monotonous and insistent in its basic forms, always tended toward rich materials, ornamental profuseness, and sensuous immediacy. The framework in which such decorative exuberance occurred was always architectural; few paintings and almost no sculpture were produced for use other than in the most direct and intimate union with architecture. The church itself was the heart of the community, and all artistic effort was directed toward its embellishment.

The colonial art of Mexico, then, is a religious art of simple content, under architectural control, but sumptuous as to form. Its overwhelming quantity defies treatment within the limits of this guide. The territory of the republic contains over 13,000 churches, each with its paintings, sculpture, and furniture. Manuel Toussaint, the eminent historian, has gathered information about some 500 colonial painters in Mexico alone. The problem of choice is almost insuperable; for present purposes, however, it will suffice to outline a few principles whereby to comprehend the bewildering variety.

The 16th century offers more architectural experiments than any other period of colonial history. It was natural that this should be so in the first years after the conquest when the forms of colonial life itself had not as yet found their expression. Speed and volume of construction were the primary requisites. The workmanship is often crude, the design amateurish. Most of it was directed by missionaries, members of the three mendicant brotherhoods, Franciscan, Dominican, and Augustinian, and in spite of its naïveté their work shows a vitality lacking in Europe, where rather less building was done than at any time during the previous four centuries. In Mexico the fortress church usually prevails, with its crenelated silhouette and the immense mass of its walls, as at Tepeaca (begun 1553) or the church of San Francisco at Huejotzingo (begun 1529), at Actopán (c. 1551) and Acolman (1555). The plan of churches is compact; the outer walls are unbroken except for a few small windows high above eye level. The churches are often roofed with rib vaults in late Gothic fashion.

Most but not all of the churches of the 16th century were fortress churches. Several examples of three-aisled edifices with wooden roofs and with Renaissance ornament recalling Tuscan work still survive, notably at Tecali (1569) in the state of Puebla, at Zacatlán de las Manzanas (begun 1555), and at Cuilapam (1555-75) in Oaxaca. Besides medieval and Renaissance forms this architecture displays elements of Moslem derivation, as in the Capilla Real (Royal Chapel) at Cholula (finished 1608), with seven aisles and scores of domes, evoking the mosque of Cordova. The form of the crenelations of the Mexican churches of this period is often rather more Moorish than European, and the artesonado or carved ceilings of Tlaxcala and of San Diego in Huejotzingo are also Moorish in their intricate geometric interlacings. Certain moldings are specifically Islamic, such as the rectangular alfiz surrounding an arched doorway.

Other monuments reveal an unusual degree of free invention. Such was the cathedral intended by Bishop Vasco de Quiroga for Pátzcuaro in Michoacán (in construction 1550), one of the strangest edifices ever designed for Christian ritual. It was to have five naves, only one of which was built, radiating outward from a central altar. Elsewhere other forms also display originality. There was, for instance, the churchyard with its open chapel. The churchyard, surrounded by crenelated walls, was the community center. Since the church was often too small to accommodate the immense congregations of the time a special chapel was built, facing out to the yard. Mass was celebrated in the chapel before great outdoor congregations. Such open-air worship evokes both the mosques of Islam and the great outdoor crowds of the pre-conquest Indian religious cults assembled at the base of a pyramidal structure over whose surfaces unfolded a processional ritual.

All this variety of solutions prevails, however, only in the architecture by friars, produced for Indian use. In the construction of cathedrals, stimulated by the bishops in the European cities of New Spain, a radically different attitude prevailed (with the exception of Pátzcuaro, the work of an independent genius, Bishop Vasco de Quiroga). Most bishops were opposed to the friars on many issues, and among these was the question of architectural style. The first cathedrals, before 1550, were impermanent, unpretentious constructions; but after 1560, when the colony had achieved some form and order, the bishops projected large edifices which reveal not the eclectic and inventive style of the missionaries but a classicizing formula derived from the style developed by Juan de Herrera in the Escorial (1562-84, built for Philip II of Spain). The cathedrals of Mexico City and Puebla show more or less faithful variants of Herreran classicism of an extraordinary severity and harmony of form. The style is in direct opposition to the amateurish solutions of the friars; it represents Hispanism as against Indianism, the authority of the crown—since bishops were nominated by the king—as against the tender paternalism of the mendicant missionaries.

Few 16th-century buildings for civilian use survive today. The house which Hernán Cortés built for himself at Cuernavaca is a good example, a small palace of quasi-military character, with gracious colonnades flanked by heavy outer wings.

Both inside and outside the buildings a rich painted and carved decoration was displayed. The painting was done either as fresco decoration extending over large masonry surfaces or on canvases set into the framework of a retablo or altarpiece. Characteristic examples of both kinds may be seen in the church of San Francisco at Huejotzingo, Acolman, or Cuauhtinchan, where the walls of the conventual buildings and churches were adorned with designs borrowed from European book illustrations. The names of several painters have been preserved; for example, Juan Gerson painted in a style reminiscent of Dirk Bouts at Tecamachalco in 1562; Simón Pereyns painted the Italianate scenes in the altarpiece in the church of San Francisco at Huejotzingo in 1580, and many Indians, trained in the Flemish and Italian manners, were active throughout New Spain and New Galicia. The façades were treated with many styles of carved ornament: a Gothic rose window sometimes occurs, as at Yecapixtla in Puebla or Atotonilco de Tula in Hidalgo; Renaissance frontispieces are more than common, done in a manner close to the Spanish Plateresque (Acolman in Hidalgo; Tlalmanalco in the state of México), while in the church of San Francisco at Huejotzingo the façade was treated with forms derived from the luxuriant Manueline style of Portugal.

From southern Peru to New Mexico the 17th century was an era of extraordinary building activity. The control of religious life passed from the friars, who withdrew to the border provinces, into the hands of the secular clergy. Thousands upon thousands of parish churches were built. The great shift, therefore, was from the sumptuous monastic establishment of the missionaries to the much more simple parroquia or parochial church. Plan, structure, and mass remained simple (e.g., the convent at Churubusco outside Mexico City; La Merced in the capital, 1634-1703). Few Baroque spatial experiments were undertaken; an exception is the façade of La Soledad in Oaxaca (1682-90). The object was rather to provide a serviceable shell upon which a rich decoration might be displayed. The plan was normally cruciform, with extensive transepts in the larger buildings, where towering altarpieces could be erected. The great novelty was the uniform use of the dome at the crossing of nave and transept; through the windows of its drum floods of light streamed down into the church. The façade was treated with massive towers, of which only one was usually completed. The dome and the tower were the most characteristic forms of the century. The dome, a device intended to secure dynamic lighting of the interior, was the only concession made to the Baroque taste of contemporary Europe. The dome is the most ubiquitous trait of the Mexican architectural scene; its profile marks the landscape everywhere, and it has become the form upon which townsmen lavish their most costly attentions, covering it with gold-leaf or glazed tiles even after the church itself has fallen into ruins.

At the same time great demands were made upon the painters of the day. As the thousands of parochial churches were built paintings were needed to decorate the walls and altarpieces. The painters were organized in well-defined guilds, but it remained a question, as in Spain, whether painting were a liberal or a mechanical art. The painter occupied an uncertain social position; the tendency was to regard him as a craftsman rather than as an artist, and the mediocrity of his work was related to the excessive volume he was required to produce. Yet the 17th century has been called the golden age of Mexican colonial painting, and indeed the technical level of the work was high. Its content expressed the ascetic mysticism of the Spanish school, and the painting was genuinely Baroque in its formal values, more so than the architecture it decorated. Several large altarpieces were done by Juan de Arrue (1565-1637) early in the century and by the erudite Biscayan painter Baltasar de Echave Orio (1548-1630), whose work reveals the influence of the Italian Baroque painters, the Caracci and Caravaggio. His pupils Luis Juárez (died 1635), José Juárez (active 1642-60), and Baltasar de Echave Ibia (1583-16?) depended more upon Spanish traditions than did their master. Thus José Juárez, as well as Sebastián de Arteaga (1610-36?) and Juan Tinoco (active c. 1680-90), show the effects of a close study of the work of the great Spanish painter Zurbarán. The work of Alonso López de Herrera (active 1609-50), a Creole—white of race, but born in America—shows some preoccupation with strong perspective effects and reveals perhaps the influence of a follower of Leonardo da Vinci in Valencia, Juan de Juanes. Pedro Ramírez (active 1666-78) and Baltasar de Echave Rioja (1632-82, the last of the Echave sequence of painters) borrowed from the work of Rubens, then available in prints. Juan de Correa (in Mexico after 1674; died c. 1738) and Cristóbal de Villalpando (1649-1714) both worked in the sacristy of the cathedral of Mexico City, producing gigantic canvases of a somber style. Other painters, Nicolás Correa (late 17th century) and Diego Becerra (late 17th century), were Creoles also, but it is curious to note that in Creole work no specifically Mexican subjects were thought worthy of representation, although the writers of the time revealed an intense love of Mexico, shown in many passages of the ecclesiastical histories. A curious exception, however, may be seen at Ozumba near Amecameca, where an anonymous painter depicted scenes from the early activity of the missionaries in a style strangely suggestive of the modern Mexican mural style.

Mexican sculpture of the 17th century rarely achieved independent plastic authority. It consisted of low-relief decorations for inner and outer walls, often of an amazing richness and complexity of design, as in the chapel of the Rosary in Santo Domingo at Puebla (decorated, 1632-59, by Pedro García Durán and Juan Bautista Alarcón). Rich color and gilding were extensively used, but the compositions betray no energetic inventiveness; rather do they represent interminable variations upon a few basic themes. The individual forms have rich body and substance; they extend indefinitely over the wall surfaces, never really disguising those surfaces, but offering a festive gilded screen, behind which the sense of a solid, simple wall remains intact. In the altarpieces the character of the style is clearly seen as a simple arrangement of columns and entablatures gilded, carved, and painted on every possible surface. The structural form is never disguised; only its surfaces are attacked.

The term Ultra-Baroque has long been used to describe the style of the churches and civil buildings of the middle of the 18th century in Mexico. It is an apt term, for it expresses two ideas, that of a Baroque style even more dynamic than its European predecessors of the 17th century, as well as the idea of an overseas style; America, indeed, was often described as the ultramarine domain of the Spanish crown. Unlike the European Baroque the Mexican style rarely offers the spectacle of a complicated treatment of real space; the walls inclose a volume that is usually clear and simple in all its extensions, and the exceptions are few, such as the lovely Pocito chapel near the Guadalupe shrine outside Mexico City, built by Francisco Guerrero y Torres (between 1777 and 1791). The ornamental language of the Ultra-Baroque, however, is of great intricacy, specially in the façades, altarpieces, window profiles, and balustrades. On the façades an exceptional use of color prevailed. In the valley of Mexico a deep red stone of volcanic origin called tezontle was used to contrast with the white trim. In Puebla colored tiles covered the entire façade, their brilliance alternating with the blinding whiteness of a stucco ornament treated as if it were confectioner's sugar (Casa del Alfeñique, Puebla, 1790, attributed to Antonio de Santa María Inchaúrregui). Worth close attention in the churches is the variety and depth of the ornamental forms of the altarpieces. The wall is lost in a screen of gilded pedestals, shafts, moldings, and scrolls standing out in several planes of relief from a background which is like a golden cave of unknown depth and structure (La Enseñanza, Mexico City, 1754). The gold leaf is sometimes burnished, sometimes dull, sometimes overlaid with other metallic colors, and its use is always calculated to impress the spectator with the sensation of a new kind of reality having nothing to do with the world outside the church; it is the atmosphere of ecstatic devotion and mystic rapture; the altar assaults the senses with its towering antigravitational masses, compelling the eye upward and driving the spectator's knees to the floor, inclosing him within an aura of gilded light and color. The traditional criticism of this architecture has been that it is lawless and profligate, tasteless and over-ornate. But it is the opposite of lawless; such forms were organized by one of the most carefully calculated ornamental disciplines that man has ever devised.

It is difficult to identify the originators of the Ultra-Baroque style in Mexico. In all likelihood many of its postulates were formed in a long anonymous tradition of cabinetmaking, woodworking, and gilding in which certain ornamental suggestions, derived perhaps from contemporary European publications on furniture, were translated into a monumental scale and organized by a consistent esthetic principle. A few architects are closely associated with the style in the decades just before and after the middle of the century. Lorenzo Rodríguez was the most notable artist of this group; to him may be credited the remarkable Sagrario (1749-68) flanking the east side of the cathedral in Mexico City, as well as the façades of La Santísima Trinidad in Mexico City (1755-86) and the Jesuit church at Tepozotlán (built 1670-82; restored 1750; new façade 1760-62), about an hour's drive north of the capital. The church of San Sebastián and Santa Prisca in Taxco

(1751-59) cannot be attributed to any single architect, for both Diego Durán and Juan Caballero, as well as others, are mentioned; but its ornamental forms are Ultra-Baroque, presenting great homogeneity and distinction of workmanship.

Important regional differences existed, nevertheless, in 18th-century architecture. The style of Guadalajara (Palacio del Gobierno, 1774) differs from that of Morelia (museum of Michoacán, 1775); Oaxaca and Puebla have quite distinct manners, and the differences are usually to be attributed to local materials, such as the tile industry in Puebla, the fine green stone of Oaxaca, and the golden flesh-colored rock of Morelia. Each region, furthermore, has its quota of survivals from older styles. Guadalajara (Santa Mónica, finished 1730) and certain northern cities such as Zacatecas maintained the ornamental profusion of the 17th century until long after 1750. Civil and domestic architecture deserve a special study. Notable traits in the residential buildings are the subtle, almost perverse skill of the stonecutters in fashioning moldings and arches. In the cities the courtyards of the palaces or town houses invariably possess studied proportions and an ample splendor. An excellent example is the so-called Casa Iturbide in Mexico City by Francisco Guerrero y Torres. Stairwells are always nobly proportioned, and the window treatments reveal great ingenuity and variety of form, while the ornamental language is vigorous, containing forms like those of the altarpieces.

Apart from the anonymous craftsmen of the altarpieces few sculptors as such are known in the 18th century. In Puebla three craftsmen were active toward the middle of the century, José Antonio Villegas Cora, Zacarías Cora, and José Villegas. Their work consisted of figures of saints and of the Virgin for the churches of Puebla and Mexico City in a style which sometimes might pass for that of the Spaniard, Alonso Cano. In Querétaro a similar school of sculptors was active about the same time; this group was composed of Mariano Perusquia, who also worked in Guadalajara, Mariano Arce, and Mariano Montenegro. Their work may be seen in the churches of Santa Clara and San Felipe in Querétaro.

The painting of the 18th century is in general as facile and empty as the architecture is complex and dense. The typical emplacement for painting was as a decoration in the altarpiece; here and there pieces of canvas were used as points of rest, as flat surfaces of an agreeable tonality, affording relief from the surrounding vortex of gilded ornament. Often, of course, canvases were painted for independent display as paintings without reference to the altarpiece, but in either case the painting shows haste and facility, shallow content, and derivative forms. At the very beginning of the century two brothers were active, Nicolás Rodríguez Juárez (1667-1734) and Juan Rodríguez Juárez (1675-1728), the sons of Antonio Rodríguez and the grandsons of José Juárez. Nicolás was known chiefly as a portraitist and was overshadowed by Juan, called the Mexican Apelles, whose brilliant and luminous manner, achieved toward the end of his life, became decisive for other Mexican painters in the latter part of the century. José Ibarra (1688-1756), a pupil of Juan Correa, developed a style which was based, like that of his master, on engravings of the work of Rubens and was later qualified by a close imitation of Murillo, under the influence of a Spaniard, Francisco Gómez de Valencia, who arrived in Mexico about the middle of the century. Miguel Cabrera (1695-1768) enjoyed the patronage of the Jesuits and was by far the most prolific painter of his time, maintaining a large workshop from which countless canvases went to ecclesiastical clients throughout the colony. His work shows casual, thinly painted forms, expressive of tenderness and pathos, in a technique that has withstood time very poorly indeed. Rather more conscientious than Cabrera was his pupil José de Alcíbar (born 1731), who became one of the first members of the Academy of San Carlos (founded in 1783). Another member of Cabrera's large school was Francisco Antonio Vallejo (active 1761-74).

As always in Mexico, alongside such activity there existed a strong tradition of popular art; 18th-century examples may be seen in various collections throughout the republic, notably in the National Museum in Mexico City, the Academy of Fine Arts in Puebla, the Museum of Michoacán in Morelia, and the State Museum in Guadalajara. It is likely that the present strength of the modern Mexican school derives more from such a long tradition of popular, nonacademic arts than from the affluent and active imitators of European style whose names have been preserved.

The great movements that caused Spain's American empire to break away from her in the early 19th century were reflected in the work of several artists who began life as viceregal subjects and ended their careers as citizens of the new Mexican republic. Francisco Eduardo Tresguerras (born in Celaya 1759; died 1833) was perhaps the most gifted architect Latin America ever produced. His works of the last quarter of the 18th century contain the final complications of viceregal style and reveal an original use of French rococo elements. Rocaille motives were used at Santa Clara and Santa Rosa in Querétaro on an enormous scale within the framework of the Ultra-Baroque façades and altarpieces. Later Tresguerras rejected this language of form and passed into a realm of classicizing monumentality where he worked with a distinction entitling him to a high position among the architects of the world in his generation (El Carmen in Celaya, 1804). The Spaniard, Manuel Tolsá (1755-1816), whose adult life was largely spent in Mexico, also underwent a change of style, between his ornate additions to the façade of the cathedral of Mexico City and his severe later style as represented in the school of mines (Palacio de Minería, 1797-1813). Tolsá produced the equestrian statue of Charles IV located at the head of the Paseo Reforma, the first large bronze figure cast in America, in 1803. Among the painters of the first third of the 19th century, José Luis Rodríguez Alconedo (1761-1815), also active as a silversmith in Puebla, participated in revolutionary movements and was exiled in 1810. In Spain he learned to do portraits in pastel which show some acquaintance with the work of Goya.

During the 19th century the arts were maintained in Mexico by the professors and members of the Academy of San Carlos, founded in 1783. Many of them were mediocre; yet they nursed a tradition and many techniques through the interminable political disorders of the time. Thus, for instance, the long-abandoned art of mural painting was resumed by a director of the academy, Rafael Ximeno y Planes (1761-1825), in the dome of the cathedral. The academy, however, was not without its troubles, undergoing reorganization in 1843 and being staffed with transient talents from Europe. Lorenzo de la Hidalga

(1810-72) came from Spain and replaced the Ultra-Baroque high altar of the cathedral of Mexico with a mediocre neo-classic tabernacle. Xavier Cavallari brought from Italy the archeological information of a revival stylist and executed the Florentine façade of the academy about 1857. Among the painters of the middle of the century were Pelegrin Clavé, the Italian Landesi, Cordero the muralist, and many others.

As in the preceding century, beside the professional artists brought to Mexico by a landed aristocracy more at home in Europe than in America, there flourished an extensive popular art. Lithography, for instance, introduced by Claudio Linati of Parma in 1826, rapidly became the vehicle for many modes of popular expression, its peculiar technical qualities allowing it a wide diffusion not possible for engravings or etchings. Ever since, lithography has been cultivated in Mexico, and it is important to note its resurgence as a medium for genuine artistic expression at the hands of such modern masters as Jean Charlot, Carlos Orozco Romero, Carlos Mérida, Dosamantes, and most of all José Clemente Orozco, the great muralist. A comparable phenomenon is the extraordinary quantity of popular portraiture done during the 19th century. The most direct and appealing master of this class was José María Estrada (active in Guadalajara, 1830-60). Estrada's psychological penetration overcame the limitations of his provincial technique. The sitters were generally members of the urban middle classes to whom the aristocratic privilege of having one's individuality recorded had previously been denied. It is likely that Estrada's portraits and those by his anonymous contemporaries were stimulated by the same demand that led to the invention of photography, namely the wish of large numbers of the middle classes to have inexpensive likenesses. With such painting as Estrada's and with photography, introduced only after 1840, the Mexican people became the true patrons of the arts of form. Lithography likewise represents a democratic art at low cost, capable of wide distribution and controlled by popular sentiment; witness the immense production of José Guadalupe Posada (active 1877-1913).

As for the academic painters of the end of the century, the men who taught Diego Rivera were not possessed of the vitality of their pupil, although their work prepared many phases of the modern school. Julio Ruelas (1870-1907) had a feeling for gruesome caricature and burlesque. Santiago Rebull (1829-1902) allowed his students the privilege of studies from nature as well as subject matter taken from Mexican history. The individual qualities of the Mexican landscape were first defined by José María Velasco (1840-1912), whose technique and scholarship were of a high order. Félix Parra (1845-1919), finally, had a vivid appreciation of Mexican archeology.

If colonial art was dominated by architecture, since 1910 it is the painters who have occupied the pre-eminent position in Mexican art. When the first great murals were painted in 1922 they were done in the corridors of colonial and neo-colonial buildings; the coherent expression of a modern attitude toward architecture was not realized until about 1929, almost 20 years after the first stirrings of the revolt in painting. Staffed by a remarkable group of talents, of whom the unquestioned leader is Juan O'Gorman (born 1905), many direct, clean designs for schools, markets, and civic buildings were carried out between 1929 and 1935. Since 1935, however, the movement has been beset by reaction; little building of the high quality of O'Gorman's School of Industrial Technics (Calle Tresguerras, Mexico City) has been achieved, and O'Gorman himself has lately turned more and more to painting. The current taste is for ornate versions of the colonial tradition, and the criticism is often heard that modern Mexican architecture is colorlessly international. Juan Legarreta's workers' housing projects (1930-34) with their immense windows were unsound, it is true, as regards the brilliant sunlight of Mexico City and the secluded family life of most Mexicans, yet his impulse was correct: to build simply and efficiently with the new materials of modern technology. Some straightforward building is being done in Mexico even now, and the neo-colonial trend of recent years is probably a vogue expressive, for the time being, of vigorous nationalist sentiments.

Sculpture as a separate vocation for artists has not had a numerous following in Mexico. The work of Luis Ortiz Monasterio has been favorably received, as well as that of Guillermo Ruiz, who attracted much attention some years ago when the School for Direct Carving was founded by him in the former convent of La Merced in Mexico City. Recently Ruiz designed the imposing monument to Morelos (1933-35) on the island of Janitzio in Lake Pátzcuaro.

Thus it is in painting that Mexican artists have excelled for more than 20 years. And if painting has had vitality and has retained meaning anywhere in the world it is in Mexico. The sudden birth of a Mexican style about 1922 is one of the most enigmatic phenomena in the history of art. It was first expressed in murals, for which Diego Rivera, Roberto Montenegro, and others had been preparing themselves through experiment and studies in Europe for about 10 years. The earliest murals were done by Roberto Montenegro and Xavier Guerrero in the church of San Pedro and San Pablo and by Ramón Alva de la Canal in the National Preparatory School in 1921. Diego Rivera also executed mural decorations in wax (encaustic) in the Bolívar Amphitheater of the National University of Mexico about this time. Rivera was most competent to undertake direction of the Mexican efforts at true fresco because of his long and deliberate technical preparation. In effect he dominated the scene until the mid '30's as Orozco has dominated it since 1935. The frescoes for the Secretariat of Public Education were begun by Rivera in 1922, and within the following five years he executed not only most of the panels (124 in number) in that building but also achieved the moving designs in the chapel of the agricultural school at Chapingo. This immense production reveals consistent unity of vision; the huge program was steadily controlled by an insistent if extravagant political doctrine, and endless new forms were created to equip his monolithic and partisan view of the world. A similar fixity of purpose dominated Rivera's conceptions for the murals in the loggia of the palace of Cortés in Cuernavaca (1929) and in the stairway of the National Palace in Mexico City (1934). Since 1936, however, Rivera has painted no further murals but has withdrawn to his studio, where he produces smaller works in an astonishing variety of techniques.

Orozco's version of the world is antithetic to Rivera's. Where Rivera maintained the grand outlines of a single ideology Orozco has been a philosophical anarchist. No doctrine animates his work; he portrays the endless variations of suffering and aspiration in compositional patterns which, unlike the centralized, stable designs of Rivera, insist on broken forms, contradictory movements, and unresolved harmonies.

Although he was a nominal member of David Alfaro Siqueiros' Syndicate of Technical Workers at the time he painted the noble frescoes of the National Preparatory School in 1922, he took part in none of its political manifestations, unlike the other artists of the group, who needed its ideological unity to express the common impulse behind their very diverse talents. Since 1935 Orozco has been awarded many great commissions for murals, in Guadalajara (the university and Cabañas Hospital), in Jiquilpan, and in the new Supreme Court building in the capital. Constantly urged by his vivid and tragic sensibility, Orozco has never been attentive to technical niceties in his painting; the will to express an entire pathology of the human spirit has led him to invent a gigantic profusion of forms which, in his recent work, are becoming less contingent, more universal.

It often happens in the history of art that when activity is most energetic and original, pairs of artists emerge to realize the opposite and contradictory possibilities of the art of their time. Such was the case in the late Renaissance with Michelangelo and Raphael and again in the 17th century with Rubens and Poussin. To understand the whole time the student cannot afford to take sides with one or the other of the pair; he must comprehend them as a single principle, one exploring what the other leaves untouched, and both together as a unit constituting the most sensitive expression of their age. Another such pair in modern Mexican painting might be defined in the persons of David Alfaro Siqueiros and Francisco Goytia. As with Rivera and Orozco, these two men constructed a whole perspective in Mexican sensibility. Siqueiros is a violent inventor of new techniques; his restless materialism drives him from sporadic artistic production of extremely high quality to a turbid political activity, while Goytia, shunning groups, cliques, and coteries, has gone deep into his own awareness of suffering for form and content, rather than to new techniques or ideologies.

PRACTICAL INFORMATION

HOW TO REACH MEXICO

From the U. S. Minimum first-class one-way steamship fare between New York and Veracruz is $100 (1941); from New Orleans to Veracruz, $50. Railroad fare from San Antonio, Tex., to Mexico City is $37, and plane fare from Brownsville, Tex., to Mexico City is $35.

BY STEAMER. New York and Cuba Mail Steamship Co.; New York office: foot of Wall St. Sailings from New York to Veracruz via Havana, Cuba. Voyage takes 5 days.

Standard Fruit and Steamship Co.; New York office: 11 Broadway; New Orleans office: 140 Carondelet St. Sailings to Veracruz from New Orleans, voyage taking 3-4 days depending on whether service is direct or via Tampico.

BY AIR. Pan American Airways; New York office: 135 East 42nd St. Has service between Brownsville, Tex., and Mexico City via Tampico, a distance of 463 miles flown inside of 3½ hours, including the stop at Tampico. This service continues from Mexico City via Tapachula to Guatemala City, where connection is made with Central American, Caribbean, and South American services of Pan American Airways.

Another Pan American Airways service is by Clippers leaving Miami, Fla., for Mérida via Havana, Cuba. Trip takes 4½ hours. At Mérida connection can be made with the Compañía Mexicana de Aviación to Mexico City.

The Compañía Mexicana de Aviación has a plane, the Californian, from Los Angeles for the following Mexican centers: Mexicali, Hermosillo, Mazatlán, Guadalajara, Mexico City, Veracruz, Minatitlán, Villahermosa, Ciudad del Carmen, Chetumal, Campeche, and Mérida. From Los Angeles to Mexico City the flight takes about 12 hours.

BY RAILROAD. Laredo, Tex., to Mexico City, via Monterrey, San Luis Potosí, and Querétaro. Air-conditioned trains run from Laredo to Mexico City (30 hours), carrying through sleeping cars from St. Louis, Mo.

Los Angeles-Mexico City, via El Paso, Tex.; Chihuahua; Torreón; Zacatecas; Aguascalientes, and Querétaro (73 hours).

Los Angeles-Mexico City, via Nogales, Ariz.; Hermosillo; Culiacán; Mazatlán; Guadalajara; Irapuato; Celaya, and Querétaro (85 hours).

BY ROAD. It is possible to drive in comfort from any part of the United States to Mexico City and some miles beyond.

The new Laredo, Tex.-Mexico City highway, a link in the great Pan American Highway which will connect all the continental nations of the Americas, extends 762 miles from the border of the United States to the Mexican capital. It is paved all the way and is in excellent condition.

From Guatemala. For railroad connections see the guide to Guatemala (p. 44); air service as above.

From Other Central American Countries. Air service as above; also coastwise vessels.

AIDS TO TRAVELERS

Mexico's Representation in the U. S. The Embassy is at 2829 16th St.,

Washington, D. C.; office of the financial attaché, 70 Pine St., New York.

Mexican consular officers are in Mobile, Ala.; Douglas, Naco, Nogales, Phoenix, and Tucson, Ariz.; Calexico, Fresno, Los Angeles, Sacramento, San Bernardino, San Diego, and San Francisco, Calif.; Denver, Colo.; Washington, D. C.; Miami, Pensacola, Salvador Aguayo, and Tampa, Fla.; Chicago, Ill.; Louisville, Ky.; New Orleans, La.; Boston, Mass.; Detroit, Mich.; Kansas City and St. Louis, Mo.; Albuquerque, N. M.; Buffalo and New York, N. Y.; Cincinnati and Cleveland, Ohio; Oklahoma City, Okla.; Portland, Ore.; Philadelphia and Pittsburgh, Pa.; Providence, R. I.; Alpine, Austin, Brownsville, Corpus Christi, Dallas, Del Rio, Eagle Pass, El Paso, Fort Worth, Galveston, Houston, Laredo, McAllen, San Antonio, and Zapata, Tex.; Salt Lake City, Utah; Norfolk, Va.; Seattle, Wash.; Milwaukee, Wis.; Colón, C. Z.; San Juan, P. R.

U. S. Representation in Mexico. The Embassy is at Calle Niza 53, Mexico City. Consular officials are maintained at La Paz, Mexicali, and Tijuana, in Lower California; Ciudad Juárez and Chihuahua, Chihuahua; Piedras Negras and Torreón, Coahuila; Manzanillo, Colima; Mexico City, D. F.; Durango, Durango; Acapulco, Guerrero; Guadalajara, Jalisco; Monterrey, Nuevo León; Salina Cruz, Oaxaca; San Luis Potosí, San Luis Potosí; Mazatlán, Sinaloa; Agua Prieta and Guaymas, Sonora; Matamoros, Nuevo Laredo, Reynosa, and Tampico, Tamaulipas; Puerto México (Coatzacoalcos) and Veracruz, Veracruz; and Mérida, Yucatán, as well as Nogales, Ariz., on the border.

Sources of Information. The Mexican national government has a Departamento de Turismo (Department of Tourism) under the Secretaría de Gobernación (Secretariat of the Interior). Its office is at Avenida 5 de Mayo and Calle Filomeno Mata, Mexico City. Other cities throughout the republic have offices of this bureau; some also have municipal tourist bureaus which will be helpful to travelers. Local chambers of commerce and branches or affiliates of the Mexican Automobile Association can be referred to. In Mexico City the Asociación Mexicana de Turismo (Mexican Tourist Association) has its headquarters at Av. Juárez 76 and the Mexican Automobile Association at Paseo Reforma 46.

Mexican petroleum distributors have organized the Pemex Travel Club for the sole purpose of giving help to U. S. automobilists. Offices are at C. Bucareli 35, Mexico City. Among the services to which a free membership in the Pemex Travel Club entitles visitors are information about tourist cards and other legal requirements; the condition of highways in Mexico and arrangement of itineraries to suit individual requirements; a list of garages, boarding houses, furnished apartments, tourist camps, and hotels; advice on shipping of baggage and packing and crating of purchases; supervision from the border to destination of convention or group tours; assistance in reserving tickets for amusements and for public functions; aid to students or others interested in special research work; care of correspondence.

Other agencies with offices in Mexico City which help travelers are the American Chamber of Commerce, Suites 18-21, Edificio Cook, C. San Juan de Letrán 24; Aguirre's Guest Tours, Av. 5 de Mayo 20; Wagons-Lits-Cook, Av. Francisco Madero 1; Wells Fargo & Co., agents for the American Express Co., Av. Francisco Madero 14; Pan American Tours, Av. 5 de Mayo 20; Reforma Travel Bureau, Hotel Reforma;

Mexico Tours, Suite 303, C. Balderas 68; Kedry's, C. Balderas 108 B; Jutra, Office 7, Av. 6 de Mayo 23.

In the United States information can be secured from the Mexican Tourist Association in the offices of the National Railways of Mexico at 11 W. 42nd St., New York, and at local offices in Chicago, El Paso, San Antonio, Los Angeles, San Francisco, and New Orleans; the Mexican Department of Tourism, 630 5th Ave., New York City; the Mexican Chamber of Commerce, 60 Wall St., New York; or Mexican consuls.

Climate. Mexico has two seasons, the rainy season (summer), June-September inclusive, and the dry season (winter), the rest of the year. Variations are great according to altitude. The lowlands are hot and steamy; the region in altitudes of 3000-6500 feet, which includes Mexico City, is temperate; the higher regions are cold. The rainy months are usually considered the least desirable for visiting Mexico. Showers occur daily, and heavy rains fall from time to time. The temperate region is generally comfortable despite the rain; the showers last only about an hour, and July and August are considered by many the most desirable months on the plateaus. But October-May is usually thought best for travel in varying climatic regions.

Clothing. The wardrobe need not be elaborate, but clothes for both warm and cool weather are essential. For Mexico City, the central plateau, and other areas of high altitude spring or fall clothing worn in the United States is suitable. A raincoat is essential for the summer rainy season, while chilly evenings make a warm topcoat or heavy sweater necessary. In the winter a warm coat is indispensable. White suits are seldom worn in and near Mexico City except in the country clubs. At lower altitudes, as at Cuernavaca, Guadalajara, and Taxco, summer sports clothes are comfortable during the day. Sports shoes are suggested for hilly and cobbled villages and for short walks. Occasions necessitating evening clothes are rare unless the traveler attends governmental and diplomatic functions or visits homes where dressing for dinner is the custom.

Health. Vaccination and antityphoid injections are advisable. It is best to eat lightly and to adopt the siesta custom, resting after the heavy meal at noon. Indulging indiscriminately in native foods and fruits is likely to lead to digestive upsets. Raw vegetables and fruit without a peel should be avoided. The water and food in Mexico City and most other large cities and the chief resorts are healthful, since proper precautions are taken. In all other places bottled drinks and mineral water should be used. It is not well to overexercise at high altitudes, and the head should be covered with a sun hat when walking under the Mexican sun. The traveler will do well to accustom himself to the slower tempo of Mexican life.

Hospitals exist only in the capital and other large urban centers; they are staffed with capable doctors and have modern scientific equipment. Those in Mexico City include the Hospital de Jesús Nazareno, Avenida Piño Suárez 35; American Hospital, Calle Gabino Barreda 34; Lord Cowdray Sanitarium, a British hospital, Av. Chapultepec, near the park; French Hospital, Av. Niños Héroes 50; General City Hospital, Av. Niños Héroes 148. Names of doctors, dentists, nurses, and drugstores can be obtained from consuls and at hotels.

Sports and Recreations. SWIMMING in Mexico is ideal because of the agreeable temperature of the waters and the long stretches of clear, golden sand. Acapulco, Guaymas, and Mazatlán are among the best of the Pacific resorts; on the Atlantic, Tampico and Hotel Mocambo at Boca del Río near Veracruz offer excellent bathing.

At Cuernavaca, inland, most of the hotels have outdoor swimming pools fed by streams of fresh mountain water; so do some of the hotels at Taxco. Lake Chapala, a few miles from Guadalajara, is known for its fine swimming opportunities. Many hot springs, including Aguascalientes and Olímpico, both on the outskirts of Mexico City; Aguas Hediondas, hot sulphur springs, near Cuautla; the Agua Azul baths near Puebla, and those of San José Purúa beyond Zitácuaro on the way to Morelia, all afford excellent bathing. There is good swimming in many rivers in the highlands.

GOLF. The Chapultepec links and those of the country club near Churubusco, considered the best near Mexico City, are excellent 18-hole courses. Visiting players can obtain temporary membership cards. There are good links at country clubs in Cuernavaca and elsewhere at which visitors can secure permission to play.

TENNIS. The large cities have many courts. Arrangements can be made to play by obtaining guest cards at private clubs through friends or from hotel managements and travel agencies.

HORSEBACK RIDING. In Mexico City the best stables are Pensión Victoria, Calzada Morales 361; Pensión Madrid, Calzada Tacubaya; and Pensión Welton, Calle Agrarismo, Colonia Escandón. Rates are low.

BOXING. The largest ring is the National Arena in Mexico City.

BULLFIGHTING. The bullring of Mexico City, on Plaza de Toros, seating 25,000, is one of the largest and most famous in the world. Leading bullfighters of Spain and South America as well as Mexico can be seen there. Bullfights are held on Sunday afternoons, beginning at 4 p.m., weather permitting. The regular season begins late in October and lasts until March. During other months young bullfighters serve their apprenticeship. Tickets can be purchased at the bullring, at the office at C. López 68, or at hotels or travel bureaus.

FISHING. Mexican deep-sea fishing is famous, and there is excellent fresh-water sport in the inland lakes and rivers. Due to the efforts of the government hatcheries millions of black bass and rainbow trout are rapidly reproducing in the fresh-water streams of central Mexico. The rainbow trout rival those of New Zealand in size and beauty.

Deep-sea fishermen are rewarded along the Pacific coast and the Gulf of Mexico with a catch that ranges from the giant ray to mackerel. Excellent fishing opportunities exist at Presa Don Martín, famous for black trout and bass, off the Pan American Highway, 45 miles S of the U. S. border; Tampico, tarpon and other fighting fish; Hacienda de Hueyapán and Hacienda de Tlaxcaltengo, trout hatcheries near Mexico City; Acapulco on the Pacific, marlin, sailfish, and many other kinds; Veracruz, excellent deep-sea fishing; and Lake Chapala, near Guadalajara, bass and trout.

For licenses see Hunting.

HUNTING. Hunters must obtain permits at Mexican consulates to import arms and ammunition. Information concerning the number of guns, types, amount of ammunition, and fees is provided there. Hunting regulations are somewhat strict, but licenses are easily obtained and are good throughout the republic. They authorize the hunting of bears; wild boars; white, dark, and burred-tail deer; rabbits; coyotes; wolves; pumas; jaguars; wild turkeys; quails; doves, and other species. Hunting is good in the regions crossed by the Pan American Highway between Laredo, Tex., and Mexico City, as well as elsewhere in the mountains.

Licenses for fishing and hunting can be secured from the Departamento de Caza y Pesca (Department of Hunting and Fishing) in Mexico City, as well as through Mexican consulates, and cost little.

HIKING AND MOUNTAIN CLIMBING. Excursions to a number of pleasant places are made regularly from Mexico City by members of the Club de Exploradores (Explorers' Club), Calle Palma 40; Ixtapopo Club, C. Brasil 11; Everest Club, C. Donceles 94, and others. Usually these are made in the valley of Mexico and the surrounding region. Orizaba (18,696 feet), which ranks as the third highest peak on the North American continent; Popocatépetl (17,883 feet), and Ixtaccíhuatl (17,338 feet) are the most frequent goals of mountain climbers. Further information concerning hikes and mountain climbing can be obtained from Otis McAllister, honorary president of the Explorers' Club, or from the Y.M.C.A. at C. Balderas and C. Morelos in Mexico City.

ROUGHING IT. The Travel Division of the Pan American Union suggests that only experienced campers and hardy youths should plan to rough it in Mexico. A gasoline stove, a sleeping bag, and a tent are essential, as well as a working knowledge of first aid. A basic understanding of Spanish is desirable.

LOTTERY. The national lottery is conducted by the Board of Public Welfare (Asistencia Pública). Drawings are held three times a week. Ordinary prizes vary from the price of a ticket up to 5000 pesos (1941); special holiday prizes may run as high as 1,000,000 pesos. After all expenses are deducted, approximately 6,000,000-7,000,000 pesos a year are distributed among hospitals, orphanages, and charitable organizations. In addition to the Federal District lottery each state has local drawings administered under the same system.

Currency. Mexico employs the decimal system. A peso or Mexican dollar ($) is divided into 100 centavos. The half peso is called a tostón. Copper coins worth 1 and 2 centavos and coins of cupronickel worth 5 and 10 centavos are issued. The peso is of silver, and silver coins worth 20 and 50 centavos are also in use. Bills are issued for 5-1000 pesos. The rate of exchange is about 4.85 pesos to $1 U. S. currency (1941). Travelers' checks can be changed at border towns and at most of the larger cities.

Cost of Living. The current rate of exchange (1941) is favorable. Actual costs depend on several related factors, such as length of stay in Mexico; method of travel, whether by car or train; class of hotel accommodation and meals, and the amount spent for extras.

In Mexico City, Monterrey, and other important cities the best hotels charge 8 pesos and up apiece for room with bath. In many clean and comfortable small hotels in the principal cities prices are as low as 4 pesos a person, with private bath. Good rooms in private homes can be rented for 2-3 pesos a day. Almost all hotels make substantial reductions for a stay of a week or longer. Hotels in the country and in the popular resort places, many of which are good in every respect, charge 6-16 pesos a person for room with bath and meals. A room with twin beds, occupied by two persons, is always considerably cheaper than a single room for each.

Meals in the principal cities average as follows: desayuno or breakfast, 75 centavos to 1.50 pesos; comida or dinner, 1.50 pesos up; cena or supper, the same as dinner or slightly less. Most of the large hotels maintain first-class dining rooms. In many of the smaller hotels in the cities and almost always in the country meals are covered by the charge for a room. Country rates are generally much lower than those in the cities.

Banks. The Banco de México, corner of Avenida 5 de Mayo and Calle Juan Ruiz de Alarcón in Mexico City, is the official government bank. This institution and the Banco Nacional de México, Av. Isabel la Católica 44, have branches in the larger cities and towns. Other prominent banks in Mexico City are the Banco de Londres y México, Av. 16 de Septiembre and C. Bolívar; Banco Mexicano, corner of Av. 5 de Mayo and C. Motolinía; National City Bank of New York, Av. Uruguay and Av. Isabel la Católica. Travelers coming into the country by the Pan American Highway find the Crédito Industrial de Monterrey convenient.

Transportation. ROADS. During the last few years several important highways and branches have been completed which make it possible for the motorist to visit points of interest that heretofore could be reached only by railroad, as well as some that were formerly accessible only on horseback. Mexico will make even greater progress in road-building in the next few years because of a loan extended for that purpose by the United States in an agreement concluded by President Avila Camacho and Ambassador Castillo Nájera with U. S. Secretary of State Cordell Hull.

The monthly bulletin of the Pemex Travel Club includes a condensed table of road information. The bulletin can be obtained without charge by writing to Pemex Travel Club, Calle Bucareli 35, Mexico City. In a recent number it was pointed out that with but few exceptions "major highways of Mexico start from the capital, where they radiate forth in various directions like spokes from the hub of a wheel. The mileposts commonly seen along most Mexican highways are in reality kilometer posts, conveniently marking the distances, in kilometers, from the National Palace in Mexico City, which is the official starting point for all major highways. Branch highways are an exception to this rule, in that the distances marked along such roads always begin from the point where they branch off the main routes. Incidentally most of the new highways recently completed are roads which branch off the major arteries. . . . The famous Pan American Highway which runs from Laredo, Texas, to Mexico City is finished, paved, and in splendid condition over its entire length. Throughout the mountainous sections, strong steel guard-rails remove any possible hazard for the driver unaccustomed to mountain driving." The survey concludes: "Many secondary roads, while not paved and too numerous to list, are hard-surfaced and in fair condition, and may be traversed even during the rainy season. In fact, the motorist who likes to explore the by-ways can drive almost anywhere in Mexico except during the wet months of summer; obviously roads of this secondary class cannot be officially recommended except to motorists who are willing to put up with an occasional bit of dust and a few road bumps in the interest of visiting unusual places unknown to the majority."

The international Pacific highway, via Nogales, Ariz., is not recommended, since the road is not in good condition all the way. From Nogales to Guaymas via Hermosillo the highway is graveled and is maintained in good condition. From Guaymas to Guadalajara the road is not improved, but is passable except during the rainy season. From Guadalajara pavement is continuous via Zamora, Morelia, Zitácuaro, and Toluca to Mexico City.

Some of the more important highways serving the larger towns and cities are:

Laredo, Tex.-Mexico City ·(764 miles), via Monterrey, Linares, Ciudad Victoria, Valles, Tamazunchale, and Jacala.

Veracruz-Mexico City (286 miles), via Jalapa, San Hipólito (junction with Mexico City-Córdoba highway), Puebla, Río Frío Pass.

Mexico City-Acapulco (281 miles), via Cuernavaca, Taxco, and Chilpancingo.

Mexico City-Guadalajara (422 miles), via Toluca and Morelia.

Mexico City-Córdoba (243 miles), via Puebla, Garci-Crespo, and Orizaba.

ROAD	TOTAL LENGTH	PAVED TO	REMAINDER
PAN AMERICAN HIGHWAY (C.N. 1)			
Laredo, Tex.–Mexico City	760 miles	All paved	
McAllen, Tex.–Monterrey	140 miles	All paved	
Monterrey–Saltillo–Torreón	234 miles	All paved	
El Mante–Tampico	95 miles	All paved	
Antiguo Morelos–San Luis Potosí	304 miles		See below
Ixmiquilpán (Km. 167)–Querétaro	85 miles		See below
PACIFIC HIGHWAY (C.N. 4)			
Mexico City–Morelia–Guadalajara	422 miles	All paved	
Guadalajara–Tequila	37 miles	All paved	
Tequila–Guaymas	883 miles		Not rec.
Guaymas–Nogales, Ariz.	265 miles	16 miles	A-W road
Km. 60–Tenancingo	27 miles		A-W road
Quiroga–Pátzcuaro	14 miles	All paved	
Carapan–Uruapan	43 miles	All paved	
Guadalajara–Chapala	30 miles	All paved	
Guadalajara–Barra Navidad	209 miles	17 miles	A-W to Autlan
ACAPULCO HIGHWAY (C.N. 3)			
Mexico City–Taxco–Acapulco	280 miles	All paved	
Tres Cumbres–Zempoala Lakes	12 miles		A-W road
Buena Vista–Tepoztlán	9 miles	All paved	
Cuernavaca–Cuautla	31 miles		A-W road
Alpuyeca–Cacahuamilpa Caves	30 miles	All paved	
Alpuyeca–Tequesquitengo–Tehuixtla	15 miles	Zacatepec	A-W road
Iguala–Teloloapan			A-W road
VERACRUZ HIGHWAY (C.N. 2)			
Mexico City–Veracruz (via Jalapa)	270 miles	All paved	
Km. 18–Texcoco	13 miles	All paved	
Santa Bárbara–Amecameca–Cuautla	47 miles	All paved	
San Martín Texmelucan–Tlaxcala–Apizaco	20 miles	All paved	
Puebla–Atlixco	19 miles	All paved	
Atlixco–Matamoros	23 miles		A-W road
Perote–Teziutlán	24 miles		A-W road
Jalapa–Coatepec	12 miles		A-W road
Puebla–Tehuacán–Córdoba	118 miles	All paved	
Tehuacán–Oaxaca	175 miles		Not rec.
Matamoros–Oaxaca	240 miles		Not rec.

ROAD	TOTAL LENGTH	PAVED TO	REMAINDER
MISCELLANEOUS HIGHWAYS			
Mexico City–Teotihuacán pyramids	16 miles	All paved	
Mexico City–Tulancingo (via Pachuca)	90 miles	All paved	
Mexico City–Tepozotlán	26 miles	All paved	
Mexico City–Desierto de los Leones (via San Angel)	22 miles	All paved	
El Paso, Tex.–Chihuahua	201 miles	Part paved	A-W road

Abbreviations: C.N. = Camino Nacional (National Highway). Not rec. = not recommended. A-W road = all-weather road.

Branch roads to San Luis Potosí and Querétaro are not recommended at present.

AUTOMOBILES. A driving license and registration card or certificate of ownership are required at the Mexican border. Upon payment of a small sum a permit is issued by the border customs authorities covering the entry of the car. Trailers are subject to similar requirements. Permits are good for 90 days; for extension, consult the A. M. A. (Mexican Automobile Association), Paseo Reforma 46, Mexico City. There are good repair garages in the larger cities and service stations are frequent. A temporary membership in the A. M. A. may be secured. This organization offers automobile insurance, road service, information, maps, and guides. Fine road maps are also put out by the Pemex Travel Club.

Mexico's tourist camps provide ample space for parking house trailers. Excellent accommodations are found in Monterrey, Valles, and Mexico City. However, trailers are best confined to the main highways in order to avoid the sharp curves and narrow bridges that are frequent on other roads.

RAILROADS. Leading railroad routes between the United States and Mexico City are:

Laredo-Mexico City, via Monterrey, Saltillo, San Luis Potosí, and Querétaro.

Los Angeles-Mexico City, via El Paso, Tex.; Chihuahua; Torreón; Zacatecas; Aguascalientes, and Querétaro.

Los Angeles-Mexico City, via Nogales, Ariz.; Hermosillo; Guaymas; Culiacán; Mazatlán, and Guadalajara.

From Celaya to Mexico City via Querétaro these routes coincide.

Important railroad routes within Mexico include Mexico City-Veracruz, via Orizaba and Córdoba; Mexico City-Veracruz, via Jalapa; Mexico City-Guadalajara, via Querétaro and Celaya; Mexico City-Tampico, via San Luis Potosí; Mexico City-Suchiate on the Guatemalan border, via Jalapa, Veracruz, and Tapachula; Mexico City-Oaxaca, via Puebla and Tehuacán.

Further information will be supplied by offices of the National Railways of Mexico, 11 W. 42nd St., New York; 201 N. Wells Building, Chicago; 541 Monadnock Building, San Francisco, Calif.; Pacific Electric Building, Los Angeles, Calif.; Smith Young Tower Building, San Antonio, Tex.; Room 9, Union Depot, El Paso, Tex. The Mexico City office is at Calle Bolívar 19.

AIRLINES. Mexico City and all the principal points in the republic are served by modern planes. The extensive international network operated by Pan American Airways and its Mexican affiliate, the

Compañía Mexicana de Aviación, provides four services which converge on Mexico City from Los Angeles, Calif.; Brownsville, Tex.; Miami, Fla.; and Central and South America.

On the 12-hour flight from Los Angeles to Mexico City (1619 miles) the beautiful cities of Hermosillo, Mazatlán, and Guadalajara are touched. From Miami an overwater route is followed to Havana, Cuba, from which the planes continue to Mérida, Yucatán; Veracruz, and Mexico City. The distance between Miami and Mérida is 748 miles; between Mérida and Mexico City, 734 miles. On this route the picturesque SE cities of Campeche, Ciudad del Carmen, Villahermosa, Minatitlán, and Veracruz are linked with the capital.

Pan American Airways' frequent service from Brownsville places this Texas gateway at a distance of only 3½ hours from Mexico City, including a brief stop at Tampico; total distance covered is 463 miles. The route extends from Mexico City to Guatemala, the Canal Zone, and South America. The Mexico City office is at the corner of Avenida Madero and Calle Filomena Mata.

Líneas Aéreas Mineras, S. A. (Lamsa), operates from Ciudad Juárez, across the border from El Paso, Tex., to Chihuahua and Torreón, where connections can be made for Mazatlán and Mexico City. The Mexico City office is at Av. 5 de Mayo 15.

Aeronaves de México operates air service from Mexico City to Acapulco on the W coast. The Mexico City office is at Av. Juárez 80.

The Compañía Aeronáutica Francisco Sarabia operates from Mexico City to Oaxaca, Tuxtla Gutiérrez, Tapachula, and interior points of the state of Chiapas. This company likewise operates a line between Mérida, Cozumel, and other points in Yucatán, the territory of Quintana Roo, and Belize, British Honduras. The Mexico City office is at C. Gante 6, Pasaje Iturbide.

A number of other Mexican aviation companies operating independently serve various cities. The traveler should confer with travel agencies or offices of operating companies for latest information about routes, schedules, and rates.

Postage. Letters to the United States require 10 centavos' worth of stamps, those within Mexico 11 centavos; postcards, 4 centavos; airmail, 20-40 centavos (1941). The main post office in Mexico City is E of the Palace of Fine Arts, at Calle Tacuba and C. Teatro Nacional. The best way to receive mail is in care of a tourist agency, a U. S. consulate, a hotel, Wells Fargo & Co. Express, or Pemex Travel Club.

Telegraph and Cable Services. Western Union, situated on the corner of Calle San Juan de Letrán and Avenida Independencia in Mexico City, handles telegrams to the United States and foreign points. The National Telegraph, on C. Tacuba across from the main post office, serves all fairly large towns within the country and handles international radiograms.

Telephones. There are two telephone systems in Mexico, the Ericsson and the Mexicana. Calls can be made throughout the republic and to the United States on either system.

Souvenirs and Handicrafts. Indians make and sell the many articles necessary for their household and personal use. These are so carefully fashioned and so tastefully decorated that a simple water jug is often a true work of art. The machine does not yet compete with the crafts in Mexico; machine-made products are more costly as well as less pleasing than handicraft articles serving the same purposes. The crafts had reached a high point of development before the conquest. Each village produced its specialties. Families devoted themselves to a particular type of ware and developed their own technique. The Indian crafts that so impressed the Spaniards have endured to this day, some in a pure state, others modified by methods adopted from the Spaniards.

POTTERY, one of the oldest of human craft products, is made everywhere in Mexico. Pottery is still turned on the potter's wheel, decorated by hand, and baked in primitive wood-burning kilns. Each region produces its distinctive type, of characteristic style, color, and form. Typical Indian pottery is made of unglazed earthenware, plain or decorated. Glazed pottery is a Spanish modification of the indigenous craft.

The villages of San Pedro Tlaquepaque and Tonalá on the outskirts of Guadalajara, which produce a large portion of Mexico's pottery, are noted for their blue-gray and buff tableware adorned with delicate designs and for their glazed yellow pottery decorated with palm motifs. Natural terra-cotta pottery with white flower and animal designs comes from this region also, as well as vases, toys, and figurines.

Puebla's famous Talavera ware, durable and well turned, reflects Spanish influence more strongly. It is commonly of a majolica type in bright colors or cobalt blues against a cream base. Puebla is noted also for exquisite and colorful decorative glazed tiles produced entirely by hand. These tiles are sometimes used singly and sometimes arranged in panels whose polished, vivid-colored figures tell a complete story.

Oaxaca pottery is created in various types. The black-colored wares, produced both in bright glazed and in unglazed finishes, are the most interesting. Most of the pottery made today is of two colors or various tones of one color which merge into each other, and it is highly glazed. The old type, seldom produced any more, is very thin, highly glazed, and dark green in color, decorated only with engravings or raised designs. It is worth scouring the potters' homes in Oaxaca to unearth an example of this rare work. Clever pottery toys, animal forms, and water bottles are a specialty.

Michoacán produces an unglazed orange-sienna clay pottery which takes its color from the rich earth of the lakeside hills.

BASKETRY is an amazing art in Mexico. With maguey fiber, grass, fine bamboo, henequen, and horsehair the craftsmen produce a wide range of colorful articles—sleeping mats, hammocks, earrings, sandals, toys, and gay baskets of all shapes and sizes. The centers for this craft are Toluca, Iguala, Oaxaca, Mexico City, Aguascalientes, and Querétaro.

LACQUER WORK was a Mexican handicraft before the conquest, but it has been greatly influenced by the models and new techniques which the Spaniards introduced. Gourds, calabashes, and sweet-smelling linaloa wood are lacquered. There are many styles and techniques, depending on the region, and each has its distinctive beauty. The lacquering, like all craft processes, is fascinating to watch. Two methods are chiefly employed. In one the design is painted with various-colored lacquers on a solid-color lacquer base; in the other, a series of coats of lacquer of solid colors are applied to the object and a fine point is used to cut the design through the layers. Both methods are laborious. Each coat must be carefully rubbed in before the next is applied, and when the cutting has been completed a final colorless coat must be thoroughly rubbed in. The first or incrusted type is typical of Uruapan in the state of Michoacán; the second or cutting method is used in Olinala in the state of Guerrero. These two towns are the great centers of the lacquer industry in Mexico. Genuine lacquer work feels and looks like engraving.

TEXTILES. The making of handwoven fabrics was an Aztec art. Like pottery-making, the technique exists both in the pure and in a modified form. The Indian weaves his own blankets and, in many regions, the materials for his clothing. Rebozos or shawls are often handwoven, and so are bags, sashes, table linens, and towels.

As with pottery, various sections of the country produce characteristic types. The chief article of apparel for the male is the sarape, a woven blanket with a slit in the center, which can be slipped over the head during the day and used as a covering at night. It is possible to recognize an Indian's town by the color, weave, and design of his sarape. In Toluca it is of wool in natural tones woven in geometric designs; in Texcoco it is tightly woven with a diamond center on blue, white, or brown background; in Oaxaca it is either dashing—striped, with a figure like an idol squatted in the middle—or a somber gray, black, fawn, or white background with a simple red or black design in the center. Those from Oaxaca are excellent for rugs or wall hangings. The man from Saltillo wears an old-fashioned sarape in rich, deep natural tones or, if he is gay and young, a blanket of many-colored stripes.

The rebozo or shawl, a basic article of apparel for the Indian woman, is draped gracefully over her head during the day and wrapped around her body at night; slung over the shoulders, it becomes a cradle for her infant. Rebozos are woven in almost every town. Santa María in the state of Puebla is a leading center of rebozo manufacture; here rebozos are made of cotton and silk in white and varying shades of blue, fawn, mauve, brown, and gray.

METALS, GLASS, ETC. The traveler should visit the tin and silver shops that line the cobbled streets of Taxco and also the glass factories of Mexico City and Guadalajara. Mexican glassware, blown by a technique that has been handed down from father to son for centuries, has much the same quality as that which distinguished Stiegel, Cambridge, Sandwich, and other early North American glass; yet its cost is moderate. Among the most beautiful specimens are those of soft cactus green, golden Tarascan amber, and rich cobalt blue.

Inexpensive handmade jewelry and trinkets of native onyx, opals, obsidian, jade, and turquoise abound in the shops of Mexico City and Puebla. Wooden furniture, knickknacks, canes, and picture frames, carved or painted, are sold in the Mexico City curio shops and at markets and fairs. Mexico City, Puebla, and Amozoc are the centers for finely made spurs, other horseman's accessories, and knives of wrought iron. Fine tooled leather goods can be purchased in Mexico City and Mazatlán. Mexican toys deserve a volume in themselves. There are seasonal, holiday, and regional toys. They have humor and fascinating individuality.

Archeological Sites. Mexico is a great storehouse of archeological treasures, with many mysterious remains of ancient civilizations scattered in forests and sierras throughout the country.

El Pedregal, 10 miles S of Mexico City, is a rocky waste formed in ancient times by successive lava waves, presumably from the now extinct volcano Xitle. Surrounded and partly buried by the lava is the very ancient pyramid of Cuicuilco, a series of superimposed truncated cones.

In and around Mexico City are many remains of Aztec and Toltec structures. Off the Zócalo, a block from the cathedral, are the foundations of an Aztec temple. Elsewhere in Mexico, Aztec architecture and sculpture can be studied in the pyramids of Tenayuca, 9 miles from Mexico City; the pyramid of Santa Cecilia, a mile N of Tenayuca; and the pyramid of Teopanzolco, about a mile from Cuernavaca.

San Juan Teotihuacán (Place Where the Gods Reside), 28 miles NE of Mexico City, is one of the most important archeological sites on the North American continent. A zone covering 8 square miles contains majestic pyramids and buildings constructed many centuries ago. The pyramid of the Sun, built in five sections or terraces, rivals the celebrated Egyptian pyramid of Cheops in size. Other interesting structures at this site are the pyramid of the Moon, the temple of Quetzalcoatl, the temple of agriculture, and superimposed buildings.

Within easy reach of Oaxaca are the celebrated ruins of Mitla and Monte Albán. In the rock tombs of Monte Albán have been found more than 500 objects, including necklaces of gold, pearls, jade, and turquoise; goblets of rock crystal, breastplates, and masks of beaten gold, and numerous other ornaments and carvings that throw light on the early civilization of this region. The ruins of Mitla, once an important city of the Zapotecs, are very extensive and are unique because of their remarkable columns without bases or capitals, their beautiful mosaics, cruciform tombs, temples, and underground chambers.

In SE Mexico the temple-studded peninsula of Yucatán, though difficult of access, is one of the most fascinating regions because of the amazing ancient Maya cities. A journey of $2\frac{1}{2}$ hours by car inland on the new road directly from Mérida, capital of the state of Yucatán, takes the traveler to the pyramid city of Chichén-Itzá. Among the outstanding ruins are the House of the Nuns, one of the most remarkable structures of Maya architecture; the temple of Kukul Can; the temple of the Warriors; the ball court; the Hall of a Thousand Columns, covering a tremendous area, and the cenotes or sacred wells into which sacrificial victims and treasures were thrown. The ruins of Uxmal, another sacred city reached from Mérida, though not so extensive as those at Chichén-Itzá, are as important archeologically because of the richness of the sculptures.

Other ruins include those of Itzamal, Kabah, Zayi, and Labná in the state of Yucatán; those of the sacred city of Palenque in Chiapas; Chalchihuites and La Quemada in Zacatecas; and the almost inaccessible Tres Zapotes, in the state of Veracruz, unearthed by a U. S. expedition of the National Geographic Society in 1940.

The ruins of El Tajín, lying near the Gulf coast N of Papantla in the state of Veracruz, are the remains of what was very probably the most beautiful of the temples erected by the Totonacs. These people were exceedingly skillful architects and sculptors, as evidenced by their pyramids excavated here and at Yohualinchán in Puebla. A fine plaster model of El Tajín as originally built can be seen on the second floor of the National Museum in Mexico City.

Permission to visit ruins that are difficult to reach must be secured from the Direction of Archeology of the Secretariat of Public Education in Mexico City, whose staff will aid in planning excursions.

Food. Mexican dishes are rich and highly spiced, and for this reason the traveler making his first visit is wise not to indulge too freely at first. This is particularly advisable in Mexico City and in the central plateau region, where the high altitude slows digestive processes. U. S. style food can be secured in the larger hotels and restaurants.

Chile is the savory base used to flavor most Mexican foods, especially meat dishes. There are many types of chile, each variety with a distinct flavor. Some are mild, others like fire. Mole, a dietary classic of Mexico, is a sauce blended of several varieties of chile. Chile jalapeño, commonly stuffed with meat and pickled, has a fine flavor. Serrano and piquín are delicious varieties, though very hot. Chilpotle, dark brown in color, is another favorite. Chile con carne, commonly believed to be a typical Mexican dish, originated in Texas; S of the border it is usually found only at restaurants catering to U. S. trade. What might be termed the national dish of Mexico is mole de guajolote or turkey covered with a rich dark sauce made of several varieties of chile, tomatoes, sesame seeds, and sometimes chocolate. Also popular are mole verde or a sauce of spiced green chile served with meat or fowl; albóndigas or meat balls stuffed with hardboiled egg and spices, served with a tomato sauce; cabrito al horno or roast kid basted with a rich sauce.

The humble tortilla, a thin pancake made of corn that has been soaked in lime water and ground, is the bread of the common people. Filled with chopped meat, fowl, or cheese, rolled up and fried, it becomes a taco or sandwich. When a taco is covered with sauce and sprinkled with grated cheese it becomes an enchilada. As tostada, which is much favored, a tortilla is fried crisp and spread with diced chicken or other meat. The quesadilla is a tortilla filled with hash, cheese, chicken, chile, or squash flowers, pinched together like a turnover and fried in lard; sold everywhere in the streets of the capital, it is as popular as the hamburger is in the United States.

The great variety of fish that abound in Mexican waters has resulted in an elaborate range of seafood cookery. Most popular is the huachinango or red snapper, served in many different ways. Róbalo and sábalo are also very appetizing. Trucha or trout is common; it is generally served fried. An unusual delicacy is young pulpo or octopus, usually served in its own rich juice.

Rice and beans are prominent in the Mexican diet. As usually prepared, arroz or rice is first boiled, then fried. A standard dish is a plate of rice surrounded with fried eggs. Several types of frijoles or beans are common; the brown and black varieties are the most popular. They are ordinarily boiled until soft, when they supply their own thick sauce; fried in lard after boiling, the beans are spoken of as refritos.

Almost all vegetables common in the United States are found in Mexico. Others relatively unknown to the American palate are garbanzos or chickpeas; chayote, a vegetable which resembles the prickly pear; nopalitos, the young leaves of the nopal cactus; and flores de calabaza, yellow squash flowers.

Tropical fruits are abundant: banana, orange, lime, mango de Manila, chirimoya, guayaba, zapote, papaya, aguacate or alligator pear, and pineapple. Two unusual fruits of the highland regions are excellent: tuna, the flavorsome fruit of the nopal cactus; and pitahaya, the fruit of the saguaro cactus.

Pan dulce or sweet bread is favored for breakfast, as a tea or luncheon bread, and as a simple desert.

Drinks. The common alcoholic drink of the poorer classes of the plateau region is pulque, the fermented juice of the maguey. A thick, sirupy liquid with an alcoholic content slightly less than that of beer, it is sold very cheap. It is often mixed with fruits. Foreigners usually think the taste somewhat rancid. Mexican beer is good.

Tequila, distilled from the fermented juice of a variety of cactus similar to maguey, is a fiery liquor much esteemed throughout Mexico. It derives its name from the town of Tequila, near Guadalajara, where it is produced. Tequila blanca or white tequila is aged only for a short time and hence is very strong. Tequila añeja or aged tequila, the color of whisky, is much milder. Mezcal, another strong liquor distilled from the juice of a cactus, is somewhat like tequila, but usually milder. The mezcal of Oaxaca, which comes in round black clay jars, is especially esteemed.

Aguardiente, brandy distilled from sugar cane, when fresh, is sweet but raw and fiery. Aged somewhat and with burnt sugar added, it is known as habanero and is popular throughout Mexico. When habanero has been redistilled and thoroughly aged it becomes ron or rum.

Good wines are produced in Mexico. The best are the red varieties of Parras in the state of Coahuila and of Ensenada in Lower California.

The mineral waters known as El Riego and Garci-Crespo, bottled at the famous springs at Tehuacán, and Agua de Lourdes are among the most popular.

Holidays and Fiestas. A fiesta is going on somewhere in Mexico every day, for all the villages celebrate the seasons, patron saints' days, and some day of the Virgin. These occasions combined with market days are often the equivalent of U. S. county fairs, with merrymaking, showers of fireworks, and native songs. Dancers attired in fantastic masks and elaborate costumes, with plumed headdresses and silver girdles, often weave through the streets to dance in front of the churches. Other features are competitive sports, games of chance, carpas or tent shows, and puppet shows.

In addition to these celebrations, religious in origin though often pagan in expression, civic holidays are occasions for simultaneous fiestas throughout the republic.

The summer months bring many local fiestas with interesting ceremonies and dances. Each town has its characteristic method of celebration. Native dances are of all types. In some of the social dances Spanish and Indian elements have fused in a characteristic Mexican expression. Primitive ritual dances which the Aztecs performed centuries ago to propitiate their gods are performed today to insure a good harvest or to drive off evil spirits. Religious dances almost completely medieval in spirit exist side by side with totemic dances imitating the bird, snake, iguana, rabbit, or jaguar. The dances, songs, and instrumental music are incredibly rich. Depending on the town, a fiesta may include bullfights, cockfights, or rodeos. There is always a lively market to which Indians from far and near bring their wares.

The fiesta gives an excellent opportunity for observing native customs and indigenous life. It is an introduction to the Mexican people. The traveler should inquire of some Mexico City travel agency about any particular occasion that he is interested in, since any given celebration may be canceled and dates are sometimes shifted. The following list of fiestas and national holidays is necessarily limited.

JAN. 1. New Year's festivities throughout the land. Island of Janitzio, a quaint fisherman's island in Lake Pátzcuaro, Michoacán: famous native dances of Los Viejitos (Little Old Men) and Los Moros (Moors). San Bartolo Oztolotepec, a little town of Otomí Indians near Toluca, México: dance of Los Concheros, representing Moors and Christians.

JAN. 1-6. Chalma, México: minor festival at the sanctuary, reached only by horseback or on foot.

JAN. 1-7. Jojutla, Morelos, on a side road E between Cuernavaca and Taxco: picturesque fiesta and market.

JAN. 6. Epiphany (Día de los Reyes) is celebrated widely, wherever the customs of Santa Claus and Christmas trees and presents in stockings have not penetrated. Little Mexican children place their shoes on the balcony in the hope of finding them filled with toys.

JAN. 15. Zimatlán, Oaxaca: colorful fiesta, especially noteworthy for the beautiful plume dance as well as other native dances typical of the region. Tenango del Valle, México, a few miles from Toluca: fiesta.

JAN. 17. St. Anthony's day (San Antonio Abad). In many towns this day is set aside for the ancient ceremony of blessing the animals, which are usually brought to the church decorated with flowers and ribbons. Xochimilco, near Mexico City: typical ceremonies in the church of San Bernardino. Tlalpam, also near Mexico City: interesting ceremony.

JAN. 17-25. León, Guanajuato: celebration of the founding of the city.

JAN. 25. Palmatlán, Puebla, a small isolated town in the mountains: fiesta outstanding for its elaborate spectacle of Los Voladores, originally an Aztec game. As this town can be reached only by train followed by a 3-hour trip on horseback special arrangements should be made beforehand. The primitive character of this fiesta makes it particularly rewarding for the student of folklore.

JAN. 25-28. Cuilápam and Mitla, Oaxaca: colorful fiesta with plume dance.

FEB. 1. Tzintzuntzan, Michoacán: typical fiesta in honor of Our Lord of the Rescue (El Rescate), with rodeos and Tarascan dances.

FEB. 1-2. Coatlinchán, México: fiesta with dances.

FEB. 2. Candlemas (La Candelaria). Tlacotalpán, Veracruz: fiesta in honor of the Virgin; dances and tug-the-bull contest.

FEB. 5. National holiday, anniversary of the constitutions of 1857 and 1917.

MONDAY BEFORE LENT TO AFTERNOON OF ASH WEDNESDAY. Amecameca, on the Mexico City-Cuautla road, 39 miles from the Federal District: pilgrimage-fair at the hill shrine of the Lord of El Sacromonte, where there is a highly venerated image said to have been brought by an unidentified riderless mule; dances, bullfights, cockfights, etc.

CARNIVAL WEEK, immediately preceding Lent, is gay with song, dance, and general revelry all through the country. Huejotzingo, an interesting village 2 hours out of Mexico City on the Puebla road: drama enacted from dawn to sundown of Shrove Tuesday by men, representing in part the famous victory over the French forces at Puebla on May 5, 1862, and also the elopement of a bandit with the daughter of a Spanish grandee; sham battles, burning down of a thatched hut, elaborate costumes, dance interludes. Mazatlán, Sinaloa; Mérida, Yucatán; Oaxaca; Taxco, Guerrero; Tepoztlán, Morelos; Veracruz: other notable carnival celebrations.

FIRST FRIDAY OF LENT. Fiestas at Tepalcingo, Morelos, and Chalma, México, in honor of Our Lord of Chalma.

FEB. 9. San Juan Teotihuacán, about 30 miles NE of Mexico City: fiesta.

FEB. 14. National holiday, death of Vicente Guerrero, hero of the war of independence and one of the early presidents.

FEB. 22. National holiday, death of Francisco I. Madero, leader of the revolution of 1910 and presidential successor to Porfirio Díaz.

SECOND AND FOURTH WEEKS OF MARCH. Taxco, Guerrero: large and colorful fiestas with numerous native dances. On the fourth Friday of Lent special ceremonies are held at the church of La Santa Veracruz and in the streets around it. In near-by towns fiestas are held every Friday, beginning with the first Friday of Lent.

MARCH 9-13. Etla, state of Oaxaca: fiesta in honor of Our Lord of the Cliffs, the patron saint of the locality.

MARCH 12. San Gregorio Acapulco, in the Federal District a few miles from the capital, between the towns of Xochimilco and Tlachuac: fiesta in honor of the patron saint of the village; native dances such as Los Vaqueros (Cowboys) during the daytime; fireworks in the evening.

HOLY WEEK is an inspiring and deeply religious period observed with fiestas and passion plays. Tzintzuntzan, the ancient Tarascan capital on the shores of Lake Pátzcuaro: pious Indians re-enact the Last Supper on Maundy Thursday and represent scenes of the Passion on Good Friday. During Holy Week in all the markets of Mexico vendors sell papier-maché Judases 1-10 feet high, painted to resemble bogeymen and criminals, with gunpowder and fusing to be set off on Holy Saturday to the unrestrained delight of children and adults alike. Santa Anita, just outside Mexico City: a beautiful and extremely popular flower festival on Good Friday in honor of the Virgin of Sorrows (Los Dolores), with flower-decked canoes on the main canal; regional costumes, bullfights, and races. Tlacolula, a village on the road between Oaxaca and Mitla: one of the finest of Mexican fiestas on Good Friday, centering around the church; many native dances, including the magnificent plume dance. Zacuatilpam, Hidalgo: a Good Friday procession of natives carrying an image of Christ which has hinges that permit it to kneel and walk. Ixtapalapa, a small town near Mexico City: Maundy Thursday and Good Friday, fiesta with a passion play of the Via Crucis.

APRIL 20-MAY 5. Aguascalientes, capital of the State of the same name: fiesta at San Marcos on the outskirts, held each year since the early 17th century to commemorate the founding of San Marcos in 1604; one of the most interesting fiestas of the N central plateau; regional dances in costume, mariachis or itinerant musicians, indigenous and popular Mexican songs, bullfights, fireworks, parades, serenades, contests, and large and interesting market.

MAY 1-4. Amatlán de los Reyes, Veracruz: religious fiesta.

MAY 1-8. Acapulco, Guerrero: gay fair and fiesta celebrating the historic victory of May 5, 1862.

MAY 3. Day of the Holy Cross, fiesta of masons and builders, celebrated throughout the entire republic. Crosses adorned with fresh flowers are placed on buildings under construction. Firecrackers are set off from early morning. There are usually native dances and dinners of mole and pulque.

MAY 5. National holiday, anniversary of the victory over the French troops of Napoleon III and Maximilian at the famous battle of Puebla in 1862.

CORPUS CHRISTI, the Thursday after Trinity Sunday, is celebrated especially in the cathedral in Mexico City with a beautiful procession in which many children take part. Generally they carry on their backs little wooden boxes laden with fruits and other products in imitation of the Indians in the marketplaces. The procession begins about 9:30 a.m. Little toy mules made of banana or other leaves are sold in front of the cathedral as souvenirs.

JUNE 10-18. Río Verde, San Luis Potosí: fair in honor of St. Anthony; religious ceremonies and popular festivities, typical dances, cockfights, horse races.

JUNE 10-20. Calpulalpán, Tlaxcala: grand market day in honor of the patron saint, St. Anthony, with dances, including the dance of Moors and Christians.

JUNE 13-29. Uruapan, Michoacán: fiesta with exciting dances; most important is Los Negritos (Little Black Men), one of the most original of all Mexican dances. Another interesting feature of the fiesta is the procession of the sowing of the crop, with oxen decorated with fruits and flowers and with large round loaves of bread hung on their horns; behind come girls in native costume carrying on their heads trays filled with fruit, symbolizing the dinners that women take to their men working in the fields.

JUNE 23-JULY 7. Guanajuato, in the state of the same name: annual fiesta at the reservoir Presa de la Olla, with athletic events and swimming competitions in which athletes from all the republic participate; popular dances and a fair.

JUNE 24. St. John the Baptist's day, celebrated particularly in small villages in central Mexico and in certain streets of Mexico City with bathing festivities. It is believed that water is free of evil spirits on this day and that anyone may bathe with impunity. People throw flowers on the water and take their household and church saints to be bathed in the purified water.

JULY 3. National holiday, death of Miguel Hidalgo y Costilla, father of Mexican independence. Oaxaca: outstanding fiesta with the plume dance.

JULY 8. Teotitlán del Valle, 15 miles from Oaxaca: fiesta with plume dance and fireworks.

JULY 8-16. Motul, a Maya town near Mérida, Yucatán: fiesta in honor of Our Lady of El Carmen.

JULY 16. Oaxaca: harvest fiesta centering about Cerro del Fortín, a hilltop on the outskirts, and harking back to ancient pre-Spanish ceremonies in honor of Centeotl, the harvest goddess.

JULY 17. National holiday, death of Alvaro Obregón, military hero of the revolution of 1910-20 and president of the republic 1920-24.

JULY 18. National holiday, death of Benito Juárez, president and victorious hero of reform, civil war, and the French invasion.

JULY 19. Juchitán, Oaxaca: harvest fiesta in honor of St. Vincent de Paúl.

JULY 24. Torreón, Coahuila: harvest fiesta of St. James (Santiago).

AUG. 1-6. Saltillo, Coahuila: fiesta in honor of the image of Christ which stands in a small chapel of the cathedral; fireworks, dances, and a large fair.

AUG. 2-9. Tulancingo, Hidalgo: annual fiesta in honor of Our Lady of the Angels; dances, serenades, bullfights.

AUG. 8. Teziutlán, Puebla: fair and fiesta.

AUG. 10-17. Zacatlán, Puebla: fiesta. Delicious apples are grown near the town, and stands are set up in the principal square where the by-products of the apple are sold, as well as regional articles such as pottery, tooled leather, sarapes, and iron articles with silver incrustations. There are fireworks and other attractions.

AUG. 10-18. Atemajac del Valle, Jalisco, near Zapopán: fiesta in honor of the Virgin of the Assumption and of St. James; interesting native dances representing the conquest, including a sham battle imitating those fought by Spaniards on Spanish soil against invading Moors.

AUG. 12-21. Huamantla, Tlaxcala: fiesta with bullfights, horse races, and cockfights.

AUG. 15. Day of the Assumption of the Virgin. Milpa Alta, F. D.; Santa María Tonantzintla and Amozoc, Puebla; Santa María del Río, San Luis Potosí: notable fiestas.

AUG. 21. Cuauhtémoc Day. Mexico City: commemoration of the bravery and loyalty of Cuauhtémoc, young Aztec leader, with services at monument in his honor at Paseo Reforma and Calle Insurgentes, including interesting native dances.

AUG. 22-26. Córdoba, Veracruz: popular civic fiesta to commemorate signing of the treaties of Córdoba; evening entertainments, sports events, horse races, bullfights, picnics, balls, and many other diversions.

SEPT. 1-8. San Bartolo Naucalpam, near Mexico City: fiesta of the Virgin of Remedies (Los Remedios), an ancient and highly venerated image, patroness of the Spaniards in Mexico; with native dances, a fair, and fireworks. September 8 is the important day. Tepoztlán, Morelos: fiesta in honor of both Our Lady of the Nativity (La Natividad) and El Tepozteco, an Aztec deity who nevertheless is locally said to have been a favorite son of the Virgin; intensely interesting native dance-drama on the afternoon of the eighth.

SEPT. 5-15. Zacatecas, in the state of the same name: fiesta.

SEPT. 8. Los Remedios, México: religious fiesta celebrated by native dances, a fair, and fireworks. The image of the Virgin of Remedies (Los Remedios) here is highly venerated. This Virgin was appointed generalissimo of the Spanish forces during the revolution of independence, while the Virgin of Guadalupe was pressed into service on the side of the insurgents. Cholula, Puebla: fiesta of the Virgin of Remedies.

SEPT. 10-15. Chihuahua, in the state of the same name: fiesta.

SEPT. 14-15. Dolores Hidalgo, Guanajuato: traditional celebration in the town where Hidalgo, father of Mexican independence, started the movement for freedom from Spain on Sept. 15, 1810. Querétaro, state of the same name: religious fiesta celebrated at the monastery of La Cruz with a fair, fireworks, and native dances.

SEPT. 16. National holiday commemorating Hidalgo's declaration of independence, the Mexican equivalent of the U. S. Fourth of July. An impressive ceremony occurs at 11 p.m. of the fifteenth, when the president of Mexico stands on the central balcony of the National Palace in Mexico City and repeats Father Hidalgo's Grito de Dolores, the revolutionary call to freedom. The throngs in the square facing the palace take up the cry as bells toll and fireworks are set off. The ceremony is duplicated throughout the republic. Independence Day is observed with parades, bullfights, and general gaiety.

SEPT. 27-Oct. 14. Mérida, Yucatán: fiesta in honor of the Christ of the Blisters (Las Ampollas), to whom there is an altar in the cathedral.

SEPT. 29. Taxco, Guerrero: gay and colorful fiesta in honor of the patron saint, St. Michael (San Miguel); large fair, many interesting regional dances, fireworks.

OCT. 1-12. Pachuca, Hidalgo: fiesta of St. Francis of Assisi (San Francisco de Asís).

OCT. 12. National holiday, Columbus Day (Día de la Raza—Day of the Race), a general civic holiday of the Spanish-speaking nations of the Western Hemisphere; colorful procession, accompanied by singing, in which an image of the Christ Child is carried to the local church.

OCT. 29-Nov. 2. Zacualtilpam, Hidalgo: fiesta; fair and native dances.

NOV. 1-2. All Saints' Day and All Souls' Day, celebrated throughout the republic. Though dedicated to the dead, these days are converted by the gay Mexican spirit into festive holidays. The Indians have little fear of the dead. During the last days of October gay placards in the bakeries announce supplies of dead men's bread, tasty round loaves surmounted by twists representing bones. Children beg their parents for the sugar skulls with bright tinsel decorations that peer from shop windows and market stands. Dapper skeletons with plumed hats beckon, and toy skeletons leap out of coffins at the pull of cleverly arranged strings. As a fascinated youngster turns the crank of a little box, a toy funeral passes in and out of a cardboard cathedral. Improvised altars decorated with black and white paper cutouts are arranged in Indian homes. Food is especially prepared for the dead of the family, who are expected to return at night to eat with their loved ones. When children are expected to return, foods such as milk, honey, fruits, and cakes are placed lovingly on the altar; a heartier meal is spread for the adult dead. The graveyards are visited by picnic parties who decorate the tombs with yellow calendulas, the flowers which Indians always use to cheer the dead. The ceremony on the island of Janitzio in Lake Pátzcuaro, Michoacán, with Tarascan chants at midnight, is an unearthly spectacle; the narrow graveyard becomes a sparkling fairyland where candles cast a magic light over mounds garlanded with fruits and flowers.

NOV. 3-12. San Martín Texmelucán, Puebla: fiesta of St. Martin, with typical dances, bullfights, and an extensive market where the renowned Choluteca and Tlaxcalteca sarapes are sold.

NOV. 20. National holiday, commemorating the beginning of the 1910 revolution.

NOV. 20-DEC. 15. Atotonilco, Jalisco: fiesta and fair, with bullfights, cockfights, and mariachis or wandering musicians. The town is in a livestock region famous for its charros or horsemen.

DEC. 1-10. Puente de Ixtla, Morelos: fiesta of the Immaculate Conception; native dances, mystery plays, cockfights.

DEC. 3-13. Virgin of Guadalupe, patron saint of the republic. There is a national and even international religious pilgrimage to the shrine of Guadalupe on the hill of Tepeyac in the outskirts of Mexico City, with dancing in front of the church, oboe and drum music day and night, and huge fairs. The most important day is the twelfth. The Virgin of Guadalupe was on Hidalgo's flag during the revolution of independence.

DEC. 5-15. Iguala, capital of Guerrero, on Mexico City-Acapulco highway: fair, with traders arriving from everywhere in the state and from the W coast; famous as a horse fair and for cockfights, bullfights, and plays.

DEC. 12-26. Monterrey, Nuevo León, on the Pan American Highway: N Mexican fiesta and fair in honor of the Virgin of Guadalupe; dances, bullfights.

DEC. 16-25. Christmas season. Nine nights of festivities precede Christmas, with dances in private homes and in the eentral plazas of small towns. These nine posadas, or literally inns, reflect the search of Joseph and Mary for a shelter in which the Christ Child might be born. In the cities parties are interrupted for the guests or pilgrims, as they are called, with candles in their hands, to circle the patios of the houses singing old hymns. In remote towns the custom persists of groups of revelers going from house to house knocking on doors, where they are refused admittance until they come to the ninth house; there the doors are flung open and they are made welcome. In almost every home, rich or poor, there is a piñata, a clay jar filled with goodies and covered with bright tissue paper on which are figures of angels, sirens, sheep, toreadors—anything pretty or dashing, regardless of religious significance.

DEC. 22. National holiday, anniversary of the death of José María Morelos, hero of the revolution of independence, in 1815; all flags at half-mast in mourning for his execution. San Cristóbal Ecatépec: special memorial services.

DEC. 28. Holy Innocents' Day (Día de los Inocentes), corresponding to April Fool's Day in the United States.

REGIONAL GUIDE

The principal Mexican port of entry is Veracruz on the Gulf of Mexico, and this city is considered first in this guide for that reason, followed by the railroad and motor routes from it to the national capital (p. 56, p. 59). Ships from the United States also serve Tampico (p. 64). The Pan American Highway makes it possible to reach Mexico City directly from the United States by car over a very interesting route from Laredo, Tex. (p. 67). To those who would make the trip to Mexico City all the way by railroad three choices are open: from Laredo, Tex. (p. 74); from El Paso, Tex. (p. 79); and from Nogales, Ariz. (p. 84); completion of the Pacific highway will also make the capital accessible from the United States by car through the W part of the country. Mexico City (p. 94) is of course reached quickest by air. It is the country's travel center (p. 93).

VERACRUZ

Veracruz was the original starting point of the Spanish conquest, and it is the oldest of Mexico's colonial settlements. Hernán Cortés landed at the Indian village here on Good Friday, April 27, 1519, and called it the Rich Town of the Holy Cross (La Villa Rica de la Veracruz); the Indians called it Chalchiuhouecan. Here the proud representatives of Moctezuma met the Spaniards; from here the conquistadores went inland to the Aztec capital. In later years Veracruz was repeatedly sacked by buccaneers and bombarded by foreign fleets. Today, with 70,000 inhabitants, Veracruz is an odd mixture of the ancient and modern, with old small-windowed houses, quaint courts, and picturesque, narrow cobbled streets contrasting with new buildings or wide, bustling thoroughfares.

Visitors like to wander around Plaza Constitución in the center of the town because of its historic interest and its animation, especially in the evening, when it is thronged with townspeople out to listen to the military band. Another interesting walk is along Avenida Independencia, a busy main thoroughfare which forms the W side of the plaza and the side streets. In the evening the carpas or tent shows in the streets, the hum of eager voices, the seashore night clubs with soft, gay Latin American music and the catchy rhythm of such dances as the danzón and the huapango are entertaining.

Plaza Zamora or the Alameda, at the S end of Av. Independencia, contains a statue, erected in 1892, of Manuel Gutiérrez Zamora, one of the noteworthy governors of the state; there is also a statue of Liberty. In Parque Porfirio Díaz, surrounded by coconut trees, stands a monument to Benito Juárez, built to commemorate the Reform Laws.

The most striking buildings in the city are the fortress of Santiago, one of the last vestiges of the colonial city; the lighthouse building, often visited at night, a handsome modern structure that accommodates the port authority, the meteorological observatory, and the immigration offices; the federal sanitary bureau; the customhouse; the post and telegraph offices; the railroad station and Hotel Terminal; the city hall, Palacio Municipal; the naval school; and the parish church, built in 1721, on Plaza Constitución.

Probably the chief point of interest is the old Castillo de San Juan de Ulúa, which was built in 1565 and served as a fort and political and general prison until 1914. On Gallega Island, a mile from the mainland, it is reached by launch from the customhouse. On the island now are a naval repair shop, arsenal, drydock, shipyard, and marine signal station. The prison, once surrounded by a shark-infested moat, is reminiscent of ancient horrors. Inmates were often flogged and tortured in special torture chambers; sometimes their cells were flooded or they were fed to the sharks. The old building is now part of the breakwaters around the reefs, constructed with stone quarried from Mt. Peñuela.

A short distance from the old fort is the Isla de los Sacrificios (Isle of Sacrifices), so named by Juan de Grijalva in 1518 when he found remains of human sacrifices there. The island contains archeological ruins and is a resort spot. It is reached by tugboat on certain days.

The carnival at Veracruz, the 5 days preceding Lent, is gay, colorful, and exciting.

SOURCES OF INFORMATION. The tourist bureau in the city hall, on Plaza Constitución, and the Chamber of Commerce assist travelers.

FISHING. Juan Chambonnet at Hotel Diligencias will furnish information concerning complete equipment for fishing in Gulf waters for the tasty huachinango or red snapper and the flashing tarpon. On near-by Isla Verde (Green Isle) are cliffs from which octopus and shrimp can be caught.

BANK. Travelers' checks and U. S. currency can be converted into Mexican currency at the Veracruz branch of the Banco Nacional de México in the port section.

HOTELS. Colón**; Diligencias**; Imperial**; Jardín Astoria; México; Miramar; Oriente; Rex; Terminal. Mocambo**, on the shore at Boca del Río, 2 miles S of the main highway, is a new resort hotel on a beautiful beach.

NOTE. Hotels are here classified by rates. Two stars indicate the higher rates for the country in question. One star means rates in the medium brackets; no star means low rates or no information available. An effort has been made to list hotels in all the towns mentioned. In a highly developed tourist country like Mexico, these are usually of good quality, and in Mexico City and other centers they compare favorably with those found anywhere in the world. In some of the out-of-the-way places, however, as in other Latin American countries, the hotels often do not come up to the standards expected by U. S. and European travelers.

EXCURSIONS FROM VERACRUZ

Alvarado, named for Cortés' lieutenant, is a picturesque fishing village situated at the mouth of the big Río Papaloapam, 45 miles from Veracruz by railroad. It is famous for fish such as róbalo, as well as turtles, crabs, and oysters.

HOTEL. Olimpia.

Tlacotalpán, down the coast, set in superabundant flora, is the first big town reached from Alvarado by steamboat. The chief attraction is the tropical cruise itself.

Barra de Chachalacas, N of Veracruz, is one of the most attractive sandy beaches of the Gulf coast.

VERACRUZ TO MEXICO CITY BY RAILROAD

Three modes of travel from Veracruz to Mexico City (280 miles) exist: by Pan American Airways, 2 hours; by night or day train, about 12 hours; and by car over a new highway via Jalapa and Puebla, about 8 hours. The motor route is covered later (p. 59).

The journey over the Mexican Railway along the route followed by Cortés is justly celebrated. Anita Brenner in her book Your Mexican Holiday says, "In one day you see a condensed version of all Mexico—tropics, sierra, volcanoes, highlands, the Pyramids of Teotihuacán, and the Shrine of Guadalupe." The traveler by train usually leaves Veracruz very early in the morning in order to enjoy to the full the natural splendors along the route. It is also customary to stop overnight in Córdoba, Fortín, or Orizaba, where the finest scenery begins, in order to grow accustomed to the increasing altitude.

After leaving Veracruz the train crosses a wide plain on which are occasional fields of tobacco and sugar cane and coconut groves. Villages are passed, and workers are seen toiling in the fields. Experienced travelers on the route claim that the best views are from the left side of the train. At Paso del Macho, in the foothills, the oil-burning locomotive is replaced by one operated with electricity, since greater power is needed to scale the lofty mountains farther inland. After passing the beautiful falls of the Río Atoyac, a roaring cataract during the rainy season, June-September, the town of Potrero, famous for its sugar plantations, is reached.

Córdoba, 70 miles E of Veracruz, the first important stop, is a tropical and picturesque city of 17,000 in the hills of Huilango. A highway to Mexico City begins here.

Córdoba is the center of a region producing coffee, tobacco, sugar, bananas, mangoes, papayas, oranges, and lemons. Not far away are wild forests and clear streams. The town was founded in 1618 by order of the Spanish viceroy Diego Fernández de Córdoba, for whom it was named. Its architecture is typically colonial, like that of most of the surrounding towns. The houses have large, heavy windows, somewhat Moorish in style, with substantial iron bars; balconies of carved wood, wide corridors with rows of arches, heavy wooden gates with copper hinges and rivets, massive knockers, and roofs of red tile which form a marked contrast with the vivid green of the fields. At Hotel Zeballos on Aug. 24, 1821, the treaties of Córdoba were signed, confirming the independence of New Spain. The signers were Agustín de Iturbide and Juan O'Donojú, last of the viceroys. The Casa Quemada (Burned House) was the scene of bloody strife between the insurgents and royalists, May 15-21, 1821.

The Palacio Municipal or city hall is of recent construction. In front of it is the parish church. The church of San Antonio y Lourdes, founded in 1688 by the Franciscans, and those of Santa María, San Sebastián, and San José, the last now in ruins, are interesting. The Alameda, a park in the SW part of the town, is a favorite picnic point to which families repair on Sundays.

HOTELS. Francia; Zeballos.

Excursions from Córdoba. The San Francisco and Texpán sugar mill lies 1¼ miles NW of the city on a stone road. Close by is the San Julio bridge across the Río Seco amid beautiful scenery. W of the city is the Zapoapita sugar mill, run by a co-operative society of workers and peasants; it is situated on the bank of the Río Blanco, with Mt. Nexca or Naranjal (Orange Grove) beyond. The San Miguelito sugar mill, one of the largest in the region, is near the railroad station. Grinding season is December-May.

Atoyac, a near-by picturesque town, can be reached by the highway which crosses the Río Atoyac over a masonry bridge constructed during colonial times. This river is excellent for fishing. The falls, which are passed on the train, are near the town and can be reached by a good road. In the caverns of Atoyac, discovered on July 21, 1906, were found prehistoric instruments, fragments of pottery, skeletons, and many other relics of unknown Indian races. Stalactites and stalagmites adorn the caves. Local guides are available for exploring them.

Three miles SE of Córdoba is the interesting Indian village of Amatlán de los Reyes, easily reached afoot or on horseback. Little touched by modern civilization, the Indians cling to their own laws, customs, and language. The women are expert in needlework. The most important fiesta, held on May 3 in honor of the Holy Cross, is celebrated with gala dances and fireworks.

Fortín, the next stop on the Mexican Railway, 4 miles from Córdoba, received its name from a small fort constructed by the conquistadores for their rear-guard while marching on the capital of the Aztecs. The town is often called Fortín de las Flores (Little Fort of the Flowers) because of the enormous production of flowers, many of them exported. The visitor sees large fields of gardenias, azaleas, gladioli, tuberoses, and white lilies; orchids are also grown. The edges of the fields are marked by flowering trees which bloom the year round and show a great variety of color. Indian women appear at the station to sell tropical fruits and flowers from their baskets. Most popular are the bunches of large, fragrant gardenias packed in cartons made from banana tree bark.

HOTELS. Fortín is becoming a popular mountain resort because of its new Hotel Ruiz Galindo, which has a swimming pool, tennis courts, riding horses, bicycles, guided tours, fishing, hunting, a bar, dining tables on open terraces looking out on magnificent jungle, and mountain views. Yola is another hotel.

Excursions from Fortín. The surroundings are of unique beauty, worth a tour by car. At one point the dam and artificial lake of the hydroelectric plant at Tuxpango can be seen from a breath-taking vantage point 1000 feet above. Arrangements can be made to ride the electrically operated funicular down to the plant.

In another direction is Las Animas, a former coffee plantation now full of lofty palm trees and luxuriant gardens.

Orizaba, with 50,000 inhabitants, 10 miles beyond Fortín, is reached on the train after passing through five tunnels, across the Cañada de Metlac, a deep ravine, and across the Metlac bridge. This bridge, an excellent piece of engineering, 345 feet long, is built on a curve and has a 3 per cent grade.

Orizaba is situated in the valley of the Río Blanco at an altitude of 4028 feet. The site is supposed to have been that of an Indian village which was called Ahuaializapán (Joyful Waters) because of its multitude of streams and which the Aztecs conquered in 1457. About midway between Veracruz and Mexico City, Orizaba is a favorite resting place before going on to the high altitude of the capital. In 1553 the Spaniards built the first flour mill here, probably the only one in

America at the time, with power from the Río Blanco. The city is now one of the most important industrial centers of Mexico and has large cotton and jute mills and breweries. It is famous as a resort because of its mild climate and fine surrounding scenery. Maximilian and Carlotta chose Orizaba as a vacation spot during their brief reign as emperor and empress. Their favorite country home, Jalapilla, is located on the outskirts. When the growing of hemp was at its peak the millionaires of Yucatán made Orizaba their pleasure ground.

Orizaba's interesting churches include those of Santa María de los Ciervos, Our Lady of El Carmen, and San Juan de Dios. The city hall, constructed of iron and steel sheets from Belgium at an initial cost of $100,000, and other public buildings are impressive though not significant architecturally.

An introduction to Mexican painting can be gained at the federal school at Paseo Colón 18, which contains a fresco by José Clemente Orozco. Points of interest include the principal plaza, Parque Castillo e Hidalgo, with palm and pine trees and statues; the Alameda or Paseo Colón, and the old wrestling arena.

HOTELS. Diligencias**; Francia**; América; Cuatro Naciones.

Excursions from Orizaba. Some interesting textile mills may be reached by street cars leaving from the center of the town or by car on the road between Orizaba and Tehuacán (p. 142). Río Blanco has some big mills. Most of the citizens are workers who after forming unions set about beautifying the town. The results of their efforts are a new stadium, a fine moving-picture house, the offices of the unions, and several schools. In front of the stadium is the Club Río Blanco, which has excellent tennis courts, a swimming pool, baths, and a bar. Along the roads are cottages of California and other U. S. types.

Nogales, another industrial suburb, has a pond formed by a great number of springs that flow from a hill. The deep blue of the water, the leafy trees, and the paved roads make it attractive. At the pond are bathhouses and springboards. Ciudad Mendoza, until recently called Santa Rosa, is another workmen's town in a beautiful setting.

The hydroelectric plant at Tuxpango, which supplies electric current to the cities of Veracruz and Puebla, can be easily reached from Orizaba as well as from Fortín.

For walking or climbing around Orizaba high boots or leggings are useful as protection against insects.

Orizaba to Mexico City. After leaving Orizaba the train threads its way through a canyon, El Infiernillo (Little Hell), and then climbs to Maltrata (5544 feet). More bridges are crossed and more tunnels traversed, the train climbing steadily and swiftly in a series of wild loops. From the observation platform roads and rivers appear as silver threads below. In 15 minutes the train arrives at Alta Luz, which affords an awe-inspiring view of the lower plains; in its valley encircled by mountains Maltrata looks like a toy village on a checkerboard.

After bridging a gigantic gorge the train winds up to Boca del Monte (7924 feet), having climbed more than 5000 feet in 42 miles. At Esperanza, a few miles farther on, the electric locomotive is replaced by an oil-burner, for the grades now are easier. At Esperanza the great Pico de Orizaba is seen at its best, rising sharply from the plain—the only place in the world where orchids bloom against a background of snow. The Indians call this peak Citlaltépetl (Mountain of the

Star). Over 18,000 feet high, it ranks next to Mt. McKinley in Alaska as the highest mountain on the North American continent. The mountain is generally climbed from Esperanza.

From Acocotla, the highest point reached by the railroad, the train descends to cross a great plateau through fields of corn, wheat, and maguey, from which pulque is made, the Mexican national drink which is gradually giving way to beer.

There are occasional glimpses of the snow-capped, majestic mountains of Malinche, also called Malintzín, 14,740 feet high; Popocatépetl, 17,888 feet, probably the third highest peak in North America, called the Vesuvius of America; and its twin volcano Ixtaccíhuatl, 17,343 feet, called by the Indians Sleeping Woman because the three peaks resemble the head, breast, and feet of a slumbering woman.

Apizaco is the next stop. Native vendors sell canes finely carved with the national emblem and snakes, eagles, and other Aztec forms painted in Aztec colors.

Continuing across the plain, the train passes the impressive pyramids of the Sun and the Moon at San Juan Teotihuacán; the Villa de Guadalupe, now officially called Villa Gustavo A. Madero, with the shrine of the famous Virgin of Guadalupe; enters the suburbs of Mexico City, and shortly afterward reaches the Buenavista station.

VERACRUZ TO MEXICO CITY BY CAR

The highway from Veracruz to Mexico City, National Highway (Camino Nacional) No. 2, passes through tropical jungles filled with palms and orchids, past quaint villages, coffee fincas or plantations, and orange groves, climbing 75 miles to Jalapa, the first important city on the highway. The whole route is 270 miles.

Jalapa, with 35,000 inhabitants, capital of the state of Veracruz, is a coffee, orange, sugar, and tobacco center and a resort. The approach to it is through miles of coffee plantations. Jalapa is reached also by railroad from Mexico City (San Lázaro station) and is connected with Córdoba (p. 56) by the National Railways.

Since the beaten track avoided it until recently, Jalapa has retained its old-time charm unspoiled. The visitor sees a quiet city of old stone houses, walled gardens, and luxuriant flowering vegetation. It is often called the flower garden of Mexico. The fine wide avenues of the newer section are in marked contrast to the winding, narrow cobbled streets of the older parts. For centuries Jalapa was a principal stop on the route between Mexico City to Veracruz. Cortés is said to have halted here on his way from the coast to the capital of the Aztecs. For 200 years after the conquest it remained a purely Indian town, until the Spaniards, attracted by the richness of the land, came in in considerable numbers. Jalapa was designated in 1720 as the place for the huge fair held each year after the arrival of the merchant fleet from Spain. After that for 60 years it was for a few weeks annually the greatest trading center on the continent, the goal of merchants from all New Spain. As much as $30,000,000 changed hands at each fair. The influx of foreign merchandise worked a change in the people. They began to discard their native dress for the finery of the Europeans and to adopt European manners and customs, including European vices. Few full-blooded Indians remain.

Points of interest include the state capitol, Palacio del Gobierno

(Government Palace), a modern stadium, Parque Juárez and Parque Hidalgo or Berros, and a teachers' college, Escuela de Maestros, which contains frescoes by José Chávez Morado.

HOTELS. Juárez*; Limón*; Posada Jalapa*; Plaza; Principal.

Jalapa to Puebla. A number of interesting little towns are scattered along the 120-mile route. Near Banderilla, at a point where the road climbs out of the valley of Jalapa, is Jardín Lecuona, a famous orchid and gardenia garden. Perote, 23 miles from Jalapa, is of interest for its 18th-century fort of San Carlos de Perote, now a military prison, and for the view of the volcano Cofre de Perote. Acatzingo, an old Indian colonial village 55 miles farther, has a beautiful 16th-century church. About 7 miles beyond Acatzingo the highway is joined by a road which runs S to Tehuacán (p. 142) and Hotel Garci-Crespo and thence to Orizaba (p. 57) and Córdoba (p. 56).

Tepeaca, on the main road 4 miles from this junction, was an important halting place in colonial times for arrieros or mule drivers and stage coaches. Here are the ruins of one of the first fortified monasteries built in Mexico. The Moorish tower is ornamented with carved heads, and the plaza contains ancient sculptured dogs. Amozoc, a quaint Indian village 12 miles beyond, is noted for its silver inlaid spurs and miniature earthenware toys.

PUEBLA

Lying in the foothills of the Sierra Madre within view of four snow-capped volcanic peaks, Puebla, with 125,000 inhabitants, 84 miles SE of Mexico City, is capital of the state of this name and the third largest as well as one of the wealthiest of Mexican cities. Numerous fabric, glass, cigarette, match, shoe, and other factories are located here, but the town is best known to tourists for sombreros, leather goods, embroideries, tecalí or transparent marble, miniatures, gold and silver articles, and clay modeling. Ceramic products are highly developed, notably loza de Talavera or Talavera pottery ware, unique for its finish and the variety of its colors.

Laid out by the Spaniards in 1531, La Puebla de los Angeles is the most characteristically Spanish city in the republic, its architecture typically colonial. Legend has it that the plans for the building of the city were brought to the friars in charge by angels coming down from heaven. Always regarded as the military key to Mexico City, Puebla has played a prominent role in the history of the country. In 1821 it was captured by Agustín de Iturbide in the struggle for Mexican independence. The French army of Napoleon III took the city in 1862, and later it was the scene of battles between the imperial forces of Maximilian and the loyal Mexican armies. On April 2, 1867, Gen. Porfirio Díaz took the city and thus ended imperialist rule.

CHURCHES. Puebla is called the city of churches and the Rome of Mexico because of the number and importance of its churches. There are more than 60, some with domes overlaid with the colored tiles for which Puebla is famous.

The most imposing is the cathedral of La Inmaculada Concepción, across from the new city hall on the chief square, Plaza Constitución. It was started in 1552 and completed in 1664. Second in importance only to the cathedral in Mexico City, it is notable for its carved façade and great doors; its high altar of gray Puebla onyx by Manuel Tolsa;

woodcarvings of extremely fine workmanship by Pedro Muñoz; paintings by the Zapotec Indian artists Miguel Cabrera, José Ibarra, and Zendejas; the gold-leaf decorations of the sacristy, and the old Flemish tapestries presented to the cathedral by Charles V. The choir may be visited with permission of the sacristan. The towers command an interesting view of the city and the surrounding country.

The church of Santo Domingo, near the same plaza, built in 1659, is a good example of tile decoration, but is chiefly interesting for its extremely ornate chapel of the Rosary, whose walls and ceiling are covered with beautiful tiles. There are sculptured figures and other carvings and gilded Churrigueresque altars. The figure of the Virgin has exquisite jewels.

The church and monastery of El Carmen, near the corner of Avenida 17 Oriente and Av. 16 de Septiembre, has a gleaming tile exterior and an unusual façade.

The Jesuit church of La Compañía formerly had connected with it a school which is now a state college. Classrooms, laboratories, museum, and library can be visited. A plaque at the entrance to the sacristy marks the burial place of the china poblana, a Chinese princess of whom it is related that she was seized by pirates and spirited away to Mexico. She became a devout Christian, adopted the name of Catalina de San Juan, laid aside her elaborate finery for a red flannel skirt, and devoted her life to helping the poor. The people revered her memory as that of a saint and even imitated her dress. From this imitation came the china poblana costume: a red skirt with a green border, usually flowered in yellow, white, and black; a blouse of fine white or light cream color embroidered in brilliant silks; lockets and necklaces of coral and bright beads; bracelets, and a thin rebozo or shawl jauntily draped.

MUSEUMS. The convent of Santa Mónica, Av. 18 Poniente 103, exposed in 1935 after it had existed secretly since the Reform Laws of 1857 abolished monasteries and convents in Mexico, was taken over by the authorities and reopened as a museum of religion. Of unusual interest, this museum is worth the couple of hours required to inspect it carefully. It is entered through a residence and a secret passageway. The 39 rooms, with intricate passages and other secret contrivances, are filled with religious paintings and relics from this and other secret conventual retreats. Guides are available. Open 11 a.m.-1 p.m. and 4-6 p.m.

The Casa del Alfeñique (Almond Paste House), 2 blocks N and 2 blocks E from Plaza Constitución, one of the most striking of the many mansions which have survived from colonial times, is now a state museum. Dating from the 17th century and owing its name to its elaborate ornamentation, with lavish white stucco trim, blue and white tiles set in the rosy ground of the façade, and wrought-iron balconies, the building was often used as a guest house by the viceroys. The first floor now contains archeological and historical collections; the second is furnished like a typical colonial house, with an attractive kitchen; and the third has been outfitted in a manner befitting viceregal guests. Open 10 a.m.-1 p.m.

The Academia de las Bellas Artes (Academy of Fine Arts), on Av. 2 Oriente, founded in the 19th century by José Antonio Jiménez as a school of drawing, is housed in an engaging 17th-century building, of which the staircase, with its alabaster windows, is quite notable, although the rest of the structure has been heavily remodeled. On the second floor facing the street is a choice gallery of Mexican colonial painting. Puebla has always had a lively artistic life, and the classes held in the building are most interesting.

LIBRARY. The Biblioteca Palafoxiana (Palafox Library) in the city hall, founded in 1648, has a valuable collection of more than 24,000 volumes on general history.

FORTS. Splendid views of the city open out from the forts of Guadalupe and Loreto. Here 2000 heroic Mexican soldiers under Gen. Ignacio Zaragoza, on May 5, 1862, repulsed an invading French army of 6000 men, who had the reputation of being the best soldiers in the world. The date is celebrated as a national holiday. In Puebla the Cinco de Mayo celebration includes an Indian fiesta and a colorful sham battle.

HANDICRAFTS. Talavera ware is the most durable and finely turned in all Mexico. From Puebla also come quaint tiles, highly glazed, sometimes used singly and sometimes arranged in panels; their polished figures usually tell a complete story in vivid colors. Puebla is also famous for its onyx. A visit to one of the factories producing Talavera ware can be arranged. Also sold in the daily market are many-colored straw mats.

MOVING-PICTURE HOUSES. The Reforma has a splendor of a kind familiar in New York. There are many other film theaters.

SWIMMING. About half an hour by bus or car from the center of the city are the popular Agua Azul sulphur springs and an immense swimming pool which is among the finest in the country.

HOTELS. Colonial**; Arronte*; Gran*; Italia*; Argentina; Jardín; Pasaje; Terminal.

Puebla to Cholula. Two interesting churches, lying off the main road beyond Puebla, are San Francisco Acatépec, an ornate 17th-century building with a façade of Puebla tiles, its towers decorated with majolica serpents, and Santa María Tonantzintla, with an interior colorful with Indian decorations and ornate altars.

Cholula, 8 miles beyond Puebla, was once the center of a Toltec civilization. At the time of the Spanish invasion in 1519 it had a population of 100,000 and 400 shrines and temples. Cortés razed the city and destroyed the teocallis or pagan shrines, with the promise to erect a church for every teocalli. He almost succeeded, for in Cholula and the tiny villages that dot the valley around it there are more than 160 churches. Many of them are very picturesque, with many-colored domes.

The town centers around the pyramid of Quetzalcoatl, dating from Aztec times, but only recently uncovered by the Mexican government Department of Archeology under the direction of Señor Eduardo Noguera. It is greater in base area than the famous pyramid of the Sun at San Juan Teotihuacán. Excavations have revealed a honeycomb of passages, galleries, and stairways; many archeological relics of early civilizations superimposed upon each other; and remains of ancient burials, some of which the caretaker shows. On top of the pyramid stands the sanctuary of Los Remedios, a colonial church in which is a small image of the Virgin of Remedies, particularly revered by the Indians.

The church of San Gabriel is interesting for its architecture, particularly the buttresses and doors. Next to it stands the famous Capilla

Real (Royal Chapel), showing strong Moorish influence; the structure has 47 domes and contains many large canvases.

Huejotzingo, 8 miles beyond Cholula, is noted for its stately church and monastery of San Francisco, erected sometime after 1529 by Friar Juan de la Alameda, one of the first 12 Franciscan missionaries to come from Spain. Situated immediately in front of the chief plaza, the building is of fortresslike construction with magnificent carved doors. The paintings adorning its imposing Plateresque altar are among the best works of Simón Pereyns, a distinguished colonial religious painter. Very interesting decorations in black and white fresco, somewhat dimmed by the passing centuries, embellish the walls of the monastery corridors.

Huejotzingo is also celebrated for its annual carnival fiesta on Shrove Tuesday in which all the male inhabitants take part. Rodney Gallop describes one such fiesta: "In its present form the carnival partly commemorates the victory won at Puebla in 1862 over the French forces on what has now become the national holiday of May 5. The French had newly embarked on the military intervention which culminated in the ill-fated imperial venture of Maximilian and Carlotta, and their forces in the carnival are led by a mounted general, whose whitewash contrasts oddly with the Indian brown of his hands. The French forces are divided into two groups—the Zapadores, who wear black beards and aprons and the tall busbies of 19th-century Sappers; and the Zouaves, who seem to have made an impression on the Mexicans. As portrayed in the carnival, the zouaves wear red and blue uniforms, leather masks which are a clever caricature of white features, and knapsacks with the legend: Viva Francia.

"The Mexicans are a more motley crew. First come a group rather misleadingly called Apaches whose costume imitates that of ancient Aztec warriors. They wear plumed headdresses and skirts, and their faces or masks are daubed with gruesome war paint—they are accompanied by their own musicians whose robes are embroidered with the Eagle and Serpent device of Mexico. The instruments which they play are a strident clarinet and a drum of pre-Columbian type called the huehuetl.

"Two other groups are included in the Mexican forces: the Serranos and the Zacapoaxtlas. The Serranos wear battered hats and rough hairy masks, utter raucous cries, and carry on their backs the stuffed skunks associated with the folk-fools who accompany many Indian dancers. The Zacapoaxtlas are incongruously clad in broad hats with bunches of paper streamers and in skirted tunics of black, white, and green, cut short to reveal frilly white drawers.

"Intermittent battles between the various groups are fought throughout the morning, but towards noon a counter plot is introduced concerning Agustín Lorenzo, a semi-mythical bandit who used to pillage travelers from Mexico City to Veracruz at Río Frío. According to legend the bandit used to keep a white maiden captive, sealed up in a cave. One day he did not return, and his mistress died of starvation.

"The capture of the lady, or rather her elopement with the bandit, is enacted at Huejotzingo. She is dressed in an elegant pink skirt and

---

NOTE. Quotation from The Musical Quarterly, January 1940: Otomi Indian Music from Mexico, by Rodney Gallop. Reprinted by permission.

petticoats, while a white plume and a piece of butter-muslin transforms a man's sombrero into a smart toque. A long white veil conceals her decidedly masculine features. The robber band rides up in a swirl of dust and the lady lowers herself by a rope from the first-floor balcony onto a waiting horse.

"From this point the rival armies are united in opposition to the eloping couple. Firing revolvers, with the lady in the rear, the bandits gallop off under heavy fire. In the afternoon, however, fate overtakes them. The troops have traced them to a straw hut in the middle of the plaza. They close in with a deafening fusillade, and the hut goes up in flame and smoke, thus bringing to an end one of the liveliest and most entertaining fiestas of Indian Mexico."

San Martín Texmelucan, 9 miles beyond Huejotzingo, has two interesting conventual buildings, Franciscan and Carmelite. The colorful Indian market is held on Tuesdays.

Excursion from San Martín Texmelucan. Tlaxcala, capital of the state of the same name, is 15 miles NE of the highway. It is a quiet but interesting Indian town, important as a wool-weaving center. Sarapes and beautiful woolen cloth are made by the Indians on handlooms. The Tlaxcalans, fierce enemies of the Aztecs, waged war against them over a long period. Their hatred for the Aztecs made them the principal allies of the Spaniards in their campaign against Tenochtitlán. Tlaxcala's chief attraction is the church of San Francisco, founded in 1521, which contains the pulpit from which the gospel was first preached on the American continent. Here also four native Tlaxcalan chiefs were baptized, the first converts to Christianity in America.

The sanctuary of the Virgin of Ocotlán, a half hour's walk from the town, located on a hill commanding a wide and beautiful view of the valley, commemorates a legend similar to that of Guadalupe. It took more than 20 years for the Indian artist Francisco Miguel to execute the rich and beautifully carved decorations.

HOTELS. Parque; San Carlos; Tlaxcala.

About 4 miles from Tlaxcala by car, horseback, or on foot the traveler can view Aztec murals containing scenes of Aztec mythology and cosmogony in the partly excavated pyramid temple of San Esteban Tizatlán. A number of years ago one of the villagers had a dream in which Xicotencatl, a young prince and Tlaxcalan warrior who fought against the Spaniards, appeared with a royal treasure. The villager persuaded his neighbors to join him in hunting for it, and with their picks and shovels they uncovered the ruins of the temple. The national Department of Archeology took over the job in order to avoid damage.

San Martín Texmelucan to Mexico City. The highway now penetrates gracious pine forests in a series of sharp bends to the continental divide at an elevation of 10,486 feet. Among the Indian villages passed is Río Frío, 17 miles beyond San Martín Texmelucan; it was notorious in early times for its bandits.

TAMPICO

Another port of entry is Tampico, reached from New Orleans by Standard Fruit and Steamship Co. ships. With 82,000 inhabitants, the city is Mexico's largest oil center and one of its busiest ports on the Gulf of Mexico. There are railroad connections with Mexico City, which can also be reached by car W to Valles and thence by the Pan American Highway (p. 72). Monterrey (p. 67) can be reached by railroad (416 miles).

Situated on the N bank of the Río Pánuco, Tampico existed before Cortés set out on his historic march from the shore at Veracruz in 1519. When in 1530 the Franciscan friar Andrés de Olmos, a student of Mexican dialects, reached Tampico a year after his arrival in Mexico, he found it almost in ruins. Through perseverance and by the extraordinary power of his personality he drew the Indians into the town, and in 1532 he founded a Franciscan monastery. In 1683 the pirate Lorencillo destroyed most of the city, and the Spaniards did not rebuild it. Gen. López de Santa Ana in 1823 ordered that a town should be set up on the site, and 26 merchants from Altamira settled here. This was the start of modern Tampico. Petroleum was known to the Indians before the arrival of the Spaniards, but the modern oil industry here dates from the beginning of the 20th century, when rich deposits were rediscovered near the town. The period 1901-22 was the era of wildcat oil. Tampico grew to a city of paved streets with gamblers, soldiers of fortune, prostitutes, mechanics, drillers white-collar workers, engineers, and financial wizards playing movielike roles of hero and villain. Intrigue and murder were commonplace. Then the oil fever subsided, and the population steadily diminished.

The visitor finds himself in a large city of modern aspect, with important stone and concrete buildings, beautiful parks and plazas, and large residential areas. Docks and warehouses care for a vast movement of shipping. Most of the oil fields are at some distance, with the city serving as the center for refining and shipping. Tampico's chief attractions are the swimming at Playa de Miramar, a beach resort reached by a good paved road, with excellent restaurants, dance halls, casinos, and roomy bathhouses, and excellent fishing and hunting near by. The climate is fine in spring and autumn; in winter cold northers lasting 2-3 days make heavy clothing necessary. The tropical heat of summer is tempered by a prevailing SE breeze. The rainy season extends approximately from the middle of June to the end of October. The beach at Tampico is considered one of the safest in the world. For a distance of more than 50 feet from shore the water reaches only to the knees; beyond, it deepens gradually.

FISHING AND HUNTING. Tampico is a favorite haunt of fishermen. The most important catch is the sábalo, tarpon or silver king; Tampico waters are full of big ones. The sun glistening on a silver king's scales is a sight that will live long in a fisherman's memory. Tarpon season is November-May; the best months are January-April. Other fish include pargo, crevallo, róbalo, jewfish, channel bass, shark, bonyfish or 10-pounder, drum, grunt, sheepshead, weakfish, croaker, mangrove snapper, pompano, sea trout, perch, and bass. The Río Pánuco, the Río Tamesí, and the lagoons or salt-water lakes in the vicinity have long been famous for sporty fish. In the rainy season, when the rivers are high, fishermen prefer the lagoons and the piers on the ocean front. The Tampico Tourist Committee (Comité Pro-Turismo de Tampico), at the corner of Calle Isauro Alfaro and Avenida S. Díaz Mirón, organizes deep-sea fishing trips by steam launch or motorboat with complete crew and expert pilot. Tampicans say that their ocean fishing is unsurpassed.

The region around Tampico offers plentiful wild turkeys, deer, wild hogs, coyotes, jaguars, mountain lions, wildcats, and smaller game. Wild ducks, geese, and other waterfowl are abundant from November until March or April. The Tampico Tourist Committee organizes hunting trips of approximately 24 hours to a distance of 80 miles or so, where chances for deer, turkeys, wildcats, coyotes, and even jaguars and mountain lions are good. A trip in deliberate quest of big game should be planned for 6 days or longer, since jaguars and mountain lions cover a lot of ground in a night and are often hard to run down.

The dry months, January-May, are open season for game, though predatory animals—jaguars, wildcats, and so on—may be killed at any time. Licenses for fishing and hunting are inexpensive and can be secured through hotels or the Tampico Tourist Committee. Efficient English-speaking guides for both fishing and hunting are available at moderate rates and can furnish tackle, guns, and ammunition.

OTHER SPORTS AND RECREATIONS. Golf, tennis, baseball, boxing, dances, and lagoon and river launch outings are all possible.

HOTELS. Brístol**, Mexican style; Inglaterra**, Av. S. Díaz Mirón and Av. Olmos; Imperial*, Av. Carranza and Av. Aurora; Rivera*, C. Rivera and C. Colón.

EXCURSIONS FROM TAMPICO

All that is left of the old Magdalena, a freighter loaded with brick which ran aground in 1920 about 10 miles N of the Río Pánuco, makes a favorite fishing and picnic spot on the beach. Banks of sand and shell have accumulated around the vessel. In the dry season, by a mirage, the land near by appears as a lake stretching out endlessly. The sunlight shimmers on the salt beds, and smoked or amber glasses are desirable. In the rainy season the wreck cannot be reached.

La Barra de Chavarría, 27 miles N on the coast from Tampico, where the Laguna de San Andrés joins the Gulf of Mexico, is a fine fishing ground. The oyster beds are famous; in the dry season many parties camp on the banks to enjoy oysters and other seafoods. The trip is made comfortably in sea-going craft.

El Bernal, a mountain NW of Tampico on the road to El Mante on the Pan American Highway (p. 72), rises majestically 3000 feet above the surrounding plain. Undoubtedly of volcanic origin, thrown up during some great upheaval in the remote past, it presents a rugged face riven into gigantic crevices and cliffs. The bare crown is a challenge to mountain climbers.

Laguna del Pueblo Viejo, Laguna de Tamiahua, and Estero de la Llave, S of Tampico, are fine places for fishing and hunting.

Dos Bocas, 67 miles S of Tampico, is what remains of the greatest oil well the world has ever known. The well came in on July 4, 1908, caught fire, and burned continuously for 57 days, with flames mounting as high as 1500 feet. Estimated consumption of oil was 500,000 barrels a day, a total loss of 28,500,000 barrels. The light could be seen for 100 miles at sea, and at night newspapers could be easily read 17 miles away. Finally the ground caved in, forming a hot salt-water and sulphur lake several acres in extent, with traces of oil still issuing from the earth. The activities of the boom days have left traces all along the route to Dos Bocas.

NORTHERN MEXICO

The most interesting approach to Mexico City is by the Pan American Highway from Laredo, Tex. Alternative routes are by railroad from Laredo (p. 74) and from El Paso, Tex. (p. 79). The railroad from Nogales, Ariz., parallels the Pacific coastline most of the way (p. 84).

PAN AMERICAN HIGHWAY TO MEXICO CITY

The magnificent Laredo, Tex.-Mexico City highway, a link in the projected Pan American Highway, is now paved throughout its entire length to Mexico City (762 miles) and is the most practical motor route to the capital. Laredo, on U. S. Route 81, is on the S border of Texas. Mexico is proud of its National Highway (Camino Nacional) No. 1, its section of the international road. Many call the Pan American Highway the Road for Democracy because it helps to cement friendship among the American nations. National Highway No. 1 was opened in 1936.

Travelers usually break the journey at Monterrey, 146 miles from the border, and again either at Valles, 322 miles farther, or at Tamazunchale, 66 miles beyond Valles.

Nuevo Laredo, with 22,000 inhabitants, port of entry, is a town of mixed Mexican and U. S. characteristics just across the international bridge from Laredo, Tex.

The road directly S of Nuevo Laredo traverses an arid country very much like the mesquite and cactus lands of Texas. Here is one of the longest stretches of straight highway in the world, about 50 miles. The road then winds over mountains. Off the Pan American Highway, 45 miles S of the U. S. border, is the Presa (Dam) Don Martín, noted for its black trout and bass fishing.

Vallecillo, with 500 inhabitants, 65 miles S of Nuevo Laredo, is the largest town between the border and Sabinas Hidalgo.

Sabinas Hidalgo, with 10,000 inhabitants, 16 miles S of Vallecillo, is a mining and farming town. At Powers Midway Café, Curio Store, and Tourist Courts good meals, U. S.-style coffee, and Mexican curios and novelties can be secured. After leaving Sabinas Hidalgo, the road crosses the Río Salinas and begins an easy climb over the Mamulique pass (2280 feet).

MONTERREY

An ancient and picturesque city, Monterrey is Mexico's most important industrial center, with 180,000 inhabitants, and capital of the state of Nuevo León. It lies in a great valley at the foot of Cerro de la Silla (Saddle Mountain) and Cerro de la Mitra (Miter Mountain), 146 miles S of the U. S. border and 65 miles S of Sabinas Hidalgo on the Pan American Highway. It is also reached by railroad from Laredo, Tex. Narrow streets call for one-way traffic in Monterrey. Blue and white arrows on the walls of buildings on each corner indicate the direction of traffic. Parking of cars on one-way streets is allowed only on the left side. The sign "No estacionarse" means "No parking." There is no time limit for parking except that cars may not stand overnight. Guides can be hired for sightseeing in and around the city.

Monterrey hums with steel rolling mills, smelters, flour and cotton mills, and factories turning out soap, cigars and cigarettes, electric bulbs, cement, shoes, furniture, tiles, and electrical equipment. The locality has seen much change since a Spanish outpost was founded here in 1579 around the springs of Santa Lucía, which the Indians had used as a gathering place for unnumbered generations. The city itself was founded on Sept. 20, 1596, by the captain general Diego de Montemayor, who stood at the point which is now the intersection of Calle Cuahtémoc and C. 5 de Mayo, near the springs, and solemnly named it the Metropolitan City of Our Lady of Monterrey in honor of the viceroy of New Spain, Gaspar de Zúñiga y Acevedo, Count of Monterrey. The Spanish colonial atmosphere is retained in the narrow streets, flat-roofed houses with colorful patios, churches, and government buildings. The center of commercial and social life today is Plaza Zaragoza, a beautiful old-fashioned square full of trees and flowers. On Thursdays and Sundays at 9 p.m., when the municipal band plays, the young people promenade here in typical fashion characteristic of the ancient Spanish mode of courtship. Plaza Hidalgo, another handsome shaded square, opposite Plaza Zaragoza, contains a large bronze statue of Miguel Hidalgo y Costilla, hero of the war of independence, which the townspeople erected in 1910.

Tours through the Cervecería Cuauhtémoc, the largest brewery in Mexico, are conducted regularly daily except Saturdays and Sundays at 9, 10, and 11 a.m. and 2 and 3 p.m., with free beer served in the garden.

PUBLIC BUILDINGS. The city hall, Palacio Municipal, between Plaza Zaragoza and Plaza Hidalgo, has the city's coat of arms carved on the façade.

The state capitol, Palacio del Gobierno, on C. Zaragoza and C. 5 de Mayo, 6 blocks N of Plaza Zaragoza, is a majestic building of red granite with stately columns, a Spanish-style patio, and halls beautifully furnished and decorated. The Red Reception Room contains the first printing press in N Mexico, set up in 1813 by Father Servando Mier, an advocate of republican principles who was among the first to answer the call of Hidalgo. This press is famous for the insurgent manifestoes that were printed on it. Among the other relics are three of the carbines used by the Nuevo León firing squad who executed Maximilian in 1867.

The federal building, Palacio Federal, a block N of the state capitol, illustrates the modern trend of construction in Mexico. It is a glistening edifice in which are housed offices of the national government including the post and telegraph offices and health department laboratories. A splendid view of the city is obtained from the tower.

The Obispado, the old bishop's palace, on the hill of Chepe Vera at the W side of the city, reached on C. Bolívar by street car, was built in the latter part of the 18th century, during a time of drought and famine, to give work to unemployed Indians. It served as the bishop's residence during the final phase of the colonial period and as a barracks and military hospital during the revolution of independence. In 1864, during the fighting with the French, it once more became a fort, and later the Villa and Carranza forces used it for the same purpose.

The Hospital Muguerza, on the hill of Chepe Vera, is one of Latin America's leading hospitals. The building is modern and handsome.

The Campo Militar, an army post and aviation field, is immediately N of the city on the Pan American Highway. The largest army post in the republic, it was commanded by Gen. Juan Andreu Almazán prior to his unsuccessful campaign for the presidency in 1940. The barracks, offices, residences with flower gardens, clubs for officers and enlisted men, and swimming pool were built by the soldiers under Almazán's direction. The whole is like a huge park.

CHURCH. The 18th-century cathedral, facing Plaza Zaragoza, is typically colonial. Its fine tower, carved stone façade, and interior with sculptures and valuable murals are noteworthy. The most important painting is a copy of Murillo, an Assumption of the Virgin, above the high altar.

CENTERS OF HIGHER LEARNING. The state university of Nuevo León is at C. Washington and C. Colegio Civil. The Escuela Industrial y Técnica Alvaro Obregón (Obregón Industrial School), at the E end of Calzada Madero at C. Gómez, has a modern building with complete equipment for training in arts and industries.

MARKETS. Mercado Colón is 4 blocks W of the Chamber of Commerce, which is at Avenida Morelos Oriente 347. Pottery and other native wares are sold. A block S of this market is that of San Luisito.

SPORTS AND CLUBS. The chief bullfighting season is November-March. Two huge rings, each seating 10,000, were recently opened; one has a modern floodlight system for night performances. Bullfighters of international renown appear here. Programs of the events are obtainable at hotels.

The Chamber of Commerce and the Mexican Automobile Association issue cards permitting visitors to play golf and tennis at the Monterrey Country Club. The club is situated 3 miles S of the city on the Pan American Highway at the foot of a mountain, Cerro de la Silla. The links are excellent. Other fine tennis courts are at the Club Deportivo Monterrey, a sportsmen's club in a beautiful setting on the hill of Chepe Vera; at the Campo Militar, and at the Railroad Club.

The surrounding country offers limitless opportunity for hunters and fishermen. Fishing is especially good in the rivers S of Monterrey and at Hacienda Santa Engracia, about 165 miles S on the highway and thence 11 miles W on a side road.

At the California Courts, at the N edge of the city, guests have the use of riding horses. The Escondida Colonial Mountain Club, 6 miles out of town, has 30 miles of trails; horses can be hired by the hour or the day.

The swimming pool at C. Allende and C. Zaragoza is fed with spring water, with a complete change every 3 hours.

Polo matches are held occasionally at the Campo Militar.

Wrestling matches are held, usually on Thursdays, at the Arena Obrero, Av. Madero, and at the Coliseo, C. Treviño.

The Círculo Mercantil Mutualista, on C. Zaragoza a block S of Plaza Zaragoza, is a social and athletic institution with a membership of more than 5000. It is housed in a fine modern building. Its gymnasium, perhaps the best in the republic, is the scene of international basketball games in the winter. Visitors are welcome.

NIGHT LIFE. Cabarets include the Foreign Club, Aztec Obispado, and Terpsícore. The Casino Monterrey, N of the cathedral on Plaza Zaragoza, is an exclusive social club which admits visitors with cards obtainable through the Chamber of Commerce or the Mexican Automobile Association. Dinner dances are held on Sunday evenings on a beautiful open-air terrace in the summer and in an elaborate dance hall in the winter; there is no gambling.

FIESTAS. The Monterrey fair, lasting the entire month of May, is a succession of picturesque events, bullfights, dog races, pageants, a parade, an athletic meet, fireworks. The N Mexico fair and fiesta honoring the Virgin of Guadalupe is held December 12-26.

SOURCES OF INFORMATION are the Chamber of Commerce, Av. Morelos Oriente 347; Club de Monterrey, affiliated with the Mexican Automobile Association, Av. Morelos Oriente 547; hotel managements, and the U. S. consulate.

BANK. Crédito Industrial de Monterrey.

RESTAURANTS. Sanborn's, air-conditioned, is at C. Escobedo 920, convenient to hotels. A branch of the popular Sanborn's in Mexico City, it has a soda fountain, cocktail bar, and handicraft shop.

HOTELS. California Courts**, at the N entrance to the city on the Pan American Highway, private tiled baths with showers, spacious grounds, swimming pool, free use of saddle horses, attractive café, accommodations for trailers; Gran Hotel Ancira**, facing Plaza Hidalgo, one of the largest hotels in N Mexico, with a mural by Salvador Tarazoma in the patio depicting the founding of the city; Monterrey**, in the heart of the city at the corner of Av. Morelos and C. Zaragoza, new, large, and very modern; Regina Courts**, at the N edge of the city on the Pan American Highway, offering all the comforts and conveniences of a hotel and with accommodations for trailers; Colonial*, Plaza Hidalgo, all modern conveniences, garage, and sports facilities; Continental, C. Cuauhtémoc and Av. Colón; Geneva, Calzada Madero 243; Ritz, C. Hidalgo Oriente 214; Terminal-European, Av. Colón 544.

EXCURSIONS FROM MONTERREY

Topo Chico has hot springs that are very popular, 4 miles NW of Monterrey.

The Salto de Caballo (Horsetail Falls) is reached by driving about 21 miles on the Pan American Highway and then 4 miles from El Cercado along a dirt road where a small toll is charged. The road winds up a mountain, offering a succession of beautiful views; passes three cascades, one above another, and comes out on a mesa or tableland, where cars must be left. From here a rustic path winds upward ¾ mile to the falls. Burros can be hired at the parking area, and lunch and refreshments can be obtained at Hacienda Vista Hermosa, in whose grounds the falls lie.

Chipinque Mesa, a beautiful mountain resort built by General Almazán, is 15 miles from Plaza Zaragoza, a 45-minute drive over a paved road up the slopes of the Sierra Madre to 4200 feet altitude. The route is 3 miles S on the Pan American Highway, then left over a low ridge of hills, and up to the mesa. A toll is charged for the use of this road. Night driving on the mountain is dangerous. The resort has bungalows and a restaurant surrounded by pines. Fine entertainment by native singers, the imposing view of the valley of Monterrey, and the exhilarating atmosphere make this an exceptional excursion.

The canyon of Huasteca, 10 miles W of the city on the Saltillo road and thence 2 miles S of Santa Catarina on a gravel road, is an awesome rocky gorge with sheer towering walls 750-1000 feet high. In places the softer rock has been eroded into curious formations. As the innermost parts of the canyon are reached the impression is that of a huge crater. The canyon is a good camping spot; the swift, cold waters of the Río

Santa Catarina are ideal for bathing in the summer. Refreshments, meals, and a few rooms are available at a resort in the canyon.

Las Grutas de García (García Caves), full of stalactites and with an underground lake, are 3 miles beyond Santa Catarina, then 17 miles N to Villa García, where it is necessary to obtain a guide before continuing up the mountainside on foot or on horseback. It is best to hire a guide and make other arrangements in Monterrey through a hotel, the Chamber of Commerce, or the Club de Monterrey, affiliated with the Mexican Automobile Association. The caves, only partially explored, have huge chambers with beautiful formations. Flashlights are necessary, since there is no lighting system.

Saltillo and Torreón can be reached by a road W (p. 75, p. 80).

(p. 75, p. 80)

About 4 miles S of Monterrey the Pan American Highway leads through the beautiful Huajuco canyon and for the next 75 miles through fine citrus fruit country.

Montemorelos, with 6000 inhabitants, 48 miles SE of Monterrey, is in the heart of Mexico's most productive orange and lemon belt. The flowering trees and orchards make the region very beautiful. A large fair and fiesta is held at Montemorelos, July 15-25.

Linares, with 10,000 inhabitants, 32 miles beyond Montemorelos, is a trading town in the center of a rich farming and grazing district, formerly the bishopric of San Felipe Linares. The town was founded in 1712. It has two churches of interest, the parochial church and that of the Lord of La Misericordia (Mercy.) There is a handsome casino.

HOTELS. Chester Courts*, with a swimming pool, on the N outskirts of the city, is on the highway at Km. 864. Hardwicke's Canada Courts*, on the N edge of the city, can be reached by following direction signs. The Ramal is in the city.

Ciudad Victoria, with 18,000 inhabitants, capital of the state of Tamaulipas, 97 miles S of Linares, is the trading center of a rich agricultural region. The city was founded in 1750 and named in 1825 in honor of Mexico's first president, Félix Fernández, who called himself Guadalupe Victoria in homage to the Virgin of Guadalupe. Points of interest are the Tamaulipas state agricultural college and its farms; the state capitol, Palacio del Gobierno; the cathedral; the Jardín (Garden) Juárez; Plaza de Armas; and near-by spots like La Peñita, known for its rustic beauty, and the falls of Juan Capitán. The region is known for good hunting, fishing, and swimming.

HOTELS. Sierra Gorda**, air-conditioned; Hacienda Santa Engracia**, 11 miles W on a road branching off the highway about 24 miles before reaching Ciudad Victoria, a guest ranch with Spanish colonial atmosphere but 20th-century comforts and good hunting, fishing, and swimming; the Dude Ranch**, operated by Mrs. Kona Reeder, 7 miles left of the highway a short distance beyond Ciudad Victoria; Campo Victoria*; Palacio*; Zozaya Tourist Courts*, left of the highway at the N entrance to the city; Estación; González; Modelo.

Thirteen miles S of Ciudad Victoria the highway crosses the Tropic of Cancer into the Torrid Zone and descends into a low, hot country of dense forest, lush with orchids and masses of vines.

El Mante, with 7000 inhabitants, known also as Ciudad Mante and as Villa Juárez, lies in the center of the sugar-cane country 82 miles beyond Ciudad Victoria. It has one of the largest and most modern sugar refineries in the republic; visitors can inspect it during the operating season, November-April. There are good hunting, fishing, and swimming in the neighborhood.

HOTEL. El Mante*.

Excursion from El Mante. Tampico, on the Atlantic coast, can be reached by a 96-mile paved road. In returning to the Pan American Highway the 63 miles between El Mante and Valles can be saved by taking the road directly W out of Tampico which runs into Valles. Tampico has been described (p. 64).

Valles, with 3000 inhabitants, on the Pan American Highway 63 miles S of El Mante, is a popular stopover. A railroad center connected with Tampico (p. 64) and San Luis Postosí (p. 76), Valles is a pleasant town with an attractive plaza and white adobe houses. Los Baños de Taninul, 9 miles away, are sulphur baths. The near-by rivers provide good swimming opportunities and the Sierra Madre fine hunting.

HOTELS. On the N edge of the town on the highway are three hotels: Casa Grande**, hacienda style; Palma Courts*; Valles*, with facilities for swimming, tennis, riding, hunting, and fishing. In the town itself is the Condesa*.

Stops between Valles and Tamazunchale can be made at towns like Pujal and Xilitla, an Indian coffee-growing center 13 miles W from the highway at Km. 404-405.

Tamazunchale, another popular stopover, is a small, picturesque town 66 miles S of Valles. Indian language and customs are kept almost intact. Tamazunchale, lying in the foothills of the towering Sierra Madre Oriental and nicknamed Thomas 'n' Charlie by tourists, is an old Aztec town with additions of gas stations, hotels, and restaurants. Hunting is excellent in the mountains, and fishing is good in the Río Moctezuma.

It is not advisable to leave Tamazunchale for the journey through the mountains before the clouds of early morning have lifted. Fogs are usually less frequent between 10 a.m. and 4 p.m.

HOTELS. DZ Courts**, on the main street at the S end of the town; Pemex Tourist Camp**, on the highway at the N end; El Sol Tourist Courts*, 2 miles N at Km. 371; Los Ríos*; Progreso*, on the highway at the N end of town; Tamazunchale Inn*, on the highway at the N end of town; Central; Davis; Gandy; Vega; Victoria.

From Tamazunchale the highway climbs in tortuous curves through magnificent scenery. Guardrails of heavy steel have been set up for protection.

Chapulhuacán, 20 miles beyond Tamazunchale, a quaint Indian village, has a road camp of the government highway department at which gas, oil, and water can be obtained. There are a restaurant and post, telegraph, and telephone offices. Four hundred yards E is another Indian hamlet, Tancanhuitz, in a beautiful tropical setting.

Jacala, with 2500 inhabitants, 39 miles beyond Chapulhuacán, is a delightful spot in the broad, fertile mountain valley of the Río Quetzalapa. There is a small tourist camp, and food can be obtained at the Russ White Cafeteria.

The road beyond Jacala climbs 10 miles through pine and oak forests to an elevation of 7500 feet and 10 miles farther S enters the beautiful Barranca de los Mármoles.

Zimapán, 41 miles beyond Jacala, is a charming colonial mining town of Otomí Indians. To the left on entering the town is a huge cypress tree measuring 42 feet around the trunk. The large parish church has curious towers and an elaborate entrance facing the plaza. The city

hall, Palacio Municipal, and the Sunday market are quite interesting.
HOTELS. Patio Colonial*; Fundición.

The Tasquillo bridge, of modern design and graceful single-arch construction, spanning the deep gorge of the Río Tula 17 miles past Zimapán, is a favorite camera subject. The near-by village of Tasquillo lies among walnut groves.

Ixmiquilpán, 30 miles beyond Zimapán, is a handsome old native town situated on the mountain rim above the valley of Mexico. Once the Otomí Indian capital, it is believed to be at least 10 centuries old. The natives are much occupied with weaving beautiful wool bags and fine oyates or carrying-cloths. This is the maguey zone, and the Indian women spin maguey fiber into balls of string as they make their way along the highway. Market is held on Sundays. A massive stone bridge built in 1654 spans the Río Tula near the town.

The H. R. Dobbs Restaurant and Service Station on the highway at Km. 159, open 24 hours, serves good U. S. food and sells local handicraft objects.

Excursion from Ixmiquilpán. At Km. 167 a road branches off the Pan American Highway to Querétaro (p. 77). It is not in good condition.

Actopán, with 3000 inhabitants, 24 miles beyond Ixmiquilpán, is another Otomí town. A rugged 16th-century Augustinian monastery here is sometimes compared with the San Agustín Acolman church and monastery, though the building in Actopán is conceded to be the more beautiful. The ancient frescoes, beautiful patio, Renaissance doorway, and Gothic cloisters are much admired, and the roof affords an excellent view. Actopán's market is held on Wednesdays.

Just past Actopán the traveler sees crags on the mountain peaks to the left called Los Frailes (The Monks). The highest point on the road (8209 feet) is at Hacienda de la Concepción at Km. 92; here Pachuca comes into sight, E. About a mile farther is the Friendly Relations Monument (Monumento de Buena Amistad), erected by the U. S. colony of Mexico City in 1936.

EXCURSION TO PACHUCA

Capital of the state of Hidalgo and one of the oldest and largest silver-producing centers in the world, Pachuca, with 45,000 inhabitants, is 5 miles E of the highway at Colonia, which is 22 miles S of Actopán. Lying among hills scarred with the openings of mines, Pachuca has steep, narrow, crooked streets. Near the city are big ore reduction plants. Through a great shaft connected with all the mines electric trains transport 5000 tons of ore daily.

According to early chroniclers the Aztecs mined silver here long before the arrival of the Spaniards. Shortly after the conquest a shepherd discovered the silver workings, a mining camp soon sprang up, and in 1534 Pachuca was made a town. In 1557 Bartolomé de Medina invented here the so-called patio process for the amalgamation of silver ore. Among the more famous of the fabulous old mines was La Trinidad, from which was extracted 40,000,000 pesos' worth of silver over a period of 10 years. In 1739 Pedro José Romero de Terreros, a Biscayan, having acquired a fortune of $60,000 in mining in Querétaro, started home to Spain. On his way to the capital he passed through the Pachuca district and was impressed so favorably that he invested his capital in a mine here. It proved a bonanza, and the owner eventually became so wealthy that he was able to lend the king of Spain a million pesos and to present him with several warships fully equipped. In return the king gave him the title of Count and afterward Duke of Santa María de Regla.

Points of interest in Pachuca are the historic building of La Caja on Calle Cajas, a handsome stone structure surmounted by towers, built in 1670 by Sebastián de Toledo, Marquis of Mancera, as a treasury for the royal tribute; the state capitol, Palacio del Gobierno; the Independence clock and tower in the main plaza; the Banco de Hidalgo, a modern bank building; and the church of San Francisco, dating from 1596.

Permission can be obtained to visit the silver mines. El Real del Monte and El Chico are the most noted for their fabulous wealth. Within the city limits of Pachuca a visit can be made to the Loreto silver refining plant, the foremost of its kind in the world.

HOTELS. Los Baños*; Camino; Colonial; Doria; Grenfell; Hidalgo.

EXCURSIONS FROM PACHUCA

Buses and autos leave Pachuca at regular intervals for places of interest.

El Chico is one of the most noted silver mines. On the way to it a path leads up to the Peña del Cuervo (The Crow's Rock), from which there is a vast panorama of mountains and forests, the magnificence of which is comparable to the natural beauty of the Swiss Alps. Set in a forest in the valley below is the village of El Chico, an attractive spot with a hotel and restaurant.

San Miguel Regla and Santa María Regla, the big hacienda and the picturesque castle once owned by the Count of Santa María de Regla, can be visited by special permission. The estate has underground dungeons in which the mine laborers were locked up at night. It overlooks huge basaltic cliffs inclosing a ravine and river.

Tizayuca is a small town farther along the Pan American Highway. Past it the two great snow-capped volcanoes of Ixtaccíhuatl and Popocatépetl can be seen on clear days. Each mile closer to Mexico City improves the view.

Venta de Carpio, beyond Tizayuca and 17 miles N of the capital, is the point of junction for the main highway and the 12-mile branch road to San Juan Teotihuacán with its famous pyramids (p. 118).

San Cristóbal Ecatépec, 3 miles beyond Venta de Carpio, is of historic interest because it was the scene of the execution of José María Morelos, hero of the revolution of independence. The Casa de los Virreyes, the old colonial house of the viceroys in which Morelos was held prisoner, has been converted into a small museum of Morelos relics. In front of the building stands a monument to his memory.

Santa Clara, 8 miles short of the capital, is the point from which a new road, now part of the Pan American Highway, leads into the heart of the city, avoiding most of the heavy local traffic on the old road via Villa Gustavo A. Madero. In casetas or shelters along the way at various points are representatives of the tourist department who will answer questions. If the traveler accepts the services of a guide he should ask to see the guide's license or registry credentials from the tourist department.

LAREDO, TEX., TO MEXICO CITY BY RAILROAD

Of the three great railroad routes into Mexico from the north the shortest is the one from Laredo, Tex., operated by the Missouri Pacific Lines in conjunction with the National Railways of Mexico (803 miles). The San Antonio-Mexico City train crosses the international bridge from Laredo, and it continues through cactus country to its first important stop, at Monterrey (p. 67). The next large city reached is Saltillo.

SALTILLO

Capital and leading industrial city of the state of Coahuila, long a cattle-raising and mining region, Saltillo, with 60,000 inhabitants, 68 miles beyond Monterrey by railroad and connected with it also by road, has had a long history. It was originally occupied by Indians, probably of the Nahua family, who were driven out by the Spaniards. The founding of the present city in 1575 is attributed to the captain Francisco de Urdiñola. During the early 17th century it was the jumping-off point for explorations of the country N of it. In 1824-36 it was the capital of a vast territory which included Texas as well as the present state of Coahuila.

Today Saltillo is a modern city with cobbled streets, wide avenues, and hundreds of picturesque colonial mansions. It is famous for its sarapes or bright blankets worn as shawls throughout the republic. Very old ponchos and sarapes from here are highly valued and can be obtained only at stiff prices in the better stores in Mexico City. Because of its healthful climate, its elevation of a mile above sea level, and its almost constant sunshine, Saltillo is a popular summer resort. The days are never hot enough to be uncomfortable, and the evenings are always cool. Facilities exist for golf, tennis, polo, swimming, and hunting. The Casino is the social center of the city.

The cathedral of Santiago, facing the central plaza, was built during the latter part of the 18th century and is one of the best examples of ecclesiastical architecture in N Mexico. Its façade and central doors are richly carved, and it has a 200-foot tower. The state capitol, Palacio del Gobierno, across the plaza from the cathedral, is decorated with murals by Tarazona; although portions of earlier structures remain, most of the present building dates from 1929.

The Alameda is a beautiful park with statues, tiled fountains, palm and cypress trees, and a small lake. Conspicuous is an equestrian statue of Gen. Ignacio Zaragoza, hero of the battle of Puebla in 1862, who was born in Saltillo. Calzada de los Héroes (Highway of the Heroes) leads off the Alameda. On this avenue is the monument to Emilio Carranza, well known for the first non-stop flight from Mexico to New York; on the return flight the aviator met his death.

Parque Porfirio Díaz and Parque Zaragoza are favorite promenades.

Saltillo has a fine theater, a public library, and a museum containing material of local interest. Among its educational institutions are a state normal college, Roberts College, and a preparatory school.

MARKET. In the center of the city, fronting on a little plaza, is one of the most interesting markets in N Mexico. Here are sold sarapes, pottery, tin masks, and innumerable other items. The plaza holds a statue of Manuel de Acuña, a Mexican poet born in Saltillo who was popular for his exquisite love lyrics.

FIESTAS. Picturesque ceremonies and dances, fireworks, outdoor banquets, a regional fair and carnival, and bullfights are highlights of the October fiesta season. In the first week of August homage is paid to an image of Christ which stands in a small chapel of the cathedral. Indian dances are features of the fiestas of May 3 and August 30 in the poorer section of the city.

HOTELS. Arizpe*, Calle Victoria 122 on the Monterrey-Torreón highway, is new and fireproof and has a patio and flower gardens with illuminated fountain, tennis courts, and ballroom with dancing Saturday evenings; Casa Colonial*, C. Hidalgo Sur 134, 2 blocks W of the cathedral, an old Spanish mansion converted into a small modern hotel, with opportunities for swimming and horseback riding; Huizache Courts*, at the E edge of the city on the Monterrey-Torreón highway, with all conveniences and a café serving U. S.-style food; Coahuila; Fronterizo; México; Roma.

EXCURSIONS FROM SALTILLO

Diamante Pass, which is accessible 11 miles S along a gravel road, is 7800 feet above sea level, 2200 feet higher than Saltillo. As it winds to the pass, the road affords remarkable views of Saltillo and the surrounding country. The land around Saltillo is very arid, but the valley beyond Diamante is fertile. The road is rough and difficult, and it is advisable to take a guide.

Torreón can be reached by a road W (p. 80).

San Luis Potosí, with 80,000 inhabitants, capital of the state of the same name, 242 miles beyond Saltillo by railroad, is situated in a rich mining and agricultural district.

After the territory N of the valley of Mexico was opened to the Spaniards through a treaty with the Indians, the Franciscan friar Diego de la Magdalena founded a mission at San Luis in the late 1580's. About the same time a military outpost was established under the command of a Captain Caldera who was well liked by the Indians because his mother was an Indian greatly esteemed by her own people.

It is related by an early source that "to Fray Diego came secretly an Indian chief, who loved greatly that venerable father in God, and discovered to him in the nearby Sierra a very rich mine, which was the San Pedro mine, afterward most famous. Then this blessed monk, desirous that the King our master should possess this treasure, and that the wealth thereof should quicken with a larger life the missionary work among the barbarians, gave to Captain Caldera (having thereto the Indian's consent) notice of what the Indian had told him. So was discovered the treasure—producing Cerro del Potosí, to which this name of Potosí was given because both the configuration of the mountain and the greatness of the riches stored there, made that place resemble the mines of Potosí in Peru"—in a part of the Peruvian viceroyalty which is now Bolivia.

Other mines were discovered, and Philip IV in 1658 raised the town to the rank of city. Many of its impressive churches, public buildings, and residences date from this time. It is a pleasant city, though not a frequent travelers' goal. In it is the former headquarters of Gen. Saturnino Cedillo, the one-time strong man of the state, whose revolt in 1939 was swiftly quelled by President Cárdenas. Interesting churches include the cathedral, on the E side of Plaza Hidalgo in the center of the city; the church of San Francisco, SW from the cathedral, on the W side of the Jardín (Garden) Guerrero, with a magnificent blue and white tiled dome; and that of El Carmen, a short distance E of the cathedral, in Plaza Morelos, with an elaborate façade and a fine tiled dome. S of Plaza Hidalgo is the state capitol, Palacio del Estado.

The best-known local product is the opals which are offered for sale on the streets, in the shops around the plaza, and at the railroad station.
    HOTELS. Colonial Nuevo**; Colonial*; Progreso*; Buen Tono; Fénix; Imperial; Nacional; Nicoux; Palacio.

San Miguel Allende, with 33,000 inhabitants, 109 miles S of San Luis Potosí, is a city of ancient colonial towers and belfries, a relic of the splendor of colonial rule. It was founded about 1560 as a military outpost against the Chichimec Indians.

The city has an important place in the history of Mexican independence. Ignacio José de Allende, associated with Miguel Hidalgo y Costilla in the leadership of the independence movement, was born here in 1779, and when independence was achieved his name was incorporated into that of the town. One of Hidalgo's first overt acts was to march on San Miguel. A royal regiment that was quartered in the town and had Allende as one of its officers went over to the revolutionary cause in a body.

Aristocratic Spanish colonial families chose San Miguel as their home. The carved stone of the conventual buildings, the splendid arcades of the seignorial palaces, the escutcheons sculptured over doorways, all witness to the wealth of the period. A Society of the Friends of San Miguel has been organized to preserve the city's ancient charm. On the initiative of Dr. Felipe Cossío del Pomar, Peruvian exile, former diplomat, writer, and artist, and with the support of this society, a school of fine arts has been founded where once stood a stately ancient convent.

Interesting churches include those of Our Lady of La Soledad; the parochial church, with a beautiful façade and tower strongly suggesting the Gothic; the oratory of San Felipe Neri, which, with its chapel of the Santa Casa de Loreto, seems to sprawl over a dozen blocks of terraced gardens on the Cerro del Chorro (Hill of the Spring), just S of the town. Other points of interest are the homes of the revolutionary heroes Allende and Juan Aldama; the hot springs of Taboada; and the tiny village of Atotonilco, in whose famous church are impressive frescoes executed in the Mexican manner with red, black, and gray earth.
    HOTELS. Granja de Santa Mónica**; Posada de San Francisco*; Central; Reforma.

QUERÉTARO

Querétaro, with 40,000 inhabitants, capital of the state of Querétaro, 51 miles beyond San Miguel Allende, is a beautiful colonial city 5947 feet above sea level. It can be reached by railroad on all three routes to Mexico City from the United States. An 85-mile road to it from the Pan American Highway branches off near Ixmiquilpán (p. 73).

Querétaro has preserved an air of antiquity more than most cities of Mexico. It is full of beautiful colonial residences, ancient churches, and old public buildings. Events of historic importance which occurred here include early gestures toward independence, the ratification of the Treaty of Guadalupe-Hidalgo which ended the war with the United States in 1848, and the surrender of Maximilian. In 1910 Querétaro was the capital of the republic for a short time, and today it is popular for national political conventions. The name is derived, according to some historians, from Queréndaro, a corruption of the Tarascan word querenda, meaning the place of the stony peak. Presumably the reference was to a rocky hill near the city. A more popular and plausible theory is that the city's name is simply the Tarascan word meaning a game of ball or, more explicitly, the place where ball is played. The exact date of the founding is not known to historians. At the time of the conquest the city was inhabited by Otomí Indians. It submitted in 1446 to the rule of Moctezuma the Elder, tribal chieftain of the Aztecs, who made Querétaro a dividing point between his domains and the Tarascan kingdom. In 1531 Fernando de Tapia, an Otomí Indian chieftain from near-by Xilotépec and a zealous convert to Christianity, gained permission to Christianize the Otomí population of Querétaro. He was appointed a captain general and recruited a small army for an attempt to capture the city in the name of Charles V. To economize in blood, attackers and defenders agreed that no weapons should be used. After a fist fight had raged for 12 hours, so the story goes, the Apostle James was seen in the sky riding a snow-white horse and brandishing a flaming sword. The strong light that streamed down from the apparition blinded the warriors of both sides, and the defenders were awed into surrendering. This miracle is said to have occurred on July 25, 1531, the day of St. James, and the Christian town was called Santiago de Querétaro because of it.

In 1810 Señora Josefa Ortiz de Domínguez, wife of the governor, became an active propagandist for the revolutionists. Her husband, though an official of the royalist party, secretly approved. A general uprising was planned for October 1, but the conspiracy was discovered well ahead of time, and many leaders and adherents of the nationalist party were arrested. Señora Domínguez at once dispatched a mounted courier with a warning to Juan Aldama and Ignacio José de Allende, who reported the news to Father Hidalgo. They decided on an immediate uprising, and on Sept. 16, 1810, the priest called his parish to arms.

The struggle of the democratic Mexican forces headed by Benito Juárez against those of imperialism and monarchy headed by Maximilian met its climax in Querétaro. On his military defeat at San Jacinto on Feb. 9, 1867, Gen. Miguel Miramón, commander of Maximilian's soldiers, retreated to this city and ordered trenches dug. Soon the imperialists were surrounded by the republicans, and though Miramón strove to break through the besiegers' lines, he failed. Finally after a siege that lasted 68 days the city was seized by the republicans. The surrender of Maximilian, who yielded his sword to Gen. Mariano Escobedo, was very dramatic. On June 19 after a speedy trial the Austrian archduke and self-styled emperor of Mexico was executed, along with General Miramón and General Mejía, by a firing squad at Cerro de las Campanas (Hill of the Bells), a short distance from the town. A chapel was erected on the hill to commemorate the triumph of democracy.

POINTS OF INTEREST. The city's history comes alive in visits to the room of Señora Domínguez in the old building which was her home, the Palacio Municipal or city hall on Plaza Independencia; the house at Calle Descanso 14, where the revolutionary conspirators met ostensibly as a society for the study of the fine arts; the house at C. Hidalgo 29 where the U. S.-Mexican treaty was ratified, and many other places which have been the scene of historic events.

Plaza or Jardín Zenea, center of the commercial life of the city, 2 blocks W of Plaza Independencia, is flanked by markets. There is a bandstand, and concerts are given on Sunday evenings and occasionally during the week. Plaza Independencia, 2 blocks E of Plaza Zenea, has a handsome fountain, statues, plaques, and attractive trees and flowers.

Many of the beautiful buildings in the town are the work of Francisco Eduardo Tresguerras, a simple mason who in the 18th century became one of Spanish America's most famous architects. It was he who designed the handsome Federal Palace, which was originally a monastery of San Agustín; he also did the work of reconstruction in the church of Santa Clara and the splendid convent of Santa Rosa de Viterbo.

The Regional Museum of Querétaro, situated in the Federal Palace, C. San Agustín, contains paintings by Miguel Cabrera and other works of art, the blood-stained coffin in which Maximilian was laid after his execution, and other souvenirs of the war of independence and the third empire.

The church and monastery of La Cruz, in Plazuela Cruz, mark the first church built in Querétaro, erected by the Spaniards to celebrate the outcome of their conflict with the Indians. The church served as headquarters for the Franciscan monks who converted the natives of this vicinity and who afterward, in missions established from Nicaragua to California, left valuable records of their work of conversion in America during Spanish domination. The strategic position of this monastery, its strong stone walls, and its great size have made it useful at times as a fortress. In it can be seen the cell in which Maximilian was imprisoned; a gallery of portraits of famous missionaries, among whom Friar Junípero Serra, founder of the mission in San Diego, Calif., is conspicuous; and the humble cell where the friar prayed.

HOTELS. Gran**; Jardín*; Ferrocarril; Hidalgo; Internacional.

EXCURSIONS FROM QUERETARO

The Cerro de las Campanas, where Maximilian was executed, is within walking distance. The view from the hill is magnificent. Also within walking distance is a handsome, sturdy aqueduct built in 1726 which still supplies water to the city. About 5 miles long, it is one of the largest in Mexico. Before entering the city the aqueduct forms a beautiful arcade of 37 tall arches supported by enormous pillars.

Near Querétaro are several interesting towns which can be reached over country roads by car during the dry season.

San Pedro de la Cañada has hot springs.

El Pueblito is the site of noteworthy archeological remains.

San Juan del Río is on the branch road connecting Querétaro with the Pan American Highway. It is an interesting town noted for its native baskets. Near it are the celebrated opal mines of La Trinidad. At Hacienda de la Llave the work of opal cutting and polishing can be observed. The fire opals from this region are among the finest and most beautiful found anywhere.

EL PASO, TEX., TO MEXICO CITY BY RAILROAD

From El Paso, Tex., to Mexico City by railroad is 1226 miles, covered in approximately 48 hours. Trains of the National Railways of Mexico pass through the fairly large cities of Chihuahua, Torreón, Zacatecas, and Aguascalientes and the somewhat smaller ones of León, Silao, Irapuato, Celaya, and Querétaro.

Ciudad Juárez, opposite El Paso, Tex., has 50,000 inhabitants. Air service is operated by the Líneas Aéreas Mineras between Ciudad Juárez, Chihuahua, and Mexico City. A good road connects Ciudad Juárez and Chihuahua.

President Benito Juárez stayed in this town during the dark days of the French intervention when Maximilian's troops held most of Mexico.

HOTELS. Kopper; Palacio; Río Bravo.

Chihuahua, with 60,000 inhabitants, 227 miles S of Ciudad Juárez, is the center of a mining and cattle region. It can be reached by car from Ciudad Juárez as well as by railroad. In the old days the haciendas or ranches on the plains around it were not unlike medieval strongholds; little cities in themselves, they sheltered hundreds of peons. In the early decades of the 19th century Chihuahua was the seat of a considerable trade between N Mexico and the United States. Annual caravans plied between the town and Santa Fe, N. M. In the second decade of the present century Chihuahua figured prominently in the exploits of Pancho Villa. Contrasting with the innumerable picturesque adobe structures in it now are modern smelters, iron foundries, factories, and mills. There are silver mines in the vicinity.

The important plazas, with trees, flowers, and bandstands, are Jardín del Porvenir (Garden of the Future), Plaza Merino, Parque Lerdo de Tejada, Alameda Cuauhtémoc, and Plaza Constitución. The busiest streets are Calle Libertad and C. Victoria. The handsome cathedral, formerly the parish church of San Francisco, faces Plaza Constitución. The fine building was begun in 1717 and completed in 1789 with the proceeds of a tax of 1 real on each half pound of silver taken from the celebrated Santa Eulalia mine and 200 others in the vicinity. Statues of St. Francis and the apostles adorn the richly ornamented façade. In the recesses of the supporting arches of the domes are bas-reliefs of the Fathers of the Church, and in one of the towers is a bell broken by a cannon ball during the bombardment of the city by the French in 1866. There is a magnificent view of the countryside from the towers.

Other points of interest include the sanctuary of the Virgin of Guadalupe, at the end of Alameda Cuauhtémoc near the notable statue of St. Ignatius Loyola, the founder of the Company of Jesus; the Jesuit church of La Compañía, built under the patronage of Manuel de Santa Cruz in 1717; the oratory of San Felipe Neri; a handsome monument to Miguel Hidalgo y Costilla in Plaza Hidalgo; the modern Federal Palace on C. Libertad, which includes the old tower of the Capilla Real (Royal Chapel) in which Hidalgo was imprisoned and from which he was taken to be executed; and the immense aqueduct which brings water into the city from 3½ miles away.

Famous in Chihuahua are the miniature dogs which in the United States are called Mexican hairless. In Mexico such a dog is called Chihuahueño or perro pelón, literally meaning bald dog.

HOTELS. América; Apolo; Azteca; Francés; Iberia; Maceyne; Nacional; Palacio (A.A.A.); Regis; San Carlos; San Luis; Victoria; Vidal (A.A.A.).

Torreón, with 80,000 inhabitants, 4 miles S of Chihuahua by railroad, is an important mining, industrial, and agricultural center in the famous reclaimed Laguna cotton and wheat region. From it a road runs E to Saltillo (p. 75) and Monterrey (p. 67).

Torreón is new as cities go in Mexico, since it was elevated to that rank as recently as 1907. Founded in 1887 on a ranch known as El Coyote, the town received its name from a watch tower set up to guard against Indian raids. The main square, Plaza Principal or Plaza Mayor, center of the social and commercial life of the city, is flanked by arcaded shops, government buildings, hotels, places of amusement, banks, and churches.

Torreón is the setting of an interesting social experiment. Clarence Senior of the department of history and political science of the university of Kansas City describes it in his monograph, Democracy Comes to a Cotton Kingdom: The Story of Mexico's La Laguna (Centro de Estudios Pedagógicos e Hispano Americanos, 1941). "On an irrigated oasis in a corner of a Mexican desert, the world's largest attempt at collectivized agriculture on a voluntary basis is being worked out," he writes. "One hundred and sixty thousand peasants, until recently near serfs, on 300 collective farms are building a new pattern for rural civilization, based on collective ownership, cooperative work, and economic self-government." The Laguna region provides an excellent opportunity for a study of one of Mexico's chief problems, the distribution and working of the land. The Center of Pedagogical and Spanish American Studies (Centro de Estudios Pedagógicos e Hispano Americanos), at Calle Tapachula 87, Mexico City, which published Senior's study, sponsors an annual conference in Torreón during which trips are made to the ejidos or lands held collectively as well as to cotton gins, schools, hospitals, irrigation works, and offices of the co-operative farms.

HOTELS. Francia*; Galacia*; Salvador*; Iberia.

Zacatecas, with 35,000 inhabitants, capital of the state of the same name, is an important mining, agricultural, and cattle-raising center, 267 miles beyond Torreón by railroad.

The name is apparently derived from that of a tribe of Indians, the Zacatecs, and from the Aztec Zacatlán (Place Where the Grass Called Zacate Grows). Dominating the city is a curious ridge, La Bufa, on which stands the little church of Los Remedios, founded in 1728, containing an image of the Virgin which is regarded by the Indians as possessing miraculous healing powers. A battle was fought on La Bufa on March 2, 1871, between a revolutionary army and the forces of Benito Juárez, which were victorious. The view from the hill is excellent. Other points of interest are the elaborate Churrigueresque cathedral; the handsome church of Santo Domingo, built by the Jesuits; the smaller churches of San Juan de Dios, San Augustín, San Francisco, and La Merced; Plaza Hidalgo with its statues; the mines, and the near-by ruins of La Quemada and Chalchihuites.

Zacatecas is known for its fine sarapes, which can be purchased at shops, in the market, and at the railroad station.

HOTELS. París*; Francia; Perla.

Aguascalientes (Hot Waters), with 80,000 inhabitants, capital of the state of the same name and important chiefly for its mineral hot springs, is 75 miles S of Zacatecas by railroad. It is a drowsy, pleasant provincial city, once an important smelting and railroad center, on a fertile, well-watered plain. Because of its mild yet refreshing climate and its gardens, trees, flowers, and vineyards, Aguascalientes is one of the most delightful cities of Mexico. Immense catacombs exist here, constructed by some unknown ancient Indian tribe according to a well-defined plan. The city has attractive plazas; a Palacio del Gobierno, the state capitol; a Palacio Municipal or city hall; good schools, hospitals, public libraries, and churches; large pottery factories, and an important drawn-work industry.

HOTELS. Francia*; México; Palacio; París; Regis; San Carlos.

León, with 85,000 inhabitants, built on a fertile plain, is 105 miles S of Aguascalientes by railroad. The town has many pleasant squares and a cathedral and several other churches. An agricultural center, León is of industrial importance also for its leather products such as shoes and purses and for its rebozos or shawls. These can be purchased in the Mercado Hidalgo, a busy market.

HOTELS. Condesa; Francés; Imperial; México.

Silao, with 30,000 inhabitants, 21 miles S of León by railroad, is accessible from there by road as well. Points of interest are the principal plaza; the market; the parochial church and those of La Tercera Orden, Jesús Nazareno, and San Nicolás, and Aguas Termales de Comanjilla, hot springs near the city. Horsehair belts, sarapes or blankets, toys, and inlaid boxes can be purchased.

HOTEL. Gran Hotel Central Victoria.

EXCURSION TO GUANAJUATO

Ranking with Taxco as one of Mexico's most picturesque cities, Guanajuato, with 30,000 inhabitants, may be visited as a short excursion, a few miles E of Silao by railroad or by car.

The city lies in a mountain gorge, and its narrow, twisted, hilly streets, one of them so narrow that it is called Callejón del Beso (Alley of the Kiss), are rich in historical background and architectural treasures. The native population, consisting of Otomí and Aztec Indians and mestizos, some of whom have Andalusian and Basque blood, are gay and friendly. In the evening serenades with guitar accompaniment are common among the young people. The name of Guanajuato is a corruption of Guanaxhuato, a Tarascan Indian word meaning Hill of the Frogs. The name was given to the settlement because of the frogs which once abounded in the neighborhood and because the Indians found here a large frog-shaped stone which they worshiped. According to legend silver was accidentally discovered by some muleteers in 1548. Today it is a mining center.

The Alhóndiga de Granaditas, near the entrance to the city, built originally as a grain market at the order of the Spanish intendente or provincial governor Juan Antonio Riano, is as fascinating in appearance as it is interesting historically. The battle-scarred structure, used for years as a fortress by the Spaniards, is now the city prison. In 1810 the revolutionists under Father Hidalgo took the city. This building was the last stronghold to fall to them, and when they gained it, they slaughtered most of the Spanish troops. When Hidalgo left the city a few days later over 200 defenseless royalist prisoners were killed by a mob which broke into the fortress. Later Hidalgo and his associates Aldama, Allende, and Jiménez were captured and executed at Chihuahua and their heads brought to Guanajuato and hung from hooks at the corners of the Alhóndiga as a warning to other revolutionists. Ten years later, after Mexican independence was gained, the heads were placed in the Mexico City cathedral and later were removed to the base of the Independence monument in the Mexican capital. The hooks on which the heads were hung remain outside the old building in Guanajuato.

Guanajuato has some fine old churches on which silver millionaires lavished their wealth: the Jesuit church of La Compañía, facing Plaza Compañía, an 18th-century structure; the church of San Diego, Plaza Unión, whose portal is one of the best examples of the Churrigueresque style in Mexico; and the church of San Francisco, Calle San Francisco, with an interesting image of a Spanish Virgin on the high altar. In the catacombs in the Panteón, the ancient cemetery on the summit of Cerro del Trozado, W of the city, can be seen natural mummies which have escaped the ravages of time because of the peculiar properties of the very dry air. Jardín de la Unión, a lovely park; the principal square or Plaza Mayor, and Alameda del Cantador are all popular promenades. Other points of interest include the state college; the imposing Juárez Theater; the Club or Casino Guanajuato, open to visitors through guest cards secured from hotel managers; the Legislative Palace; the Presa la Pastita, a dam with a huge electric plant that supplies the city with light and power, and the Bustos mine.

HOTELS. Luna**; Palacio*; La Unión.

EXCURSION FROM GUANAJUATO

La Valenciana, 3 miles from Guanajuato, is noted for its church, one of the most famous in Mexico, which is near the Valenciana mine, at one time the largest silver mine in the world. Churrigueresque in style, with suggestions of the pure Moorish in its lavish ornament, it was built by the Count of Rul, one of the principal holders of mining rights in the region. The church is cruciform in shape and has a single belltower. It was dedicated in 1788 and is well preserved today. The interior is lavishly carved. It is said that silver was built into the foundations and that the Count of Rul sent to Spain for fine wines to be used in mixing the mortar. The peons who worked the mines for a daily wage of $.06 spent their religious holidays working on the building for nothing. Even so, the cash outlay on it was enormous, possibly 1,000,000 pesos altogether. There were a thousand miners at La Valenciana, and each gave the church a piece of ore every week. This was known as the piedra de mano, a block the size of a man's fist. In consequence the church had an income of some 50,000 pesos yearly, and its services were maintained with great pomp.

Mrs. John Wesley Butler, in her book Historic Churches in Mexico, gives further details about the building.

Irapuato, with 32,000 inhabitants, 18 miles S of Silao on the railroad, is a charming old city with fine buildings. The strawberries grown in the vicinity are unusually big and fine-flavored. The Compañía Manufacturera de Cigarros El Aguila has the largest cigarette factory in the republic here.

From Irapuato there are railroad connections W to Guadalajara (p. 89) and the Pacific coast.

HOTELS. Hidalgo; Rioja; Roma.

Celaya, with 25,000 inhabitants, 38 miles S and E of Irapuato, at the junction of the Laredo-Mexico City and El Paso-Mexico City railroad lines, lies in the fertile agricultural Bajio valley, 2 miles from the Río Laja. It was founded on Oct. 12, 1570, by 16 families and 17 bachelors. The settlers, mostly Biscayans, named the town Zalaya, a Basque term meaning Level Land. The fact that Philip IV raised Celaya to the rank of a city in 1655 long before a similar dignity was conferred upon Guanajuato is a source of great satisfaction to the local Celayan chroniclers.

Celaya is noted for its dulces or sweets, its pleasant surroundings, a momentous battle between the Villistas and Carrancistas, and especially because it was the birthplace on May 13, 1765, and the home of Francisco Eduardo Tresguerras, Mexico's great architect, sculptor, painter, and poet. The architectural beauty of the city is due to this remarkable personality. A Creole, he was the last of the old Mexican school, and by his amazing industry he left monuments to his skill and taste in church and conventual buildings, theaters, bridges, and other public structures throughout the republic. Anita Brenner in Your Mexican Holiday writes that as "architect and sculptor he was beyond doubt a master, in the sense that his work is new, vigorous, personal and often illumined by the flare of genius; very Mexican in his daring use and control of monumental and heroic proportions."

Tresguerras is buried in the chapel of the parish church of San Francisco, which he built, and which was originally dedicated to Our Lady of Los Dolores. His admitted masterpiece, famous throughout the republic, is the church of El Carmen in Celaya, erected in 1803-07 and notable for its size, its beautiful simplicity combined with dignity, and its lightness and stately grace. The extraordinary beauty of the tower and the dome of glazed gold and green tiles has won them the reputation of being the finest of their type and period in Mexico. In the chapel of the Last Judgment (Capilla del Juicio) are some of his notable frescoes, his painting in oils of Our Lady of Mt. Carmel, and self-portraits at the ages of 35 and 63. In the church proper there is a large painting by Nicolás Rodríguez Juárez, The Triumph of Mary, done in 1695.

The city has an interesting market, pleasant plazas, theaters, and public buildings; an Independence monument on the main plaza; a great bridge across the Río Laja, and a federal agricultural school for Indian boys.

HOTELS. García*; Central; Gómez; Guadalupe; México.

After leaving Celaya the train's next objective is Querétaro (p. 77). It then climbs to the valley of Mexico and Mexico City.

WESTERN MEXICO

Mexico's Pacific highway, when completed, will run from Nogales, at the Sonora-Arizona border, through Hermosillo, Guaymas, Mazatlán, Tepic, and Guadalajara to Mexico City (1102 miles). At present an all-weather stretch of the projected highway from the border as far as Guaymas and a paved section between Mexico City and Guadalajara are completed. Formidable construction difficulties due to the harsh topography make progress slow. When the highway is finished motorists will be able to retrace the romantic old Spanish mission trail from the one-time Aztec capital to California. At present, however, the journey from Nogales, Ariz., to Mexico City is best made by train. The Southern Pacific Railroad's W coast of Mexico route is in some respects the most spectacular of the overland approaches to Mexico City. It was finished in 1927 when Southern Pacific engineers succeeded in overcoming the forbidding gorges of Nayarit and thus completed the line through to Guadalajara, where it joins the National Railways of Mexico line to Mexico City. Many W points attractive to visitors are covered by this route.

Crossing the international border at Nogales, the W coast railroad route passes through great stretches of cactus growth in the state of Sonora and enters rich agricultural districts of semitropical products such as oranges, limes, and pomegranates, which gradually give place to bananas, coconuts, and mangoes. S of Mazatlán it climbs the slope of the Sierra Madre Occidental and near Tepic begins the final ascent through the awesome gorges of Nayarit to the high plateau on which Guadalajara lies. From Guadalajara to Mexico City is an overnight trip.

The principal train on the W coast route, the Coaster (El Costeño), carries air-conditioned Pullmans and de luxe trains of a type familiar in the United States. There is through Pullman service between Los Angeles and Mexico City. Passengers from the E United States board this train at Tucson, Ariz. Leaving Tucson, the train cuts S through vivid desert country to Nogales, Ariz., which is separated from Nogales, Mexico, only by a wire fence. The Mexican Nogales is of no special interest to the general traveler. Leaving it, the train climbs through wild, rocky country to Encina and Casita and enters the valley of the Río Magdalena, where it passes through Magdalena, 62 miles S of Nogales, a rich and attractive colonial mining and agricultural town. After that the train crosses the great desert of N Sonora. Here are forests of saguaro or organ cactus, so named because they resemble pipe organs; their tips are favorite resting places for the enormous zopilotes or black buzzards of Mexico. The train then descends gradually to Hermosillo.

Hermosillo, with 30,000 inhabitants, capital of the state of Sonora, is the prosperous center of a rich agricultural district growing oranges, limes, figs, dates, peaches, pomegranates, guayabas or guavas, avocados, papayas, mangoes, and bananas. Mining is important. Hermosillo's name, meaning Little Beauty, is well deserved. The original settlement bore the namo of Pitic, which in the local Indian dialect signifies Confluence or Joining, because on the E edge of the city the Río Sonora and the Río San Miguel merge. Parque Madero, containing many subtropical trees and plants, is a promenade which comes alive with the evening.

HOTELS. Cohen; Ramírez. Casa Turista is a boarding house.

Excursions from Hermosillo. Hunting and fishing near by are excellent.

Tiburón Island is the home of the vanishing Seri Indians, a nomadic tribe who roam the mainland and are frequently seen in the vicinity of Kino Bay, 68 miles from Hermosillo. The Seris offer a good subject to students of ethnology. They are distinctly Asiatic in appearance and speak a dialect different from that of any other tribe in the state. Their mode of life is most primitive, and though they are not fierce, they have refused to accept modern civilization and are fast becoming extinct from the ravages of disease and high infant mortality. A few years ago the tribe had several thousand members; at present it has a scant 300.

Numerous vestiges of ancient inhabitants exist in the region, particularly paintings and hieroglyphs on rocky-faced mountains. Their makers were undoubtedly Indians who held the secret of indestructible paints.

Empalme, the next principal stop on the railroad, is the junction for the line to Guaymas, 6 miles W.

GUAYMAS

A famous desert resort by the sea is located at Guaymas, with 20,000 inhabitants, lying on the Gulf of California on a landlocked bay surrounded by brilliantly colored mountains and easily reached by railroad from Empalme; the road from Nogales, Ariz., is gravel. The town is charming and friendly. The country around it is famous for its spectacular sunsets and for its sports, swimming, fishing, and hunting. The climate is semitropical. Winters (October-April) are warm and clear with little or no rain; summers (April-October) are quite warm, with the heat tempered somewhat by breezes from the Gulf of California.

HOTEL. Playa de Cortés** on Bocochibampo Bay, 4 miles NE of Guaymas, is a famous resort. Every room has outside exposure and a bath and is furnished in Spanish style; there are suites and also detached bungalows. The restaurant specializes in seafood and game. The hotel is open from November 1 to the middle of July.

Horses can be rented at the hotel for riding through the desert and by the sea. Swimming is excellent in the large outdoor salt-water pool in the hotel court, as well as in the bay. There are two double tennis courts and a badminton court.

The Gulf of California in the vicinity of the hotel is held to be one of the three finest places in the world for marlin and sailfish and the only place where totoaba is caught. The hotel rents cruisers specially constructed for big-game fishing; it also has several fishing launches for hire. The boats carry experienced fishing guides. Licenses are arranged for by the hotel. The fisherman's summer catch may yield marlin, average weight 180 lb.; sailfish, 90 lb.; albacore, 15 lb.; bonito 8 lb.; dolphin, 20 lb.; giant ray, 1500 lb.; moonfish, 20 lb.; needlefish, 7 lb.; red snapper, 5 lb.; rock bass, 15 lb.; roosterfish, 20 lb.; shark, 250 lb.; skipjack, 5 lb.; Spanish mackerel, 3 lb.; triggerfish, 2 lb.; tuna, 50 lb.; yellowtail, 15 lb. In winter he may take totoaba, 80 lb.; jewfish 250 lb.; pompano, 3 lb.; red snapper, 5 lb.; rock bass, 15 lb.; silver sea trout, 8 lb.; Spanish mackerel, 8 lb.; spotted rock bass, 3 lb.; yellowtail 15 lb.; giant ray, shark, etc.

Hunting trips can be arranged from the hotel to many points, including Ciudad Obregón, 80 miles S of Guaymas, where duck, geese, quail, snipe, doves, cranes, deer, wild pigs, ocelots, and pumas can be bagged.

Navojoa, S of Empalme on the W coast railroad route, lies along the Río Mayo in a fertile valley. It is one of the several Mayo Indian villages in Sonora. The Indians here are noted for their excellent baskets and handwoven sarapes or blankets patterned with vegetable dyes that do not fade. Every train is met by Indians who offer their blankets for sale, and prices often drop abruptly as the train is about to leave. The sarapes, distinctive in color and weave, are among the best in Mexico. Important fiesta days in the village are those of the Holy Cross on May 3 and St. John the Baptist on June 24.

HOTELS. García; Jardín.

San Blas, S of Navojoa on the railroad, is a small town on the Río Fuerte.

Excursions from San Blas can be made by railroad to Los Mochis, 25 miles W, a popular winter resort with a considerable U. S. colony, and to Topolobampo, a small port on the Pacific coast that is popular as a fishing resort.

From San Blas the train proceeds through country that looks more and more tropical. Exotic products are offered for sale by the Indians at the stations.

Culiacán, with 21,000 inhabitants, S of San Blas on the railroad, is a town on the Río Culiacán that is rapidly growing in importance. It is capital of the state of Sinaloa and modern in appearance though it dates from the 12th century, when it was a stronghold of the Colhua Indians. In the lower part of the city on the river is the attractive Jardín Rosales, a beautiful park full of tropical trees, flowers, and birds. Beyond Culiacán the train crosses the Tropic of Cancer and enters the Torrid Zone.

Mazatlán is reached in 3 hours, S of Culiacán on the railroad. It marks the halfway point on the W coast route and is a city of rare charm as well as an important Pacific port.

A favorite stopover, Mazatlán, with 31,000 inhabitants, is a miniature edition of Rio de Janeiro. It lies on a peninsula overlooking the waters of Olas Altas Bay. In many outward characteristics it suggests a South Sea island village. On one side of the peninsula is a beach fringed with tall coconut palms sheltering thatched huts. Hollywood has filmed many South Sea island dramas near Mazatlán. The broad boulevard on the other side of the peninsula is lined with substantial buildings. The climate is pleasantly warm, and Mazatlán is a good place to loaf. Galleons from China used to unload rich cargoes on the wharves, and ships from the Orient still land their merchandise here. Life moves at a very leisurely pace. There are many automobiles, but most travelers like to jog through the cobbled streets in horse-drawn arañas, rickety two-wheeled carts whose name means spider. Fruit, fish, brilliant tropical birds, and articles made of coconut shells and alligator hide are for sale in the market.

Facing the main square, Plaza República, are the parochial church and the Palacio Municipal, the city hall. An old Spanish fort and the little park around the observatory on the Vigía promontory are interesting. El Faro, the great lighthouse that crowns Crestón Island, has a lantern 515 feet above high water, with a beam visible 31 miles at sea. Paseo Olas Altas, a boulevard along the waterfront, has some little rocky perches inviting a stop to admire the view.

There is excellent bathing at the beaches, which are strewn with countless colored shells. Game fish are plentiful in the waters near the shore. Boats can be hired for a cruise to Cocos (Coconut) Island, as well as for fishing. From the bay a number of lagoons reach inland dotted with islands that are covered with coconut palms. Many varieties of wild birds—flamingoes, cranes, herons, pelicans—haunt the mangrove swamps fringing the lagoons. Alligators are found near the city; a license is required for shooting them, and hotel management will assist in securing it.

Carnival in Mazatlán, during the last few days before Lent, is one of the most famous of Mexican fiestas because of its extraordinary brilliance and gaiety. The town is thrown wide open to parades, garden parties, fireworks displays, costume balls, and general hilarity. The big day is Shrove Tuesday.

HOTELS. Belmar**, with flower-filled patios; Central*.

Tepic, with 18,000 inhabitants, 185 miles S of Mazatlán on the railroad, capital of the primitive state of Nayarit, is one of the most picturesque cities in Mexico. Situated on a broad plain at the base of the extinct volcano of Sangangüey, Tepic can hardly have changed since Cortés occupied it in 1524. Many of its streets and houses in mudéjar or Spanish Moorish style, with long balcony windows, and some of its customs recall the days of the conquistadores. In the evening the crowded streets are gay with laughter and music. Groups of mariachis or street musicians move about, singing and playing for a few centavos. The market is extremely attractive on Sundays. Cora and Huichol Indians come in from the sierras in picturesque costume, the women wearing four-cornered pre-conquest embroidered blouses called quexquemitles; the men unbleached suits with strings of hand-woven bags around their waists and over their shoulders.

Near by is the old Aztec town of Jalisco with a federal normal school. Information concerning the school can be secured at the federal office of education in Tepic.

HOTELS. Bola de Oro; Brandes; Imperial; Palacio.

Leaving Tepic, the train enters the sierra of Nayarit, speeding through tunnels and over gorges in the depths of which rivers roar and churn on their way to the sea. The scenery of the sage and purple mountainsides ranks with the finest in the Americas. The 62 miles of track between Tepic and La Quemada cost $14,000,000 and represent the heroic toil of thousands of men for four years. Fifteen miles of the track rest on ties of solid ebony.

Compostela, with 13,000 inhabitants, founded by the conquistadores in 1535, lies amid wild scenery. The town has a 16th-century church of Santiago, built of the red tezontle which was so popular in the early period in Mexico. Compostela was the first capital of the province known as the kingdom of New Biscay. An expedition was organized here to explore the Pacific NW region as far as the Columbia River.

Ixtlán marks the entrance of the gorges of Nayarit, one of the most awe-inspiring stretches of scenery in the world. The tracks cling to a mountainside, 1000 feet below the peak and 1500 feet above the bottom of the gorge. The train twists and turns, climbing steadily. New limitless majestic vistas keep opening out. The Jesuit José Ortega wrote of this region in 1754: "It is so wild and frightful to behold that its ruggedness, even more than the arrows of its warlike inhabitants, took away the courage of the conquerors, because not only do the ridges and the valleys appear inaccessible, but the extended range of towering mountain peaks confused even the eye."

Leaving these rugged gorges, the train climbs through the state of

Jalisco to the high Mexican plateau. The air becomes crisper with the increase in altitude.

GUADALAJARA

The second city of Mexico in size and importance, Guadalajara, capital of the state of Jalisco, has 200,000 inhabitants. It is 380 miles NW of Mexico City, which is reached by air, by the National Railways of Mexico in 14 hours, or by an excellent 411-mile highway via Morelia and Toluca; near this highway lies the lake region (p. 132).

Guadalajara is sometimes called the Dresden of Mexico because of its artistic characteristics and pleasant social life. It was founded in 1530 by one of Cortés' captains, Juan Oñate, who named it, in courtesy to his immediate commander Nuño de Guzmán, for the old Moorish city of Guadalajara in Spain, where Guzmán was born. At first it was used as a base for exploration and conquest up the W coast. It grew rapidly, and when the rebellious Indians of the surrounding regions had been conquered it was made the seat of the W bishopric and capital of the rich region long known as the kingdom of New Galicia.

THE CITY. Guadalajara was laid out in the old Spanish fashion with a main plaza lined with the cathedral and important public buildings. This flower-filled square, Plaza Mayor or Plaza de Armas, is an attractive promenade. The cathedral on the N side faces on a street that runs past the plaza. The state capitol occupies the E side of the square. The State Museum is in the block NE of the cathedral; a couple of blocks E is the huge and famous old Degollado Theater with the church of San Agustín across from it. Streets running E from the main plaza meet the wide Calzada Independencia, which runs NE-SW across the city. The part of this boulevard lying SW of the market, which is almost directly E of the main square, is called Calzada Independencia Sur; NE, Calzada Independencia Norte. The large and beautiful park of the Alameda faces Calzada Independencia Norte a few blocks above the market.

Guadalajara lies on a plain. The streets as a rule cross each other at right angles. Many of them are lined with trees which never lose their foliage; flower gardens and restful little plazas beautify the city. The old housefronts have grilled windows and overhanging balconies. The people live much in the open, for the climate, though semitropical, is not hot; they sit in their secluded patios or stroll the streets with a pause at a sidewalk café. In the main plaza, 7-9 p.m., the military band plays in a costly bronze kiosk made in Paris. The people prefer waltzes, perhaps because the famous waltz composer Juventino Rosas lived here. The young men turn out in charro or horseman costumes with sarapes and umbrella-sized sombreros or in the latest styles from Savile Row; the girls, among the most beautiful in Mexico, dress in fashions ranging from the gracious mantillas and high combs of viceregal days to the current offerings of Fifth Avenue. At the markets Indian musicians play stringed instruments and sing their songs. The markets offer a great variety of native handicrafts. Multitudes of natives from neighboring towns flock into the city on fiesta days to sell their wares. Elaborate bags and textiles are brought by Huichol Indians; woolen fabrics, hats, baskets, sarapes or blankets, toys, and novelties are also offered. The city is famous for its blown glass in blue, green, amber, and amethyst; there is an endless variety of table and decorative pieces. In the markets and shops can also be found beautiful black, ivory, and blue pottery; leather articles, homespuns, silver and gold work, and tequila and delicious regional dishes like pozole, made with corn, pork, and chile sauce.

PUBLIC BUILDINGS. The Palacio del Gobierno, the state capitol, on the main plaza, was built in 1743 and is an excellent example of the exuberant Churrigueresque style in colonial architecture. The interior patio is magnificent. The frescoes by the great muralist José Clemente Orozco on the stairway are particularly noteworthy.

The Hospicio is a very unusual orphanage located on Calle Hospicio, E of the main plaza, a couple of blocks past Calzada Independencia Norte. The institution includes a girls' industrial school and a home for aged women. The immense building has more than 20 lovely patios, some of them filled by gardens and others by playgrounds or athletic fields for the 600-700 children who live here. Conducted along modern progressive lines, the orphanage is pleasantly free of the dull institutional atmosphere common to such places; the smaller children look happy and well cared for, and there is a high percentage of vocational placements among the older ones. The former chapel, now a library and moving-picture theater, was decorated by José Clemente Orozco in fresco with motifs suitable to the character of the institution.

The Hospital Belén near Parque Alcalde, N from the main plaza, was opened in the last decade of the 18th century. It occupies another unusually fine building, a great square structure more than 1000 feet on each side. In the large central court are a chapel and cemetery.

The state penitentiary, just outside of the city, is a model institution especially interesting to students of penal methods. Humane methods and intelligent direction are producing fine results in the regeneration of delinquents. The prisoners, paid modest sums for their labor, are taught trades to make them self-supporting when they leave. The building is modern and contains swimming pools, a moving-picture theater, and a library.

CHURCHES. The huge cathedral, facing Avenida Alcalde, with a wide entrance on the main plaza, has been rebuilt and remodeled so many times that almost all known styles of ecclesiastical architecture are represented in it. The beautiful dome was added as late as 1908. The whole is a mixture of Byzantine, Greek, Gothic, and Arabic elements with a superb cupola and two Byzantine towers 200 feet high with delicate spires. The towers provide an eagle's-eye view of the surrounding country. The cathedral's ornate interior contains beautiful details in its carved doors and choir stalls. Sumptuous vestments can be seen. Paintings include a splendid Assumption of the Virgin by Murillo, presented by Charles IV of Spain in gratitude for the city's financial help against Napoleon; this treasure, highly valued, is in the sacristy. Near the high altar is a curious legendary coffin, the tomb of the bishop Francisco Mendiola. The story goes that this sainted man died in Zacatecas about 300 years ago, and his body was being carried home to Guadalajara in a coffin on the back of his mule when, to the bewilderment and dismay of the faithful mourners, the mule and its burden suddenly disappeared. Later the animal materialized at the cathedral door and knocked loudly with its hoof three times. It stood patiently while being unloaded and then dropped dead on the steps. The church authorities accepted the event as a sign that the bishop's body was to remain in the cathedral. The coffin is much scarred as a result of its wild trip; it is further worn because those who pray for miracles knock on it three times and the devout frequently kiss it.

The church of Santa Mónica, on the street of the same name 8 blocks W of the Alameda, is the handsomest building in the city. It has an elaborately carved Plateresque façade. The church of Our Lady of El Carmen, on the W side of Plaza Carmen, 1 block S and 6 blocks W from the main plaza, has a severe, heavy façade, but an interesting interior with paintings by native artists.

The Baroque church of San Francisco, on the plaza of the same name, 4 blocks S of the main plaza, was built in 1550. E of it is the church of Our Lady of Aranzazu, a charming ancient structure with a rich Churrigueresque interior. Between the church of San Francisco and the railroad station S of it is the Jardín San Francisco, full of roses, fountains, and fine trees.

The popular church of San Juan de Dios is on Calzada Independencia Sur, just S of the central market. The old weather-beaten church of San Juan Bautista is in the Mexicaltzingo section of the city, S of the railroad station. The front part of the atrium of this church is now a market. This is a poorer part of the city, and the tents in the streets are the people's theaters of an evening. Mariachis or itinerant musicians stroll through the streets, ready to oblige with a song.

MUSEUM. The Museo del Estado (State Museum) is in a building which occupies a whole block diagonally NE of the cathedral. It was erected in 1700 as a religious seminary but now contains the state library, with ample collections on archeology, ethnography, history, and folklore. Outstanding is a collection of paintings by Bartolomé Esteban Murillo and some of his students illustrating the life of St. Francis. The 11 large canvases were originally intended for the Franciscan monastery in Mexico City, for which they were ordered by Philip II. Notable colonial paintings represent Joseph Emerging from the Cistern, by Cristóbal de Villalpando; St. Anne Teaching the Virgin, by Juan Rodríguez Juárez; Marriage of the Virgin, by Sebastían de Arteaga; St. Bruno, by Ramón de Torres, and St. Theresa, by Luis Juárez.

CENTERS OF HIGHER LEARNING. A contrast to the old religious paintings is found at the university. Powerful murals in the modern manner by José Clemente Orozco deal with the progress of science and labor. There are others by Amado de la Cueva and David Alfaro Siqueiros. The university is housed in a fine French-style modern building.

THEATER AND MOVING-PICTURE HOUSES. Opera and dramatic performances are sometimes given in the famous Degollado Theater, built between 1855 and 1866. It is an immense structure conceived in the grand manner, its classic style differing strikingly from most· of the city's architecture. The main portico is Corinthian in treatment. The magnificent arched ceiling of the interior is decorated with frescoes on themes from Dante's Divine Comedy. The Colón, Reforma, and Roxy Theaters show moving pictures.

SPORTS. The season for bullfights is November-March inclusive. Excellent 18-hole golf courses are to be found at the airport and at the Country Club, and there are tennis and swimming at the Country Club. Parque de Agua Azul in the S suburbs is a beautiful little park with four swimming pools; dances are held here.

BOOKSTORE. Librería Font, Leopoldo Font's bookstore, Av. Colón 14, is the largest in W Mexico.

BANK. Banco Nacional de México, Av. Juárez.

NIGHT CLUBS. Quinta de las Rosas is especially favored by U. S. visitors. Others are American Club, C. 1 No. 162; Club Como, Av. Corona; Valentina, very Mexican, in the markets, Mercado Alcalde and Mercado Libertad.

RESTAURANTS. Francés and Imperial, European cuisine; Roma, Mexican; Guadalajara, U. S.

HOTELS. Del Parque**, Av. Juárez 845; Guadalajara**, Av. Colón 180; Imperial**, Av. Colón 258; Virreinal*, Av. Corona 229; Roma, C. Pedro Moreno 219.

GUADALAJARA'S ENVIRONS AND NEAR-BY EXCURSIONS

Hotel managements in Guadalajara assist the traveler in planning country trips, horseback jaunts, fishing excursions to Laka Chapala, hikes, and mountain climbing expeditions.

San Pedro Tlaquepaque and Tonalá, NE suburbs reached by street car or bus, are pottery towns where descendants of the Tonaltec Indians make their famous very fragile, highly glazed and decorated earthenware pottery. Each family has its own craft secrets handed down from generation to generation. Among the best is the product of the Panduro family and El Arte Tonalteca. These towns are also popular with the people of Guadalajara for rest and relaxation and are especially lively during warm evenings.

Zapopán (Among Zapotes), reached NW from Guadalajara by street car, bus, or car in little more than half an hour, is a small town whose chief claim to distinction is a 17th-century Plateresque church from which the founding fathers of the California missions were sent out. Indians come from all over the state to honor the miraculous Virgin of Zapopán. During these pilgrimages, especially on October 4, when a beautiful fiesta is celebrated, roads leading to the town are thronged with heavily laden burros and Indians garbed in the various colors of their tribes.

Barranca de Oblatos, 6 miles NW of Guadalajara and reached by bus, car, or horseback, is a magnificent gorge reminiscent of the Grand Canyon. It is one of the stupendous sights in Mexico. The 2000-foot sides of the yawning canyon are covered with rich tropical vegetation. At the bottom the Río Santiago flows toward the sea; above it, lining the walls, are little farms where tropical fruits and vegetables, impossible to raise on the plains above, are grown for the city market. Guides conduct visitors to the bottom. The climb back sometimes proves difficult for women.

Tequila is reached by a pleasant drive of 48 miles NW from Guadalajara over a good road. Here the visitor can see tequila made from a special variety of the maguey cactus. Near the town are great fields of the small bluish-leaved plants. A waterfall near by is an excellent setting for picnic lunches.

Salto de Juanacatlán (Juanacatlán Fall), probably the leading scenic attraction of the vicinity, is 15 miles SE of Guadalajara on the road to Chapala, then 8 miles off the highway on a dirt road from El Castillo. The famous falls, second in size only to Niagara on the North American continent, pour over a mammoth horseshoe 524 feet wide to drop 70 feet to the foaming chasm below. A cloud of mist rises, catching the rays of the sun and turning them into a gorgeous rainbow. There is a restaurant near by.

Lago de Chapala (Lake Chapala), 40 miles SE of Guadalajara, is the largest and most important lake in the republic, 70 miles long and averaging 15-20 miles wide. It is a favorite resort region, particularly with honeymooners. The town of Chapala on the N shore, reached by a good road from Guadalajara, is very popular with vacationists from there and from Mexico City. The beaches of fine clean sand and the balmy air are invitations to spend hour upon hour alternately sun-bathing and dipping into the water. Chapala has gardens and prome-nades and strolling bands of musicians. The natural beauty of the region is almost unmatched. Scenically the lake compares favorably with those of Switzerland and N Italy, but it is much larger. Canoes and barges are the chief conveyances in evidence, though in recent years the Indians in their lakeside villages have had to adjust themselves to the startling sputter of motor launches. Boats of all sizes can be rented at reasonable rates.

The lake teems with fresh-water fish, including the popular pescado blanco or white fish. The region is the winter refuge of many rare North American birds, including the snowy egret. For fishing the natives use nets, some of them 300 feet long, which they weave them-selves. In the early morning the men of the lakeshore villages hasten to the waterfront and scramble into their battered boats. By midday mounds of fish can be seen glinting in the sun along the shore and the village streets are walled with nets stretched on poles like great cob-webs. As day fades the villagers busy themselves at repairing old nets or making new ones; their hands fly like shuttles over the shapeless mass of cords. The villages bear such musical names as Jocotepec, Tuscueca, Tizapán, La Palma, Pajacuarán, and Jamay. The inhabitants seem as primitive in their culture, customs, and fiestas as in the days of Moctezuma. They are the direct descendants of the Indians whom the Spaniards found here four centuries ago. Capping a hill on Mescala Island in the lake is a castle with crumbling dungeons and broken battlements. By turns it has been a prison, a fortress, and a stronghold of brigands.

HOTELS. Arzapalo; Nido.

CENTRAL MEXICO

Mexico City, the capital, is the natural travel center for the country as a whole. All the routes that have been described converge on it, and the traveler who comes by air or who takes the Pan American Highway or one of the railroads direct to the central plateau can con-veniently visit many points of interest along these routes as excursions out of Mexico City. Several railroads, airlines, and a network of modern automobile highways radiate from the city in all directions.

Puebla and other cities passed on the way inland from Veracruz, already described, can become the objectives of journeys from Mexico City as a base. Acapulco, S on the Pacific coast, is an occasional port of entry by freighter from North and South America, but the town's present importance is rather as a resort, and for this reason it is pre-sented after Mexico City as the end of a journey in which some of the country's most interesting towns may be visited (p. 122). Guadala-jara can be made the terminus of a drive through the lake region, described here after the capital (p. 132). Oaxaca, the ruins of Monte Albán and Mitla, and Tehuantepec are grouped as S Mexico (p. 142), while Yucatán with its great Maya ruins and Chiapas are considered as SE Mexico (p. 152). All of these points can be reached more or less directly from Mexico City.

MEXICO CITY

Mexico City, which the Mexicans write as México—with a million and a quarter inhabitants, capital of the republic, vibrant with more than six centuries of dramatic history, tradition, romance—is the oldest metropolis on the continent. It is the most important city in Mexico politically, culturally, and commercially and one of the largest and most modern cities of all Latin America. Its setting is majestic. It knows neither heat wave nor cold wave; the weather is uniformly pleasant the year round. The valley of Mexico in which the capital lies, 7415 feet above sea level and containing more than 1,235,000 acres, is in the very heart of the great cordilleras that cross the country N-S. Its configuration is that of a wide elliptical basin, the sides formed by great rugged mountain ranges. The peaks of Popocatépetl and Ixtaccíhuatl rise SE. From the crest of the cordillera that forms the S boundary of the valley emerges the volcano Ajusco, which thousands of years ago poured out a burning sea of lava under which archaic man and all his works within the valley were buried.

Legend relates that one morning in 1325, many years after the seven Nahua tribes who came from the hypothetical land of Aztlán had settled in the valley, some Aztec fishermen on the largest of the lakes spied on the rocks of a little island an eagle perched on a cactus and trying to swallow a snake. They took this for a sign from the war god Huitzilopochtli that they should establish their home here. Consequently the Aztecs erected a shrine to their principal deity on the island, and all around this primitive structure they soon covered the waters with chinampas or floating gardens on rafts, which little by little became rooted to the bottom. This formed the nucleus of their city, which they called Tenochtitlán after Tenoch, their high priest. A century after the founding of Tenochtitlán the Aztecs had become a powerful nation exacting tribute from the neighboring tribes, and their capital grew to be the richest and most magnificent on the continent. The islands, connected with the mainland by three broad masonry causeways, had been amply extended by means of floating gardens.

When in 1519 Cortés came to Mexico with an army of 500 men he obtained, after considerable intrigue and many fierce battles, the assistance of the Tlaxcalans, a nation of sturdy warriors, and marched inland toward the city of canals called Tenochtitlán. It was during the reign of Moctezuma II that the handful of bold Europeans made their appearance. As they passed the city's ramparts and encountered the exotically dressed inhabitants their amazement was indescribable. Bernal Díaz del Castillo, one of Cortés' captains, who with some companions ascended the great temple, described the scene below. The houses, he related, were connected by drawbridges, and their walls glittered "like silver plate"; here and there rose temples, shrines, and towers, some of them resembling fortresses, and many palaces. The canals were crowded with canoes. The market was "a plaza so well traced, so symmetrical and large, and so crowded with people, as they had never seen the like anywhere before."

After almost two years of fighting, during which Moctezuma II was killed, Tenochtitlán fell to Cortés. Teocallis or truncated pyramids supporting shrines of the strange and bewildering Aztec religion, markets that resembled beehives, botanical gardens full of rare specimens of the rich and diversified Mexican flora, zoological parks where examples of America's fauna were gathered, palaces and mansions with elaborate decorations in which virile craftsmen had crystallized their ideals of art and beauty—all was mercilessly annihilated. The canals were filled with blood-soaked debris, and on this as a base the Spaniards started to build a new city, tracing plazas, streets, and avenues for the capital of the colony, a precious gem offered to the crown of Charles V. Two years after its foundation the emperor did not hesitate to confer the title of Very Noble, Faithful, Renowned, and Imperial City on it.

The first structures had the aspect of fortresses, with thick walls, turrets and battlements, armories, and large stables. The churches and monasteries, also massive, displayed a Franciscan simplicity in their architectural lines. Some material from the original buildings was used; other material was carried from distant places on the patient backs of the surviving natives, who pined in slavery and could expect no liberation save death. Friar Toribio de Benavente, one of the first chroniclers of Mexico, wrote: "The seventh plague was the construction of the great city of Mexico, in which they used more people at the beginning, than in the erection of the temple of Jerusalem, being indeed so great the number employed in the works, that one could hardly walk in the streets and causeways, notwithstanding their width; while working some were struck by logs, others fell from a height and others still were buried under the ruins of buildings that were demolished, especially when the principal temples were razed to the ground. Here died a great number of Indians, and they usually go singing." The stream of Spanish colonizers lured by the golden rumor of the West Indies gave a great impulse to the growth of the city. The first buildings were little by little replaced by splendid mansions, sumptuous palaces, and magnificent churches ornamented with elaborate and capricious Spanish forms of decoration which acquired their fullest expression in the colony, thanks to the extraordinary ability of the Indian craftsmen and the fanciful inspiration of those who designed them.

The fenced inclosure of the great teocalli became the site of the Plaza Mayor or principal square, now known as the Zócalo, on which the most important buildings were erected. Cortés built his first residence on the ruins of the old palace of Moctezuma. The N side of the plaza was occupied by the cathedral, and E rose the large building of the audiencia or high court on the site of the present National Palace. The Zócalo—its name derived from an Arabian word zoc, which means marketplace or square—remains the very heart of the city. The monastic brotherhoods gave the city as a whole its characteristic physiognomy. In enjoyment of exclusive privileges, they were able to erect innumerable monasteries which, like those of San Francisco and Santo Domingo, sometimes covered several blocks; large colleges like the Franciscans' of Tlaltelalco, the Dominicans' of Portacoeli, and the Jesuit institutions of San Pedro y San Pablo, San Gregorio, and San Ildefonso; hospitals like that of Jesús Nazareno which was founded by Cortés himself, the Hospital Real, and that of San Hipólito; finally a great number of churches—the magnificent cathedral, the handsome Sagrario Metropolitano, and the churches of Santo Domingo, La

Profesa, San Francisco, San Agustín, the basilica of Guadalupe, and many more.

The civilization which the Old World introduced into New Spain got off to a flourishing start during the administration of Antonio de Mendoza, the first viceroy, who ruled in 1535-50. He is regarded as the founder of the institution which survives as the National University of Mexico, notwithstanding the fact that the royal ordinance which authorized it was not issued until later. In 1534 the Italian Juan Pablos (Giovanni Paoli) was authorized to start the first publishing house in America; he established it at the corner of Calle Moneda and C. Licenciado Verdad, where a commemorative tablet has been placed. Two years later the first book was published, and in 1722 the first newspaper, La Gaceta de México (The Gazette of Mexico). The city's growth was rapid. In 1600 the population included 7000 Spaniards; by 1746 it amounted altogether to 90,000. During this last century of peaceful colonial life the city underwent little change except for the gradual embellishment of the churches.

Mexico City's modern phase was initiated by the viceroy Juan Vicente Güemes Pacheco, Count of Revillagigedo (1789-94), an eccentric but able administrator. Before he became viceroy the city had been permitted to fall into a condition mean and foul beyond all description —unlighted, unpaved, and infested by footpads. Under the Count of Revillagigedo's government the city was cleaned and drained, its principal streets paved and lighted, an effective police force established, and the custom of building handsome and substantial dwellings firmly reestablished. The census which was taken at his order recorded a population of 112,926. At the end of the second decade of the 19th century Mexico had gained its independence, but Mexican society dwelt in the atmosphere of the past. The city fell into a long decline again as a result of political chaos. It was not until after the reform period that colonial relics were safeguarded and modern embellishment begun.

THE CITY. The modernistic influence of contemporary civilization has been transmitted to the new architecture of Mexico and, according to some, threatens to change the artistic physiognomy of the town. But the government, alarmed by the invasion, has made provision for the preservation of its peculiar Mexican character and has given a strong impulse to the harmonious adaptation of modern means of construction to traditional plastic rules. Largely because of its large foreign colonies the city has many cosmopolitan features. Its older streets are bright and colorful, with many old colonial churches and mansions to give them variety. The new residential districts have houses and apartment buildings of functional design embowered in trees and flowers. The city's fascination is enhanced by the varied dress of the people, ranging from the latest modes of Paris and New York to the graceful Spanish mantilla and to the native garb of the Indian workers. Mexico City, in short, is a pleasing combination of old and new, a contrasting fusion of 16th- and 20th-century civilizations, of stately ancient palaces and venerable churches surrounded by clean-cut business buildings. Some narrow winding streets, called callejones, are reminiscent of former days, still with their ancient cobblestones. All the principal arteries are broad paved avenues. There is a marked trend toward replacing the old religious names of streets and plazas with names of secular heroes, dates of important events, or other more or less topical allusions.

The heart of Mexico City, the area traversed oftenest by visitors, lies just beyond the Zócalo or central plaza, between it and the park of La Alameda. A street of smart shops, restaurants, and hotels is Avenida Francisco I. Madero, which starts at the Zócalo and several blocks W becomes Av. Juárez. The center of night life is Av. 16 de Septiembre, which becomes Av. Independencia as it runs W. Parallel with Av. Madero and a block N of it is Av. 5 de Mayo; on this central avenue are the offices of the principal steamship and railroad companies, banks, bookstores, and commercial houses.

One of the most beautiful boulevards in the world, comparing favorably with the Champs Elysées of Paris, is Paseo Reforma, which starts a little W of the Alameda. This stately avenue, 3 miles long and 200 feet wide, is shaded by a double row of trees and lined with the most luxurious residences. Pride of the capital, the Paseo owes a large part of its beauty to the tragic Maximilian and Carlotta who did much to adorn the city in the few years of their rule. Carlotta planted great cypress trees here, most of which have been replaced by smaller trees because the soft earth could not support the great weight of the cypresses. The Paseo widens into six glorietas or circles, in some of which monuments have been erected. The pedestal which upholds a figure of the last Aztec emperor, Cuauhtémoc, is of world-wide repute.

CENTRAL ZONE. The Zócalo, the main square, is also known officially, though not in ordinary usage, as Plaza Constitución. At the E end of the main business district or central zone, it occupies the site of the great Aztec plaza which held a magnificent teocalli or temple and Moctezuma's palace. This plaza is the heart of the city, both historically and in present fact, since most of the bus and street-car lines start here. On the N side of the Zócalo, over the ruins of the old Aztec temple, stands the cathedral. It was erected three centuries ago and to this day is the largest and finest structure of its kind in the Western Hemisphere. Opposite the cathedral, on the S side, is the handsome colonial city hall, while on the W side of the square have stood portales or arcades sheltering the place of business of innumerable tradesmen ever since the conquest. The National Pawnshop is housed in a palatial ancient building at the NW corner. The entire E side of the Zócalo is occupied by the extensive façade of the National Palace.

The cathedral, consecrated as the church of La Asunción de María Santísima, is a gigantic structure of basalt and gray sandstone with very thick walls. According to tradition, it not only stands on the site of the main temple of the Aztecs, that of the war god Huitzilopochtli, but was partly built with materials from it. Actually only a comparatively small Christian church was begun at this location in 1525; this church was raised to the dignity of a cathedral, and the feeling grew that a grander structure was needed. Philip II obtained permission from Pope Clement VII for the destruction of the first modest church so that a new and larger one might be begun. The cornerstone of the present building was laid in 1573, and construction was completed almost a century later in 1667. The twin towers which rise 203 feet above the atrium were not finished until 1791. The exterior is a composite of Doric, Ionic, and Corinthian styles, freely treated and richly ornamented. Designed in the neo-classic manner, the building is 374 feet long and 198 feet wide. One of the bells weighs 27,000 pounds; the clapper is 8 feet long and weighs 500 pounds. To Manuel Tolsa, the great Mexican silversmith, are attributed statues on the façade of the cathedral and the design of the lantern-shaped domes which were completed in 1813. Outstanding treasures of the interior are paintings by Murillo, Baltasar de Echave Ibia, and Juan Rodríguez Juárez. The most interesting altars are those of El Perdón (Pardon), near the S door, and Los Reyes (The Kings), immediately behind the high altar, both in the best Mexican Churrigueresque style. The chapel of Los Santos Reyes is a replica of a chapel in the cathedral at Seville where several Spanish kings are buried. The cathedral is never closed.

The Sagrario Metropolitano is a distinct church although it adjoins the cathedral. It houses a museum of ecclesiastical art. Dating from

KEY TO MAP OF MEXICO CITY, CENTRAL DISTRICT

1. Plaza San Fernando
2. Plaza Ciudadela
3. Plaza 23 de Mayo (Santo Domingo)
4. Parque Carranza
5. San Fernando church
6. San Hipólito church
7. San Juan de Dios church
8. Santa Veracruz church
9. La Concepción church
10. San Francisco church
11. San Felipe de Jesús church
12. La Profesa church
13. Santo Domingo church
14. Cathedral
15. San José de Gracia church
16. San Pedro y San Pablo church
17. La Santísima Trinidad church
18. Jesús María church
19. Loreto church
20. La Soledad de Santa Cruz church
21. Casa de los Azulejos (House of Tiles)
22. Las Vizcaínas (The Biscayans)
23. La Ciudadela (The Citadel)
24. Western Union
25. Palacio de Correos (post office)
26. Edificio de Communicaciones y Obras Públicas (Communications and Public Works building)
27. Palacio de Minería (Palace of Mining)
28. Senate
29. Iturbide Palace
30. Chamber of Deputies
31. Monte de Piedad (National Pawnshop)
32. Palacio Municipal (city hall)
33. Secretariat of Education
34. National Palace
35. Supreme Court building
36. Palace de Bellas Artes (Palace of Fine Arts)
37. Biblioteca Nacional (National Library, formerly San Agustín church)
38. El Caballito
39. Jesús Nazareno hospital
40. National Preparatory School Colegio de San Ildefonso)
41. National University of Mexico
42. National Museum (in National Palace)
43. Escuela Nacional de Bellas Artes (National School of Fine Arts, formerly Academy of San Carlos)
44. Flower market
45. Mercado San Juan
46. Mercado Abelardo L. Rodríguez
47. Mercado Merced
48. American Club
49. National Theater (in Palace of Fine Arts)
50. Fabregas Theater
51. Lírico Theater
52. Arbéu Theater
53. Banco de México
54. Banco Nacional de México
55. National City Bank of New York
56. San Lázaro railroad station
57. Hotel Regis
58. Hotel Luxor
59. Hotel Ritz
60. Hotel Majestic

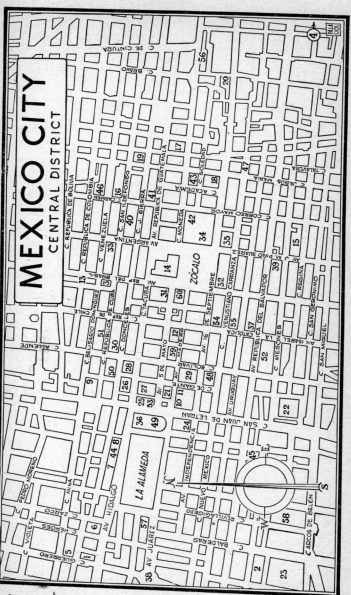

MEXICO CITY
CENTRAL DISTRICT

the middle of the 18th century, one of the three important examples of Churrigueresque church exteriors now in existence in the capital, it is remarkable for both its S and E façades, elaborately and intricately decorated. The interior is nobly proportioned.

Aztec ruins have been excavated at the corner of Av. Guatemala and Plaza Seminario, opposite the NE corner of the cathedral. These ruins are believed to be part of the foundations of the teocalli or principal temple of the Aztecs. They can be seen from the street level at any time.

The National Palace, erected over the foundations of Moctezuma's great palace, is austere in design, faced with rust-red tezontle and gray-stone Plateresque decorations, and fills a whole block. The site was also that of Cortés' house, which remained in the possession of the conquistador's heirs until 1562, when it was bought by the crown and used as the viceregal residence until it was destroyed in the riots and fire of 1692. The present building, begun in that year, has seen frequent and extensive reconstruction. The official residence of the Spanish viceroys from 1698 until the establishment of the republic, it now houses government offices, including the president's executive offices, the national archives, the treasury, and the war ministry. Over the central portal hangs Mexico's independence bell, which is sounded by the president at 11 p.m. on the night of September 15 in a dramatic re-enactment of the Grito de Dolores as part of the popular festivities commemorating Mexico's liberation from Spain. Splendid murals by Diego Rivera line the walls of the main staircase. Guides are available. Open weekdays 9 a.m.-6 p.m., Sundays 10 a.m.-1 p.m.

The Palacio Municipal or city hall, on the S side of the Zócalo, opposite the cathedral, at Av. 16 de Septiembre and C. 5 de Febrero, houses the offices of the government of the Federal District. The site was selected by the conquistadores for the use of the municipal government, but actually several houses were constructed here for other purposes before the present building (1720-24). In the library are portraits of rulers of Mexico from the time of Cortés and valuable documents relating to the history of Mexico City. Open 9 a.m.-1 p.m., 4-6 p.m.

Portal de los Mercaderes (Arcade of the Tradesmen), on the W side of the Zócalo, opposite the National Palace, houses shops and itinerant vendors offering cheap jewelry, notions, haberdashery, food, and drink. At the N corner behind the arcades is the Hotel Majestic, which fronts on Av. Madero.

OLD QUARTER. The streets radiating from the main square and the near-by smaller plazas are among the oldest and historically most interesting parts of the city.

The National Museum, in the National Palace, is entered on the N side of the huge building, on C. Moneda, a street named for the royal mint formerly at this location. The museum contains what is probably the world's finest collection of American archeological objects. Mexican history is strikingly illustrated by many ancient relics. These include the famous Aztec Sacrificial Stone, on which thousands of human beings were slaughtered ceremonially. There is also a great variety of stone images, monoliths, sculptures, and other prehistoric objects from all parts of Mexico. Of all the remarkable relics of pre-Spanish civilizations in the Americas the Aztec Calendar Stone, now in the museum, is probably the best known to visitors to Mexico. The huge monolithic block of basalt from which it was sculptured was hauled from quarries several miles away; how this was done is not known, since the Aztecs used no beasts of burden. Here in the heart of the Aztec city it was carved with a skill and precision that provoke wonder today. In its present form it is 12 feet in diameter, 3 feet thick, and weighs in excess of 24 tons. The stone from which it was produced is so hard that the elaborate detail of the carving is still clean and sharp after several centuries. The design is perfectly symmetrical and harmonious. In the center is the face of the sun god Tonatiuh, one of the principal deities of the Aztecs. Surrounding it are four large rectangles containing symbols generally believed to represent four world epochs. Next comes a series of concentric bands filled with symbols, the first band containing hieroglyphs representing the 20 days of the Aztec calendar month. The succeeding bands, broken by four large pointers indicating the cardinal points of the compass, contain an elaborate series of hieroglyphs symbolic of the four elements—fire, water, earth, and air—as well as conventional representations of deities and the Aztec months. On the outermost band are designs representing the butterfly Itzpapalotl, symbolizing the heavens. Sculptured at the bottom of the stone and facing each other are two elaborate plumed serpents with human faces. Had the Aztecs left behind them no other relic of their civilization, this stone would be sufficient to establish conclusive proof of the high degree of culture they attained. The bold but delicately wrought motifs, the superb handling of the design, and the exquisite artisanship of the carving make the Calendar Stone a monumental work of art. The stone has had a curious history. Buried at the time the Aztec capital was destroyed by the Spaniards, it was uncovered in the main plaza toward the end of the 16th century. But it was again buried, this time by order of the Catholic archbishop, for fear that it might have a dangerous effect upon the conquered Indians who had been deprived of their pagan deities. Two centuries later, in 1790, the forgotten stone was again accidentally discovered in the main plaza during some excavation. It was placed at the base of the W tower of the cathedral, and in 1885 it was moved to the museum, where it has been ever since. Other relics in the museum include suits of armor of the conquistadores, including that worn by Pedro de Alvarado, Cortés' lieutenant; relics of the colonial and imperial periods such as maps, books, documents, paintings; an extensive exhibit of historical objects associated with the heroes of Mexico's revolution of independence and with Maximilian's reign; collections of ceramics, antique furniture, jewelry, and native arts and handicrafts. Open Mondays-Fridays, 9 a.m.-2 p.m.; Sundays 10 a.m.-1 p.m.; closed Saturdays and holidays.

The **Escuela Nacional de Bellas Artes** (National School of Fine Arts), the old Academy of San Carlos, at C. Academia 22, around the corner from the block beyond the National Museum on C. Moneda, has a noble collection of old paintings, including works of Murillo and Rubens. Most of the best-known paintings of Mexico's old masters, some dating from the early 1600's, are to be found here. The academy, founded by a royal order of Charles III in the latter part of the 18th century, grew from a small beginning to an institution which exerted a profound influence upon the art of the country, numbering among its faculty and students the best of Mexico's artists, sculptors, and architects. Paintings dating after 1850 are in the Palace of Fine Arts. Open 10 a.m.-1 p.m. daily including Sundays; closed holidays.

The church of **La Santísima Trinidad** (Most Holy Trinity) is a block beyond the National School of Fine Arts, at Plaza Santísima. The second church of a foundation dedicated to good works, it dates from 1677 and was remodeled in 1755. The building is noted for its rich Churrigueresque façade and fine towers.

The church of Our Lady of La Soledad de la Santa Cruz (Solitude of the Holy Cross) is at the end of C. Soledad, 4 blocks E and 2 blocks S of the church of La Santísima Trinidad. The original church is said to have been built around 1534 by early Aztec converts to Christianity. The present building was completed in 1731. The church is of special interest because the image of the Virgin of La Soledad on the high altar is greatly venerated as the protectress of devout unfortunates of the underworld.

The church of Our Lady of Loreto, on a small plaza, is 2 blocks N of that of La Santísima, at C. San Ildefonso and C. Rodríguez Puebla. The original church at this location was a little building dedicated to St. Gregory. About 1675 plans were drawn for a new church to be dedicated to Our Lady of Loreto, but it was not begun until 1809 by Manuel Tolsa and a collaborator. Almost immediately after its completion in 1816 the building began to sink because of the use of solid stone in the E wall and porous stone in the W wall. The E wall settled to such an extent that the towers are perceptibly out of line.

The church and monastery of San Pedro and San Pablo, at C. San Ildefonso and C. Carmen, present an unusual example of the early church without side aisles. Converted into a lecture hall, its wall decorations and a great stained-glass window are by Roberto Montenegro. The monastery now contains a government school; in its spacious patios are interesting frescoes by Roberto Montenegro and Dr. Atl (Gerardo Murillo) depicting reconstruction following the revolution, regard for the popular arts, and a scene of the fiesta of the Holy Cross.

The National University of Mexico, whose many buildings are scattered about the city, has its headquarters at C. Justo Sierra 16. This university opened its doors as the Royal and Pontifical University of Mexico in 1553, five years before Elizabeth ascended the English throne and 54 years before the founding of Jamestown, Va. One of the oldest institutions of higher learning in North America, it was closed about the middle of the 19th century after a long and distinguished career; 60 years later it was reopened as the National University of Mexico. The administrative building contains the Bolívar Amphitheater, with interesting frescoes on each side of the stage by Diego Rivera and at the back scenes from the life of Simón Bolívar by Fernando Leal. Several of the university's colleges are housed in stately buildings dating back to the viceregal period. The summer school building, at the corner of Av. Ribera de San Cosmé and C. Naranjo, was erected by a nobleman, the Count of the Valley of Orizaba, in 1766, and its elaborate stone façade is representative of Spanish American colonial architecture. The university at present comprises 27 schools and departments and covers all branches of learning. It is attended by 15,000 students.

The National Preparatory School, on C. San Ildefonso between C. Carmen and Av. Argentina, is a handsome, massive Baroque building whose inner courts have been decorated in recent years by Mexico's outstanding mural artists. This institution, founded in 1749 by the Jesuits as the Colegio de San Ildefonso, has as its main function the preparation of advanced pupils from the lower schools for professional careers. The main patio walls on three floors, as well as on the stairways, are covered with many striking frescoes on revolutionary themes by José Clemente Orozco. The last two murals at the top of the main stairway are Fernando Leal's Fiesta at the Chalma Sanctuary and Jean Charlot's The Murder of Indians at the Cholula Temple. A mural by Fermín Revueltas in one of the entrances off the main patio depicts the planting of the cross in Mexico; opposite is a scene from the conquest by Ramón Alva de la Canal. On the walls of the stairway in the patio at C. San Ildefonso 43 are several frescoes, some unfinished and some defaced, by the revolutionary painter David Alfaro Siqueiros. A helpful Interpretative Guide to the Frescoes in the National Preparatory School is published by Frances Toor. The salon called El Generalito contains beautiful choir stalls and a pulpit with biblical scenes carved by Indian artists from the monastery of San Agustín, which now houses the National Library.

The Secretaría de Educación Pública (Secretariat of Education), at Av. Argentina and C. Luis González Obregón, occupies a building erected in 1922 which is one of the best known in the city because of its murals by Diego Rivera, José Clemente Orozco, and other fine artists depicting the struggles, sorrows, and hopes of Mexico's Indians and workers from the earliest times to the present day. These murals are on the walls of the two large patios of the building. Other paintings, exciting, satirical, or informative in theme, are to be found on the walls of offices, in the little theater, the library, and elsewhere. These are the work of Roberto Montenegro, Francisco Goitia, Carlos González, Carlos Mérida, Jean Charlot, David Alfaro Siqueiros, and Amado de la Cueva. A helpful Interpretative Guide to the Frescoes in the Ministry of Education is published by Frances Toor. The building houses the principal offices of the federal educational department, an open-air theater, and a children's branch of the public library. Concerts, popular festivals, lectures, and exhibitions are presented here. Open weekdays 9 a.m.-6 p.m.; closed Sundays.

The church of Our Lady of La Encarnación, adjoining the building of the Secretariat of Education on C. Luis González Obregón, is a 17th-century church whose chapel was converted into the Biblioteca Ibero-Americana (Latin American Library) by José Vasconcelos in 1922. The frescoes are by Roberto Montenegro.

Plaza 23 de Mayo or Plaza Santo Domingo, on Av. Brasil, W from the Secretariat of Education building, is one of the city's old and interesting public squares. On the W side are portales or arcades where for hundreds of years public letter-writers plied quill or steel pen for the benefit of poor people unable to read or write. Their successors, about 50 in number, use typewriters. Here artisans and fortune tellers also carry on their trades. In the plaza is a statue of doña Josefa Ortiz de Domínguez, heroine of the war of independence.

The National School of Medicine, on the NE corner of Av. Brasil and C. Venezuela, occupies the grim building of the Holy Inquisition, dating from 1736 and still containing the old tribunal and cells.

The church of Santo Domingo, in the center of the plaza at C. Venezuela, stands on the site of the first church established by the Dominicans. The present church, dedicated in August 1736, is Baroque with Plateresque echoes and has a fine Churrigueresque interior.

The church and convent of La Enseñanza, on C. Doncelos near Av. Argentina, were consecrated in November 1754 under the ample and imposing name of Nuestra Señora del Pilar de Religiosas de la Enseñanza, Escuela de María. Well preserved, the Baroque church is regarded as one of the finest of its kind in the city. The civil courts of the Federal District occupy the adjoining convent, now known as the Palace of Justice, which has beautiful patios.

The Casa de los Condes de Heras Soto, now the express office of the Mexican National Railways, at Av. Chile and C. Donceles, is an old colonial mansion, formerly the home of the Counts of Heras Soto. It is distinguished by an interesting Churrigueresque façade and arch.

The Monte de Piedad (National Pawnshop) is on the NW corner of the Zócalo at Av. 5 de Mayo, opposite the cathedral. This institution, in a building of pure colonial architecture, was founded for the benefit of the poor in 1775 by Pedro José Romero de Terreros, Count of Santa María de Regla, whose wealth came from the Real del Monte silver mine at Pachuca. He allowed the poor to obtain loans at nominal rates of interest in order to combat the usurious rates prevailing among private pawnbrokers. The Monte de Piedad is now part of the public charities administered by the government; it has many branches. Loans are made for six months on personal property of all kinds. Unredeemed property is sold at periodical auctions which are announced in the papers. Occasionally valuable articles can be bought at attractive prices; between auctions unredeemed pledges remain on view with prices marked. Open weekdays 9 a.m.-2 p.m. and 4-7:30 p.m.; Saturdays 9 a.m.-2 p.m.

The Supreme Court building, new and handsome, is located on the site of an old market, Mercado del Volador, on Av. Piño Suárez at the SE corner of the Zócalo. The Volador market has been moved NW to C. Mixcalco.

The Hospital of Jesús Nazareno (Jesus of Nazareth), at Av. Piño Suárez and Av. Salvador, is the oldest hospital in the Americas, founded by Cortés in 1524. It is maintained by an endowment bequeathed by the conquistador; all attempts by governments and individuals to break his will in this respect have failed. The building has been restored to some extent, but some ancient parts, among them the patio and stairway, remain.

The Casa del Conde de Santiago (House of the Count of Santiago), Av. Piño Suárez 30, at the corner of Av. Salvador, is an ancient and imposing colonial residence with a façade of pink tezontle. Massive carved doors lead into a spacious patio with a fountain and chapel.

THE ALAMEDA SECTION. The Alameda, the city's oldest park, lies some blocks W of the Zócalo, between Av. Juárez and Av. Hidalgo. The name of Alameda is applied throughout Mexico nowadays to any large park or playground. Luis de Velasco, eighth viceroy of Mexico, conceived the idea of laying out the E half of the present Alameda for the purpose of adding to the beauty of Mexico City and for the recreation of its citizens. In 1592 the area was planted with alamos or poplar trees, from which comes the name of Alameda; it was adorned with fountains and flowers and was inclosed by a wall pierced by gateways. During the reign of the viceroy Carlos Francisco de Croix (1766-71) the Alameda was enlarged to its present size, a rectangle 1483 feet by 712, by adding the old Plaza Quemadero to it. The viceroy ordered the removal of the stone platform in the open space of Plaza Quemadero where victims of the Inquisition had been burned. Since that time the park has undergone many changes and substantial improvements. Many of the great ash, elm, and eucalyptus trees are two to three centuries old. In the early morning the park is much frequented by students who come to study in its seclusion. During the day citizens of all classes resort to it, and in the evening its benches are filled with romantic couples. It is especially colorful on Sundays, when band concerts are given, 11 a.m.-1 p.m. On the S side facing Av. Juárez is a striking monument to Benito Juárez, erected in 1910 in commemoration of the first centennial of Mexican independence.

The Palacio de Bellas Artes (Palace of Fine Arts) is at the E end of the Alameda, facing Av. Juárez. This massive, ornate white marble building with yolk-yellow domes was begun by Porfirio Díaz partly for the centennial celebration of Mexican independence scheduled for 1910 and partly as a luxurious social setting for himself and his circle. Unfortunately for him, the revolution called a sharp halt to construction. Because of its tremendous weight and the porous character of the soil, the building began to settle. Many millions of pesos were spent by the postrevolutionary governments to prop it up and many more to finish it with modern facilities such as central heating, air-conditioning, and indirect lighting. The Mexican architect Federico Mariscal is responsible for adding a third balcony and completing the building (1934-35) in spite of the fact that by this time it had sunk almost 6 feet. The total cost has been 35,000,000 pesos. The building contains the National Theater, other auditoriums, galleries containing some of the best of Mexico's art since the middle of the last century, an excellent museum of popular arts, a conference room, bar, dining room, ballroom, and rehearsal salons. On the third floor are frescoes by José Clemente Orozco and Diego Rivera. The state sponsors all the concerts, lectures, operas, and exhibits presented here, usually at low prices. Lectures are often free. The Mexican Symphony Orchestra (Orquesta Sinfónica de México), under the direction of Carlos Chávez and sometimes internationally known visiting conductors, gives its concerts here. The theater's famous curtain of glass mosaic depicting the two great Mexican volcanoes Popocatépetl and Ixtaccíhuatl was designed by Dr. Atl (Gerardo Murillo) and made by Tiffany of New York at a cost of $47,000 U. S.

The Palacio de Correos, the main post office, across from the Fine Arts Palace, at the corner of C. Tacuba, occupies a building erected in 1904 in a mixed style of antique Spanish and Plateresque elements with Italian details. Designed by the Italian architect Adamo Boari, who also designed the Fine Arts Palace, it is one of the largest post offices in the world. It is never closed.

The Palacio de Minería (Palace of Mining), around the corner from the post office, on C. Tacuba, is one of the city's most famous old secular buildings. It houses the engineering college of the National University (Facultad Nacional de Ingeniería). Of almost perfect neo-classic design, dating from 1797, this palace was planned by Manuel Tolsa, the famous architect and sculptor. It also contains the offices of the Secretariat of Agriculture and Development (Fomento), a library, and a mining museum.

The Edificio de Comunicaciones y Obras Públicas (Communications and Public Works Building), across from the Palace of Mining on Av. Tacuba, holds the national telegraph office and public works agencies including the national highway commission. Erected in 1910, this was the third of the great public buildings designed by the Italian architect Adamo Boari.

The Cámara de Senadores (Senate), across from the Communications Building, on C. Santiago Felipe Xicotencatl, and the Cámara de Diputados (Chamber of Deputies), a block away from the Senate, on the NE corner of C. Donceles and C. Allende, are the halls in which the houses of the Mexican Congress meet.

The Secretaría de Asistencia Pública (Public Welfare), across from the Chamber of Deputies, on the SE corner of C. Donceles, occupies one of the beautiful colonial mansions of the city. The work conducted from this center claims the special attention of those interested in Mexico's social welfare administration.

The church of La Profesa, at Av. Madero and Av. Isabel la Católica, is a Jesuit church founded in 1595 and designed by the Spanish architect Pelegrín Clavé and three of his pupils. Its high altar is one of the most notable creations of Manuel Tolsa. The church was the meeting place of the council of absolutist grandees and bishops who induced Agustín de Iturbide to subvert the revolution of independence to their own ends.

The Iturbide Palace, Av. Madero 17, was the mansion of Agustín de Iturbide during his ephemeral reign as first emperor of Mexico (1821-23). In the 18th century the extremely wealthy Countess of San Mateo Valparaíso, who already had one mansion, built this four-story palace with the beautiful patio and graceful arches, one of the tallest buildings of the colonial period. After Iturbide's time it was a fashionable hotel. Today it is occupied by a brokerage house, other business concerns, and shops.

The Casa de los Azulejos (House of Tiles), Av. Madero 4, now occupied by Sanborn's Restaurant, is the most noted of the numerous colonial houses in Mexico City whose façades display the old coats of arms. The palace is as blue as the blood of its first owners. One of the oldest structures in the city, it was the residence of the Count of the Valley of Orizaba in the 16th century. The exterior, of blue and white Puebla tiles, is both unusual and beautiful. The explanation for this luxurious tile façade is a favorite story in Mexico City. The count who built the house was a prodigal in his youth. The heir of an enormous fortune, handsome and dashing, he attached more importance to his fine clothes, his stable, and his exclusive parties than to the voluminous account books of the family's many plantations, sugar mills, and other business affairs. His father used to quote the old Spanish saying to him, "You'll never build a house of tiles." The young man ended by taking his father's words as a challenge, and the result is evident in the beautiful mansion that he left to posterity. From the 1890's till the revolution of 1910 it was the headquarters of the Jockey Club, a highly select social organization. Today it houses Sanborn's drugstore, gift shop, and restaurant. The walls of the stairway are covered with murals by José Clemente Orozco.

Callejón de la Condesa (Alley of the Countess), a narrow street which borders the mansion on the W side, was once the scene of a curious event. Two noblemen riding in their carriages entered the alley from opposite directions. For either to pass through, the other would have had to back his horses out of the alley. Believing that retreat would constitute a stain upon his honor, each stood fast. This would have been a perfect excuse for a duel, but instead, the hidalgos held their places three days and three nights until word of the deadlock reached the viceroy, who settled the dispute. The Alley of the Countess is now a one-way street.

The church of San Francisco, on Av. Madero diagonally across from Sanborn's Restaurant, founded in 1525 by the first 12 Franciscans to arrive in New Spain, who are usually spoken of as the 12 apostles of Mexico, was for a long time the greatest church in the country, the center of Catholicism in America, and headquarters of the powerful Franciscan brotherhood. In the beginning it was under the direction of Friar Pedro de Gante, Mexico's first great educator. Thomas A. Janvier wrote of it in 1890 in his Mexican Guide: "The history of this foundation almost may be said to be the his.ory of Mexico; for contained in it, or linked with it, is almost every event of importance in the colonial or national life. From this centre radiated the commanding influence of the Franciscan order—the strong power that kept what was won by military force, and that by its own peaceful methods greatly extended the territorial limits of New Spain." Cortés for a time was buried here; the viceroys for hundreds of years attended services at the church; here a Te Deum was sung for Mexican independence, and here Iturbide was interred. The old group of buildings, churches, monastery, gardens, and hospital, altogether covering almost four entire blocks, has been whittled down to the main church, now in Protestant hands, with a well-proportioned Churrigueresque façade and beautiful Baroque doors, and the adjoining chapel, Capilla de Balvanera.

The church of San Felipe de Jesús, E of the church of San Francisco, on Av. Madero, is dedicated to the patron saint of Mexico City, the only Mexican canonized, a result of his missionary labors in Japan. One of the original structures of the Franciscan center, this church has been remodeled.

Las Vizcaínas (The Biscayans) is a magnificent Baroque building on C. Vizcaínas, E of C. San Juan de Letrán. An immense building, occupying a full block, it was constructed in the 18th century by three Biscayan merchants as a school for girls. In it are a handsome chapel dedicated to St. Ignatius, a series of fine patios, and a colonial garden.

The Biblioteca Nacional (National Library), at Av. Isabel la Católica and Av. Uruguay, occupies the former church of San Agustín, a massive colonial structure. The library was established by Benito Juárez in 1867 with books taken from the university, the cathedral, and the libraries of monasteries and other ecclesiastical institutions, in accordance with the reform laws. The library, under the direction of the National University, contains more than 900,000 volumes in Spanish, English, French, Italian, and Latin; rare works and paintings describing and portraying the early races of Mexico; some of the first books printed on the continent, and books in Indian languages dating from the 16th century. Open Mondays-Fridays 9 a.m.-8.30 p.m.; Saturdays 9 a.m.-2 p.m.

The Casa de la Condesa de San Mateo Valparaíso (House of the Countess of San Mateo Valparaíso), on the corner of Av. Isabel la Católica and C. Venustiano Carranza, is a magnificent Baroque colonial palace. It now contains the main office of the Banco Nacional de México. The building is notable for its fine façade, doors, and coat of arms, its patio and double spiral stairway.

The Colegio de Niñas (Girls' School), with an adjoining church, at the corner of C. Venustiano Carranza and C. Bolívar, was founded in 1548 by Friar Pedro de Gante as a free school for poor girls of good family. It passed into the hands of the government under the reform laws. The school building has now been converted into a theater.

The church of San Hipólito, at Av. Hidalgo and C. Zarco, NW of the Alameda, was first built of adobe in 1546. The present building dates from 1602 and was repaired in 1758 after damage from earthquakes. An inscription on the front may be translated: "So great was the slaughter of the Spaniards by the Aztecs at this place on the night of July 1, 1520, called for that reason the Dismal Night, that having in the following year re-entered the city in triumph, the conquerors resolved to build a chapel here, to be called the Chapel of the Martyrs, and which should be dedicated to St. Hippolytus because the capture of the city occurred on that saint's day." Notable features of the church are its tiled Churrigueresque dome and simple façade.

The church of San Fernando, W of the church of San Hipólito, on Plaza San Fernando, was dedicated April 20, 1755, by the monks of the brotherhood of San Fernando, who belonged to the Franciscan apostolic college, called the Propaganda Fides. It has a massive Baroque façade which is of interest, but its original rich Churrigueresque altars and many paintings have been removed. Behind it lies a cemetery, Panteón San Fernando, in which are buried such national heroes as Benito Juárez, Vicente Guerrero, Ignacio Comonfort, Ignacio Zaragoza, and Tomás Mejía. In the plaza is a bronze statue of Guerrero.

PASEO REFORMA. Paseo Reforma, Mexico City's splendid residential boulevard, begins at the end of Av. Juárez, W of the Alameda, and runs SW to the large park, Bosque Chapultepec.

El Caballito (The Little Horse) is an equestrian statue of Charles IV standing at the head of Paseo Reforma. Modeled by Manuel Tolsa, it was cast from 30 tons of bronze in a single operation by Salvador de la Vega. Since it was set up in 1803 it has been regarded as the finest equestrian statue in the Americas and one of the very finest in the world. It is said to mark the geographical center of the city.

The monument to the Revolution, in the center of the handsome Plaza República, a block W of El Caballito and N from Paseo Re-

KEY TO MAP OF MEXICO CITY, PASEO REFORMA DISTRICT

1. Bosque Chapultepec (park)
2. National Association of Charros
3. Plaza República
4. Plaza Ciudadela
5. San Cosmé church
6. U.S. Embassy and Consulate
7. Edificio de Salubridad (Health Building)
8. Frontón Mexico (jai alai)
9. Museum of Natural History
10. Monument to Mexican Independence
11. Cuauhtémoc statue
12. Columbus statue
13. El Caballito statue
14. University summer school
15. Centro Escolar de la Revolución (School of the Revolution)
16. English Hospital
17. American Hospital
18. San Cosmé market
19. Juárez market
20. Mexican Automobile Association
21. Buenavista railroad station
22. Mexican Railways station
23. Insurgentes station
24. Shirley Courts
25. Hotel Geneve
26. Hotel Reforma
27. Hotel Imperial

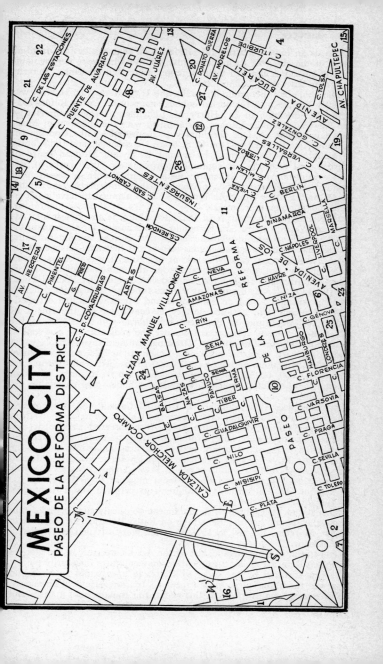

MEXICO CITY
PASEO DE LA REFORMA DISTRICT

forma, is an imposing structure 250 feet high that can be seen from all parts of the city. At each corner just below its immense copper dome are allegorical sculptured figures representing Independence, Reform, Agrarian Laws, and Labor Laws.

The Biblioteca Benjamín Franklin, the U. S. library in Mexico, was recently opened in a remodeled colonial mansion at Paseo Reforma 34 under the direction of Dr. Harry M. Lydenberg, formerly director of the New York Public Library. Established with the approval of Mexican government officials, the library is sponsored by the Coordinator of Inter-American Affairs, the U. S. State Department, and the Library of Congress and is operated by a joint U. S. and Mexican board of trustees and directors. It contains approximately 5000 works of reference and non-fiction in many fields together with a selection of standard and popular novels, particularly those interpreting the United States or the other American republics. It is planned to have a microfilm and photographic service.

C. Puente de Alvarado, N of Plaza República, is an extension of Av. Hidalgo W from Plaza San Fernando and is named for the conquistador Pedro de Alvarado, who the legend says escaped the Aztecs during the Dismal Night by a tremendous leap across the canal along here.

La Tabacalera, so called because at one time it was used as a cigarette factory but now headquarters of the national lottery, at C. Puente de Alvarado 50, is a historic mansion designed by Manuel Tolsa, built in 1800. It was occupied at various times by such national figures as Gen. Antonio López de Santa Ana and Marshal Bazaine of Maximilian's reign. The national lottery is conducted by the Board of Public Welfare (Junta de Beneficencia Pública) and sanctioned by the government because its proceeds finance the philanthropic and public welfare agencies of the country. Drawings are held three times a week, and prizes vary from the price of a ticket up to 5000 pesos. Holiday prizes are sometimes as high as 2,000,000 pesos. After all expenses are deducted 6,000,000-7,000,000 pesos remain each year for distribution among the hospitals, orphanages, special schools, and charitable organizations.

La Ciudadela (The Citadel), S from El Caballito by way of Av. Bucareli and E from the glorieta with the Chinese clock on that street, is a large building dating from 1700. It has served as a cigar and cigarette factory, warehouse, armory, fortress, and munitions factory. It was the scene of important action and was bombarded during the Ten Tragic Days (Decena Trágica) when President Francisco Madero was killed by counterrevolutionaries in 1913. Today it houses the Federal munitions factory and the national museum of artillery. In the park before La Ciudadela is a children's playground and a monument to José María Morelos.

The statue of Columbus, a monument to the great navigator and discoverer, is another notable statue on Paseo Reforma, in the glorieta at Av. Morelos. Erected in 1877, it is the work of Charles Cordier, a Frenchman.

The statue of Cuauhtémoc, last of the Aztec emperors, in the glorieta on Paseo Reforma at Av. Insurgentes, commemorates the sturdy patriot who was tortured by the order of Cortés in an attempt to force him to reveal the hiding place of Moctezuma's treasure. He held his silence. On August 21, anniversary of this event, the Indians hold a fiesta and dance around the statue.

The U. S. Embassy and Consulate are a short distance S from Paseo Reforma, at C. Niza 53.

The monument to Mexican Independence, in the glorieta on Paseo Reforma at C. Florencia, is notable for its beautiful 150-foot column surmounted by a gilded winged figure of Victory. The work was begun in 1901 and finished in 1910. At the base are superb statues representing Law, Justice, War, and Peace, and the monument includes also statues of Mexican patriots. An eternal light and a daily guard of honor for the heroes of independence are other features.

The National Association of Charros (Horsemen) has a field almost at the foot of Paseo Reforma which is the scene of riding exhibitions on Sundays, 11 a.m.-1 p.m. The public is admitted.

The Edificio de Salubridad (Health Building), at the very end of Paseo Reforma, is the handsome modern building of the federal health department. It is of special interest to visitors because of the Rivera frescoes in the council room or Salón de Actos and the two stained-glass windows on the second floor by the same artist representing the four elements, Earth, Fire, Water, and Air.

BOSQUE CHAPULTEPEC, one of the world's largest and most beautiful parks, is reached by car or by the Lomas de Chapultepec bus on Paseo Reforma. The park contains well-kept drives, an avenue of palms, shaded walks beneath giant centuries-old ahuehuete trees, large flower gardens, a remarkable cactus garden, a zoo containing specimens of wild life, and small lakes where boats can be hired. On a high bluff is Chapultepec Castle, formerly the residence of the Mexican president, from which a magnificent view of the city and the valley of Mexico is gained.

The first point in the valley of Mexico occupied by the Aztecs was this beautiful height, which they termed Chapultepec (Grasshopper's Hill). Around it was a forest of hardy ahuehuete trees. The Aztecs fortified themselves in spite of their trespass on the estates of the cruel chieftain of Atzcapotzalco, who had allied himself with neighboring sovereigns against the invaders. Later the Aztecs established Tenochtitlán and by degrees extended their power and domain. This first bulwark in the valley was never forgotten, and Chapultepec was the favorite resort of the Aztec emperors.

Chapultepec Castle, crowning the hill, was begun in 1785 by the viceroy Matías de Gálvez, who intended it to become the residence of the viceroys. The purpose was never realized because it was not completed until 1840, 19 years after the consummation of Mexico's independence from Spain, when it was fortified and made the home of the military academy.

The Don Quijote fountain memorializes Cervantes' hero, whose story is pictured in the tiles of the near-by seats.

On Sunday mornings the largest crowds, mostly workers, visit the park. A concert is given by a fine military band. The ponds are filled with boats. Playgrounds, athletic fields, a merry-go-round, gardens, beautiful drives, and bridle paths are crowded. Members of the National Association of Charros, both men and women, are seen riding in picturesque Mexican costume.

President Cárdenas converted Chapultepec Castle into a museum. Maximilian and Carlotta made the castle their royal residence, and many relics of their occupancy may be seen. Open 9 a.m.-2 p.m. except Mondays.

A new museum of tropical flora and fauna was opened by the Department of Forestry, Hunting, and Fishing of the federal Secretariat of Agriculture on Feb. 15, 1940. The museum is housed in specially designed new buildings. Here are many strangely beautiful flowers from Mexico's fantastic tropics, birds whose brilliant plumage seems almost unreal, and many strange animals unfamiliar to inhabitants of temperate climates.

Lomas de Chapultepec (Chapultepec Heights), reached from the city by Paseo Reforma along the N side of the park, is a new residential district distinguished by luxurious homes.

SOUTH SIDE. Other residential sections, with sports resorts and modern schools, lie S in the city, and some specially notable workers' homes SE. S of Paseo Reforma and converging toward it at the great park of Bosque Chapultepec lies Av. Chapultepec; the E end of the thoroughfare, at the arsenal of La Ciudadela, is some blocks S from the foot of the Alameda. Ruins of the colonial aqueduct completed in 1779 still exist on this avenue, between C. Praga and C. Varsovia. The aqueduct brought water from the great spring at Chapultepec to the SW quarter of the city. An inscription states: "The course of this aqueduct is the same as that of the aqueduct made by the Aztecs in the reign of Chimalpopoca, who was granted the right to the water of Chapultepec by the king of Atzcapotzalco: to whom the Aztecs were tributary until the reign of Itzcohuatl (A.D 1422-33), when they achieved their independence."

Plaza de Toros, where the principal bullfights are held, is on Av. Oaxaca, which strikes off SW from Av. Chapultepec, at C. Valladolid and C. Colima.

The National Stadium, at the end of C. Orizaba, S from Av. Chapultepec, was constructed of concrete in 1924 and is capable of seating 80,000 persons. It is used for school festivals, athletic events, and important civic ceremonies, including the inauguration of the president. On the façade Diego Rivera has painted two huge figures of Indian types. The stadium was planned by José Vasconcelos as Secretary of Education with the idea of creating a sports center to replace the bullring. The project had substantial popular support.

Plaza Antonio M. Anza, in front of the stadium, named for one of Mexico's outstanding educators, contains a unique fountain presented by the National University.

The Escuela de Orientación, just W of the stadium, is a modern school, formerly the Juárez primary school, which was built by José Vasconcelos during his term as Secretary of Education. In addition to its fine facilities for youthful sports which include large playing fields, the school has interesting mural decorations by Roberto Montenegro.

The Centro Escolar de la Revolución (School of the Revolution), near La Ciudadela, at the corner of Av. Niños Héroes and C. Arcos de Belén, is the largest and best-equipped school in the Federal District. Built for children and adults at a cost of 2,000,000 pesos, it has modern workshops, laboratories, playing fields, a swimming pool, and an outdoor theater. The building's modern design and the fine frescoes and stained-glass windows by Fermín Revueltas are impressive.

The Sarmiento open-air school, in Parque Balbuena in the SE part of the city, another interesting primary school, is made up of a series of one-room buildings open on one side. In the grounds are shops, a theater, a large swimming pool, and gardens. The frescoes depicting school life on some of the classroom walls are by the Otomí Indian Máximo Pacheco, who in his youth assisted Fermín Revueltas and Diego Rivera.

Parque Venustiano Carranza, adjoining Parque Balbuena at its N end, was laid out in 1929 for the comfort and recreation of the workers of the district. It contains a day nursery, moving-picture theater, concert hall, gymnasium, swimming pools, playing fields, and a large open-air theater.

The federal penitentiary, reached from Parque Carranza, N on Calzada Balbuena 7 blocks and E on C. Penitenciaría for 5 blocks more, was constructed at the beginning of the century. Its progressive and humane administration aims at the rehabilitation of the inmates. Provision is made for vocational training as well as general education, and prisoners receive part of the amount realized by the sale of objects made in the shops. Ample opportunity for recreation in the open air and normal family life is provided. Visitors are permitted daily.

NORTH SIDE. The church of Santiago Tlaltelalco, on the plaza of the same name, at the end of C. Santa María la Redonda, reached from the Alameda section, lies directly N from the W side of the main post office. Here, on the site of the Aztecs' chief market, the Franciscans established a chapel in 1524, one of the numerous institutions inspired by Friar Pedro de Gante, and in 1537 the celebrated Colegio de la Santa Cruz, a school for Indians. In 1811 the school was closed and the building turned into a prison barracks. A good idea of the original appearance of the building can still be formed although it is now a customs warehouse.

IMPORTANT COLONIAL BUILDINGS AND CHURCHES. Palacio Municipal, S side of the Zócalo; Hospital de Jesús Nazareno, Av. Piño Suárez and Av. Salvador; Iturbide Palace, Av. Madero 17; National Palace, E side of the Zócalo; El Monte de Piedad (National Pawnshop), NW corner of the Zócalo; National School of Fine Arts (San Carlos Academy), C. Academia 22; cathedral, N side of the Zócalo; church of Our Lady of La Concepción, Av. Santa María la Redonda near Av. Cuba; church of La Enseñanza, C. Donceles near Av. Argentina; church of La Profesa, Av. Madero and Av. Isabel la Católica; church of La Santísima Trinidad, Plaza Santísima; church of Our Lady of La Encarnación, C. Obregón, next to the Secretariat of Education; church of Our Lady of La Soledad de la Santa Cruz, C. Soledad; church of Our Lady of Loreto, C. San Ildefonso and C. Rodríguez Puebla; church of San Agustín, now occupied by the Biblioteca Nacional (National Library), Av. Uruguay and Av. Isabel la Católica; church of San Francisco, Av. Madero opposite Sanborn's Restaurant; church of San Hipólito, Av. Hidalgo and C. Zarco; church of San Pedro and San Pablo, C. San Ildefonso and C. Carmen; church of Santa Veracruz, E of the flower market facing the Alameda; church of Santo Domingo, Plaza 23 de Mayo; Colegio de San Ildefonso, C. San Ildefonso near Av. Argentina; house of the Count of Santiago, Av. Piño Suárez 30; house of the Counts of Heras Soto, Av. Chile and C. Donceles; Casa de los Azulejos (House of Tiles), Av. Madero 4; Las Vizcaínas (The Biscayans), C. Vizcaínas, E of C. San Juan de Letrán.

PUBLIC BUILDINGS. Chamber of Deputies, C. Donceles and C. Allende; Communications and Public Works building, Av. Tacuba; Departamento de Salubridad (Health), Paseo Reforma and C. Lieja; National Lottery (La Tabacalera), C. Puente de Alvarado 50; National Palace, E side of the Zócalo; National Preparatory School, C. San Ildefonso between C. Carmen and Av. Argentina; Senate, C. Xicotencatl; National University, headquarters at C. Justo Sierra 16; Palace of Fine Arts, E end of the Alameda facing Av. Juárez; post office, across from Palace of Fine Arts, on Av. Tacuba; Sarmiento primary school, Parque Balbuena; School of the Revolution, Av. Niños Héroes and C. Arcos de Belén; Secretariat of Education, Av. Argentina and C. Obregon; Supreme Court, Av. Piño Suárez at C. Carranza.

MUSEUMS. Commercial and industrial, in Secretariat of Agriculture building, C. Filomeno Mata 8; paintings since 1850 and popular arts, in Palace of Fine Arts, E end of the Alameda; National School of Fine Arts, C. Academia 22; natural history, C. Chopo 10; archeology, history, and ethnology, in National Museum in National Palace (N side).

LIBRARIES. Biblioteca Nacional, Av. Uruguay and Av. Isabel la Católica; National School of Fine Arts, C. Academia 22; art and archeology, in National Museum in National Palace (N side); Benjamín Franklin, Paseo Reforma 34.

CENTERS OF HIGHER LEARNING. National University, headquarters at C. Justo Sierra 16; National School of Fine Arts, C. Academia 22; school of engineering and mining, in Palacio de Minería, Av. Tacuba; school of medicine, Av. Brasil and C. Venezuela; summer school, Av. Ribera de San Cosmé and C. Naranjo.

HOSPITALS. American, C. Barreda 34; Lord Cowdray Sanitarium (British), Av. Chapultepec; General, Av. Niños Héroes 148; Juárez, Plaza San Pablo.

MARKETS. In smaller towns a day each week is set aside for market, but in Mexico City every day is market day. Trading in the Mexican market is a social as well as a business affair. Everybody comes to look, to admire, to discuss politics, to exchange gossip, to pass the time of day lazily and pleasantly—and incidentally to buy or sell. A Mexican market is both an esthetic experience and a shoppers' paradise. Strange tropical fruits—shiny red, deep orange, violent green—gleam in the sunlight. Yellow Chinese pomegranates, the red hearts of some cut open, and the curious deep coral flesh of the mamey fruit contribute to the symphony of color. Calla lilies, orchids, roses of all hues, marigolds, and gladioli are heaped in generous profusion, their fragrance mingling with the exotic odor of herbs used for spicing Mexican dishes and for treating all sorts of ailments. Enormous radishes and bunches of artichokes arranged like bouquets of flowers nestle beside incredibly golden carrots. Native handicrafts—pottery the color of soft, rich earth; textiles in brilliant shades; tawny leather products; basketry in bold, gay colors; handblown blue glassware; embroideries—blend exquisitely.

Mercado Abelardo L. Rodríguez, named for the ex-president, a few blocks N of the church of Our Lady of Loreto, is the newest and cleanest, decorated with arresting frescoes by the vanguard of Mexican artists. The themes of the mural decorations in the patio, corridors, and stairways are drawn from the life of peasant and worker. They were painted by Ramón Alva de Guadarrama, Pedro Rendón, Angel Bracho, Miguel Tzab, Girón Passage, Antonio Pujol, the young U. S. artist Paul O'Higgins, and the Greenwood sisters, Marian and Grace.

Mercado Merced, several blocks E of the Zócalo and a little S, between C. Carranza and Av. Uruguay, the largest and one of the most picturesque in the city, spills out of a central building over an area of several blocks. Here foodstuffs of all sorts—fruit, vegetables, meats—are sold at the equivalent of wholesale prices. Fine handicrafts are brought by Indians from distant states.

Mercado San Juan, C. Ayuntamiento at C. Dolores, lies a block W from C. San Juan de Letrán, a few blocks S of the Alameda. It is a smaller edition of Mercado Merced, but equally colorful. There are fine arrays of fruits and a magic street of flowers. In addition to fruit, vegetables, and other foods, pottery, clothing, hardware, and other wares are sold. On narrow C. Dolores which runs from the market to the Alameda is Mexico City's Chinatown with numerous Chinese restaurants.

The flower market, Av. Hidalgo at the Alameda, one of the most picturesque of its kind, is noted for funeral wreaths and pieces.

La Lagunilla, Av. Isabel la Católica, is a silk and textile bazaar. Overhead dangle elaborate costumes in china poblana style with flashing sequins gleaming on bright red and green satin.

Mercado San Lucas, Av. Piño Suárez, has the city's largest collection of finely tooled saddles, handbags, belts, cigarette cases, and luggage.

MUSIC. Orquesta Sinfónica de México (Mexican Symphony Orchestra), weekly concerts July-August at Palace of Fine Arts; National University concerts, auditorium at C. Justo Sierra 16.

ART GALLERIES. Central, Av. Juárez 4; Palace of Fine Arts, E end of the Alameda; Mexican, C. General Prim 104; National University, C. Dolores 11.

THEATERS AND MOVING-PICTURE HOUSES. National Theater, in Palace of Fine Arts, E end of the Alameda; Lírico, Av. Cuba 8; Teatro Arbeu, Av. Salvador; Fabregas, C. Donceles 24; Hidalgo, C. Regina 52; Ideal, C. Dolores 8. Moving-picture houses include the Alameda, Av. Juárez across from the Alameda; Balmori, C. Alvaro Obregón 121; Magerit, Av. Juárez 58; Olimpia, Av. 16 de Septiembre; Palacio, Av. 5 de Mayo 30; Regis, Av. Juárez 77; Rex, Av. Madero across from Ritz Hotel.

SHOPS. Artes de México, Av. Juárez 48; Fred Davis (Sanborn's), Av. Madero 4; De la Peña y Lascurain, Av. 5 de Mayo 6; El Sol, Av. Juárez 71; El Tesoro, Av. Madero 17; George Plateau, Av. Juárez 22; Industrias Típicas, Av. Juárez 60; Maciel, C. Sadi Carnot 6; Mayan Art, Av. Madero 17; National Pawnshop, NW corner of the Zócalo; Native Arts, Av. Madero 6; Ortega, Av. 5 de Mayo and Callejón de la Condesa; Alex Taylor, Av. Madero 10; Frances Toor Studios, C. Manchester 8; Weston's, Av. Madero 13.

SPORTS. See under Practical Information (p. 36).

COUNTRY CLUBS. Chapultepec Golf Club, Lomas de Chapultepec; Chapultepec Sporting Club, Bosque Chapultepec; Polo Club of Mexico, Lomas de Chapultepec; Reforma Athletic Club, Lomas de Chapultepec.

TELEGRAPH OFFICES. National Telegraph, Av. Tacuba and C. Xicotencatl; Western Union, C. San Juan de Letrán and Av. Independencia.

U. S. EMBASSY AND CONSULATE. C. Niza 53.

TRAVEL BUREAUS. Aguirre's Guest Tours, Av. 5 de Mayo, 20; Mexico Tours, C. Balderas 68; Pan American Tours, Av. 5 de Mayo 20; Pemex Travel Club, C. Bucareli 35; Wagons-Lits Cook, Av. Madero 1; Wells Fargo (American Express and Raymond-Whitcomb), Av. Madero 14.

TRANSPORTATION OFFICES. Mexican Railways, Av. 5 de Mayo 18; National Railways of Mexico, C. Bolívar 19; Atchison, Topeka and Santa Fe, C. Bolívar 24, Illinois Central, Av. 5 de Mayo 24C; Missouri Pacific, Av. 5 de Mayo 23; Pennsylvania Railroad, C. Bolívar 22; Southern Pacific, Av. 5 de Mayo 32; Pan American Airways, Av. Madero and C. Filomeno Mata.

SOURCES OF INFORMATION. See Practical Information (p. 35).

BANKS. Banco de Londres y México, Av. 16 de Septiembre and C. Bolívar; Banco de México, Av. 5 de Mayo 2; Banco Nacional de México, Av. Isabel la Católica 44; National City Bank of New York, Av. Uruguay and Av. Isabel la Católica.

NIGHT LIFE. El Patio, C. Atenas 9; Grillon, Colonia del Valle; Reforma (Hotel); Regis Hotel (Don Quixote Salon); Rossignol, C. López and Av. Juárez; Waikiki, Paseo Reforma and C. Bucareli.

RESTAURANTS. Acapulco, C. López 9; American Club, C. Bolívar 31; Butch's Manhattan Café, Av. Juárez 58; Café Colón, Paseo Reforma and C. Artes; Chapultepec, Paseo Reforma at entrance to Bosque Chapultepec; El Danubio Azul, C. Tabasco and Av. Insurgentes; El Oriental, Av. Brasil 44; El Retiro, Av. Oaxaca and C. Valladolid; Fornos, Av. 16 de Septiembre and C. Bolívar; Fronton Restaurant, Fronton building; Lady Baltimore, Av. Madero 5; Majestic (Hotel); Manolo, Av. Juárez and C. López; Mitla, Av. Chile 46; Mrs. Thimgren's Coffee Shop, Av. Madero 1; Paolo, C. Gante 11; Peña Montañesa, Teatro Olimpia; Prendes, Av. 16 de Septiembre 4; Reforma (Hotel); Reforma Pharmacy; Regis (Hotel); Regis Pharmacy; Ritz (Hotel); San Angel Inn, outside the city at Villa Obregón; Sanborn's, Av. Madero 4.

BARS. Antonio, C. Niza and C. Liverpool; Broadway, C. San Diego 21; Casino Americano, C. Filomeno Mata 15; Colón, Paseo Reforma across from Hotel Imperial; Fornos, C. Bolívar and Av. 16 de Septiembre; Fronton, Fronton building; La Cucaracha, C. Gante 3; La Opera, Av. 5 de Mayo 10; Paolo, C. Gante 11; Papillon, Callejón de la Condesa; Reforma (Hotel); Regis, Av. Juárez 88; Ritz (Hotel).

HOTELS. Castleview Apartments**, C. Ganges 44; Departamentos Washington**, Plaza Dinamarca 42; Geneve**, C. Londres 130; Guadalupe Courts**, Av. B 918; Guardiola**, Av. Madero 5; Majestic**, Av. Madero 73; María Christina**, C. Lerma 31; Montejo**, Paseo Reforma 240; Prosperity Courts**, C. Martí 214; Reforma**, Paseo Reforma and C. París; Ritz**, Av. Madero 30; Royal Courts**, C. Luz Savignon 611; United States Courts**, C. Mazatlán 121; Waldorf**, Av. Chapultepec and C. Oaxaca.

Carlton*, C. Mariscal 32; Casa Real*, C. Nápoles 9; Casa Rul Courts*, C. Tenochtitlán 1220; Danky*, C. Donato Guerra 10; Edison*, C. Edison 106; L'Escargot*, C. Filadelfia and C. Oklahoma, Colonia Nápoles; Florida Tourist Mansion*, Av. Insurgentes 381; Gillow*, Av. Isabel la Católica 17; Hunter*, Calzada Villalongín 12; Imperial*, Paseo Reforma and Av. Morelos; Isabel*, Av. Isabel la Católica 63; Loly*, C. Buenavista 4; Los Angeles Courts*, Av. Insurgentes 786; Mancera*, C. Venustiano Carranza 49; Ontario*, Av. Uruguay 87; Plaza*, C. Dr. Mora 3; Regis*, Av. Juárez 77; Royalty*, C. Eliseo 21; Villa Internacional*, C. Pánuco 10.

Avenida, C. San Juan de Letrán 38; Biltmore, C. Ramos Arizpe 38; Buenos Aires, C. Motolinía 21; Canadá, Av. 5 de Mayo 47; Coliseo C. Bolívar 28; Colonia Roma, C. Jalapa 110; Colonial, C. Sor Juana Inés de la Cruz 40; Cosmos, C. San Juan de Letrán 12; Hipódromo Av. Insurgentes 287; Humboldt Mansion, C. Humboldt 45; Luxor, C. Revillagigedo 92; Montecarlo, Av. Uruguay 69; Palacio, Av. Isabel la

Católica 38; Pánuco, C. Ayuntamiento 148; Pennsylvania, C. Mariscal 15; San Angel Inn, C. Las Palmas 50, Villa Obregón; Tivoli, C. Ramón Guzmán 6; Toledo, C. López 22; York, Av. 5 de Mayo 31.

Shirley Courts*, Calzada Villalongín 151, is a place where trailers can find agreeable and convenient shelter.

MEXICO CITY'S ENVIRONS AND EXCURSIONS

Atzcapotzalco (Ant Hill), so named in primitive times because of its large population, is 5 miles NW from the center of Mexico City by bus or street car. Little remains of this town, the Tepanec capital, except giant ahuehuete trees and a 17th-century parish church on the site of an ancient slave market. On the side of the church tower facing the plaza is engraved the image of an ant, symbol of the town's name. Inside the church are canvases by Rodríguez and Cabrera. It is said that Malinche, the Indian girl who was Cortés' interpreter and mistress, haunts the ahuehuete groves and lures men to destruction by her siren songs.

Tlalnepantla, 5 miles N of Atzcapotzalco, was founded by Otomí Indians but later conquered by the Aztecs. The church, begun in 1583 by the Franciscans, contains one of the first images brought to the New World, a Christ of La Merced (Mercy). The baptismal font is supposed to have been a cuauhxicalli or sacred vessel used by the Aztecs to receive the hearts and blood of sacrifices.

Tepozotlán, 15 miles from Tlalnepantla, has a church and monastery regarded as one of the most beautiful examples of the Churrigueresque style in the republic. Founded by the Jesuits in 1584 with an endowment provided by an Indian cacique as a school for priests, the buildings were completed in the 18th century. The monastery, set in a formal colonial garden, is austere in effect. The church and chapels are rich with gold-leaf altars and decorations. Paintings by Cabrera, Rodríguez, Juárez, Villalpando, and other famous artists are here. The monastery is preserved as a national monument.

The basilica of Our Lady of Guadalupe, in Villa Gustavo A. Madero, 4 miles N of Mexico City by car or street car, is the most famous of Mexico's shrines. What Benares is to the Hindu and Mecca to the Moslem this shrine is to the devout Mexican Indian. For here, according to tradition, the Virgin spoke to the poor Indian Juan Diego and caused her image to appear on his mantle. The large church is said to occupy the site of an Aztec temple dedicated to the goddess of earth and corn, Tonantzín, for whom the Indians mourned after the Spanish conquest. On Cerrito Tepeyac, the hill where the goddess's temple had stood, the Virgin appeared to Juan Diego three times on Dec. 9, 1531. As a proof of her visitation she miraculously imprinted her likeness on his tilma or blanket in the guise of an Indian princess and requested that a shrine be erected on the mountainside in her honor. Widespread conversions to Christianity resulted. The present church, the fourth, was begun in 1695.

The Virgin of Guadalupe was credited with halting the great plague of 1736. A few years later she was named the patroness and protectress of New Spain and her image became the venerated symbol of the Mexican people. The mantle of Juan Diego, set in a heavy frame of pure gold and inclosed by a solid silver railing said to weigh 24 tons, occupies the center of the altar, a magnificent structure of marble and bronze. The Carrara marble portal cost 91,000 pesos. Just beneath the miraculous painting is a kneeling statue of Juan Diego. On important occasions a jeweled crown, presented by the women of Mexico and valued at more than $30,000, is placed over the picture. The mantle is well preserved. During December 3-13 as many as 100,000 Indian pilgrims come from all parts of Mexico to worship at the shrine. During this great fiesta, a combination of religious and tribal ceremonies, they encamp for miles around, and the plaza outside the church resembles a great country fair.

Near the shrine is the Capilla del Pocito (Chapel of the Well), built over a spring which is said to have gushed forth from the rock at the spot where the Virgin appeared. All day long Indians can be seen filling their pitchers with the water, which they believe to have miraculous healing qualities. At the top of Cerrito Tepeyac in back of the church is the Capilla del Cerrito (Chapel of the Little Hill), marking the spot where Juan Diego gathered flowers that sprang up from the barren soil in testimony to the Virgin's having manifested herself. Close by is the Tepeyac cemetery, containing the tombs of some of the leading personalities of Mexico's history, including General Santa Ana. There is a splendid view of Mexico City and the surrounding countryside from Cerrito Tepeyac.

In the near-by Colonia Industrial is a federal primary school designed by Juan O'Gorman along modern lines, with frescoes by Paul O'Higgins.

The pyramid of Tenayuca, 9 miles N of Mexico City, is an outstanding example of Aztec construction, 140 feet square and 50 feet high. The serpent, which dominates Aztec mythology, was greatly stressed at Tenayuca. R. H. K. Marett in his book Archeological Tours from Mexico City writes that Tenayuca presumably resembles the great temple at the Aztec city of Tenochtitlán: "On three sides of the base of the monument are low platforms, upon which are many S-shaped serpents ranged side by side. Compared with the delicate sculpture of Teotihuacán, or Xochicalco, these snakes are very crudely modeled . . . They perhaps represent a belated attempt to emulate the ample serpent-wall which surrounded the courtyard of the great Mexican temple." Excavations have revealed interior structures believed to have been erected at some earlier period. A magnificent view of the surrounding valley is gained from the top of the pyramid.

The pyramid of Santa Cecilia, a smaller but apparently contemporary replica of Tenayuca, not as fully excavated, lies a mile N from Tenayuca.

San Juan Teotihuacán, 28 miles NE of Mexico City, contains some of the most remarkable remains of an ancient civilization that exist anywhere in the world. The ruins are reached either by car or by railroad to a station within half a mile of them.

Today a well-kept government reservation, Teotihuacán is believed to mark the center of an extensive prehistoric city. The ruins occupy a huge rectangle containing about 8 square miles. Immense temples, pyramids, and extensive courts are arranged in a splendid design. The structures were executed on a mammoth scale with an engineering skill and a precision that are baffling. According to some authorities the great pyramids of the Sun and the Moon were built by the Toltecs. Other authorities insist that they are much older and may have been built 2000 years ago; still others are of the opinion that they are 6000 years old. Unlike the pyramids of Egypt, they were not designed as places of burial, but as temples dedicated to the worship of two principal deities, the Sun and the Moon.

The imposing pyramid of the Sun, one of the largest artificial mounds in America, is almost square at the base, 765 by 725 feet, and nearly 220 feet high. It consists of five sections or terraces which produce a series of symmetrical ascending walls sloping inward toward the top. Before excavation was begun the entire structure was covered with a heavy layer of earth and debris overgrown with vegetation. The original structure, which had deteriorated, has now been restored. The top affords a comprehensive view of the entire plain. Covered in olden times with gleaming red pyrite, the pyramid must have been a gorgeous spectacle

Not far from the pyramids of the Sun and Moon are several temples believed to have been erected by the Aztecs, including the great temple of Quetzalcoatl, which has remarkable stone carvings representing mythological deities. These are in the Citadel, a quarter-mile quadrangle. The absolute precision with which this court was laid out, the architectural beauty of the temples and surrounding structures, and the sculptural work are amazing in view of the primitive methods that must have been employed. A short distance away is a structure supposed to have been the mansion of some ancient dignitary. It contains large halls, stairways, polychrome decorations, a chapel and altar, and a bath which was supplied by a deep well still in existence.

The regional museum at Teotihuacán contains an extensive and fascinating collection of objects unearthed in the ancient city—pottery, idols, ornaments of jade or nephrite and obsidian, weapons, agricultural implements, and many minute representations of human faces. A manual training school in the immediate vicinity has a fine exhibit, largely of pupils' handicrafts.

In a large natural cave near the museum there is an excellent restaurant, the Grotto.

San Agustín Acolman, about 10 miles SW of San Juan Teotihuacán, has one of the oldest churches still standing that were built by the Spaniards immediately following the conquest. A strong, fortresslike structure completed in 1560 and later restored by the Mexican government, its façade is designed in modified Plateresque style. Mural decorations along the upper corridor of the patio and around the high altar depict the life of St. Augustine and represent popes and other ecclesiastical dignitaries. The church was built in connection with a monastery.

Chapingo, 23 miles E of Mexico City, is the seat of the national agricultural college. The building occupied by this school was formerly the plantation house of Manuel González, at one time figurehead president for Porfirio Díaz. The institution is completely equipped with dormitories, modern laboratories, and large experimental grounds. In the main building and chapel are frescoes of Diego Rivera which rank with the best of his work. The theme revolves around the revolution in relation to agriculture and the life of the people. On one of the frescoes along the stairway of the main building is a text: "Here we teach exploitation of the earth and not of man." For more detailed descriptions, see Interpretative Guide No. 3, published by Frances Toor Studios.

Texcoco, 25 miles E of Mexico City, beyond Chapingo, in pre-conquest times was the capital of the Acolhua kingdom, one of the most powerful in ancient Mexico. During the century preceding the coming of the Spaniards, Texcoco equaled the city of Tenochtitlán and was the cultural center of the Aztec domain. Netzahualcoyotl (1431-72) was the Tezcucans' most distinguished monarch. The Mexican historian Orozco y Berra sums up his character thus: "Just, yet clement, compassionate of misfortune, generous, intelligent, an intrepid warrior, a philosopher, poet, engineer, legislator, the father of his people, he filled with his fame the world of Anáhuac. . . . The Texcoco of his time may be called the Athens of America."

A monument at the entrance of the town marks one base of Cortés' operations against Tenochtitlán. Here the flat-bottomed boats built in Tlaxcala and brought across the mountains in sections were reassembled and launched. The town today, an agricultural and crafts village, is very pleasant. Places of interest include the 16th-century church of San Francisco, a handsome colonial fountain, and several colonial homes.

Huexotla, 3 miles SE of Texcoco, can be reached by road from Chapingo. It is an interesting archeological site that has been only partially excavated. A pre-conquest wall 35 feet high and over 200 feet long is its outstanding feature. There are also a number of small pyramidal structures. A village church is situated on one of them.

Coatlinchán, 3 miles S of Texcoco and a mile E, is a village notable chiefly for an idol that lies in a ravine some 3 miles SE. This huge monolith, known as the idol of Tecomates, is about 18 feet long by 4 feet across, weighing perhaps 300 tons, and was probably intended to represent the deity Tlaloc or Xicaca, goddess of waters.

Texcotzingo (Laughing Hill) is about 7 miles E of Texcoco on a dirt road. The summer palace of Netzahualcoyotl here, though in ruins, is an enduring monument to the skill and taste of the Tezcucan ruler. On the road to it, 3 miles from Texcoco, is Molino de Flores, a public park with attractive flower gardens and streams, a favorite picnic place. Texcotzingo was originally laid out in terraced walks or hanging gardens, with stairways of several hundred steps winding around the hill from base to summit. Baths were hewn out of the natural rock near the top. An aqueduct carried water for the gardens and the baths. Near the top of the hill are two broken idols called the King and Queen. The view from the summit is majestic. A guide is almost essential for this trip.

Chiconcuac, 2½ miles from Texcoco on the road to San Andrés, with a left turn at the church, is a pleasant village where the celebrated Texcoco sarapes or blankets are woven.

The floating gardens of Xochimilco, constructed long before the conquest and often described as Mexico's Venice, are 14 miles SE of Mexico City and best reached by taxi. In a lake which existed here the Aztecs constructed a settlement on chinampas, small floating islands of twigs and reeds interlaced, covered with earth and planted with gardens; later the plants took root in the bottom of the lake so that the islands were held fast. On them the Indians cultivated flower and vegetable gardens from which they supplied Tenochtitlán. Today their descendants similarly supply fruit, vegetables, and flowers to the Mexico City markets as well as to a large local market. The former islands are now surrounded by a network of canals. Tall trees grow in abundance. On Sundays and holidays Xochimilco attracts hosts of pleasure seekers and picnickers. Indians who speak the ancient Aztec tongue among themselves propel along the canals among the beautiful gardens large flat-bottomed boats resembling Venetian gondolas, decorated with flowers. Minstrels who sing and play songs of old and new Mexico can be engaged at very little cost. The rose-colored 16th-century church in the village is interesting. On Saturdays Indians from surrounding villages bring their products to the market.

Churubusco, 6 miles S of Mexico City, reached by street car or by bus marked Coyoacán or Tlalpam from the Zócalo, is an old Aztec religious center. The picturesque monastery, built in 1678 by the Franciscans, is now deserted and crumbling. It contains some interesting paintings, a library, and relics of the battle fought here during the Mexican-U. S. war, in 1847. Opposite is a monument with an inscription that signifies: "Erected 1856 to the memory of those brave Mexicans who gave their lives for their country at this spot, August 20, 1847. President Ignacio Comonfort and the Mexican nation gratefully dedicated this monument to their honor and glory."

The Churubusco Country Club has a membership composed largely of U. S. residents. The grounds, admirably laid out, include a fine golf course and tennis courts. The clubhouse is a handsome building in Spanish mission style.

Tlalpam, 10 miles S of Mexico City, an old and beautiful suburban town with orchards, brooks, fountains, and villas from the days of the Spanish viceroys, lies on the slope of the extinct volcano Ajusco, which is believed to have caused the lava flow of El Pedregal. The picturesque old parochial church of San Agustín de las Cuevas, near Plaza Constitución, was built in 1532 and has a fine Churrigueresque altar and some interesting paintings by Miguel Cabrera.

The pyramid of Cuicuilco, 1½ miles W of Tlalpam near the village of Peña Pobre, is thought to be the oldest so far discovered on the continent. It is surrounded and partly buried by the lava field of El Pedregal.

Villa Alvaro Obregón, formerly San Angel, 8 miles SW of Mexico City, is a popular residential suburb containing fine modern homes. It is reached by express street car in 20 minutes.

Near the main plaza are the church and monastery of the Virgin of El Carmen, begun in 1615. The church has three magnificent domes of colored tiles, making it a favorite subject for painters. A crypt beneath one of the chapels holds a number of well-preserved mummies of the colonial period. A monument to Gen. Alvaro Obregón, revolutionary military genius and a president of Mexico, stands at the end of Calzada Nueva on the spot where he was assassinated. Half a mile from the plaza is Diego Rivera's ultramodern home.

HOTEL. San Angel Inn, opposite Rivera's house, is very attractive for luncheon parties and for those seeking the quiet of the countryside.

El Pedregal, a prehistoric volcanic lava field covering about 15 miles, is near Villa Alvaro Obregón. In it are imbedded human remains and primitive ancient articles. The visitor should not venture into it without a guide.

Coyoacán, adjoining Villa Alvaro Obregón so closely that it is hard to tell where one begins and the other ends, is a suburban district popular with U. S. visitors. This beautiful ancient town was inhabited even before the Aztecs came to dominate the valley. Cortés used it as the base for his attack upon Tenochtitlán and later made it the first seat of Spanish government. Here he built his first private residence, and here in 1757 his descendants completed the building on the main plaza which is now the city hall, Casa Municipal or Casa de Cortés. Local legend, heedless of dates, points out a room in this building where the great conqueror is said to have tortured Cuauhtémoc, the last of the Aztec emperors, in the effort to make him reveal the hiding place of Aztec treasure.

At the entrance of the town are botanical gardens which are open to the public. On the main street is an old rose-colored Spanish mansion said to have been built by Pedro de Alvarado, lieutenant of Cortés. It was long owned and inhabited by the celebrated archeologist Mrs. Zelia Nuttall, who died in 1933. She made it a veritable museum of Mexican art of all periods. The big garden behind it is superbly beautiful. Also of interest are the parish church of San Juan Bautista, S of the plaza, built in 1583, and the adjoining Dominican monastery, built in 1530.

Desierto de los Leones (Desert of the Lions), 18 miles SW of Mexico City on an excellent highway, is not a desert and has no lions. The name refers to the solitude of the place, and León in this case is a family name, like Lyon in English. In this charming park on the edge of a pine forest are the ruins of a Carmelite monastery built in 1606, with strange underground labyrinths and vaults, secret chapels, ghostly dungeons, and an old glass factory. The ruins are surrounded by a beautiful garden cut by many paths. On Sundays and holidays the place is full of refreshment stalls and booths, picnic tables, and gay crowds.

Popotla, 20 minutes W of Mexico City by street car or bus, is celebrated for the Tree of the Dismal Night (El Arbol de la Noche Triste), beneath which Cortés sat down and wept during the Spaniards' terrible retreat from Tenochtitlán.

Tacuba, a suburb 3½ miles W of the center of Mexico City, is a pleasant little village. In ancient days, as Tlacopan, it was part of the Aztec empire. The parish church of San Gabriel has an attractive exterior.

San Bártolo Naucalpam, 8 miles W of Mexico City via Tacuba by bus or street car, is notable for the church of Our Lady of Los Remedios, the patroness of the Spaniards in Mexico, which once rivaled the shrine of Guadalupe. The church in this dusty little Indian village is said to have owed its origin to a miracle associated with a roughly carved wooden image of the Virgin, one of several brought by Cortés' soldiers. The miracles continued, and during the Mexican revolution of independence some astonishing incidents occurred while the likeness of this Virgin was on the banners of the Spanish loyalists. Today the image is enshrined in a glass case on the altar. The great fiesta of Los Remedios starts September 1 and lasts through September 8, which is the big day.

MEXICO CITY TO ACAPULCO

National Highway (Camino Nacional) No. 3 runs almost due S from the capital to Acapulco on the Pacific coast. It is paved as far as Chilpancingo and improved for the 90-odd miles from there to the ocean. There is good bus service. Cuernavaca and Taxco, two of the most engaging towns in the republic, lie on this road, which first passes the great volcanoes that dominate Mexico City, Popocatépetl and

Ixtaccíhuatl, and then rises to the pass across the mountain rim of the plateau at El Guarda (9990 feet), where even in summer it is often very cold. Descending, the route enters the semitropical valley of Morelos and is lined with flowers.

An alternative route as far as Cuernavaca follows National Highway No. 2 at first. It is longer, but it offers rewarding views of the volcanoes closer at hand. It also gives glimpses of the towns of Amecameca and, with a little detour, Cuautla. The road out of Mexico City to Amecameca is straight and level. The small towns of Los Reyes and Santa Bárbara are passed in quick succession. At Santa Bárbara the route strikes S off National Highway No. 2 to Chalco.

Tlalmanalco, 8 miles beyond Chalco, is noted for its 16th-century Franciscan church and monastery. There are frescoes in the cloisters, and the open-air chapel has remarkable Plateresque decorations.

E of the highway, 5 miles before reaching Amecameca, the San Rafael paper mill is passed. The road rises somewhat, running through a semiarid valley.

Amecameca, with 10,000 inhabitants, is an important and interesting old Aztec town near the foot of Mexico's two most famous volcanoes, Popocatépetl and Ixtaccíhuatl. It is 37 miles from Mexico City by road.

The sanctuary of the Lord of El Sacromonte (Sacred Mountain), a small church built around a cave atop a 300-foot hill back of the railroad station, is the most venerated spot in Mexico except only the shrine of Guadalupe. The cave was once the dwelling of a saintly hermit and missionary, Friar Martín de Valencia, who came to Mexico from Spain in 1524. A strange miracle is said to have occurred here, when an unidentified riderless mule came bearing the image which has long been regarded with such veneration. A chapel now shelters the life-sized figure of Christ. Holy Week and November 2, All Souls' Day (Todos los Muertos), are interesting here. The leading annual fiesta begins on the Monday preceding Lent and continues until the afternoon of Ash Wednesday. The hill, which it is possible to drive up, offers a magnificent view.

The parish church of Amecameca dates from the 16th century. Market is held on Sundays, the best day for a visit.

HOTELS. Central; Sacromonte.

Excursions to Popocatépetl and Ixtaccíhuatl. Amecameca is the usual base for the difficult climb to these summits. Guides and horses can be secured in the town. It is best to make all arrangements with the advice of experienced persons such as members of the Explorers' Club in Mexico City. About a mile S of Amecameca a good but dusty gravel road leads SE 16 miles up the side of Popocatépetl. Fifteen miles in on this road another road strikes off 12 miles toward the summit of Ixtaccíhuatl.

The climb of Popocatépetl (17,883 feet) is usually started after an early breakfast. A halt is made in the foothills for lunch, and the ascent continues on horse or muleback to Tlamacas (12,782 feet), from which there is a beautiful view. The night is passed in a hut here. The next morning the ascent is resumed; the horses are left at La Cruz (14,104 feet), and if little snow is encountered a good climber should reach the summit by 1 p.m. In clear weather the view is indescribably grand, encompassing the entire valley of Mexico, domes and spires of the capital, and several towns, including the city of Puebla, together with highlands and lowlands. Popo, as the great mountain is endearingly called, has had many violent eruptions in the past 400 years. As lately as 1921 it exhaled great volumes of smoke and gases for months. Shortly after the arrival of Cortés the Spaniards scaled it and extracted sulphur from the crater for the manufacture of gunpowder. Since that time it is said that more than a million tons of sulphur have been taken from the volcano. The crater, about 2700 feet across, is more than 550 feet deep. Experts estimate the floor to consist of an immense deposit of sulphur a thousand feet deep.

The ascent of Ixtaccíhuatl (17,338 feet) presents few difficulties such as the big Alpine peaks do; yet the mountain has never been so popular with climbers as the higher Popocatépetl. The surrounding sierras, however, are of great interest to the naturalist and geologist.

Ozumba, with 3100 inhabitants, 6 miles S of Amecameca, is the nearest town to the volcano Popocatépetl, only 5 miles distant. An old Franciscan church in the town contains some 17th-century paintings of unusual interest, especially one depicting a meeting of Cortés, some of his men, and some missionaries with Cuauhtémoc. There are beautiful orchards and on Tuesdays an interesting market.

Excursion from Ozumba. A mile and a quarter away is Chimalhuacán, with picturesque gardens and a Dominican establishment possessing the font where the great Mexican poetess Juana Inés de la Cruz was baptized, a nun who was born in the neighboring village of Nepantla. Near by is the Cascada de Chimal (Chimal Fall).

Excursion to Cuautla. Twenty-one miles S of Ozumba a road branches off 2 miles to Cuautla. This town, with 6000 inhabitants, lies in a tropical valley and is a popular resort because of its hot sulphur springs and baths. Even before the conquest the springs here were famous among the Indians, who came from distant places to bathe in them. Many drive out from Mexico City for the week end. Aguas Hediondas, sulphur springs some 2½ miles from the town, have a modern outdoor swimming pool, bathhouses, and a pavilion.

A heroic incident of the revolution occurred here in 1812 when the famous priest José María Morelos y Pavón, standard-bearer of the revolution after Hidalgo, was besieged by Gen. F. M. Callega's royalist army. After three months of furious attacks and a strict blockade Morelos succeeded in withdrawing secretly. Lucas Alamán, the famous Mexican historian, wrote: "If at the siege of Cuautla victory fell to Calleja, the honor and glory fell to Morelos."

A century later Cuautla was the center of the revolutionary activities of the agrarian leader Emiliano Zapata, idol of the peasants, who was treacherously assassinated in 1917 at a little town near by. An imposing monument has been erected to mark his tomb. On April 10 a fiesta is held in his honor; on September 30, one in honor of Morelos.

HOTELS. San Diego*; Vasco*; Francia; Morelos; Quinta Amalia.

Excursion from Cuautla. Oaxtépec, a short distance from Cuautla, can be reached on foot, on horseback, or by car. A federal normal school which prepares Indian boys and girls to teach in the rural schools is lodged in a 16th-century monastery decorated with interesting paintings of saints. One of the famous gardens in which Moctezuma is supposed to have cultivated medicinal plants is near by.

CUERNAVACA

An extremely attractive town, Cuernavaca, with 10,000 inhabitants, capital of the state of Morelos, can be reached direct from Mexico City by National Highway (Camino Nacional) No. 3, running through to Acapulco on the Pacific coast. By the other route that has been described it is 26 miles W from the turnoff for Cuautla. On this road huge fields of sugar cane are passed, dotted with neglected old plantation houses. Beyond the Cañon de Lobo (Wolf Canyon), Cuernavaca is reached. Cuernavaca's quiet environs and even, temperate climate make it a year-round health resort and the fashionable week-end playground of Mexico City's smart set. Week-end reservations should be made in advance. July-February is the favorite season.

For centuries prior to the conquest of Mexico the ancient Tlahuicas, a race of Nahua origin, prospered in Cuauhnahuac (Near the Woods), on the site of the present Cuernavaca (Cow's Horn). They erected pyramids and dwellings, vestiges of which remain as testimonials of their skill and ingenuity. The Tlahuicas became tributaries of the Aztecs; in 1521, after a bloody fight, they succumbed to Cortés. The difficulty of pronouncing and spelling Cuauhnahuac caused the Spaniards to change the name to Cuernavaca. The king of Spain granted Cortés the greater part of the present state of Morelos as a gift. In 1530 the conqueror returned from the mother country to Mexico to assert his rights over his lands and subjects. He introduced the culture of sugar cane and installed the first sugar mill in America. Charmed by the mild climate of the place, its natural beauty, and the fertility of the soil, he chose Cuernavaca for a resting place and built here for his second wife, doña Juana Ramírez de Arellano y Zúñiga, a palatial mansion with beautifully decorated salons, galleries, and gardens, whose splendor was a symbol of his own magnificence. While the palace has undergone a number of changes and repairs, its imposing exterior remains intact, and it is a good example of early colonial architecture. It now houses state offices. The building is W from the cathedral.

The amazing story of the Spanish conquest of Cuauhnahuac is strikingly depicted in Diego Rivera's murals which adorn the Cortés palace. These were painted in 1930 on commission of the late U. S. Ambassador Dwight Morrow. The N lateral wall is concerned with Indian life and customs in pre-Hispanic days. The large main wall develops the story of the conquest in rich, bold colors. From right to left the subjects are: the Spaniards attacking an Aztec temple; a battle between the Indians and Spaniards; the Spaniards crossing a ravine in order to take the town; the taking and occupation of Cuernavaca; construction of the Cortés palace and Cortés receiving tribute from the conquered Indians; beginning of the sugar-cane industry; Father Toribio de Motolinía teaching the Indians; revolution, and portrait of the agrarian leader Emiliano Zapata. In the middle panels, facing each other, are portraits of José María Morelos and of Zapata. On the S lateral wall the horrors of the Inquisition and the complete submission of the Indians are graphically portrayed. Reproductions and detailed information concerning these famous frescoes are contained in an inexpensive booklet, Frescoes in Cortés Palace, Cuernavaca, with critical notes by Carlos Mérida, published by Frances Toor, which can be obtained in Cuernavaca and Mexico City bookstores.

CHURCHES. The cathedral of Cuernavaca has been but little altered during the 400 years since its construction. The ancient weather-beaten structure, with a high tower and a low dome, was built for military as well as for religious purposes. Its grim, massive lines suggestive of a medieval fort and its naïve Indian decorations are typical of early

Franciscan architecture. The first Franciscan monks arrived in Cuernavaca in 1529 and in that year began construction of the monastery and chapel of San José. Mass was celebrated on the roof of this chapel for an open-air congregation of thousands of Indian converts; within, Cortés himself attended Mass. At the entrance to the atrium of the cathedral is the chapel of La Tercera Orden de San Francisco. The Indians with rude chisels cut naïve animal and plant designs on the sacred walls. The cloister of the cathedral, that of the first priests' seminary in America, now houses a secular elementary school.

Other churches include those of San Pedro and of La Asunción; a tiny chapel called La Ermita de Guadalupe; the church of Our Lady of Guadalupe, across the street from the cathedral, built by a son of José de la Borda; and the delightful little Indian church of Los Topetates, which is flanked by two cypress trees higher than itself.

OTHER POINTS OF INTEREST. A building opposite the cathedral which is now a boarding house is reputed to have been the first residence of Cortés in Cuernavaca.

The fine colonial Casa de Mañana, near the cathedral, was the home of Ambassador Morrow. In February 1940 former President Lázaro Cárdenas donated his summer residence in Cuernavaca for an orphanage and children's hospital. With the property went a gift of 100,000 pesos for the equipment of dormitories and infirmaries.

The federal secondary experimental vocational school, a block from the chief plaza, Jardín Juárez, at Calle Rayón and C. Comonfort, has interesting co-operatives. The auditorium contains several frescoes by Máximo Pacheco.

Band concerts are held in the plaza on Thursdays and Sundays. Boys and girls promenade while the music goes on.

MARKET. Gaily painted rush-bottomed chairs, terra-cotta pottery the color of the sun-baked earth, and well-made huaraches are typical of the crafts that flourish here.

CLUBS. The Country Club, to which the managers of the hotels can secure temporary admission for the visitor, was built by a group of residents to provide a social and recreational center. It has a tiled bar, ballroom, swimming pools, and an 18-hole golf course.

RESTAURANTS. Lunch in the Hotel Jardín Borda is a pleasant experience. The gardens were part of the estate of José de la Borda, who in the early days of the 18th century amassed a mining fortune estimated at 40 million pesos and built an ornate mansion here. The estate was a tropical Versailles such as Marie Antoinette might have planned. The clear waters of two exquisite pools reflected graceful swans. Luscious fruits and flowers spilled over into orderly paths. When Carlotta and Maximilian visited the place in 1864 they were enchanted with its elegance and beauty. It became the imperial residence, and a period of regal splendor, of gay parties and French fêtes and masques, ensued. Carlotta and the ladies of the court swam in the tepid waters of the artificial lake, while on the broad terraced descent to the pool court musicians played sarabandes and gigues.

HOTELS. The Cuernavaca hotels range from venerable remodeled monasteries and mansions to modern edifices. Some of the older buildings retain their original woodwork, masonry, and tiling. Many have swimming pools. The hotels include Chula Vista**; Mandell's Inn**; Astoria*; Bellavista*; Jardín Borda*; Butch's Manhattan Inn*; De la

Selva*; Marik*; Los Canarios, a tourist camp; Moctezuma; Morelos; Rex; Roma; Savoy.

EXCURSIONS FROM CUERNAVACA

San Antonio is a tiny, charming potters' village on a ledge above a waterfall, a little W of Cuernavaca, across the ravine in back of Hotel Jardín Borda. Its single street is lively. The pottery-making craft has been handed down from father to son for generations. The graceful water jugs which are always on sale in the plazas of Cuernavaca are made here. The waterfall, less than a mile from Cuernavaca and reached on foot or by car, drops a hundred feet into a deep pool. A walk cut into the rock behind it enables the visitor to see what a waterfall is like from the inside. Wild orchids cling to the perpendicular trees whose roots pierce the surrounding boulders.

Tepoztlán, a primitive village occupied by the Aztecs for centuries, can be reached by a road which, about 3 miles N of Cuernavaca, branches 11½ miles E. This isolated town with its native language and old traditions figures prominently in Robert Redfield's book Tepoztlán, Stuart Chase's Mexico, and Carleton Beals' Mexican Maze. The village, one of the most picturesque and friendly in Mexico, is beautifully situated on a hilly bit of land surrounded by awe-inspiring peaks. Since there are neither hotels nor good restaurants, the visitor should carry lunch or be prepared to eat the simplest Mexican food. Near the plaza are the massive church and monastery of Tepoztlán, dating from the 16th century. On a cliff overhanging the village is the pyramid of Tepozteco, built centuries before the advent of the Spaniards, probably by the Tlahuicas, in honor of Ometotochtli, god of pulque. The caretaker of the ruins or a boy in the village will serve as guide. A 2-hour climb through dense foliage leads to the summit from which the Spaniards hurled Ometotochtli's image. When the idol did not break the monks smashed it with hammers. Only then did the simple villagers accept the credo of the conquerors and the overthrow of their own pagan divinity. The view is perhaps more rewarding than the pyramid itself. On the evening of September 7 a colorful fiesta is held; its climax is a dance-drama in Aztec performed in full regalia and representing the victory of the native god-hero El Tepozteco over the surrounding villages.

The seven lakes of Zempoala form a chain of gleaming beauty set in rugged mountains 10,000 feet above sea level. The first of the lakes, surrounded by balsams, is reached on the road to Mexico City as far as Tres Cumbres (Tres Marías), then a 40-minute drive W. Abrupt mountain slopes and mossy banks outline the lakes' shores. This Alpine region of Mexico is excellent for brief or extended camping and fishing trips. Rainbow trout are caught.

Tempanzolco is a small pyramid temple which was discovered on the outskirts of Cuernavaca, NE of the railroad station, during the 1910-20 revolution, when the mound was used as a base for a cannon. It has a double stairway. Thought to be Aztec, though it may date from the time of the earlier Tlahuicas, it somewhat resembles the Tenayuca pyramid. Tempanzolco can be reached in 5 minutes by car or by a walk of less than half a mile. About 200 yards short of the pyramid the road narrows to a small path which climbs the hill. The deep ravine separating the pyramid from the town may be said to divide the ancient from the modern culture.

Chapultepec, a short distance E of Cuernavaca, is a village with a delightful bathing pool fed by cold mountain springs, modern bath-houses, and a pavilion surrounded by giant cypresses and lush foliage.

Atlacomulco, 2 miles E of Cuernavaca, is the place where Cortés planted the first sugar cane to be grown in America and established the first American refinery. Part of the aqueduct constructed to bring water to the mill remains. A Spanish inscription on it is translated: "Hernán Cortés, Conqueror of the great Tenochtitlán."

Acapacingo, a few miles S of Cuernavaca, is an exquisite tropical village. It is said that when Maximilian wearied of the gaieties of the Borda gardens he secluded himself at Acapacingo. A quaint chapel sur-rounded by flowering trees faces the tiled gateway of this rural retreat. It bears the inscription: "Antigua Casa del Emperador Maximiliano."

Xochicalco (House of the Flowers), ruins of an ancient city on a hilltop, is reached by driving 5½ miles on the road S toward Taxco, then 2 miles W at the sign reading Xochicalco. The ruins are the re-mains of a fortified town and of a pyramid. The latter is decorated with seated priests entwined by serpents. The subterranean passages under the pyramid bear traces of paintings. Undoubtedly important at one time, the place was evidently abandoned before the conquest. The pyramid can be scaled, and it is well to go equipped for climbing and for protection from the sun. No water or refreshments can be found at the ruins.

Zacatepec, the most modern and important sugar refinery in Mexico, can be reached by driving 12 miles over a fair road that branches off the highway at Alpuyeca, 16 miles S of Cuernavaca. The refinery was established by the government and is co-operatively run by Mexican workmen.

The Grutas de Cacahuamilpa, 28 miles beyond Zacatepec, are caves discovered in 1835, the largest in Mexico. They were used by ancient Indians as shrines and for military purposes and later by outlaws as hideouts. The caves are cared for by the government. They have been described as forming a series of pleasure domes and palaces wrought by nature herself to rival the architectural achievements of Indians and Spaniards. The endless labyrinth of vast chambers, some 100-150 feet high, 200 feet long and almost as wide, has been only partially explored, and is said to be connected with the Xochicalco caverns 20 miles away. More than 50 forms of stalactites and stalagmites achieve strange deco-rative effects and fantastic formations, chiefly in green, orange, and white. Two rivers which flow under the caves unite at the entrance to form the large and beautiful Río Amacruzac. The caverns are open 1-5 p.m. daily. Cars must be at the caves before 12:30 p.m. on Sun-days and the following holidays: January 1, February 5, Holy Thurs-day, Good Friday, September 15 and 16, October 12, and November 20. The grottoes are partially lighted by electricity, and there is guide service.

Lake Tequesquitengo, an hour's drive S out of Cuernavaca, is a favorite spot for catching large-mouth bass and for dove, quail, and deer hunting. About 50 years ago the village which formerly stood here sank and was covered by the lake. During the dry season it is said to be possible sometimes to see the belfry of the submerged cathedral.

Las Estacas is on the Río Yautepec, about 30 miles from Cuernavaca. The royal palms, mangoes, oranges, limes, and aguacates with which it is overgrown make it an idyllic picnic spot.

TAXCO

A town of 3600 inhabitants, Taxco lies 50 miles S of Cuernavaca. Emerging from a semiarid tropical valley dotted with primitive thatched Indian huts, the road winds into the mountains. About 10 miles short of Taxco a detour can be made to Puente de Ixtla, a small Indian village known for its luscious melons. Though Taxco is located in a warm zone, its elevation of more than 5600 feet gives it a temperate climate the year round.

The original Indian town was founded in 1445. Later the Aztec chieftain Moctezuma the Elder conquered the Tlahuica region and forced the inhabitants to pay tribute in the form of gold bricks. Previous to the discovery of Taxco by the Spaniards, the country around it was called Tlacho (Ball Game). It was conquered in 1531 by Cortés' officers, and silver mines were discovered shortly afterward during a search for tin to be used in making bronze for cannons. The first shipment sent from Mexico to Spain was extracted in 1534 from this place. Taxco claims as her native son Juan Ruiz de Alarcón, renowned Spanish poet and dramatist who lived in the 17th century, the golden age of Spanish literature. To fix its claim to being his birthplace the town is called Taxco de Alarcón.

In colonial days Taxco attained great prosperity when the Frenchman Joseph le Borde was active here. He lives in Mexican memory as José de la Borda. The story is that one day, downcast over a streak of bad luck, Borda was on his way to Mexico City when his mule's hoof sank into the ground and stuck there. Borda dismounted and, examining the ground, discovered the vein of silver from which he was to amass an immense fortune. The incident restored his faith, and he decided to erect a church dedicated to San Sebastián and Santa Prisca; hence the Mexican saying, "God gives to Borda, Borda gives to God." Taxco has changed little in appearance since Borda's time. Because of its colonial character the government has made it a national monument and prohibits modern structures. The town's steep, narrow cobbled streets, its fountains, its quaint white houses with red-tiled roofs on different levels, attract artists and writers from all over the world. It has an increasing number of U. S. residents.

The profusely ornamented church of San Sebastián and Santa Prisca, which dominates the town even today, was completed in 1757 at a cost of 8,000,000-10,000,000 pesos and was said to be at that time the most complete monument of ecclesiastical art on the new continent. The huge dome, decorated with glazed tiles in vivid colors—ultramarine, orange, green, and white—sparkles in the intense sunlight. Its façade is Baroque; the altarpieces within are Churrigueresque. The chapel of Todos Muertos (All Souls) contains three altars. The pulpit and two confessionals are richly carved in dark wood. The floor, which in recent years has been relaid with polished light wood, was originally entirely covered with an India carpet brought from Manila via Acapulco. A fragment of it can be seen in the sacristy. The pendentives of the dome are occupied by reliefs in gold representing the legend of the Virgin of Guadalupe. The walls are covered with huge canvases painted by the famous Miguel Cabrera, one of the most prolific painters of the 18th century; these are probably his best work—a beautiful Nativity, an Assumption of the Virgin, and 12 scenes of the life of Christ. The furniture in the sacristy is extraordinarily rich, and in the chapter room are portraits of Borda and other personages, all by Cabrera. An organ built in 1806 blends with the church surroundings. By climbing one of the towers it is possible to get a remarkable view over the countryside. Cactus, bougainvilleas, and beautiful flowers abound everywhere.

Other points of interest are the monastery of San Bernardino de Sena, of historic importance because it sheltered Agustín Iturbide, later emperor of Mexico, while he was working out an amicable agreement with Vicente Guerrero, hero of the revolution of independence, in 1821; the mines; the house in which the famous naturalist Baron von Humboldt lived for a short time; the market in the plaza, and the stands and shops occupied by skillful weavers and tin and silversmiths. At William Spratling's shop, Taller de las Delicias, can be seen the hand manufacture of old-style sarapes or blankets, tin candlesticks, mirrors, silver objects, and furniture. Taxco is not a bargain hunter's paradise; prices are the same as in Mexico City. On Sundays the plaza is alive with throngs of Indian vendors at the weekly market.

Hotel managers will secure guides and horses for trips into the hills. Attractive villages dot the slopes.

HOTELS. Arcos**; Chapultepec**; Posada de la Misión**; Rancho Telva**; Victoria*; Casa Grande; Meléndez.

On the highway to Acapulco a waterfall is passed, 6 miles out of Taxco, which at the height of the rainy season is comparable to the falls of the Columbia River above Portland, Ore.

Iguala, 22 miles S of Taxco, is a market town noted as the cradle of Mexican independence, because the Plan of Iguala was proclaimed here in 1821, with Agustín Iturbide's three guarantees of unity, religion, and independence. The town has a plaza with superb tamarind trees. Points of interest are the house where the Plan of Iguala was proclaimed and the parish church.

Chilpancingo, also known as Ciudad Bravo, with 8500 inhabitants, 66 miles S of Iguala, is capital of the state of Guerrero and an important agricultural center. Mexicans regard the place affectionately because of its historical associations. It was headquarters of the hero of Mexico's revolution of independence, Vicente Guerrero. The first Mexican congress met here in 1813. Points of interest include the Palacio del Gobierno, the state capitol; the house of the first revolutionary congress; a 16th-century bridge, and an old cemetery.

HOTEL. Trepieddi.

Chilpancingo marks the end of the paved highway. From here to Acapulco (91 miles) the road is improved. A couple of tunnels are traversed. The most beautiful part of the drive is after crossing the Río Balsas at Mexcala, when it runs through the Cañada del Zopilote (Buzzard's Ravine), with a long stretch of wild scenery.

Nearing Acapulco, the road dips and climbs, always losing altitude and reaching at last a ridge which affords a dramatic view of the bay of Acapulco encircled by green hills. Then it descends through a curious blend of dense forest and the tangled exotic foliage of the tropics to the town.

ACAPULCO

Acapulco, with a population of 7000, is the oldest port on the North American Pacific coast. Discovered in the 16th century by Hurtado de

Mendoza, it has played an important part in the development of the country. In Marquez Bay just outside the harbor Miguel López de Legazpe constructed the ships in which he sailed on the voyage which resulted in the conquest of the Philippines. Sailing galleons brought their rich cargoes to Acapulco from China, cargoes that were loaded on burro trains to travel on rock-paved highways over the sierras to Mexico City or to Veracruz for transshipment to Europe. Castillo San Diego, a fort at the entrance to the harbor, was built in the 17th century to guard against pirates. A new phase of life opened in this idyllic little port on completion of the Mexico City-Acapulco highway (281 miles). It is becoming an unrivaled vacation resort. Winter and spring are the ideal seasons, although the climate is enjoyable at all times. Swimming and fishing seasons are the year round.

The market is interesting, and in the town can be seen native goldsmiths at work on their wares.

There are two main beaches. Playa Caleta, shielded from heavy tides and breakers, where the water is always pleasantly warm, is generally preferred in the morning. Playa Hornos or Anáhuac is excellent for surf bathing in the afternoon. Playa Manzanillo and La Angosta are other beaches. Moonlight bathing is very popular.

FISHING. Acapulco's deep-sea fishing is world-famous. Sharks, swordfish, sailfish, giant rays, and turtles are abundant; fishermen come from all parts of the world to hook these fighting fish. The amateur, too, can enjoy a fishing trip. Launches with trained fishermen are for hire.

HUNTING. Marshy country N of the town, around the Laguna de Coyuca, abounds with wild fowl, and there are alligators on which to test marksmanship. Deer, wildcats, and small game are found in the mountains and wooded country near by. Hunting parties are organized at Aguas Blancas, a guest hacienda managed by Orrin Beebe of Hotel Tropical.

HOTELS. Flamingos** is beautifully situated on a cliff 350 feet above the ocean. Mirador**, in La Quebrada, perches on a rocky cliff 150 feet above the ocean, a short walk from the center of the town; it has individual cottages with baths, private porches, and hammocks. Papagayo**, a mile N of the town on Playa Hornos, has modern and comfortably furnished bungalows of 1-4 bedrooms, each with tiled bath, ceiling fan, telephone, living room, and private porch. Other hotels are Las Palmas Courts**; Marina**; Colonial*; Quebrada*; Monterrey*; Tropical*; Villa Julieta*; Acapulco; América; Del Monte; Los Hornos; Jardín; México; Recreo Quebrada; Quinta Eugenia.

EXCURSIONS FROM ACAPULCO

Brilliant-colored parakeets and flamingos, water hyacinths and luxuriant tropical flowers, make excursions from Acapulco by motorboat exceptionally interesting. Arrangements should be made in advance at the hotels. Wells Fargo frequently sponsor excursions. Undersea marine life can be seen from glass-bottomed launches. A scenic boat trip can be taken to Puerto Marquez, just outside the harbor, on a bay with good swimming. Castillo San Diego, the fort at the entrance to the harbor, commands a fine view.

Las Playas offers a circular drive that is a favorite, passing the highest point of the peninsula, Cumbre de las Playas. There is a splendid ocean view from the steep cliffs of La Quebrada. Eleven miles N at Pie de la

Cuesta (Foot of the Mountain) a beautiful beach lies at one side, where breakers 10 feet high pound thunderously; at the other, the Laguna de Coyuca, a long, narrow fresh-water lagoon bordered by coconut groves.

Tecpán is in a very primitive countryside; excursions to it by open bus, arranged at the hotel, are good. Although the trip is rough, it is extremely interesting.

THE LAKE REGION

The excellent National Highway (Camino Nacional) No. 4, the Pacific highway, has a paved stretch of 422 miles ending at Guadalajara (p. 89), the most interesting means of reaching the lake country from Mexico City, though there are also some rather roundabout railroad routes. The first stage, to Toluca, 40 miles W, may be covered conveniently by railroad; there is also bus service over the highway.

Either of two routes may be taken in driving out of the capital. Officially the route is on Paseo Reforma to the entrance of the park Bosque Chapultepec, then diagonally left a block across the large circle, 2 blocks on Calzada Tacubaya, then right to the highway. The highway passes the S side of Bosque Chapultepec and the large cemetery Panteón de Dolores where many of Mexico's national heroes are buried. The alternate exit, simpler and more direct, is from Paseo Reforma at the entrance to Bosque Chapultepec diagonally right into a continuation of the Paseo along the N side of the park. This route enters the new residential section called Lomas de Chapultepec; continues along the main street, which is still called Paseo Reforma; and passes into the country, where it intersects National Highway No. 4.

Some interesting excursions from this highway are possible. A branch road from Km. 13.2 runs to Santa Fe, the site of the first home for foundlings and hospital for Indians, established in the 16th century by Vasco de Quiroga, later famous as the bishop of Michoacán. Thousands of young trees have been planted by the government near here for reforestation and erosion control. Just beyond La Venta, at Km. 24 on the main highway, a paved side road leads to the Desierto de los Leones (p. 122) and then leads back to the capital via Villa Obregón (San Angel, p. 121).

The main road enters the mountains shortly beyond the fork at La Venta and climbs steadily. At several points magnificent panoramas of the valley of Mexico unfold, with the capital nestled in the center. The view is especially good on clear nights. The summit is reached at Las Cruces, at Km. 32, at an altitude of 10,381 feet or almost 2 miles. Here the road leaves the Federal District and enters the state of México, dropping gently to the large meadows known as the plains of Salazar. Beyond, the descent is more abrupt. At Km. 35.8 the highway passes a simple shaft of marble surmounting a large rock and inclosed by an iron fence, a modest memorial to the great inciter of Mexico's independence José María Hidalgo. Here on Oct. 30, 1810, Father Hidalgo won an important battle against the Spanish royalists. The surrounding hills are now a national park. The road continues through meadows and beautiful woods.

About Km. 40 the first view is gained of the great valley of Toluca, dominated by the magnificent snow-capped volcano Nevado de Toluca or, in Aztec, Xinantecatl (Nude Gentleman). Immediately on descending to the floor of the valley the road crosses a large swamp fed by springs, out of which the Río Lerma flows, to empty finally into the Pacific as the Río Santiago after forming Lake Chapala (p. 92) and crossing several states. Lerma, on the far side of the swamps, though once an important city, now has less than 1200 inhabitants. It was granted a city charter as early as 1613. The parish church contains an interesting painting by Miguel Cabrera. On leaving the town the highway crosses a 17th-century stone bridge noteworthy for its three arches, enormous buttresses, and massive breastwork. This is the beginning of a 9-mile straight stretch that ends at the outskirts of Toluca.

A side road left from Km. 60 leads to the village of Metepec, notable for its craft objects, and to the important town of Tenango del Valle, beyond which it descends through pine forests to subtropical Tenancingo, a pleasant summer town little visited by tourists. From Tenancingo delightful trips can be taken on horseback to Malinalco, remarkable for Aztec ruins; to the famous sanctuary of Chalma, which recently celebrated its 400th anniversary; to the Desierto de los Leones, noted for an old Carmelite monastery hidden deep in the forest; and, in another direction, to the falls called El Salto Chico and to La Cañada de Moisés (Moses' Glen), so named from a point where water springs from a rock. From Tenancingo a 20-mile road, usually negotiated by stage, leads to the famous medicinal hot springs of Ixtapan de la Sal.

Toluca, with 50,000 inhabitants, capital of the state of México, is an important commercial and crafts center. The market on Fridays is one of the liveliest in all Mexico; extending over several blocks, it is famous for bright basketry, natural color wool blankets with geometrical designs, and girdles embroidered with animal and bird motives.

The Palacio del Gobierno, the state capitol, is on the main plaza. The Biblioteca Pública (Public Library), near by, contains 15,000 volumes, many of which are rare. The Museo del Estado de México, the state museum, contains archeological, colonial, and modern pieces. Interesting churches include the parish church of La Tercera Orden, near the arcades; El Carmen, near the market, and El Calvario de Toluca, on a hill reached by Paseo Colón.

HOTELS. Gran; Gran Sociedad; Imperial; San Carlos.

Excursions from Toluca. The volcano Nevado de Toluca, 32 miles SW, is reached by car. In the crater of this extinct volcano, called Xinantecatl (Nude Gentleman) in Aztec, lie the lakes of the Sun and the Moon. The view from the summit is awe-inspiring.

The archeological zone of Calixtlahuaca, an ancient city, is 4 miles NW of Toluca, reached by car or afoot. Here are ruins of buildings and many scattered mounds and monuments. The most important so far unearthed are a rectangular ball court, the priests' college in the shape of a beehive, and a rounded pyramid. The culture indicated is similar to that of the Toltec and other mixed civilizations.

Beyond Toluca the highway continues into the state of Michoacán (Country of the Fish), home of the Tarascan Indians. Covered with thick woods and dotted with green and blue lakes and rivers, this countryside abounds in fruits, fish and game, gold, silver, copper, tin, and obsidian. Because of variations in altitude it is divided into zones of hot, temperate, and cold climate. Michoacán has several extremely colorful cities and villages within a short distance of each other, all with good hotel accommodations and reached by railroad or car.

Morelia, the capital, is the largest. Pátzcuaro, a short distance away, is an exquisite little town built on a hill overlooking the lake of the same name. Janitzio, on an island in Lake Pátzcuaro, is one of the most picturesque of villages. Also on the lake shore is an interesting old Indian village with the sonorous name of Tzintzuntzan. Uruapan, a few hours distant from Lake Pátzcuaro, is a town of narrow cobbled streets and flower-filled plazas and patios. The landscape and life; the folklore; the lacquer ware and featherwork; the shooting, hunting, and fishing, and to a lesser degree the archeological sites make the entire state intensely interesting to the visitor.

According to legend the seven tribes after leaving their caves in the N country came to Pátzcuaro. A few stopped to bathe in the lake; while they were swimming the others, advised by their gods, stole their companions' clothes and quickly moved on. When the bathers discovered the trick they were so indignant that they decided to settle here rather than travel with thieves. Actually nothing is known of the first inhabitants of Michoacán, though all the original tribes coming into Mexico from the north must have traversed this region. It is certain that the Toltecs and the Chichimecs did and that the Aztecs lived here for a while. It is believed that before the Tarascans arrived the country was occupied by the Tecos, related to the Nahuas. The wanderings of the Tarascans are recorded in paintings on the Lienzo de Jujutacato, a piece of cotton cloth preserved by the Mexican Society of Geography and Statistics, at Calle Justo Sierra 19, Mexico City, but not yet satisfactorily deciphered.

Michoacán has been called the most romantic of all Mexican states. Local customs and even the ancient religion have undergone little change. The Tarascan language, very soft and melodious and one of the easiest of the Indian tongues to pronounce and write, is spoken in many parts of the state. Popular arts, particularly music and dancing, have remained alive and vigorous, and the greatest variety today exists in Michoacán.

Usually executed to the music of the teponaxtle or wooden drum, a flute, and sometimes a fiddle, the dances are taken very seriously. Costumes must be correct to the last detail, and masks are carved with infinite pains. Spectators must take care not to obtrude themselves in any way, since many of the Indians resent feeling that they are on display.

The dance of Los Viejitos (Old Men) is one of the most original and characteristic. In spite of its religious spirit, since it is essentially a rain propitiation ceremony, it has a humor usually lacking in such rituals. The dancers wear very low-crowned, wide hats with bright-colored ribbons and cover their faces with clay masks which, although they represent old men, have a healthy look and a definitely laughing expression. The dancers' pantaloons, very wide at the bottom, are decorated with 2-inch lace. The dance is performed on January 1 at Janitzio.

Los Sembradores (Planters), a dance of joy in work, is performed at harvest time. It is elaborate and is marked by strong rhythm. The draft animals are brought in by the workmen. One man cracks a whip in time to the music, while another on horseback directs the steps with loud shouts. Men and girls dance around the animals, and at a signal the girls throw petals on the ground with gestures of sowing. These girls, chosen as the most beautiful in the neighborhood, are dressed in their best, with paper flowers and colored ribbons braided into their hair. The grand finale is the famous Jarabe dance of Michoacán. The special day for this dance is February 2.

Los Apaches is a dance performed on February 4 in the atriums of the churches. The cast includes the devil, but it is more warlike than religious in character. The performers wear cardboard crowns adorned with little pieces of mirror and beads and upholding panaches of green and yellow. Little pieces of colored paper are hung all over them. Eight of the dancers paint their faces red; the other eight, white. Two children wearing cardboard monkey masks take part; their clothes are hung with bells, and they clutch dried pieces of squirrel.

Los Negritos (Little Black Men), indigenous to Tzintzuntzan, is supposed to be danced only on February 2, but it is a favorite, and is usually executed on all fiesta days. It is probably of colonial origin, since it represents the ceremony of paying tribute to the Spanish representative. First it is danced in the atriums of the churches and then before the house of each of the performers and musicians. There is a pause after each performance for refreshments consisting of favorite local foods. The dancers wear red kerchiefs on their heads, and around their necks are hung long strings of coral with little balls of silver and good-luck charms carved like fish. Their white trousers are tight above the knee, but flare out below in starched ruffles. One of the leading characters appears in a black charro suit, a fancy riding habit.

Los Moros (Moors) is one of the most beautiful and interesting of all the dances. It is performed in the neighborhood of Lake Pátzcuaro during carnival and at religious fiestas. In Janitzio and Iguatzio it has remained authentic in every detail. There are three or four dancers, one of whom is known as St. James (Santiago), distinguished by a little silver-handled ebony staff tied with colored ribbons. In some localities the dance is performed first in the atrium of the church and later in the patios of the houses, where the neighbors provide presents for the performers. The dancers continue their rounds until noon, when they go to the house of the high magistrate of the town, who, besides providing food and drink for them and the other inhabitants, presents St. James with an offering. A dance of colonial origin, it has no religious significance. The costume includes a turban made of reed grass, lined with emerald green or red silk and decorated with braided strings of pearls and corals; pinned to the side of the turban is a triangular silk kerchief which covers the face except for the eyes.

The fishermen's dance, belonging to this district, is performed only at fishermen's weddings. The bridal couple dance inside a fish net.

Las Canacuas (Crown Dance), the classic ritual of hospitality, is performed on Corpus Christi Day in Uruapan and the vicinity, where the natives are noted for their friendliness and hospitality.

The fandango, as danced in Uruapan, is performed by a man and a woman and is merely social in character. Throughout the dance the man balances a glass of aguardiente on his head and carries a sword. The woman holds a great bunch of fruit in her hand. They go round and round until suddenly the man, stopping, makes a great swing with his sword.

MORELIA

Morelia, with 40,000 inhabitants, capital of the state of Michoacán, has the reputation of exceeding all other Mexican cities in the beauty of its architecture. It can be reached from Mexico City by car or bus in 6 hours over mountains and valleys by way of the excellent National Highway No. 4 over its paved stretch.

The city was founded by the viceroy Antonio de Mendoza on May 18, 1541, in the picturesque valley of Guayangareo. The site was chosen for its strategic location. From here the conquest of the Indians of Michoacán and neighboring Jalisco could be easily undertaken. Originally called Valladolid after the viceroy's native city in Spain, the city was renamed Morelia in 1828 in honor of the great general of the Mexican revolution of independence, José María Morelos y Pavón, who was born here.

The entry into the city is past the ruins of an aqueduct built 1785-89 at the order of the bishop of Michoacán at a cost of 100,000 pesos in order to provide work for the unemployed during a famine. It conducted the water from the springs on the hills of Carindapaz, El Moral, and San Miguel del Monte through clay tubes. The structure is composed of 254 arches and is 27 feet high by 18 feet wide. Throughout, Morelia has an Old World atmosphere reminiscent of the 18th century. Most of the buildings are constructed of pink trachyte, and the whole city has a pinkish glow. It is laid out around two central garden plazas, Jardín de los Mártires (Garden of the Martyrs) and Plaza de la Paz (Peace Plaza), with the cathedral between. Most of the interesting buildings are on or near these principal plazas. There are fine drives and promenades.

CHURCHES. The cathedral, between the main squares, one of the most beautiful churches in Mexico, was a century in building. Constructed of pink stone, it was started by Marcos Ramírez del Prado in 1640 and was finished in 1744. An outstanding example of Plateresque ornamentation, it is particularly notable for its rose stone façade; its towers 210 feet high, affording a fine view of the valley; its stately domes and pillars, and the colonial wrought-iron fence and gates. Inside, the organ case above the main entrance is finely carved. The two unsigned pictures above the choir have been attributed to José Ibarra and Miguel Cabrera. The sacristy contains an excellent unsigned painting of the crucified Christ. Morelos and the emperor Iturbide were baptized in the same font here.

Other churches include those of San Francisco; Our Lady of El Socorro, also known as San Agustín; the former monastery of San Diego; Our Lady of El Carmen, containing pictures by José and Nicolás Juárez and a portrait of Bishop Palafox y Mendoza, supposedly by Miguel Cabrera; and Las Monjas Catarinas.

LIBRARIES AND MUSEUMS. The state capitol, Palacio del Gobierno, facing the cathedral, a fine old colonial building, houses the state library, Biblioteca del Estado, which contains many volumes of rare historical interest.

In the library of the Confederación Obrera (Workers' Federation), near the market, are works of the well-known artists Paul O'Higgins, Leopoldo Méndez, Alfredo Zalce, and Raul Anguiano.

The Museo Michoacano (Michoacán Museum), near the main plaza, contains an interesting collection of Tarascan ceramics, sculptures, idols, other historic relics, and frescoes by the young New York artists Grace Greenwood and Ryah Ludins. It also contains a famous image of Christ which is supposed to have appeared miraculously outlined on a tree trunk.

HOUSES. Colonial houses in the city include many beautiful mansions and several simpler buildings of historical interest, among them two houses associated with Morelos. His birthplace, near the church of San Agustín, belonged to a friend of his mother, who took refuge there when her labor began very suddenly. The house is marked by a plaque. Inscriptions are found also on Morelos' home, the birthplace of Agustín Iturbide, and houses which sheltered other notable figures of the independence movement. Relics of Morelos' career are preserved by the city with reverent care.

CENTERS OF HIGHER LEARNING. The Colegio de San Nicolás, founded in 1540, was the second educational institution established in the Americas. It is the oldest surviving, for the Colegio de Santa Cruz Tlaltelalco, founded in Mexico City in 1537, has long been out of existence. Originally started in Pátzcuaro by the famous bishop Vasco de Quiroga, the Colegio de San Nicolás was moved to Morelia in 1580 when the episcopal see was transferred. Miguel Hidalgo, called the father of Mexican independence, studied here and later taught theology and philosophy; Morelos was one of his pupils. Iturbide was also a student here.

In the university of Michoacán there is a patio with some frescoes by Marion Greenwood.

A school of arts and one of arts and crafts are located in a former Jesuit monastery.

At the Huerta railroad station near by is a federal agricultural school for Indian boys and girls.

MARKET. On Thursdays the market becomes an open-air restaurant. On sale besides all sorts of food are absurd painted clay toy animals, a specialty of the district; lacquer ware; pottery; sarapes or blankets; woodcarvings, and jewelry.

HUNTING AND FISHING. It is possible to procure a guide, usually from a hotel, to Lake Cuitzeo for duck shooting or fishing. There are lodgings on the shore.

HOTELS. Alameda**; Virrey de Mendoza**; Iturbide*; Posada de la Montana*; Bella Vista; Central; Oseguerra; Palacio; Roma; Valetti.

PATZCUARO

Pátzcuaro (Place of Delights), with 10,000 inhabitants, is 26 miles W of Morelia on National Highway No. 4 and then 15 miles S, off the main road. At an altitude of 6900 feet, it is the principal town on Lake Pátzcuaro, one of the highest and most beautiful lakes in the world. The town is typical of the 16th century. The houses have projecting roofs and wooden balconies, and the narrow streets are cobbled. The architecture is so pure and quaint that visitors have difficulty in believing such a town can exist on the North American continent.

According to tradition Pátzcuaro was founded by a great tribal chieftain Curátame. He organized four powerful armies and sent them to conquer the four corners of the earth; four is the sacred number among the Purépecha, the Tarascans' name for themselves. Above all, this chieftain wanted to found a city that would be a worthy capital for the kingdom he was planning. One day when Curátame and his followers were going through a forest they found four enormous rocks. The king cried out: "Here are four rocks that are none other than the Petátzecuaro [cement], and which represent the four stars that form the doorway of the palace of God. Let us found a holy city and call it Petátzecuaro." His followers set to work and built the city which is now known as Pátzcuaro. Eventually, after wars of succession and other troubles, the throne of Pátzcuaro became vacant, and Tzintzuntzan, a few miles N, was made the capital. Pátzcuaro became the religious center and the place of recreation for the kings.

When the armies of Spain penetrated this region they were captivated by its extraordinary beauty. They filled their chronicles with glowing reports of the "bounteous gifts which the Creator hath bestowed upon his favored terrain." Pátzcuaro, bravely defended by a handful of patriots led by an ancient nobleman and his daughter, was the last stronghold of the Tarascans against the Spaniards. But it was finally conquered, and the Spaniards, realizing its strategic and practical value, soon began the construction of a new town over the ruins of the old.

The town owed its second period of greatness to Vasco de Quiroga, the bishop whose deeds have become a legend. The emperor Charles V sent Quiroga, an able and eminent lawyer, to correct the severe wrongs caused in New Spain by the cruelty of the first audiencia or high court. The Indians had fled from the towns and were hiding in the mountains. Quiroga with infinite patience and wisdom managed to convert them to Christianity. At the same time he took holy orders and quickly rose through all the grades of the priesthood to the rank of bishop. In 1540, when the episcopal see was moved to Pátzcuaro from Tzintzuntzan, he imported 30,000 Indians and 28 Spanish families to repopulate and reconstruct the town. He organized work throughout the state so that each town was dedicated to a single occupation. For instance, in Uruapan only lacquered bowls were produced; in another village trunks were made; in a third town all the workmen were carpenters.

Pátzcuaro is built around two plazas surrounded by giant trees. The main plaza serves as a market on Fridays. In addition to the usual market products there is a wide assortment of Indian handicraft articles of unusual beauty. The handmade pottery; lacquer work; sarapes or blankets, sashes, and other handwoven textiles, and articles hammered out of native virgin copper, as well as woodcarvings, are especially attractive. Whole families of Indians from the surrounding villages arrive at Pátzcuaro in huge dugout canoes early on Fridays.

CHURCHES AND OTHER POINTS OF INTEREST. The basilica was built by Quiroga, who planned it originally, before Morelia was designated as the seat of the bishopric, as an enormous cathedral in the form of an extended hand with five naves representing fingers. This design is still to be seen in the escutcheon of Pátzcuaro. When one of the naves had been finished and only the foundations laid for the other four, the colonial government became alarmed by the magnitude of the project and persuaded the king of Spain to stop it, with the plea that the soil would not stand such a tremendous weight. In 1563 the church, with only one nave, was finally dedicated. It contains the image of Our Lady of La Salud (Health), modeled with a paste made from the pith of corn stalks by an Indian convert—though legend states that it was miraculously discovered floating in a canoe on Lake Pátzcuaro by a poor Indian. The image is very much venerated as the patroness of the ailing, for whom she is supposed to have accomplished many miracles. Thousands of pilgrims come on December 8 to pay homage to her.

The sanctuary of Guadalupe, designed by the Mexican architect Francisco Eduardo Tresguerras, was built with funds provided by Feliciano Ramos, who came to Mexico from Havana as a slave in a Spanish family. After some time Ramos managed to obtain his liberty and eventually amassed a great fortune. He built the sanctuary and endowed it because of a vow made to the Virgin. He died in 1830, three years before the church was finished. The Fuente del Toro (Bull's Fountain), near the sanctuary, is supposed once to have faced the other way. According to legend, many years ago people who happened to be strolling near it were horrified to see a horse galloping down the street, running away with a poor Spaniard who was doing everything he could to stop it. In one of these efforts he headed it straight toward the fountain; the horse only brushed against it, but the rider was killed, and the authorities later condemned the fountain to lose its place. Apparently it carried out its sentence by turning round without human aid.

The church of San Francisco, built in 1545, was burned by republican troops on Jan. 5, 1857, and later reconstructed. In it is a figure of Christ crucified, sculptured with a paste of corn pith. It is said that this figure at first hung straight on the cross, but in 1566 it began to move about until finally it was crooked. The image is supposed to have miraculous powers.

The chapel of El Calvario is situated on the hill, Cerro del Estribo, 15 minutes' walk from the center of the town. According to tradition this ancient chapel, built in 1666, stands on the site of the town of the early chieftain Tariacuri. It offers a magnificent view of the lake and its five islands.

Near the 16th-century church of San Juan de Dios is the old fountain of San Miguel, so called because it is decorated with an image of the saint, painted at the order of Vasco de Quiroga to frighten away the devil, who, it is said, often appeared here.

El Humilladero, an ancient chapel set among cypresses, is a short distance out of the town on the road to Morelia. The chapel was built in 1553 to house an Indian sculpture of Christ. On the façade are sculptured images of Tota Huriata and Nana Cutzi, Father Sun and Mother Moon.

The Jesuit church of La Compañía, now in ruins, contains the remains of the illustrious bishop. In the tower of this church is a very old clock which, according to legend, was sent out of Spain because it struck the fatal hour of Philip II.

On Calle Alcantarillas are the ancient ruins of the bishop's palace. Near them is a vault covering the spring that provides drinking water for the town. This spring is another of the great Quiroga's contributions. According to the story, after some digging had been done without striking water the Virgin of La Salud was brought to the scene. After solemn prayer Quiroga struck the ground with his staff, and a spring gushed forth. The bishop's staff is preserved in the cathedral at Morelia.

Two houses are particularly worth visiting, the house in which Vasco de Quiroga lived and the Casa del Gigante (House of the Giant), so named because of a huge sculptured figure in it. Former President Cárdenas had a summer home close to the station called Quinta Eréndira, named for a Tarascan princess.

MUSEUM. Near the bishop's palace, in the building where in 1540

Vasco de Quiroga founded the Colegio de San Nicolás, which was later transferred to Morelia, is a Museum of Popular Art and Archeology. The collections were made under the supervision of the young Mexican artist Rodolfo Ayala.

FISHING AND HUNTING. The lake, N of the town, yields five kinds of fish; whitefish is the best. October and March, with the best weather, are also the season of most abundant game. The duck season opens November 1 with natives in hundreds of canoes killing the birds with long throwing sticks.

HOTELS. Posada de Don Vasco*; Concordia; El Lago; Ocampo; Plaza.

EXCURSIONS FROM PATZCUARO

Janitzio (Corn Flower), 2 hours from Pátzcuaro by motorboat, is one of several islands in Lake Pátzcuaro and is the one most visited, because of its picturesqueness and the excellence and variety of the fish in the waters near it. Motorboats can be hired by the hour for tours of the lake. It is pleasanter to use one of the native dugouts; the Indians who paddle them supply fishing tackle for any who may want to fish. Nets are everywhere on Janitzio, either drying, stretched out on high poles along the hilly streets, or in the process of weaving. On the summit of the island is a memorial to José María Morelos with a huge modern statue sculptured by Guillermo Ruiz and presented by former President Cárdenas. The artist Ramón Alva de la Canal is responsible for the decorations in the interior, which outline the life of Morelos and historical themes connected with it. A long stairway leads to the top of the statue. The little church of San Gerónimo crowning a hill over some caves contains idols worshiped by the Indians. November 2, All Souls' Day (Todos Muertos), is the leading fiesta day on the island. The chief ceremony takes place at midnight of November 1, when the natives, men, women, and children, dressed in their best, bring offerings of food, baskets decorated with flowers, and candles to the cemetery near the church. The scene by candlelight is beautiful, and the singing of the men and boys is impressive. It is best to go accompanied by a guide.

The other islands include Jarácuaro, the most thickly settled, where the occupations are farming and making palm-leaf articles; La Pacanda, with fishing and fruit-growing; and Yuyuán and Tecuén, with fishing settlements.

Iguatzio (Place of the Coyote) is a little town on the mainland, a short distance NE of Pátzcuaro, reached by motorboat in 20 minutes. Its inhabitants make objects of grass and the pith of corn stalks. The town is connected N with Tzintzuntzan by a causeway built by the Indians before the conquest. Of the many historic ruins in the vicinity the most interesting is the fortress of Queréndaro, also called the Ciudadela de Iguatzio (Citadel of Iguatzio), a kind of stadium with two pyramids or temples. This is the only archeological monument of the Tarascans so far discovered. Here the Tarascans formerly congregated to ask the assistance of their father the Sun and their mother the Moon before going to war.

Tzintzuntzan (Place of the Humming Bird) is 10 miles NE of Pátzcuaro, on the shore of the lake. Though it is passed on the automobile road before reaching Pátzcuaro, most travelers prefer to visit it by boat as an excursion from Pátzcuaro. Originally known as Huitzilil, the town was founded by the Aztecs and later became the capital of the Tarascan kingdom. It was noted for the objects produced by the natives with hummingbird feathers. The parish church erected by Franciscan missionaries was very important until Vasco de Quiroga transferred the episcopal see to Pátzcuaro. It contains a famous painting, The Descent from the Cross, which has been attributed to Titian, José Ibarra, Miguel Cabrera, and even El Greco. Facing the entrance to the church is an enormous stone cross which has been there since the time of the conquest, when it was the meeting place for the Indians who came to be baptized.

In the little Calle Magdalena are the ruins of an old Franciscan monastery which was closed early in the 18th century. Near it is an olive grove, probably the oldest on the continent, with the bells of the monastery church in the branches of the trees. They were put there long ago for greater safety in case of earthquake.

Tupátaro is a small village about 10 miles from Pátzcuaro, reached only on horseback or afoot. It is advisable to take a guide. The tiny church which houses the image of the Christ of the Little Pine, said to have been found on a tree, is amazing for its lacquering, which seems definitely Oriental.

Uruapan (Place Where Flowers Bloom), with 20,000 inhabitants, is reached from Pátzcuaro by returning to the main highway, driving 50 miles W to Chilchota, then S over the mountains. The last stretch is somewhat rough, but scenically beautiful. Uruapan can also be reached from Pátzcuaro by railroad. The city is set against a background of green orchards, streams, and waterfalls. The vegetation is bright with tropical birds, and the locality is called the Paradise of Michoacán. The inhabitants are extraordinarily hospitable. The city was founded in 1540 by the Franciscan friar Juan de San Miguel, who traced out the streets, laid the foundation for the church which still exists, planted many flowers and fruit trees, and taught the Indians to improve their gardens and farms. Uruapan is the metropolis of the Indian pueblos in the vicinity. Three large central plazas distinguish the city plan. Perhaps the most attractive of these is the plaza called Jardín de los Mártires (Garden of the Martyrs), with the church facing on it. The square contains monuments to the patriots José M. Arteaga, Carlos Salazar, Jesús Díaz, and Juan González, chiefs of the republican army during the French intervention, who were executed in October 1866. Uruapan is the birthplace of the well-known painter Manuel Ocaranza.

Sundays are market days. Typical objects are brought from neighboring villages by the Indians. Many of them make their living by manufacturing the celebrated lacquered gourds. The lacquer workers may be seen at work in the Barrio de San Pedro and at the co-operative in the center of the town. Bright-colored bateas or painted trays are made by drying and splitting the gourds and covering them with lithomarge; then fanciful designs are scratched on the surface with a sharp instrument and the incisions filled with a pigment made from plant lice of a certain kind. The method for concocting the gay colors is known only to the Indians. It takes a long while to finish this ware.

HOTELS. Progreso**; París*; Annex; Europa; Imperial; Mirador; Palacio.

Excursions from Uruapan are many. Hikes over the hard dirt footpaths are popular, and horses can be hired. Beaten paths lead to quaint Indian villages and to farms, banana and coffee plantations, and the orchards of Quinta Ruiz, Quinta Hurtado, and La Camelina. A popular excursion is to the beautiful waterfall of Tzaráracua near by, a good place for picnics. In the dry season it is possible to motor 200 miles over a good dirt road to the Pacific Ocean.

Paracho (Where Instruments Are Made), between Uruapan and the main highway, is famous for the manufacture of guitars and harps and for the ancient and beautiful folk music played and sung here.

San Juan de las Colchas, or Parangaricutiro, is 25 miles from Uruapan by a poor road. In the village is the sanctuary of the miraculous Santo Cristo, an 18th-century church in which, tradition says, the visitor is immediately overcome with an irresistible desire to dance and has no power to stop himself as long as he remains under its roof; many, however, have overcome the temptation. There are beautiful lacquered panels depicting the various miracles performed by this Christ.

SOUTHERN MEXICO

The Pan American Highway below Mexico City is as yet largely visionary. When it is completed it will supply a direct route S through Amecameca, Oaxaca, Tehuantepec, Juchitán, and Tuxtla Gutiérrez in the state of Chiapas, and Tapachula to Guatemala. At present the distance to Oaxaca from the capital can be covered by car, via Puebla, to Tehuacán and thence by railroad, or all the way by railroad; to Tehuantepec the route is by car or railroad to Córdoba or Veracruz and thence by railroad. The quickest and most convenient way to reach either Oaxaca or Tehuantepec from Mexico City is by air. Although Acapulco also may be regarded geographically as belonging to S Mexico, the trip to it is interesting largely because of possible stopovers or short excursions, and it has been described under Central Mexico (p. 122).

The celebrated ruins of Mitla and of Monte Albán are near Oaxaca. One of the most remarkable archeological discoveries of modern times was made not long ago at the latter of these sites. Oaxaca is also of great interest itself and may be regarded as the capital of S Mexico because of its ancient grandeur, the beauty of its public buildings and churches, its size, and its importance as a business center. It is 358 miles SE of Mexico City by the Mexican Railway of the South, part of the National Railways of Mexico; the journey takes 15 hours. To avoid a hot trip, it is good to go by bus or car as far as Puebla (p. 60), then by day train to Oaxaca via Tehuacán. Air service between Mexico City and Oaxaca takes 2-3 hours. Reservations can be made at the Compañía Aeronáutica Francisco Sarabia, Pasaje Iturbide 8, in Mexico City, or at tourist agencies. At present it is difficult to reach Oaxaca by road.

Tehuacán, with 16,000 inhabitants, often spoken of as the Mexican Carlsbad, 210 miles SE of Mexico City, can be reached by car from Mexico City via Puebla or by the National Railways of Mexico via Puebla. A stop here makes a delightful break in the journey to Oaxaca. The town is noted for its fine climate and its mineral waters. In the picturesque country around it there are many large fruit farms.

HOTELS. Near the town is the Hotel Garci-Crespo**, built by Gen.

Abelardo Rodríguez, ex-president of Mexico. This is one of the famous resorts of Mexico. It has attractive surroundings and excellent facilities for tennis, golf, hiking, hunting, horseback riding, and motoring. Outstanding attractions are the large swimming pool and artificial bathing beach at the famous mineral springs. Hotels in Tehuacán itself are Villa Granada**; El Riego*; México*; Iberia; La Española.

OAXACA

Oaxaca, with 40,000 inhabitants, capital of the state of the same name, lies in a beautiful valley at an altitude of 5108 feet, reached by railroad through the marvelous country beyond Tehuacán, with mountains, valleys, canyons, sugar plantations, and little Indian farms. Boasting a mild and uniform semitropical climate comparable to that of Cuernavaca, Oaxaca is an attractive, well-kept city situated in one of the most imposing cordilleras of Mexico, with the bright vegetation and fresh flowers of an eternal spring. The valley of Oaxaca was the home of the ancient and highly civilized Zapotec and Mixtec Indians, whose cities and religious buildings, covered with the dust of many centuries, are now being unearthed to reveal dazzling riches of jewels, sculptures, and native handicrafts. Near by and easily reached by car are the ruins of Mitla, which testify to the highly artistic inspiration of their Mixtec builders, and the ruins of the pyramids and tombs of Monte Albán, spread out over a hill that overlooks the entire valley.

The city of Oaxaca was founded by the Aztecs. During the reign of Ahuitzotl the Aztecs established a military post here in 1486 in order to watch the troop movements of the Zapotecs. In 1521 the conquest of Oaxaca or Huaxyacac (Place of the Gourds) was achieved by Francisco de Orozco. Oaxaca has played an important role in all periods: colonial times, the revolution of independence, the reform era, and the interval of foreign intervention. It is and always has been an important link between the Isthmus of Tehuantepec, the Gulf of Mexico, and the central plateau. The official name of the city is Oaxaca de Juárez, because Benito Juárez, a Zapotec Indian, was born in a near-by village. As governor, Juárez made Oaxaca one of the most progressive states of the nation before he entered the national scene. Porfirio Díaz was born in Oaxaca, studied law under Juárez here, and achieved most of his spectacular military victories within the state.

From the near-by hill Cerro de Fortín, on which stands a great statue of Juárez, an excellent view of the city can be obtained—picturesque streets and avenues with their old houses and gardens, the domes and towers of the churches glittering in the bright sunshine. Down in the town the visitor cannot help admiring the elaborate carvings of the façades of the colonial buildings and the stately arcades of patios and cloisters and enjoying the charmed quiet of old abandoned monasteries. The architectural gems of Oaxaca are remarkable in spite of the havoc wrought by numerous earthquakes. All the buildings are massively constructed; yet it is doubtful whether any ancient structure in Oaxaca has survived entire from the time of its erection. The important colonial buildings date for the most part from the 18th century. This fact, together with the many different colors of stone used, imparts a special character to the architecture. The buildings are very low and sprawling, and the walls are exceedingly thick. Windows and doors are few and small, and corners are generally strengthened with massive buttresses. The forged ironwork presents an extraordinary and beautiful variety of design.

PALACES AND PUBLIC BUILDINGS. The Federal Palace, on the main plaza, formerly the palace of the archbishop, is a stately building erected in 1580 and reconstructed in the last century. Its façade resembles those of the Mitla ruins. In its interior is a large court surrounded by beautiful arcaded galleries.

Other public buildings are the Palacio del Gobierno, the state capitol; the Palacio Municipal or city hall, and the Instituto de Ciencias (Scientific Institute), the last containing a state library and the State Museum, with collections of regional archeological interest. These buildings are all on or near the main plaza. Elsewhere are found the courthouse, on Calle 65; the mint, and the old Alhóndiga or granary.

CHURCHES. The cathedral, on the main plaza, is a massive two-towered structure, probably begun in 1610 and dedicated in 1730; the dates are open to question, and authorities disagree. The façade consists of a beautifully carved and intricate Baroque frontispiece flanked by two plain towers. The interior consists of five stately aisles with a transept that supports a huge dome covered outside with polychrome glazed tiles. The building has suffered from earthquakes and shows the scars of war.

The church and monastery of Santo Domingo, completed in the 17th century, make up one of the most imposing works of art of the vice-regal period, as well as the costliest, at more than 13,000,000 pesos. Its massiveness vies with the richness of its decoration. The elaborate entrance, suggestive of an altarpiece, can be better appreciated because of the raised platform before the building. At the sides are two towers. Close by is the chapel of El Rosario, dating from 1731, built in the form of a Latin cross. Although these buildings have suffered damage from earthquake and war, the interiors are among the most splendid in Mexico. On some of the ceilings a curious conception has been carried out in the shape of a luxuriant many-branched tree of gold bearing the heads of saints and, in one case, the Virgin. The walls, altars, vaults, and pillars are literally covered with paintings, sculptures, and thick gold-leaf ornamentation.

The church of the Virgin of La Soledad, patroness of the state of Oaxaca, dates from the late 17th century. Its fine frontispiece, its nave and adjoining chapels, and its buttressed dome are on an immense scale. The ironwork that adorns parts of the building is noteworthy, and some of the sculptures rank among the finest of the colonial period.

The churches of Las Nieves, with a detached belltower; the Jesuit church of La Compañía; San José; San Felipe; San Francisco, and many others are remarkable for their beautiful architecture, decorations, and valuable old pictures.

MUSEUM. The Museo Regional de Arqueología del Estado (State Museum), near the main plaza, contains impressive archeological treasures. The priceless jewels from Tomb No. 7 at Monte Albán are on view here.

THE MARKET, one of the most interesting in Mexico, has great displays of fruits, vegetables, and strangely varied wares, even pigs and burros. There are at least a dozen Indian tribes living in the state, with Zapotecs and Mixtecs the most numerous; many of them are represented at the market on Saturdays. Oaxaca is famous for cheese which is rolled up like ribbon and for tamales of distinctive flavor wrapped in banana leaves. Handmade articles in the market and shops include bright-colored sarapes or blankets from Teotitlán del Valle, first known capital of the Zapotec tribe; fine steel knives and other excellent steelware; black pottery, especially water jars from Coyotepec and green pieces from Ozumba; pottery in Mitla designs; embroidered huipiles or blouses; fiber baskets and bags; handwoven table cloths, napkins, and aprons embroidered in bird designs; belts and pocket-books, and woodenware.

FIESTAS. Among the many local fiestas an observance of the Christ-mas season is especially charming. Beginning with the afternoon of December 23 delicious buñuelos, Christmas pastries served with mo-lasses, are offered at stands set up in the main plaza. The buñuelo is sold together with its plate. The buyer may keep the plate, but local custom is to drop and break it. This custom is limited to Oaxaca and is probably due to the fact that the plates are imperfect specimens from the famous local potteries.

HOTELS. Monte Albán**; Ruiz**; Francia*; Hispano-Americano*; Modelo*; Juárez; México; París.

EXCURSIONS FROM OAXACA

Monte Albán (in Mixtec, Green Hill) is reached in 20 minutes by car over an excellent road from Oaxaca. The road is up a mountain, and the panorama that unfolds below is very striking. In prehistoric times almost the entire mountain was built or worked over by the natives, and today their terraces, walls, pyramids, and mounds erected above tombs are clearly distinguished even at a distance. The main plaza, a rectangle 1000 feet long by 650 feet wide, is surrounded by platforms from which pyramids rise. In the opinion of some authorities a city was built on the lower part of Monte Albán, while the summit was a sort of sacred city used as the burial place of chiefs, priests, and noblemen.

The researches at Monte Albán suggest that the tombs here were originally constructed by the Zapotecs and later used by the Mixtecs. Further study on these lines may do much to illuminate some dim reaches in Mexican prehistory. Almost no one but specialists in ancient Mexican history is aware of more than three civilized races who were in the country before the conquest, the Aztecs and Toltecs on the plateau and the Mayas in Yucatán and Central America. Actually there were other independent peoples who developed cultures that were in some respects superior, among them the Zapotecs and the Mixtecs. These two distinct and even antagonistic races probably constitute the link between the peoples of the central plateau and those of Yucatán and Central America.

Alfonso Caso, director of the department of archeology at the National Museum in Mexico City, organized an expedition to Monte Albán in the early 1930's. His excavations in the ancient tombs on the mountain uncovered the remains of several Mixtec nobles, together with jewelry of gold, jade, and pearls and goblets of crystal and quartz. On clearing away vegetation and earth from the N side of the main plaza Professor Caso discovered the lower steps of a grand stairway leading to a building. This stairway was almost 130 feet wide and 42 feet high, with 33 steps.

"It is a curious fact," Professor Caso has written, "that the general rule of native Mexican ruins shows one structure built over another, leaving the first hidden. Thus, in the great stairway of the north platform, we found three separate periods of construction, or, rather, three stairways superimposed. It is still a mystery to us why the indigenous Mexicans executed these superimposed works, which apparently do not serve any practical ends, but represent a tremendous expenditure of time and energy.

"To understand this fully, it is necessary to remember that by means of the superimposition of the three stairways the total height of the edifice was increased by less than 2 feet, while it was twice necessary to cover the previous stairs with mud and rock. Probably some religious motive caused the ancient people of Monte Albán to renew their monuments periodically. . . .

"One of the strangest finds at Monte Albán was relief sculptures of human beings, all of whom have some bodily deformity. Some show the heads too flat, while others show them extraordinarily elongated. In some the extremities, usually the feet, are twisted; others are bent, and in some I found hermaphrodite characteristics.

"These sculptured stones were utilized in the north platform merely as construction material and show that they were torn from some older edifice. Since they do not present the characteristics of Zapotec sculpture, I do not believe that they belong to the same civilization that constructed the great platform. Although some bear hieroglyphs, they cannot be deciphered by any of the keys to the writing so far known in Mexico and Central America.

"Who were the authors of these writings and why did they prefer to show cripples on their sculptured stones? Here are two problems that confront Mexican archeologists. . . . Was it the intent to ridicule certain enemies? Or should we see in these sculptures a representation of the sick who came to a temple in which there was a god who performed miraculous cures? Could Monte Albán have been at one time a kind of Lourdes? For the time being we can offer only hypotheses, for we still lack sufficient data to solve the problem."

The ruins include the temple of the Dancers, so called because of the rhythmic attitudes of the sculptured figures, at the W side; E is a ball court.

From most of the tombs unearthed and explored, Professor Caso and his associates took human skeletons, pottery, clay vessels, and some articles of jade, shell, and obsidian. Tomb No. 7 yielded the greatest treasures, and more than 500 articles from it have been catalogued. Included are exquisite pieces of gold jewelry, eagle-headed rings, bracelets of gold and silver, obsidian earrings, knives, a belt clasp of hammered gold ornamented with the figure of a spider, small flat pieces of turquoise that originally composed a rich mosaic, and a breastplate representing a jaguar knight. There was also a rock crystal urn measuring $4\frac{1}{2}$ inches in height by 3 inches in diameter, with the side 2/5 inch thick. Since rock crystal is one of the hardest of substances and exceedingly difficult to work, it is inexplicable how the Mixtec lapidaries succeeded in creating an object which even today would challenge a sculptor possessing tools of a refinement and precision unknown to the ancient natives.

"From a scientific viewpoint," Professor Caso writes, "the most important finds of all are the carved bones, which cast much light on the writings and history of the Mixtecs. They are the bones of some large animal, probably a jaguar or deer, but their use is still a mystery to me. The bones are cut in high relief, and the work is so exquisite that it could not be surpassed by the finest products of China and India in ivory. Many had the background incrusted with turquoise, which made the design stand out more effectively. Others were simply carved and used as religious daggers for the sacrificial rites, which consisted in drawing blood from different parts of the body."

Hundreds of tombs at Monte Albán, some perhaps as rich as Tomb No. 7, remain unexplored. It is believed that magnificent edifices are still covered by vegetation and rubble.

Cuilápam and Zachila are two small villages in the same direction as Monte Albán. Cuilápam is of Mixtec origin, built in Zapotec territory when the Zapotecs needed an alliance with the Mixtecs to fight the Aztecs. With stone taken from the ruins of Monte Albán the Spanish missionaries started to erect a church and monastery here, but the work was never concluded. This was due to the opposition of Cortés, who claimed that the missionaries had invaded his possessions, since the valley of Oaxaca, except for the town itself, had been granted him by Charles V with the title of Marquis of the Valley of Oaxaca. In the patio of the monastery Gen. Vicente Guerrero, one of the foremost heroes of the revolution of independence, was executed on Feb. 14, 1831.

Zachila is a simple village with a charm of its own. The plaza is shaded by wild fig trees, and there is an interesting church. Market is held on Thursdays.

Santa María del Tule, 6 miles from Oaxaca, on the road to Mitla, is a little village in whose churchyard stands one of the few largest trees in the world. Belonging to a cypress species, Cupressus disthica sabina, it is an ahuehuete, like so many other trees associated with Aztec history, but more venerable than any other. The natives used to worship this tree as the god of growth, and it is certainly one of the oldest living objects in the Americas as well as one of the biggest, measuring 162 feet in circumference and about 140 feet in height. It was ancient and awesome even at the time of the conquest, when it sheltered Cortés and his men.

Tlacochahuaya, beyond Santa María del Tule on the road to Mitla, is an ancient Zapotec town, with a 16th-century church, the most imposing church near Oaxaca. The interior is decorated with 200-year-old frescoes showing native influence. The ingenuity and vividness of the Indian designs, with simple motives like the sun, moon, stars, and flowers, show not only artistic ability but also the pagan influence of the ancient religion.

Tlacolula is the last town before Mitla. The Sunday market here is colorful. The church is of interest chiefly for its chapel dedicated to El Santo Cristo. The gilded walls are covered with amazing sculptures in high relief. The unique wrought-iron pieces date from the 16th century and like much other ironwork in Mexico are the work of Spanish craftsmen brought over in the early days of Spanish domination.

Mitla, 26 miles E of Oaxaca, presents a magnificent sight which has been visited by the most famous archeologists in the world during the last century. It is a matter of guesswork when the enormous buildings now in ruins were erected, by whom, or to what use they were dedicated. In the Zapotec language Mitla means Place for Repose of

Souls, and for this reason it has been thought that the ruins were originally tombs.

Mitla was laid out on a plain. The buildings, magnificently adorned, are constructed of hard cut stone, fitted to make solid walls of great thickness and length without the use of mortar. They are embellished with what from a distance appears to be sculptures. A closer examination discloses beautiful designs in 14 different motives of amazing mosaics, the pattern formed with small, perfectly cut stones. The designs make up frets that extend all around the buildings, both inside and out, as well as numerous panels in the side walls. Even subterranean apartments and tombs contain such designs. So adeptly and so precisely were the small pieces of stone cut and fitted without binding material that the beautiful designs resemble the work of a master sculptor.

The present village church stands in the center of what was one of the largest and perhaps the most ornate group of ancient edifices. The old walls were painted, and in some places there are remains of beautiful and delicate filigree-work which probably portrayed historical events. Part of the front wall of the church is built on a section of the ancient wall. The ornamentation of the fragment and the magnificent mosaics in the walks of the inclosure in the rear of the church suggest that this may have been the dwelling place of the king or the high priest of the ancient inhabitants.

The most prominent building now standing, called the Palace, is approached by a flight of steps. The building remains beautiful in spite of its great age. The great Hall of Columns fronting on the ancient plaza is a remarkable sight. Six gigantic columns, each fashioned from a solid block of stone, stand equally spaced down the center of the area. What the significance of these pillars may have been no one knows. It is evident that they supported no roof, since their tops are rounded. There are other columns scattered about the ruins.

The entrance to another large building is by three wide doors. Over each doorway is a great lintel of a single piece of stone about 20'x4' x5'6", estimated to weigh 30 tons. They are thought to have been quarried in the mountains some 3 miles distant. How the ancients transported them to the site of the temple and raised them perhaps 30 feet to their place in the wall is a mystery.

Below this building are subterranean chambers and a cruciform tomb. A panel over the door of the tomb bears some hieroglyphs which have not been deciphered. Under a near-by building in the same court is a passage leading to another cruciform tomb. In the center of the junction of the arms of the cross is a great column called the Pillar of Death. It is about 8 feet high and of about the same circumference as the pillars in the Hall of Columns. The visitor is invited to embrace it, whereupon the guide, by measuring the space left between his hands, predicts how long he will live.

The Zapotec Indians are convinced that the ruins of Mitla are the tombs of their ancestors. Every New Year's Eve they bring candles and flowers as offerings to the departed.

The small town of Mitla is of no particular interest in itself. The village is composed of a collection of adobe and bamboo huts, each having its own garden plot surrounded by a hedge of organ cactus. On a truncated pyramid some 500 yards from the main ruins a small

Catholic mission chapel has been erected. Beyond it is a conical hill fortified with trenches and a rampart called La Fortaleza (The Fortress).

HOTEL. There is an old inn in Mitla with good service and satisfactory meals.

TEHUANTEPEC

Tehuantepec, with 11,000 inhabitants, near the Pacific coast in the narrowest part of S Mexico, the Isthmus of Tehuantepec, is not impressive in itself, but its lush setting at a great bend of the river of the same name, its fringe of orchards and gardens and its lovely flowering trees and graceful palms, its intensely green vegetation against whitewashed tiled roofs, more than compensate for its lack of notable architecture. Perhaps most fascinating are the people, their customs, history, and legends. These amply compensate for the inconveniences of tropical heat, bugs, and primitive accommodations. The trip requires careful planning, and most travelers find it best to consult a tourist agency. The city is reached from Mexico City by train via Córdoba (p. 56) or Veracruz (p. 54) or by air; from Oaxaca it is a week's horseback trip. The train passes through tropical country with vegetation of endless exuberance and colorful villages. Beyond Jesús Carranza, 24 hours from Mexico City, where many travelers break the journey, is the so-called land of the butterflies. The jungle thins as the Pacific is neared.

The Aztec word Tehuantepec means Mountain of the Man-eaters. The town got its name from the legend that long ago the hills behind it were infested with man-eating jaguars. A powerful wizard from the Huave tribe was brought to the town. As if by magic he caused a huge turtle to appear from the sea; it confronted the man-eaters as they came down the hills, and they were turned into stone. Then the magician, fearful of the turtle himself, changed it also into stone. And there they remained, stone beasts on the hills and stone turtle at their feet.

Today single-story stucco buildings in white or soft pastel shades, with heavy walls as protection against earthquake, surround a great tree-shaded square. Most of the inhabitants are Zapotecs, speaking their own language and pursuing the traditional life of past centuries. They differ much in character, however, from the Zapotecs who live in the valley of Oaxaca. The Tehuana women give the town distinction because the Zapotec social system here makes them the more important of the sexes. Their native beauty, characteristic dress, and independence establish them as belles indeed. Most are tall and well proportioned and carry themselves with stately grace, thanks to their practice of bearing burdens of flowers, fruit, and other products in bowls balanced on their heads. They wear their hair in braids crossed on top and tied with bright ribbons. Their dress is gay. It consists of a full skirt, deeply flounced and long enough to cover the wearer's bare feet, and a square-necked huipil or blouse, short-sleeved and generously embroidered. They adorn themselves with gold jewelry, in which strings of U. S. gold pieces often figure prominently.

Life in Tehuantepec centers about the river and the market. The versatile Tehuana women monopolize both, for besides their household concerns, their sewing and embroidery, and their activities in orchards and gardens they pre-empt the town's commerce. The visitor to the market is so struck by the extraordinary sight of these women bedecked in all their finery and squatting on the ground in the midst of heaps of produce that he may not notice at once the almost complete absence of men. The complexion of the market varies with the hour. In the early morning vegetables are brought in. These are followed by exotic fruits and rare flowers and later by crayfish, turtle eggs, and Oaxaca tamales incased in banana leaves. Still later in the day toasted tortillas appear, borne aloft in stacks 3 feet high. Women come and go constantly, bearing their wares for sale and carrying away purchases balanced on their heads. Each new group brings fresh gossip. A steady drone of conversation rises in the singsong Zapotec dialect. If a man appears, he is likely, unless a stranger, to be the target of taunts.

The industriousness of the Tehuana is as phenomenal as her charm, In both work and play her every movement expresses poetic grace, and despite her variety of occupations she is ever serenely gracious. The river, like the market, is under her domination. Here she comes to bear away, like Rebecca of old, jars of water for household purposes, to do the laundry work for her family, and to perform her personal ablutions. The Tehuana is no prude; she bathes naked, the warm sun glinting on her olive skin. Though conspicuous by their absence from the market and the riverside, the men nevertheless are also busily engaged. Some cultivate orchards and gardens, but the majority work as artisans. Their tasks are to weave the exquisite fabrics which comprise the Tehuana's costumes, to mold the fine black clay pottery, and in the talabarterías or saddleries to produce elaborate pieces of tooled leather. In contrast to other parts of the country male dress is casual and drab; the glories of adornment are left entirely to the female.

The city comprises 16 barrios or districts, each with its own church and patron saint. A fiesta is in progress almost constantly. The more important fiestas occur in the barrios of Liesa, Santa María, Santa Cruz, and Laborillo during the months of January and February in honor of their patron saints. These celebrations, lasting several days, are noted for parades and pageantry, feasts, music and dances, fireworks, and frolics. The best time to visit Tehuantepec is Holy Week, when the women display their finest costumes and jewels. The fiestas are eagerly awaited, and the pretty Tehuana sews and embroiders her colorful dress long ahead of time. Busiest of all on fiesta days are the mayordomo, the host or master of ceremonies, and his wife, chosen at the festivities of the preceding year. Since most of the events are held at his home only the owner of a large house and patio can be mayordomo. Before the fiesta he collects what money he can by sending pieces of cake covered with squares of chocolate to other inhabitants of his barrio; the number of chocolate squares indicates the amount the recipient is expected to contribute.

FIESTA. One of the principal fiestas is in honor of St. John the Baptist, observed in towns and villages throughout the republic. Usually it is celebrated here June 22-25. It opens with a procession at 10 p.m. on June 22 in which musicians and women with torches go from one church to another dancing old pre-Spanish Zapotec dances. They swing their shawls rhythmically to the movements of their feet. The ceremony lasts until about midnight. The chief attraction on the following day is the paseo de flores or parade of flowers to the palo grande, an age-old tree at the entrance to the town. The parade takes place in the morning. Men, women, and children participate—youths with wreaths on their hats, maidens carrying palm leaves. Under the old tree they stop for a short dance accompanied by rhythmical swinging of palm leaves. About 5 p.m. or as soon as the day cools the most remarkable procession of all takes place. Even the oxen parade, and the boys dress them with gaily colored ribbons for the occasion. They pull carts full of branches, twigs, and palm leaves. The boys sit in the midst of the greenery, then follow the girls on foot in their beautiful Tehuana costumes with snow-white stiffly starched olanes or ruffles and a flaring headdress called huipil grande falling over the shoulders. Flags and huge bouquets are carried. It is the custom to throw a large fishing net over unsuspecting onlookers. At night a public dance is held in the plaza. A dance at the mayordomo's house begins on June 24 at 10 a.m. and lasts until 6 p.m. Anyone may take part without being thought intrusive. The houses are adorned with bunches of coconuts, palm leaves, and colorful paper hangings. Marimba and brass bands, taking turns, play without interruption. It is customary for the hostess, the wife of the mayordomo, to send a traditional meal, consisting of mole and local dishes, to friends and relatives. Women are seen all over town carrying trays on their heads. The portions are small, but the sender would not be without the trouble of sending them and the recipients would feel hurt if they were not sent.

On the twenty-fifth a paseo or procession in the morning is led by a queen elected for the occasion. She carries a green standard and is attired in typical embroidered Tehuana dress. Then follow two maids of honor, also beautifully dressed, each carrying a white flag on which is the likeness of the saint. They all go barefoot. In the evening the fiesta terminates. This time the maidens carry on their heads enormous gourd bowls up to 2 feet in diameter, painted with flowers, full of fruit, toys, and sweets. The church bells ring at their approach, and marimbas and other musical instruments are played on the church porch. The occasion is eagerly expected by the children, for all the fruits, toys, and sweets are thrown to them, and they scramble to catch as much as their hands will hold.

EXCURSIONS FROM TEHUANTEPEC

Salina Cruz, a Pacific port, 21 miles S, is located at the narrowest point of the North American continent above Nicaragua. It is the Pacific terminus of the Tehuantepec National Railway, which joins it with Puerto México (Coatzacoalcos) almost directly N. The huge docks of Salina Cruz, representing a triumph of engineering skill, were installed by Sir Weetman Pearson, British railroad concessionaire and oil man, an engineering genius. Two converging breakwaters provide a harbor of several hundred acres. The ruinous competition of the Panama Canal, which shortened the route between the oceans, followed by the Mexican revolution and the first World War, resulted in abandonment of many of the great fruit ranches and disuse of the docks. At one time 40 freight trains ran between Puerto México and Salina Cruz each day; now perhaps a couple of mixed trains daily are enough. Dredging has been started recently in the harbor.

Juchitán is one of the Indian towns which can be reached by car or on horseback from Tehuantepec. It is extremely old. Here the visitor can see salt manufactured by the simple process of evaporation. The town has a large market. On July 19 a brilliant pagan fiesta celebrating the harvest is held in honor of St. Vincent de Paul.

SOUTHEASTERN MEXICO

This part of the country comprises the state of Yucatán, the N part of the peninsula of the same name, which contains also the state of Campeche, bounded N by the Gulf of Mexico and S by Guatemala; Tabasco, W of Campeche on the Gulf Coast, and Chiapas, on the Pacific and bordering on Guatemala. The territory of Quintana Roo occupies the E coast of the peninsula above British Honduras. The peninsula is the most SE part of Mexico and is one of the least visited because of its inaccessibility. Yet its beauty, mystery, remarkable pre-conquest ruins, and unusual peoples make it to many visitors the most fascinating region in Mexico. This temple-studded land is the ancient seat of the Maya civilization, one of the greatest of native American cultures.

Trips to Yucatán and Chiapas are described here.

YUCATAN

The most comfortable method of travel to Mérida, capital of the state of Yucatán and its travel center, is by air from Mexico City or from Miami, Fla., via Havana, Cuba. Boats of the New York and Cuba Mail Steamship Co. normally make a weekly stop at Progreso (1941). It is possible to reach Progreso by boat also from New Orleans, Tampico, and Veracruz, but the service is irregular.

In Yucatán (Land of the Yucca), in the midst of what was until recent years an impenetrable jungle, still stand in much of their original and incredible splendor the gleaming buildings of the ancient Maya civilization. The Mayas at the height of their development are believed to have numbered 2,000,000. In addition to constructing remarkable buildings. they evolved an elaborate calendar of amazing accuracy, taking into account the movements of the moon and sun cycles; they invented a system of picture writing and were beginning to make historical records centuries before Columbus set foot in America.

An extensive plain slopes gradually to the N coast of the peninsula. In the SE portion there are low hills known as Sierra Baja (Low Ridge) and Sierra Alta (High Ridge). The soil throughout is mostly rocky and bears poor and scanty vegetation except in the south, where dense jungle blocks off the peninsula from Mexico proper and Guatemala. Since only shallow lakes and water holes exist in the S and E parts of the peninsula, the essential source of water supply for the population here is underground water accumulated in natural caverns called cenotes—deep, circular, vertical-walled, curiously beautiful holes in the limestone. In spite of its dry appearance the state is important agriculturally and is one of the great henequen regions of the world. It produces also corn, the main foodstuff of the people; beans, and sugar cane. The forests contain an abundance of dyewoods. Along the coasts are found turtles which yield the highly prized carey or turtle shell. Fine sponges are found in the sea. Among the handicrafts of the region are jewelry, with gold and silver filigree frequently worked in with coral; beautiful hamacas or hammocks, as sturdy as the best linen and as delicate as the filmiest lace; and very fine straw hats of the Panama type.

The bulk of the population is Maya, by nature peaceful but strongly tribal and proud of their ancient culture. Though short, the Mayas are robust and well proportioned. Yucatán has often been called Mexico's Ireland. Separated from the rest of Mexico by distance and tropical forests and withdrawn from physical contact with other cultures, the inhabitants regard themselves as different from the other people of Mexico, usually referring to themselves as Yucatecans rather than as Mexicans. Movements to break away from Mexico have met with considerable favor at various times. While Spanish is the official language of the state, Yucatecan Maya is the common tongue.

Yucatán's climate, in accordance with the low altitude, is warm and fairly moist. The prevailing E winds have some refreshing qualities. May-August is marked by high temperatures, cloudiness, thunderstorms, and heavy rainfall. January-February is relatively dry; there are many clear days and no thunderstorms, and nights and mornings are generally cool and agreeable. Light summer clothing can be worn throughout the year. During the cooler months a light wrap or top-coat is useful for late evening and early morning. High outing shoes or boots and knickers for women make exploratory jaunts around the ruins easier. A light raincoat is useful during the rainy season, and medication for insect bites is welcome in the jungles. Sun glasses and strong gloves also prove helpful.

The region is excellent for hunting. Deer, mountain lions, wild boars, quail, and wild turkeys are plentiful. Deep-sea fish are caught near Progreso and other points along the shores.

Typical dishes in Yucatán include puchero, prepared with vegetables and rice; a chicken pie baked under the ground and generally served on All Souls' Day; rolleno negro, a spicy dish made of ground peppers served with black sauce; a hot drink called posol, made of ground corn and water and often flavored with honey; beans; red peppers, and tortillas.

Air service from Mexico City to Mérida (6½ hours) is maintained by frequent planes of the Mexican Aviation Co. (Compañía Mexicana de Aviación), a subsidiary of Pan American Airways. The plane from Mexico City flies first E past the majestic volcanoes Popocatépetl and Ixtaccíhuatl, which overlook the road used by the conquistadores on their march from Veracruz to Mexico City. In a short while the traveler is elbow to elbow with the peak of Orizaba, Mexico's highest mountain. After leaving the airport of Tejerías near Veracruz, the first stop, the scenery changes. The plane passes over sea, jungle, lakes, and numberless rivers, a stupendous spectacle. The second stop is at Villahermosa, a town of 1600 inhabitants, capital of the state of Tabasco, a famous banana region. The flight continues over Ciudad del Carmen, on an island in the remotest corner of the bay of Campeche.

Campeche, with 16,000 inhabitants, a stop on the air trip from Mexico City, is the capital of the state of the same name and the second city of the peninsula. It is a very interesting old town with crumbling church and pink and yellow houses mellowing against the blue sea. Historically noteworthy as the city where the Spaniards first set foot on Mexican soil in 1517, Campeche is Mexico's only completely fortified city, surrounded by walls built in the 16th and 17th centuries as protection from the pirates attracted by the town's wealth and its beautiful women.

Progreso, with 13,000 inhabitants, on the Gulf of Mexico, at the NW corner of the peninsula, is the chief port, 1580 miles from New York, 420 from Havana, 600 from New Orleans, and 390 from Veracruz. Travelers to Yucatán who land at Progreso can take railroad, bus, or car to Mérida, 24 miles inland, a journey of less than an hour. Since the state is relatively isolated almost all entries and departures except by air are normally through this port.

Progreso's most distinguished features are its attractive driveway along the breakwater, its summer cottages, its broad streets, and Plaza Hidalgo and the Palacio Municipal or city hall. There is good surf bathing on the sandy beach. The fishing is excellent.

MERIDA

Capital and most important city of the state of Yucatán, Mérida, with 100,000 inhabitants, is reached by air from Mexico City or from Miami, Fla., via Havana, Cuba, or by boat to Progreso on the Gulf of Mexico. The city was founded in 1542 on the site of the ruins of the prehistoric Maya city of Ti-Ho by an army of Spanish conquistadores led by Francisco de Montejo the younger after a dozen years of almost continual fighting with the native defenders. Today its fine colonial buildings dating from the 16th century are surrounded by modern business and residence districts. It is a quaint, extremely clean city with substantial white houses and thousands of windmills used for pumping water from deep wells.

The principal plaza, one of the most beautiful in Mexico, with well-kept walks shaded by beautiful Indian laurels and tropical trees, is near the geographical center of the city. In the evening this plaza is gay with music and promenading youth. The mestizas in particular catch the eye. They wear loose blouses embroidered in colors, with rebozos or shawls crossed on their breasts; their skin is bronze, their eyes shining black. E of the main plaza is the cathedral, the largest and most impressive church on the peninsula. Completed in the 16th century, it has old wooden doors swinging on pivots instead of hinges and is full of interesting statues and curious ornaments. Flanking the plaza S is the famous Casa Montejo, erected in 1549. On the façade of this mansion is an escutcheon cut in stone which depicts two Spanish knights with their booted feet on the heads of two kneeling Mayas, symbolic of Spanish dominion over the natives. Though the mansion is occupied, it may be possible for the traveler to see the interior by inquiring at his hotel. W of the plaza is the Palacio Municipal or city hall, N the Palacio del Gobierno or state capitol.

The central business section surrounds the plaza. Here are shops, banks, import and export offices, large wholesale houses, insurance agencies, department stores, automobile dealers, garages, modern hotels, theaters, and restaurants.

MONUMENTS. In the cemetery on the outskirts and elsewhere in the town are monuments to Felipe Carrillo Puerto, Maya agrarian and labor leader who successfully organized the League of Resistance of the Socialist Party, a labor organization of 100,000 members who during the revolution attacked the feudal system in which the large planters held absolute power over the Maya people. Before the revolution

Puerto had been imprisoned for reading the constitution aloud to the Indians. In 1920 he became governor of the state, and with the assistance of his League he made Yucatán one of the foremost states in distribution of land and social advancement. He made many improvements in the city and promoted diversification of crops in the hope of making his people economically independent. His program aroused the bitter hatred of the reactionary planters, and in 1923 during the Huerta revolt he and three of his brothers were killed.

MARKETS are models of cleanliness and as colorful today as they must have been in ancient times. The Mercado Lucas de Gálvez and the Mercado García Rejón, the most important, are in the main business section of the city; others are to be found in the suburbs. Women in dresses embroidered in gay colored designs do most of the selling. Squatted on the ground, they are surrounded by neatly piled peppers and tomatoes, baskets of beans and corn, jars of honey, and mounds of salt from the marshlands. For sale also are woven hammocks, straw hats, and pottery. The markets represent Mérida's strongest link with its Indian past. Early morning is the best time for visiting them.

MUSEUM. The Museo Yucateco, the state museum, near the cathedral, is held by the Yucatecans to be the second in importance and grandeur in all Mexico. Careful study of Maya relics in the museum will repay those who expect to visit the ruins. In the collection are Maya idols, monoliths, animal figures, statues, mural paintings, bowls, beads, jewels, weapons, pottery, bones, and deformed skulls. Open 9 a.m.-12m., 3-5 p.m.

CENTERS OF HIGHER LEARNING. The National University of the Southeast, established in 1922, gives degrees in law, medicine, and pharmacy. Facilities for study of the fine arts are offered by an art school. The municipal archives in the city hall are rich in books and manuscripts relating to Yucatán.

SPORTS during the last few years have experienced a great impetus in Yucatán. The Casa del Pueblo (People's House), headquarters of the League of Resistance of the Socialist Party; the Club Mérida; the federal barracks, and the Escuela Modelo (Model School) hold baseball, basketball, and football games on their playing fields. The Country Club has facilities for tennis. There are excellent swimming pools at Hotel Colón, the Club Mérida, Quinta Cuestar, and elsewhere. Cenote Geyser and Cenote Volopoch are good pools. The city has two bullrings, Circo Teatro Yucateco, where boxing matches also are held, and the modern Plaza de Toros.

FIESTA. The carnival, the pre-Lenten period beginning on Ash Wednesday, is the most colorful of all fiestas in Mérida, celebrated with great enthusiasm and splendor. Confetti and flower battles, elaborate floats and parades, masked balls and other dances, make the holiday riotous. Indians arrange their own dances and music.

THEATERS AND MOVING-PICTURE HOUSES. The Peón Contreras Theater, modern and elaborate in architecture, in addition to its regular attractions holds dances twice a week in its lobby. The Colonial Theater is devoted to revues and musical comedies. Novedades, Principal, and Cantarell, moving-picture houses, are in the main section of the city; there are others in the suburbs.

BANKS. Banco Nacional de México; Banco de México; Banco de Londres y México; Banco Refaccionario de Yucatán.

RESTAURANTS. The hotels have up-to-date restaurants. Other restaurants are La Panificadora, Versalles, El Regalo, and El Centenario. Many cafés serve grecas or small cups of good coffee; these include La Sin Rival, La Tacita de Oro, and Louvre.

HOTELS. Gran**, Calle 60 No. 496-8; Itzá**, C. 59 No. 495; Colón*, C. 62 No. 483; Imperial, C. 58 No. 488; Reforma, C. 59 No. 508; Sevilla, C. 62 No. 511.

EXCURSIONS FROM MERIDA

More than 50 dead Maya cities throughout Yucatán are known to archeologists. The principal two are Chichén-Itzá and Uxmal, both easily accessible. The buildings which in part remain standing today are believed to have been temples, palaces, and tombs of the rulers of the ancient Mayas. The common people probably lived in dwellings similar to those of the peasants of today. Buildings were erected on artificial mounds. Outside walls were faced with highly ornamented figures; the significance of many of these is understood, that of others conjectured. Bird, animal, reptile, and human forms served to express religious ideas, to celebrate a victory, or to commemorate a peace. These ornaments were placed on the buildings in the manner of mosaics; a design seldom appears complete on a single stone. Admiration mounts for the sturdy race who selected this apparently sterile locality for a home, yet prospered there and developed into a mighty nation. These ancient people, though they probably were hardly scientific farmers, were doubtless more highly skilled than their successors today. However, there is evidence of a slow progressive drying up of the region, and this offers an explanation not alone of the comparative prosperity of the ancient inhabitants, but also of their ultimate decline in numbers and in power.

Much is known of the Maya civilization, but far more remains unfathomed, for no key to the countless hieroglyphic inscriptions and carvings has yet been found. It is believed that the Mayas occupied some 250,000 square miles of territory, including the Yucatán peninsula, Tabasco, Chiapas, and a large portion of Central America. Their culture dates back several hundred years before the beginning of the Christian era. At the time of the birth of Christ the highest Maya culture was centered in the N part of Guatemala, but it was cut short some 500 years later when the Maya race abandoned their remarkable cities and betook themselves to the jungles. The Maya culture reappeared in Yucatán with the cities of Uxmal, Chichén-Itzá, and others which manifest an even greater architectural knowledge and sculptural skill than had existed in Guatemala. The Maya tribes were now more warlike. They fought among themselves until the 13th century, when the powerful leader Kukul Can, known to the Aztecs as Quetzalcoatl, merged them into a single empire. He made the city of Mayapán the civil capital of the peninsula, while Chichén-Itzá remained the religious center. The two peaceful centuries that followed saw a great revival of the arts. This empire dissolved in the 15th century because of tribal wars and pestilence.

Chichén-Itzá is 77 miles SE of Mérida by a combined railroad and automobile route or entirely by car (2½ hours). Points of interest along the highway are the henequen plantations of San Pedro and Ticopó and the villages and towns of Tahmek, Hoctún, Socchel,

Kantunil, Holcá and Pisté. Going by railroad, the traveler changes to bus or car at Dzitas. The country is flat, with extensive forests and large plantations of henequen. Another important industry is the production of chicle, used for making chewing gum.

The celebrated ruins in the deep jungle are the most important and extensive yet brought to light on the peninsula. They lie in an extensive government reservation. Large sums are being spent to restore the magnificent buildings under the direction of archeologists from the Carnegie Institution and experts appointed by the Mexican government. Thousands of forest trees that have encroached upon the old city are being cleared away. Chichén-Itzá, founded sometime between A.D. 360 and 430 by migrants from Guatemala, remained a provincial town of the first Maya empire until the seventh century, when it was abandoned. Three centuries later it was reoccupied, and this time it grew steadily, to become one of the major cities of the league which centered in Mayapán. Internecine strife destroyed the league, and in the 15th century Chichén-Itzá was once more abandoned in the retreat of the Mayas to Guatemala.

Chichén-Itzá was a sacred city to which thousands of pilgrims came from all parts of Mexico and Central America. When the Spaniards arrived in the early 16th century they found it deserted and in ruins. A few squatters told them of its past glory. Here are found the remains of superbly constructed and beautifully decorated temples. The structures evince an amazing mastery of the laws of architecture and engineering. Expert craftsmanship is evidenced in the high, broad cornices and in the profusion of bas-relief decorations carved in stone on the massive walls. In size and construction the temples and other edifices rival those of ancient Egypt and India. Curiously, in spite of all their inventiveness the Mayas never worked out the principle of the segmental keyed arch, and as a result a characteristic of Maya interiors is the flat arch.

The great temple of Kukul Can, called the Castillo now, is conspicuous among the ruins. The name of Kukul Can, the tutelary deity of the ancient city, means Plumed Serpent. The structure is composed of two pyramids, one inside the other. The exterior rises in nine terraces, decreasing in size, with a wide central staircase on each side and a beautiful temple at the top. In this outer structure Toltec influence is evident, but the inner pyramid is pure Maya. The famous crouching red stone jaguar discovered upon excavation of the two chambers in the superstructure of the inner pyramid is incrusted with 74 green jade disks representing the animal's spots; the eyes are green jade half spheres. The tusks are of highly polished flint, and the teeth, painted white, are of limestone.

The temple of Los Guerreros (The Warriors) is E of the temple of Kukul Can. In it was discovered the famous mosaic of turquoise, coral, and jade which was put on exhibition in the National Museum in Mexico City. This temple, of monumental proportions, is adorned with altars and sacrificial stones. In connecting subterranean chambers four successive periods of Maya art can be clearly distinguished.

The Grupo de la Mil Columnas (Group of the Thousand Columns), S of the temple of the Warriors, consists of more than 1000 columns 8-10 feet high inclosing a central plaza of 5 acres, with colonnaded halls, sunken courts, and pyramided temples within it. Many of the columns, formed of mosaics, bear distinctive polychrome carvings.

The Cenote Sagrado (Sacred Well), lying some distance N of the temple of Kukul Can, is 350 feet long, 150 feet wide, and 70 feet deep. In times of national danger, pestilence, or drought the ancient Mayas sought to propitiate their gods by casting beautiful maidens and jewels into this famous pool fed by subterranean springs. Some years ago the pool was dredged and a fortune in gold and jade ornaments was taken out, as well as frail bones of girls and young women who had been offered to the gods.

Several ball courts are scattered among the ruins. The largest, NW of the temple of Kukul Can, is a cemented area of enormous proportions. Here the Mayas once played their game called tlachtli and perhaps also performed important civic rites. The ball court is notable for its extraordinary acoustics.

Between this ball court and the temple of Kukul Can stands the temple of Los Tigres (Tigers), guarded by two enormous plumed serpents whose deep-set eyes were once inlaid with precious jewels. A great procession of carved jaguars gave the building its name. The creation of the universe is vividly represented on two stones here, and a frescoed chamber shows scenes from the life of the people, presumably religious or civic festivals.

SE from the temple of Kukul Can lie numerous buildings among which El Osario (Ossarium), a tomb, may be singled out. Within the small pyramid a perpendicular shaft leads to a subterranean chamber. It is supposed that passages from this chamber led to other structures.

El Caracol (Snail), shaped like a turret and standing on an artificial mound, has a winding stairway inside which is responsible for its name. The building was used as an observatory and as such demonstrates the high stage of astronomical knowledge achieved by the Mayas.

The Casa de las Monjas (House of the Nuns) may actually have been a palace of the high priests. Richly sculptured, the building is well preserved and is one of the most beautiful of the ruins. It has indeed been called the most perfect example of pre-Columbian art in the Americas.

Other points of interest are the temple of Los Retablos (Pictures); El Akab-Dzib (House of the Dark Writing); Chichán-Chob, also known as the Casa del Venado (House of the Deer); the Casa Colorada (Red House); the market, where slaves were probably traded; and Las Aguilas (Eagles).

HOTEL. Mayaland Lodge, next to the ruins, is operated by the Mayaland Tours. Arrangements should be made in advance for accommodation in its picturesque bungalows with modern facilities. There is also a boarding house, doña Victoria's.

Old Chichén is a mile from the major ruins by a path through the jungle. Among the palaces and temples, mostly unexcavated or unrestored, are a phallic temple, with a carving on a lintel indicating the year A.D. 619; the Paul Martin temple, dating back to the fifth century; a temple carved with little heads and one with notable lintels, the latter the only completely restored temple in the Maya area.

Uxmal, SW of Mérida by bus or car over 49 miles of paved highway 2½ hours), has some ruins on a broad plain surrounded by a picturesque range of hills. By railroad the route from Mérida is to Muna (3 hours), where board and lodging can be secured at moderate rates, and thence 15 miles by car to the ruins. The Mayaland Tours, with offices in Mérida, conduct travelers through the ruins.

Uxmal, once the aristocratic center of the noble family of Tutal Xiu, contains exceedingly beautiful examples of Maya architecture. While the buildings in Chichén-Itzá are spread over a large area, the Uxmal structures are compressed into a comparatively limited space. They have an air of mystery and strange grandeur. The buildings date about A.D. 1000, but indications have been found of earlier structures. Uxmal means Three Times Sacred. The Xius had become the second most important people of the peninsula, and Uxmal rivaled Chichén-Itzá and Mayapán, the other major cities of the Maya federation. During a period of wholesale migration the Xius abandoned their magnificent capital and moved to Mani, 30 miles away. The new capital never equaled the old. Today Mani has few traces of the pre-conquest period.

The Casa del Gobernador (House of the Governor) is the best preserved of the ancient structures of Uxmal and the most beautifully ornamented. This long, narrow, dignified building rises on an artificial mound of triple terraces. Its thick walls are covered with an intricate array of finely sculptured human heads and animals.

E of this ruin is the Casa de las Tortugas (House of the Turtles), containing six rooms. It owes its name to the ornamental row of bas-relief turtles on the upper cornice of the façade.

The temple of El Adivino (Prophet), ornamented with hieroglyphic carvings, crowns a great pyramid. From its ledges all Uxmal, a breath-taking panorama, comes to view.

The Casa de las Palomas (House of the Doves), N of the pyramid supporting the temple of the Prophet, draws its name from the intricate fretwork of the crest, which from a distance resembles a row of dovecotes. This building is probably the oldest of the main group.

The Casa de las Monjas (House of the Nuns), a great building W of the temple of the Prophet, consists of four large rectangular structures around a richly decorated patio from the S side of which a beautiful archway looks toward the House of the Governor. The nunnery is believed to have been a seminary rather like a Christian convent in which dwelt the young girls dedicated to the service of the gods. In its 88 rooms are masks of Yum-Chac, the rain god, one of the principal deities; entwined serpents, symbols of divinity; Greek keys, and rosettes.

Ruins of a large ball court are S of the nunnery. Near by is a cemetery with its own court and temples and the very old Casa de la Vieja (House of the Old Woman), so called because of the mutilated statue of an old woman discovered near it. Several other incomplete ruins are in the vicinity.

Oxkutzcab is a center from which many scarcely explored ruins can be visited on horseback. Two or three days should be set aside for a visit to these places. To reach them, the traveler goes by train or car to Oxkutzcab, beyond Muna, about 4½ hours out of Mérida. From here the traveler usually goes by horseback accompanied by a guide through the beautiful Yucatán forests. Hardly less interesting than those already described are the ruins of Labná, Zayi, Kaba, and the grottoes of Loltun. The arch of Labná and the palace of Zayi are masterpieces of architecture. The arch of Labná is one of the finest in any Maya building. The grottoes of Loltun are unusual. Their stalactite-covered galleries resemble magnificent royal halls. Labná lies S of Oxkutzcab; Kaba and Zayi W, the first on the way to the second. Oxkutzcab has accommodations for an overnight stay.

Izamal (Place of the Itzáes), 50 miles E of Mérida by railroad or car, is believed to be older than Chichén-Itzá and was the goal of aboriginal pilgrimages. Believers came from the four cardinal points by four sacbés or white roads, of which traces remain. At Izamal are the ruins of a great mausoleum in which the bones of Itzamna, the leader of a migration, are supposed to rest.

Today Izamal survives as a picturesque colonial city of some importance. On one of the main hills where the Maya temples used to stand the bishop Diego de Landa built an immense monastery with a famous cathedral. The ruins are a short distance from the modern town.

Mayapán, about 30 miles S of Mérida and reached by railroad, was the capital of the Maya federation and victim of the fury of the great Maya civil war. It has almost disappeared. The central pyramid of these ruins is replete with idols and remains of temple columns.

Other ruins are at Chacmultun, Kewich, Mecanxoc, and Chunconab, minor sites notable in some details of architecture and sculpture. This group and the grottoes of Sabacha can be reached by train (Mérida-Peto), S via Tekax, an important and prosperous agricultural city which has a beautiful church and an ancient hermitage. The ruins are visited by horseback from Tekax. A guide is essential.

The Oxkintoc labyrinth and the grottoes of Calcehtoc, singularly beautiful, are reached by the Mérida-Campeche train to the San Bernardo station (2 hours). A neighboring tramway leads to Calcehtoc, where horses are provided for completion of the excursion.

Valladolid, E of Mérida and reached in a few hours by railroad, is a historic and interesting city, scene of bloody native uprisings in 1847.

Colestun, Sisal, and Dzilam are small, picturesque port towns. The clean and sandy shore provides good bathing beaches near them, and the region is excellent for hunting and fishing. In Sisal there are a church and monastery dating from colonial times and a large and beautiful cenote or pool.

CHIAPAS

Barricaded by mountains, Chiapas, the state farthest S, has remained backward until recently and is little visited. The Compañía Aeronáutica Sarabia operates air service from Mexico City via Oaxaca to Tuxtla Gutiérrez (5-6 hours) and Tapachula. By railroad the traveler can go from Mexico City via Veracruz to Arriaga (45 hours), then by car or bus to Tuxtla Gutiérrez (4 hours), a superb drive. The Compañía Aeronáutica del Sur offers air service to local points, while the Pan American Highway provides an all-weather road from Arriaga through the highlands to Tapachula on the Guatemalan border, also reached by railroad.

Tuxtla Gutiérrez, with 14,000 inhabitants, is the capital, a modern city. Situated 2000 feet above sea level, it enjoys a perfect climate. Of particular interest are the Museo del Estado (State Museum), housing archeological relics and an extensive library, and the market, where the visitor will find earthenware vessels, painted gourds, fire-works, religious sculpture, cigarettes, textiles, lace, and other native products.

Tuxtla Gutiérrez is the center of a cattle and agricultural region, famous for its cheeses, fine horses, double-eared corn, and a species of cotton which protects itself from the boll weevil. It is also rich in mahogany, dyewoods, anise, cacao, coffee, tobacco, tropical fruits, and henequen.

El Sumidero is a gorge lying near the bus route from Tuxtla Gutiérrez to Chiapa de Corzo. About halfway to Chiapa a modern bridge spans the Río Grijalva or Nandechia, which here enters the Huitepec mountains, a few miles from the gorge. El Sumidero is one of the great natural wonders of Mexico. At the time of the Spanish conquest the ruling race ended its existence by drowning here rather than lose its freedom.

Chiapa de Corzo, a half hour's bus ride from Tuxtla Gutiérrez, is built on the site of Nendiume, the pre-conquest Indian capital. Beautifully situated on a high bluff overlooking the Río Grijalva, Chiapa is a colonial city of great charm, noted for its pretty women. In the plaza is a handsome fountain built by Friar Rodrigo de León in the 16th century. Nothing recalls the past glory of Chiapa so fully as the old cathedral, whose colossal bell weighs 4½ tons and has the temper of Venetian glass. Surmounting the belltower are four statues, three representing saints and the fourth a Falstaffian figure of uncertain identity. Looking down from the tower, one sees the Río Grijalva far below, dotted with primitive piraguas or dugout canoes.

San Cristóbal de las Casas, commonly called Las Casas, with 12,000 inhabitants, capital of the state until 1890, can be reached from Tuxtla Gutiérrez by car (5 hours) or by plane (½ hour). Founded in 1538 at Ciudad Real by Diego de Mazariegos, Las Casas was the colonial capital. In an ever-cool mountain valley 7000 feet above sea level, it was given its present name in honor of Bartolomé de las Casas, Protector of the Indians, the first bishop of the diocese. In its old churches, arcaded palaces, low tile-roofed houses with grilled windows and patios, and tortuous cobbled streets the city preserves its colonial aspect. Dashing charros or horsemen in embroidered sombreros and skin-tight pants ride spirited horses whose bridles and saddles are incrusted with silver. Las Casas is famous for its silver saddles, worth three or four times as much as a horse.

The market is intensely interesting. Thousands of Indians come daily with their wares from villages such as Zinacantan, Chamula, Larrainzar, Cancuc, Huistan, San Bartolomé, and Tenejapa. Overflowing the market building, they fill the streets, creating a blaze of color with their brilliant costumes, the natives of each village distinguished by the tribal dress. The Zinacantecs wear a wide-brimmed palm-leaf hat bedecked with long ribbons, the colors of which indicate whether the wearer is married or single. The Huistecs' hats imitate halos. The huipiles or blouses of the women of Larrainzar are woven with the designs carved in the sculptures of Palenque. The caites or sandals of the men have high leather backs, indicating caste, also as shown in ancient Maya art. The tiny stalls in the main street cater primarily to the Indians. Here are found earthenware utensils, candles, palm-leaf rain capes, tasseled kerchiefs, embroidered shirts, woolen and cotton cloth, woven head ribbons and belts, straw hats with peaked crowns, sandals, monkey hides, and guitars. The guitars have 14 strings and are inscribed with such legends as "Precious Princess," "I think only of thee," and "I seek my beloved." The Indians carry their guitars wherever they go.

Las Casas has many churches, every street leading to a plaza with a church, monastery, or chapel. Two hills dominate the city. These are topped by the churches of San Cristóbal, a crumbling ruin, and Guadalupe, shining white and intact. Two of the finest churches in Las Casas are the cathedral and the church of San Nicolás, while the church of Santo Domingo, begun in 1547, with its delightful façade, gilded rococo interior, and time-darkened paintings, is one of the outstanding examples of the colonial period in Mexico.

Excursions from Las Casas. Chamula, reached by horseback in half an hour, is a typical Chiapan Indian village. The municipality consists of a church, school, jail, and a few circular thatched huts. Its 20,000 Indians are scattered over an area of 650 square miles. The women are shepherdesses; the men, craftsmen, dyers, weavers, and farmers, cultivating the soil as their pre-conquest ancestors did, without steel, wheel, or domestic animals. Tourists should ascertain the days on which local markets or fiestas are held before visiting this or any similar Indian village.

Other near-by towns worthy of note are Cinjalapa; Comitan, a textile center, and Ocosingo, on the edge of the Lacandon country. E Chiapas is inhabited by the Lacandons, the most primitive tribe in Mexico, living in the unexplored jungles. Possessing no towns, they live in isolated family groups, hunting game with blowpipes and bows and arrows. Both sexes wear their hair long and dress alike in long cotton shifts. At prescribed intervals they visit the ancient ruins to worship the spirits of their ancestors.

Palenque, an archeological site in the NE corner of the state, can be reached by plane from Tuxtla Gutiérrez to Ocosingo or to the Indian village of Palenque and from there by horseback.

The Palenque ruins are the highest expression of ancient Maya culture. Unlike other Maya sites, the principal edifice is not the temple but the palace. Raised upon a stone-faced terrace, it is built in vaulted galleries about four inner courts and contains a maze of chambers and long galleries which provide magnificent perspectives. Its most spectacular feature is a square tower four stories high, the only one of its kind in the Maya area. The temples, grouped around the palace, are gems of architecture. But Palenque is most celebrated for its sculptured wall panels and roofcombs. Modeled in stucco rather than cut in stone, these sculptures, like the buildings they adorn, represent the final achievement of a great cultural epoch.

INDEX TO THE REGIONAL GUIDE

THE REPUBLIC OF GUATEMALA

GUATEMALA

BY NATALIE RAYMOND

The republic of Guatemala, most populous of the Central American republics, is a country where spectacular contrasts of topography and climate have been paralleled in its strange and dramatic history. The impenetrable jungles of the north hide the ruined cities of the ancient Maya empire, where one of the great civilizations of pre-Columbian America developed. These cities have been nearly obliterated by the jungle; their inhabitants are gone, and a few chicle gatherers roam the wilderness. On the rugged highland plateau among still smoking volcanoes, the present Indian inhabitants live bound to their past by many traditions. In their beautiful villages, now made accessible by modern roads, they have developed a colorful and harmonious life within the framework established by the colonial culture. On the rich coastal plains is yet another Guatemala—the realm of sugar cane and banana plantations.

HISTORY

PRE-CONQUEST. Somewhere about the beginning of the Christian era, the Mayas seem to have spread out from their home on the coastal plain of the Gulf of Mexico. The term Maya does not refer to any specific tribe, but groups together people who spoke related languages. They pushed westward into other parts of Mexico, eastward into what is today British Honduras, southward into Honduras, and southeastward into what is now the inhospitable jungle of northern Guatemala, where the remains of their civilization can still be seen. They found and conquered, killed, or absorbed thousands of Indians whose remote forefathers may well have come to the American continent from Asia and about whose archaic agricultural mode of life very little is known today. Much, however, is known about the Mayas. During the first period of their culture, the Old Empire, they built such elaborate and beautiful cities as Uaxactún, Tikal, Chaculá, and Quiriguá in Guatemala and Copán in Honduras.

The people of the Old Empire were far advanced in architecture and mathematics, astronomy, the arts, and philosophy. Not only did they master writing in hieroglyphs, examples of which are still preserved at Quiriguá and Copán as well as other places, but they developed and used a calendar fully as accurate as the Gregorian. Maya writing made use of some 400 characters representing objects or ideas rather than sounds. The hieroglyphs which have been deciphered relate to dates, such as an eclipse or astronomical conjunction, but most of the glyphs have not yet been read. Authorities disagree as to whether the Mayas had writing in our sense of the word; whether they did or did not, it may be that when the key to these glyphs is discovered we shall know more about the ritual, history, and life of the Mayas. The correlation of Maya and Gregorian calendars is still in dispute. At Uaxactún scientists of the Carnegie Institution discovered a monument bearing the earliest date recorded in the Maya area; it has been interpreted as June 10, A.D. 68. Here also is the latest date recorded in the whole region of El Petén, A.D. 639. During the six centuries between these

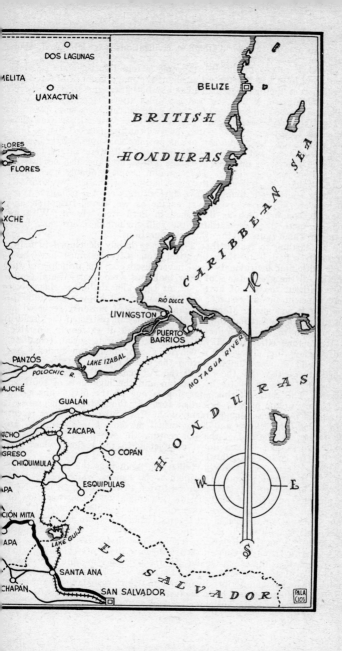

two dates one of the world's highest civilizations was elaborated, flourished, and passed away.

The chief record of this great people is found in their cities, which even now show some of the grandeur of the magnificent sculptured and painted stone temples, palaces and public buildings, and stelae or carved stone columns, of which the best examples are at Copán. They were skilled artisans, and vestiges of their jade cutting, weaving, painting, and pottery have been found. Fragments of a vase with a true glaze and some thin porcelainlike pottery with beautiful painted figures have been discovered. Less is known of the people themselves, partly because their cities were not lived in all the time, but were rather used as gathering places for markets, festivals, and games, and also because no cemeteries have been found. The common people probably lived much as the Indians do today, in thatched houses surrounded by cornfields which provided their living. Maya agriculture was of a primitive type. There were no horses, no cows; as far as we know, irrigation and regional economy such as flourished in Peru were absent. With no effective method of replenishing the soil, dwindling crops may have been the chief cause of the Mayas' migrations.

It is startling to realize that a people so highly developed in many ways never had iron—their beautiful stone carvings must have been made with flint instruments—and never discovered the principle of the wheel. All the great stones of their buildings were quarried and set in place without the aid of horse, ox, or cart. The buildings themselves were deficient in one respect; the Mayas did not know the true arch. Their arch was made of overlapping courses of masonry, covered at the summit by a flat flagstone. This construction restricted the breadth of the arch to about 16 feet and often made it extremely unstable. In their stone cities the Mayas set up an elaborate social, economic, and religious life. They had a warrior group, though no evidence has been found of wars fought during the Old Empire. Yet they abandoned their cities. By the end of the 7th century they had migrated to the north, to new sites in Yucatán and the highlands of southern Mexico. The cause of this migration is one of the major puzzles in the history of the Mayas. Scientists formerly thought of it in terms of an almost overnight abandonment of the Old Empire, but more recent data point to a slower and more casual movement to the north. In either case, by the end of the 7th century the system of caste and of public works had broken down completely in the regions where the Old Empire culture had flowered.

The next centuries of Maya civilization, known as the New Empire, brought a second period of brilliant achievement which reached its greatest height in the 11th-14th centuries. The history of the New Empire lies outside the territory of Guatemala, with the exception of one Maya group, the Itzá house of Yucatán, which migrated back from Yucatán to the Petén lake forests shortly before the arrival of the Spaniards and which maintained Maya culture in Guatemala until 1698, when it was finally conquered by Spanish forces.

The major tribes in Guatemala in the immediate pre-colonial period are spoken of as the Maya-Quiché, grouped together because they spoke related languages. Several records of these people have been found, among them a manuscript discovered in Chichicastenango known as the Popol Vuh, written by a convert to Christianity soon after the Spanish conquest. Its author gives an appealing account of Maya legend and history. He goes from the origin of man and the super-human but often quixotic doings of the Maya gods to the wandering of the Maya chieftains along the Río Usumacinta, bordering Guatemala, to intertribal wars and the establishment of kingdoms. The last section of this remarkable manuscript brings the story up to the time of the Spanish conquest and Pedro de Alvarado's destruction of the ancient cities. The Maya-Quiché were well organized into distinctive tribes, with the Quiché, Cakchiquel, Zutugil, Pocoman, and Mam tribes pre-eminent. The Quiché seem to have settled in the region about the 6th century; the Cakchiquels came later. About A.D. 1000, with the break-ing up of the Toltec empire in Mexico, the group must have received an infiltration from the north. The great nations set up kingdoms, established capitals, and instituted complicated royal lines and a dis-tinctive social, economic, military, and religious life. Yet they did not have such cultural riches and great public works as the people of Yucatán more or less contemporaneously or those of the Old Empire. For example, they possessed a calendar, but its form was Aztec, not Maya, and it did not have the astronomical accuracy of the Maya calendar. Wars between the Cakchiquels and the Quiché, occasionally also the Zutugils, were almost continuous for several centuries, chiefly over boundary disputes. In addition, many other smaller tribes, allied by blood, were from time to time conquered by one or the other of the larger nations.

The Quiché were supreme in power, statesmanship, and art, and they dominated this whole region at the time of the conquest. Nevertheless the nation was not strong enough to withstand the bitter civil wars which depleted its wealth, man power, and prestige. In addition, shortly before the advent of the Spaniards, the Maya-Quiché lands were rav-aged by locusts, fire, and epidemic. Although in sheer numbers there must have been a total of several hundred thousand Indians, the sepa-rate tribes, conquered from within by want and pestilence, disunited, outmaneuvered in strategy and cunning, and terrified by armored horsemen and artillery, were an easy prey for the small band of Span-ish invaders.

THE CONQUEST. The conqueror of Guatemala was Pedro de Alvarado, a daring young lieutenant of Hernando Cortés who had distinguished himself in the conquest of Mexico. He was handsome, with such bright hair that the Aztecs called him Tonatiuh (Sun). Courageous, cunning, and ruthless, he was well equipped to carry on the Spaniards' unre-lenting warfare against the Indians. Although he was sent by Cortés to carry out the crown's New World policy to "bring the people to peace without war and to preach matters concerning our Holy Faith," he was primarily intent upon warfare, power, and the acquisition of gold. Alvarado was only 28 years old when he left Mexico in December 1523 with 135 horsemen; 300 foot soldiers, of whom 120 possessed crossbows or muskets; and some 200 native auxiliaries. Even before entering Guatemala he encountered an Indian force of 6000 men. The Indians were terrified, since they had never seen horses or guns, and they were easily defeated.

Alvarado proceeded to the neighborhood of present-day Quezalte-nango. Here the real fighting began, against the powerful Quiché. In the midst of a battle against the Quiché, said to have been 30,000 in number, the Quiché war chief Tecúm Umán was killed. The civil chief of the nation and his advisers decided at this point to resort to strategy;

so they pretended submission and friendship and invited Alvarado and his men to their capital Utatlán, a city with a reputed population of at least 60,000. When the Spaniards entered the city, they suspected a ruse, lured the chiefs to the plains outside, seized them, forced them to confess trickery, and burned them to death. The Quiché resistance was broken.

Alvarado established his first capital at Iximché in 1524. He had been received by the Cakchiquel chiefs with great friendliness, and on July 25, the day of St. James, patron of Spain, the Spaniards took possession of the Cakchiquel city and named it the Very Noble and Very Loyal City of St. James of the Knights of Guatemala (La Muy Noble y Muy Leal Ciudad de Santiago de los Caballeros de Guatemala). Almost every authority has his own interpretation for the meaning of the name Guatemala. Undoubtedly the Spaniards took it over from some Indian source. Among the derivations suggested are Mountain Which Vomits Water, in reference to the volcano Agua; Abundance of Trees, and Captive Eagle. Using Iximché as a base, Alvarado went on to Lake Atitlán, where he succeeded in conquering the Zutugils. Because of his demands for a heavy tribute of gold, his friends the Cakchiquels turned against him, harassed the Spaniards with guerrilla warfare, and eventually drove them out of the first Guatemalan capital. They then settled briefly at a town called Xepau whose exact location is not known. With reinforcements Alvarado proceeded to subdue the Cakchiquels and to burn Iximché.

During the next few years Alvarado was able to defeat the remaining tribes of the country and at the same time to subdue the continuous uprisings in conquered territory. He set off for Spain to answer charges of appropriating crown funds, leaving the country in charge of his brother Jorge de Alvarado. Under Jorge's direction, a new capital, again called Santiago de los Caballeros de Guatemala, was established in the valley of Almolonga, at the foot of the volcano Agua, on Nov. 21, 1527. This place, now known as Ciudad Vieja (Old City), is about 3 miles from present-day Antigua. At the Spanish court, Alvarado managed to pacify the emperor Charles V, and he was named governor and captain general of Guatemala, his territory including lands that are today Chiapas, Honduras, El Salvador, Nicaragua, and Costa Rica. To secure his position further, he married doña Francisca de la Cueva, niece of the powerful Duke of Albuquerque. On the return trip to Guatemala, however, his wife died of fever in Veracruz.

Alvarado's return to America was followed by years of Indian uprisings and dissension among the Spaniards. Most of the time Alvarado was in high disfavor both in Mexico and among his own people in Guatemala. At strategic moments he would return from his current conquest, re-establish order in his capital, and subdue some Indian revolt. His power was too great for any concerted opposition to thrive. He was restless, and the comparatively settled life of the capital irked him; so he went far and wide conquering, subduing, and getting into the territory of other conquistadors. He even led an expedition in 1534 to present-day Ecuador, where he hoped to acquire some of the hoards of gold and silver that the Pizarros were reputedly taking from the Incas. After he reach Ecuador, Alvarado found that his dream of conquest was not to materialize. He was bought off by Diego de Almagro, Francisco Pizarro's lieutenant, and left behind him that remnant of his force which had escaped death during the disastrous passage through Central America.

After a second trip to Spain to strengthen his political fences, Alvarado married doña Beatriz de la Cueva, sister of his former wife, with special papal dispensation. Alvarado, his second wife, and their numerous retinue arrived safely in Guatemala in 1539. Still restless, in 1540 he decided to go to the Spice Islands with 850 soldiers and a large number of Indians. On the way, in Mexico, he was diverted by a local uprising near Jalisco and went to help subdue it. Here he was mortally wounded when his scribe's horse stumbled and fell on him, and he died soon after. The city of Guatemala heard of Alvarado's death on Aug. 29, 1541, and nine days of rigorous mourning were ordained. The deep mourning, however, did not prevent doña Beatriz from considering other matters, and on September 8 she called the municipal officials to the palace and ordered them to name her governor and captain general of Guatemala. In signing the decree, on September 9, she wrote "The unfortunate doña Beatriz"; then she crossed off "doña Beatriz," and the signature remained "The unfortunate."

The palace built by Alvarado and occupied by his widow was a three-story stone building, high on a mountainside in the mouth of a deep, broad gully. On September 8 a storm began, which was regarded as a punishment for the iniquitous acts of doña Beatriz. The storm raged for two days, and on September 10 an avalanche of water overwhelmed the city. There is still some question whether this event was caused by an earthquake which released the waters of a lake in the crater of an extinct volcano. Perhaps, in accordance with an Indian legend, the Maya ruler Quicab had been buried in the crater and had taken his revenge on the foreigners who had overrun his nation. Six hundred people, including doña Beatriz, her maids of honor, and several of Alvarado's illegitimate children, perished in the flood. A few months afterward, in October 1541, a resolution was adopted to move the colony about 3 miles to the valley of Panchoy, and the Holy Sacrament was carried to the fourth capital on Corpus Christi in 1543 and placed in the hermitage of Santa Lucía. This new capital, now known as Antigua, was one of the most beautiful and prosperous cities of the colonial era. The buildings, which at one period included more than 60 churches, were fine examples of the Spanish architecture of the times, a provincial adaptation in which both Italian and Moorish influences were strongly felt.

The capital at Antigua was not untroubled. During the 16th and 17th centuries there were memorable earthquakes and volcanic eruptions which caused much damage and loss of life. In 1717 there was some talk of moving the city, but nothing was done about it. Finally, on July 29, 1773, there was an earthquake which destroyed practically the entire city. Following this catastrophe, the king of Spain in 1775 authorized the removal of the capital to the valley of Las Vacas, some 25 miles away. Here in 1776 the present capital of Guatemala was established, on a site once occupied by the hamlet of La Ermita. Even the present city has had its disasters; in December 1917 and January 1918 it was practically destroyed by a series of earthquakes, though there was little loss of life. Since 1917 almost the entire city has been rebuilt.

THE COLONIAL PERIOD. Life in the New World did not prove easy for the Spanish conquerors. First they appropriated the hoards of gold that the Indians had amassed; then they levied a tribute on new production, and such levies were a frequent cause of Indian insurrections. Soon the alluvial sands that were easily reached were washed out, and gold was no longer obtainable. The agricultural staples were corn, beans, cacao, chile, squash, pineapples, tobacco, cotton, and honey. Wheat, oats, barley, and rye were unknown to the pre-conquest peoples. Sugar cane was introduced from Santo Domingo soon after the conquest. Bananas were brought in, somewhat after 1531, probably from Santo Domingo and Mexico, and by 1600 most European subsistence crops had been established: grains, Spanish vegetables, grapes, limes, oranges, figs. However, even today the pre-colonial crops are still the staple foods.

The problem of labor was of course acute. Under various guises the Indians were reduced to a state approaching slavery. The abuses were modified but not abolished by the work of Bartolomé de las Casas, bishop of Chiapas, who went to Guatemala in 1535 and tried to humanize the Spaniards' treatment of the Indian population. In 1537, to prove that the brutal Spanish methods were unnecessary, he went unarmed among fierce, unconquered tribes who inhabited a region known as the Land of War. His success in pacifying and converting the Indians was so great that the region was renamed Land of True Peace (Verapaz), a name which still survives. Las Casas returned to the Spanish court in 1539 to protest against the treatment of the Indians. He was able to secure some improvement in methods of dealing with them. However, during the early colonial period, the encomienda or royal grant was the keystone of economic activity. These grants apportioned the natives among the Spaniards, with the right to force the Indians to work and to contribute produce. Theoretically the Indians were repaid through the obligation of the encomendero or holder of an encomienda to care for his natives and to see that they embraced Christianity. The end of the 16th and the beginning of the 17th centuries slightly changed this system and brought in two new practices. One was the mandamiento or order issued by magistrates, compelling Indians in their districts to work for 16 weeks a year. The other was debt servitude; money loans were made to the Indians, to be paid off by future work. These two methods of securing forced labor were the foundation of economic life for the next 250 years.

INDEPENDENCE. On Sept. 15, 1821, Guatemala declared its independence from Spain. There followed a brief period of annexation to Mexico, then under the rule of the emperor Agustín de Iturbide. In 1823 Iturbide was forced to abdicate, and when Mexico became a republic Guatemala was free to choose its own form of government. A constitutional assembly on July 1 issued a declaration of independence and created the United Provinces of Central America, comprising the present republics of Guatemala, Honduras, El Salvador, Nicaragua, and Costa Rica. Chiapas, however, which had been a part of Guatemala, joined Mexico. A constitution adopted on Nov. 22, 1824, abolished slavery, encouraged immigration, and formulated a popular, representative, and federal government.

Francisco Morazán established a military dictatorship in Guatemala City in 1829. Elected president of the Central American confederation in 1830, he promoted education, increased immigration, and abolished most of the monastic orders. A drastic struggle with Rafael Carrera as leader of the Conservatives opposing Morazán's regime began in 1839, following the collapse of the confederation and declarations of independence by Nicaragua, Honduras, and Costa Rica. In April 1839 Guatemala established an independent government. Victorious against Morazán in 1840, Carrera began a general massacre of Liberals throughout Central America. In 1842 Morazán tried again to unite the several Central American states, but his plans were unsuccessful and he was captured and executed. In March 1847 the country became the republic of Guatemala.

The problems of political adjustment were complicated by an economic crisis. The chief income crops of the early 19th century were cochineal, which flourished near Antigua, and indigo, which grew in the lowlands near the Pacific coast. About the latter part of the 19th century this trade was ruined by the introduction of aniline dyes, and in sudden need of new sources of revenue the country turned to coffee-growing. Coffee had been introduced in the middle of the 18th century from the French West Indies, but it had not been extensively grown. With an assured supply of Indian labor, guaranteed by money advances, coffee-growing now flourished and soon became Guatemala's most important industry.

During the next three-quarters of a century there was continued strife between the Conservatives and the Liberals, the Conservatives of one Central American nation uniting with those of another to destroy the Liberals. There were also sporadic attempts to form another union of the republics, and in various combinations the republics into which the old captaincy general of Guatemala had been broken went to war four or five times; on two other occasions they escaped war only as a result of foreign arbitration. The outstanding figure during the mid-19th century was Rafael Carrera, the Conservative leader under whom the separate republic of Guatemala was formed, after the dissolution of the Central American confederation in 1839. In 1843 and again in 1851 when a new constitution was promulgated, Carrera was elected president, and later he was given the office for life. Following his death in 1865, his successor continued the Conservative regime until 1871, when a revolutionary army under the leadership of Miguel García Granados and Justo Rufino Barrios entered the capital and took over the government by force.

Barrios, who is regarded as the Lincoln of Guatemala, took office as president on June 4, 1873, and governed for 12 years. He did away with the remaining religious orders, abolished monasteries, and brought to an end the economic and political influence of the Church. He increased the power of local governmental agencies and promoted education and communications. He encouraged agricultural development; gave free land to growers of rubber, cacao, and cattle; and aided the banana and coffee industries. He dreamed of a reunited Central America and proclaimed a new union, and in his efforts to enforce it over the protests of the other republics he invaded El Salvador. In April 1885, at the head of his army, he was killed in the battle of Chalchuapa.

The next important president was Manuel Estrada Cabrera, who was elected in 1898 and for 22 years gave his chief attention to increasing crop yields and industrial development, extending communications, and improving public education and public health. In 1920 a popular uprising and a brief but lively revolutionary campaign, confined to the capital, forced him to relinquish his office. Carlos Herrera, a Conservative and a unionist, followed, but was overthrown by the Liberals in 1921. José María Orellana succeeded him and held office until his death in 1926. Lázaro Chacón was elected for the term 1926-32, but became ill and retired in 1930. In February 1931 Gen. Jorge Ubico was elected president of the republic.

CONTEMPORARY PERIOD. During his first 10 years in office, President Ubico strengthened the powers of the administration and the public finances. He supported the currency, kept gold in the country, and balanced the budget. Public works were built and paid for. Guatemala has a very small internal debt, and its external debts have been reduced or retired. President Ubico instituted and enforced the so-called probity law requiring that anyone assuming public office must take inventory of his assets at the beginning and end of his term; if a discrepancy between salary and assets cannot be accounted for, a rigorous penalty is imposed. President Ubico also developed and reorganized the national police and gave the country peace and order. Guatemala is practically free from crime, and its people are perhaps more law-abiding than those of any other modern nation with the exception of Iceland. Primary education has held the president's interest. He has improved and diversified agriculture and done much for public health and national sanitary control. Highways are one of his chief concerns. He personally inspects every road and local government office in Guatemala at least once a year. Traffic laws are strict and are rigidly enforced.

A great recent achievement of the government has been the betterment of the Indians' condition. Indians' property rights and the jurisdiction of their own courts have been extended. After 250 years of debt slavery, this practice was abolished in May 1936, when all outstanding debts were canceled after two years' warning. To compensate for the old method of getting labor for the seasonal coffee crop, a vagrancy law of 1934 provided that a man must do a certain amount of work by taking a labor contract or cultivating a minimum amount of land. In practice the amount of work is 150 days a year. A tax of $2 for road-building has been levied on all men, and Indians are permitted to put in two weeks' work on the roads in lieu of payment. A liquor law of 1938 forbidding the sale of liquor except by the bottle is markedly reducing the incidence of drunkenness among the Indians, especially during fiestas.

GOVERNMENT. The legislative body of Guatemala is the National Assembly. Each member, representing 30,000 people, is elected for four years by popular vote. The Assembly declares war, governs national finance, and controls concessions. The president is elected by direct vote for a term of six years and is not eligible for immediate re-election. President Ubico's term of office has been extended to 1949, following plebiscites in 1935 and 1941. The Council of State, an advisory body, has seven members, four nominated by the president and three elected by the Assembly: the ministers of agriculture, finance, foreign affairs, interior, public education, public works and communications, and war. The Supreme Court has a chief justice and four associates who are elected by the people. Primary education is free and compulsory.

Guatemala is divided into 22 departments, each of which is again subdivided into municipios or townships. The jefe político, appointed by the president, is the highest authority in the department. The alcaldes or township administrators are elected by direct vote, and so are the regidores or aldermen.

THE LAND

The northernmost of the Central American republics, immediately adjoining Mexico, Guatemala has a N seaboard of about 70 miles on the Atlantic and a S coastline of about 200 miles on the Pacific. The country is slightly smaller than New York State, with an area of 45,452 square miles and a population of somewhat over 3,280,000. Guatemala is conveniently divided into four regions: the lowlands of the Pacific and the Atlantic coastal plains; the volcanic mountains of the Sierra Madre; the highlands, and the low plateaus of El Petén.

The Pacific lowlands constitute a strip of flat terrain about 30 miles wide which extends into Mexico and Salvador. This is tierra caliente —hot, fertile, tropical lands in which are found many jungle animals such as tapir, honey bear, armadillo, wild pig, cougar, and jaguar. The best beef cattle are produced in these lowlands. Here, too, grows much of the native cotton, known as criollo, which is exceptionally white and strong; there is also a native brown variety, and legend says that before the conquest cotton grew in all colors. Sugar cane, bananas, pineapples, and other tropical fruits flourish in the low country of both Pacific and Atlantic coasts.

From the Pacific there is a rather abrupt rise to the mountain ranges, running NW-SE, which constitute the most prominent and spectacular feature of the country. The range near the Pacific coast forms part of the volcanic chain which extends along the entire W coast of Central America and continues into Mexico. There are 27 volcanoes in Guatemala. They appear to rise from the heart of the Sierra Madre, but actually their bases are farther S. Among the volcanoes are the highest peaks in Central America: Tajumulco and Tacaná, near the Mexican border; Santa María, near the town of Quezaltenango; and Agua, Fuego, and Acatenango, which tower above the city of Antigua. Few of the volcanoes are still active. Fuego erupted in January 1932, scattering ashes as far as El Salvador. Santa María burst out in 1902, causing considerable loss of life, and it has given evidence of activity since then, the last time in 1928. Pacaya erupted in 1870. The rest have long been dormant. This volcanic mountain area, up to about 5000 feet altitude, is unexcelled coffee terrain.

The highland region really consists of high valleys inclosed by mountains. Many important towns are located in the highlands at elevations of 5000-8000 feet. Most of the corn and beans, the dietary staples, are grown at these elevations. Sheep, especially black sheep, are raised in the highlands, and wheat is grown above 6000 feet.

From the Sierra Madre the land slopes more gradually down to an Atlantic coast strip of lowland 30-60 miles wide, with climate and crops similar to those of the Pacific lowlands. N lies El Petén, a limestone plain covered with dense tropical shrub, covering about a third of the area of Guatemala, with a population density estimated at less than two to the square mile. This region is still relatively unknown and undeveloped, although a number of expeditions have gone into it in the last few years. Its chief product is chicle, the basis of chewing gum, which is obtained from a tree called the sapodilla. Other important trees also grow in these forests: Spanish cedar, mahogany, ebony, logwood, walnut, and wild rubber (Castilla elastica). The problem of developing these resources is one of transportation, for the dense jungle can be penetrated successfully only by mules and airplanes. A road is being built from Cobán to Flores, but is not yet completed (1941).

Guatemala has several important rivers, chief among them the Río Motagua, which flows 250 miles into the Gulf of Honduras and is navigable to within 90 miles of the capital. The Río Polochic, 180 miles long, passes through the Golfo Dulce on its way to the Gulf of Honduras and forms part of an important N waterway. The most spectacular river, the Usumacinta, formed from the Río Chixoy, the Río Lacantún, and the Río de la Pasión, flows along the Mexican border and eventually into the Gulf of Mexico.

The largest lakes in Guatemala are Lake Izabal, 36 miles long, and Lake Flores, 27 miles long, both rather inaccessible. The most beautiful is Lake Atitlán, surrounded by great volcanoes. Lake Amatitlán, small but lovely, noted for its summer homes, is only some 16 miles from Guatemala City.

Guatemala is primarily an agricultural country, with chief emphasis on coffee, bananas, sugar cane, and corn. The country is almost self-sufficient with regard to staples and imports only beef and a few other special foods. Exports consist chiefly of agricultural produce: coffee, sugar, bananas, timber, and chicle. Coffee and bananas constituted about 90 per cent of the total foreign trade in the years through 1941. The economic welfare of the country is directly tied up with the coffee market. Guatemalan coffee, some of the finest grown anywhere in the world, is used chiefly for blending purposes. All exports to the United States have increased greatly of late; in 1938 they amounted to 70 per cent of the country's total, in 1940 to 91 per cent of the total.

Very little is known about mineral deposits, which are almost entirely undeveloped. Gold has been found near Lake Izabal and along the valley of the Río Motagua, silver in the departments of Santa Rosa and Chiquimula. Salt is mined in Santa Rosa and Alta Verapaz. There are also unknown quantities of coal, iron, lead, tin, zinc, copper, sulphur, and manganese. There have been rather extensive efforts to find oil in El Petén, and surveys still continue.

INDIAN LIFE

According to the 1940 census, 55 per cent of Guatemala's 3,280,000 inhabitants are pure-blooded Indians. The rest are either pure white or of mixed blood, both locally called ladinos. Ladinos here, as elsewhere in Latin America, predominate in the fields of finance and government. It is the Indians, however, who give the country its unique and picturesque interest. The Guatemalan Indian is a dignified person, proud of his history and in many ways true to his ancient customs. Throughout the four centuries of white rule many communities of Indians have retained their racial purity, language, distinctive costumes, and much of their former religion. The Indian is usually very poor, and he cannot always be convinced that it is worth his while to do more than a very small amount of money-earning labor; but he has an honesty which is in keeping with his pride of race and the formal dignity of his life.

costume. Guatemala is one of the few countries in the Western Hemisphere in which bright native costumes persist, not only for ceremonial occasions but for everyday use. Unfortunately, it is also a country in which one can watch, month by month, the slow disintegration of native dress under inroads of cheap imports and locally made factory clothing. Formerly costumes were tribal, but with the breakdown of the old political divisions the people became village-minded rather than tribal-minded. Often villages only a few miles apart have garments wholly distinctive in coloring, weave, shape, and length, differing completely from those of neighboring villages. The experienced eye can pick out different costumes from among a confusing welter of color, but in this discussion it is not possible to go into intricacies of weave or design. The serious student of textiles is referred to Lilly de Jongh Osborne's book Guatemala Textiles.

Though the form and design of the village costume is roughly predetermined, infinite variations occur. In almost all villages certain articles are woven by hand on portable looms of the most primitive construction, while other parts of the costume are purchased from centers of native industry where slightly more developed equipment is used. For the handwoven articles no pattern is drawn, even for the most intricate design. Weavers are guided only by memory, experience, and wide imagination, with the result that each garment is completely individual. Occasionally designs are added to the garment after the weaving has been completed, as true embroideries. More often, though the same general effect is produced, patterns are worked into the fabric as weaving progresses. The tie-dye technique used for many skirt materials is a special and intricate form of design-making. To produce these patterns, a hank of yarn is tied tight at intervals and then dyed. The part of the yarn that was tied remains uncolored, and in the weaving it forms a preconceived pattern.

Many designs are symbolic, though the original meaning may have been forgotten. The double-headed eagle, often very stylized, is usually referred to the Hapsburg influence, for the reigning Spanish king at the time of the conquest was the emperor Charles V, of Germanic extraction. Also recognizable are sun and lightning symbols; figures of tigers, eagles, wasps, and hornets, and the favorite man-and-horse unit. In Chichicastenango, zigzags represent mountains; stripes are cornfields, and the diaper pattern represents corn kernels. Colors still have reference to old Maya symbolism: thus black represents weapons, which were made of black obsidian; yellow is food (corn); red is blood; blue, royal lineage.

Present-day costumes represent adaptations of those worn for generations, rather than substitutions. A fundamental change introduced by the Spaniards is the use of wool. Cotton weaving antedates the earliest records, but sheep and wool looms came with the conquerors. Though there is wide variation, the basic plan of dress is quite similar in all parts of the republic. Women's dress consists of a loose huipil or blouse and a long skirt. The huipil, the most varied and striking article of clothing, is woven in two or three straight panels and worn long or short, gathered or loose. An extra huipil is folded and thrown over the shoulder to serve as head-covering, for carrying a baby, or for wrapping food for long hauls. Perrajes or shawls are often substituted for the huipil as wrap, head-covering, or carry-all. These show great variation, but on the whole do not have the intricacy or interest of the huipil. A refajo or skirt, also varying in length and color, is worn either wrapped tight or gathered. A skirt length of material is called a corte, and this word is often used loosely to mean the skirt itself. A faja or belt of varying size, plain or figured, is wrapped around the skirt, sometimes visible, sometimes hidden under the loose blouse. Cintas or tocoyales, which are headbands, show tremendous variation, from a simple braided cord or narrow ribbon to a work of art such as that of women of Atitlán or Totonicapán, whose specialized headband is outstanding. Jewelry, especially chachales or necklaces, is worn more in some villages than in others and is often a characteristic part of the costume.

In general, men's dress has changed more in recent years than women's. Furthermore, although women retain the costume of their native village when they work on plantations or in alien villages, men away from their villages lay aside their regional costume and adopt an approximation of ladino dress. Camisas or shirts are a recent addition to men's costume, sometimes made of intricate handwoven material in bright colors and designs but more commonly of cheap cotton, imported or locally manufactured. Pantalones or trousers, often covered by a tight, short woolen skirt called ponchito or rodillera, are usually made of cotton, sometimes woven with figures. Perhaps more characteristic are the short or long tight woolen trousers, slit up the outside of the leg. Cotones or sacos, which are coats, are also adaptations of ladino costume, though local ingenuity may change them into something far more interesting, as, for example, the black and white coat of Sololá or the red of Cotzal. There is great variation in the belt or sash, called cincho or banda. Though for everyday use this is often simply a leather belt, ceremonial sashes are intricate and beautiful and must be worn in a specified fashion. The sute or tzute, a square headcloth, is gradually being replaced by the straw hat, though often both are worn, the sute beneath the hat or wound around its crown. Hats may be woven of straw or palm or fashioned from leather or wool. Zuyacales or capes are generally made of palm leaves sewed together to form a long wrap. In districts where rubber is plentiful, rain capes are made of latex; in warmer regions a wide banana leaf affords protection. The capixay, an overgarment usually of black or brown wool, is made in one piece to cover front and back and is often fringed; it may be short or long, bound at the waist or free, and is usually sleeveless. Caites are leather sandals bound simply with a thong between the toes and around the ankles. The Indian man usually carries a staff on the road and always carries a small bag to hold money and identification papers. The bag may be made of wool, sisal, or jute, in a variety of forms. Knitted bags such as are made in Sololá are both decorative and amusing.

Children's dress is usually a replica of the parents'; the little girl of the household wears a miniature of her mother's costume; it may vary from that of the township into which the mother has married. Little boys dress as their fathers do, if they do not wear long cotton trousers, shirt, and straw hat like the ladinos. The only special child's garment is a cap worn by babies, usually called gorra, often beautifully woven or embroidered. Traditionally this must be worn for the first three months of a baby's life to ward off the evil eye and it is common in the markets to see babies with caps pulled far over their eyes as protection.

MARKETS. The Indian market is more than a place to buy or sell produce. It is a great social gathering, often the only reason for a woman's leaving her house or a man's journeying from one end of the country to the other. Markets are held on different days in adjacent villages, and merchants travel from one to another. Each market specializes in the produce of the region, but local and visiting merchants bring to it all the necessaries and luxuries of the country—the corn, beans, potatoes, eggs, and pigs of the mountains; the coffee, sugar, chocolate, fruits of the lowlands; and the blankets, bags, ropes, mats, pottery, and furniture of the industrial villages. Even coffins are sold in these open markets.

Markets are strangely quiet. There is a low hum of conversation, but no strident voices raised in altercation or bickering. All produce has its proper place in an orderly scheme which may seem illogical and haphazard at first, but soon becomes evident. This scheme depends on the convenience of the merchant and not of the customer. The general plan is to group things according to source rather than character or use. It is assumed that everyone knows that choca, a spice used in sauces, comes from the north and will be found among the mats from Rabinal, while cloves, coming from Guatemala City, will be found on the dry goods stands, and that chickens, being women's business, will be found among the flowers rather than in the livestock market.

All night long preceding the opening of a market, Indians can be seen trudging along the road, loaded to capacity and often in addition driving before them recalcitrant pigs or other livestock. Women carrying babies and often with a complacent rooster or a watermelon on top of their head join the procession. Cacaxtes or square wooden frames piled high with pottery and other wares and suspended from a tumpline tower high above the heads of Indian tradesmen.

FIESTAS. Each municipality has its patron saint, as well as dozens or even scores of other saints whom it honors. The chief fiesta of any village usually celebrates its patron saint's day, though there are often additional religious fiestas of equal importance. The chief Catholic festivals—Epiphany, Holy Week and Easter, Corpus Christi, All Saints', Immaculate Conception, Christmas—are observed to a greater or lesser extent in all parts of the country.

A person entering a town where a fiesta is going on receives a first impression of overpowering noise, confusion, and color. There is a great din of marimbas, drums, and flutes playing in different sections of the town; frequent shooting off of rockets; the odor of burning copal or incense; erratic processions winding from one section of the town to another, usually bearing the image of some saint; Indians in gala attire; and sometimes a great stir and shuffle of people which may be interpreted as a dance, with the chief actors wearing red-wigged masks or animal heads. But everything has its definite and carefully prearranged place in the celebration of the fiesta. Marimbas are usually being played in a cantina or drinking place where a great crowd of Indians can be seen inside, in various stages of drunkenness, shuffling back and forth singly in the dull, repetitive dance known as El Son. Within the houses of heads of cofradías or religious brotherhoods elaborate ceremonies are taking place, and there is a procession of the cofradía's particular saint from house to house; each time the image leaves its house or enters the church, a rocket is fired. Dancers are most often dancing the Bull Dance, the Snake Dance, or the Animal Dance; the favorite above all is the dance of La Conquista, in which the red-haired conquerors play the important roles; Alvarado's red hair made a lasting impression on the Indians. Probably the significance of most of these dances has long been forgotten; as time goes on, an essential element may be dropped out or some completely irrelevant detail inserted.

THE TOWN. The municipio or township is the smallest political entity. It is also the linguistic, economic, and religious unit. Indians of a municipio think of themselves as a race of people physically and culturally distinct from their neighbors. They ordinarily marry within the municipio, dress in a characteristic fashion, and maintain a unique cultural organization. Not only from highlands to lowlands but between adjacent villages there are marked differences in customs, costume, foods, superstitions, and religious practices. Even today, 22 independent languages are spoken. Thus it is impossible to group Guatemalan Indians together in one blanket classification. Rather than attempt an overall description of different regions, the town of Santo Tomás Chichicastenango has been chosen as an example of the life of the Maya-Quiché Indian. The description of this town is based upon a study made by Dr. Ruth Bunzel, to be published under the title Guatemala Village.

There are about 1000 ladinos in the town proper. Chichicastenango is an empty village, by which is meant that most of its Indian inhabitants, estimated at 25,000, live in the adjacent hills. For five days of the week the town seems empty; the plaza is almost completely deserted, except for some few women selling corn or potatoes. Nevertheless, the Quiché is very much of the town. Though for the most part the town is merely a stage for public performances—market, fiestas, and judicial proceedings—the more important Indians maintain town houses. On Sunday, the big market day of Chichicastenango, there is much activity. Indian homes are open for the day, and their patios are full of women and children. Booths are erected, awnings and tents set up, and the plaza becomes a busy commercial center.

INDUSTRY AND AGRICULTURE. The chief industry in Chichicastenango is the weaving of woolen and cotton textiles. Bricks and tiles, tallow candles and tapers, are produced in small amount. However, the great function of men is as middlemen for other regions. They are found on every road, driving laden mules and carrying merchandise suspended from tumplines. Love of the land is the root of family life and of social structure. Land is conceived of as belonging to the ancestors. A man does not own his land; it is merely lent to him as his lodging in this world, and for it he must continually make payment in the form of candles, incense, and roses to the ancestors, the real owners. Fields have their own small shrines so that the ancestors need never be neglected.

The general rule of inheritance is division of land and other property among male children. The oldest son must remain in the ancestral home to carry on the line. Women marry and go to the homes of their husbands. Younger sons must build their own homes, sometimes on land located miles from the village. Quarrels over land are the most frequent cause of bitterness and deep resentment. Though good friends during childhood, brothers may become rivals in later life, so bitter that they practice sorcery against one another, burying bones under the doorstep, burning salt, or burying crosses marked with the victim's name, with solemn curses and incantations.

Corn and beans are the staple foods. Corn is served as tamales, tortillas, or atole, a gruel. These, with squash and potatoes, chile, salt, eggs, a little fruit, coffee, and occasionally meat, constitute the Indian's diet. Food is never regarded as a serious problem even though many Indians live at a bare subsistence level. It is unimportant compared with clothing and housing, which are the real difficulties. Fertilizers and crop rotation are used to maintain soil fertility, both practices probably learned from the Spanish. Agricultural implements are the hoe and machete. Plows are not in use; the ground is broken laboriously with a hoe and seeds dropped in and tamped down. There is an early planting in February to tide over until the main crop is ready. The big planting is in May, after the first rains. Harvest begins in September and is at its height in December. In April the fields are burned over, and the countryside is white with smoke.

There is much agricultural folklore. During earthquakes women run to the storehouse and knock at the door, calling to the corn, so that the spirit of the corn may not be frightened and run away. White and yellow corn are not allowed to lie in the same place for fear that they will mate and the ears be speckled. The farmer does not eat onions or avocado when he is planting; onions cause the corn plant to be broken by wind, for the stem of onions is soft, while avocados fill the corn with fungus.

All outside work and heavy work is done by men; women contribute cooking, washing, the tending of small animals, and weaving. The woman owns and has complete control of whatever she has made or received by inheritance or gift. If it is sold, the money is paid directly to her, even if the man has had the care of the property.

MUNICIPAL ORGANIZATION. Chichicastenango has a completely dual social organization. There is a ladino alcalde or mayor and an Indian alcalde, and each individual lives under the jurisdiction of one or the other. The ladino alcalde has supreme authority; he rules over the Indians not directly, but through the medium of their own officers. The two racial groups maintain formal relations, but the line between them is clear and sharp; they remain two separate bodies with clear distinctions of language, custom, economy, and social, religious, and political structure. The Indians have a definite schedule of service to their own community, expressed in service to the church, to the municipality, and to the cofradía or religious brotherhood. In the organization of the town, church and state are almost equally important. Whether in municipal or churchly tasks, a boy starts at the lowest grade and works up gradually toward the top rank of alcalde of the administrative or of the religious group. The highest positions carry the title of principal—that is, civil administrator—and involve helping determine town policy.

The household as a unit is liable for community service. Each year the principales prepare a list of boys eligible for public service. From this list are chosen sacristans, servants of the monastery, and alguaciles or boys who take care of streets and buildings. There are about 40 sacristans, who begin their church work at six or seven and from then on spend one week at it out of every four. During their service their families are exempt from all taxes and work levies. The boys learn to assist at the Mass and to make responses in Latin; they receive small fees at baptisms and other functions. The first manly service occurs about the age of 20, in a cofradía. This is the start on the path toward dignity and honor; it confers status and implies allotted duties. The concept of the cofradía originally derived from Seville, where the cofradía was a voluntary religious society devoted to the worship of a particular saint, and processions, when they occurred, were penitential in nature. The Guatemalan Indians have taken over the form of this group but have altered the significance so that membership in a cofradía has become a compulsory religious duty for each man in the community. Each cofradía has an image of its particular saint, which is kept in the town house of one of the alcaldes and is cared for by them in turn. The six or eight alcaldes are appointed by the principales. Serving in this capacity is merely an extension of the civic duties which little boys discharge when they take care of the appearance of the town and run errands.

There are a number of honorable learned professions. The secretary is the one person in the community who is distinguished by special dress. On formal occasions he is entitled to wear a special type of long fringed black robe which is folded and draped around the body and over the left shoulder. He is not the secretary of anything, but since he is literate he holds a lifelong position of influence and power. The kalpul or judge, a man learned in tradition, acts as mediator or arbitrator, especially in family matters. The musicians of the town comprise a special group. They are treated with great respect and are paid in money and food. Another semiprofessional group is the coheteros, the men who fire rockets at fiestas and ceremonies. Each stage in the life of an individual—birth, baptism, marriage, initiation, death—is marked by ceremonies, and at each of these there are rockets. Rockets are always fired by specialists. The coheteros have their own organization and a series of ceremonies. They also have their special patron Tsijolaj, whose fiesta comes during the All Saints' celebration.

RELIGION. Throughout the life of the Quiché runs a tangled web of superstition and taboo inherited from his ancestors and overlaid with the Christianity of the conquerors. In Chichicastenango as in no other town the commingling of the Catholic and native religion may be observed. The beautiful church and the chapel of El Calvario are devoted to the worship of the Christian God, but in addition there are several hundred shamans or medicine men who intervene for the people directly with their own pagan gods. In general Christian ceremonies are group activities, replacing the old temple worship, while pagan ceremonies are individualistic.

It can be said that Christ and the galaxy of saints has merely been added to the group of gods worshiped by the Indians. This was facilitated by the concept of the nahual held by the ancient Maya-Quiché and by the Indians of today throughout Guatemala. This is the belief that to each soul is allied some wild creature, bird or animal. This creature's misfortunes have direct consequences to the related human soul. If a man's nahual is a lynx and that lynx hurts its foot, the man will inevitably suffer an injury to his foot. When death comes it is because the nahual has died. The saints of the Catholic Church fitted nicely into this concept. It was described by the salty Thomas Gage in 1648: "Because they see some of [the saints] painted with beasts, as Hierome with a lion, Anthony with an ass, and other wild beasts, Dominic with a dog, Blas with a hog, Mark with a bull, and John with an eagle, they are the more confirmed in their delusions, and think verily those saints were of their opinion, and that those beasts were their familiar spirits, in whose shape they also were transformed when they lived and with whom they died."

Another basic idea of Guatemalan paganism is the idea of destiny incorporated in their concept of time. They use the old Maya calendar of 260 days, each of which has a special significance. The days are named and numbered, and there are good and evil days, strong and weak days. There are days that are lucky for crops or business or marriage, days on which one is in danger from sorcery. The shamans know the use of this calendar and manipulate it for their clients.

When sickness or misfortune overtakes a person, it is due to his own sin, to sorcery on the part of someone else, or to an act of the gods. It is the function of the shaman, through ceremonies and divination, to interpret events and foretell the future, to diagnose the cause and conduct the cure. So completely is this state of affairs accepted that the shamans practice their profession even on the steps of the church itself, where their fragrant copal incense burns almost constantly.

Title to the church building in Chichicastenango is held by the Indian municipality, which is responsible for its maintenance. Although the Dominicans were expelled with the other religious orders in 1871, their monastery here is still maintained in good condition as the residence of the parish priest, and each district contributes yearly a certain amount of corn, firewood, and fodder for the animals kept at the monastery. The cost of Masses and processions for certain important fiestas is also borne by the Indian municipality. Expenses of other fiestas are borne by the cofradías, from $50 for a small one up to $250 for a large one.

There are practically no church marriages. Since the law requires a civil marriage and the Indians cannot afford both, they have neither. Instead, they have a series of formal negotiations between the prospective bridegroom and the bride's parents. Neither are there any church funerals. However, every child who lives any length of time is baptized. The church is not merely a place to visit on state occasions; it is very much a part of each Indian's life. At all times of the day and often at night there are groups in the church, praying, lighting candles, and burning incense. In addition, there are altars and shrines everywhere around the town, along the roads, in the woods, on any hillside.

Food and drink play a very important part in all ceremonies. The ceremonial gift or sacrifice is always food; eating and drinking constitute a major part of the ritual. First place as ceremonial food is accorded to cacao; its presence on the table is a guarantee that one is following in the ways of the ancestors. Cacao is a taboo tree. The myth about it is the only one told in Chichicastenango. This relates that when Jesus was being pursued by His enemies, He took refuge under a cacao tree, and the tree let fall a blanket of white blossoms over Him and concealed Him, wherefore Jesus blessed the tree and decreed that its wood should never be used for firewood and that its seed should be on the table at all ceremonies.

ART AND ARCHITECTURE

BY ROBERT C. SMITH

Colonial architecture in Guatemala had a development distinct from that of Mexico to the north, a development that had a direct influence on the local schools of Central America to the south. Time and again the land suffered from earthquakes, until finally in the catastrophe of 1773 the city of Antigua was nearly obliterated. This series of disasters had its effect upon the national architecture. As a result what might be termed an earthquake style or better an anti-earthquake style was produced. To safeguard buildings against destruction walls were constructed of unusual thickness and were often reinforced with solid buttresses. Low, compact structures were the rule, and architectural elements were correspondingly small. A typical church façade is that of La Merced of 1760 in Antigua, which has miraculously remained unharmed. The angle towers, placed wide apart, are low and solid. The columns of the frontispiece are short and stocky. The arch above the central window is broad and depressed. In comparison with such a contemporary structure as the church at Taxco in Mexico the whole façade looks as though it had been sawed off. Most of the churches of the region conform to this pattern. Angle towers, rare in the area, are correspondingly low at the church of San José in Antigua and at the cathedral of Almolonga. The same diminutive columns on high bases are found at the ruined churches of Santa Cruz, El Carmen, San José, La Candelaria, and San Juan de Dios and in the cloister of the Escuela de Cristo, where short pilasters are placed above to increase the vertical accent. Similar broad, depressed arches were used in other church façades, the mighty galleries of the palace of the captains general, the arch of Santa Catalina, and the ruined cloisters of Santa Clara, La Merced, and the Escuela de Cristo. Again it is interesting to contrast these latter buildings with courtyards and cloisters in Mexico and Cuba, where, as the 18th century wore on, there was a tendency to exaggerate the height of the arches. That Guatemalan buildings, though low, could be designed on a vast plan is proved by the large area covered by these same cloisters and conventual buildings. An exception to this general convention of low proportions is found in the lofty 18th-century façade of the Antigua church of San Francisco, where the façade columns are exceptionally elongated, and in the high vaults of this church and of the cathedral itself, which, as was to be expected, were among the buildings most seriously damaged by the earthquake of 1773.

The Antigua churches possess several interesting local ornamental characteristics. In general it may be said that they are unusually colorful. Multicolored tiles were not used here as they were in Mexico, but the buildings were frequently painted in a variety of brilliant hues. Hence the local architecture has a close affinity to the provincial Mediterranean Baroque, especially the Portuguese. This peculiarity may be connected in some way with the colorful fabrics of the local Indians. The architects of the region in their church façades frequently used groups of coupled columns surmounted by individual pediments or segments of arches (El Carmen, La Santa Cruz, San Francisco). These columns, generally built of brick, are often covered with vigorous plaster decorations, highly individual but lacking in delicacy. At La Merced there are spirals and masks in the upper order, a twisted vine with curious pendant flowers in the lower. These patterns fill the friezes of the entablatures, penetrate the moldings and the soffits of windows and doors, and sprawl across every inch of the flat wall surface (El Carmen, La Merced, La Santa Cruz). This all-over low-relief decoration may be a crude reflection of an element of Maya design. At La Santa Cruz the columns are given highly ornamented exotic ogee bases which in turn are complemented by ogee forms in the entablature above. Occasionally, however, columns are omitted altogether from a church façade, as at the cathedral of Almolonga, Santa Clara in Antigua, or the provincial church of Chiquimula, where what might be described as contorted banisters or superposed urns are substituted. This peculiarity has been explained as the result of imitation of the title pages of Spanish books printed in the 16th and 17th centuries, where this motive occurs with great frequency, framing a series of niches holding figures of saints exactly as on these church façades. It should be remembered, however, that this is one of the principal elements of the so-called Churrigueresque Baroque of Mexico, where it culminated in the buildings of Lorenzo Rodríguez. Other local elements of design at Antigua are the use of a prominent splayed window or portal, necessary for such thick walls, given perspective decoration by a series of radiating lines (La Merced, Santa Teresa, San Juan de Dios, El Carmen, La Candelaria) and by doorways in the form of ogee and other exotic arches. The trefoil arch motive is found in pure mudéjar or Spanish Moorish form in the arcade of the beautiful cloister of the old university of San Carlos, now the museum of Antigua.

Indigenous influence is rare in colonial Guatemalan architecture beyond the examples already cited. Occasional low-relief angels with markedly Indian physiognomy and stylized gestures are found in the spandrels of the arched portal at La Santa Cruz and in the pendentives of the dome of the ruined cathedral at Antigua. Both are reminiscent of the colonial Andean style in Peru and Bolivia. The large pointed leaves in the spandrels of façade arches at Santa Teresa and La Merced at Antigua are a realistic touch that betrays Indian influence.

Very few secular buildings survived the great earthquake in Antigua. The two fine government structures in the Plaza de Armas follow the classic double arcade model of the typical Spanish and Portuguese American cabildo or city hall. Neither, however, possesses a central façade belltower, so common in such buildings elsewhere in Latin America. Of these buildings the finer is undoubtedly the palace of the captains general, notable for its well-articulated piers and bold cornice designed to suggest crenelation. The building was completed in 1764, on plans of the military architect, J. Diez de Navarro. La Casa de los Leones (House of the Lions) has an unusual angle window with sculptured post and stone window seat which seems to have been another feature of the local architecture, for it is found in several colonial houses of Antigua. This motive was occasionally copied elsewhere in Central America. In the ruins of the 17th-century hospital of Belén extensive gardens typical of the period have been cultivated.

The new capital, Guatemala City, was constructed in the correct neo-classic style of the later 18th century under the direction of the Spanish architect Marcos Ibáñez (1738-84). His masterpiece was the noble cathedral of Guatemala City, begun by him in 1784, but completed in 1815 by another architect, Santiago Marqui. It is a large, well-proportioned building of local golden stone decorated with the rare Composite order. Stylistically it is closely related to the severe rectilinear architecture of the cathedrals of Montevideo and Santiago de Chile, prime examples of the classical revival. The other churches retained in general the proportions of those at Antigua, but in spite of this they were severely damaged in the earthquakes of 1917-18. The church of Santo Domingo (1792-1802), by Pedro Garci-Aguirre, is in a sense a small reflection of the cathedral. Palladio's distinctive Renaissance style served as model for the churches of San Francisco and La Merced (1813); the latter recalls especially San Giorgio Maggiore in Venice. It has a cold, handsome cupola covered with modern yellow tiles. At present the colonial style in somewhat simplified form is enjoying a revival in Guatemala, thanks to such buildings as the Secretaría de Obras Públicas (Public Works) by Pérez de León (1940) and the beautiful houses of Roberto Durón in the Aurora district.

Guatemala early in the colonial period became a center for ecclesiastical wood sculpture. By 1543 a large amount was being sent annually to Mexico. The majority of these figures, designed slightly under life size, were cut from a single block of wood taken not from the trunk but from the roots of such trees as cedar, sapodilla, and tacisco. The wood was seasoned for four years under water and then exposed to the sun for two more. After being carved it was covered with gesso and then gold or silver leaf and finally painted by a special enamel process. Stylistically this sculpture followed closely Spanish Baroque models; there was almost no Indian influence. Some critics find in it, however, a local poignancy and special delicacy of expression.

One of the inaugurators of the school of Antigua was Juan de Aguirre, who came from Spain via Lima. His masterpiece, Christ with the Cross, of 1563, can be seen in the church of La Candelaria in Guatemala City. His contemporary, Quirio Cataño, born in Antigua, made the famous miraculous Christ for the sanctuary of Esquipulas (1595) and the Christ of Compassion in the Antigua cathedral. All three of these works are absorbing Renaissance interpretations. More Baroque are those of the celebrated Alonzo de la Paz (1605-76), author of the realistic, haunting Christ with the Cross of the church of La Merced at Antigua and the technically brilliant San Francisco de Paula of the Guatemala City cathedral, the San Pedro Nolasco at La Merced, and the St. Joseph of the Dominican church in Guatemala City. The 18th-century Evaristo Zúñiga's genius for the pathetic is revealed in his masterpiece, a Virgin of Sorrows, now at the church of La Merced in the capital. Colonial art works from Antigua are often removed to Guatemala City, to the churches there and to the colonial museum.

Less interesting were the colonial painters of Antigua, Tomás Merlo, Antonio de Montúfar, and Francisco de Villalpando of the 17th century, whose works may best be studied at the colonial museum in Guatemala City. In the mid-18th century José de Valladares worked for the great church of La Merced at Antigua, where his 1759 Apotheosis, the largest painting in Guatemala, is preserved. In 1797 a school of drawing was opened in the capital under the direction of the distinguished engraver and architect, Pedro Garci-Aguirre. His best-known pupil was the miniaturist Francisco Cabrera (1780-1845), who painted in the style of Ingres the beautiful cosmopolitan early 19th-century world of Guatemala, ladies and gentlemen of the families of Batres, Montúfar, and Aycinena. Most of these miniatures have remained in Guatemalan private collections.

A modern school of painting in Guatemala is still in process of formation. Carlos Mérida, its most brilliant element, lives permanently outside the country. When he returned from Paris to Mexico in 1920, a year before Diego Rivera's historic return, he brought with him the ingredients of a new style, based upon Maya forms and tropical color. Entirely without modeling but strongly outlined in white, he presented the beautiful forms and patterns of Indian figures and landscape, put together with the most delicate geometric balance. Less spectacular than some of his Mexican contemporaries, Mérida has produced watercolors, book illustrations, and albums of the dances and the costumes of Guatemala and Mexico. Having passed through a period of profound abstraction, he is now entering a kind of Baroque phase, using for his principal inspiration the ceramic figurines of pre-conquest Mexico. Mérida has had practically no influence in Guatemala. Native painting has not yet reacted from the realist-Impressionist habit of painting picturesque Indians in picturesque costumes. The work of such men as Humberto Garavito and Alfredo Suárez, which is primarily illustrative, is occasionally exhibited at the Academia de Bellas Artes in Guatemala City. The director of this school, Yela Gunther, is a conservative sculptor who has continued the old Guatemalan tradition of woodcarving.

PRACTICAL INFORMATION

HOW TO REACH GUATEMALA

From the U. S. Minimum first-class one-way steamship fare (1941) from New York City to Puerto Barrios is $100; from New Orleans, $60. One-way plane fare from Brownsville, Tex., to Guatemala City is $88; from Los Angeles, $157.

BY STEAMER. United Fruit Co.; main office: Pier 3, North River, New York; New Orleans office: 321 St. Charles St. Sailings from New York via Havana, Cuba, and Tela or Puerto Cortés, Honduras, in alternate weeks; voyage takes 6 days. Sailings also from New York via Kingston, Jamaica; Cristóbal, C. Z.; and Puerto Limón, C. R., returning to New York via Havana; cruise takes 12 days. Sailings from New Orleans to Puerto Barrios; voyage takes 3 days.

BY PLANE. Pan American Airways; main office: 135 E. 42nd St., New York. The Mexico Flyer leaves Brownsville, Tex., for Guatemala City via Tampico, Mexico City, and Tapachula, Mexico; trip takes 8½ hours; continues from Guatemala City to other Central and South American countries. Two other plane services, one from Los Angeles and one from Miami, also reach Mexico City, where transfer can be made to the Pan American Airways lines. See guide to Mexico (p. 34).

BY RAILROAD. To Mexico City, where the National Railways of Mexico gives connections to Suchiate, near the Guatemalan border; trip takes 2 days. The Mexican and Guatemalan railroad systems do not connect (1941). It is necessary to cross the Río Suchiate in a small boat, then walk about half a mile to Ayutla, Guatemala, where the International Railways of Central America start. Baggage is rechecked at this point. An overnight stop is necessary at Suchiate or Ayutla. The trip from Ayutla to Guatemala City takes about 10 hours.

BY AUTOMOBILE. There is no through road from the United States to Guatemala City, since a long stretch of the Pan American Highway route in lower Mexico is impassable (1941). A car can be shipped from Mexico City to Tapachula, Mexico, in a box car, which can be arranged for only at Mexico City. Alternatively, a car can be driven as far as Córdoba, Mexico, and then shipped to Tapachula, but no box cars can be obtained in Córdoba; therefore there is often a long delay. From Tapachula to the Guatemalan border (9 miles) the road is paved. From the border to Guatemala City is 195½ miles by all-weather dirt road.

From Mexico. Services as indicated above.

From Other Central American Countries. United Fruit Co. and Pan American Airways services as indicated above. Also occasional sailings by other companies from Cristóbal, C. Z., to San José and Champerico.

The International Railways of Central America connect Cutuco on the Gulf of Fonseca and San Salvador, the capital of El Salvador, with Guatemala City; actual trip takes 17 hours, with 17 hours stop in Zacapa, Guatemala.

The Pan American Highway between San Salvador and Guatemala City is an all-weather road.

AIDS TO TRAVELERS

Guatemala's Representation in the U. S. The Guatemalan Legation is at 1614 18th St., Washington, D. C. Consuls and vice-consuls are found in Mobile, Ala.; Los Angeles, Oakland, and San Francisco, Calif.; Miami and Tampa, Fla.; Chicago, Ill.; New Orleans, La.; Baltimore, Md.; Boston, Mass.; St. Louis, Mo.; New York; Portland, Ore.; Philadelphia, Pa.; Brownsville, Dallas, Galveston, and Houston, Tex.; Seattle, Wash.; Balboa and Cristóbal, C. Z.; San Juan, P. R.

U. S. Representation in Guatemala. The U. S. Legation is in Guatemala City, at the N end of Bulevar La Reforma; the Consulate General, at 4 Avenida Sur No. 14. There are no U. S. consuls in other cities.

Sources of Information. Within the United States the Guatemalan consulates, travel agencies, and the United Fruit Co. or Pan American Airways offices are helpful. In Guatemala City the National Tourist Committee, at 6 Avenida Norte No. 6, an agency of the Secretariat of Foreign Relations (Relaciones Exteriores), under the direction of Delfino Sánchez Latour, is organized to help visitors in every way. Clark's Tours, on 12 Calle Poniente, next to the Palace Hotel, handles all shore excursions for the United Fruit Co. and is equipped with every kind of information.

Climate. There are only two seasons in Guatemala, dry and wet. The dry season is November-May; then the rains begin and the country becomes green. The rainy season, May-November, is wettest during the months of June and September. During June-July, rains occur usually in the afternoon. Rainfall varies greatly from region to region and is especially heavy on the Atlantic seaboard. In Guatemala City the average is about 50 inches a year. In spite of the rains, the sun is said to shine 2250 hours during the year, which is an average of more than 6 hours a day.

On both coasts it is hot and damp, with a mean temperature of 80° F., but the highlands are agreeable at all seasons, and the nights are always cool. There is little temperature variation during the year. In Guatemala City, for example, the average is 60° F. for the coldest months, December-January, and only 67° for the hottest, March-April.

Clothing. If a stay of some length at either coast is intended, tropical clothing should be included in the wardrobe. In the highlands, men usually wear light-weight clothing at all seasons. A light-weight top-coat is useful in the evenings during December-January A raincoat is necessary during the wet season.

Clothing worn by women in the highlands is similar to that worn during spring and fall in the United States, light-weight woolen dresses, sports clothing, and afternoon dresses. A raincoat and umbrella for the rainy season and a topcoat for all seasons are essential. During the dry months a coat similar to the old-fashioned duster is useful, since dust on the roads is very troublesome and enters even closed cars. Flat-heeled walking shoes should be carried. Open sandals are discouraged since a vicious little insect known as the nigua bores under the skin of the toes and causes great trouble. Informal clothes such as playsuits and slacks look ridiculous to Guatemalans on city or village streets.

Health. In general, health and sanitation are good. The two dread diseases of smallpox and yellow fever have been eradicated. Measures are being taken to combat malaria, which is confined to the low regions, and hookworm, acquired only by those who go barefoot; the foundation for this work has been laid under President Jorge Ubico's direction. Since 1934 there has been a widening of scope and authority by the national Department of Public Health (Sanidad Pública), including dispensaries for remote regions, sanitary inspection of foods and their handling, and special sanitary commissions in most of the departments. The Department of Public Health in Guatemala City gives inoculations and vaccinations and has modern equipment.

There are 19 government hospitals, located in the capitals of the departments. Independently owned and U. S.-operated hospitals of the United Fruit Co. are at Quiriguá and Tiquisate. In Guatemala City is the American Hospital, partially supported by the Presbyterian Board of Foreign Missions; it maintains traveling clinics which visit various parts of the republic each year.

There are many doctors and dentists of good standing, most of them in Guatemala City. The majority are Guatemalans who have had at least part of their training in the United States.

If travel is to be confined to the usual routes and larger cities, there is practically no danger from typhoid or dysentery. In all major restaurants and hotels food is well cooked; water and milk are filtered or boiled. On the other hand, if out-of-the-way places are to be visited, it is probably best to take typhoid injections and also to carry various antidysentery medicines and chlorinated tablets to purify water. Fruits and vegetables that do not have a thick peel, such as strawberries and lettuce, always constitute a hazard when eaten raw.

Sports and Recreations. GOLF. There are two golf clubs within easy reach of Guatemala City: the Guatemala Country Club, 5 miles from midtown, and the Maya Golf Club, 3 miles from town. Arrangements can be made to play at either club through sponsorship by a member. Hotels, the United Fruit Co., Pan American Airways, Clark's Tours, and other agencies will arrange for such sponsorship.

TENNIS. The Tennis Club in the heart of Guatemala City, at 15 Calle Poniente No. 28, offers tennis and swimming. Access to the club is secured in the same way as to the country clubs.

SWIMMING. There is good swimming at Lake Amatitlán and Lake Atitlán; at the ports of San José, Puerto Barrios, and Champerico; and at Iztapa, where there is both salt- and fresh-water bathing. Guatemala City has several good pools: San Antonio, at 8 Avenida Norte (prolongation); Sauce, at 1 Calle Poniente (prolongation); Lo de Bran, at 3 C.P. (prolongation); El Tuerto, at 10 C. Oriente (prolongation); Ciudad Vieja, at 12 Av. S (prolongation). Hot springs are widely patronized both for sport and medicinal purposes, especially at Escuintla, Antigua, Chimaltenango, Fuentes Georginas, and Almolonga near Quezaltenango. There is a swimming pool at Chichicastenango, but the journey to reach it overshadows the pool itself.

RACES are held in Parque Aurora, Guatemala City, during the National Fair in November, and also in Antigua at La Recolección racetrack. Especially during the fair, good horses are brought from adjoining countries, and competition is keen. Motorcycle and bicycle races are frequent throughout the year.

THE LOTTERY is government-sponsored, the proceeds being used to maintain the National Orphanage. Drawings normally occur on the first Sunday of each month, open to the public, at 10 Avenida and 9 Calle in Guatemala City. Tickets with a full face value of $4 (1941) are sold in eight parts, each costing $.50. The grand prize is $16,000, and there are many lesser prizes. Four times a year, in January, April, July, and October, tickets cost $6, and the prize is $30,000. Winning ticket numbers are listed at the lottery office, in newspapers, and with the many ticket vendors on the streets.

PHOTOGRAPHY. People, scenery, and color are a real challenge to the photographer. It is very important to have an exposure meter, since lights and shadows in brilliant sunshine are very deceptive, and pictures are usually overexposed. Filters, too, are required, since many of the most beautiful effects are those of clouds, smoke, etc. Films can be brought into the country in moderate amount and can also be bought and developed in Guatemala City; equipment and service may be secured there of Beiner, 6 Avenida Sur No. 3; Eichenberger, 6 Av. S. No. 5; and Foto Serra, 6 Av. S. No. 11.

RIDING is a major recreation in Guatemala City, where there are several good stables and an infinite number of trails through the parks and adjoining countryside. Good horses can also be secured at the hotels at Lake Atitlán and at Chichicastenango. For long trips mules or horses are usually obtained through local municipal officers.

FISHING is good off both coasts, at Puerto Barrios on the Atlantic and San José or Iztapa on the Pacific. Iztapa especially is becoming a favorite vacation resort with Guatemalans. Deep-sea fishing is very good at Puerto Barrios, where it is held to be equal to that off the Florida coast. Boats and guides can be hired on either coast for about $5 a day (1941). There are tarpon, barracuda, sailfish, and sometimes giant ray; also jackfish, snook, mullet, bonito, and red snapper. Fish are plentiful in Lake Petén-Itzá, Lake Izabal, and the Río Dulce, all rather inaccessible. Most of the lakes of the country are fed by volcanic waters which do not favor the growth of fish. Lake Amatitlán has mojarra, a small fish of good flavor, and at Lake Atitlán there are in addition triponcito, pepezca, and fresh-water crabs.

HUNTING is very good in the wooded areas—almost any woods, picked at random from the map. It would be hard to miss getting satisfactory returns almost anywhere outside of Guatemala City if a good guide is chosen and expectations are not too high. El Petén, of course, is the wildest region, but it is hard to reach. The back country of Huehuetenango and the district bordering on Honduras are heavily wooded, and the Cobán region is rich in game.

There are deer in all parts of the country, but they are naturally commoner in the less settled areas. There are two kinds, both more like what U. S. hunters call antelopes than deer, one small and reddish, and the other larger and tan in color. Wild turkeys, doves of many kinds, chachalacas or pheasants, peccaries, and monkeys are fairly easy to find. Jaguar, tapir, and puma are rarer. Duck hunting near San José is good in October-December, at the end of the rainy season. There are crocodiles on the Río Dulce.

If the traveler is fortunate enough to be invited to a finca or plantation, he can hunt under the most favorable circumstances. Such invitations cannot be paid for, but depend entirely on personal contacts.

There is a closed season on large game, except dangerous and destructive species, September-January. It is not always possible to get permits for .30 caliber rifles or for .45 revolvers. Shotguns and .22 rifles are adequate for most hunting and require no permits. Permits must be secured before bringing firearms into the country, and hunting licenses must be arranged for with authorities at Guatemala City or on the coast. Shooting the quetzal, Guatemala's emblematic bird, is forbidden.

MOUNTAIN CLIMBING. To climb volcanoes, go to the nearest large town at the foot of the mountain and ask for guides and mules.

The volcano Agua, 12,307 feet, is the most frequently climbed, and a rest house has been built inside the crater for hikers. Most people go up in the evening (5 hours), spend the night there, and wake before dawn to see the sunrise and the shadow of Agua on neighboring Fuego. It is cold, and there is no water; provisions must be taken along. The trip starts from Santa María de Jesús, where guides and horses can be secured.

The climb of Acatenango, 12,986 feet, starts from Calderas, a coffee plantation reached by car from Antigua. The trip takes about 8 hours.

Fuego, 12,851 feet, is usually reached from adjacent Acatenango. However, the climb can also be started from Alotenango, near Antigua.

Pacaya, 8345 feet, is most quickly reached from the village of San Vicente on its slope. A more sporting climb is from Calderas.

Atitlán, 11,499 feet, is climbed from San Lucas Tolimán in about 10 hours. Tolimán, 10,750 feet, is reached from the same town in about 6 hours.

Santa María, 12,361 feet, is reached from Quezaltenango via Suipache. Zunil, 11,590 feet, is ascended starting from the town of Zunil.

Tajumulco, 13,812 feet, and Tacaná, 13,332 feet, are both ascended starting from San Marcos.

ROUGHING IT. Travel in out-of-the-way rural districts in the dry season is highly recommended to the more adventurous and adaptable who delight in discoveries. Villages in the highlands are not far apart, and there is always something to eat, though the only food that can be counted on is tortillas, beans, eggs, and coffee—monotonous but filling. If this does not seem adequate, it is necessary to carry supplies. In a village of any size, the kindly townsfolk will always provide food—not because their hospitality can be bought, but because they wish to. Often a roll of bills is the worst possible introduction to a community, though a tactful offer of payment for services should not be omitted. Water is a problem. Chlorinated tablets are sold in the United States which will purify water, but the taste is a little unpleasant. Perhaps easier is to carry a canteen of boiled water.

Warm bedding should be taken, including a mattress, if a solid wooden or earth bed does not seem soft enough. Instead of traveling with a pack animal, it is easier and quicker to send equipment from town to town by native porters, who can be secured through municipal officers. These porters are cheap and dependable; they never lose things along the way. It will be necessary to change porters and perhaps guides at each day's end, but town officials will always provide local men for the next lap of a journey.

Passers-by on the roads always compute in leagues. By taking several such observations and averaging them, some idea can be obtained of the length of the journey. In general, a league (3 miles) an hour is all that can be counted on.

The mules and horses are sturdy. They eat grass and corn in wet seasons, zacate or corn fodder in dry seasons. On a journey of any length corn should be carried for the animals, for there is no certainty that one will find it at the day's end unless a fair-sized village is reached. A mule or horse will need 2-4 pounds of corn a day.

Currency. The official monetary standard of Guatemala is the quetzal, which exchanges at par for the U. S. dollar (1941). The quetzal (written Q) is divided into 100 parts called centavos. Coins are of ½, 1, and 2 centavos in brass and 5, 10, and 25 centavos in silver. Paper money is issued in notes worth 50 centavos and 1, 2, 5, 10, 20, and 50 quetzales. There is no charge for exchange. Guatemalan currency will be exchanged for U. S. currency at the Banco Central de Guatemala, in Guatemala City, also without charge.

Especially among Indians, the peso is still spoken of, though there are no peso coins; 60 pesos equal 1 quetzal. The real is sometimes mentioned; it corresponds to ⅛ peso. These obsolete units add confusion to bartering with Indians, but usually some helpful bystander will translate into terms of centavos.

Cost of Living and Travel. Expense of hotels, transportation, and so on (1941) come to about $75 a month if the traveler lives modestly and uses buses. In a pensión or boarding house, traveling little, a stay of some duration may cost $40-$60 a month, without allowing for clothing or incidentals.

Cars with drivers can be rented from Clark's Tours in Guatemala City for about $15-$20 a day and are not expensive for group travel. The taxis which stand on the S side of Parque Central can be rented somewhat cheaper for short or long trips. The cost of driving one's own car is about the same as in the United States, with the difference that gasoline and oil are somewhat more expensive. Repairs are approximately the same as in the United States; inexpensive labor and expensive materials cancel out. The cost of garaging a car in Guatemala City is about $5 a month.

Banks. Practically all banking is concentrated in the Banco Central de Guatemala, the only bank of issue. Its headquarters are at 7 Avenida and 9 Calle, Guatemala City; there are branches in the important cities of the country. An English-language bank in Guatemala City is the Bank of London and South America, at 9 C. Oriente No. 4. At these banks one may cash letters of credit and do general banking business. There are no U. S. banks in Guatemala. Banking hours are 9 a.m.-12 m. and 2-4 p.m. on weekdays, 9-11 a.m. on Saturdays.

Transportation. ROADS. The Pan American Highway (Carretera Internacional) is open to all-year traffic throughout its entire 300 miles (483 km.) in the republic of Guatemala. It is the most important of all highways in the country, since it forms the backbone of the highway system. Running W-E, it passes through the principal centers of population, connects the capital with the important towns of the interior, and gives access to the intensively cultivated central districts dependent entirely on highways for transportation. The highway is of historical and archeological interest as it follows practically the same route that the Spaniards took during the conquest. Its termini are at the Talismán bridge on the Mexican border and San Cristóbal Frontera on the Salvadorean border. In 1938 all highways in Guatemala were classified and given numbers according to their importance. The Pan American Highway was divided into W and E sections, numbered

Routes 1 and 2 respectively. At the close of 1941, Guatemala had about 3900 miles of roads, of which some 400 were macadamized. About half the roads are serviceable throughout the year. Apart from the Pan American Highway, the most important Rutas Nacionales (National Routes) are Route 3, Guatemala City to San José; Route 4, with 121 miles now open, which runs out of Guatemala City and will eventually reach Puerto Barrios; Route 5, with 190 miles now open, which runs N out of Guatemala City and will reach El Petén.

AUTOMOBILES. Clark's Tours, on 12 Calle Poniente near the Palace Hotel in Guatemala City, manages the Guatemalan end of the United Fruit Co. tours through which most visitors today see Guatemala. Standard trips of 3½ or 7 days are made through the highlands in luxurious cars with expert chauffeurs and guides. Longer tours can be arranged, either before leaving the United States or after reaching Guatemala. Clark's Tours also arranges all details of special trips anywhere in the country.

Bringing one's own car is easiest from Mexico. See notes under How to Reach Guatemala: By Automobile (p. 26). By ship from the United States, a car can be sent cheapest to San José, on Guatemala's Pacific coast. The charges for a light car are $180-$200 (1941). From San José to Guatemala City there is a good road.

On entering Guatemala, a deposit is required covering duty on the car. This amount is refunded when the car leaves Guatemala. The amount of duty is calculated at 20 per cent of the cost up to $1000, with 1 per cent increase for each $100 of value over $1000, minus a given amount for depreciation: 20 per cent for one year; 30 per cent for two years; 40 per cent for three years and over. Customs inspection takes place at Guatemala City. Getting a car into and out of the country is facilitated by using the services of agencias de aduanas or customhouse agencies, several of which are located near the customhouse in Guatemala City.

It is well to find out before leaving the United States whether an insurance company will cover a car that is to be driven in Central America; probably it will not cover it.

An automobile map of the republic is issued by the national highway commission, Dirección General de Caminos, 7 Avenida and 17 Calle, Guatemala City, under the direction of Gen. Miguel Ydigoras Fuentes. A road map by Rubio is for sale at stationery stores in Guatemala City.

International driving licenses are not recognized in Guatemala; however, upon presentation of a U. S. driving license, a local license will be issued without the necessity of taking a road test. U. S. license plates may be used for 30 days. After that the car must be registered in Guatemala.

The freedom-loving and adventurous traveler will find his own car a great convenience, permitting trips that would be very expensive by hired car. However, driving in Guatemala is not for the timid; preferably a driver should have a background of mountain driving. In the rainy season, chains must be carried and perhaps a tow line. There is a law against driving through towns with chains on; they must be removed before entering any town. During the rainy season the secondary roads are often deeply rutted and pitted, which endangers axles and demands relatively high clearance. Traffic laws in the large cities must be investigated; they are very different from those in the United States.

BUS SERVICE is widespread. Camionetas or buses and camionetas de sport or station wagons provide service at very low rates between Guatemala City and all important towns of the republic. Prices are not standardized but are a matter of individual agreement between the passenger and the bus company. For example, from the capital to Quezaltenango the trip may cost $.75-$2. In general, higher price means faster service.

These buses are only for the hardy. The driver may pick up his passengers as early as 4 a.m. It is bad form to object to waiting while one passenger finishes his breakfast or another is routed out of bed. The bus is sometimes hours late in starting; it may stall in transit or break down in the mud. On the other hand all buses seem to arrive without serious accident. The drivers are expert and completely good-natured. Perhaps there is no way of seeing the country and the people in it, no way of appreciating their patience and courage and friendliness, that can equal a 12-hour trip from one town to another with 10-30 fellow travelers. Spanish is spoken; there is seldom anyone who can speak English. Stops are made for breakfast and lunch.

Some of the larger bus lines in Guatemala City are those of Valerio Letona, at 10 Calle Oriente No. 8; La Sonrisa, 19 C. Poniente No. 36; León y González, 10 C.O. No. 11; and Garage Guatemala, 7 Avenida Sur No. 14.

RAILROADS. The International Railways of Central America (Ferrocarriles Internacionales de Centro América—IRCA) operates 795 miles (1280 km.) of track over three main routes.

From Puerto Barrios, on the Atlantic, to Guatemala City the train passes through Zacapa, where connections are made for San Salvador, the capital of El Salvador, and through El Rancho, where there is a bus connection to Cobán. The trip from Puerto Barrios to Guatemala City takes 10½ hours. There is no dining car on the train. A stop is made for lunch at Zacapa.

From San José, on the Pacific, to Guatemala City, the fast train takes about 5 hours.

Between Guatemala City and Ayutla, at the Mexican border, where a change can be made to the National Railways of Mexico, the trip takes about 10 hours. Meals are not served on the train, which passes through Santa María, Mazatenango, and Retalhuleu. Connections can be made to San Antonio; San Felipe, near Quezaltenango; and the Pacific ports of Champerico and Ocós.

The IRCA station in Guatemala City is at 10 Avenida and 18 Calle. Tickets and information are also obtainable at the ticket office at 12 C. Poniente No. 4; at Palace Hotel and Hotel San Carlos Gran; and at Ascoli & Co. in Hotel Astoria.

The Ferrocarril Verapaz operates a N rail-and-water route that gives connections between Cobán and Puerto Barrios, through the beautiful Lake Izabal and Río Dulce waterways. The trip takes a minimum of 2 days, with overnight stops at both Panzós and Livingston unless a special boat is hired for the stretch beyond Livingston. The distance from Cobán to Pancajché is covered by bus, from Pancajché to Panzós by bus or train. From Panzós to Livingston takes 8½ hours on one boat; another boat leaves Livingston several times weekly, arriving at Puerto Barrios in 1½ hours. The Guatemala City agent for the Ferrocarril Verapaz is Sapper and Co., at 10 C.P. No. 3.

AIR TRANSPORT. Aerovías de Guatemala (Guatemalan Airlines) maintains bi-weekly schedules on three routes: W route, Guatemala City to Santa Cruz Quiché, with intermediate stops at Quezaltenango, Huehuetenango, and Retalhuleu; N route, Guatemala City to La Tinta, via Rabinal, Salamá, and Cobán; El Petén route, Guatemala City to Puerto Barrios, via Flores, Paso Caballos, Carmelita, Uaxactún, and Dos Lagunas, all in El Petén. Rates are reasonable. By special arrangement, trips are made by air to Copán in Honduras, the site of some of the greatest Maya ruins in this whole area.

Postage. Regular mail between the United States and Guatemala takes 10-14 days. From the United States it costs $.03 an ounce; airmail, $.12 a half ounce, taking 2-4 days for delivery (1941). From Guatemala regular mail is $.04 for 20 grams, airmail $.19 for 10 grams (1/3 oz.); it is illegal to send money in letters. The only express service in Guatemala is air express; other parcels must be sent as mail or as freight, preferably by ship.

Telegraph and Cable Services. Cables may be sent from Guatemala City by the Tropical Radio Co., at 12 Calle Oriente No. 16, or All America Cables, at 6 Avenida between 9 C. and 10 C. If a message is sent from a remote point in Guatemala, there is no additional charge for telegraph service to Guatemala City if the sender specifically marks the message for transmission by either of these cable companies.

All points of the republic are connected by telegraph service, which is both fast and reliable.

Telephones. The local dial telephone system in Guatemala City is owned by the government. Long-distance service is also maintained to many points in the country. Distant points, such as cities in the United States, can be reached from Guatemala City only, by radio-telephone of the Tropical Radio Co., at 12 Calle Oriente No. 16.

Souvenirs and Handicrafts. Baskets, pottery, and silver are made in Guatemala, but by far the finest handicraft is the weaving of textiles, in which the Indians excel. Locally grown wool and cotton are the bases of weaving, though imported cotton, silk, and rayon are sometimes found and are often used to accent the duller fabrics. Many Guatemalan Indian towns have costumes which vary in design, fabric, weave, and shape from those of other towns. After some experience, one can differentiate between costumes and can tell from them the wearer's town and perhaps even his family. Even though in some regions there is an increasing manufacture of articles for tourists, often of inferior design and weave, fine weaving remains a matter of extreme pride, and as a rule the Indians buy or make the finest garments they can afford. There is, however, a rapidly accelerating abandonment of the native garments in favor of cheap cotton machine-made shirts and trousers, and in some regions the traditional costume is now seen only on ceremonial occasions. See Indian Life: Costume (p. 14).

These textiles are bought in the shape of some article of apparel, a woman's blouse, skirt, carrying cloth, etc., or a man's blouse, belt, or head-covering. Most of these are made on hand- and footlooms; they are rectangular in shape and can be used as table covers and for upholstery. Especially adaptable are the women's skirts made in Totonicapán and Quezaltenango, which come in a piece 5-12 yards long. Size, shape, and colors are limited only by the buyer's preferences.

The most beautiful and intricate weaving is done at San Antonio Aguas Calientes, near Antigua. Another center which makes a superficially similar product is San Martín Jilotepeque, about 2 hours' drive from Guatemala City.

A center for wool blankets and rugs is the Sunday market at Momostenango. A very fine representative selection of these goods can be bought on Fridays at the market in San Francisco el Alto. In the large native markets at Antigua, Totonicapán, Quezaltenango, San Francisco el Alto, Cobán, etc., woven goods are sold, but it is necessary to speak Spanish in order to trade. In most of the larger towns there are one or more stores carrying local merchandise, but the buyer needs a trained eye, since cheaply woven articles are prevalent.

Probably the only sure way for one who does not speak Spanish to obtain textiles of fine quality is to buy in shops that specialize in them. In Guatemala City are some excellent shops under U. S. ownership: Mrs. Tocsika Roach, El Patio, and Dyer's, all near the Palace Hotel; the native stores that border the large central market near the cathedral are also good. In Chichicastenango there are three stores. Miss Knittel, in San Francisco el Alto, has a beautiful selection of woolen goods.

Guatemalan dolls, dressed in regional costumes, are very charming souvenirs. They are found in most stores in Guatemala City and in the native market at Totonicapán.

Pottery, glazed and unglazed, is found in all markets. It is manufactured principally in and near Antigua, Totonicapán, and Chinautla. All pottery is handmade, some in crude fashion, the more perfect articles on the potter's wheel. Often the designs are very interesting stylized figures.

Gourds are made into bowls, dippers, cups, and even masks and may be engraved and painted. The articles most highly prized have white designs on a black background.

Baskets are woven from wicker, reed, or rush, in every size and shape. They are sold in all market places. Those without handles are called canastos; those with, canastas.

Bags and hammocks are made from locally grown henequen, agave, and maguey and are found in all markets, though they originate chiefly near Cobán and Huehuetenango. They are sold in quantity in the general market in Guatemala City.

Petates or mats are woven from rushes or reeds and in some regions from palmetto leaves. They are often gaily colored, are exceptionally strong, and are found in most markets.

Woodwork is confined chiefly to the making of masks and boxes, although in Guatemala City there are some shops that sell fine carved frames, bag tops, candlesticks, and book ends. The two outstanding mask makers are both Indians: Miguel Chuj, in Totonicapán, and Diego Ignacio, in Chichicastenango. The latter town is also the chief market for crude painted wooden chests which are sometimes also carved.

Leather goods such as bridles, saddles, suitcases, sandals, and belts are sold in the Guatemala City market and in some local native markets, notably at Chichicastenango and San Francisco el Alto. In the former town there is a lively trade in made-to-order shoes and sandals, dyed and styled to specifications.

Much Maya jade is sold both in stores and by individuals, but only an expert can distinguish good specimens. The finest collection of

Maya jade is in the home of Father Ildefonso Rossbach, in Chichicastenango. Other examples may be seen in the Archeological Museum in Guatemala City.

Modern and antique silver is sold in stores chiefly in Guatemala City. The commonest silver articles consist of obsolete coins made into necklaces or bracelets. Very lovely old beads of colonial design and workmanship are found from time to time, chiefly near Cobán and San Marcos.

It is forbidden to take archeological or colonial antiques out of the country. Baggage is thoroughly inspected at airport or seaport, in addition to an inspection at the customs office in Guatemala City.

Food. Guatemalan food is not hot with chile like Mexican dishes. Instead, chile is served separately with a meal and can be added at pleasure. Tamales are made of corn meal finely ground and turned into a sort of dough to which is added pork, turkey, or chicken meat, dressed with a red chile sauce for red tamales or with a black sauce made of burnt plantain skin garnished with raisins, prunes, and some sweet spices; the whole mixture is wrapped in banana leaves and boiled over a slow fire in a clay pot. Chuchitos are small red tamales boiled in corn husks. Enchiladas are toasted or fried tortillas over which a layer of ground meat or other material is placed in a conical shape; the whole top is then covered with chile sauce and powdered cheese. Gallo en chicha is chicken cooked in a dark sauce made of richly spiced fermented corn mash. Frijoles or black beans, one of the staple foods, are eaten boiled, mashed, or fried. Huisquil is prickly pear, eaten as a vegetable, boiled or fried. Yucca is sweet cassava, eaten boiled, fried, or in fritters. All starch in Guatemala is obtained from the yucca; a very fine medicinal flour used for making gruels is also produced from this plant, which bears no relation to the U. S. plant of the same name. Fiambre, eaten on All Saints' Day, is a mixed salad richly garnished with chicken, sausages, sardines, olives, etc.

Other native foods are chilaquilas, tortillas with cheese inside, dipped in egg before cooking; revolcado, tripe in sauce; bananas and plátanos or plantains, cooked in a variety of ways; flor de isote, cooked flower of the yucca of the U. S. west; guacamol, mashed avocado with onion and spices; chilacayote, candied squash; buñuelos, similar to Swedish timbales, cooked in city streets on December 8, fiesta of the Immaculate Conception.

In Guatemala the somewhat familiar tropical fruits are found in abundance: mango; papaya; granada or pomegranate; anona or sweetsop; granadilla, the fruit of the passionflower; níspero or loquat, and piña or pineapple. In addition there are countless excellent fruits that are rarely seen in the United States: mamey; injerto; pitahaya, the fruit of the night-blooming cereus; jocote; jocote marañón, the fleshy edible stalk on which the cashew nut is borne; caimito or star apple; icaco or coco plum; acerola, a tart cherry.

Holidays and Fiestas. January 1, New Year's Day; January 6, Epiphany (Día de los Reyes), the gift-giving equivalent of the U. S. Christmas; carnival, three days preceding Lent; February 14, President's Day, when President Ubico took office; Holy Week; March 19, St. Joseph (San José); Ascension, Pentecost, and Corpus Christi; May 1, Labor Day; June 24, St. John (San Juan); June 29, St. Peter and St. Paul (Santos Pedro y Pablo); June 30, anniversary of the 1871 revolution, when Granados and Barrios took over the government; August 15,

Assumption (Asunción de la Virgen, patroness of Guatemala City);
September 15, Independence Day; October 12, Columbus Day; November 1 and 2, All Saints' Day and All Souls' Day; November 10, President Ubico's birthday; the National Fair (Feria Nacional) in Guatemala City, a week starting the third Sunday in November, with two or three days' holiday; December 8, Immaculate Conception; December 12, Virgin of Guadalupe, celebrated to some extent in Guatemala, although it is primarily a Mexican holiday; Christmas; December 28, the equivalent of the U. S. April Fool's day (Día de los Santos Inocentes); December 31, bank holiday.

REGIONAL GUIDE

The Spaniards assigned patron saints to all Indian towns and regions; these saints' names were placed before the original Indian names. Full names are generally given in this guide with parentheses around any part not in common use. Puerto Barrios, main port of entry, and the trip to Guatemala City (p. 42) are covered first; then Antigua (p. 52) and travel possibilities SW (p. 59), principally to Lake Amatitlán; N (p. 62) to Lake Izabal (p. 64) and Cobán (p. 65) with the wilderness of El Petén (p. 66) as an ultimate goal; S (p. 67) to El Salvador; W (p. 68) toward lovely Lake Amatitlán (p. 71) and the notable Indian town Chichicastenango (p. 76). In W Guatemala (p. 84) routes open out from Quezaltenango to the Pacific (p. 86), N to Huehuetenango (p. 87) and the Cuchumatanes mountains (p. 89), and W to Mexico (p. 92).

PUERTOS BARRIOS TO GUATEMALA CITY

Puerto Barrios, 198 miles (319 km.) from Guatemala City, is capital of the department of Izabal and chief port of Guatemala. All bananas and chicle and much coffee, fruit, wood, and other exports pass through here, as well as three-quarters of Guatemala's imports. Customs inspection takes place at Puerto Barrios. There are a United Fruit Co. commissary and government and shipping offices, but little else. The climate is very hot, but fishing and swimming are good.

There is a motorboat service to Puerto Cortés, Honduras, and to Livingston (p. 65), where trips up the Río Dulce start. A motorboat also gives service to Belize, British Honduras. Planes from Guatemala City, via El Petén, are scheduled biweekly.

HOTEL. Del Norte.

NOTE. Hotels are here classified by rates. Two stars indicate the higher rates for the country in question and also, in nearly all cases, mean good accommodations. One star means rates in the medium brackets; no star means either low rates or no information available. An effort is made in all these guides to list hotels in the various cities and towns, but travelers who are accustomed to North American or European accommodations should use the information with care. In the capitals and larger Latin American centers hotels usually have standards comparable with those found elsewhere and at times on a par with those anywhere in the world. In the smaller centers throughout Latin America hotels are often more nearly boarding houses whose standards of accommodations and food make them unacceptable to all but the most adaptable.

At first the train to Guatemala City passes through a dense tropical jungle filled with unseen birds and animals, then through banana fincas or plantations, with their exotic yellow and purple blooms. Heavy cactus hedges line the tracks, and the Río Motagua winds through the country. The traveler sees an occasional crocodile and sometimes natives washing clothes or traveling in their handmade cayucos or dugouts. The elevation increases slowly. There are many little settlements and fruits are peddled while the train stops. In December the Motagua valley is full of the fiery blossoms of liquidambar trees, very tall.

Bananera, 37 miles (60 km.) from Barrios, headquarters of the United Fruit Co., has all the conveniences of a small U. S. town.

Quiriguá, 23 miles (37 km.) beyond Bananera, is the site of the only easily accessible Maya ruins in Guatemala. They were discovered by Stephens and Catherwood in 1840. In his fascinating Incidents of Travel in Central America, John L. Stephens describes Quiriguá as it was a hundred years ago, and Catherwood's incredible lithographs depict each tiny detail of the uncovered stones. The men unearthed two rectangular spaces, like plazas, formed by obelisks or stelae sculptured with human figures and hieroglyphs. There are also great rocks carved with reptiles and other animals, chief among them the tortoise. The sculptures are in high relief and resemble those of Copán in Honduras.

The ruins are cared for by the United Fruit Co., which also maintains here one of the best hospitals in Guatemala. There is no hotel; so visitors wishing to remain overnight to view the ruins must make arrangements to stay at the United Fruit Co. rest house.

Good detailed descriptions of the excavations at Quiriguá can be found in Sylvanus G. Morley's Guide Book to Ruins of Quiriguá and in Herbert J. Spinden's Ancient Civilizations of Mexico and Central America.

(San Miguel) Gualán, 20 miles (32 km.) SW of Quiriguá, was formerly an important port reached by small craft on the Río Motagua. The creation of Puerto Barrios as an Atlantic port destroyed Gualán as a shipping center, and it is now only an agricultural district. The town celebrates the fiesta of St. Michael, September 29, and the apparition of the archangel, May 8. La Cueva de doña María, 20 miles from town, is a vast cave which is reported to open also into the department of Izabal. The cave, which is very damp, is full of elaborate stalagmites and stalactites. The automobile road, Route (Ruta) 4, planned from Guatemala City to Puerto Barrios, reaches Gualán (1941).

(San Pedro) Zacapa, capital of its department, is midway between the Atlantic and Guatemala City. Trains both to and from Guatemala City stop here at noon, and luncheon can be bought at the hotel. This stopping place provides the first close view of native fruits; near the hotel grow papayas and cashew nuts.

The city has a rich native life. Market is held Sundays. Fiestas are St. Peter's, June 29, and the Immaculate Conception, December 1-10. On April 30 and May 1, Indians conduct rites with an admixture of horseplay to secure good rains, for the region is dry and hot. Local products are palm hats, cheese and butter, crude sugar, and cigars. N of the city are baths, Baños de Santa Marṭa, at a sulphur spring reputed to cure rheumatism. The church has the solid construction and style of the colonial period, but was badly damaged by earthquakes of June 1765.

HOTELS. Ferrocarril (Railroad); France.

From Zacapa there is railroad service to El Salvador. A highway leads to Chiquimula and Esquipulas, the latter the goal of a great pilgrimage each January 15. Local buses travel between the station and the city of Zacapa, 2 miles away. To insure transportation to Esquipulas, arrangements should be made in advance with Clark's Tours, Guatemala City, or with local municipal officers in Zacapa.

EXCURSION TO ESQUIPULAS

A side trip well worth making from Zacapa is to the pilgrimage town of Esquipulas, 70 miles (113 km.) SE, via Route 20 and Route 18. The town can also be reached by car from Guatemala City. The road from Zacapa winds through a beautiful valley flanked on either side by mountains. The country is low and hot, as well as dusty in the dry season.

Chiquimula, 17 miles (27 km.) from Zacapa, capital of the department of the same name, is a prosperous town, noted for cattle and fruit, with a daily market. Its great fiesta is Epiphany (Día de los Reyes), January 6. Ruins of the colonial church, destroyed by the earthquakes of 1765, are to be seen. There is a fine Protestant mission school. Gasoline is sold. Travelers to the Esquipulas fiesta may do well to spend the night in Chiquimula, since Esquipulas is very crowded at this time.

A recently completed road, Route 21, branches NE from Route 20 at Vado Hondo, a short distance E of Chiquimula. This road, continued into Honduras via Jocatán, leads to the great Maya ruins at Copán.

A good road, Route 18, goes from Chiquimula to Guatemala City, via Ipala, Jilotepeque, San Pedro Pinula, Jalapa, Mataquescuintla, and San José Pinula. This road, 126 miles (203 km.), winds up and down valleys and mountains and requires 8 hours' hard driving, justified by the sweeping view of the countryside—forests, volcanoes, mountains, streams, and valleys.

HOTEL. Pensión Suiza is clean and attractive, with good food.

(San Francisco) Quezaltepeque is 19 miles (31 km.) from Chiquimula. Market is held Sundays and Thursdays. Fiestas are those of St. Francis, October 4 and December 19 (San Francisco Conquistador). Each year on April 23 there is a procession of Indians to the source of the Río Conquista. Sacrifices of birds are made, and a cross is added to the many already there.

The colonial church has noble proportions, but is rather barren inside; however, there are good silver around the altar and some gold-leaf decorations.

Regional products are mats, baskets, brooms, excellent fish nets, crude sugar, and coffee.

Buses pass daily to Chiquimula, Esquipulas, and Concepción. The road to Concepción will ultimately be continued into El Salvador.

HOTEL. Pensión Torres.

Esquipulas is 34½ miles (55 km.) from Chiquimula over a good but dusty road which in its latter part overlooks the beautiful and fertile valley of Esquipulas, with the white sanctuary visible many miles away. The sanctuary of Esquipulas has a Black Christ of such sanctity that each year pilgrims come from great distances, even Mexico and Costa Rica, to worship it, and dozens of churches in Central America have been dedicated to it. Only two or three shrines in the Western Hemisphere attract more pilgrims, for miraculous cures are said to have been effected at this sanctuary. Formerly only the Día de Esquipulas, January 15, was celebrated, but so many merchants came during Lent and Holy Week that since 1840 this period also has seen a notable celebration.

In 1595 the image of Christ Crucified by Quirio Cataño was placed in the town of Santiago Esquipulas, so named for the Indian chief who ruled here before the conquest. The image, carved from dark orange wood, has darkened further with age and the smoke of candles and incense. From the first it was worshiped with avidity by the Indians, perhaps partly because black was the sacred color of their ancestral religions. It is about 5 feet high, clothed in jeweled white satin, and inclosed in a glass case above the gold- and silver-incrusted altar of the sanctuary.

The image was formerly located in the parochial church which faces the sanctuary from the opposite end of a mile-long cobbled street. In the middle of the 18th century Pedro de Pardo de Figueroa, archbishop of Guatemala, came to ask for the return of his health. Cured of a contagious disease, he began the present sanctuary, but it was not finished before his death. It is a magnificent structure, topped by four domed towers 150 feet high, above which stands the tall cupola. The huge portals at front and sides are of beautiful proportion and design. The Christ was moved in 1758 to its present location with great ceremony.

The celebration of Esquipulas is more than a religious pilgrimage. Gay booths line the single street, food and baubles are sold, traveling merchants exchange their wares, and aguardiente flows freely. Great public Masses are conducted at the sanctuary, but Indian worshipers, their tiny candles placed on the floor of the vast temple, are more concerned with their private devotions. When they return to their homes they wear special wide straw hats decorated with bright painted gourds and red flowers; they may be seen wearing these hats on roads far at the other end of the republic.

Esquipulas is a center of commerce, for merchants pass through it on their way to Mexico or the south. It stands near the junction of Guatemala, El Salvador, and Honduras, into which roads are now being built.

From Zacapa the train for Guatemala City runs to El Rancho. By car it is more interesting to take a parallel road slightly N which passes through some interesting old villages.

Teculután, 18 miles (29 km.) from Zacapa by car, celebrates the fiesta of Candlemas (La Candelaria) on February 5 instead of February 2, the day on which the Church honors the purification of the Virgin, because of competition from a near-by village.

San Cristóbal (Acasaguastlán), 13 miles (21 km.) from Teculután, celebrates the fiesta of St. Christopher (San Cristóbal) on July 25. It has an interesting old colonial church with an arched roof of stone and lime, quadrangular towers of Spanish Renaissance design, a carved façade with a sunburst and saints, and fine bells. The interior, which has suffered from earthquakes, contains a gold-leaf altar, silver lamps, and many pictures.

San Agustín (Acasaguastlán), 10 miles (16 km.) N of San Cristóbal, has one of the oldest churches in the region. The structure is vaulted and contains ornate gold-leaf altars. There is also a parochial church which contains an image of Jesus of Nazareth (Jesús Nazareno), visited on Easter because of its reputed miracles. San Agustín has notable Lenten observances and a fiesta of St. Augustine on August 28. There is a small market daily, a large one on Sundays.

In this region are found traces of advanced Maya civilization—remains of pottery, temples, and palaces. The olla of San Agustín now in the Heye Museum of the American Indian in New York is probably the most beautiful Maya ceramic ever found in Guatemala.

El Rancho, whose full name is Rancho San José, 4½ miles (7 km.) from San Agustín, marks the junction of railroad and highway; from El Rancho to Guatemala City the routes run more or less parallel. El Rancho is hot. Tropical fruits from the lowlands are sold here in abundance. The fiesta of St. Joseph is celebrated on March 19. Gasoline is sold in cans.

From El Rancho a motor road leads N to Cobán, center of a rich industrial and coffee region. Buses cover this route frequently, but advance reservations should be made with William Bird, De León y Gonzáles, or Gonzalo Reyes, all in Cobán, in order to insure transportation.

The road from El Rancho to Guatemala City (70 miles, 113 km.; a 4-hour drive) continues level for a time, then climbs rapidly, and the heat decreases. The road passes through Progreso, capital of the department of the same name, a place of minor interest for tourists. Gas is sold here in cans.

Travelers on the train reach Guatemala City just as the sun is lowering. Suddenly against the clear sky are seen the silhouettes of three great volcanoes, climax of a journey of ever-changing scenery. The highlands of Guatemala, beautiful and magnificent, lie ahead.

GUATEMALA CITY

Martín de Mayorga, captain general of Guatemala, arrived in Antigua, the capital, just before its wrecking by earthquake in 1773 made the civil authorities wish to move it to a new site. They were opposed by the churchmen. Following years of dissension, the deadlock was broken by the Spanish king Charles III, who decreed in 1775 that

KEY TO MAP OF GUATEMALA CITY

1. Parque Central
2. Plaza J. R. Barrios
3. Plaza 11 de Marzo
4. Botanical Garden
5. Cathedral
6. Santo Domingo church
7. Merced church
8. San Francisco church
9. Concepción church
10. Belén church
11. Capuchinas church
12. San Agustín church
13. Santa Catarina church
14. Santa Clara church
15. Guadalupe church
16. Presidential Palace
17. National Palace
18. Municipalidad (city hall)
19. Correo Central (post office)
20. National Assembly
21. Hospicio Nacional (orphanage)
22. National University
23. La Aduana (customhouse)
24. Polytechnic School
25. Railroad station
26. National Museum
27. General Hospital
28. Mercado Central (Central Market)
29. Mercadito (Little Market)
30. Mercado Colón (Columbus Market)
31. Hotel Palace
32. Hotel Gran

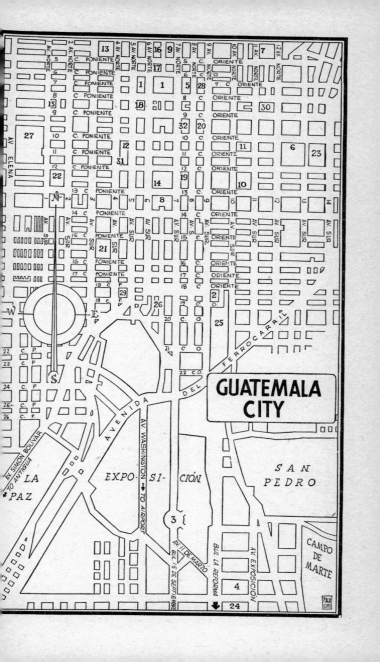

the capital should be moved 25 miles N. The new town was established in 1776 at La Ermita, at the foot of the Cerrito del Carmen, because the church built there 150 years previously had come through the earthquakes undamaged. After a short time the capital was moved again, to the adjoining valley of the Virgin, and named Nueva Guatemala de la Asunción in honor of the Virgin of the Assumption, whose image had long been worshiped by the Indians of that locality. Gradually the inhabitants of Antigua traveled across the mountain and took up their residence in the new city. This capital, the fifth, never gained such glory as Antigua. Florid heaviness took the place of the simple lines of the old buildings and churches. Now even most of this has been lost, for in 1917-18 a succession of earthquakes almost completely demolished Guatemala City, and it was rebuilt along modern lines.

Today Ciudad Guatemala, locally called simply Guatemala, at an elevation of 4897 feet, neatly laid out, has modern stores, movies, and buses. Some of the old churches were not destroyed; a few others have been reconstructed in whole or in part. Aside from its markets, Guatemala City with its 165,000 population might be found almost anywhere in Latin America. The city is located in a narrow valley, with ranges of hills crowding it E and W. Its center is Parque Central (Central Park), a plaza covering about 2 blocks and divided in two by 6 Avenida. The E half, called Plaza de Armas, contains a monument to Columbus, erected in 1896, and another commemorating the centenary of Guatemala's independence. This is the popular promenade. Evening concerts are given here, often broadcast on long or short wave to the United States. Parque del Centenario on the W side has a beautiful fountain, lighted in color at night. Formerly this was the location of the palace of the captains general. N of the park a palace for the central government is being erected; S are arcades with small shops; E is the cathedral, and W a cuartel or barracks.

THE CITY is laid out with numbered avenues and streets, the former running N-S, the latter E-W. The E-W dividing line is 6 Avenida, which runs down the center of the city through Parque Central. This avenue is the most important shopping street in Guatemala City; the principal theaters and stores also are on it. The N-S line of demarcation is 8 Calle, at the S end of Parque Central. Addresses are given thus: C.P. (Calle Poniente or West Street), W of 6 Av.; C.O. (Calle Oriente or East Street), E of 6 Av.; Av. N. or Av. S. (Avenida Norte, North Avenue; Avenida Sur, South Avenue), N or S of 8 C.

The city's main shopping district lies immediately S of Parque Central on 6, 7, and 8 Avenidas and between 8 and 13 Calles. In this district also are located the principal hotels and boarding houses. Immediately S of this major business district is an area of small shops and business houses extending to the tracks of the International Railways of Central America, which run diagonally across the S part of the city. The railroad station is at 10 Av. and 18 C. In the small park in front of the station, called Plaza Barrios, is a bronze statue to President Rufino Barrios, reported to be one of the most beautiful statues in Central America. The National Museum of History and Fine Arts is 2 blocks W, on the corner of 18 C. and 6 Av.

S of the railroad begins the suburban residential district of the city, with a prolongation of 7 Av. running into Plaza 11 de Marzo. Here, in a small area, the streets run diagonally SE into the main boulevard, Bulevar La Reforma, where the city's finest homes are located. Along this spacious tree-lined thoroughfare are several monuments: Monumento del Ejército, the army monument; a statue of Gen. Miguel García Granados, erected to celebrate the victory of the Liberals in the revolution of 1871; an equestrian statue of Gen. José María Reina Barrios, in Plaza Reina Barrios; a statue of Miguel Hidalgo y Castilla, honored as the father of Mexican and Central American independence; and finally toward the S end the impressive monolithic statue to Guatemalan independence in Parque de los Próceres (Park of the Fathers of Independence). At the N end of Bulevar La Reforma are the Botanical Garden, with a valuable collection of orchids, cacti, begonias, and other flowering plants of the country, and the Polytechnic School, the national military academy. The U. S. Legation is immediately S. Three blocks E of the Botanical Garden is Campo de Marte, a broad parade ground with a reviewing stand, which is also used for various sports and games; some of the city's best riding academies are in the immediate vicinity. Two blocks S, facing Plaza Reina Barrios, is the Escuela de Artes y Oficios (School of Arts and Trades), with the old Military Hospital immediately E. A block W of Bulevar La Reforma is Plaza España, with a monument to Charles III, dating from colonial times and originally located in the city's central square.

At the S end of the city is Parque Aurora, with beautiful gardens, a zoo, the Archeological Museum, the observatory, and a racetrack, in addition to the excellent airfield and La Aurora airport, perhaps the finest in Central America. The National Fair is held in Parque Aurora in November.

The area N of Parque Central is devoted mainly to residences. Many legations and consulates are located in this modern district.

Parque Minerva, N of the city, contains the Temple of Minerva, one of many buildings erected during the regime of President Estrada Cabrera. E of the Temple is a monumental relief map of Guatemala, covering more than 2500 square meters, constructed by the engineer Francisco Vela in 1905. It should be studied by all visitors before venturing into the highlands, since it gives an admirable conception of the mountains, plateaus, and roads of Guatemala. The vertical scale is five times as large as the horizontal, so that the height of the mountains is exaggerated. The Hipódromo del Norte, a racetrack, encircles the map and the Temple of Minerva.

CHURCHES. Treasures of colonial painting and sculpture from the old churches and monasteries of Antigua have in many cases been moved to the churches of Guatemala City. The traveler who feels special interest in these works of art should bear in mind the possibility of their being moved about among the churches of the capital or to the Museum of History and Fine Arts.

The cathedral, on Parque Central, was designed by the Spanish architect Marcos Ibáñez. It was begun in 1782 and completed in 1815, though the towers were not added until 1867. Partially destroyed by the earthquakes of 1917-18, its towers and main dome are new. It has five arched naves, crowned by domes, and 16 altars. Many of the paintings and statues from ruined Antigua have been placed in the cathedral, among them a Crucifixion by Rosales and a Virgin of La Concepción de los Espinos and a St. Sebastian by Juan de Chávez. To the right of the high altar is the chapel of the Virgin of El Socorro (Aid), brought from Antigua, and to the left El Sagrario. Next to the cathedral is the palace of the archbishop of Guatemala, one of the few remaining colonial mansions in the city.

A hermitage, La Ermita del Cerro del Carmen, stands on the Cerrito del Carmen. In the early 1600's a Franciscan friar, Juan Corz, arrived in Guatemala bearing an image of a Virgin which had been given to him by the nuns of St. Theresa in Spain. He placed the image in a cave on a small hill, and he himself lived in another near by. News of the miraculous powers of the image spread among the population. A chapel was built for it, but it is said that the image always returned to the cave in which Juan Corz had placed it. In time the hermit built a chapel. It was finished and dedicated on Aug. 15, 1620, and on the same day the hermit disappeared and was never seen again. A small village at the foot of the hill was called La Ermita in his honor, and it was here that the dispossessed people of Antigua first settled while they were seeking a location for the new capital. The chapel was destroyed by the earthquake of 1917, but the image was not harmed, and a new chapel has been built along similar lines. The stone cross before it is modern. The view of Guatemala City from this hilltop is exceedingly beautiful. The hillside has been turned into a small park with walks and trees. The fiesta of La Ermita in September is one of the city's gayest.

The church of Santo Domingo, 12 Av. and 10 C., was started in 1782 and completed in 1808. The mortar for it was mixed with cane sirup, cow's milk, and white of egg to give greater strength. The church was reconstructed after the 1917 earthquake. The venerated image of Our Lady of the Rosary, generally regarded as the queen of Guatemala, is here, as well as several sculptures by Alonzo de la Paz, including a figure of Christ (Cristo Yacente) and the beautiful Apotheosis of St. Thomas Aquinas.

The church of Our Lady of La Merced, at 11 Av. and 5 C., was finished in 1813, and its altars, the most beautiful in all Guatemala, were brought from Antigua in 1815. The church is known for its costly jewels and its colonial art treasures, among them the Virgin of the Conception by Ramírez and masterful sculptures by Evaristo Zúñiga and Alonzo de la Paz. The church was rebuilt after 1917 and its bell-towers removed.

The church and monastery of San Francisco, at 6 Av. and 13 C., date from the 18th century. In 1773, following the destruction of Antigua, Friar Cristóbal Navarro was commissioned to look for a new site for the brotherhood. The cornerstone of the monastery was laid at the end of the century, but it was not completed until 1851. In this building, as in Santo Domingo, sirup, milk, and egg whites were reputedly used in the mortar. In 1829 the Franciscans were expelled, and the monastery was used as a barracks, leaving only the church for public worship. Many treasures have been brought from Antigua to this church, which was one of the finest in the country until the earthquake of 1917, when it was badly damaged and its underground chapel completely destroyed.

Other churches or chapels of interest are those of Our Lady of La Asunción, 7 Av. N. near 7 C., in Jocotenango, a N part of the city, containing the image of the patroness of Guatemala City; Belén, 10 Av. and 13 C., its cloisters now housing a normal school for girls; Las Capuchinas, 10 Av. and 10 C., containing carved and gilded altars from Antigua, some of the finest in the country; Our Lady of La

Candelaria, Av. Candelaria, housing the Jesús de la Candelaria from Antigua, the scene of a notable fiesta on Holy Thursday; Our Lady of Los Remedios, 18 C. and Callejón Concordia, with a Virgin of Los Remedios and a Virgin of the Rosary from Antigua; La Recolección, 3 Av. and 3 C., being rebuilt (1941); San Agustín, at 5 Av. between 10 C. and 11 C., with images from the Antigua church of the same name; Santa Catalina, at 4 Av. and 5 C., whose image of Cristo Yacente from Antigua, presumably discovered by Pedro de Betancourt, is said to have performed many miracles; Santa Clara, 6 Av. and 13 C., a fashionable church with a sculptured group by Evaristo Zúñiga; Santa Rosa, 10 Av. and 8 C., which contains colonial paintings and which for 26 years served as cathedral; Our Lady of El Carmen, 8 Av. and 10 C., where many fashionable weddings are held. The sanctuary of Guadalupe, 1 Av. and 9 C., is the scene of a gay fiesta on December 12; the church has been completely rebuilt.

PUBLIC BUILDINGS worth seeing include the Presidential Palace, 6 Av. N. The streets around it are closed to traffic after 9 p.m. The National Palace, being built (1941) N of Parque Central, will accommodate government offices and a municipal theater. The National University, at 2 Av. and 12 C., originally in Antigua and known there as the university of San Carlos Borromeo, was moved to the new capital in 1777. La Aurora airport, with a customhouse, is in Parque Aurora at the S end of the city. La Aduana, the main customhouse, is at 13 Av. and 10 C., a modern building of reinforced concrete. The building of the Secretariat of Agriculture is in a beautiful garden at 12 Av. and 19 C., containing a coffeehouse where visitors may sample Guatemala's finest product. The Palacio de la Sanidad Pública, the national health department offices, is a new building at 9 Av. and 15 C. The Biblioteca Nacional (National Library) is at 9 Av. and 10 C. The Archivo General del Gobierno (General Archives of the Government), 4 Av. and 6 C., contains priceless documents of the colonial era. The Escuela Politécnica (Polytechnic School), on Bulevar La Reforma, is the nation's military academy. The Hospicio Nacional, an orphanage, at 4 Av. and 16 C., was founded in 1854 and taken over by the Sisters of Charity of St. Paul in 1864.

MARKETS. Especially in early morning, roads into the city are crowded with Indians carrying cooked and raw produce to the three markets. Vendors may come by bus or driving their tiny mules with heavy loads of merchandise from the four corners of the country. Even in the busy midtown section the patter of jogtrotting bare feet is heard as the un-self-conscious natives go about their trade with little thought of the modern paved streets.

The great Mercado Central (Central Market), behind the cathedral, provides ever-changing and fascinating scenes. Its merchants sell fruits, vegetables, and flowers from all over the country. Great bunches of orchids and gardenias compete with flamboyant nameless weeds; live iguanas lie near great bins of pineapples or mangoes; loofas or vegetable sponges, armadillos, spices, rice, dried fish, all have their place. Around the sides are stalls where leather, textiles, rope, and bags of all kinds are made and sold. A large section is given over to the preparation and sale of cooked food, and native dishes are offered at extremely low prices. The small stores outside the market, W and S, are largely devoted to textiles, including woolen goods from Momostenango and Totonicapán.

The Mercadito (Little Market) in the S end of the city, on 18 C.P. between 5 Av. and 6 Av., specializes in fruits and vegetables.

The third market is an open square called Mercado Colón (Columbus Market), bounded by 8 C.O., 11 Av., 9 C.O., and 12 Av. Pottery, gourds, and baskets abound here, but there is less variety in foods. At Christmas this market is filled with Christmas trees, flowers, and decorations.

MUSEUMS. The Museo Nacional de Historia y Bellas Artes (National Museum of History and Fine Arts), at 6 Av. and 18 C., sometimes called the Colonial Museum, occupies the former church of El Calvario, one of the first churches built in the new capital. Opened as a museum in January 1935, the building contains old religious paintings by Montúfar, Merlo, and Villalpando, Antigua's greatest painters, in addition to woodcarvings and other religious art of the colonial period.

The Museo de Arqueología (Archeological Museum), in Parque Aurora, contains Maya relics from all parts of the country. The best examples of the Maya arts unearthed in the 19th century now rest in museums all over the world, but an embargo on further exports will retain in Guatemala whatever is discovered in the future. In addition to stelae, beautiful pottery and jades from Uaxactún, Kaminal Juyú on the outskirts of Guatemala City, and the newly explored Pacific coast region of Santa Lucía Cozumalguapa, the museum contains the largest single piece of jade in America (216 pounds).

FAIRS. La Gran Feria Nacional (Grand National Fair), held the third week in November, brings games, racing, exhibits of agricultural produce and textiles, band concerts, dances, and other amusements. An interesting feature is the Indian village in which Indians from all parts of the country exhibit and sell their finest textiles and other products.

The fiesta of Jocotenango is celebrated by a popular fair held in Parque Minerva on August 14-21, in honor of the Assumption of the Virgin.

CLUBS. The American Club, founded in 1896, has its own building, at 8 Av. S. No. 26, with game and reading rooms; visitors must be sponsored by a member. The Club Guatemala, at 6 Av. S. No. 17, has a primarily Guatemalan membership. Country clubs are the Guatemala Country Club, 5 miles out of the city, and the Maya Golf Club, 3 miles out. Arrangements can be made to play at either club through sponsorship by a member.

HOSPITALS. American Hospital, 8 Av. N. (prolongation); General Hospital, 1 Av. and 10 C.

GARAGES. Storage: San Agustín, 5 Av. S. No. 30; San Francisco, 13 C.O. No. 5; Fiat, 14 C.P. No. 19; Nuevo, 9 C.P. No. 3. Repairs: El Cielito, 7 Av. and 18 C.

RESTAURANTS. Aside from hotels, the chief restaurants are the Grace Inn, 7 Av. S. (prolongation), and El Patio, 11 C.P. No. 6, U. S.-owned and operated and very attractive, with fireplace and open patio. Mexican food is served at the Xochimilco, 12 C. between 9 Av. and 10 Av. The Salon Granada, 6 Av. and 11 C., is a popular restaurant and ice-cream parlor.

HOTELS. Palace**, 4 Av. and 12 C., is the center of public social life, especially at cocktail dances Thursday and Sunday afternoons. San Carlos Gran** is at 8 Av. and 9 C. Pensión Guéroult*, 4 Av. and 9 C., is quiet, with a patio garden; the management is very helpful. Other hotels and boarding houses are Astoria*, 6 Av. and 9 C.; Pensión

Fernández, 4 C.P. No. 1; Pensión Shaffer, 9 C.P. No. 11; Pensión Royal Home*, 13 C.P. No. 31. The best apartments in the city, including some equipped for housekeeping, are San Francisco**, 6 Av. and 14 C., with American baths and pingpong tables. It is also possible to stay in a private house or apartment and take meals at one of the hotels or at El Patio.

GUATEMALA CITY'S ENVIRONS

(Santa Cruz) Chinautla, 6 miles (10 km.) N of Guatemala City, is reached by a pleasant road which winds down the ravine beside the Río de las Vacas most of the way. Chinautla was formed in 1526 by those Pocoman allies of Mixco Viejo who survived the war with Alvarado. It is a center for homemade pottery, especially water jars, used throughout the country, and comales or flat round pottery pieces on which tortillas are baked. Here one can watch the various processes of pottery-making in individual households. First earth is bought from merchants, mixed, and molded by hand, then dried in the sun and polished, then decorated and dried out over a fire half a day or more. Most men of the town work at gathering wood and preparing charcoal to sell in the capital; women make most of the pottery.

E is a hill called Cerro Vivo, at the foot of which and facing the village is an old cave some 40 yards deep, which the Indians regard with superstitious awe. There is no market. Fiestas are those of the Holy Cross (Santa Cruz); Esquipulas, January 15; and the Rosary, October 7. The church was destroyed by earthquake, and the present one is very new.

Buses arrive daily from Guatemala City. No gas is sold, and there is no place to eat.

Excursion from Chinautla. San Pedro Ayampuc is reached by a branch road E. The town was founded on June 29, 1549, and given as an encomienda to Bernal Díaz del Castillo, author of the classic Verdadera y Notable Relación del Descubrimiento y Conquista de la Nueva España y Guatemala (Truthful and Remarkable Story of the Conquest of New Spain and Guatemala). In those times there were rich deposits of gold N of the city, but the easy supply of gold pebbles has long since been exhausted. On May 3, the day of the Holy Cross, the Indians of San Pedro go to the mountains and burn candles to their gods, petitioning for ample rain for the coming season.

San Antonio las Flores, 5 miles beyond Chinautla, is a very small, completely Indian village situated at the junction of the Río de las Vacas and the Río Zapote. The road from Guatemala City, good during the dry season, always suffers in heavy rains and should be inquired about before starting. The church is very small and new. E of the plaza are the old walls of an ancient chapel, in front of which stands a huge amatle tree. About 1¼ hours from the town by foot is a crater inclosing a lake about 100 by 300 yards, where swimming is excellent. The climb to the lake is a fairly easy continuous ascent.

Fiestas are those of St. Anthony, June 13, and the Rosary, October 7. The chief occupation is agriculture, including cultivation of yucca, sugar cane, and fruit.

There is bus service from Guatemala City.

San Pedro (Sacatepéquez) is a high, flourishing village lying 9½ miles (15 km.) NW of Guatemala City. It is reached by a side road, Route

5, which begins 4½ miles (7 km.) from the center of the capital. In its lower part this is one of the most colorful roads in the country, especially in early morning when a stream of gaily costumed women trot briskly toward the city, bearing on their heads great baskets of fruit and flowers for the day's markets. From San Pedro, whose Indian name means Hill of Grass, there is a beautiful view over the whole valley of Guatemala and N over mountain ranges and valleys. The chief occupations are agriculture and the making of tiles. Women make textiles for several surrounding villages. Their own huipiles are unique, with the design of a tree of life in red and purple on a white background. A larger huipil is used folded for a head-covering. Market is held daily; those on Sundays and Thursdays are the most important. Fiestas are carnival, preceding Lent, and St. Peter's, June 29. The church, which suffered in the 1917 earthquakes, has been reconstructed. It contains two beautiful silver lamps and an image of the Christ of Esquipulas to which a pilgrimage is made each year from all parts of the country. Another large image, the Christ of the Crown (La Corona), remains in the house of one of the Indian municipal officers, and each March 15 when new officeholders are inducted it is moved with great ceremony. A fiesta is held in May in honor of the image. In processions images are clothed with native costumes and adorned with painted feathers. In this village it is said that the Indian women do not talk Spanish to ladinos except in the course of trading; at other times they must speak only their native tongue. There is frequent bus service to Guatemala City, and gas is sold. Food can be obtained, but there is no boarding place.

Excursion from San Pedro. About 5 miles (8 km.) away by trail is (Santo Domingo) Xenacoj. This village is seen as a white spot N of the Pan American Highway in traveling between Sumpango and Chimaltenango. The horseback trip to Xenacoj is pleasant and offers beautiful views as it passes through pine forests and discloses sudden spectacular scenes. At one point 10 volcanoes are visible: Agua, Fuego, Pacaya, Acatenango, Atitlán, Tolimán, San Pedro, San Pablo, Zunil, and Santa María. Xenocoj is mostly Indian. It has a small daily market. Fiestas are St. Dominic's, August 4, and Suriano, November 27. The local women's costume is interesting: a huipil of red and brown stripes rather widely spaced, red servilleta or carrying cloth, and for ceremonial occasions garments heavily figured on a white background or on brown and red. The church, simple in style, was built about 1750; it has a new roof, but old walls. It contains a beautiful painting of the Virgin of Guadalupe and lovely silver banners, lamps, and candlesticks. The monastery has been completely destroyed in recent years. The colonial historian Francisco Ximénez lived in it while he wrote his history of the province of Chiapas and Guatemala. Food can be obtained from the hospitable townspeople. There is no boarding place.

San Juan (Sacatepéquez), 4 miles (6 km.) beyond San Pedro, is reached on a descending road which passes terrace after terrace of flowers under cultivation for the Guatemala City markets. Ninety per cent of the inhabitants are Indians, and the afternoon market is very gay. There are many fiestas: St. John, June 24; Esquipulas, January 15; St. Joseph, March 19; Sangre de Cristo, August 24; the Rosary, October 7; the Immaculate Conception, December 8. This is the center of a rich agricultural district abounding in sugar cane and coffee plantations. Many textiles are woven here. The costume is interesting: red and yellow striped blouse, often with bright yellow and purple figures or other designs on the shoulders or at random over the garment. The church was rebuilt in 1933; it has a silver and gold altar and altar screen and several beautiful silver lamps. Frequent buses leave for Guatemala City. Gas is sold.

HOTELS. París is the boarding house that has the best food.

Beyond San Juan, Route 5 turns to the left toward the Río Motagua, Santa Cruz el Chol, Rabinal, and Cobán (pp. 62-66).

San Raimundo (de las Casillas), 8 miles (13 km.) from San Juan Sacatepéquez, has a large and festive Sunday market which is widely patronized by Indians in their native costumes from all near-by regions. A small market is held on Thursdays. The township is one of the oldest in the department, dating from the end of the 16th century. The church was completed Sept. 15, 1604. It has an ornate façade, a domed roof, striking gold-leaf altars, and old paintings. The fiesta of the patron saint is January 23.

Occupations are the making of jugs and textiles, agriculture, and firewood cutting.

Buses arrive from Guatemala City twice a day. No gasoline is sold.

HOTELS. El Torigal is a boarding house.

Excursion from San Raimundo. (San Pedro) Chuarrancho is a charming village 10 miles (16 km.) away, via Vuelta Grande. The road is beautiful, overlooking brown and green checkered hills, with blue hills in the distance. The population of Chuarrancho is entirely Indian, including the mayor. A relatively isolated town, it retains many of its old customs. Market days are Sundays and Thursdays. Fiestas are St. Peter's, June 29; the Rosary, October 7; and Guadalupe, December 12. The tiled houses are hidden in a series of little hills separated by barrancas or deep hollows. The beautiful plaza, on a hilltop overlooking valleys and mountains E and W, is wind-swept and cool. E the mountains of Jalapa are seen, with the volcano Jumay standing out; N is the mountain range of Baja Verapaz; S, Nacahuil; W, the Pichol mountains in San Raimundo.

The natives wear unique pink and purple blouses with many figures, of which a double-headed dragon is the favorite. The ground fabric often has a raised white welt which makes a wide crossbar.

A footpath leads from Chuarrancho to the Cobán region. Along it are seen many trotting Indians bearing great loads of Rabinal's fine oranges to the Guatemala City markets. There is no bus service. Food can be secured only from friendly natives.

GUATEMALA CITY AS A TRAVEL CENTER

The Pan American Highway is generally followed W from the capital as Route 1 (pp. 68-76, 80-84) to Quezaltenango. Important side trips can be made, as to Antigua, described below, and Chichicastenango (p. 76). The road continues from Quezaltenango into Mexico (p. 92). E and S from Guatemala City the highway runs to El Salvador as Route 2 (p. 67).

A route formerly well known to travelers is Route 3, between the Pacific port of San José and the capital (p. 59).

Visitors less often use Route 5, N to Cobán (p. 62), and Route 4,

NE toward Puerto Barrios (p. 38). From the latter route an excursion can be made to the pilgrimage town of Esquipulas (p. 40).

ANTIGUA

In a unique category, from the traveler's point of view, is the old capital of Guatemala, now known as Antigua, 25 miles W from Guatemala City. It is a delightful place to stay in. Antigua can be reached from Guatemala City by Route 10 from Mixco (p. 68) or roundabout through Amatitlán, Palín, and Santa María de Jesús (pp. 59-60). Route 14 leads from Antigua to Chimaltenango (p. 69), on the Pan American Highway, and thus makes it possible to reach the highlands without returning to Guatemala City. Roads radiating S from Antigua include Route 10, which ultimately circles N to San Lucas Tolimán on Lake Atitlán (p. 72).

Antigua, whose name means Ancient, is a city of ruins—the impressive remains of some 85 churches, monasteries, and public buildings, which were built in the flourishing days when this city, called Santiago de los Caballeros de Guatemala, was Guatemala's fourth capital. Partially destroyed in 1717, the city was almost wholly demolished in 1773 and never regained its power or beauty. Today one sees fragments of chapels, arches, naves—some churches rebuilt, some repaired, some left alone in their ruins. The beautiful paintings and sculptures have for the most part been dispersed or lost, and the tourist must use a vivid imagination to recapture the grandeur of the old Spanish capital. Many of its art treasures are now in Guatemala City, in churches or in the Museum of History and Fine Arts. So many shifts are made that it is difficult to report the location of these works of art accurately.

Following the inundation in 1541 of the third capital at Almolonga, now called Ciudad Vieja, the authorities resolved to move the city to the valley of Panchoy. Here the new capital was built, under the direction of the engineer Juan Bautista Antonelli, partly with materials from the ruined city. In this valley grew up one of the most beautiful cities of the New World. In the succeeding centuries it was visited by flood, earthquake, volcanic eruption, pestilence, and drought; yet it was the center of learning, of arts and crafts, and of magnificent churches which had few equals in the New World. Baroque, mudéjar or Spanish Moorish, and Italian styles were blended in the construction of churches and public buildings. Houses, following the model of Spanish homes, were built around patios and adorned with ironwork, heavy furniture made of rare woods, carved ceilings, magnificent rugs, and silver. Public festivals, games, bullfights, and tournaments occupied the cavaliers of Guatemala. The fiestas of the patron saints, St. James and St. Cecilia, were very elaborate, and Holy Week and Christmas were observed with great solemnity.

Sculpture was given special prominence. Marble, stone, wood, stucco, and plaster all were used in creating images of great beauty, and from the colonial period emerged works of rare excellence, especially those of Quirio Cataño, Alonzo de la Paz, Juan de Aguirre, and Juan de Chávez. Painters on the whole showed less originality than sculptors, and not much of their work has survived the centuries. However, works by Correa, Tomás de Merlo, especially his Passion of Christ, and Antonio de Montúfar are excellent, and in addition, many a forgotten colonist and nameless Indian artisan added to the vast collection found today in churches throughout the republic.

In 1660 a printing press and printer were brought to Antigua, and more than 2000 books were printed during the colonial regime. The historian Bernal Díaz del Castillo spent his declining years in Antigua and there wrote and published one of the finest accounts of the conquest. Francisco Antonio de Fuentes y Guzmán and Antonio de Remersal contributed their share to the literary record of Guatemala. Thomas Gage left a spicy account of the capital in his book The English American; a New Survey of the West Indies, which, written in England after his retirement from priestly affairs, is one of the most interesting contemporary sources of information about the colonial era. Music flourished in the capital, spurred by church choirs and organs. Orchestral instruments were both imported and made in Guatemala, and music, though seldom original, was an indispensable accessory to all important functions. The iron workers, leather workers, silversmiths and goldsmiths, tile makers, and artisans of all classes were banded into guilds which had great importance and influence. They had their own patron saints, and their fiestas enriched the pageantry of colonial life.

Earthquakes in 1717 and later damaged the city, and it was almost completely demolished on the day of St. Martha, July 29, 1773. By royal decree the capital was moved to its new location, the present Guatemala City, in 1776, but many of the Spanish and the Indian inhabitants preferred to remain in Antigua. At first they lived in the ruins of their former homes and other buildings; then gradually they built a new city on the remains of the old. Antigua is today surrounded by beautiful coffee plantations. Some of the finest coffee in the country is produced here, since climate and elevation combine to create the perfect environment. For the sake of protection from too much sunlight, the rows of bushlike coffee trees with their cherry-red fruit alternate with great shade trees; in Antigua the gravilea predominates, a tall, stately tree with a special beauty of its own. Some of the important ruins are briefly described here. For a more complete picture of Antigua, see Four Keys to Guatemala by Vera Kelsey and Lilly de Jongh Osborne or Santiago de los Caballeros de Guatemala by Dorothy Popenoe.

THE CITY. Life is centered around Plaza de Armas. Formerly called Plaza Real (Royal Plaza), it was the setting for the market, bullfights, and public hangings. Today it is a shaded square in the center of which is a fountain some of whose stones have been in place since 1614. The ruins of the great cathedral stand at the E side of the plaza. S are the ruins of the palace of the captains general. The N side of the plaza is occupied by the Palacio del Muy Noble Ayuntamiento (Palace of the Very Noble Municipal Government). The Portal de los Mercaderes, a row of small shops, is the arcade bounding the W side of the plaza. Antigua is not large, and visitors have no difficulty in locating points of interest.

CHURCHES. The magnificent cathedral, now partly rebuilt, was begun in 1543 under the direction of the bishop Francisco Marroquín and reputedly cost 150,000 gold pesos. It had three aisles and eight chapels along each side. Two of the latter, El Sagrario and the chapel of Our Lady of El Socorro (Aid), were as large as ordinary churches. Seven great doors and 70 windows opened into the cathedral. Above the façade was a statue of the Virgin of the Conception. The high altar, the work of the famous sculptor Mateo de Zúñiga, rested on a decorated many-sided bronze base. The Virgin of El Socorro, which first graced the cathedral at Almolonga and later the hermitage of Santa Lucía, was placed here with the special function of warding off public disasters. Paintings and sculptures by the finest colonial artists filled the cathedral, which in addition was adorned by quantities of gold, silver, and bronze ornaments. From the ruins of two of the chapels, El Sagrario and that of the Virgin of Guadalupe, the church of San José has been constructed. Its façade is new, but the three doors are old. It contains Quirio Cataño's Christ of Compassion (El Perdón), probably his best work. A special celebration for this image, on the first Friday in Lent, is an impressive occasion. The tombs of Pedro de Alvarado, his wife doña Beatriz, the historian Bernal Díaz del Castillo, and Bishop Marroquín were placed in the cathedral, but they have been destroyed or forgotten during the many reconstructions. Currently there is much interest in recovering the tomb of Alvarado.

The church of Our Lady of La Merced (Mercy) is one of the few that survived Antigua's many earthquakes. Until 1760, when the church was finished, the Mercedarians had lived on a very modest scale, first in Almolonga, where they arrived in 1537, and later in Antigua. The great temple was two stories high, with three naves, two patios, spacious rooms, an oratory, and a hospital. In 1745 a clock was placed in one of its two towers. Its façade, still standing, is heavily carved with figures and designs. The church was decorated with paintings and magnificent statues, especially one of Our Lady of Mercy, wearing a gold and jeweled crown, and the image of Christ with the Cross made in 1616 by Alonzo de la Paz. The monastery of La Merced, much older than the church and now destroyed, contained a library and cells. It has a magnificent fountain, the most beautiful in Antigua. Another fountain, surmounted by a marble bust of Bartolomé de las Casas, has a base of colonial origin. A stone cross, before which colonial officials swore allegiance to the crown of Spain, now stands in front of the church.

The church and convent of Our Lady of La Concepción was established in 1578 by four nuns from Mexico City. It was the first of the capital's convents and was to be the largest and richest of all. It housed more than 1000 women, servants, children, and nuns, including the much-discussed doña Juana de Maldonado, whose notoriety was delicately touched on by Thomas Gage. Of the church only the walls remain. The convent was partially repaired in 1694. Two of its fine figures, St. Jerome and a pregnant Virgin, La Concebida, are the work of the Spaniard Juan de Aguirre. There are underground passages through which the nuns could pass without exposing themselves to the eyes of men, as well as peepholes through which they could speak without being seen.

The Franciscan church and monastery were originally set up in Almolonga in 1538 under the direction of four priests. After the transfer of the foundation to Antigua, the monastery was built in 1543, the first in the new capital. It was a magnificent structure, with the nave very high and the roof a series of domes, of which only one remains. The principal dome, painted inside, was one of the highest in the city. The high altar had shrines containing images of St. Michael, St. Francis of Assisi, and the Virgin of the Conception. Sculptures by Alonzo de la Paz and Juan de Aguirre and paintings by Tomás de Merlo and Francisco de Villalpando, especially 44 pictures of the life of St. Francis, were set off by gold, silver, and precious stones. The church possessed a reputed piece of the True Cross. Its single chapel survived the earthquake and now is the only portion still in use. It is important as the tomb of Friar Pedro de Betancourt, much beloved holy man of colonial days, who set up a brotherhood known as the Bethlehemites to serve children, the sick, and the poor. Friar Peter also built a home for invalid women and founded the hospital and church of Belén.

The church and convent of Las Capuchinas were founded by five Capuchin nuns in 1725. A primitive church was first built, then replaced by an elaborate stone structure, finished in 1736. The solid Romanesque cloister still supports the heavy roofing stones that are the floor of the cells above. Today the dark stone rooms hold the cooking fires, laundry, and looms of families who live there. The cloisters are among the best in Antigua, and the cells in which the nuns spent periods of seclusion are well preserved.

The ruins of the great church of Santo Domingo, bright with flowering vines, stand among the cornfields of small householders who have built their houses against the old walls of the great inclosed area. In 1535 the order was established by four Dominican friars from Nicaragua. A few years later the great Dominican friar Bartolomé de las Casas came to Guatemala, and largely because of his work in converting the local Indians the Dominicans enjoyed high favor. Their monastery in Antigua became very rich. The church had a fine façade with towers at either side. The arches were heavily ornamented; there were many paintings, sculptures, carved wooden altars, and silver candelabras. Art treasures included a silver Virgin of the Rosary; a Jesús Sepultado, brought from England after Henry VIII's differences with the Church; and a St. Dominic by Alonzo de la Paz. One patio contained a library and music hall. The monastery has been completely destroyed by earthquakes.

The Jesuit church of La Compañía now serves as a magnificent background for Antigua's public market. The Company of Jesus was established in Guatemala in 1582, and in 1626 its church was dedicated. The walls, towers, arches, and cupolas were all well proportioned and it contained 70 statues and 40 pictures. Even now one can see stucco figures and murals of red and green. When the Jesuits were expelled in 1767 the church and college were given over to the dean of the cathedral. The most famous Jesuit priest was Rafael María Landívar, poet and author of Rusticatio Mexicana.

The great ruins of the church of La Recolección, on the outskirts of modern Antigua, are seen through the tall shade trees of coffee groves lying on either side of the road. A turret stairway to the roof has been opened, and the roof commands a delightful view of the valley and of the volcano Agua. One can look down into the ruined church, dominated by the single remaining arch, its floor littered by the immense fallen fragments of the roof. The first simple building of the Recollect friars was built in 1701 and later replaced by the magnificent structure whose remains are seen today. Its library and archives were among the best of the period. A great 50-foot open-air oval bath is recent, built in 1910.

The visitor who remains some time in Antigua will be interested in visiting other churches and ecclesiastical buildings.

The bishop's palace is two stories high, with great arches, enormous balcony, and door adorned with bronze. A palace was built by Bishop Marroquín in the 16th century, but the present structure is comparatively modern.

The chapel and hospital of San Juan de Dios were the first stone ecclesiastical buildings erected after the 1773 earthquake.

The church and convent of Santa Clara were finished in 1734, the foundation having started with six nuns from Puebla, Mexico. The main entrance to the church does not open on the street, but on the interior of the convent; thus the nuns could enter without being seen. Little of the church now remains, but the court of the convent, with a massive fountain and a double tier of arches, is interesting.

The church of La Santa Cruz has a portal which, though in ruins, indicates its ancient beauty. It contained a Christ with the Cross, later taken to the church of La Merced after its restoration, and a Virgin of the Rosary that is now in Guatemala City.

The school of Las Beatas Indias, with a church, under the protection of the Virgin of the Rosary, was founded in 1550 for Indian girls.

The small church and convent of Santa Rosa de Lima were built in 1570.

La Candelaria, a hermitage in charge of the Dominicans, was built in 1550 and later almost completely destroyed. It sheltered the famous image of Christ with the Cross, called Jesús de la Candelaria, the work of Juan de Aguirre, now in the church of La Candelaria in Guatemala City.

The church of San Sebastián was built in 1565 but was rebuilt on a different site in 1580. Today only the side walls are intact, but the procession of St. Sebastian is still held on January 20.

The hermitage of El Calvario, built in 1618, is simple. It contained fine paintings, many by Antonio de Montúfar and Tomás Merlo, and included a Virgin of Sorrows which has been taken to Guatemala City and a Passion of Christ. It was not destroyed by the earthquakes and is one of the few colonial buildings that have the authentic stamp of their original character.

The church and monastery of San Agustín were founded in 1615 on a site occupied earlier by a convent of Santa Catalina. The church contained magnificent paintings of St. Augustine, St. Peter, and St. John the Baptist by Montúfar. The monastery is now used as a blacksmith shop, and only the façade of the church remains.

Of the church of El Espíritu Santo, inaugurated in 1559, only part of the façade remains.

The church of Our Lady of El Carmen has its façade still standing, but almost nothing remains of the convent. A great fiesta is celebrated here on July 16.

The church and convent of Santa Teresa were established in 1677 by three Carmelite nuns. The convent now serves as a women's prison.

The church of Santa Catalina Mártir was founded by four Conceptionist nuns in 1606 on the site later occupied by that of San Agustín. In 1613 it was rebuilt at its present location, and later an annex was constructed across the street, connected with the convent by a hollow arch containing a stairway.

The Escuela de Cristo (School of Christ), with a church and monastery, was built in 1664 by the brotherhood of St. Philip Neri. The church, two stories high, with arches and pillars, is still in use. It contains a Christ Crucified by Quirio Cataño, an Adoration of the Magi brought from Barcelona during the past century, and a painting erroneously attributed to Murillo. The courtyard of the monastery is impressive.

The Bethlehemites, established in 1563 by Pedro de Betancourt, built a hospital for women, with a painting of Bartolomé de las Casas in one of the wards, and a church and monastery, finished in 1670. The church was simple, but it had a fine organ and four silver lamps, and in the monastery was a library with historical documents. The church was restored in the 19th century by Capuchin monks.

The cemetery of San Lázaro is at the side of the lepers' hospital which was in charge of the friars of St. John of God (San Juan de Dios).

The church of San Felipe de Jesús, in the outskirts, was founded by Indians who abandoned the town of San Juan Perdido in 1670 because of an epidemic and a plague of bats. They took with them their image of Jesús Sepultado and built it a modest church which later burned down. The new church was built in 1870 and restored after 1917. The celebration of the first Friday in Lent, by Indians and ladinos alike, is very impressive.

PUBLIC BUILDINGS. The palace of the captains general, a wide two-story building with arcades across the whole front, held colonial offices and salons including the hall of the audiencia or high court and the mint. The present building, replacing the original Casas Reales (Royal Houses) of the colonial government, was completed in 1764, but was badly damaged in the earthquake nine years later. The façade still bears the coat of arms of the Spanish king Charles III. Some of the rooms have been converted into a post office and offices for agencies of the government of the department, but the back of the building is still in ruins. The upper arched balcony has beautiful lines, and two gracious fountains are found in the patio at the rear.

The old colonial cabildo or city hall, Palacio del Muy Noble Ayuntamiento, is still used by municipal officers of Antigua. Its double arcade has suffered relatively little damage. The building contains interesting old portraits, including one of Bartolomé de las Casas.

The university of San Carlos Borromeo was founded in 1678 with funds left by Bishop Marroquín; in its day it was the greatest seat of learning in Central America. It is of mudéjar or Spanish Moorish architecture and is in good condition even to its great hexagonal windows. The stone portal is not colonial, however. The building is now used as a colonial museum and contains important paintings and relics of the period.

HOUSES. Several famous old houses are worth visiting. The Popenoe house, built in 1634 by Luis Mendoza y Venegas, later known as Casa del Capuchino, was the subject of Louis Adamic's book The House in Antigua. The large and beautiful colonial home was restored by the late Dorothy Popenoe with great attention to exact colonial details. It can be visited by permission. The Casa de las Campanas (House of the Bells), a beautiful old mansion, was reconstructed by Mr. and Mrs. Lewis Palmer, U. S. residents of Guatemala City. El Alcázar is now a hotel. The home of Bernal Díaz del Castillo, conqueror and author, is at 5 Calle Oriente No. 14. The birthplace of Rafael Landívar, poet, is also interesting. The Casa de los Leones (House of the Lions) has some stone lions guarding its entrance.

OTHER POINTS OF INTEREST. The market, held Mondays, Thursdays, and Saturdays in the old Jesuit church, is a focus of vivid and picturesque activity as the center of commercial life for miles around. This is an excellent place to see the beautiful costumes of San Antonio Aguas Calientes, Comalapa, and San Martín Jilotepeque, in addition to the colorful displays of foodstuffs brought up from the tropical lowlands. Modern Antigua is noted for its pottery and ironwork, as well as fruit and vegetable produce, especially castor beans.

SWIMMING POOLS. The hot springs of El Cubo and Medina are attractive to swim in.

FIESTAS. The Holy Week celebrations in Antigua are among the finest in the country. The church of San Felipe de Jesús, on the outskirts, has a spectacular fiesta the first Friday in Lent.

HOTELS. Aurora* built around a central patio, serves interesting and authentic Guatemalan dishes, which are hard to find in most hotels. Manchen* (Old Tree) occupies a colonial site on Calle de los Herreros, Antigua's most active street in its time. El Alcázar* is a restored colonial home with fireplaces and patios; it is somewhat formal, but very attractive.

ANTIGUA'S ENVIRONS AND EXCURSIONS

For climbs of Acatenango, Fuego, and Pacaya see p. 30.

Ciudad Vieja (Old City), 3½ miles (5 km.) SE of Antigua, is the old Almolonga, founded in 1527, third capital of the Guatemalan captaincy general. Though little is left but some relics of Pedro de Alvarado's palace and of the church, it was once an impressive city. The parochial church, said to have been the first in the new country, was begun in 1529 and finished in 1537 under the direction of Francisco Marroquín, first bishop of Guatemala. It housed an image of the Virgin of La Piedad, later called the Virgin of El Socorro (Aid), which reputedly accompanied the Spanish conquerors from Mexico. Another very old image was the Virgin of the Conception, called also La Chapetona, meaning the Spanish Virgin, because it was brought from Spain.

San Juan del Obispo, located on the slope of the near-by volcano Agua, was founded in 1547 by Bishop Marroquín, who also supervised the building of the church with its elaborate altars and paintings. The ancient paintings have disappeared, but a few of the altars have survived. Even more impressive is the view from the church balcony. The dance of La Conquista (The Conquest), dedicated to Bishop Marroquín, had its origin in this town in 1558.

Jocotenango, on the N outskirts of Antigua, was founded in 1542 by Quiché and Cakchiquel Indians whom the Spaniards had added to their following. The church possesses some fine images, including one of Christ with the Cross which is brought out on Holy Monday. As in Thomas Gage's day, "The high altar within is also rich and stately, being all daubed with gold." The fiesta of the Virgin of the Assumption, patroness of the town, is celebrated on August 15.

San Antonio Aguas Calientes, 4 miles (6 km.) E of Antigua, is the village where Guatemala's finest weaving is done. Blue predominates, but all colors are used in the magnificent huipiles of this region.

Babies' caps are very attractive, and servilletas or carrying cloths are often decorated with amusing animals and birds. The church contains an image of St. Anthony of Padua which is honored by a fiesta on June 13. In this town there are also elaborate rites on All Saints' Day (Todos los Santos), November 1, and on Dulce Nombre de Jesús (Sweet Name of Jesus), usually the first Sunday in January. There is bus service to Antigua several times a week. The village has no market.

Santa Catalina Barahona, a mile from San Antonio Aguas Calientes, is an almost completely Indian village. Its principal building is the church with its image of St. Catherine, honored on November 25. The fiesta of Esquipulas, January 15, is also observed. In the plaza is a very old and interesting fountain.

SOUTHWEST FROM GUATEMALA CITY

From Guatemala City SW to Puerto San José, on the Pacific coast, is 76 miles (121 km.) by narrow-gauge railroad, or 64 miles (103 km.) by car over a good road, Route 3. The descent from the highlands is abrupt. During the first 55 miles (89 km.) the elevation drops from 4900 feet to 400 feet, with corresponding change in vegetation. Pineapples, sugar cane, and great trees dominate the lower stretches of road, and rare bright flowers dot the tropical vegetation. The jungle is not dense here, as on the Atlantic side, for most of the land is under cultivation. A strip about 30 miles wide and 200 miles long, the most fertile in the country, is given over to cotton, cacao, sugar cane, kapok, livestock, and tropical fruits.

Amatitlán (Abundance of Amatle Trees), a small village located on Lake Amatitlán, is 16 miles (25 km.) from Guatemala City over a fine road. The lake affords excellent swimming, boating, and fishing; on its shores have been built summer and week-end homes of Guatemalan families. The S shore is lined with hot springs and steam jets used for washing clothes and for bathing.

Produce is sugar, coffee, and fruit. Formerly this was a cochineal center, and the dye is still used in small quantities for manufacturing rouge. The church, built in 1635, but badly damaged in the 1773 earthquakes, is noted for its image of the Niño de Atocha (Child of Atocha), which has a reputation for curative powers. With a merry pilgrimage to this image the fiesta of the Cross (La Cruz) is held each year on May 2-3.

There are frequent buses to and from Guatemala City and some to the coast port of San José. The railroad also passes through Amatitlán, crossing the lake at a narrow part. Gas is sold.

HOTELS. Aurora; Nacional; La Cataluña.

Excursions from Amatitlán. The park of El Filón, overlooking the lake from a point about 1½ miles N, provides an observation point and rest house in the midst of gardens and walks and presents a beautiful view of the lake and its surroundings. It is a pleasant trip on foot or by car.

A scenic highway girdles the lake. The road is good and provides an easy hour's ride.

From the S shore road, 8 miles (13 km.) E of Amatitlán, a road turns sharply S toward the volcano Pacaya. From the turn to the summit and Lake Calderas is 5½ miles (9 km.); to San Vicente, a small Indian village, 6½ miles (10 km.) more. This road presents beautiful views of the volcanoes Pacaya and Agua, as well as of the Salvadorean mountains and volcanoes. San Vicente does not amount to much; there is no market, no church. To climb Pacaya one starts from the aldea or hamlet of San Francisco; the summit is 1-1½ hours away by horseback. Horses can be secured through the municipal officers of San Vicente. A road W to Palín, 4 miles (6 km.), has recently been completed.

From Amatitlán the lake road leads 15 miles (23 km.) E to Morán. This is a town of ladinos, with a small Sunday market patronized by Indians of near-by villages as well as by ladinos. The fiesta of the Seña de la Agonía (Sign of the Agony) is celebrated during Lent. From Morán it is 14½ miles (23 km.) to Guatemala City, via La Aurora airport, over a good road.

Palín (Steep Water, from the Michatoya falls, S of the town) is a small, interesting Indian village 8 miles (13 km.) beyond Amatitlán. It is chiefly noted for its market, held Wednesdays, Fridays, and Sundays until midafternoon under the shade of a 400-year-old ceiba tree with a 180-foot spread. The women wear an interesting huipil, very short and loose, which has a coarse white background covered with designs of birds and animals.

The church, built in 1570, was partially destroyed by the earthquake of 1773. It contains a silver altar and figures made in the colonial era.

Palín celebrates several fiestas: Corpus Christi, with the Bull Dance; St. James, celebrated along with that of St. Christopher on July 30; St. Theresa, October 15; All Saints' (Todos los Santos), with the dance of the Devils, November 1. At fiestas men wear the old picturesque costume which is not seen on everyday occasions.

The Michatoya falls provide power for an electric plant just below the town. This is a rich agricultural region specializing in kapok, sugar, and pineapples and marks the beginning of the great plain that stretches down to the Pacific. From the town there are magnificent views of the surrounding mountains and especially of the volcano Agua, immediately above. Looking W, 40 miles of ranches, plains, and virgin forest stretch to the Pacific.

Buses pass daily between Guatemala City and San José. Food is procurable, but there is no boarding place.

Excursion from Palín. A back road leads to Antigua via Santa María de Jesús. This is a longer but more colorful route from Guatemala City to Antigua than via Mixco (p. 68). The volcano Pacaya is on the right during the ascent from Palín.

Santa María de Jesús, on the side of the volcano Agua, offers magnificent views of Fuego and Pacaya. It is a thatch-roofed, almost completely Indian village, its streets lined with cornstalk fences. Women wear a striking huipil with diagonal, zigzag, and diamond patterns on a white or colored background. Men wear woven red shirts, sutes, and sashes. Occupations are weaving and agriculture; vegetables, corn, and beans are grown. There is no market. Fiestas are Dulce Nombre de Jesús (Sweet Name of Jesus), usually the first Sunday in January; St. Anthony, June 3; Sagrado Corazón de Jesús (Sacred Heart of Jesus) and Santísima Trinidad (Holy Trinity), which are movable feasts; and the Immaculate Conception, December 8.

The church, built in 1560 by Franciscan monks, has a 16th-century altar, 400-year-old organ, woodcarvings, a replica of the Black Christ of Esquipulas, and a very old image of the Virgin of Guadalupe. There are also ruins of the older church of El Calvario, ½ mile N, whose foundations alone remain.

The ascent of the volcano Agua by foot or mule starts from this village. There is frequent bus service to Antigua. On the road descending to Antigua there are sweeping views of the volcanoes Agua, Fuego, and Acatenango; the valley of Panchoy, and the city of Antigua. For description of Antigua, see above (p. 52)..

(Concepción) Escuintla (Abundance of Dogs), at 1100 feet elevation, 10 miles (13 km.) beyond Palín, is a winter resort in the center of a rich tropical valley below the volcano Agua. Escuintla is also reached by railroad from Guatemala City (48 miles, 77 km.) and San José (28 miles, 45 km.). At Santa María, a hamlet S of Escuintla, the railroad branches W to Mexico. There is a landing field in the outskirts of Escuintla, but no planes stop there regularly.

Escuintla was a pre-conquest town which was most prosperous during the 17th and 18th centuries, when indigo was of utmost commercial importance. Today the city is noted for its medicinal baths, especially those of Aguas Vivas and Aguas de Zarza. It is the center of a rich agricultural district of coffee, sugar cane, and banana plantations. All sorts of fruits and tropical plants grow here: mangoes, breadfruit, coconuts, pineapples. There is a daily market, and the fiesta of the Immaculate Conception, December 8-12, is celebrated.

Bus service is maintained with Guatemala City and San José. Gas and air are procurable.

HOTELS. Ferrocarril (Railroad) ; Central.

Puerto San José, 30 miles (49 km.) S of Escuintla by road, is an important shipping center, especially during the coffee season. An iron wharf leads to the pier head, and passengers and freight are carried by crane from ship to shore.

The region is tropical and hot, but swimming, hunting, and fishing are excellent. San José is well patronized as a resort, especially during Holy Week. Launches can be secured for the trip through the Chiquimulilla Canal, a waterway paralleling the coast and separated by a long narrow strip of land from the Pacific Ocean. This canal has been dredged to Ahumado, 36 miles (58 km.) distant. The scene is vivid with jungle vegetation, red and white herons, egrets, macaws, monkeys, pumas, and alligators. The surface of the water is almost covered with the balón, a kind of lotus with immaculate white blossoms. The passage of the boat pulls loose masses of the plants with a noise like ripping silk.

Two trains make daily round trips from Guatemala City to San José. The fast train takes 4¾ hours. Buses also run to and from Guatemala City. Gas is sold.

HOTELS. Miramar; California.

Iztapa, reached by car from Guatemala City (75 miles, 121 km.) or by launch from San José, is a small village on the Río María Linda, famous as a resort. Here are fishing, swimming, and boating in the midst of tropical jungles of great beauty. In addition, a launch trip along the Río María Linda (Pretty Mary) affords superb views of vegetation and wild life. Immense ceiba trees, 60 feet or more to the lowest branch, and mahoganies hung with moss and orchids stand in dense thickets of palms, tree ferns, and trailing water vines which contain a pint of liquid to each foot of vine. The brush is full of game —small deer, herds of peccary and tapir, monkeys, sometimes jaguars— and birds and butterflies of all kinds and colors.

Iztapa in olden times was a port. Alvarado sailed from it on his disastrous expedition to present-day Ecuador, whose wealthy kingdom of Quito he hoped to conquer.

NORTH FROM GUATEMALA CITY

The easiest way to reach Cobán, 100 miles N of the capital as the crow flies, is by plane from Guatemala City in 40 minutes, as against many hours of hot driving. Until recently it was necessary to go to El Rancho (p. 42) by car or train and on to Cobán by bus or car. The completion of an alternate route has lessened both time and distance. The new Route 5 passes through San Juan Sacatepéquez (p. 50). The trip to the Río Motagua, 21 miles (33 km.) from San Juan Sacatepéquez, is hot. Beside the road are patches of wild teocintle, presumably the precursor of corn. Corn existed in its present form many centuries before the discovery of America and undoubtedly was the dominant food crop of the aboriginal peoples, as well as of the present-day Indians. Teocintle is similar to corn in many respects, but has never been made to produce ears. It can be recognized by its cornlike tassel. Route 5, one of Guatemala's important highways, continues 9 miles (15 km.) to Granados; 7 miles (11 km.) to Santa Cruz el Chol; and 15 miles (25 km.) to Rabinal. Beyond Rabinal it passes through Salamá, from which Cobán is reached over the old road. The grades at Cachil and Santa Rosa, between Salamá and Cobán, are bad in wet weather.

(San Pablo) Rabinal is the first place of importance, 53 miles (84 km.) beyond San Juan Sacatepéquez. Founded by Bartolomé de las Casas, Rabinal is situated on the Río Rabinal in a beautiful valley surrounded by mountains. Primarily Indian, it raises rice and fruits of all kinds and makes petates or mats, hats, ollas or pots, and gourds. Market is held daily; Sundays and Thursdays are the most important days. The patron saint's fiesta is that of St. Paul on January 25; there is also a celebration for St. Peter and St. Paul, June 29.

The large church, rebuilt after earthquakes, contains a silver and gold altar and is interesting for its arches. Rabinal is sometimes locally called Rabinal Achí, the name not of a place, but of a dance which was last performed in this town. The ruins of Tinamit, a pre-conquest city with well-preserved buildings, are about 2 miles from town, and those of Cajyup a little farther.

Thomas Gage described Rabinal as a town "which hath all that heart can wish for pleasure and life of man." His idea of the "pleasure and life of man" was restricted apparently to foodstuffs: oranges, lemons, citrons, pomegranates, grapes, figs, almonds, dates, beef, kid, mutton, fowl, turkey, quail, partridge, rabbit, pheasant. What has become of this great wealth of local foodstuffs in the ensuing centuries is a mystery, for although Rabinal produces bananas and the best oranges in the country, there are today few other attractions for gourmets.

San Miguel Chicaj, 11 miles (17 km.) due E of Rabinal, has an attractive tree-filled plaza with a fine central pila or fountain. A daily market is held in late afternoon; the fiesta is that of St. Michael, September 29. The white and pink huipiles used as head coverings and as servilletas or carrying cloths are unique. There is no bus service, no gas, and no place to eat.

(San Mateo) **Salamá,** at 930 feet elevation, capital of the department of Baja Verapaz, is 6 miles (9 km.) farther E. This is hot country; olives, cane, and livestock are produced. Market is held daily. The main fiestas are those of Corpus Christi and of St. Matthew, September 15. The colonial church contains many altars of the finest workmanship, carved and gilded, including a figure of Christ by Evaristo Zúñiga, the noted colonial sculptor.

HOTELS. Pensión Victoria. Better lodgings can be secured with doña Esperanza.

Excursion from Salamá. Route 17, SE to El Rancho, is the road which formerly gave the only access by car from Guatemala City to Cobán. Two great mountains and hot, level desert country lie between Salamá and El Rancho, a total distance of 41 miles (66 km.).

San Jerónimo (Verapaz) is the only town of importance. In the 17th century, as a property of the Dominican monastery at Antigua, it was known for its sugar, slaves, and excellent horses. Dominican friars built aqueducts and made the town a famous wine-producing center. Later wine was replaced by aguardiente, for which the town is still noted.

Market is held Thursdays and Sundays. The fiesta of St. Jerome is observed, September 30.

There is frequent bus or truck service to El Rancho. Gas is sold.

Tactic is 25 miles (40 km.) N of Salamá on Route 5. E of this road, a few miles beyond Salamá, the Río Cahabón is seen gushing from the mountainside. The road forks just before Tactic, going W toward Cobán, E toward Panzós on the route to Lake Izabal (p. 64).

Tactic holds an interesting market on Sundays and Thursdays. The chief fiesta is that of the Assumption, August 15. Occupations are weaving, agriculture, and soap- and candle-making. The huipiles here are remarkable; they are made in three pieces, the central piece heavily woven in an all-over pattern on a blue or green background, the outer two panels less heavily decorated. With the huipil a bright red skirt is worn.

In this town quaint small clay animals or other figures are perched on the ridgepoles of houses. The church is attractive, with carved wooden crossbeams and an elaborate carved altar covered with gold leaf.

An entertaining sight is a small pool called pozo vivo or live well, reached by going somewhat more than a mile W of the plaza and then across a field N of the road. The pool is supposed to respond to the sound of voices; when people come near it and begin talking, it soon starts roiling and bubbling, and the quiet sandy bottom and calm surface are converted into a great boiling pool, sometimes so active that it throws submerged logs far into the air. Left to itself, it presumably subsides.

A bus goes to Cobán irregularly, but there is no gas. Food can be purchased.

Excursion from Tactic. San Cristóbal (Verapaz), 12 miles (19 km.) away, lies W off the road to Cobán. Its vivid market is well worth seeing on Sundays and Thursdays. Fiestas are those of St. Christopher, July 25, and St. Sebastian, January 20. Agriculture, especially sugar cane and coffee, and hides provide the chief occupations. Leather goods and shoes are made. There is a colonial church which contains good silver and an old figure of St. Joachim (San Joaquín). Laguna de San Cristóbal, on the outskirts of town, is a lake locally esteemed for its fishing, swimming, boating, and, in season, duck hunting. It is also supposed to have been a sacrificial lake of the Mayas and to contain vast treasures that cannot be recovered. An ancient Indian site, Caj-Caj, lies S of the town.

There is no regular bus schedule and no gas.

W of San Cristóbal a road extends toward the Río Chixoy. Eventually this will run farther W to connect with Sacapulas (p. 79), via Uspantán and Cunén; a stretch of 10 miles (16 km.) is finished (1941). It is worth traveling to the end of the road for the spectacular views of mountains and valleys.

EXCURSION TO LAKE IZABAL

A trip to the Atlantic coast above Puerto Barrios, via large Lake Izabal, is possible from Tactic. Route 7E winds E along the Río Polochic through several small towns to Panzós, terminus for small river boats which traverse Lake Izabal.

(Santa Catalina) Tamahú, the first place of interest, is 9½ miles (15 km.) from Tactic on a descending road. It is noted for its hot springs, each with different properties, and for its no less important fine onions. Market is held Saturdays and Wednesdays; notable fiestas are those of St. Catherine, November 25, and St. Paul, January 25. Women of this town have a very interesting hair arrangement of braids wound with red ribbon and crossed in front over the forehead.

(San Miguel) Tucurú, 9½ miles (15 km.) farther, grows excellent bananas. Market is held Thursdays, Saturdays, and Tuesdays. Fiestas are those of St. Michael, September 29; St. Catherine, November 25; and the Immaculate Conception, December 8. Women's huipiles are similar to those of Tactic, and their skirts are brilliant red. The hair is worn in a red roll. The simple church contains a Black Christ, much revered, and other images that are heavily dressed in huipiles of the region.

A bus passes daily, but not at a scheduled time. There is no hotel and no gas.

Pancajché, 9½ miles (15 km.) from Tucurú, is the starting point of the Verapaz Railway, which runs from here to Panzós, where connections for Livingston are made by water. Pancajché is very hot. A small, informal market is held beside the railroad tracks, where lowland produce is sold: mangoes, avocados, pineapples, and so on.

Lago de Izabal (Lake Izabal), azure and forest-lined, the largest lake in Guatemala, abounds in fish and crocodiles. At its E side it narrows to a stretch called La Angostura, then widens again to form the Golfete Dulce, out of which the Río Dulce flows to the sea. At the beginning of the narrows is the ancient castle of San Felipe, partially hidden by dense undergrowth. This was once a fort of great importance, garrisoned to prevent inroads by pirates in the 17th century. A chain was stretched from the fort to the opposite shore, under the water, to prevent ships from entering the lake. However, in 1666 a party of buccaneers landed and burned the castle, after which it was abandoned as a fort. For a time it was used as a state prison for political prisoners, but now it is deserted and overgrown.

The Río Dulce is one of the most beautiful stretches of water in the world. It emerges from the Golfete Dulce as a thin, curving line of water bordered by dense jungles alive with animals and exuberant tropical flowers. The river makes such abrupt turns that its course seems to be lost in forests. Along its shores are occasional small villages alternating with towering cliffs of greenery or great white stones that look like the leaves of an opened book. The natives of the region say that there is an enchanted cave in which dwells a mysterious cow with the power of regulating rains.

The palm-shaded city of Livingston is situated on a low promontory at the mouth of the Río Dulce. This was the Atlantic port before the construction of the railroad and of Puerto Barrios, and even now some ships stop at its customhouse. Its trade today consists in bananas, India rubber, and sarsaparilla; there is also some boat building and mahogany cutting. The inhabitants are Caribs whose forebears came from the island of St. Vincent and who even today maintain their independent customs and life. Ten miles SE of Livingston, Puerto Barrios can be reached by launch.

COBAN

(Santo Domingo) Cobán, at 4281 feet elevation, capital of the department of Alta Verapaz, is 19 miles (31 km.) from Tactic. The N center of the coffee industry, Cobán is a city of considerable size and importance. The climate is much wetter than that of most of the country, and produce is exceptionally good; the city is surrounded by plantations of coffee, tea, cacao, vanilla, and so on. Since shipping via the Río Polochic and Livingston from here is cheaper than by railroad through El Rancho, Cobán has a semi-independent industrial life.

Cobán was founded by Bartolomé de las Casas, the peripatetic friar who reorganized the Verapaz region, and it was named for an Indian chief, Cobaón. The colonial church, built in 1650, is well preserved. A more beautiful edifice is the church of El Calvario, high on a hillside, which dates from 1559. It contains a beautiful image of Christ Crucified by the colonial artist Evaristo Zúñiga.

The huipiles of Cobán women are charming and distinctive. For everyday use, small stylized figures are woven on a colored background, usually green or blue. For special occasions the huipil is woven with white figures on a lacy white background, giving a very airy appearance. The headdress is also interesting; colored wool is wound tight around one braid of hair, then around the head. For more elaborate occasions, the woolen strands are woven into two long braids that hang down the back and end in great tassels. Indian women wear beautiful silver necklaces, often made of very old coins or figures.

Market is held daily, lasting half a day on Sunday, in a semi-inclosed space near the plaza. It is rich in food and textiles from far and near. Vanilla beans, strange spices, nets, ropes, and colored hammocks are specialties of this region. A shop in the town, El Indio, has a good supply of local textiles. Fiestas are those of Holy Week and St. Dominic, August 4.

The whole district extending as far as the source of the Río Negro is a potentially rich field for archeologists. There are innumerable artificial mounds, and many beautiful examples of Maya arts, including polychrome work, have been recovered from pools and caves, though no serious excavations have been undertaken.

Buses and trucks leave frequently for El Rancho. Ordinarily train connections to Puerto Barrios are good, but there is a long wait at El Rancho for the train for Guatemala City.

HOTELS. La Posada**, famous for its cooking; Progreso; Central.

EXCURSIONS FROM COBAN

San Juan Chamelco, a small Indian village which is 6 miles (10 km.) SE from Cobán, holds a small market each weekday and the fiesta of St. John on June 24. Fine woven string bags and hammocks are made in this village. The colonial church contains much beautiful silver and is especially known for its bells. A local Indian legend says that the bells were left in the tower by the king of the bats when he was frightened away. Until recently women were not allowed near them lest the tone be spoiled. Near by are some caves, consisting of great galleries, caverns, and intricate waterways.

San Pedro Carchá is an almost completely Indian village, 5 miles (8 km.) E of Cobán. It holds a daily market, with those of Fridays and Mondays most important. The patron saint's fiesta is that of St. Peter, June 29. The town specializes in agriculture and weaving and is a noted pottery center. It is situated on or near a pre-conquest site, and many bits of pottery, figures, and stones are found in the caves and hillsides in the immediate vicinity and are sold by the Indians. There is no regular bus service to Cobán. Gas and food are not on sale.

EL PETEN

Entry to the great N plain of El Petén, in area almost a third of the entire country, is very restricted. A road NE from Cobán to Flores, capital of the department, is under construction; 36 miles (58 km.) have been completed beyond San Pedro Carchá. At present, however, access to Flores is only by plane detouring en route from Guatemala City to Puerto Barrios.

Flores, capital of the department of El Petén, occupies an island in Lake Petén, surrounded by dense tropical jungle. Well into the colonial period a nation of Maya stock, the Itzás, maintained their independence in the country around the lake. They numbered at least 80,000 and were ruled by the admirable native chief Canek from his capital at Tayasal, which is now Flores. In 1697, after some five years of preliminary work, this native kingdom was brought under the rule of Charles II, king of Spain, by Martín de Ursúa y Arizmendi, the governor of Yucatán, aided in his dramatic conquest by the Franciscan Father Andrés de Avendaño y Lóyola. Philip Ainsworth Means tells the story in his book, The Spanish Conquest of Yucatán and of the Itzás.

The region provides unexcelled hunting and fishing, since the waters and forests abound in animal life, with jaguars, tapirs, peccaries, alligators, and manatees.

Uaxactún, site of the great Maya ruins, is reached by plane from Guatemala City via Flores. A chicle camp is located here.

Uaxactún (Eight Stones, to commemorate the finding of the early stela dated A.D. 68) dates from the Old Empire period. The ruins, discovered in 1916, were excavated under the auspices of the Carnegie Institution. Here were discovered the earliest monuments in the whole region of El Petén, as well as the latest, dated A.D. 639. During the six centuries between the two dates, one of the world's highest civilizations arose, flourished, and passed away. Flat-topped and highly ornamented stone pyramids, built in a series of terraces, surround a main plaza which was probably used as a market place. Excavations have revealed sculptures, jade pieces, and beautiful pottery.

Tikal, only 12 linear miles from Uaxactún but very difficult to reach, is another Maya site, almost unexplored. It consists of vast temples, monuments, and public buildings. It is covered in Thomas Gann's entertaining Maya Cities (London, 1927)

GUATEMALA CITY TO EL SALVADOR

Guatemala City and San Salvador are the only two Central American capitals which are connected by the Pan American Highway (1941). There is daily bus service (10-12 hours) between the two cities. From Guatemala City to the border is 104 miles (168 km.); to San Salvador, capital of El Salvador, a total of 166 miles (267 km.). The road follows the crests of high ridges much of the way. It passes through Cuilapa and Jutiapa, then drops down to skirt the shore of Lake Atescatempa before passing into El Salvador. Old inhabitants at Atescatempa say that near the turn of the century the lake dried up and disappeared, then suddenly reappeared. The lake, extremely irregular, has several grassy islands. Its surroundings are dense green forests which provide good hunting, especially for deer, cougar, ducks, and cranes.

On this road is the Río de los Esclavos (Slaves), 2 miles (4 km.) E of Cuilapa, crossed by a massive stone and brick bridge which is still in excellent condition and about which many legends center. Begun in 1592 and seriously damaged several times, the bridge is locally regarded as the work of the devil, to whom a slave had sold his soul. The devil was exorcised, but he managed to knock loose a stone, which has since left a vacancy. If it is put back in place the stone always disappears again.

In one section of the road the work on culverts and bridges was done in co-operation with the U. S. government. This is the part that begins at Asunción Mita (92 miles or 148 km. from Guatemala City). It ends at the border. Among the bridges, those of Tamasulapa and Amatal are the most important.

A number of Indian mounds and graveyards dating from pre-conquest days were discovered near Asunción Mita in 1936 while the road was under construction. The Carnegie Institution made careful studies and researches at the request of the national highway department, and valuable jade, clay, and stone objects were found, which can be seen at the Archeological Museum in Guatemala City. Asunción Mita derives its name from the Indian word Mitlan, which means City of the Dead. Presumably the district around Asunción Mita was the chosen burial ground of the Indian tribes of the region.

WEST FROM GUATEMALA CITY

Five miles W of Guatemala City on Route 1, the Pan American Highway toward Quezaltenango (p. 84) and Mexico (p. 92), is the site Kaminal Juyú, explored by the Carnegie Institution. Excavators uncovered an ancient ball field about one square mile in area, believed to have been part of a Maya city of considerable grandeur. Two carved stone parrots' heads, typical of the ball courts of several Maya cities, were dug up in the region. As the site is one of great natural beauty and easily accessible from Guatemala City, a national park will be established here and will eventually be the site of the National Museum of Archeology, already planned.

The Pan American Highway winds up a mountain from which there are magnificent panoramic views of the valley of Las Vacas, especially at night when the city lights shine brilliantly in the long valley.

(Santo Domingo) Mixco, 8½ miles (13 km.) from Guatemala City, was founded about 1526 by survivors of Mixco Viejo (Old Mixco). It owes its name, meaning Place of Clouds, to the fact that the original Mixco, on a hill, was often shrouded in mist. Following the destruction of the capital in 1773, the printing press was moved from Antigua to Mixco, and here was printed Felipe Cadena's famous work about Antigua and its sufferings in the earthquake, written in 1774.

Mixco was a thriving city when Thomas Gage knew it in the early 17th century. Gage noted one practice that has not survived: the women of the town, who made pottery of a white earth, ate great quantities of the stuff so that their skin would appear lighter. At present Mixco manufactures comales or round, flat pottery pieces on which tortillas are baked. The tortillas themselves, together with fruits and vegetables, are borne to the Guatemala City markets daily.

Market is held in Mixco on Sundays, Tuesdays, and Thursdays. The chief celebration is the fiesta of Los Morenos (The Dark Ones), during the last week of January, with Indian dances. Of second importance is the patron saint's fiesta, that of St. Dominic (Santo Domingo de Guzmán), August 2-4. That of the Rosary, October 7, is also celebrated. Every third Sunday in the month there is a religious procession.

Buses pass at all hours, since Mixco is on the main road to Antigua as well as the route W. Gas and air are procurable. Food can be bought, and there is a small boarding house.

Beyond Mixco the road continues climbing, past a Swiss chalet and hotel called San Rafael. N of the highway, across a ravine, are seen the paths and gardens of President Ubico's country estate.

Excursion to Antigua. A road branches sharply left from Route 1 at a point 4½ miles (7 km.) beyond Mixco. The first town on this side road is San Lucas (Sacatepéquez), a pre-conquest village once noted for pools reputed to produce a lasting black dye. The beautiful church, ruined by earthquakes, has been rebuilt, unfortunately with a zinc roof. The fiesta of St. Luke is celebrated on October 18. After passing San Lucas, there is a curving segment of road known as La Mano del Diablo because of its five curves in the shape of fingers. There is a sharp descent from Cuesta de Las Cañas. Then the Río Pensativo, bordering Antigua, is crossed by a stone bridge. For description of Antigua, see above (p. 52).

(Santiago) Sumpango (Place of Skulls), 14 miles (22 km.) beyond Mixco, has a lively daily market across from the church. The church, one of the few not damaged by earthquakes, contains two good images of St. James on horseback and a gold-leaf altar and images. There are carved crossbeams, and the font on the right of the entrance is primitive but of beautiful design and color. Manufactures are soap and candles. The fiesta of St. Augustine is celebrated on August 26-29 with Indian dances.

(Santa Ana de) Chimaltenango (Place of Shields), at 5869 feet elevation, capital of its department, is 6½ miles (10 km.) farther W. It is an Indian municipality, originally founded in 1526 by Pedro de Portocarrero, one of Alvarado's lieutenants. The old city was fortified and was much more important than the modern one.

The town can also be reached from Antigua; the approach then is through an avenue of pine, cypress, and eucalyptus; on the left, half a mile away, are the swimming pool of Los Aposentos and the National Agricultural School. The chief industry is brick-making. A pleasant market is held Mondays, Wednesdays, and Fridays. Fiestas are Epiphany (Día de los Reyes), celebrated January 6-9, and St. Anne, July 26. There are fine views over mountains and volcanoes. The chief interest of the town itself is its colonial fountain, situated on the continental divide; from one side the water flows to the Pacific, from the other to the Atlantic.

Buses pass at all hours. Gas and air are procurable.

HOTELS. Central; Rex; Lux; San José.

Excursions from Chimaltenango. A road leads 12 miles (19 km.) N to San Martín Jilotepeque. The road crosses barrancas or steep-sided hollows and narrow passes, but the vegetation is dotted with bright orchids, and the village is well worth seeing for its great market and beautiful costumes.

San Martín Jilotepeque (Corn Husk Mountain), 80 per cent Indian, has markets on Thursdays and Sundays that are almost unrivaled for their array of beautiful huipiles in which blue and purple predominate, though there is also much green and some brown. In superficial appearance these blouses resemble those of San Antonio Aguas Calientes, where the weaving is the finest in all Guatemala; the infinite variation of design and workmanship is fascinating. The patron saint's fiesta is that of St. Martin, November 11. Occupations are weaving, jug-making, and production of beans and eggs. The town is pre-colonial. The present church is built on the walls of the old Mercedarian church, now represented chiefly by its belltower, with fine bells, and some silver accessories. There is occasional bus service to and from Guatemala City. No gasoline is sold. There are two boarding houses.

Mixco Viejo, beyond San Martín Jilotepeque, is the ruins of the old Pocoman capital, which held out strongly against Alvarado but was eventually conquered. It is some 18 miles (29 km.) from San Martín Jilotepeque and can be reached only by horseback. An overnight stop can be arranged at Las Pilas plantation, which belongs to Francisco Martínez. The round trip requires at least 3 days.

Zaragoza, 6 miles (10 km.) W of Chimaltenango, raises cereals, avocados, and other agricultural produce. Corpus Christi is celebrated, and an interesting fiesta of Our Lady of El Pilar is held on October 12.

Excursion to (San Juan) Comalapa. About ¾ mile W a road branches

N to Comalapa, 10 miles (16 km.) away. The road is poor, and the trip takes 1¼ hours, but the town is very rewarding for its busy market and interesting huipiles. The afternoon markets held on Fridays, Mondays, and Wednesdays are among the brightest in the country. Huipiles are made on a brown or white cotton background, with broad red stripes interspersed with rows of designs in magenta, purple, and green silk or wool. The infinite variations within this scheme are amazing; quality, design, and even size are completely individual. Fiestas celebrated are those of St. John, June 24; the Immaculate Conception, December 8; and the Virgin of Guadalupe, December 12, the largest. Occupations are agriculture, weaving, and brick-making.

The church of San Juan Bautista, very rich, is one of the oldest and finest in Guatemala. Built by the Franciscans about 1600, it contains an excellent image of St. John the Baptist, beautiful lamps and paintings, a carved altar, and silver ornaments. There are also two less interesting churches, Guadalupe and El Calvario.

(Santiago) Patzicía (Near the Badger's River), 4 miles (6 km.) from Zaragoza on Route 1, is a small Indian village established in 1545. Market is held Wednesdays and Saturdays. The fiesta of the patron saint, St. James, is held July 23-26. The church, a few blocks W of the central plaza, contains elaborate and beautiful silver and a good altar. There are two small places to eat.

Beyond the town of Patzicía the road bifurcates, and the right branch goes to Tecpán and the Chichoy Pass, the left to Patzún and Lake Atitlán. The two roads come together again at Los Encuentros. The left road to Patzún leads past La Sierra, an old Franciscan wheat mill where many stone idols were found. After climbing the Cuesta de Patzún the town of Patzún is reached.

(San Bernardino) Patzún (Hide-Beating Place), 8 miles (13 km.) from Patzicía on the left road, has a church dating from 1570, with silver and gold altarpiece and red lacquer decorations, which has not suffered markedly from earthquakes, and its original beautiful carved wooden roof and doors are intact. On looking back after leaving the town, it is possible to see that the church tilts slightly to one side.

Patzún has a great stone pila or fountain of colonial construction with heraldic inscriptions. Women's huipiles of bright red and white striped cotton are very arresting. Market is held on Sundays. The patron saint's fiesta, that of St. Bernard, is held on May 20. Gasoline is sold.

From Patzún the road climbs the Cuesta de los Chocoyos, named for a bird species of the region, and then descends to cross the Puente de los Idolos, so called because certain large idols were found at the bottom of the barranca or deep hollow. There is a local legend that a cave near here was the hiding place of bandits; an earthquake caused the rock to fall in, imprisoning the bandits as well as their great store of wealth. The entrance can be seen from the road as a huge boulder suggesting a cathedral door.

Godínez, a small town 10 miles (16 km.) W of Patzún, is of interest only as a place to eat and where buses stop. A road leads S from the village to San Lucas Tolimán (p. 72) and thence to the low-lying villages and plantations of the Pacific coastlands.

Just out of Godínez the highland plateau abruptly ends. From a lookout there is a sudden and spectacular view of Lake Atitlán some

2000 feet below, one of the world's most beautiful lakes, with an infinite variation of color. Three magnificent volcanoes border the lake, their peaks often hidden by clouds. Two of these, Tolimán and San Pedro, form its S limit; the third, Atitlán, is S of Tolimán. The tiny village of San Antonio Palopó is visible far below clinging to steep mountain slopes, and cornfields seem to slide down into the water.

San Andrés Semetabaj (Round Stones), at the bottom of the hill 4½ miles (7 km.) from Godínez, is a small pre-colonial village of white plaster houses and tiled roofs set in the midst of pine forests. There is no view of the lake, but the volcanoes are visible. The old church was destroyed by earthquake, only the façade and dome in the rear remaining, and within its walls a cornfield now flourishes. There is also a modern church.

The valley of Panajachel is bordered by terraced gardens, especially of garlic and onions. A small stream, the Río Panajachel, threads through the valley. In the dry season this stream is only a few inches deep, but after several days of continued rain it becomes a raging torrent. Fortunately for drivers, there is a new bridge across it. The river empties into Lake Atitlán.

LAKE ATITLAN

The villages that lie around Lake Atitlán are familiar to many who have never seen them as being 12 in number and named for the apostles. Actually there are more than 15 settlements, and only three take their names from apostles. All can be reached by water. A launch service operates from a wharf in front of Hotel Tzanjuyú in Panajachel, with regular schedules to some of the villages; motorboats can be hired for special trips to other less frequently visited spots. Trails connect most of the villages, though there is a break between Panajachel and Santa Cruz.

Lake Atitlán (Place of the Water), 5000 feet above sea level and 1500 feet deep, is a lake of very irregular outline, approximately 17 miles across and 60-80 miles around. The bed is thought to be an ancient valley dammed by volcanic ash. The three great volcanoes near by are those of Tolimán, 10,750 feet, which has not been violent since 1852, with the small Cerro de Oro (Gold Hill) in front of it; Atitlán, 11,499 feet high, which erupted last in 1843; and far W, San Pedro, 9920 feet. The water is not cold, and the swimming is excellent. In the mornings the lake is quiet and mirrorlike, but in the afternoons a strong wind often springs up and makes canoeing or sailing hazardous. The Indians use big canoes or little cayucos, tree trunks hollowed in a special form. The lake is full of small fish that make delicious eating, mojarras and pepezcas, and there are fresh-water crabs.

Three separate language groups survive in this countryside: Cakchiquel, Zutugil, and Quiché, representing the three great Maya-Quiché nations that were at war among themselves at the time of the Spanish conquest. Each of the lake villages has a distinct costume, usually completely different from its neighbors' and often very beautiful. Red and white predominate, in checks or stripes overlaid with small figures. Men generally wear a blue or black capixay or long cloak and a straw hat.

(San Francisco) Panajachel (Place of the Matazano Tree) is the first of the lake villages reached, since the central part of it is on the Pan American Highway, 5 miles (8 km.) from San Andrés Semetabaj. It holds its market on Sundays. Fiestas are those of St. Francis, October 4; All Saints', November 1; and the Immaculate Conception, December 8. The colonial church was built in 1641 by the Franciscans, but was partially destroyed by earthquakes. Still intact are the façade, walls, and the sacristy, now used as a church. The old church was beautifully proportioned. In the shadow of its ruins the market is held, patronized by Indians in gay costumes from all over the lake region. Coffee, onions, and garlic are the principal crops.

Buses pass frequently to and from Guatemala City. Gasoline is sold.

HOTELS. Near the shore of Lake Atitlán are several hotels. Hotel Tzanjuyú* (Mountain's Nose), a little more than a mile from the Panajachel church, has a long balcony overlooking the lake, a cocktail room directly above the water, fireplaces, horses, tennis, and swimming. Casa Contenta** consists of several separate complete units; there are fireplaces, horses, and a private beach, and the food is excellent. Hotel Monterrey stands directly on the lake shore.

The other lake villages are listed here clockwise from Hotel Tzanjuyú.

Santa Catalina (Palopó) (On the Sea) is a tiny village where petates or large reed mats are woven. This is a fishing and crabbing village. By launch, 15 minutes.

San Antonio (Palopó), a very lovely mountainside village, is known for its petates or mats. Fiestas are those of St. Anthony, June 13, and St. Nicholas, September 10. The town has a fine old church. By launch, ½ hour.

San Lucas Tolimán (Where Reeds Are Gathered) is an active trading center, since it is located on the chief trade route from highlands to coast, crossing Lake Atitlán. The village can also be reached by car from the main roads. N it communicates with the Pan American Highway at Godínez and S with the main E-W road to the Pacific. Market is held Tuesdays and Fridays. The fiesta of St. Luke is on October 18. The church has two excellent paintings near the high altar. By launch, 1½ hours.

Climbs of Atitlán and Tolimán start from this town.

Doña Beatriz de Crespo has accommodations for travelers.

Cerro de Oro (Gold Hill), on the flank of the volcano Tolimán, was settled by natives from Patzicía. Petates or mats are woven here. It is a rich archeological site. There is a legend that the fabulous treasures of the Zutugils are buried somewhere in the vicinity. At Isla de los Gatos (Cat Island), presumably hundreds of Zutugils jumped into the water rather than let themselves by captured by the advancing Spaniards.

(Santiago) Atitlán, on the slopes of the volcano Atitlán, is the most interesting and colorful of the villages because of the extremely picturesque costume of its women: long red skirt; white huipil with purple stripes, decorated around the neck with red or purple; red and blue rebozo with woven fringe; and a headband 1½ inches wide and 10-12 yards long which is tied around the hair, then wrapped around the head to resemble a great red halo. The women are tall, beautifully formed, and of majestic carriage; they may often be seen sitting in groups around the edges of the lake, washing, or carrying great jugs of water to their homes.

Before the conquest this was the principal town of the Zutugils. Today it is a delightful village; with its thatch-roofed huts hidden by foliage, it has almost the appearance of an African scene. Zopilotes or buzzards are often seen perched on the peaked rooftops. Chuitinamit, directly across the bay from the town, is thought to be the ruins of the Zutugil capital destroyed by Alvarado. There are some rich archeological sites which have been little explored as yet.

On a hill behind the village is a coffee beneficio or processing establishment, readily located by the smell of fermentation. Coffee beans, when ripe, look like cherries, but the flesh is of no value and must be fermented and washed off. The seed consists of two hemispheres held together by a tough skin. The beans are dried, hulled, sorted, graded, polished, and sacked. Various stages of this process can be seen during the picking season, November-March.

The market, attended almost solely by women, is held daily on a broad plaza, 11 a.m.-2 p.m.; the one on Saturdays is the largest. The church dates from 1541 and is very picturesque with its saints' images dressed gaily in floating garments. The fiesta of St. James is on July 25.

By launch 1¼ hours.

San Pedro (la Laguna), in the lee of the volcano San Pedro, is a pre-conquest village where today a few dugouts are made. Men wear green, blue, red, or yellow shirts; the longest trousers in any of the lake villages, with colored designs; and a long, soft red belt knotted in front. By launch, 1¼ hours.

Las Cristalinas, a delightful bathing beach, is best reached from San Pedro. It lies halfway between San Pedro and San Pablo.

San Juan (la Laguna) is devoted entirely to agriculture. By launch, 1¼ hours.

Visitación and Santa Clara (la Laguna) are two small villages side by side on a plateau high above the lake. Splendid baskets are made here. The climb to the plateau lengthens the trip to the villages. By launch, 1¼ hours.

San Pablo (la Laguna), a pre-conquest village, is today a center of the henequen industry. Beautiful hammocks, much of the sisal rope used throughout the country, and fine net bags are made. There is half an hour's steep climb from the lake shore to the town. By launch, 1 hour.

San Marcos (la Laguna), rarely visited, is a fruit-growing village. By launch, 1 hour.

Tzununá, rarely visited, is noted for the quality of its oranges.

Santa Cruz (la Laguna), high on the volcano San Pedro, is reached by a stiff climb from the landing dock. The picturesque old church is visible from almost every part of the lake. By launch, ½ hour.

───────────

The Pan American Highway, W of Panajachel, rises 2000 feet in the 5 miles (8 km.) to Sololá. This steep grade is one of the most scenically beautiful stretches of road in all Guatemala.

San Jorge (la Laguna), a small village, is seen a short distance up the hill at the left of the road. It is almost completely hidden by the thick forest of jocote trees filling the gorge in which it lies.

Continuing, the road passes a beautiful waterfall, Cascada de San Buenaventura, which falls from the cliff above and continues its descent below the road.

SOLOLA

(Asunción de) Sololá (Gushing Water), capital of its department, is known chiefly for the costume of its men, especially the elders of the community, and for its gay and active Friday market held on a broad plain overlooking the lake far below. The Sololá market is a great trade center for vegetables grown in the region, with emphasis on onions, garlic from Panajachel, and anise from San Antonio. Since it is a leading market on a great trade route, merchants also sell here tropical fruits and cacao from the coast, wheat and potatoes from the highlands, pottery, soap, leather, and so on. A much smaller market is held on Tuesdays.

Sololá men wear red shirts; white trousers with many red stripes; short slipover or coat jackets made of black-and-white or brown-and-white woolen, with scrolls and other designs in black braid; and straw hats with a sute or headdress striped and figured in red. The men make and usually carry black-and-white knitted bags, gaily figured. High Indian civil and religious officials wear blouses with turned-back collar, black overpants turned up, and shiny black straw hats with squared-off crowns and decorated colored bands, underneath which the sute hangs down.

A departmental fair is held during the week preceding Holy Week. The great fiesta is the Assumption of the Virgin, August 15. Also celebrated are those of Candlemas (La Candelaria) in February and the Immaculate Conception, December 8. The church was built by the Franciscans in 1541 but was rebuilt after the 1902 earthquakes. It contains old silver and gold altars and interesting robes for the Virgin.

Many buses serve Sololá, and several begin their journey to Guatemala City from here. Gas is sold.

HOTELS. Letona; Pensión Salas.

EXCURSIONS FROM SOLOLA

A mile beyond Sololá a lovely road, newly built, goes W to Nahualá, an exceedingly interesting Indian village.

San José Chacayá is passed about 4 miles (6 km.) out of Sololá. It has a colonial church with a carved and painted wooden altar and silver treasures. There are two venerable images of the Virgin, one of Aid and the other of Sorrows.

Santa Lucía Utatlán, 5 miles (8 km.) beyond San José Chacayá, also has a colonial church with carved and painted wooden altar and silver treasures.

(Santa Catalina) Nahualá, at 8129 feet elevation, 18 miles (29 km.) W of Sololá, is an Indian village of great interest. The population of 22,000 includes only two or three ladinos, since the Indians dislike having them in the municipality. The town is unique in another way, since it prohibits the sale of liquor and pays an annual tax to the government on the amount that might otherwise be consumed. Costumes are picturesque. Black huipiles are made by men. Very beautiful wide red-striped belts are woven by women and exquisitely embroidered by men. These belts are not usually visible, nor are the short white trousers, decorated with figures; the color used for them generally runs, in contrast to most Guatemalan dyes. Sutes of blue or green are woven by both men and women.

A living is made by agriculture and weaving, especially heavy wool blankets and rodilleras, worn like aprons or wrapped around. The fame of Nahualá rests on its metates or stones for grinding corn and on its marimbas. Along roads in the most remote regions men may be seen laboring under loads of metates from Nahualá, for there are few centers with an equal reputation.

There is a stone church with beautiful altars and a hammered silver image of St. Catherine. Market is Sundays and Thursdays. The fiesta of St. Catherine is held on November 25.

No food can be secured here unless from the priest or school teacher. No buses pass here; from Nahualá to Totonicapán (p. 81) there is a footpath which is eventually to become a motor road and so perhaps put an end to the privacy of this village. There is a new motor road S to Santa Catalina Ixtahuacán, its older twin. There is great rivalry between the two towns.

Concepción (Quichelaj), at 6500 feet elevation, about 6 miles (10 km.) E of Sololá, is reached by horseback, a small, lovely Indian town lying within its surrounding mountains as in a cup. The townspeople are little touched by outside influences; the majority do not speak Spanish, and their social customs are in many respects very ancient. The church dates from 1621 and is said to be built over Maya monoliths. The chief fiesta is that of the Immaculate Conception, December 8. Onions and garlic are the chief products. There is no place to eat.

Concepción forms a rough triangle with Sololá and Panajachel, and it is possible to descend 6 miles down a very steep cliff to Panajachel instead of returning to Sololá.

Los Encuentros (Meeting Place), 7 miles (12 km.) N of Sololá, is, as its name suggests, little more than a junction for two well-traveled roads: Route 1, from Lake Atitlán, which continues W more from this point to Totonicapán and beyond, and Route 15, coming more directly from Guatemala City via Tecpán and the Chichoy Pass and continuing N beyond this point to Chichicastenango and other towns described below. Los Encuentros consists of some few houses huddled together on the top of a mountain. There are a telegraph office and a place to eat where buses often stop. At 8038 feet elevation, wind-swept and always cold, Los Encuentros is not an enjoyable stopping place even in the best of weather, although the views are very fine on a clear day.

An alternate route to Los Encuentros can be taken from the bifurcation of the road a little past Patzicía (p. 70). The right branch, Route 15, continues W from there to Los Encuentros via Tecpán and the Chichoy Pass. Each route has its distinctive beauties of scenery; if possible, both roads should be traversed, depending somewhat upon the weather. The beauty of the Chichoy Pass is often completely obscured by heavy fog or rain, whereas that of Lake Atitlán is never completely hidden by the elements.

(San Francisco) Tecpán, at 7492 feet elevation, 12 miles (20 km.) NW of Patzicía, is the site of Alvarado's first capital. The old Cakchiquel capital of Iximché lay about 2 miles from the present city. Few vestiges of Iximché survived its destruction by the Spaniards. Today interest centers in the handiwork of the conquerors at Tecpán, the great church with beautiful altars of silver, carved wooden pillars and magnificent ceiling, and quaint images. The woodwork of the altars is almost completely covered with gold leaf. On the ceiling are seen the familiar double eagle, reminiscent of the Hapsburg influence; the clothed arm of St. Francis linked with the bare arm of Christ, a familiar Franciscan symbol; and various sun symbols.

The costume of the women is very striking. Brown huipiles are made from native brown cotton with red stripes of varying size intermingled with fine yellow and blue stripes. Market is held on Thursdays. It is a colorful scene, for this is a rich agricultural district which also boasts flour and lumber mills. The fiesta of St. Francis is celebrated October 1-8. Other fiestas are those of the Cross, May 3, and the Immaculate Conception, December 8. There are frequent buses to Guatemala City and some W to Quezaltenango (p. 84). Gasoline is sold.

HOTELS. Iximché* and Marta are boarding houses.

After leaving Tecpán, the road rises suddenly and spectacularly 3000 feet to the summit of the Chichoy Pass (Above the Lake), 10,000 feet high. On clear days the pass is spectacularly beautiful. First the volcanoes Agua and Fuego are seen across a broad valley, later Lake Atitlán and its surrounding volcanoes. A curious shrub looking like bamboo is seen everywhere on the pass, as well as occasional orchids. At Los Encuentros the road meets the Pan American Highway from Lake Atitlán; Route 1 continues W (p. 80).

EXCURSION TO CHICHICASTENANGO

If only one Indian town in Guatemala is visited, that one should be Chichicastenango. It can be made the point of departure for trips into all highland country; moreover, the Mayan Inn here is the best hotel in Guatemala. The easiest way to reach Chichicastenango from Guatemala City is with Clark's Tours or by plane to Quiché (p. 78), then by bus or private car. An extremely colorful town, Chichicastenango is a representative highland Indian community. See section on Indian Life (pp. 18-21).

(Santo Tomás) Chichicastenango (Place of Nettles), about 7000 feet elevation, 10 miles (15 km.) N of Los Encuentros, is a town of white plaster houses and red tiled roofs, the center for hundreds of traders and agriculturists who come each week for the market. Although tourists invariably call the town by its Indian name, natives more often refer to it as Santo Tomás, and indeed the villagers are commonly called Maxeños, a name derived from the last syllable of Tomás. The town is situated in the midst of hills which contribute greatly to its beauty. Because of the altitude the weather is cool in summer and cold during the winter months. During the rainy season it is often cloudy and foggy.

Costumes are extremely picturesque. Men wear a black woolen jacket and short black trousers with a winglike side flap elaborately decorated with braid and embroidery. On their heads they wear sutes of rich reds and purples; the finer examples have beautiful texture and color as well as striking design. Almost all men carry a black blanket with red and white checked ends. Women wear heavy huipiles with red figures woven on a white or brown background, usually finished off with rosettes of silk at the neck. Servilletas or carrying cloths are extremely fanciful and amusing. The skirt of dark blue stripes is bound about the waist with a thick belt. Men of Chichicastenango weave the material for their costumes on footlooms and do all the making except the final embroidery. Women do hand-weaving which includes men's sutes as well as their own huipiles.

Sundays are the chief market days, and there is also a small market on Thursdays. The great fiestas in order of importance are those of St. Thomas, December 18-21; Holy Week; and All Saints', November 1. There are smaller fiestas of St. Sebastian, January 20, and St. Joseph, March 19; on St. John the Baptist's day, June 24, there is a special celebration for shepherd boys.

The fiesta of St. Thomas here is one of the greatest celebrations in the whole country. The market place overflows with people from all parts of Guatemala in their gayest costumes. Processions with dancers, bearing saints' images, wind their way through the crowds, preceded and followed by men drumming on the tun and others playing on the chirimía or flageolet. Marimbas from near-by regions are brought into the city, and dozens of them are played night and day. Rockets are set off at all hours, and their acrid smell, together with that of copal incense from the church, is added to all the odors of the market. From the church belfry hangs a rope on which Tsijolaj, a little figure of a man mounted on a horse, rides up and down, never quite reaching either earth or heaven. The exact status of this figure is obscure, but apparently he is a kind of patron saint of rockets and fire. At one end of the plaza a volador—a high pole around which players swing themselves in rope loops in ever-increasing circles, presumably to imitate flying—may be set up, and though the ceremony has not the splendor here that is sometimes associated with it, the men swinging high up in the air add to the general stir and holiday feeling. Throughout the several days of the fiesta, dances are conducted in the houses of the cofrades or members of religious brotherhoods and in the plaza. Of these the most popular is that of La Conquista (The Conquest). Men wearing pink masks with elaborate curled mustaches and long red wigs and mounted on hobbyhorses are the Spanish conquerors. The Quiché and Cakchiquel war chiefs prepare for battle against the invaders. There is a ritual of preparation and sacrifice, together with a dance by the daughters of the chiefs. Alvarado and his men engage in battle, and the Quiché chief is killed. The victory of the Spaniards is celebrated. A religious note is introduced with the baptism of the Indians.

The present church and sacristy are splendid examples of Spanish colonial architecture. The church is amply proportioned, with immensely thick walls. The façade unfortunately has been modernized, but the two belltowers and the narrow gallery between them, reached by a spiral staircase in the wall, are old. The church is built on rising ground, and the door, many feet above the level of the plaza, is approached by an impressive flight of stone steps which lead to a large semicircular terrace or platform before the door. This platform is extremely important in Indian ritual. There are 18 steps leading up to it. Near the foot of the stairs, directly in line with the door of the church, is a boxlike structure some 3 feet long by 2 feet wide, built into the staircase and covered by a flat slab of rock with ashes always smoldering on it. This is the quemador, the place of burning, where copal incense is offered to non-Christian gods. Adjoining the church is the cloister of the old Dominican monastery built in 1542. Across the plaza is another church, the chapel of El Calvario. This building is much smaller and less pretentious; the steps are higher and the platform wider, and the quemador is on top of the platform, almost in the doorway of the church. It is against every local tradition for ladinos to enter the chapel of El Calvario or to take photographs within the church.

Father Ildefonso Rossbach of Chichicastenango, perhaps the best-known priest in Guatemala, has gained a unique appreciation of the Indians through his 50 years' association with them. His remarkable collection of jade and other Maya objects, housed in the monastery, is open to the public on market days when he is in residence. In this same monastery the Popol Vuh was discovered, the most valuable document that has survived to tell of the life of the Maya-Quiché.

A visit to the house of Diego Ignacio, maker and importer of masks, is interesting. Diego's wife Juanita does beautiful weaving and does not mind being watched. Beside the house a path leads to Turkaj, the chief idol and shrine of the region, also known as Pascual Abaj (Pascual's Stone). Farther up the same path is the shrine of Poquojil (To Open the Heavens). The latter trip takes about 2½ hours on horseback.

About a mile from town on the Quiché road a path descends to a deep ravine where there is a swimming pool. The pool can be reached only by horseback or on foot over very steep ground.

Chichicastenango is served several times a week by the buses run by Hermanos Botrán from Guatemala City to Quiché. A correo or mail bus regularly travels between Chichicastenango and Los Encuentros. At the latter point connections may be made with buses both W to Quezaltenango and E to Guatemala City. There is often a wait of 1-7 hours at Los Encuentros, and the journey is advised only for the determined traveler.

The trip to Quezaltenango (p. 84), 50 miles (80 km.) via Los Encuentros, takes about 3 hours. Another road to Quezaltenango is by Quiché to Totonicapán (p. 81); this road is less interesting but also less curving and is therefore sometimes preferred. Huehuetenango (p. 87), 80 miles (129 km.) N and W from Chichicastenango, is reached in about 4 hours in dry weather.

Gas is sold in Chichicastenango.

HOTELS. Mayan Inn** has excellent food and service; fireplaces in most rooms and private baths in many; beautiful colonial furnishings; gardens, pingpong, and private stables. Reservations are necessary at the height of the tourist season. Pensión Chugüilá has baths, fireplace, and an inner court for cars.

EXCURSION TO QUICHE

(Santa Cruz) Quiché (Many Trees), at 6616 feet elevation, 11 miles (18 km.) N of Chichicastenango, is capital of the department of El Quiché. It is situated near Utatlán, the ancient capital of the powerful Quiché nation which at the time of the conquest extended N and W through Chiapas and parts of Socunusco and E to Tecpán. It is said that with the downfall of the Quiché empire, the nobility migrated to Chichicastenango.

Market is held Sundays and Thursdays. The principal fiesta is Fiestas Elenas, instituted in honor of St. Helena and extended to a great fair, August 16-20. Also celebrated is the day of the Cross, May 3. In the town are the mineral baths of Pachitak. The Dominican church has been rebuilt; vestiges of its past glory are found in silver halos, images, and a few beautiful pictures.

Occasional buses give service to Chiché, Joyabaj, and Sacapulas (below), and there is scheduled service several times weekly to and from Guatemala City, via Chichicastenango. Gas is sold in Quiché.

HOTEL. España.

EXCURSIONS FROM QUICHE

Utatlán (Abundance of Wild Reeds), site of the old capital, is 2 miles from Quiché. Royal palaces were built of cut stone, most of it now removed to Quiché, and the ruins have little to show beyond the layout of the old city. There are two caves, one of which, according to local tradition, is an ancient passage leading underground to Totonicapán. The passage is dark and airless. Probably no one has ventured far enough into it to verify the tradition.

(Santo Tomás) Chiché, 7 miles (11 km.) E of Quiché, is interesting for its large Saturday market, where attention is centered on livestock. The fiesta of St. Thomas, December 21, is prolonged for a week. There are Indian burial mounds in the vicinity.

Excursions from Chiché. Zacualpa, 10 miles (16 km.) E, is an old town noted today for its small woolen bags woven by the Indians. Market is Sundays and Thursdays; fiesta, Pentecost (Espíritu Santo). There are interesting Maya ruins near by; Maya idols can be reached by mountain trails. The church is very large and has a façade notable for its beautiful lines. A bus runs occasionally to Quiché and Guatemala City.

Joyabaj (Stone Head), 7½ miles (12 km.) from Zacualpa, was formerly on the old Spanish trail from Mexico into Guatemala. Market is Sundays and Thursdays. The fiesta of the Virgin of the Assumption, August 15, is celebrated with a fair beginning a couple of days before and with the Snake and Deer Dances. The ruins of Cabulco are near the town. Men wear gay red jackets and white homespun shirts. A bus called La Gaviota makes the trip to Guatemala City once a week.

(Santo Domingo) Sacapulas, at 4003 feet elevation, beyond Quiché and 42 miles (67 km.) N of Chichicastenango through wide valleys and hills, is located on the Río Negro, an imposing river whose banks are here lined with natural mineral baths. Remains of a colonial bridge across the river can be seen even today. There is a marked change in vegetation from the colder regions of Quiché. In the market, held in the shade of a great mango tree in the plaza, are sold zapotes, mangoes, anonas, and matazanos, as well as more familiar fruits. The town is famous for its candy, alfeñique, made with molasses. Market is Sundays and Thursdays; the fiesta of St. Dominic is celebrated August 1-4. Women wear many elaborate silver necklaces; the headdress is of bright red and white tasseled bands.

Sacapulas is a pre-conquest city. Its chief industry now, as long ago, is the making of salt. Thomas Gage wrote of the salt "which they gather in the morning from the ground that lieth near the river"; the same procedure is followed today. Each morning a rime forms on the ground; this is gathered, washed, drained of mud, dried in fires and finally formed into hard round cakes. The salt beds are somewhat E of the main plaza. Other occupations are agriculture, especially the growing of fruit, sugar, and chile, and the production of excellent tumplines. Most Guatemalan Indian handmade silver necklaces and rings come from Sacapulas.

The colonial church, built in 1554, has a high altar with a front of 18th-century hammered silver and a galaxy of Indian-made images, some very noble. There are several large pyramidal mounds between the road and river that have not been investigated yet.

Bus service is undependable. Food and lodging can be secured.

Excursions from Sacapulas. A road is being built to Cobán (p. 65) via Cunén, but it is completed (1941) only to Cunén, the site of a mammoth cave. The trip E to Cobán can be completed by horseback over good trails, but the route does not pass through any colorful Indian towns. The interesting villages of Nebaj, Cotzal, and Chajul NW of Sacapulas, are reached by a newly completed road. At Chajul on the second Friday of Lent there is a tremendous Indian pilgrimage to the shrine of El Cristo del Golgota (Christ of Golgotha).

Aguacatán (Abundant Avocados), at 5479 feet elevation, is 23 miles (37 km.) W of Sacapulas by Route 7W, which presents magnificent views as it winds among valleys and hilltops. Aguacatán is primarily an Indian municipality, a so-called empty village, which is resorted to on market days and celebrations. Near by are the ruins of Chalchitán and of Pueblo Viejo, a pre-conquest town. About 2½ miles E of Aguacatán the Río San Juan is seen gushing from the foot of a mountain. At the top of the mountain is the village of San Juan Ixcoy, where the river has its source. Occupations are agricultural, especially production of rice and avocados. It is somewhat surprising to see great avocado trees, 50 feet high or more, laden with fruit which is often eaten by pigs for want of better fodder. Textiles and thread are manufactured, and there are gypsum mines near by. Market is Sundays and Thursdays. Fiestas are those of the Incarnation and of St. Stephen (San Esteban), August 3. Women's headbands are very interesting—red, woven with fine designs in so-called blind weaving, which does not show on the back of the fabric. These bands are braided with the hair and wound around the head. The colonial church is in ruins. Beside it stands a modern church which contains many relics of former times. Food can be purchased, but there is no hotel.

Route 7W continues due W for 15 miles (25 km.) to Huehuetenango (p. 87); the latter part affords spectacular views of the great Cuchumatanes mountains (p. 89). From Huehuetenango a road runs S to join the Pan American Highway at Quezaltenango (p. 84).

WEST FROM LOS ENCUENTROS

Route 1 beyond Los Encuentros (p. 75) crosses the mountain María Tecúm and the high, desolate region of Los Desconsuelos (The Disconsolates) at 11,000 feet. Legend says that María Tecúm was the sister of the great Quiché war chief Tecúm Umán. Upon hearing of his death at Pedro de Alvarado's hands, she retired to this mountain where she perished of cold and hunger. Before she died, she cursed its earth, its water and air. The curse was effective; the land is an arid barren waste with few dwellings. In one of the highest parts there is said to be a great white stone where at every full moon María Tecúm returns to sit and weep. Her cries, it is said, are heard many leagues away.

Suddenly the view opens upon the beautiful valley of Totonicapán, with the white buildings of San Francisco el Alto in the far distance and the volcano Santa María shadowing the west. The descent is rapid, and in a short time the red roofs of Totonicapán are seen.

(San Miguel) Totonicapán (Place of the Birds), at 8214 feet elevation, capital of the department, is 23 miles (37 km.) from Los Encuéntros. It is a delightful Indian city known for its thriving industries and beautiful women. Agriculture is here subordinated to other occupations. Almost every house has its footloom, since this is one of the largest skirt-weaving centers in the country. At the Saturday market one can buy the beautiful textiles of these regions, especially skirt lengths and the fine white ceremonial huipiles of Totonicapán itself. There are also glazed pottery, furniture, and leather goods. Even drums and ceremonial masks can be bought in outlying homes. The annual fair of the department, September 26-30, which grew up around the fiesta of St. Michael, September 29, is an elaborate occasion, arranged more for tourists than for Indians, but extremely interesting and colorful. Many of the festivities take place in Totonicapán's modern theater. The fiesta of St. James (Santiago), July 25, is celebrated. On ceremonial occasions women wear elaborate headbands made of silk with silver-wrapped tassels which dangle to the shoulder.

The climate is cold and clear with sometimes a light drizzle called la salud del pueblo (health of the village). Half a mile from the plaza there are sulphur and hot springs with baths. Also interesting are pottery works and some long-abandoned colonial silver mines.

A unique industry run by Miguel Chuj is that of making and supplying masks and costumes for native dances throughout the country. He conducts a complicated and intricate business which involves keeping track of the many details of fiestas of all kinds in all regions. There is nearly always a contingent of Indians from some remote section calling on him in the course of arranging business and social details of their fiestas.

In Totonicapán in 1817, after 300 years of Spanish rule, the Indians revolted and crowned an Indian king Paúl. Several ladinos were killed, but the insurrection was put down and Paúl was beheaded. According to legend the grave of Tecúm Umán is in this Quiché stronghold, but it has never been located.

The church, rebuilt, is large and plain, of good proportions. There are many silver altars and two statues of St. Michael in silver and gold.

Buses pass frequently to Quezaltenango and Guatemala City. Gas is sold.

HOTEL. Berna.

San Cristóbal (Totonicapán), 9 miles (15 km.) W of Totonicapán, is famous for its fine colonial church, one of the largest and richest in the country. Built by Franciscan friars, it is still intact in spite of eruptions and earthquakes and holds many valuable works of art. Its gilded altars are exceptionally beautiful. There are also hand-hammered silver lamps and screens, sculptured silver saints—outstanding among them the elaborate Virgin of El Socorro—and portraits of colonial celebrities. The high altar has been removed for safekeeping. The side altars are of intricate rococo style.

The town is noted for its textiles. Many of the skirts worn by Indian women of other villages are woven here. The region from Totonicapán to Quezaltenango specializes in tie-dye weaving. Other industries are the making of silk cloth from imported silk, wool weaving, and flour milling. El Moro here supplies masks and costumes for fiestas, though the business is not as active as the one in Totonicapán.

Market is held on Sundays and Wednesdays on either side of the river which winds through the center of town. On the E outskirts of San Cristóbal there is a hot stream in which women can usually be seen washing or bathing.

Bus service to Quezaltenango is very frequent, and buses often pass through on the way to Guatemala City. Gas is sold. There is a restaurant, Brisas de Samalá.

Excursion to San Andrés (Xecul). A predominantly Indian hamlet, San Andrés is 2½ miles (4 km.) W of San Cristóbal. Market is held Thursdays. The fiesta of St. Andrew is on November 28-30. The community is agricultural; no weaving is done. The church has an interesting façade carved with grapes, statues, and jaguars, and inside are great new columns. The roof is of the rare vaulted type. There are a silver altarpiece and a small Black Christ with silver crown and bellyband.

Excursion to San Francisco el Alto. This Indian village, 3 miles (5 km.) N of San Cristóbal, is most interesting. High, at 8661 feet, with a clear atmosphere, it overlooks the beautiful valley of Samalá, the towns of Totonicapán and San Cristóbal, the volcanoes Tajumulco and Tacaná in the far distance, and the majestic conical Santa María. The Friday market, held in the central plaza, is patronized by Indian merchants from all parts of the country, who come to buy woolen goods produced here and in near-by Momostenango. The best market is on the first Friday in Lent, but any Friday provides a fine show. A livestock market is held on the hill back of the plaza; here Indians and ladinos gravely speculate on the qualities of pigs or mules. The road to San Francisco is a special hazard on market days, for it is crowded with people driving and carrying animals to market. The fiesta of St. Francis is celebrated, October 4.

The church, a particularly fine example of colonial workmanship, has a vaulted roof. There are a beautiful silver altar, lamps, crucifix, and image of St. Francis. In the sacristy Father Carlos Knittel discovered old frescoes of St. Francis which had been covered over with lime.

A fine selection of blankets and other woolen goods can be procured from Miss Knittel, sister of Father Knittel, who not only chooses the best and most interesting things from the native market, but will order special pieces from the local weavers. Luncheon is served by Miss Knittel for a limited number of people on advance notice.

A bus operated by Socol Rivera makes a round trip between Quezaltenango and San Francisco el Alto on market days.

Excursion to (Santiago) Momostenango. At 7283 feet elevation, 10 miles (16 km.) N of San Francisco el Alto, Momostenango is a mostly Indian town which is a wool center. Market is held Sundays, and on Saturday nights Indians gather about a mile N of the town at the Río Paúl to bathe and wash their blankets and rugs in the hot springs. The river at this point lies at the bottom of a steep slope. The streets of Momostenango are spread with wet woolen articles demonstrating that the colors do not run.

The cold, high land is barren; even corn grows poorly. As in many places where women's skirts are woven on footlooms, men weave women's skirts and huipiles as well as their own sutes.

By far the most important ceremony is that of the Uajxaquip Báts, celebrated in some smaller villages as well as in Momostenango. Uajxaquip Báts means Eight Monkey and represents a definite day in the 260-day sacred Tzolkin calendar which has been handed down from the time of the Mayas. In Momostenango this day is observed with religious ceremonies of great intensity and significance. In prosperous years, Momostenango may be flooded with 10,000-20,000 Indians from all over the country. Anyone born in the town is supposed to return for the celebration, under penalty of ill fortune.

With the coming of the Spaniards a Christian ceremony was added; this is conducted late the preceding night in the church. Early in the morning after it, people leave for their altars in the surrounding hills, along paths lined with booths selling food, incense, and candles. The place of worship, whose name means Little Broom, is about half a mile W of the city. The altars are really mounds formed of broken pottery, for any broken or discarded object is saved and returned here to the god who made it break. At the bases of these mounds of potsherds fires are built, and before them stand the shamans, the intermediaries between the people and the gods, and small groups of people who give thanks to the gods or pray for good fortune or remission of sins. The shamans place little offerings of copal on the fires and perhaps aguardiente as well, and in return for a penny or two earnestly solicit divine help from the World God, known as Hurakan or Mundo. In Momostenango, sorcerer, fortune teller, and physician are indistinguishably fused in the office of shaman. There are perhaps 300 shamans, both men and women. They are distinguished by a little woven bag containing ritualistic objects such as small red seeds, bits of quartz and jade, pebbles, and semiprecious stones. When a shaman dies, his successor cannot take over his office until the bag containing his sacred paraphernalia has rotted away.

At nightfall the groups move farther W on the hills to a place whose name means Big Broom, where ceremonies are conducted through the night. The following two days are given over to ceremonies and to celebrations in the town's crowded cantinas or drinking places.

Uajxaquip Báts celebrations are scheduled for March 10 and November 25, 1943.

Momostenango also celebrates the fiestas of St. James (Santiago), July 30, and St. Anthony, June 13. The colonial church has interesting silver work, a fine altar and accessories, and an unusual monstrance. More veneration is accorded St. Anthony than the patron St. James.

E, within easy walking distance, are riscos or curious formations of eroded sand which resemble great stalagmites.

On Sundays a bus makes a round trip from Quezaltenango.

Amalia de Cifuentes has a good place to eat.

HOTEL. Escobedo.

Excursion from Momostenango. Santa María Chiquimula is about 9 miles (15 km.) E by a picturesque trail winding through pine forests (2-3 hours by horseback). It is an almost exclusively Indian town of traveling merchants, of the empty village type; most of the natives come into town only for market and fiestas. Feeling against ladinos is strong here. Market is Thursdays and Sundays. Fiestas are those of

Esquipulas, January 15, and the Nativity of the Virgin, September 8. The market here is exceptional in drawing many more men than women. The women's costume is outstanding because of the black wool braided headband, with long tassels which hang down in back and which, with expert winding, form an elaborate headdress.

In the vicinity of the town are altars and quemadores, where incense is burned. A small hill N of the city is the scene of ancient rituals; visitors are definitely not invited.

There are no food and no lodgings.

(San Luis) Salcajá (White Water, from the clay content) is on Route 1, 3 miles (5 km.) from San Cristóbal and only 6 miles (10 km.) short of Quezaltenango. It is a small town of ladinos, with market on Tuesdays. Fiestas are those of St. Louis, August 25; Epiphany (Día de los Reyes), January 6; and the Virgin of El Carmen, July 16. The country's best native liquor, commonly called olla, is made here; there are three grades, the best of which is olla de leche. An artificial lake lies 150 yards from the center of the town. There are mounds near by but no distinguishable ruins. An old colonial church, reputed to be the first built in the country, is of little interest save for its antiquity.

Buses pass through regularly, to and from Quezaltenango.

WESTERN GUATEMALA

The city of Quezaltenango, the second most important in the republic, can be made the base for several trips in the W part of the country, since all the roads in this section radiate from it. The port towns of Ocós and Champerico, the latter via Retalhuleu, can be visited on the Pacific coast (p. 86). For travelers willing to brave inconvenience for the sake of new experiences the Cuchumatanes mountain region, N of Huehuetenango (p. 87) and without motor roads or railroads, is full of beauty (p. 89). It is also possible to reach Mexico from Quezaltenango (p. 92); the first important town beyond the border is Tapachula, from which there are railroad connections for points N.

QUEZALTENANGO

Possibly the only Spanish city in Guatemala founded exactly on an Indian site is Quezaltenango, at 7656 feet elevation, capital of the department of the same name. The old Indian town was called Xelahú (Under the Ten, from the 10 Quiché lords who ruled over the region). On the road E of Quezaltenango is a stone marking the place where the Quiché war chief Tecúm Umán was killed by Alvarado. Some 5 miles from the city, on the summit of a mountain called El Baúl (The Trunk, because of its shape), a gigantic statue has been erected in his honor. The city's present name means Place of the Quetzal, a native bird of extravagant plumage which abounds in this region and which had great symbolic importance among the Mayas. Since it usually dies at once in captivity, it was adopted as the national symbol when Guatemala became a republic. It has a fiery red breast and green tail feathers half a yard long and is said to be so vain that it drills two holes in the tree in which it nests, one for going in and the other for coming out, so that its tail feathers will not be injured in turning around. In 1835 a local political uprising resulted in the secession of

Quezaltenango from the United Provinces of Central America and the formation of an independent Estado de los Altos (Highland State) with Quezaltenango as its capital. The revolt of the highland state was soon suppressed, however.

Quezaltenango is the center of a densely populated region. It is a modern city, almost entirely rebuilt during the present century; yet it retains much of its colonial atmosphere, with narrow streets, broad avenues, and imposing public buildings and plazas. It is Guatemala's second industrial and trading center, handling most of the produce and manufactures of the W regions. In the 19th century its commercial importance was greater, but the destruction of the city in 1902 and the rise of Puerto Barrios to supplant the Pacific ports of Champerico and Ocós took away much of its commerce. Quezaltenango's population is 80 per cent Indian. The market, held daily, with the largest attendance on Thursdays and open half the day Sundays, is extraordinarily bright and colorful, for people from the entire W region come to trade here, and there is a very wide assortment of purely Indian handicrafts. Quezaltenango does much weaving for other parts of the country, and its own full-skirted costume is particularly fine. The women are noted for their beauty.

The city lies among high mountains and volcanoes. One of the volcanoes, Santa María, is today a graceful symmetrical cone overhanging the city, but in 1902 it erupted and destroyed Quezaltenango and many of the neighboring towns. Its latest activity occurred in 1928. This mountain is held sacred by the Indians, and from time to time mysterious rites are conducted at its summit. Opposite Santa María is the volcano Cerro Quemado, now extinct, formerly one of the highest volcanoes in the world. In the lee of Santa María is Santiaguito, a new cone gradually building up beside the old one. Volcanoes in this region emit cinders and ash oftener than lava and form cones with evenly sloping sides. The old church was badly damaged in 1902. Its modern part, built after the city's destruction, is overcrowded with pillars, but inside are old silver altarpieces and beautiful silver crosses which testify to its ancient beauty. Here rest an image of El Padre Eterno (The Eternal Father), inclosed in a hammered silver case, and one of Our Lady of the Rosary, the city's patroness, with a rosary of pearls and diamonds.

The chief holiday is Independence Day, September 15. The most important religious ceremonies are those of the first Friday in Lent; Pentecost (Espíritu Santo); and the Virgin of the Rosary, October 7.

There is bus service constantly to and from Guatemala City and service to San Francisco el Alto and to Momostenango on market days. Garages with gas and air are numerous. There is a fine airport near the city limits, with biweekly transportation by air to Guatemala City.

HOTELS. Europeo*, with fireplace; Recreo*, with fireplace; Modelo.

EXCURSIONS FROM QUEZALTENANGO

(San Buenaventura) Cantel (Yellow), which is 6 miles (10 km.) SE from Quezaltenango, is a town whose importance lies in its manufacture of textiles, especially a white fabric called manta de Cantel, made in the only large mechanized factory in the country. The population consists almost entirely of Indian laborers in this industry, which is regarded as the most important in Central America. The factory, set in beautiful gardens, is interesting to visit. Market is Thursdays. Fiestas are the Assumption, August 15, and Easter, with a Passion play.

Santa María is climbed from the town of Suipache.

QUEZALTENANGO TO THE PACIFIC COAST

Two routes run in a general SW direction to the Pacific coast. The road terminating at Ocós is covered later as an excursion from San Juan Ostuncalco (p. 92).

Below Quezaltenango a road runs SE a few miles to Zunil and from there SW to Retalhuleu, from which it continues to the Pacific port town of Champerico.

(San Pedro) Almolonga (Gushing Water), not to be confused with the site near Antigua where Alvarado founded his third capital, is 3 miles (5 km.) SE of Quezaltenango on this route. It is noted for the men's beautiful and intricate costume, which, however, is rarely seen except on ceremonial occasions. The great fiesta is St. Peter's, June 29. Livelihood is gained chiefly from growing very fine vegetables and fruits. About a mile from the center of town are hot springs with reddish water; outstanding are the springs of Cirilo Flores, owned by the town, and Santa Eulalia, privately owned, both with immaculate bathhouses.

The church was banked by a deposit of several feet of ash from the eruption of Santa María in 1902, but the colonial altar, with its silver pieces and elaborate silver-plated saint, survived.

Buses pass frequently to Retalhuleu and to Quezaltenango.

(Santa Catalina) Zunil, 6 miles (10 km.) SE of Quezaltenango on Route 9S, beyond Almolonga, also is noted for its springs. Market is Mondays. The great fiesta is that of St. Catherine, November 25. The simple, beautifully proportioned church has a fine belltower and elaborate carved façade; the carved beams inside are painted white. The dome of the nave is painted with well-preserved designs; the carved altar is elaborate with gold leaf, and St. Catherine wears a silver gown. The side altars vary, some with elaborate silver saints such as the Virgin and St. Anne, others plain and new.

Near the town is the volcano Zunil, noted for hot springs and for a mercury mine said to be known only to the natives.

Buses pass frequently to and from Retalhuleu. There is a place to eat in the village, but no hotel.

Excursion from Zunil. Fuentes Georginas, springs named in honor of President Jorge Ubico, are a little more than 5 miles SE of Zunil. The road affords a spectacular view as it winds up the side of the volcano Zunil through jungle vegetation. Below lies the valley of the Río Samalá (Muddy), stretching toward the Pacific, and the volcanoes Santa María and Santiaguito are visible. The springs have several sorts of medicinal water: azufre or sulphur (yellow); amarga or bitter (green); black; and radioactive (pink). There are inclosed baths and large and small swimming pools fed by water somewhat warmer than body temperature. There is also a stream of agua dulce fría (cold fresh water).

Off the SW route toward the coast, about a mile below Zunil, down the canyon of the Río Samalá, are some famous hot geysers whose steam can be seen from the road. One of these, Los Vahos (Vapors), is locally reputed to have medicinal properties. The rocks surrounding the geysers are vivid green, yellow, and red.

Some hot springs that are attracting increased attention lie on a road that branches E. These are Aguas Amargas (Bitter Waters), 5 miles (8 km.) from Zunil. Sulphur and sodium predominate in the water, 110°-140° F., which is reputed to be beneficial for rheumatism and skin troubles. There is a hotel. Bus service from Quezaltenango is operated by Rafael Andrade.

As the road winds on to the Pacific coast the air grows hot, and clothing changes from the wool of the highlands to a scanty costume of thin cotton.

Santa María de Jesús, not to be confused with another town of the same name near Antigua, is a small Indian town on the Río Samalá. The majority of the inhabitants have migrated to plantations near the coast. A great waterfall and a dam 345 feet high supplying power for the entire region enhance the spectacular view down the river canyon. This project now supplies electricity to a good part of the country; eventually even Guatemala City will use power from Santa María.

A few miles below Santa María de Jesús the descent becomes more gradual and tropical vegetation begins to appear.

San Felipe, at 2056 feet elevation, is tropical. Mangoes and other tropical fruits grow here, and there is an increasing number of royal palms, coconut palms, and almost impenetrable jungle vegetation. Orchids of all colors grow wild in crotches of trees, and deer and jungle fauna may be seen: armadilloes, tepezcuintles, iguanas, monkeys, parrots and parakeets, peccaries, jaguars, and pizotes. San Felipe can also be reached by spur line from Mulua, located on the main E-W railroad from Guatemala City to Ayutla (p. 93).

Retalhuleu, at only 787 feet elevation, capital of the department of the same name, is very hot. It is an important center of coffee- and sugar-growing, and a customhouse is located here, serving the port of Champerico, S. Retalhuleu was founded by the Spaniards by merging two Indian villages. The train stops here en route to Mexico. A large fair is held December 6-12. Casino Retalteco is the scene of social gatherings.

HOTEL. Astor.

Champerico on the Pacific is still a port of some importance, though most of its trade, except for coffee shipments from the excellent plantations in the adjacent regions, has disappeared. The fine beach is crowded by vacationers especially during Holy Week, and the country near by is a paradise for hunters and fishers, since a great variety of animal life abounds: white and red herons, ducks, crocodiles, and fish of all kinds. Champerico is situated on a spur line from the main E-W railroad.

QUEZALTENANGO NORTH TO HUEHUETENANGO

(San Juan) Olintepeque, an Indian town 3 miles (5 km.) N of Quezaltenango on Route 9N, is the presumed site of the battle between the forces of Alvarado and the Quiché war chief Tecúm Umán, who was killed in combat. The Indian name for the near-by stream means Bloody River, because of the great loss of life in that battle. Market is held Tuesdays. Fiestas are those of St. John the Baptist (San Juan

Bautista), June 24, and the beheading of St. John (Degollación de San Juan), August 29. The women's huipiles are very interesting, blue with widely spaced magenta stripes.

There is a place to eat, and gasoline is sold. Buses pass frequently to Quezaltenango and Huehuetenango.

(San Carlos) Sija, at 10,500 feet elevation, 12 miles (19 km.) farther N, lies at the foot of Cerro de Sija. From the road one sees the magnificent panorama of the W descent. The name Sija is a corruption of Ecija, a city in Spain, home of the town's founders.

In the vicinity is the famous Casa de la Mica (Monkey's House), a cave in which the ancient protector of the town was said to live. Becoming displeased with his people, he turned his wealth into stones which line the road from Sija to San Antonio before he departed for San Francisco el Alto; thus is explained the richness of San Francisco's soil and the barrenness of Sija's. Fiestas are those of St. Charles, November 4, and the Immaculate Conception, December 8; neither is elaborate, since this is a ladino town. Gas is sold.

Cumbre del Aire (Summit of the Air), 28 miles (45 km.) from Quezaltenango, presents views S to the volcanoes Zunil, Cerro Quemado, Santa María, and on the right, Siete Orejas. The grades are thick with pines, spruce, fir, and the higher passes are covered with the familiar pajón or bunch grass. During the latter part of the journey the volcano Tajumulco is visible NW, and there are magnificent views of the Cuchumatanes mountains.

Chiquibal and Malacatancito are both small ladino towns. In the former there are two places to eat, and in the latter gasoline can be bought.

(Concepción) Huehuetenango (Place of the Old People), at 6201 feet elevation, capital of the department of the same name, is 53 miles (85 km.) from Quezaltenango (3-4 hours) and 80 miles (129 km.) from Chichicastenango (4 hours; p. 76). Founded by the Spaniards after the downfall of the Indian capital at near-by Zaculeu, it is the chief trading center for dozens of villages located in the remote and rarely visited mountains N and W. The streets are bright with strange costumes from both hot and cold regions. Here one sees the red-and-white plaid trousers of Todos Santos men, the knee-length full huipiles of San Miguel Acatán women, and men from Nebaj and Cotzal in gay red coats. Market is held daily and is especially well attended Thursdays and Sundays. A racecourse near the outskirts of the city draws good horses and is well patronized. Fiestas are those of the Carmelite Virgin, celebrated with a large fair, July 12-18, and the Immaculate Conception, December 8. The church, built in 1854, has an old silver altar and ornaments.

Huehuetenango is the heart of a region rich in lead, silver, and copper, little exploited as yet. More important is its traffic in pottery, leather, and textiles. This is the only place in Guatemala where merino blankets are made.

Buses run frequently to and from Quezaltenango, but the roads are bad in mid-rainy season. The road E to Sacapulas (p. 79) is nearer level and remains in fair condition even in the rainy season. Passenger cars are numerous on this road, but there is only occasional and unpredictable bus service.

HOTELS. Maldonado*; Central.

Excursions from Huehuetenango. A mile W are the ruins of Zaculeu (White Earth), ancient capital of the Mam tribe who were conquered by the force and guile of Spaniards under the leadership of Gonzalo de Alvarado, Pedro's brother. Situated on the crest of a steep hill surrounded by a river and deep canyons, the ruins of the palace and fortress are very interesting, though they date from a rather late period and do not have the beauty of the more ancient Maya sites. Zaculeu must have been built by a people influenced by Toltec civilization, since it is similar in many respects to the famous pyramids of San Juan Teotihuacán in Mexico. Exploration was started in 1927. It disclosed two artificial mounds, the more important a pyramid which covered fragments of temple walls and stairways, badly damaged by the roots of great trees growing among them.

Chiantla, 3 miles (5 km.) N of Huehuetenango, is on a scenic road which when completed will lead N to Barillas. Chiantla is chiefly noted for a solid silver Virgin of La Candelaria to which a great pilgrimage is made on Candlemas, February 2. This is an old town. Thomas Gage passed through it in 1626 as he came from Mexico, and he described the colonial grandeur of this small, out-of-the-way village: "The church is richly furnished, but especially the high altar where the picture standeth in a tabernacle with half a dozen curtains of silk, satin, cloth of gold, thickly beset with diamonds and other precious stones. There hang before it at least a dozen rich lamps of silver; and in the vestry of the church are many gowns, candlesticks of silver, censers to burn frankincense before it, besides rich capes, vestments, ornaments for the altar, and hangings for all the church." Chiantla also has a fiesta for the Nativity of the Virgin, September 8, with a great market. Market is held daily, a large one on Sundays. The township is about half Indian, though the town itself is almost entirely ladino. Occupations are agriculture, leather tanning, and wool growing. There are 15 lead mines in the vicinity. The old Spanish mines, now abandoned, are interesting. Buses go to and from Huehuetenango frequently. Victor del Valle has a place where travelers can eat, but there are no lodgings.

On the same road, 11 miles (18 km.) N of Huehuetenango, is a lookout which is well worth visiting for the magnificent view of mountains and valleys. From this point on a clear day is seen an entire horizon of volcanoes: Agua at the far left, then Fuego and Acatenango close together, straight ahead the sharp symmetrical peak of Santa María, and to the far right the double peak of Tajumulco on the Mexican border. Just to the left of Santa María is Cerro Quemado.

CUCHUMATANES MOUNTAINS

The magnificent Cuchumatanes Mountains, N and NW of Huehuetenango, are seldom explored by travelers. There are no motor roads to them, but travel is not difficult and is completely safe. It is impossible to describe the beauty of these mountains; there are majestic vistas accented by volcanoes and low-lying farm lands or jungle. Above 10,000 feet are high wind-swept prairies where nothing grows but bunch grass and Alpine vegetation. At the other extreme is tropical vegetation with fine trees, mahogany, rubber, cacao. In between the scene gradually changes; first there is sugar cane, then coffee up to about 5000 feet, and above this firs, potatoes, and wheat. Especially at the end of the rainy season, December or January, the heights and valleys alike are luxuriant with strange and beautiful flowers.

The whole region is dotted with mounds and ruins. Some of them still serve as places of worship. The ruins are little known and for the most part have not been described in archeological literature. Curiosity is not fostered; on the contrary, the Indians would very much resent any disturbance of their sacred relics. Nevertheless, visitors are free to speculate on the gorgeous pageantry and unknown rituals for which these places were once the stage.

Guides and mules can be secured from municipal officers in Huehuetenango or Chiantla. Trails radiate in all directions from each town; there is no prescribed route to be taken. Some of the better-known villages are briefly described here, with distances given approximately in leagues. See section on Roughing It (p. 30).

Todos Santos (Cuchumatán), at 8104 feet elevation, is about 10 leagues (30 miles, 8-10 hours) NW of Huehuetenango by trail. A shorter trip can be made either by leaving from Chiantla or by going N by car some 17 miles (27 km.), to a point where guide and horses will be waiting by prearrangement, and then branching off W. From the motor road it is about 1½ leagues (5 miles) to La Ventosa (Windy Place), high up at 11,500 feet, and another 2 leagues to the town.

Todos Santos is one of the most interesting and colorful villages in Guatemala. The men are taller, more arrogant, and handsomer than most Guatemalan Indians. They wear a striking costume which accentuates their banditlike appearance: red and white striped or cross-barred trousers and cotton shirt, with woolen overpants buttoned tight around the waist and reaching to the knee; these last, when fastened up for work or travel, look like breechcloths. Over all is a dark woolen capixay. A red bandana handkerchief is worn around the head, usually covering one ear, and the whole is topped with a shallow-crowned straw hat, often with cock feathers waving jauntily in back.

Todos Santos, a settled community at the time of the conquest, was on the main road to Mexico. Today men engage in agriculture and weave wool, while women make pottery and weave cotton textiles. There is a small daily market. Fiestas include that of St. Francis, October 4; All Saints' (Todos Santos), November 1; and All Souls', November 2, when natives make trips to the cemetery with offerings of food. The church has beautifully carved beams and several large carved figures of St. Lucia, St. Isidore, St. Peter, and St. Paul.

A short distance from the central square are the ruins of Tecumanchún, 10 mounds of different sizes and shapes which have never been investigated. Here the Indians conduct their rites and ceremonies. In Todos Santos the ancient calendar is still used by the shamans.

Felipa Alonzo has accommodations for travelers.

San Juan Atitán, 4 leagues (12 miles) S of Todos Santos, is in the center of a sheep-raising region. It is an empty village, coming to life only for markets and fiestas.

(Santiago) Chimaltenango, 5 leagues (15 miles) SW of Todos Santos, is a friendly little village. Fiestas are those of St. James, July 25, and Easter.

Amalio Rojas has accommodations for travelers.

Colotenango is 6 leagues (18 miles) W and S of Chimaltenango and lies lower, at 5490 feet. Because of deposits of volcanic dust from the eruption of the volcano Santa María, this is good soil for raising corn, beans, yucca, bananas, and sweet potatoes. Pine, cypress, and oak grow in the vicinity.

(San Ildefonso) Ixtahuacán, W of Colotenango, is mainly ladino, though there are many Indians in the surrounding countryside. Coffee, fruits, vegetables, sugar cane, and peanuts are grown.

(San Andrés) Cuilco, 7 leagues (21 miles) W of Ixtahuacán, at only 2720 feet elevation, has very fertile soil, owing in part to Santa María's eruptions. There are forests of timber, medicinal plants, and deposits of copper. Sugar refining, fishing, hat-making, and cattle-raising are the chief occupations.

La Libertad, NE of Cuilco at 5700 feet elevation, is on a flat ridge at the foot of Peña Blanca, a high and precipitous cliff not far from the famous Boquerón, a deep, narrow gorge formed by the Río Selegua, NW of the village.

San Pedro Nectá has an Indian population of 4500 distributed in aldeas or hamlets. The village itself is ladino. It is located midway between La Libertad, W, and Chimaltenango, E.

San Antonio Huista, at 4000 feet elevation, is 7 leagues (21 miles) N of San Pedro Nectá, near the Río Huista. The town is mostly ladino, and Indians wear ladino clothing. Crops are corn, sugar cane, coffee, and bananas; manufactures are palm hats and rope. Market is Sundays. The great fiesta is St. Anthony's, June 13. Many pre-Columbian ruins are found scattered throughout this area, several near the town.

Laura Estrada and Felipe Escobedo have boarding houses.

(Purificación) Jacaltenango, 2 leagues (6 miles) NE of San Antonio Huista, is situated on a beautiful gorge with the Río Azul at the bottom. The town is known for its attractive Indian women. Palm-leaf hats are made by men, textiles by women. Cattle-raising and crude sugar production are the chief occupations. Forest trees abound, especially cedar and ebony. Much wild teocintle, the presumed precursor of corn, grows in the vicinity. Its origin may well have been in this very section of NW Guatemala.

Market is held daily, with most attendance on Sundays. Women wear white huipiles and narrow silk bands in their hair. The chief fiesta is Candlemas, February 2. The church is old; it has a carved altar and a few silver pieces indicating a departed glory. Indians of this region hold the ceremonial rites of the Year Bearer, which are described in Oliver La Farge's book The Year Bearer's People.

San Marcos (Huehuetenango) lies on the opposite side of the Río Azul, which is as blue as its name. Ruins are visible on the left as one enters the town. The Cerro Azul is a center for pagan rites in a big cave. Fiestas celebrated are St. Mark's, April 25, and carnival.

(San Benito) Nentón, 7 leagues (21 miles) NW of Jacaltenango, is low, at 2430 feet. Produce is sugar cane, chile, bananas, and other tropical fruits. There are rich archeological ruins, no study of which has been published.

San Miguel Acatán, at 5730 feet elevation, 8 leagues (24 miles) SE of Nentón, produces flour, hats, rope, cervatanas or blowguns, and lead. Market is held daily, the largest on Sundays. The women's costume is colorful, a very long white huipil, with deep flounces around the neck, and a red skirt. Fiestas are St. Michael's, September 27, and carnival. Ruins of a temple of the Sun are 2 leagues from the town.

Aurora González has a boarding house.

San Mateo Ixtatán, at 8300 feet elevation, 8 leagues (24 miles) NE of San Miguel Acatán, produces salt, wheat, hats, and wool. Extensive ruins are seen near the town, the massive remains of the church of El Calvario and the smaller but more ornate Catepán ruins. El Calvario is still a scene of religious rituals. The rainy season here lasts until January or February, two months longer than elsewhere.

Santa Eulalia is 5 leagues (15 miles) E of San Miguel Acatán. Its 9000 people, almost all of them Indians, are primarily engaged in agriculture, but hats, rope, and wool are also produced. A large cave near the village is used by shamans in an annual rite of prophecy for the people. The image Jolóm Conóp (Head of the Village), very sacred and very secret, is kept in state in the municipal building and is highly revered by Indians from miles around.

(San Pedro) Solomá, SE of Santa Eulalia, was the scene of the last Indian uprising in Guatemala in July 1898. The entire ladino population of about 30 was massacred.

Concepción, at 7070 feet elevation, an Indian village, raises sheep and makes hats. The village is SW of San Miguel Acatán, NW of Todos Santos.

San Martín (Cuchumatán), at 6000 feet elevation, is populated by Indians who probably emigrated from Todos Santos, but they have adopted many ladino customs, including clothing. Near the village are the extensive ruins of Tilajión and Chanjón. San Martín is located about midway between Concepción and Todos Santos.

QUEZALTENANGO WEST TO THE MEXICAN BORDER

The Pan American Highway, Route 1, leads W to Mexico via San Marcos.

San Juan Ostuncalco, at 8301 feet elevation, 9 miles (14 km.) from Quezaltenango, is the center of a fine agricultural region, noteworthy for its active and colorful Sunday market, where a great variety of native costumes are seen. The men of the township wear beautiful waistbands, seen chiefly at the elaborate fiesta of Candlemas, January 29-February 3. On important occasions music is played on rare instruments such as rabeles or rebecs made of armadillo shell, as well as guitars and violins; the town prides itself on its music. Two noted modern musicians have lived here, the pianist Miguel Espinosa and the composer Jesús Castillo, author of an opera on an Indian subject, called Quiché Vinak.

The façade is all that is left of the old church, the rest being modern except for its interior decorations. There are a very fine silver altarpiece and many carved images, including one of the patron saint, some with silver costumes. The Virgin of the Rosary has the reputation of granting prayers.

Near by is the volcano Lacandón, whose sloping sides are covered with woods and fertile coffee and sugar plantations. There is hunting in this region, and fishing is good in the Río Samalá, the Naranjo, and the Tilapa.

Buses pass from Quezaltenango and from San Marcos. There is a place to eat, but no hotel. Gas is sold.

Excursions from San Juan Ostuncalco. A road leads 65 miles (105 km.) SW to Ocós on the Pacific coast. Champerico, farther S on the coast than Ocós, can also be reached from San Juan Ostuncalco by following this road and then turning off more directly S. The turn can be made at Colomba, from which the road passes through Retalhuleu (p. 87), or Coatepeque farther on. From Coatepeque there is also railroad connection for Champerico.

Concepción Chiquirichapa is a very attractive and rich Indian town just out of San Juan Ostuncalco. The quetzal, the bird that is Guatemala's emblem, is said to abound in the woods around it.

San Martín Sacatepéquez, commonly called San Martín Chile Verde (Green Pepper), is the principal town of interest on this route, 4½ miles (7 km.) S of San Juan Ostuncalco. The town, located in a cleft between mountains, is cold and windy, but its people are extremely friendly and interesting. The men wear one of the most striking costumes in the country: shirt and trousers with thin red stripes on white background; sleeve and trouser cuffs red, intricately woven with designs in purple, green, and yellow; the long black woolen capixay familiar in cold climates, wound with a long red belt; and sometimes a long red sute reaching to the knees in back. Near the town is Lake Chicabal, cold and clear, in the crater of an extinct volcano at the foot of a mountain called Las Siete Orejas (Seven Ears) because of its seven well-formed cones. Beside this lake ceremonies and pagan rites are performed, chiefly just before the rainy season. Copal is burned on stones beside wooden crosses, and fowls are sacrificed to the accompaniment of the inevitable drum, chirimía or flageolet, and firing of rockets. It is said that the pre-conquest inhabitants of this town were attacked by jaguars and then by bats until, unable to endure any more, they moved S to the present city of Coatepeque. There is no market. The chief fiesta is St. Martin's, November 11. Buses pass daily to Coatepeque and Quezaltenango.

Coatepeque, SW of San Martín Chile Verde, at 1595 feet elevation, reached by railroad or car, is well into the hot country. Agricultural products are fine coffee, sugar, coconuts, plantains, pineapples, and other tropical fruits. A large fair is held March 10-15.

HOTELS. Europa; Ambos Mundos.

Ocós, reached by car W and S from Coatepeque or by a railroad spur from Ayutla, where the International Railways of Central America starts, with service to Guatemala City, is a port which did a brisk business in the 19th century, chiefly in indigo and cochineal. Some coffee is still exported, but Ocós has been superseded by Puerto Barrios on the Atlantic.

The road to Mexico, beyond San Juan Ostuncalco, dips and climbs through valleys, mountains, and pine forests and suddenly emerges at a high level overlooking the valley in which lie the towns of San Antonio and San Marcos. In the distance are the majestic volcanoes Tajumulco and Tacaná on the Mexican border, the former the loftiest peak in Central America (13,812 feet).

San Antonio (Sacatepéquez), at 7874 feet elevation, is 18 miles (29 km.) W of San Juan Ostuncalco. Market is held Thursdays and Sundays. Fiestas are those of St. Anthony the Abbot (San Antonio Abad), January 17, and St. Anthony of Padua, June 13. In the main plaza there is a large and interesting map of the vicinity. Near the city are unexplored ruins.

Buses pass from Quezaltenango and San Marcos.

San Pedro (Sacatepéquez), a pre-conquest city 5 miles (8 km.) beyond

San Antonio, should not be confused with the town of the same name in the region of Guatemala City. It has an interesting and colorful market on Thursdays and Sundays. The fiesta of St. Peter is held June 29. A government textile school has been established with the purpose of promoting native weaving, dyeing, and designing.

A bus passes frequently to Quezaltenango. Gasoline is sold.

HOTEL. Roma is a boarding house.

San Marcos, at 7689 feet elevation, capital of the department of the same name, the last important Indian city of Guatemala on this route and the end of the highlands, is only a mile beyond San Pedro by a wide cypress-bordered avenue. San Marcos is a city of great life and color; its Sunday markets attract merchants from all the W parts of the republic, and in it are seen costumes and textiles unique in these regions, notable particularly for the predominating yellow, which is rare in other parts of the country. The silver necklaces of the women are very fine, but it is almost impossible to buy one of them. The fiesta of St. Mark is celebrated with a big fair, April 22-30.

Center of social life is the country club, Valin T'Manek, which offers tennis, hunting, and fishing. San Marcos has an airport and a radio station.

Climbs of Tajumulco and Tacaná start from San Marcos.

HOTEL. Longo.

Six miles (9 km.) W of San Marcos the descent to the lowlands begins. In the next 11 miles (18 km.) the elevation drops from 8200 to 3525 feet at San Rafael Pié de la Cuesta (Foot of the Slope) and then to 1200 feet at Malacatán, 16 miles (26 km.) farther. Malacatán is thus not only 33 linear miles from San Marcos; it is also 1½ miles downward, a drop from the cold clear air of the highlands into pure jungle flora and fauna.

(Santa Lucía) Malacatán is the last town in Guatemala. Here a call must be made at the police and immigration office, always open. The formalities are elaborate but are conducted with great courtesy. Market is held Sundays and Thursdays; few Indians attend. The chief fiesta is that of St. Lucia, December 13.

Eight miles (14 km.) W of Malacatán is the customhouse of El Carmen, where it is necessary to report before leaving the country. Official permission for the visitor to leave is forwarded to this office from Guatemala City, and final details of clearing a car are also undertaken here. Half a mile beyond, at the sentry box of the immigration officials, final checking-out is effected before crossing the Río Suchiate over the Talismán bridge into Mexico.

INDEX TO THE REGIONAL GUIDE

THE REPUBLIC OF HONDURAS

HONDURAS

BY CHARLES PARMER

Columbus first set foot in Central America in 1502, during his fourth voyage, on the Caribbean coast of Honduras. Hernando Cortés marched into the region in 1525 with his conquistadores in pursuit of his rebellious lieutenant Cristóbal de Olid. This country which figured early in the discovery and conquest is the most mountainous in Central America. The capital, Tegucigalpa, perched high in the mountains, has no railroad, but it possesses an unequaled air service. Within a radius of 100 miles are more than 100 landing fields where passengers and freight may be taken on and off by local airlines. The Hondurans of today are largely Indian and mestizo or mixed Indian and Spanish in blood and heritage, and they are proud of the Indian qualities of courage and loyalty which their leading citizens display in high degree. Their culture is marked by contrasts of the oldest with the newest. In the country's western section lie the ruins of Copán, a great cultural center of the Maya empire. Not far from Tegucigalpa construction was started in 1941 on the Escuela Agrícola Panamericana by the United Fruit Company; this will be one of the hemisphere's most modern agricultural colleges, where students selected from the five Central American republics are to be educated without charge. About the size of Pennsylvania, Honduras' area is roughly wedge-shaped, with a long Caribbean coast and a short Pacific frontage.

HISTORY

ABORIGINAL PERIOD. By the end of the first 500 years of the Christian era no fewer than five distinct tribes of Indians had reached what is now Northern Honduras, the ancient realm of Teuzgalpa. The most important were the Mayas, who established the first true civilization in Central America. The once mighty Maya community of Copán was a city with a great court capable of holding 30,000 people. The Carnegie Institution of Washington has proceeded with the excavation and reconstruction that were begun intensively at this site by the English explorer A. P. Maudslay in 1885 and were continued by the Peabody Museum of Harvard University until 1895. Lying on an alluvial flat of the Río Copán, the city was the capital of an empire that extended over a large section of Honduras' north coast. The Jicaques were the most warlike of the five aboriginal tribes in Honduras, so ferocious that for a while the Spaniards called all hostile Indians Jicaques. They held the far western part of what is now the department of Yoro; a portion of ancient Teuzgalpa, not to be confused with the country's present capital, the city of Tegucigalpa; part of Sula-Ulúa, and the southern part of Atlántida. Only vestiges of their culture remain. Unlike the Mayas, who were builders, and the Jicaques, who were warriors, the Mexicanos were a roving, trading people, speaking a Nahua dialect. They had a colony near Naco and trading posts in Comayagua, Teuzgalpa, the gold hills of Olancho, and a coastal community on the site of today's Trujillo. They became camp sutlers for the conquistadores and paid for the privilege by acting as interpreters and guides. As traders they carried news from one center to another. The Payas, a fishing and hunting people, were discovered

3

by early explorers touching at the Bay Islands off the north coast of Honduras. This tribe occupied the mainland from the Río Patuca northwest to the Río Aguán. The Lencas, good fighters and fine potters and sculptors, lived in the great valley of Comayagua, in Olancho, and in Gracias and Intibucá; from these last two western sections they spread into today's El Salvador.

DISCOVERY. Christopher Columbus discovered Honduras in 1502 on his last voyage. He reached the island of Guanaja, one of the Bay Islands, in July and saw there a large cayuco or fishing boat laden with native goods and manned by Indians from Yucatán. A landing was made near the Trujillo of today. Doris Stone says in her study, Archaeology of the North Coast of Honduras (Memoirs of the Peabody Museum of Archaeology and Ethnology, Harvard University, 1941, Vol. IX, No. 1), that from this vicinity "the ships sailed eastward and on August 14, 1502, a landing was made and mass was said. This marks the first contact of Europeans, not alone with Honduras, but also with the mainland of Central America."

Columbus claimed for Spain the land at the mouth of the Río Tinto, which he called Río de la Posesión to commemorate the claim. Doris Stone says that the Spaniards were excited by the numbers of calabashes or gourds that came drifting down this river. Some called the land Hibueras (Calabash); others termed it Guaymura, for the town near which they made harbor in the vicinity of the present Trujillo. The water was so deep along the entire coast that the land was finally called Honduras (Depths). Discovering here a semicivilized people possessed of cunning artifacts, Columbus inquired as to the source of their gold and was referred to the east. Throbbing with eagerness for the hoped-for passage to the Indies, he raised anchor and sailed on, keeping the coast on his starboard quarter. But his luck changed, and for 40 days he battled adverse currents and head winds. At last, doubling a cape, he turned south and had the wind with him. He was so rejoiced by this good fortune that he named the point Cabo Gracias a Dios (Cape Thanks to God), and maps today still carry the name.

CONQUEST. Colonization followed quickly on some of Columbus' discoveries, but it was 22 years before white men pushed into this part of the mainland. In the interval, however, the Bay Islands off the north coast were exploited and the Indians carried off to serve as slaves in the fields of Cuba. Gil González Dávila established the first colony in this region in 1524 on a spit of land jutting off what is now Guatemala; this settlement was called San Gil de Buenavista. About the same time Cortés sent his lieutenant Cristóbal de Olid into Honduras. Olid played his master false, taking everything for himself. He defeated González Dávila and Francisco de las Casas, whom Cortés had sent in pursuit of him. Casas, however, turned the tables on Olid and had him assassinated. Meanwhile Cortés had set out after Olid himself. He marched down into Honduras, established a town called La Natividad de Nuestra Señora near the site of the Puerto Cortés of today, and pushed along the Caribbean coast to Cape Honduras, where Casas had started the settlement that was to become the present Trujillo. Here Cortés made his headquarters for a year while he explored and conquered. The quantity of gold that was found did not come up to expectations, and Cortés, fearful of losing his control of Mexico, returned to that country.

Four hundred thousand Indians were at that time scattered over

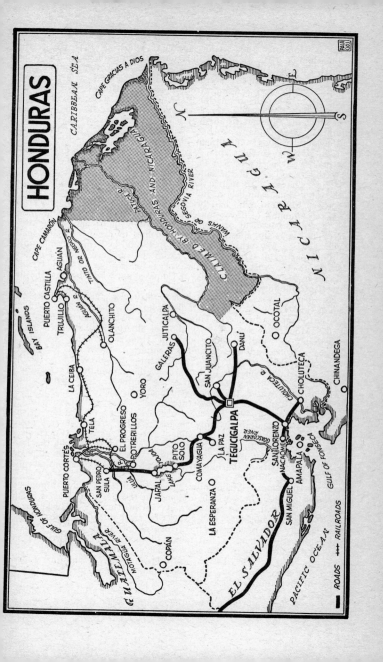

what is Honduras today—the Honduras which in 1941 had a total population of 1,109,833. The hills were rich in minerals, the valleys filled with crops. But soon the Spaniards began to fight among themselves for spoils, and henceforward Honduras was a battleground. Administrators were sent out from Spain and Mexico. But men who were strong enough to master their own kind were also avaricious and cruel to the natives. In 1530 Andrés de Cereceda was appointed governor; his rule was so harsh that the Indian workers took refuge in the hills. The Spaniards, so busy fighting one another that they could not feed themselves, sent urgent pleas to Guatemala for Pedro de Alvarado to come to their aid. Alvarado appeared in 1536 and founded the northwestern city of San Pedro Sula in the valley of the Río Ulúa, now the second city in the land. From San Pedro Sula he dispatched Juan de Chávez with instructions to "found a city between the two seas" and thus establish a hold on the land before the arrival of Francisco Montejo, who had been ordered from Mexico by the crown to take command. Chávez marched his men onto a high tableland in the present department of Gracias; there they quarreled among themselves and split up, most of them returning in disgust to Guatemala. Nevertheless a few years later Alvarado established the present capital of the department, Gracias a Dios. Montejo sent men under Alonso de Cáceres to the vast Comayagua valley, which lies east of Gracias. Cáceres in 1537 founded the city of Comayagua, which became the first capital of Honduras.

This period was marked by bloody struggles against the stalwart Indian chief Lempira, the only Indian who came near success in breaking the Spanish advance in Honduras. His name, which means Lord of the Mountain, remains a symbol of liberty and strength and is used today for the monetary unit of Honduras. After the city of Gracias a Dios had been founded Lempira rounded up 30,000 men along with their women and children and withdrew to a fortified height, generally believed to have been the mountain of Cerquín in the southeast of the present Gracias Department. Amply provisioned with corn and water, the Indians managed to make much trouble for the Spaniards for six months, threatening the very existence of the new city. Montejo, the governor, ordered Alonzo de Cáceres to take the rebellious chieftain by any means possible. After several unsuccessful tries, according to one widely accepted account, Cáceres sent a mounted soldier to parley with Lempira. Hidden behind the horse was another soldier with a loaded gun. When the chieftain appeared to talk to the envoy the hidden soldier shot him, and Lempira rolled dead down the hillside.

COLONIAL PERIOD. Spain now was exercising its rule through an audiencia or high court which first met in the town of Gracias a Dios and held Central America under its jurisdiction. The bickering of Spanish leaders continued, and attacks by freebooters complicated matters. Finally a semblance of order was established, and in 1578 the real colonization began. Great mines, especially of silver, were opened near Tegucigalpa; many colonists rushed in, and an alcalde or mayor was appointed for the district. Shortly thereafter Honduras was divided into two provinces, Comayagua and Tegucigalpa, and this resulted in more unfriendly rivalry.

The 17th century was quieter. New cities were established, Tegucigalpa grew in importance, and the Spanish way of life became the accepted mode. But there was friction with the English, operating in Mosquitia on the eastern Caribbean coast. The Spaniards succeeded in driving the English from the north coast of Honduras and in retaking the Bay Islands. The result of this was the treaty of 1786 which gave the English control, under certain conditions, of a small area between Yucatán and the Río Sarstún in the British Honduras of today.

During the entire colonial period Honduras, like neighboring provinces, maintained close social, cultural, and governmental relations with the mother country. Some provinces were relatively free from internal trouble. Not so Honduras; it was a dark ground for years, while one faction fought another. Comayagua came out on top in 1788, when the more southerly city of Tegucigalpa was placed under her control. Despite treaties the English in 1793 once more seized Roatán, one of the Bay Islands, and dumped there a number of fighting Caribs who were later shipped by the Hondurans to Trujillo on the mainland. Tegucigalpa, determined on recognition, finally was given the title of city, and in 1824, after the country freed itself from Spain, it became joint capital of Honduras with Comayagua.

INDEPENDENCE. During the later colonial period, as elsewhere throughout Hispanic America, educated groups among the young were inspired by Miguel Hidalgo of Mexico and Simón Bolívar in South America to ask themselves the old question: Why can't we rule ourselves? Following the lead of Mexico, the province of Comayagua de Honduras, as the country was officially known, announced on Sept. 15, 1821, its independence of Spain, together with the present Guatemala, El Salvador, Nicaragua, and Costa Rica. The patriot José del Valle, whose statue stands in Tegucigalpa opposite the American Legation, presented a formal declaration which was signed next day; and Central America was free from Spain.

For a time in 1822 Honduras, together with all the rest of Central America, was part of the Mexican empire. The following year, however, on the downfall of the emperor Agustín de Iturbide, Honduras became one of the states of a Central American confederation with the capital at Guatemala City. The Honduran Liberal leader Francisco Morazán became president of this confederation in 1830. The life of the confederation was brief and turbulent; Honduras withdrew from it in 1838, and the confederation collapsed the following year. At various subsequent times loose confederations were formed which included Honduras. A constitution for the independent state of Honduras was adopted in 1848. Tegucigalpa was made the capital in 1880 and remains so today.

Honduras in 1904 was among the first of the Latin American countries to adopt a constitution specifying that the president should be elected by popular vote. In 1932, after years of unrest, a strong man was elected president, Gen. Tiburcio Carías Andino, a soldier, scholar, and excellent administrator. President Carías proved himself an enlightened leader. He sought internal peace, progress, and prosperity for his people. Beginning with the children, he established compulsory free schooling. In 1935 he instituted a rural resettlement plan, giving needy families 50 acres of good land and the necessary cattle, tools, and seed. In 1941 he had United States agricultural experts survey Honduras' agricultural possibilities in search of a staple crop that would enable the individual farmer to prosper despite depressions. He also promulgated a new commercial code facilitating trade with the United

States. Legitimate debts piled up by past regimes were systematically paid off, even at a sacrifice. He consistently refused to let his government make loans for fanciful schemes. In 1939 the Congress of Honduras extended Carías' tenure of office to 1949.

The president has a cabinet of six members. The legislative branch is a single body of 38 members, one deputy to each 25,000 inhabitants, elected for six years each. The national judiciary is a supreme court of five judges appointed by the executive and approved by Congress for four-year terms. Each of the 17 administrative departments has local and departmental justices.

THE LAND

Honduras, 44,480 square miles in area, is about the size of Pennsylvania. It lies SE of Guatemala and NE of Nicaragua and has a front of 350 miles on the Caribbean and 80 miles on the Pacific. Among its possessions are the picturesque Bay Islands off its N or Caribbean coast. Its topography is a mass of saw-toothed mountains interspersed by tablelands and fertile valleys watered by spring-fed streams. In general the cordilleras spread into two ranges, with 10,000-foot elevations not uncommon, running parallel to the Caribbean and Pacific coasts.

There is a broad N coastal plain extending 60-75 miles back from the Caribbean. Here are the great banana lands, swept almost continuously by moisture-laden trade winds. Along the lower eastern Caribbean coast, stretching S from a little below Cape Camarón, is Mosquitia, a great stretch of mountains and swamps that reach far inland and comprise almost a third of the country's surface. In it are rich logging sections and wild reaches of river, with Indian huts and a few whites. The Bay Islands, where Columbus made his first landfall in this section, are inhabited by English-speaking natives. The N seaboard has several ports, Puerto Cortés, Tela, La Ceiba, Trujillo, and Puerto Castilla.

Along the short Pacific coastline the mountains decline to hills which extend almost to the water's edge. Here, almost surrounded by volcanic islands, is Honduras' one Pacific seaport, Amapala, on Tiger Island in the Gulf of Fonseca.

The country has several large rivers and countless small streams. Among those on the Caribbean side are the great Río Ulúa, which rises far W in Gracias Department, and its ample tributaries, the Lindo and Humuya or Comayagua. The Ulúa flows for 50 miles through a valley 20 miles wide, the banana empire, and empties into the Gulf of Honduras. Next in importance is the Río Aguán, flowing NE through a fertile valley 60 miles long and reaching the Caribbean below Puerto Castilla. Also important are the Río Tinto or Negro, better known in history as the Black River; the Plátano; the Patuca, which is the great waterway of Mosquitia; and the Wanks. Rivers flowing to the Pacific empty into the Gulf of Fonseca, among them the Goascorán and the turbulent Choluteca, which winds through many a mountain gorge after passing through Tegucigalpa.

In Mosquitia are several coastal lakes, some of them really arms of the sea with narrow inlets, such as Laguna de Caratasca, Micos, Elbana, and Guaymoreto. Honduras' pride is large Lake Yojoa in the NW interior on the route from the Caribbean coast to Tegucigalpa.

This lake is believed to be an extinct volcanic crater. It has no apparent outlet; there are, however, two branches of the Río Ulúa, the Lindo and the Jaitique, which flow from it through subterranean passages. Lake Yojoa is one of the great sights of Central America.

The topography accounts for the products of Honduras: bananas in the lowlands; minerals in the mountains; pineapples, oranges, sarsaparilla, and cacao in the midlands; coffee and tobacco in the highlands. Sugar cane, beans, and corn are raised on hillsides for home use. Some livestock is raised. But it is for bananas, gold, silver, and fine hardwoods that Honduras is primarily noted. Two great corporations handle the major portion of Honduras' vast banana crop, the Standard Fruit and Steamship Co., with headquarters at La Ceiba, and the Tela Railway Co., a subsidiary of the United Fruit Co., with headquarters in the company town of La Lima, not far from Tela.

The Indians have panned gold in the hills of Honduras, especially in the department of Olancho, since before the days of the conquest. Mining operations of late years have been largely carried on in Olancho Department, at the Agua Fría mines, and by the New York and Honduras Rosario Mining Co. in the fabulously rich mines at San Juancito, 20 miles NE of the capital, where about $2,000,000 worth of silver is mined yearly. Iron and copper are found in the department of Yoro, and lead, zinc, antimony, platinum, nickel, and manganese beds have been discovered in various sections. A few emeralds, diamonds, and opals have been found.

Today, logging is carried on mainly in the almost inaccessible Mosquitia. The heaviest of woods, lignum vitae, is now in demand because of a certain peculiar property; it withstands the erosion of sea water so well that it is used for bearings in ship propellers. But it is the mahogany tree that is especially sought, a tree that takes 200 years to reach full growth, is often 12 feet thick at the base, and rises to a height of 100 feet.

Honduras' imports are a little more than $10,000,000 yearly, its exports a little less (1941). The United States receives 95 per cent of the country's exports and supplies about 76 per cent of its imports. Export figures are: bananas, 66 per cent; gold and silver, chiefly the latter, 29 per cent; coffee, 2 per cent; miscellaneous, 3 per cent.

PRACTICAL INFORMATION

HOW TO REACH HONDURAS

From the United States. Minimum one-way fare from New Orleans to Honduran ports is about $60, round trip $108 (1941); from New York $110, round trip $162. Fare from Tampa, Fla., to Honduras in small ships is $25 one way, $40 round trip. Plane fare from Brownsville, Tex., to Tegucigalpa is $105 one way.

BY STEAMER. United Fruit Co.; New York office: Pier 3, North River; New Orleans office: 321 St. Charles St. Has sailings from New York and New Orleans for Honduran ports. Voyage takes a minimum of 4 days.

Standard Fruit and Steamship Co.; New York office: 11 Broadway; New Orleans office: 140 Carondelet St.; Chicago office: 111 W. Washington St. Has sailings from New York and New Orleans.

Barton H. Smith Line; general offices: Tampa, Fla. Has sailings of small 10-passenger ships from Tampa, Fla.

BY AIR. Pan American Airways; main office: 135 E. 42nd St., New York. Planes leave from Brownsville, Tex., for Mexico, Guatemala, El Salvador, Honduras, and points S. The trip to Tegucigalpa takes 24 hours, with an overnight stop in Guatemala.

From Neighboring Countries. Via United Fruit or Standard Fruit lines or Pan American Airways from stopover points on services indicated above.

Also by Transportes Aéreos Centro-Americanos (TACA), which maintains services from San José, C. R.; Managua, Nicaragua; San Salvador, El Salvador; Belize, British Honduras; and other Central American points.

The Pan American Highway will give access E from El Salvador and W from Nicaragua. In its present condition the road is passable in dry weather E of Choluteca.

From El Salvador it is also possible to reach Honduras by motor launch across the Gulf of Fonseca to Amapala.

AIDS TO TRAVELERS

Honduran Representation in the U. S. The Honduran Legation is at 2611 Woodley Place, Washington, D. C. Consuls and vice-consuls are in Los Angeles and San Francisco, Calif.; Jacksonville, Miami, and Tampa, Fla.; Chicago, Ill.; New Orleans, La.; Baltimore, Md.; Boston, Mass.; Detroit, Mich.; New York; Philadelphia, Pa.; Brownsville, Galveston, Houston, Port Arthur, and San Antonio, Tex.; Balboa, C. Z.; San Juan, P. R.

U. S. Representation in Honduras. The U. S. Legation is in Tegucigalpa. Consular offices are in La Ceiba and Puerto Cortés.

Local Sources of Information. The office of Transportes Aéreos Centro-Americanos (TACA) in Tegucigalpa is very helpful in planning air tours, such as the trip to the famous ruins of Copán, which can be reached comfortably only by air; to the Pacific port of Amapala; to the ancient city of Comayagua, San Pedro Sula, and the coastal towns of Tela and Puerto Cortés; to Belize in British Honduras, and other points. With pilots who know Honduras thoroughly, TACA planes make many special trips to various parts of the country for sportsmen,

scientists, and tourists. Further information regarding routes, regula-
tions, and laws may be obtained at United Fruit Co. offices at La
Lima and Tela, from U. S. consulates, and from the U. S. Legation in
Tegucigalpa.

Climate. Honduras' climate is ideal for the tropics, especially in the
highlands around Tegucigalpa, 3200 feet and more above sea level.
Here the rainy season or summer starts the last of May and runs
through November, the thermometer rising as high as 90° F. in midsummer; yet it does not seem excessively hot. The dry season or winter is December-May. The first two months the air is brisk during
the day, chilly at night. In February-May the days are warm.

In the midland, between highlands and coast, the climate is good
at altitudes of 500-2500 feet, with a mean temperature of 85° F. The
coastal lowlands are hot and humid; here the rainy season extends
from mid-September through February, with the temperature above
80° much of the time. From March until mid-September, the dry
season, the temperature touches 90°, and humidity adds discomfort.

Clothing. Tropical clothes are needed along the coast. Light wool-
ens, cashmeres, and tropical worsteds are appropriate in the mountains,
with warm wraps and topcoats at night, December-February, and on
the coast during chilly spells.

Health. The traveler should drink boiled or bottled water only.
Vegetables should be thoroughly cooked. Only those raw fruits and
vegetables that can be peeled should be eaten. In the lowlands it is
necessary to sleep under mosquito netting.

There is a modern hospital with English-speaking nurses on a high
tableland overlooking Tegucigalpa, the Hospital Viera, owned and
operated by Dr. Roy B. Nutter, born in Maine and trained in New
York, who has spent 30 years in hot countries. The Polytechnic Clinic
in Comayagüela, Tegucigalpa's twin city, has English-speaking as well
as Spanish-speaking doctors. There is a general hospital in Tegucigalpa, the San Felipe. The United Fruit Co. maintains an up-to-date
hospital at Tela. Other hospitals are government institutions, the
Atlántida in La Ceiba, the Santa Teresa in Comayagua, the Hospital
del Norte in San Pedro Sula, and the Occidente in Santa Rosa de
Copán. The capital has several dentists trained in the United States.

Sports and Recreations. Honduras is a sportsman's paradise. Airline
and steamship officials can assist travelers with information on hunting parties. Hunters often go out on the road to Danlí from Tegucigalpa on Saturday nights and may bring in a deer before sunrise; during the winter months they hire a plane and fly from the capital to
the Pacfic coast near San Lorenzo, where mallard ducks abound. Lake
Yojoa is another good duck-hunting ground. There are bears, pumas,
leopards, and panthers in the hills.

Fish are plentiful in Lake Yojoa. Deep-sea fishing is good in the
Gulf of Fonseca and near Puerto Cortés on the Caribbean. A mile
from Puerto Cortés there is good fresh-water fishing in Lake Alvarado.

Neither fishing nor hunting licenses are needed, and there is no
closed season.

Motorboats and sailboats can be rented at Pito Solo or Jaral on
Lake Yojoa and on other lakes.

Tennis and golf can be played at the country clubs at Tegucigalpa,
San Pedro Sula, La Ceiba, La Lima, and El Progreso. Each spring El

Progreso is the scene of a national golf meet which assumes the proportions of a gala social event.

Below Amapala on the Pacific there is a palm-shaded bathing beach; near by is a cave where Henry Morgan is said to have cached some doubloons. Lake Alvarado near Puerto Cortés provides excellent freshwater swimming, and Tela has a fine beach.

Mountain trails, especially near Tegucigalpa and the Rosario silver mines, are excellent for riding on mule or horseback.

Soccer football is the national sport.

Currency. The lempira (L) is the gold standard unit, its value stabilized at $.50 U. S. (1941). Named after the great Indian chief, it is divided into 100 centavos. Currency is issued in these denominations: silver pieces of 20, 50, and 100 centavos; nickel, 5 and 10 centavos; copper, 1 and 2 centavos. Notes are for L1, L2, L5, L10, and L20. U. S. currency circulates freely in the banana and coastal sections, and U. S. paper money is highly prized throughout the country.

Banks. Honduras has two banks, each with branches. The Banco Atlántida has headquarters in La Ceiba, a large branch in Tegucigalpa and other branches in Puerto Cortés, San Pedro Sula, Tela, and Trujillo. The Banco de Honduras has headquarters in Tegucigalpa and branches in Puerto Cortés and San Pedro Sula.

Cost of Living. Living is not cheap for transients in Honduras, judged by U. S. standards (1941). Taxis in Tegucigalpa and San Pedro Sula charge L1-L4 or $.50-$2 for an average trip. Flights from the coastal towns of Tela and Puerto Cortés to Tegucigalpa are $15, with flying time an hour or less; overland the cost is $5 from Tegucigalpa N to the town of Potrerillos, a 2-day trip by bus, and several dollars more by railroad from Potrerillos on to coastal points.

Puerto Cortés has one hotel. There is no hotel in the Pacific port of Amapala, though there are several native taverns. In Tegucigalpa the hotels are not first class, though an excellent new one is under construction in the twin city of Comayagüela (1941). Rates are rather high in the capital, L5-L12 a day or $2.50-$6, meals included. The price is $.75 and up for an average luncheon in Tegucigalpa. There i one well-known North American boarding house in Tegucigalpa, commonly spoken of as the TACA staff house; the charge is $3 a day for room and board.

Throughout the country districts, especially on the bus highway from the Atlantic to the Pacific, there are rustic roadside taverns where native foods are served. The food is usually excellent, the price of a meal $.25 and up. Food brought from the United States is expensive. Prices must cover import duties and transportation costs.

If the visitor travels by mule—the best way to explore—it is a good idea to buy an animal for a few dollars and to sell it at the journey's end.

Transportation. HIGHWAYS. The roads radiating out of Tegucigalpa are often winding and bumpy, though the government has undertaken an extensive road-building program that promises before long to result in a relatively excellent highway system. The two most important roads are the N Highway (Carretera del Norte), which, supplemented by a comparatively short stretch of railroad, connects Tegucigalpa with the N coast, and the S Highway (Carretera del Sur), which links it with the Pacific coast. The road to Danlí, running some 45 miles E from Tegucigalpa in the direction of Nicaragua, is very good. The

Olancho Highway (Carretera de Olancho) runs NE into Olancho Department. Branch roads, many of them passable only in the dry season, lead off from these main highways to various towns and settlements. An 87-mile stretch of the Pan American Highway has been laid out across S Honduras from El Salvador to Nicaragua. The best part of this road runs through the towns of San Lorenzo, from which the Pacific port of Amapala can be reached, and Choluteca. From Choluteca to the Nicaraguan border it is little more than a trail.

AUTOMOBILES AND BUSES. Because of the inadequacy of motor roads travelers seldom take their cars to Honduras. The country has extensive bus services, though some parts can still be reached only by plane or muleback.

RAILROADS. There are about 900 miles of railroad in Honduras, mainly in the sugar and banana lands on the N coast. The National Railroad runs from Puerto Cortés 66 miles S to Potrerillos. The Tela Railroad, with about 200 miles of track, has a main line from Tela 55 miles SW to El Progreso, from which there are connections to Honduras' second city, San Pedro Sula. It also connects with a line running to La Ceiba, E of Tela on the coast. The Trujillo Railroad has 241 miles of track, its main line extending from the coastal town of Trujillo to Olanchito on the Río Aguán. The Vaccaro Brothers and Co. line operates from La Ceiba 105 miles into the banana lands.

AIRLINES. Honduras is one of the most air-minded countries in the world, being the birthplace of Transportes Aéreos Centro-Americanos (TACA), which covers Central America. Tegucigalpa is TACA's headquarters. Within a radius of 100 miles of the city are more than 100 landing fields where planes call on order to pick up or deliver passengers, produce, cattle, or supplies. In addition to its regular international route TACA gives special service to such points as Belize, British Honduras; Amapala on the Pacific coast, and the N coast.

A government service, Compañía Aéreo Hondureño, operates within the republic. One of its most important routes is from Tegucigalpa to Tela via San Pedro Sula. The company also arranges special flights to many points in the republic.

Pan American Airways, connecting the United States with Central and South America, has frequent service to and from Tegucigalpa.

COASTWISE NAVIGATION. Small coastal boats plying along Honduras' N coast connect it with Guatemala and Nicaragua. Sailing dates are irregular. Passenger-carrying freight vessels from New York, Boston, Miami, Mobile, and New Orleans make regular calls at Puerto Cortés, Tela, La Ceiba, and Trujillo.

Several motor launches belonging to import-export companies operate on call in the Gulf of Fonseca and connect San Lorenzo on the mainland with Amapala on Tiger Island, 15 miles out. Light-draft vessels operate on the Río Ulúa as far inland as El Progreso (125 miles) and on the Wanks, Aguán, Negro, and Patuca. Ferry launches operate on Honduras' great inland lake of Yojoa, connecting Jaral on the north with Pito Solo on the south.

Postage. Rates from Honduras to the United States are $.03 an ounce for first-class mail (1941); delivery takes about 12 days. Airmail to the United States is $.08 for a letter weighing not more than 5 grams, about one tissue sheet and airmail envelope. Parcel post is accepted up to 22 pounds. From the United States rates are $.03 an ounce for letters and $.12 a half ounce for airmail.

Telegraph, Cable, and Telephone Services. Honduras connects with the outside world through the Tropical Radio Telegraph Co. and All America Cables. Stations are in Tegucigalpa, La Ceiba, Puerto Castilla, Puerto Cortés, and Tela. There is direct telephone connection with New York.

Souvenirs and Handicrafts. Straw rugs, earthenware, alligator leather goods, and Panama hats can be purchased. Silver from the time of the conquest is much sought after. The export of Maya and other archeological antiquities is prohibited by law.

Food. Typical native food has as its base frijoles and tortillas, or beans and corn cakes. Tapado is made of smoked beef with coconut milk and tropical vegetables. Enchiladas are tortillas with various sorts of stuffing. Tamale pie or tamale and chile, a variation of a local dish, is cooked for the foreign palate. There are many native fruits, including bananas, plantains, papayas, mangoes, tamarinds, grapefruit, and oranges.

Holidays. January 1, New Year's; July 14, Bastille Day; September 15, Independence Day; October 12, Columbus Day (Day of the Race—Día de la Raza). Many business houses close for the more important feast days of the Roman Catholic Church.

Fiestas. It is customary for communities to celebrate their patron saints' days with special ceremonies. Four such local festivals are marked by especially picturesque processions: San Pedro Sula, June 23-July 4, celebration in honor of St. Peter, the city's patron; Tegucigalpa Feast of the Immaculate Conception, December 8-January 1; Tegucigalpa and Comayagua, Holy Week, preceding Easter. A noteworthy celebration is held in honor of the black St. Benedict (San Benito) patron saint of cooks, in Tegucigalpa during Holy Week.

The development of aviation has made it possible to reach Tegucigalpa, the capital of Honduras, directly and easily, passing the customs at the Toncontín airport, a short distance out of the city. This is now the preferred means of entering the country. Coming from British Honduras, San Pedro Sula is the airport of entry. By water, entry is by any one of several ports on the Caribbean coast or by the Pacific port, Amapala (p. 27) on the Gulf of Fonseca. The Pan American Highway, passable in dry weather, gives access from El Salvador; from Nicaragua it is little more than a trail. The N ports are covered here, then the capital and automobile routes radiating out from it which are interesting to follow somewhat at leisure. Wherever the object is speed and convenience, air service is the recommended means of travel within the country.

THE CARIBBEAN COAST

Puerto Cortés, the port farthest W on the N coast, is a United Fruit Co. banana port, with good steamer service from the United States. Founded in 1896, it has a radio station, railroad car shops, a flour mill, and a soap, candle, and coconut oil factory. It is partly encircled by a palm-fringed body of fresh water, Lake Alvarado. Hernando Cortés passed through this region on his memorable march from Mexico in 1525.

HOTEL. Cosenza.

NOTE. Hotels are here classified by rates. Two stars indicate the higher rates for the country in question and also, in nearly all cases, mean good accommodations. One star means rates in the medium brackets; no star means either low rates or no information available. An effort is made in all these guides to list hotels in the various cities and towns, but travelers who are accustomed to North American or European accommodations should use the information with care. In the capitals and larger Latin American centers hotels usually have standards comparable with those found elsewhere and at times on a par with those anywhere in the world. In the smaller centers throughout Latin America hotels are often more nearly boarding houses whose standards of accommodations and food make them unacceptable to all but the most adaptable.

Excursions from Puerto Cortés. Fresh-water fishing is good in Lake Alvarado and deep-sea fishing in the Caribbean.

Tulian, halfway along the bay, makes a popular excursion. There is a fresh stream for bathing and picnicking amid beautiful tropical vegetation.

Omoa, an ancient port, is across the bay from Puerto Cortés. Boats can be rented for the trip to it. Now practically abandoned, Omoa is interesting for the remains of Honduras' oldest fort, San Fernando.

Tela, 30 miles E of Puerto Cortés and reached from it by car, railroad, or boat, is an important United Fruit Co. banana port, with steamer service from the United States. It is also connected by railroad with El Progreso, San Pedro Sula, and La Ceiba.

Trainloads of bananas are drawn onto the great pier at Tela for transfer to steamers. To the left of the pier is a sandy beach almost a mile long with a gentle slope, excellent for children. Parallel with the beach is a palm-shaded gravel walk lined with United Fruit Co. guest houses. At the end of the walk, near the pier, is the spacious United Fruit Co. clubhouse, which serves excellent meals and shows moving pictures in its dining room at least one night a week.

Behind these waterfront houses are paved streets lined with neat white green-trimmed houses set in spacious grounds, the homes of United Fruit Co. officials. Here, too, is the United Fruit Co. hospital. Almost opposite the end of the pier is the company's well-stocked commissary, and across the railroad tracks that lead onto the pier are the headquarters of the Tela Railroad Co. and the United Fruit Co. offices, set in well-kept lawns with shrubs and palms. All this is Tela Nueva (New Tela). From the offices a winding dirt road leads across half a mile of flat land and a steel bridge to Tela Vieja (Old Tela), a cluster of native wooden houses along wide streets. Tela Vieja contains a church, a school, the military headquarters of the district, and a smart Spanish clubhouse.

HOTELS. Balderach and Italia are both in Tela Vieja.

Excursions from Tela. A few miles S of Tela in the Lancetilla valley, reached by car, is the tropical experiment farm of the United Fruit Co. Here species from all parts of the world and especially from the tropics are experimented with to ascertain which plants are most adaptable to Honduras.

On the outskirts of Tela lies a snake farm that was formerly famous. Reptiles are not kept there at present, as sufficient serum has been obtained and stored for years to come.

The beautiful Lean valley, in the heart of the ancient Jicaque Indian country, can be reached from Tela by a combination car and horseback trip. It is interesting historically and archeologically. Much of the valley has gone back to the jungle, though the Standard Fruit Co. has planted a portion of it with orange groves.

La Ceiba, with 15,000 inhabitants, 40 miles E of Tela, in a lush coastal valley, is headquarters of the Standard Fruit and Steamship Co., with frequent steamer service from the United States. It is capital of the department of Atlántida. Jutting up not far from the city is the peak of Bonito, a 5000-foot mountain, part of the coastal range.

HOTEL. Royal.

Excursion from La Ceiba. The Bay Islands may be visited in an unusual and rewarding trip (p. 17).

Trujillo, E of La Ceiba, within the sheltering arm of Cape Honduras, lies near the site of the ancient village of Guaymura, now no longer in existence, where Columbus landed in 1502. Trujillo was founded in 1524 by Francisco de las Casas and was Cortés' headquarters for a while. At one time it had the only cathedral in all Honduras; unfortunately the building has been destroyed. Near Trujillo, William Walker, the U. S. filibuster, was executed in 1860 after fleeing from Nicaragua, where he had made himself president as a step in his program to create a vast Latin empire under his command. Various catastrophes have destroyed or damaged the colonial monuments.

HOTEL. Codina.

Excursions from Trujillo. Olanchito (Little Olancho), inland in the hills SW, is reached by a railroad journey of some 90 miles. It is one of the oldest settlements in the area. The church has a Virgin wearing a crown of hide. According to popular belief Olanchito was founded by the few people who managed to escape from the destruction of Olancho el Viejo (Old Olancho), in the interior between Juticalpa and Catacamos. In colonial times Olancho el Viejo or San Jorge de Olancho was one of the wealthiest cities in Honduras. It is said that the people were so proud and selfish that God destroyed the city and most of its inhabitants, perhaps by fire and perhaps by a volcanic eruption. One of the very few things that were saved was this hide crown of the Virgin, which the Indians, too poor to give gold, had presented to her. This crown was brought to Olanchito, named after the former town.

S and E lies the vast territory of Mosquitia, almost a third of Honduras, with no railroads, no roads, no cities, nothing save swamp, jungle, and mountains inhabited by blotch-faced Indians and a few white lumber workers and prospectors. Mosquitia gains its name from a corruption of Missiko, the name of the aboriginal tribe who inhabited it. Guides and good outfitting are necessary for penetration of this wilderness.

The Bay Islands can also be visited from Trujillo.

BAY ISLANDS

A unique journey is to the Islas de la Bahía (Bay Islands), the 80-mile chain parallel to Honduras' N coast which Columbus first sighted in 1502. The islands can be reached from any Honduran port on the Caribbean, but La Ceiba and Trujillo are most convenient because of their nearness to the main islands.

The archeology of the Bay Islands offers important evidences of relationship with Costa Rica. These islands are one of the farthest N and W parts of an area which was the home of a basic Central American aboriginal culture. They also served as an important stopping place for pre-Spanish trading canoes between Yucatán and Central America. Some artifacts found here may have been buried with the dead, but most of them come from old settlements covered with debris. Stone implements, including club heads, chisels, blades, and spear heads, have been found. A rare series of implements made of flaked shaly stone and fashioned like the ace of spades have been dug up; these tools are worn at the edges, an evidence of their having been used as shovels. According to the archeologist Lord Moyne nothing of this shape was discovered previously in Central America; the tools resemble stone implements found 3000 miles distant on Easter Island in the Pacific.

Soft green soapstone must have been abundant in the early days; amulets of this material pierced for stringing have been found in fair quantities, as well as some jadeite specimens. Figurines on the amulets evidently represent deities. Other figurines, particularly on pottery, more nearly resemble human figures and perhaps were conceived at a later date. Some of the vases are beaker-shaped, with two handles, and some show the motif of a weeping god in high relief.

A rare souvenir of the Bay Islands is the ocarina, a musical instrument made of clay and resembling a yam, which, when blown, gives forth a soft whistle. Ocarinas have been found in the ruins of many old settlements. A six-hole ocarina is a lucky find. A few are marked with something like a St. Andrew's cross; these are collector's items.

Roatán, the largest island and capital of the group, is only 40 miles

NW of Trujillo. Fishermen can be persuaded to make the journey to Coxen Hole on it for a small fee. The islanders are primitive but friendly. The officials speak Spanish, the natives English. England ruled the islands during buccaneering days but gave them up to Honduras in 1859. When visitors drop anchor at Coxen Hole, harbor officials come out in boats. The comandante impounds all passports until final departure from the islands. The natives who come out in their cayucos or dugout canoes offer souvenirs and rare breeds of parrots. The Museum of the American Indian of the Heye Foundation, the Smithsonian Institution, and the Peabody Museum of Harvard University have sent experts to study these islands. Today's natives are chiefly descendants of peoples brought to the islands by the British since the conquest. They claim to be English and have little intercourse with the Honduran coast, choosing instead to maintain relations with the people of Belize in British Honduras and those of the Cayman Islands.

Bonacca Island in particular still offers a rich field to the antiquary and the archeologist. It lies E of long Roatán and small Barbareta. On Bonacca are the remains of a once-powerful settlement surrounded by an earthen wall higher than a man and containing a number of mounds and monoliths.

CENTRAL HONDURAS

Tegucigalpa is easily accessible both from other countries and from points in Honduras because of its well-developed air services. Most travelers arriving at a port on the N coast proceed to Tegucigalpa by air. From Tela the air trip takes 45 minutes. It is also possible to make the trip inland by a combined railroad and motor route. Puerto Cortés has railroad connections to Potrerillos (66 miles), from which there is bus service over the N Highway to Tegucigalpa; the journey, a distance of 200 miles, takes 2 days altogether. Travelers entering the country at Amapala (p. 27) on Tiger Island in the Gulf of Fonseca on the Pacific side take a launch to San Lorenzo on the mainland (2¼ hours) and go on from there by car or bus over a good road, the S Highway (5 hours), or they may engage a special plane.

TEGUCIGALPA

Capital of Honduras, with 70,000 inhabitants, Tegucigalpa lies in a high mountain valley 3200 feet above sea level, 120 miles by air from the N coast and 60 miles from the Pacific port of Amapala. It is one of the few capitals in the world without a railroad, but its air services are outstanding. Highways make it a travel center for more leisurely trips to other cities and small towns and into rural regions.

Most historians have said that the capital traces its name to the ancient Indian realm of Teuzgalpa, whose name meant Hills or Slopes of Silver. But Alberto Membreño, former president of Honduras, has stated in his authoritative work, now out of print, Nombres Indígenas de Honduras (Indigenous Names of Honduras), that Tegucigalpa means Place of the Pointed Stones in the mixed Maya-Aztec tongue. Hills that jut up thousands of feet on three sides give the city much of its charm. To the north, modern residences are built on terraces on the sides of El Picacho, a mountain topped with a picturesque park containing a reservoir. The Río Choluteca flows between Tegucigalpa and its twin city of Comayagüela. In 1898 hilly Tegucigalpa and rolling Comayagüela were united, each part retaining its distinctive name. Since 1938 they have been administered jointly as the Central District. Physically the cities are connected by two masonry bridges, Puente Mallol near the Presidential Palace, built centuries ago by the Spaniards, and the handsome Puente Carías, constructed under the direction of President Carías in the 1930's. The streets of Comayagüela are laid out in Spanish checkerboard fashion on almost level ground. Comayagüela gets water from its own reservoir and electric current from the plant on the river's edge in Tegucigalpa; it has a great public market, normal schools, the most modern school of arts and crafts in Central America, and a great obelisk commemorating the centennial of Central American independence. Because of its elevation Tegucigalpa has a fine climate. The air is bracing; nights are cool. It has known neither earthquake nor hurricane, fire nor bombardment. Thus the city stands as originally laid out and built, even to its quaint streets of stairs which at several points connect one level with another. Built flush with the streets, without portico or stoop, each building has its own central patio. Stucco has always been the prevalent building material, and houses are frequently painted pastel green, blue, lavender, or pink. It was customary for houses to have a single entrance with thick doors and heavy bars for defense in time of revolution.

Approaching by air, the plane shoots through a wide pass in the mountains, giving a sudden view of the capital gleaming in the sunlight. The Toncontín airport is regarded as one of the best natural fields in Central America. On it are the hangars and machine shop of the Honduras air corps, the Country Club, the neat building of Pan American Airways (made of stone in natural pastel shades), and the white brick building of Transportes Aéreos Centro-Americanos with its open-air restaurant and near by the TACA machine shops and hangars. On the brow of the hill to the east, overlooking the airport, is a handsome white stone structure, the home of Lowell Yerex, the British founder and president of TACA. The house is set in a garden containing varieties of plants, trees, and vines which Mr. Yerex brought from many sections of the tropics.

The drive into Tegucigalpa from the airport is by the highway across the river and through Comayagüela, past the Central American obelisk at Calle 13 and 2ª Avenida. The road, 2ª Av., goes within a block of the Polytechnic Clinic and by the old city hall of Comayagüela; crosses C. 2ª, with the large San Isidro market 4 blocks to the left; and approaches the old Spanish stone bridge across the Río Choluteca. Some blocks to the left on C. 1ª is the San Miguel Normal Institute. The National School of Arts and Crafts is near the bridge. Avenues bear names as well as numbers.

Across the river in Tegucigalpa, to the left, is the Presidential Palace with its gardens. The palace has ornamental medieval-looking turrets and bastions. In the quarter-mile stretch beyond the bridge are some of the most important and colorful buildings of Tegucigalpa. To the left beyond the Presidential Palace are the barracks of the president's Guard of Honor; a detachment is on duty at the palace constantly.

Plaza Morazán, the city's center, lies on C. Bolívar. On or near C. Bolívar, before reaching this square, are passed the Normal School for Men, the National School of Pharmacy, the House of Congress, and the National University. The square contains an equestrian statue of the Honduran patriot Francisco Morazán, shrubbery, and walks lined with stone benches.

On the square's E side is the handsome twin-towered and domed cathedral of San Miguel, completed in 1782. It has a fine altar of gilded wood, an attractive cloister, and bells brought from Spain. The services here are colorful and lavish. On special occasions such as weddings the congregation follows the old Spanish custom whereby the men sit on the right of the nave, the women on the left. The cathedral is the focal point of the unique Holy Week services, when the figure of Christ is taken down from the Cross, anointed by chosen members of the congregation, and reverently placed in a casket for the multitudes to view. During the dry season one of the military bands plays almost nightly on the stairs before the cathedral, and the citizens turn out to promenade. Public broadcasts of news and music are a feature of the square.

Across the square from the cathedral on Av. Paz Baraona is the National Museum. It contains a scale model of the Maya city of Copán which travelers often study before visiting the remains of the ancient city. Here too are many Maya fragments and artifacts as well as other early Indian objects. One section of the museum is devoted to birds of Honduras, another to fish, another to mammals. In the patio is a small zoo containing monkeys that roar and beat their breast, as well as pumas, deer, and great condors of the hills. The flora of Honduras is well represented.

On the S side of the square is the Palace of the Central District, the modern municipal building, constructed of Honduran woods and marble. It is one of the handsomest structures in the country.

Two blocks E of Plaza Morazán, at C. 9ª, is a street of stairs leading to a lower level. These street stairs are lined with quaint and colorful houses, frequently with ancient wrought-iron fittings dating back to the 17th century.

On C. 10 stands the American Legation and Consulate, a solid two-story brick structure with the U. S. flag flying from a central window. It extends from Av. Paz Baraona to Av. Colón and faces on Plaza San Francisco. Erected only 40 years ago, this building was planned

---

KEY TO MAP OF TEGUCIGALPA AND COMAYAGÜELA

1. Old city hall
2. San Miguel Normal Institute
3. National School of Arts and Crafts
4. Polytechnic Clinic
5. San Isidro market
6. Plaza Morazán
7. Parque Concordia
8. Paseo Leona
9. Cathedral
10. San Francisco church
11. Los Dolores church
12. Presidential Palace
13. Palace of the Central District (city hall)
14. Palace of Justice
15. Ministerial Palace
16. Post office
17. Police headquarters
18. Barracks of the president's Guard of Honor
19. U. S. Legation and Consulate
20. National University
21. Normal School for Men
22. Dolores market
23. National Theater

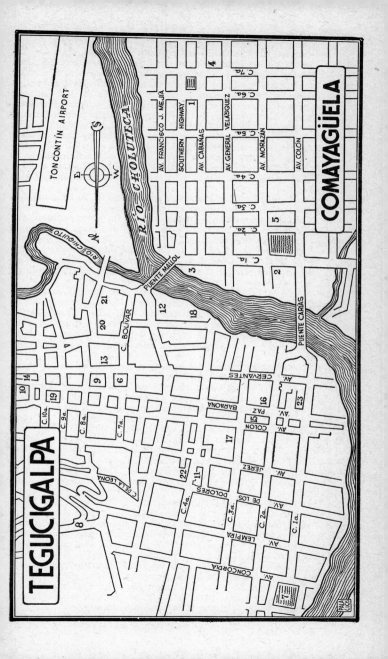

on time-proven Honduran lines. Originally there was only one entrance and exit; a separate door for the Consulate has since been cut. The original entrance is a huge wooden double door which may be barred at night and could withstand a battering-ram. In the old days Honduras had many a revolution, and it was wise to have but one entrance to a mansion, and that well barred. The building surrounds a huge patio with a fountain in the center and palms, poinsettias, and coffee trees growing along the walks. On the plot, belonging to the Soto family, a workman some years ago unearthed a cache of gold coins dating back to the conquest. Circling three sides of the second floor is a wide balcony; just back from the head of the stairs the U. S. minister, his wife, and the staff stand to receive their guests at large parties. Native marimba bands play for balcony dancing on such occasions.

The rebuilt church of San Francisco, opposite the U. S. Legation, has a fine tower containing bells of more powerful tone than any others in the city. Next to the church is a guardhouse. On festal occasions the president's military band marches to the church and plays the national anthem as the colors are raised.

On Av. Cervantes near C. 11 is the dignified Palace of Justice, where the higher court sits. A block E is the Clámer Theater. The city's one broadcasting station, HRN, at C. 12 and Av. Colón, offers Honduran and U. S. programs.

Some blocks W of Plaza Morazán, at Av. Paz Baraona and C. 3ª, are two large buildings, the Ministerial Palace, housing departments of the national government, and the national post office. In the latter, stamps of all Honduras issues are on sale. A little farther W is the National Theater, renovated in 1941, on a plaza of its own. Across from it, sheltered by trees, is the lovely ancient church of El Calvario (Calvary).

On C. 3ª, near the Ministerial Palace, is the national police headquarters in a large, somber building of green stucco. A block N and E from it is the Dolores market, facing the church of the Virgin of Los Dolores. The church has a fine 18th-century façade that recalls the style of the cathedral. Country people drive in to the market at night to bring goods ranging from live pigs to firewood. At open braziers along the streets tortillas and frijoles are cooked and sold. The market is best viewed a little before midday.

A couple of blocks N of the church of the Virgin of Los Dolores and 4 blocks W, on Av. Concordia, is Parque Concordia, with the Río Choluteca W of it. A number of replicas of Maya monuments have been erected in the park, which is one of the most photographed spots in Honduras.

On the city's N edge looms the mountain El Picacho. Paseo Leona lies a third of the way up. A park about 3½ acres in extent, it is colorful with palms and bougainvillea vines and has a concrete walk with an iron railing along its S side, overlooking the city. It is reached by a winding drive, C. Leona, along which are built some of the city's newer and most attractive homes. Still farther up is Dr. Roy B. Nutter's Hospital Viera, one of the finest in Latin America. Staffed with U. S. technicians and English-speaking nurses, the hospital draws patients by plane from all parts of Central America. Higher yet on El Picacho, in an ornamental park, is the great reservoir where Tegucigalpa's drinking water is stored for piping into the city.

THEATERS AND MOVING-PICTURE HOUSES. The remodeled National Theater was opened in 1941 for the eventual presentation of legitimate dramas and concerts. Moving-picture houses include the Clámer and Variedades.

CLUBS. The Country Club has facilities for golf and tennis.

BANKS. See Practical Information (p. 12).

SOURCES OF INFORMATION. See Practical Information (p. 10).

RESTAURANT. Café de Paris, under Hotel Honduras, facing Plaza Morazán, is a favorite rendezvous of the English-speaking colony for afternoon tea and after-theater snacks. There are no short-order restaurants like those in the United States, but in several cafés various dishes will be cooked to order.

HOTELS. Américas; Honduras; Palace; Ritz. There are also several boarding houses. Many visitors from the United States stop at the TACA staff house near the cathedral, where U. S. food is served. A new first-class hotel is under construction in Comayagüela (1941).

TEGUCIGALPA'S ENVIRONS AND EXCURSIONS

The church of the Virgin of Suyapa, 5 miles NE, is a shrine to which the faithful make pilgrimage from all parts of Honduras. The object of adoration is a small wooden figure of the Virgin about 2½ inches high, incased above the altar. This Virgin, said to have been found by a wandering peon who brought it to the church, is credited with many miracles. The Suyapa sanctuary has two adjoining chapels, one of the Señor de las Misericordias (Lord of Mercy), the other of the Sagrada Familia (Holy Family).

San Juancito, 20 miles NE of Tegucigalpa, is the site of the Rosario silver mines, operated by the New York and Honduras Rosario Mining Co. These mines were worked by the Spaniards. They have been in active production under the present management since 1882. The $2,000,000 worth of silver taken out each year is transported in bars by mule trains down the hills to Tegucigalpa. The road is so hilly that a bus requires about 2 hours for the journey. Visitors are permitted to watch mining operations. A clubhouse serves excellent food and has a bowling alley. One of the most picturesque mountain trails in Central America, for horseback and mule riding, was opened here in 1941 by the management.

Lepaterique is an Indian town some 15 miles W of Tegucigalpa, reached over a good and attractive dirt road. Much of the clay ware found in the market of Tegucigalpa is made here. The road passes the reservoir from which the city of Comayagüela draws its water and which is itself worth a visit.

THE NORTHERN HIGHWAY

The N Highway (Carretera del Norte) runs from Tegucigalpa to Lake Yojoa, which is crossed by ferry. It then continues to the important city of San Pedro Sula, from which there is a railroad to the Caribbean ports. This road is only fair but is one of the most interesting historically and scenically in the entire country. A trip along it should be planned for 2-3 days, depending on the number of places visited along the way. The first overnight stop should be Comayagua.

Comayagua, with 9000 inhabitants, was the first capital of Honduras. It is 75 miles NW of Tegucigalpa and is reached by car in a 5-hour drive. Mass was said in the village square on Dec. 8, 1537, for the famed conquistador Alonso de Cáceres, and there is a record of church services as early as 1523. The first Spanish university in Central America was established here in 1632; the cathedral was completed early in the 18th century.

The truest examples of colonial architecture in Honduras are to be found in the city of Comayagua, where nature, diverting earthquake and hurricane, has conspired to preserve them. Rows of massive white one-storied houses flank the cobbled streets where grass forces its way between the stones. Occasionally an iron grille guards one of the great square windows which open on the street. Behind the cathedral stands a crumbling wall with an iron-grilled gate marked dimly with the date 1741—all that remains of the once-great Spanish treasury of Honduras.

Scattered over the wide-spreading city, with few people to be seen on its streets, are six churches besides the cathedral. These are La Caridad, built in 1550; La Merced, 1550, on the other side of the city from the cathedral; San Francisco, 1575; San Sebastián, 1585; San Juan de Dios, 1590, where the Inquisition is said to have sat; and El Carmen, comparatively new, constructed in 1784.

Crucifixes and altar cups of ancient workmanship may be seen in the sacristy of the cathedral, and the building is renowned for holding the mummified bodies of 10 bishops of the diocese who reigned from the conquest through the colonial period. Through an opening in the cathedral's glassed-in crypt, to the right of the presbytery just beyond the transept and raised about four feet from the floor, may be seen plainly the mummy, clad in flowing robes, of Bishop Ruy López, who reigned over the see in the 16th century; the mummies of nine other bishops lie behind him. The mummy is best viewed in the morning, when light conditions inside the cathedral are good. The façade of the cathedral, massive and spectacular, shows some Indian influence in its sculptures. It is divided into four stories; the third story is particularly striking, with three massive recessed figures of saints. The square tower, untouched by decoration, stands at the left in contrast to this façade with its flowery traceries in low relief, its emblems and figures. The clock, said to be the first tower clock in the Americas, was sent from the Alhambra by Philip III of Spain in 1715. Arrangements may be made to climb the belltower for a view over the great Comayagua valley. The great processions of Holy Week come to massed climaxes in front of the cathedral. The ceremonies at Easter dawn are noteworthy.

The city of Comayagua is one of the last strongholds of the colonial way of life in Honduras. Its citizens, many of pure Spanish ancestry, often refer to the last Spanish governor, whose hillside estate overlooks the valley, as though his removal were within their personal recollection. Life here is Castilian in atmosphere despite the tropical setting, with little of the gaiety of the capital and none of the frivolity of the ports. Residents are proud of the legend which says that the seat of government was moved from Comayagua to Tegucigalpa because Comayagua society would not accept the light-o'-love whom a ruler had installed in the palace.

The little city is distributing center for the great Comayagua valley and headquarters for the manufacture of the varicolored fireworks which make a Honduran holiday night a thrilling spectacle.

HOTEL. There is an inn on the cathedral plaza.

Excursions from Comayagua. At Flores, 12 miles S on the N Highway, horses may be obtained for a trip to Tenampuá, about 1½ hours away. Arrangements should be made by telegraph either from Tegucigalpa or from Comayagua. Tenampuá is the most famous fortified archeological site in Honduras.

A good dirt road leads S from Comayagua across the plain to the department of La Paz, including the picturesque Indian towns of Ajuterique and Lejamani.

Siguatepeque is N of Comayagua. The highway climbs the steep mountain of Siguatepeque (Hill of the Little Girl), so called because the first Spaniards were said to have found nobody in the beautiful green valley and only a little girl on the hilltop, crying her eyes out for fear of the conquerors. The town, near the mountain, has long enjoyed a high repute for its cool, healthful climate.

Excursion from Siguatepeque. A dirt road leads W into the valley of Jesús de Otoro in Gracias Department.

Continuing N from Siguatepeque, the highway leads to Pito Solo at the S tip of Lake Yojoa.

LAKE YOJOA

Reached conveniently by the N Highway, Lake Yojoa, some 25 miles long by 8 miles wide, is one of the most beautiful mountain lakes in all Central America and the goal of hunting and camping excursions. There are several villages around the lake shores, and one of them, Los Naranjos, is usually preferred by campers. No lodgings can be found along or near the lake, and it is necessary to take camping equipment for overnight stays.

The Jicaque mountains rise abruptly from the E shore. The hills on the W side are less steep, and there are several villages here, including Los Naranjos. Nueva Esperanza (New Hope) lies a few miles back from the middle section of the W shore. Farther S and closer to the lake is Las Vegas, and at the extreme SW end, which is pointed, is the hamlet of Pedernales. Lake Yojoa lies at an elevation of 2000 feet, and the vegetation around it is different from that of the lowlands. The pine supplants the palm, and sturdy shrubs the white gardenia. The great condor may be seen soaring over the high hills, and the puma roams in the deep forest.

Pito Solo is the town at the S end of the lake, reached by the N Highway from Tegucigalpa. From here Isla Grande (Large Island) may be reached by boat. Another island in the lake is La Islita (Little Island). There is ferry service to Jaral.

Jaral lies on the N shore. Duck hunting is especially good at this end of the lake, where the land is comparatively low. Campers generally stay at Los Naranjos (The Orange Trees), a settlement about 20 minutes' walk from Jaral. At Los Naranjos is the largest and most important aboriginal ruin in the area.

From Jaral the N Highway continues through Potrerillos and Búfalo to San Pedro Sula.

SAN PEDRO SULA

Honduras' second city in size is San Pedro Sula, with 20,000 inhabitants. It is important in business and industry, the center of sugar and banana enterprises, and serves as a distributing point for N and W Honduras. San Pedro Sula is connected by the National Railroad with Puerto Cortés, 38 miles N on the Caribbean coast. It is an aerial crossroads for TACA planes. Here converge the air routes from Tegucigalpa, Tela and other N coast points, and Belize in British Honduras. The TACA airport is five minutes' drive from the city.

Founded by Pedro de Alvarado in 1536, the city is today briskly modern, with wide thoroughfares. It is divided into eight sections, with 22 streets and 18 avenues; the business district has modern stores and good moving-picture houses, the government's Hospital del Norte, and excellent hotels and restaurants. There are imposing modern residences with flower-fringed lawns, well-kept parks, and boulevards. In the city's center, facing a palm-filled park, is the new city hall, an ornate yellow-faced structure. On its left, occupying a full block, are the military headquarters, in walled barracks with two-story blockhouses at the corners. On the boulevard named for Francisco Morazán, the Honduran patriot, is a bust of Alvarado; in Parque Baraona are busts of two former presidents, Manuel Bonilla and Miguel Paz Baraona, and on the residential avenue that bears his name is a heroic statue of Lempira, the Lenca chieftain whom the Spanish killed by treachery. At the José Reyes Normal Institute here many of the country's leaders are trained. The Casino Sampedrano, on the edge of the residential district, occupying a modern structure with a large, cool patio, is a social rendezvous for dancing and dining. There is a country club.

Good food is found in San Pedro Sula, both in the restaurants and in the hotels. Spaghetti and macaroni are manufactured in the city; steaks are cut from Honduran beef. Superb dishes are made, including the familiar tortilla and tamale, the latter spoken of by the waiter perhaps as montouca. The frijoles are especially good.

MOVING-PICTURE HOUSES. Clámer; Colombia; Variedades. These theaters show films imported from the United States, Mexico, and Argentina and an occasional European film.

HOTELS. Internacional**; Roosevelt**.

EXCURSIONS FROM SAN PEDRO SULA

La Lima, with 4000 inhabitants, banana capital, 8 miles E of San Pedro Sula by railroad or car, is the United Fruit Co.'s Honduras headquarters. Here the company's executives live and work in an atmosphere of tropical charm, in gleaming white houses with wide screened verandas, set against the green of palms and lawns. They direct the cultivation of 38,000 acres of banana lands supporting 12,000-14,000 workers and their families. Farther inland on the banana plantations live the overseers and timekeepers.

Ruins of Travesía. Unearthed remains of the aboriginal city of Travesía are on the Sula plain near the Río Ulúa, a short distance E of

La Lima. These ruins, containing some artifacts which give evidence of Maya derivation, were discovered in a United Fruit Co. pasture in 1936 by Doris Stone. A quadrangle of what once had been stone structures was uncovered. Bowls of Lenca geometric designs and Maya shapes; various pieces of pottery, some cunningly patterned; earthen female heads and jaguar heads; a bell-shaped incense burner, and other articles were discovered in mounds and buried rooms. The most important discovery was the temple of the Carvings, thought to be part of the ceremonial section of an ancient Maya city.

El Progreso, 15 miles E of San Pedro Sula, reached by railroad, is the scene of a national golf tournament, a leading social event, in the spring. A banana town, El Progreso is headquarters for some of the United Fruit Co. officials.

Excursions from El Progreso. The town is a good base from which to explore Yoro Department, the home of the warlike aboriginal Jicaques, many of whose descendants live in the region today. The department has some fine mission churches built by the friars who followed in Cortés' train. One good example is the church at Luquiqui, 7 miles SE of the city of Yoro, the department's capital. This primitive region is of interest to students of ethnology and to the more adventurous and adaptable travelers. Transportation facilities are still inadequate. Yoro can be reached by air or mule, Luquiqui only by mule.

THE SOUTHERN HIGHWAY

The S Highway (Carretera del Sur) is a very good road leading S from Tegucigalpa to San Lorenzo, 60 miles away, on the Gulf of Fonseca. Here connections are made for the port of Amapala on Tiger Island.

Excursion to Ojojona. About 15 miles out of Tegucigalpa a fair but winding road branches off to Ojojona, some 7 miles farther. Francisco Morazán was at one time held prisoner here, and the house in which he stayed is still standing. This house is one of the most perfect examples of Spanish colonial architecture in Honduras today.

San Lorenzo marks the end of the S Highway.

Excursions from San Lorenzo. Amapala, with 4000 inhabitants, Honduras' only port on the Pacific, located on Isla del Tigre (Tiger Island) in the Gulf of Fonseca, is reached from the mainland by launch in 2¼ hours. Coastwise vessels serve the port at irregular intervals; there is also air service. The marshes in the region are excellent for duck hunting, and the waters near by provide deep-sea fishing.

Choluteca, some 20 miles SE of San Lorenzo, is reached by the Pan American Highway over one of its finest bridges. Choluteca was one of the earliest and most famous Spanish cities on the Pacific plain of Central America. It lies on the wide and beautiful flood plain of the Río Choluteca. The climate is very hot, but many horseback trips may be made into the cool neighboring highlands. The Pan American Highway continues from Choluteca to the Nicaraguan border, but it is little more than a trail.

EAST OF TEGUCIGALPA

The road to Danlí, about 45 miles E of Tegucigalpa, is good, and in a trip of 4 hours over it the center of the hacienda or farm country near the Nicaraguan border is reached. A point of great interest is the Escuela Agrícola Pan Americana, about 20 miles from the capital, in the valley of the Río Yeguare. This is the agricultural school on which the United Fruit Co. started construction in 1941. One hundred and twenty students will be taught here annually, 30 of them entering each year for a course of four years, with six picked candidates from each of the five Central American republics. Courses will include general cultural subjects, crafts, and husbandry, with emphasis on agricultural methods that will advance and improve the countries. Dr. Wilson Popenoe, noted U. S. agronomist, will be the director.

Excursion to Yuscarán. The mining center of the early days of the republic, Yuscarán lies in beautiful rolling pine country, reached by a road branching S from the road to Danlí about 30 miles out of Tegucigalpa.

The important Agua Fría mines are about 6 miles SE of Yuscarán. The trip to them is scenically impressive and passes through a sheltered valley where many Spanish colonial customs and some colonial objects, such as elaborate metal stirrups, are still encountered. However, the trip is somewhat dangerous because the road is narrow, winding, and very steep.

NORTHEAST OF TEGUCIGALPA

The Olancho Highway (Carretera de Olancho) connects Tegucigalpa with Olancho Department, whose capital, Juticalpa, is about 120 miles NE. The road is in good condition only to Galeras. This region, little known to travelers, is excellent for cattle-raising and is famous for its gold. In the dry season it is possible to continue from Juticalpa across the rich valley of Lepaguare to Catacamos, the heart of the cattle country.

WEST OF TEGUCIGALPA

La Esperanza, capital of Intibucá Department, about 80 miles W of Tegucigalpa, is the home of the Lenca Indians. The town is reached by air from Tegucigalpa or by a mule journey of 2-3 days over high mountains from Jesús de Otoro, which is connected with the national capital by road (p. 24). La Esperanza lies at an altitude of 4866 feet. In the town is a street on one side of which live only pure-blooded Indians who if they can help it do not speak to the people whose homes are on the other side. The town is the center of sheep-raising in Honduras, and its Indians weave blankets and woolen cloth by hand.

La Virtud, a hamlet some 22 miles SW of La Esperanza and reached by mule, is noted for the Fuente de Sangre (Fountain of Blood) which pours from a triangular-shaped grotto. The name derives from the fact that thousands of bats live in the grotto, and their droppings mix with the water that seeps through the roof in the rainy season. This forms a red liquid which runs into the creek outside.

THE RUINS OF COPAN

The ancient city of Copán, 85 miles NW of Tegucigalpa near the Guatemalan border, is a mecca of travelers to Honduras. This great cultural center of the Mayas is reached by air in about 45 minutes from Tegucigalpa. The name by which the site is known is borrowed from the town of Santa Rosa de Copán, E of it in a valley surrounded by high mountains. Unlike most places in Honduras, Copán is sheltered from the ever-blowing winds and lies simmering in the tropical heat. The plane lands on a field which has a terminal building with conveniences. A road runs W to Chiquimula in Guatemala; see the guide to Guatemala (p. 40).

The ruins of the former Maya center are about 1800 feet above sea level in the middle of an alluvial flat beside the Río Copán. A winding road runs a little more than a mile from the airport to the entrance to the ruins. On the road's right side at one point is a stela or pillar with an inscription; it is quite modern in effect, though erected centuries ago. It bears the figure of a human being, carved in stone, and a thumb definitely points toward Copán. The stela was dubbed Old Hitch-hiker by Carnegie Institution scientists who in 1941 completed seven years' work in restoring the ruins to a hint of their former grandeur. This work was done under direction of Gustav Stromsvik and with the co-operation of President Carías and the government of Honduras. When Stromsvik and his fellow scientists finished this work President Carías announced that the jungle would never again be allowed to encroach on the ancient city. He assigned a group of government workers to preserve the place as the scientists had left it.

The city is spread over many acres and is built on two levels, the upper one on a cliff top, mainly artificial, overlooking the Río Copán, whose course has been diverted so that the base of the cliff will not be further eroded. Entrance is by the lower level into what has been called the Great Court, a rectangular plain large enough to hold 30,000 people. This was the main gathering place of worshipers. Scattered on the plain are a number of stelae, one of which the Mayas erected every 20 years. Some date as far back as the fifth century; the last that can be dated was set up A.D. 733. These stelae range about 10-15 feet in height, and the figures on them are believed to represent real people, probably rulers or priests of the tribes or cities. Only one stela carries the likeness of a woman—Stela H, as it is now designated. The figure, clad in skirts with a jade belt, has a strikingly modern coiffure. There are small vaults under all but one stela, and Stromsvik says that when the cruciform vault under this figure was excavated the tiny gold feet of a figurine were found and also a broken necklace of fine jade beads.

The first stela seen on entering the Great Court is Stela A. At the base of the stela is a cruciform vault. The entrance, down a flight of several steps, is just large enough for the average person to get his shoulders through. The Mayas were and are small people; there are many alive today, especially in Yucatán. By getting down on all fours and using a flashlight one may view the stone-walled chamber, where offerings undoubtedly were placed. The date on this stela is interpreted as A.D. 733. The stelae are designated by both letters and figures. In front of Stela 4 is a round altar stone about 6 feet around and 4 feet high, with a cavity in the top and grooves spiraling down the sides. This has been called the sacrificial stone. It is within plain view of the three terraced sides of the plain, on which spectators could sit. It is much debated whether humans were sacrificed here. Stela C, whose cruciform vault was excavated by an expedition of the Peabody Museum of Harvard, is the best preserved of the monoliths and has the finest detail. The W side shows a figure with a full beard, the only beard seen in Copán. The stela, whose date is doubtful, was painted with a red pigment believed to have been sulphide of mercury. The color is well preserved. This stela has two altars. The one on the east is unfinished; the one on the west depicts a turtle in its pond.

Stromsvik, whose excellent work follows that of a long line of scientists and explorers dating back to Diego García de Palacio in 1676, says that Copán has "the only known example of three superimposed ball courts"—courts where the national game, possibly a forerunner of soccer, was played. The latest Copán ball court to be restored is S of the Great Court. It is rectangular, larger than a tennis court, and surrounded by tiers of stone seats. The game was played with a rubber ball, larger than a baseball, which was never touched by the hands but was batted with the body. This court now is fully restored. With the towering trees on the bluff to the south, it makes one of the great sights of Central America—a vast amphitheater, the stone of the seats gleaming in the sunlight as it must have a thousand years ago. Stromsvik, who made a special study of the ball courts, has written that a second court lies 30 centimeters under this one and that a third, the earliest, is about 1½ meters below the top pavement.

At the Great Court's E end, S of the ball court and ascending the W side of Mound 26, is one of the wonders of the ancient world. This is the Hieroglyphic Stairway, leading to the top of the bluff, the second elevation of the city, overlooking the Río Copán. On this elevation is found the vast E Court, with entrance to the Lions' Court. There is a stone figure of a laughing jaguar at the top of steps to a temple—steps of great depth leading to a main entrance representing a beast's open jaws. Another smaller entrance is just back of the framed way to the main entrance. The proportions are perfect. There are two unroofed openings on either side of the main temple, which had deep niches in the walls, undoubtedly serving as windows, almost shoulder high. At the right edge of the E Court is a sharp drop to the river. The strata at various levels reveal different periods of civilization, the archaic, the Toltec, and the Aztec. One stone of great significance is on the upper level. This is the astronomer's stone, carved in bas-relief, whereas most sculpture in Copán is an alto-relievo. This stone, 6 feet square and 4 feet high, commemorates a meeting of astronomers centuries ago. The top is divided into 36 tablets with hieroglyphics. Around the four sides are carved figures, supposed to be the tribes represented at the astronomers' convention.

The Hieroglyphic Stairway, about 20 feet wide and towering perhaps a hundred feet above the lower plain, was shaken down by earthquake at some time in the past. A Peabody Museum expedition discovered the immense pile of carved stone in 1892 and began digging it out piece by piece. Some stones were carried off to museums; others were left lying on the ground, where they were found by the Carnegie Institution scientists, who reconstructed the great stairway during the 1930's. According to Stromsvik: "The Hieroglyphic Stairway constitutes the longest known Maya inscription (each step being inscribed) and contains about 2500 glyphs. The top step is carved in the rare full-figure glyphs."

Following Palacio's first written account of the Copán ruins, Francisco Guzmán wrote a fantastic account in 1689. An Irishman, Col.

Juan Galindo, wrote of them in 1834. When President Martin Van Buren sent the traveler diplomat John L. Stephens to Central America in 1839 Stephens made an extensive study of Maya ruins, especially those at Copán. In 1885 came the noted British expedition under A. F. Maudslay in 1885, whose works on Copán archeology are authoritative, and next the Peabody Museum's expeditions and studies. A little later Sylvanus G. Morley made intensive studies of the hieroglyphics, which he embodied in his standard work, The Inscriptions at Copán, published by the Carnegie Institution of Washington. The latest scientific studies of Copán are those of Gustav Stromsvik. Scientists now agree that Copán must have been in ruins long before the conquistadores came. The ultimate dissolution of the community is attributed by at least one authority to the possibility that the Maya civilization disintegrated on contact with some tribe from South America believing in a communal way of life without leaders.

A museum not far from the ruins contains many artifacts of jade and stone and some of gold.

INDEX TO THE REGIONAL GUIDE

THE REPUBLIC OF EL SALVADOR

EL SALVADOR

BY GERALD DE AGUILAR ECHEVERRIA

Although it is the smallest of the Central American republics, El Salvador is the most densely populated. On the whole the country is modern, largely lacking the colonial atmosphere of its immediate neighbors. It is progressive and politically liberal. The capital, San Salvador, is a modern city; the extensive road system is good and is being constantly improved; accommodations for the traveler, especially in the smaller towns, are above the average for Central America. Climate, the Salvadoreans' friendly hospitality, and a number of spas and pleasure resorts combine to make it a center of attraction for tourists from neighboring countries.

HISTORY

The history of El Salvador has been one of frequent conflict and foreign intervention. From ancient times, when the Mayas and Toltecs first came to explore and settle in the territory, through the Spanish conquest and subsequent domination by the captaincy general of Guatemala and on into the confusion of the 19th century, the little country has been periodically invaded or interfered with by neighboring countries or embroiled in political upsets within its own boundaries. During the periods of peace the energies of the people have been turned to economic, social, and cultural advancement. The first quarter of the 20th century was such a time; great advances were made then in agriculture and industry, and an intensive program of public education was begun. Throughout the alternating periods of calm and conflict a liberal bias has persisted, which is now demonstrating its economic and political value.

THE ABORIGINAL PERIOD. Several important Indian strains, numbering altogether more than a million souls according to early Spanish estimates, inhabited El Salvador before the conquest. The most important and advanced, with the greatest number of tribes, was the Pipils, of mixed Toltec and Aztec origin. The towns of Sonsonate, Ahuachapán, Apanecán, and Cuscatlán were founded by the Indians before the coming of the Spaniards. Remains of the culture are plentiful and point to Toltec and Aztec origins in Mexico, but archeologists have been able to decipher very little of the hieroglyphic inscriptions that have been found. That this was an advanced culture cannot be doubted, for its relics bear witness to high artistic achievement. Some local archeologists believe that under many layers of lava will some day be discovered remains of a civilization antedating the Aztec, Maya, and Toltec cultures and equal to them in interest.

The Indians whom the Spaniards encountered in Cuscatlán raised tobacco, corn, cacao, and many other crops which, with fish and game, constituted their food. They had advanced to such a stage in commercial development that the farmers brought their produce to tangues or central markets. A caste system prevailed in all the tribes. The nobles were marked off from the workers by white trousers and shirts, sandals, and white mantles embroidered with birds and animals. They wore their hair long, and they pierced their ears and lower

3

lip in order to hang from them star-shaped ornaments of gold and silver. In the tropical coastal region the mazaguales, the working or plebeian class, wore nothing but maztlotes or loincloths; in the cooler uplands they wore long shirts with flaps which they turned up between their legs and tied about their waists. The head covering was a piece of cloth, but no shoes were used. The women wore colored skirts and embroidered huipiles or blouses and enveloped themselves completely with white shawls.

A primitive system of education prevailed among these natives, with the older women as teachers of the young. In their religion the Indians revered the sun and their ancestors and sacrificed children 7-12 years old. They were served by augurs and priests, and some tribes practiced diabolism in the belief that a man could become wealthy only through selling himself to the devil or an evil spirit. The functions of government were vested in the elders of the tribes. Political and social organization was similar to that of the Aztecs. Homicide, robbery, incendiarism, and attacks on a cacique or chief were punishable by death.

DISCOVERY AND CONQUEST. In 1486 the Aztec king Ahuitzol in Mexico seems to have made preparations for invading the territory then known as Cuscatlán and now constituting a large part of El Salvador. He sent in emissaries disguised as merchants, with instructions to settle in the land, spy it out, and pave the way for an armed force. Only six years later Columbus made his first great voyage of discovery, and the Old World exploded from centuries of pent-up pressure and spilled over into the New. The Spaniards settled the island of Hispaniola, occupied now by Haiti and the Dominican Republic. Then they spread westward into Cuba. In 1519 Hernando Cortés came to the mainland to conquer the great Indian kingdoms there; so began the stirring and bloody struggles against the great Mexican emperor Moctezuma and the subjugation of Mexico. When Cortés had completed the conquest of Mexico, he sent his companion-in-arms Pedro de Alvarado, with his lieutenants and their Indian allies, to explore the country to the south. They invaded and conquered what is now Guatemala and in 1524 came to the rich country west of the Río Lempa, now part of El Salvador.

The first tribes whom Alvarado met belonged to the great Pipil nation. These tribes treated the Spaniards with courtesy and explained that they were in a state of constant warfare with one of the Indian peoples of Guatemala. Alvarado joined them and, having defeated their enemies, proceeded to Guarapacán, where he enslaved the native population of the territory around the Río de Paz, the border between today's Guatemala and El Salvador. From there he made his way toward the Pacific coast and subjugated the Indians around what is now Acajutla. In the same year Cortés sent another of his lieutenants, Cristóbal de Olid, to take possession of Honduras. Olid not only took the country, but proclaimed himself supreme chief, and it became necessary for Cortés to go down from Mexico to subdue him. When Alvarado heard that Cortés was on his way to Honduras, he decided to go there too and assist in punishing Olid. But Cortés had accomplished his task and begun his return to Mexico before Alvarado arrived. Alvarado then marched back toward Cuscatlán. There he remained, 1525-28; he subdued all the Indians, took the stronghold of Cuscatlán, and set up a capital city, in

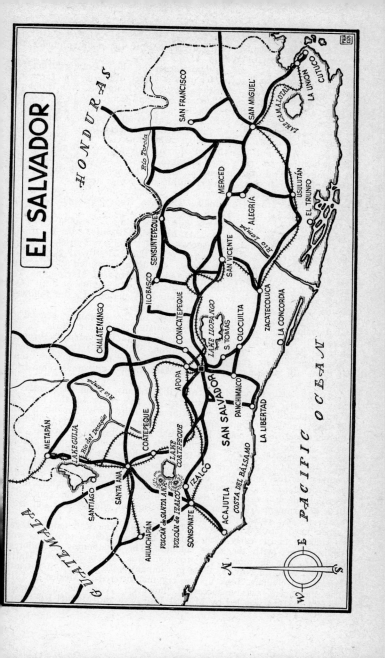

which the first regular civil government of the country under the Spaniards was established in 1528.

The political life and administration of the country during the following years was a chapter in the larger story of the captaincy general of Guatemala. Alvarado governed Guatemala and Honduras as well as the provinces of San Salvador and Sonsonate in the present El Salvador. He treated his Indian subjects with such harshness that they rebelled, and he, in turn, reduced them all to slavery. Intertribal disputes were constant, and in 1529 Alvarado sent Diego de Rojas to pacify the various Indian tribes who were at war beyond the Río Lempa. About this time, Pedrarias, governor of Nicaragua, sent an expedition to take the province of San Salvador from the captaincy general of Guatemala, on the claim that its lands were within his jurisdiction. The expedition met Rojas and took him prisoner. Then it marched toward San Salvador and there encountered troops coming from Guatemala. The men from Nicaragua were defeated and Rojas was set free.

After serving in Guatemala for some time, Alvarado went to Mexico and there, on July 4, 1541, he died. His wife, doña Beatriz de la Cueva, was appointed his successor. Her glory was brief. She was drowned that same year when a great flood destroyed the capital. Her brother Francisco de la Cueva was then appointed captain general of Guatemala jointly with the bishop Francisco Marroquín. Together Cueva and Marroquín held the reins of government until 1542, when Alvaro Maldonado was appointed. A period of calm followed, which lasted through the rest of the 16th century.

THE COLONIAL PERIOD. As provinces of the captaincy general of Guatemala, San Salvador and Sonsonate, which are parts of the present El Salvador, were ruled from the capital in Guatemala throughout the Spanish colonial administration. This was a time of intense proselyting among the Indians—a time when many churches, some of them still standing, were built. Many monks and nuns came from Spain.

Spanish settlers took land from the Indians, whom they enslaved. San Salvador was happily situated on the route to the ports of Nicaragua and Costa Rica, where Spanish ships arrived regularly, and in these ports the fruits and riches of the country were traded for merchandise from Spain. Substantial homes began to appear, and every galleon from Spain brought goods to make life pleasant. Schools were established. Many well-to-do families sent their children to Guatemala to be educated; the students remained there to finish their courses at the university of San Carlos Borromeo. San Salvador soon developed an agreeable social life and political activities of its own. It drew away from the mother country, while the conception of a government free from the domination of officials sent out from Spain became constantly more vivid.

THE REVOLUTIONARY PERIOD. When Spain's American empire began to collapse in the early 19th century, the Salvadorean provinces were ready to act with the sister colonies. The outstanding Salvadorean leader in the movement for freedom was the priest José Matías Delgado, who, on Nov. 5, 1811, in company with a group of patriotic priests and civilians, took up the cry first uttered in Mexico in 1810. The movement was unsuccessful, however. A second unsuccessful attempt in 1814 was led by Manuel José Arce and Manuel Rodríguez, who in consequence were imprisoned for several years. On Feb. 24, 1821, Mexico declared its independence of Spain by proclamation of Agustín de Iturbide and Gen. Vicente Guerrero. This proclamation was known as the Plan of Iguala; under it racial equality in political rights was declared. When the captain general of Guatemala learned of this event, he called a meeting of all the officers of government on the memorable fifteenth of September, 1821; an act of independence was then drawn up and solemnly sworn to. The governor general remained at the head of the government, in which he was assisted by a consultant body. Father Delgado, who exercised great influence in Guatemala, was sent from there to San Salvador to restore peace and order. On his way the patriot priest set free his former comrades, Arce and Rodríguez.

THE EXPERIMENTAL PERIOD. Less than four months later, the Central American provinces, now independent, were invited to join the Mexican empire created by Iturbide. Guatemala accepted, but the Salvadoreans were opposed to the move, and war was declared between them and the mother state of Guatemala. At this point, the Salvadorean congress, in order to avoid the alliance, looked to the United States for adoption, but that country, not wishing to antagonize Iturbide, politely turned down the chance. Thereupon the joint armies of Mexico and Guatemala under the Mexican Gen. Vicente Filísola defeated the opposition forces and compelled El Salvador to join the empire. The union lasted only a short time. In 1823 the Central American countries withdrew from the Mexican empire and formed a confederation of five states with the name of United Central American Provinces. Father Delgado was appointed to preside over a constitutional assembly which elected Manuel José Arce as first president of the confederation.

Several years of internal political differences followed until 1829, when Gen. Francisco Morazán, at the head of a Honduran army, established military control. The next year he was formally elected president of the confederation. A cultured, capable, and liberal-minded man, he set to work at once on a policy of social and political reform. He promoted public education, fostered industry and commerce, reorganized the administrative machinery, and made registration of births, deaths, and marriages compulsory. These reforms, together with the removal of the seat of government to San Salvador, antagonized the Conservatives to such an extent that for more than 10 years the state of El Salvador was involved both in internal struggles and in conflicts with the neighboring states. Most important was the war with the Guatemalan ruler Rafael Carrera.

In the midst of this turmoil, the congress of the confederation passed an act authorizing the various states to assume their own forms of government. Accordingly, in 1841, the state of El Salvador withdrew from the union, adopted a constitution, and became the republic of El Salvador. From that time to 1865 was a stormy period, and the government constantly changed hands as Liberals and Conservatives succeeded one another. Even the death of Carrera, who had established himself as ruler of Guatemala, did not put an end to these troubles; they continued until one more attempt at confederation was made in 1885 by Justo Rufino Barrios, then president of Guatemala. A war broke out in which Barrios was killed in action and the unionists were defeated. President Rafael Zaldívar of El Salvador, who had been backed by Barrios, was then overthrown by Gen. Francisco Menéndez, who took upon himself the leadership of the Salvadorean republic.

THE CONTEMPORARY PERIOD. The period of military leadership in El Salvador had begun. One general followed another at the head of the government until 1903, when Pedro José Escalón was legally elected to the presidency. For 25 years after the turn of the century, though one president rapidly succeeded another, El Salvador enjoyed an era of comparative peace which permitted extraordinary economic development, attended by improvements in communication and transportation. Shortly after the second quarter of the century began, however, internal difficulties commenced again and continued for several years, until they were put down by force by Gen. Maximiliano Martínez, who promptly assumed the chief executive's chair. His government, established late in 1931, was recognized by the United States in 1934. President Martínez is a strong man and a progressive. He was still in office in 1941.

THE LAND

El Salvador is relatively unknown to U. S. travelers, largely because it is the only Central American republic with no seaboard on the Atlantic Ocean. Its 160 miles of coastline are entirely on the Pacific. The country's area of some 14,000 square miles approximates that of Maryland; its 1,700,000 inhabitants give it a population density that is heavy for an agricultural country, about 125 to the square mile.

There are five readily accessible ports on the coast, La Libertad, La Unión, La Concordia, El Triunfo, and Acajutla. Two mountain chains traverse the country, with 14 mountains or volcanoes that exceed 3000 feet in altitude. The highest peak is Santa Ana, which reaches almost 8000 feet. Izalco is the most active volcano in Central America, and its almost continuous flames, about 25 miles inland from the port of Acajutla, serve as a beacon for navigators on the Pacific. Among these mountains are upland valleys of great fertility. The principal rivers are the Lempa; the Paz, which forms the NW boundary with Guatemala; and the San Miguel in the E part. They are navigable, however, by small craft only. There are numerous picturesque lakes, of which Lake Guija in the west and Lake Ilopango in the center of the country are the largest, the former about 15 miles long, the other about 10 miles. On the coastal plains the climate is hot; it grows milder in the uplands, varying from 60° to 95° F. The rainy season is May-November, and rains are sometimes extremely heavy in June and September. The pleasantest months are November-January.

San Salvador is the capital and principal city; other large centers are the picturesque old colonial cities of Santa Ana in the west and San Miguel in the east. There are numerous smaller towns, each with its own special attractions and its special reputation for some particular product. Politically and administratively, the country is divided into 14 departments.

The republic's economy is dominated by the coffee crop. There are about 118,800,000 coffee trees, and as a coffee producer El Salvador possesses the important advantages of abundant low-cost labor, low production costs, good roads and railroads in the coffee regions, and seaports accessible to its plantations. Sugar is becoming an important crop, and large tracts of land in the departments of Sonsonate and San Salvador are planted to cane. Several refineries produce sugar for local consumption as well as a small amount for export. Henequen, which was exported for years, is now used locally as the basis of a new industry. During the crisis of 1929 growing henequen meant losing money, and most of the plantations were abandoned. Some planters, however, formed a co-operative, built a bag factory in San Salvador, and began to create a domestic market for their product. Now all the coffee bags shipped out of El Salvador are made locally, and the republic is attempting to develop an export trade in the bags. The annual output is in the neighborhood of 1,200,000 bags, but the factory's capacity is double that figure. Thousands of families are now employed in the cultivation and preparation of the fiber, and the central factory employs more than 400 persons permanently. Cotton has also become a factor in the nation's economy. The government has lately encouraged the production of cotton in every way possible.

El Salvador is the only country in the world producing the so-called balsam of Peru, which is widely used in the preparation of medicines and perfumes. Reputedly through an error made by the early Spaniards, who misinterpreted the Indian word piru, meaning a pottery vessel, as the fabled Peru, or because the product became confused with Peruvian goods during transshipment in Panama, it is known universally as bálsamo del Perú. The term naturally annoys the Salvadoreans.

Cattle and allied industries are ever-increasing sources of wealth for the country, and for years the breeders, with the full co-operation of the government, have worked toward improvement of their herds, in part through imported sires. Tobacco, indigo, wheat, corn, black beans, rice, millet, peas, potatoes, and a number of fruits are grown for local consumption. Gold and silver mining are increasingly important in the departments of San Miguel and Morazán. There is also small-scale mining of copper, lead, zinc, mercury, sulphur, gypsum, alum, and lime.

Manufacturing industries, besides the bag factory at San Salvador, include three mills with an important output of cotton textiles, while four factories supply nearly all the local needs in cotton yarn. Beautiful silk fabrics are woven, but not in large quantities. Five modern mills using imported wheat meet the demand for flour. Most of the straw hats are made by one factory. The Izalco Indians are famous for their colorful textiles and artistic designs; most of these materials are handwoven or made on crude mechanical looms. Hammocks, bags, ropes, palm hats, etc., come from the small factories of Cacaopera, a town in the department of Morazán. Factories at Ilobasco and Saturno turn out some very creditable commercial pottery, as well as exquisite special items for which they have long been famous. One brewery supplies the demand for beer, and some local wines and liquors are produced which are moderately priced.

In order to protect craftsmen, President Martínez has prohibited the importation of machinery for the manufacture of shoes and other leather goods, and the tariff on such goods is prohibitive. Good, attractive shoes are commonly made at home by hand. The Salvadoreans are also expert silversmiths, and throughout Central America the best shoemakers and silversmiths are often from El Salvador. Industrial activities include also the manufacture of candles, rubber heels, soap, cigarettes, matches, and buttons, as well as an iron foundry.

ART AND ARCHITECTURE

BY ROBERT C. SMITH

Salvadorean colonial architecture is extremely simple and almost entirely religious, dating principally from the 18th century. During that period the country was a, small, obscure provincial district remote from the local seat of governmental authority and culture at Antigua, Guatemala. Like the churches of California and the southwestern United States, those of El Salvador were small utilitarian structures. Elsewhere in Latin America such unassuming churches had generally been erected in the 16th or 17th centuries, only to be replaced in the 18th by new and more monumental buildings. Like the California missions the Salvadorean churches, in spite of their simplicity, have the charm of good proportions and vigorous design. They lack, however, the originality of those of Minas Geraes in Brazil, that other region where formal architecture was an achievement of the 18th century.

The colonial churches of El Salvador have low roofs and, for their size, massive walls, as a precaution against earthquakes. A further precaution was the use of stout polygonal cupolas at the crossing and a series of small domes in lieu of vaults in the nave. Architectural sculpture is almost nonexistent either inside or on the exteriors. Indigenous influence is extremely rare, limited largely to the very interesting church at Chalchuapa, near Santa Ana. There, and in a very few other local churches, were used friezes of molded clay representing such tropical fruits as the coconut, pineapple, avocado, and ears of corn; these take the place of conventional moldings. Beyond this there was no reflection of the art of the Indian, a circumstance which is not surprising when we consider that the Pipil Indians of El Salvador were an archaic people, traces of whose advanced civilization had disappeared by the time of the conquest without leaving an artistic tradition in the country.

The principal building that has been preserved is the cathedral of Metapán, where the date 1743 appears in the vault of the choir. This seems to apply, however, to a reconstruction rather than to the original edifice, remains of whose late Gothic decoration are still to be seen over the principal door. The single-aisle nave of the cathedral is higher than usual. Between its octagonal windows are a series of uniform altarpieces, whose accessories, carried out in high relief, are the product of the silver mines of Metapán. The façade, which is surmounted by a two-story belfry of classic simplicity, is made picturesque by a single angle tower and several cupolas. The church of El Pilar at San Vicente is noted for its dodecagonal cupola and the relative elaborateness of its three-aisle nave. So similar is El Pilar church at Sonsonate that it is thought to have been built by the same architect. The old cathedral at San Miguel, another 18th-century building, has low towers that emphasize the great bare façade between them, where a single door and octagonal window among three stories of Doric pilasters provide the only ornament. At Izalco in the department of Sonsonate, the church of La Asunción has an almost identical façade. Both are related to that of the cathedral of León in Nicaragua. At Coatepeque the façade of the church is already neo-classic. Its coupled Doric columns supporting a semioval pediment recall the revival of Palladian designs that occurred in some of the Guatemalan churches of the close of the 18th century. The much smaller church of San Sebastián at Villa Delgado makes similar use of double Ionic pilasters in an extremely simple but graceful design. Characteristic of the style are the picturesque adobe walls and gateways around the church of Coatepeque and the cathedral of Metapán.

During the colonial period there were no distinctively Salvadorean painters or sculptors. After independence the first artist to receive international attention was the painter Francisco Cisneros (1823-78), who spent much of his life in Cuba, where he became the first non-Spaniard to direct the academy of San Alejandro of Havana. Both his portraits and his large dramatic canvases, like Lot and His Daughters, at the Havana National Museum, are based on a vivid contrast of light and shadow. Stylistically, Cisneros was a typical romantic painter.

Modern art in El Salvador suffers from lack of a museum or other collection of painting and also of adequate instruction in art. Nevertheless, the society of Amigos del Arte in the capital has succeeded in arousing considerable interest in contemporary art and in the painting of Salvador Salazar Arrué (Salarrué) and José Mejía Vides. The former, trained in Washington, is a distinguished writer as well as artist, whose landscapes with colonial buildings have an extraordinary linear quality and also depth of plastic penetration. Mejía Vides specializes in portraying the Indians and mestizos of Salvador in a simplified pattern style that may derive from Gauguin and Van Gogh His work represents in El Salvador the effect of the modern movement in Mexico, but it is not accompanied by either the development of a real Indian school or a revival of the folk arts. This is natural, because El Salvador is a Europeanized country, without a living Indian cultural tradition.

PRACTICAL INFORMATION

HOW TO REACH EL SALVADOR

From the U. S. Minimum first-class one-way steamship fares to the Atlantic port of Puertos Barrios, Guatemala, the port of debarkation for El Salvador, are about $60 from New Orleans and $100 from New York (1941). One-way plane fare from Brownsville, Tex., to San Salvador is $96.

BY STEAMER. No direct steamship service exists between the United States and El Salvador, but connections can be made from Guatemala or Cristóbal, C. Z.

United Fruit Co.; New York office: Pier 3, North River. Has sailings to Puerto Barrios, Guatemala, from which San Salvador is reached by railroad. Voyage from New York, 6 days; from New Orleans, 3.

BY AIR. The only direct and regular means of reaching El Salvador from the United States is by plane.

Pan American Airways; main office: 135 E. 42nd Street, New York. Mexico Flyer from Brownsville, Tex., reaches El Salvador in about 23 hours, with an overnight stop in Guatemala City.

From Other Central American Countries. BY STEAMER. There are steamship services between various Guatemalan and Honduran ports and the Salvadorean ports of Acajutla, La Libertad, and La Unión. La Libertad, the principal port of entry by sea, is only 23 miles from San Salvador.

BY AIR. Pan American Airways has planes from Cristóbal, C. Z., and other Central American cities. Transportes Aéreos Centroamericanos (TACA) operates a service in 3½ hours from San José, C. R., to San Salvador via the capitals of Nicaragua and Honduras.

BY RAILROAD. International Railways of Central America (Ferrocarriles Internacionales de Centro América—IRCA) has service between Guatemala City and San Salvador via Zacapa, 261 miles on the Puerto Barrios-Guatemala City line; time from Guatemala City to Zacapa, an overnight stop, 5 hours; from Zacapa to San Salvador 12 hours.

BY PAN AMERICAN HIGHWAY. Guatemala City and San Salvador are so far the only capitals in Central America linked by motor road. The 166-mile road has a maximum altitude of 4650 feet. The Salvadorean section is very good. The Guatemalan section is uncertain in the rainy season and dusty in the dry. There is bus service of station wagon type. The trip takes about 8 hours and is inexpensive and interesting, though often not very comfortable.

AIDS TO TRAVELERS

El Salvador's Representation in the U. S. The Salvadorean Legation is at 2400 16th St., Washington, D. C. Consular officials are maintained at Los Angeles and San Francisco, Calif.; Denver, Colo.; Chicago, Ill.; New Orleans, La.; New York; Philadelphia, Pa.; Brownsville, Dallas, and Houston, Tex.; Cristóbal, C. Z.; San Juan, P. R.

U. S. Representation in El Salvador. The United States has a Legation in San Salvador. There is also a consulate.

Local Sources of Information. The national tourist board of El Salvador, Junta Nacional de Turismo, maintains a permanent office in the Hotel Nuevo Mundo in San Salvador and branch offices in Santa Ana,

San Miguel, Sonsonate, Acajutla, San Vicente, La Unión, La Libertad, and other centers. Complete information is available in these offices on travel in El Salvador as well as the neighboring countries. The tourist board also conducts a number of excursions, information on which should be obtained locally. Managements of hotels are helpful in giving information and advice. The Chamber of Commerce of El Salvador, Avenida España 5, San Salvador, is particularly helpful to commercial travelers.

Climate. The climate varies from hotly tropical in the lowlands to warm but agreeable in the higher regions. There are only two seasons, rainy and dry. The former usually is May-November; the dry season, December-March, covers both the coolest period, December-January, and the hottest, March-April. The average 24-hour temperature is about 75° F.

Clothing. Since there is little variation in temperature throughout the year, the same type of clothing is worn at all seasons. In general, the clothes worn by men and women are of the same weight and kind as would be used in the E part of the United States in the late spring and early autumn. Linen and other light tropical suits and dresses are suitable, but are not worn as much as in other parts of the tropics. After nightfall at all seasons of the year it is considered preferable to wear woolen suits, light in weight but dark in color. Women use linen and cotton only for daytime frocks. In the capital men never need overcoats, but a light raincoat is often desirable. Light coats are essential for women, and fur scarfs are often worn. Formal and evening clothes for both sexes are the same as in the United States except that white dinner jackets are usually worn.

Health. In the lowland regions it is advisable to sleep under a mosquito net. The best hotels in San Salvador provide filtered and boiled water. Elsewhere it is well for the traveler to see to the boiling or to drink bottled water. Although there are no U. S. or European doctors in El Salvador, many of the medical men and dentists have been trained in the United States or Europe. The general hospital in San Salvador and a children's hospital there are good. Most foreigners and many Salvadoreans prefer to go to the United States, to Panama, or to the United Fruit Co.'s hospital in Quiriguá, Guatemala, for operations, except in emergency. In case of illness it is well to ask the U. S. consul to recommend a doctor and hospital.

Sports and Recreations. Swimming is a favorite Salvadorean sport. Surf bathing is excellent at La Libertad and other resorts, while several inland resorts offer lake bathing. Native ponies are available for riding on plantations on the outskirts of San Salvador and elsewhere throughout the country. There is little or no hunting or fishing within easy reach of the capital. Ocean fishing for marlin, pike, and so on is among the finest in the world, notably at La Unión on the Gulf of Fonseca. Alligator hunting is available in various parts of the country. The national tourist board will supply information.

In San Salvador there are a number of private tennis courts, as well as those of the Country Club and in the Campo de Marte, where visitors may arrange to play for a moderate fee. Golf may be played by arrangement, for a low greens fee, at the San Salvador Country Club. The National Stadium, built for the Central American and Caribbean Olympic Games in 1935, is used for soccer and baseball, which attract large crowds. Horse races are held in the Campo de Marte several times a year.

Currency. The monetary unit, the colón, is equal to $.40 U. S., colones .50 to the dollar (1941); this rate has prevailed since 1935. The colón is divided into 100 centavos. Silver pieces are issued in denominations of 25 and 50 centavos; nickel pieces of 1, 3, and 5 centavos are in circulation. Paper bills are issued in denominations of 1, 2, 5, 10, 25, and 100 colones. U. S. currency, however, circulates freely, and no exchange regulations are in force.

Banks. The Banco Central de Reserva de El Salvador is the bank of issue; like the Banco Salvadoreño it has headquarters in San Salvador and branches in other leading cities. The Bank of London and South America has a branch in San Salvador.

Cost of Living. The cost of living, for tourists and transient visitors, is relatively low. The Astoria and the Nuevo Mundo, the best hotels in San Salvador, charge a top price of $6.25 a day for room and meals, with good accommodations available about $3 (1941). Average prices throughout the country are $2.50-$3.50 a day with meals. For prolonged stays one may put up in a good boarding house in San Salvador for about $60 a month with meals. Food costs for native provisions are relatively low, though imported foods are naturally quite high. Railroad fares are about on a par with those in the United States, and sightseeing and excursions are quite reasonable.

Transportation. ROADS. El Salvador has 1605 miles of national highways, something of a record for a country whose coastline is about 160 miles and whose width averages 60 miles. All principal towns and cities are connected by highway, and the roads that link the republic with Guatemala are of growing commercial and international importance.

The Salvadorean section of the Pan American Highway, also known as the International Highway, enters the country from Guatemala at Candelaria and extends to the Honduran border. Almost all of it is surfaced.

A main trunk road N from San Salvador runs through the departments of Cuscatlán and Chalatenango and thence passes into Honduras. The asphalt road from the port of La Libertad to San Salvador makes it possible for passengers and goods to reach the capital in less than an hour from this seaport. Especially important to visitors is the road leading W from San Salvador to Izalco and Sonsonate and thence into Guatemala. From Sonsonate one branch of this road leads S to the port of Acajutla, while another runs N past the volcano Izalco and Lake Coatepeque to Santa Ana on the Pan American Highway.

AUTOMOBILES. The visitor's own car, if desired, is best shipped from the United States to Guatemala and driven to El Salvador from there. However, the process is costly and laborious, and it is not recommended, since cars are easily rented in El Salvador. Salvadorean consulates will supply details.

BUSES. Good bus services throughout the republic are being constantly extended as the government proceeds with its road-construction program. There is international service to Guatemala.

RAILROADS. The republic has two railroad systems with about 310 miles of track in use.

The country is traversed by the International Railways of Central America, whose line from Cutuco and La Unión on the Gulf of Fonseca leads to San Salvador via San Miguel. From a junction at Soya-pango, just before reaching the capital, the line continues to Texiste-peque near Santa Ana; an extension to the Guatemalan border opened in 1929 gives a through connection with the interocean system of Guatemala at Zacapa. This improvement shortened the journey to Europe and North America via Puerto Barrios by more than a week. There is a branch from Santa Ana to Ahuachapán.

One line of the Salvador Railway Co., British owned, connects the port of Acajutla with San Salvador via Sonsonate. Another line runs from the capital to Santa Ana.

AIRLINES. Pan American Airways and Transportes Aéreos Centro-americanos (TACA) give international service for passengers, cargo, and mail. Transportes Aéreos Salvadoreños is a Salvadorean line which operates regular services to the E part of El Salvador and also makes special trips to any airport in the country.

Postage. Outgoing mail to the United States goes by railroad to Puerto Barrios and thence to New Orleans and New York. Postage is about $.05 for the first ounce and $.03 for each additional ounce or fraction thereof. There is parcel post service. Airmail costs $.15 a half ounce for letters and $.10 for postcards (1941).

Communications. Telephone and telegraph service throughout the republic is supplied at low rates. There is also telephone service to Guatemala, telegraph to all parts of Central America, and radio communication by telegraph, telephone, and cable to all parts of the world. A wireless station at the capital communicates with Mexico and with the rest of Central America. There is direct radiotelephone service between El Salvador and Miami, Fla., where messages are relayed.

Souvenirs and Handicrafts. San Salvador has a number of attractive little shops where visitors may purchase quite reasonably some of the beautifully wrought articles made in all parts of the republic. Chief among these are the famous Izalco gourd bowls, made from the fruit of the jícara tree, beautifully designed and highly polished. It is said that the Indians gather these fruits only during the full of the moon. The Santo Domingo pottery is notably well made. Baskets are numerous, many of them of coconut leaves, which are said to be more delicate than reeds and to lend themselves to more intricate patterns. The Apaneca basket designs are famous. Beautiful cotton and silk textiles are woven in Panchimalco and can be bought cheap there. Handmade leather goods, especially shoes and slippers, and handwrought silver are famous. All towns and cities have annual fairs where visitors may buy distinctive local products directly from the makers.

Food. International food is served at the major hotels. Salvadorean food otherwise is like that of the rest of Central America, the native workers subsisting largely on frijoles or black beans, tortillas or corn cakes, gallons of coffee, and the fruits of the land. The urban Salvadoreans eat a more varied diet of meat, fruits, and vegetables. Corn, particularly white corn, made into tortillas, is the staple food for all. Small coffee shops are everywhere. Fruits are abundant. Oranges, lemons, pineapples, granadillas or passionflower fruit, and nearly all the tropical fruits are found everywhere. The cashew tree has in recent years acquired a high market value. Besides its nuts and fruits, it is the source of an excellent wine. The bark is used as an astringent; the wood is known as white mahogany; the nut shells are in demand for making a product used by dentists; and the gum extracted from the bark makes an excellent furniture polish. Fish abound in the lakes and rivers, and many varieties, mostly with local names, are served in the hotels.

Holidays and Fiestas. Every department of the country celebrates all the national legal holidays as well as a few special fiestas of its own, which either commemorate some historic event or have a religious significance. On such days business is forgotten; the day starts with a solemn religious ceremony at the church, and it usually ends in gaiety with dancing and feasting.

The principal national holidays are: January 1, Feast of the Circumcision and New Year's Day; four days of Holy Week; Corpus Christi; June 30, bank holiday; July 1, bank holiday; July 24-August 6, Feast of the Holy Savior; September 15, Independence Day; October 12, Columbus Day (Día de la Raza—Day of the Race); November 1, All Saints' Day (Todos Santos); November 5, Salvadorean Independence Day; Christmas; December 31, bank holiday.

The longest and most spectacular fiesta is that of the Holy Savior. In San Salvador colorful floats are driven around the streets at irregular intervals throughout this almost two-week period. Dressed in their finest clothes, the people stroll about the streets to watch the religious processions or go to the racetrack to see the races or to the clubs for dancing. The fiesta ends on August 5 with a great religious procession, when the image of the Salvador del Mundo (Savior of the World) is carried about on a very high float. The last day of the festival, August 6, is the Feast of the Transfiguration, a day devoted entirely to solemn religious ceremonies.

Holy Week and Christmas are the most universally celebrated.

One of the most colorful local fiestas is celebrated on the day of St. Ursula, October 21, in the little village of Jicalapa in the department of La Libertad. To this village perched on a high rock overlooking the sea, whose 1500 inhabitants live in houses of wood and thatch, hundreds of pilgrims stream every year to do honor to its patron saint and to fulfill their vows to her.

On the Day of the Indian (Día del Indio), December 12, children and young people dressed in authentic Indian costume walk in procession to honor the patroness of the American Indian, the Virgin of Guadalupe.

At the fiestas some of the most beautiful flowers in the country are seen, including more than 20 species of Salvadorean orchids.

REGIONAL GUIDE

For visitors from the United States, San Salvador, capital of the republic, is the country's main port of entry, even though it lies 23 miles inland from its seaport, La Libertad. This is because there is no direct steamship connection between the United States and any Salvadorean port. U. S. travelers usually reach El Salvador either by plane or by the International Railways of Central America from Guatemala.

SAN SALVADOR

The first city founded by the Spaniards in the region that is El Salvador today, San Salvador was originally located, in 1525, in the valley of La Bermuda, with Diego de Holguín as its mayor. Here, too, on April 1, 1528, was established the country's first regular government, with Diego de Alvarado, brother of the conquistador Pedro de Alvarado, at its head, subject to the captaincy general of Guatemala. The Spaniards were not satisfied with the site they had chosen, and they soon moved the city to the Valle de las Hamacas (Valley of the Hammocks). There it remains today, now a city of some 140,000, pleasantly situated on the Río Acelhuate, at an altitude of 2238 feet and within a circle of mountains, the highest of which are the volcanoes San Jacinto and San Salvador. The name of the Valle de las Hamacas suggests the many earthquakes that San Salvador has experienced, and the effects of these earthquakes in turn help to explain the city's modernity and lack of colonial atmosphere. The architecture of the outstanding government and private buildings follows a general trend toward the modern, modified for protection from earthquakes. The water system with its modern filtration plant is new. The streets are wide and well paved. The city's outmoded street-car system was replaced some years ago by a cheap and efficient local bus system that extends to the suburbs.

THE CITY. Modern San Salvador is laid out in the general form of a cross, with four beautiful broad avenues meeting at the very center. The upright of the cross is formed by Avenida Cuscatlán, S, and Av. España, N; Calle Arce is the W arm, C. Delgado the E arm. From this intersection the city spreads out in regular rectangular blocks. The streets run E-W, parallel to C. Arce and C. Delgado; the avenues N-S, parallel to Av. Cuscatlán and Av. España.

Even-numbered avenues are E of Av. Cuscatlán and Av. España. S of C. Delgado they are called Sur, and on the other side of the main intersection they are called Norte; for example: 2ª Avenida Sur and 2ª Avenida Norte, 4ª Avenida Sur and 4ª Avenida Norte, to be read as Segunda Avenida Sur (South Second Avenue), etc. Similarly, the odd-numbered avenues lie W of Av. Cuscatlán and Av. España and are divided into N and S parts by C. Arce.

The even-numbered streets lie S of C. Arce and C. Delgado and are divided by Av. Cuscatlán into E and W parts; for example: 2ª Calle Oriente (East Second Street), 4ª Calle Poniente (West Fourth Street), etc. The odd-numbered streets are N of the main intersection.

The heart of the city formerly lay farther S, and there were many quaint, crooked streets and uneven blocks.

PARKS AND PLAZAS. Parque Barrios, a block S of the center of the city and on the E side of Av. Cuscatlán, is the principal square. Eight main walks converge on a central point where a fine equestrian statue of General Barrios stands. This statue faces W and is in a direct line with the main entrance of the National Palace on Av. Cuscatlán. Looking N from the monument, the visitor can see the great central doors of the cathedral. Hotel Astoria is opposite the SW corner, at the intersection of Av. Cuscatlán and 4ª C.O. Also visible from the park are the buildings of the National University and the central post office (Departamento General de Correos), which occupy the block bordered by Av. Cuscatlán and C. Arce, opposite the cathedral.

Parque Dueñas is a block E of Parque Barrios and a block S of C. Delgado. Its walks are laid out in the usual star-shaped pattern, and in the exact center is the monument to Liberty, which was dedicated on Nov. 5, 1911, during festivities commemorating the centennial anniversary of the first Central American movement for liberty. This imposing monument of bronze and marble stands a little over 50 feet high. Atop the tall pillar is a winged figure of Glory and at the base one of Liberty; on the sides are busts of Delgado, Arce, and Rodríguez and the national coat of arms. Appropriately, the monument faces the church of El Rosario, where Father Delgado is buried, on the E side of the park. The Palacio Arzobispal (Archbishop's Palace) is next to the church. The S side of the square is filled by the Municipal Palace, the city hall.

Plaza Morazán, containing a monument to General Morazán, is a block E of the central intersection and N of C. Delgado. S of it, across C. Delgado, stands the National Theater. Hotel Nuevo Mundo also faces this square. W from it, on the NE corner of the main intersection, is the imposing Tesorería Nacional (National Treasury), diagonally opposite the post office.

Plaza Carretas is 4 blocks N of C. Delgado, at the end of 6ª Av. N. The large church of San Francisco is a block W of this square and Parque Rodríguez 2 blocks E.

Parque Bolívar is 6 blocks W of the main intersection and a block S of C. Arce. Facing its W side and occupying a whole city block is the municipal jail. The Imprenta Nacional (National Press) fronts it S; N is the Departamento General de Sanidad, the health department, with the large basilica of El Sagrado Corazón de Jesús across from it on C. Arce.

Campo de Marte, the largest and most popular of the city's many parks, lies in the NW part of the city, on 7ª Av. N., 4 blocks N of C. Arce. A pleasure resort where races are held every fortnight during the summer season, it is the favorite rendezvous for the young people of the city. The track is one of the best in Central America. There is ample space for motorists to park in a semicircular area and view the races from their own cars. El Salvador breeds fast horses, and both native and foreign horses are entered in the events. The tennis courts can be used for a moderate fee.

Parque Atlacatl, one of the Salvadoreans' favorite parks and a training ground for the city's garrison, is also on the N side of the city. In the park is a statue of the famous warrior Atlacatl, bow in hand, looking over the whole city of San Salvador.

The National Stadium, built especially for the Central American and Caribbean Olympic Games in 1935, is some 5 miles SW of San Salvador and is easily reached from the heart of the city by an excellent road that winds through picturesque hills.

PUBLIC BUILDINGS AND INSTITUTIONS. Architecturally the public buildings of San Salvador, though modern in construction, show the strong influence of the Spanish Renaissance. Other buildings, notably the churches, some of the luxurious private residences, and the Hospital Rosales, have a Spanish colonial flavor.

The National Palace, the capitol, is one of the most imposing buildings in the city. Facing Parque Barrios, this handsome building with a beautiful interior court occupies an entire block. It is designed in the Renaissance style and is two stories high. Stately fluted columns with Corinthian capitals adorn the four main entrances. The offices of the national government and the National Assembly are housed here.

The National University, just across 2ª C.P. from the National Palace and next to the post office, has a simple concrete building.

The Casa Presidencial (Presidential Mansion), on C. Delgado, 4 blocks E of the main intersection, between 5ª Av. N. and 8ª Av. N., is quite different in style from the National Palace, with wide overhanging eaves. It is surrounded by beautiful gardens.

The barracks of the First Artillery Regiment, opposite the Presidential Mansion, is a long, low structure, obviously a military building, in the form of a hollow square. It has rather an austere look because of its few windows, its crenelated flat roof, and its four battlemented corner towers.

The Biblioteca Nacional (National Library) occupies the building at 2ª Av. N. No. 16.

The National Theater was built for plays and large social and musical gatherings, though as a rule it shows motion pictures. On the S side of Plaza Morazán, it was designed by the Salvadorean architect José María Peralta and is regarded as one of the best on the continent because of its excellent acoustics.

The U. S. Legation, on C. Arce at 19 Av. N., is a modern building showing strong Spanish influence, set well back from the street in a beautiful garden. Near by are many beautiful residences.

MARKET. The Mercado Público is immediately behind the National Palace. It is an excellent place to buy woodenware, silverware, shoes, and so on and an interesting place to observe. Visitors should remember that the Salvadoreans do not like to bargain; they expect to be paid what they ask.

CHURCHES. San Salvador has no churches that are colonial in the

---

KEY TO MAP OF SAN SALVADOR

1. Parque Barrios
2. National Palace
3. Cathedral
4. Hotel Astoria
5. Parque Dueñas
6. Rosario church
7. National Theater
8. Hotel Nuevo Mundo
9. National Treasury
10. Post office
11. Plaza Carretas
12. San Francisco church
13. Parque Rodríguez
14. Parque Bolívar
15. Sagrado Corazón basilica
16. Market
17. Presidential Mansion
18. U. S. Legation
19. Hospital Rosales

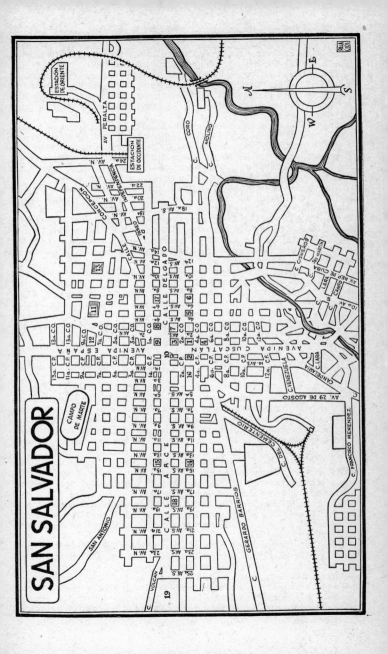

sense of having been built and decorated before the era of independence. The following are the city's more prominent churches.

The cathedral, fronting on Parque Barrios, has several interesting features. Spanish Gothic in style and constructed entirely of wood to protect it from earthquakes, this church was commenced in 1881 and consecrated seven years later. The beautiful woodcarvings of its nave and choir are notable.

The basilica of El Sagrado Corazón de Jesús (Sacred Heart of Jesus), on C. Arce at 15 Av. N., is one of the republic's greatest churches and a fine example of Spanish Gothic. Its imposing façade, divided into three parts, corresponds to the three-aisled plan of the interior. Over the large central door is a handsome rose window, above which rise two tall spires resting on the strong shaft of the tower below.

The church of El Rosario, on the E side of Parque Dueñas, built in the middle of the 19th century, is a famous landmark in the capital city, for here is buried José Matías Delgado, the first to promulgate in El Salvador the idea of independence from Spain. The church is a good example of the Spanish colonial style of architecture, with a fine central porch. In front of it a bronze monument commemorates the deeds of Father Delgado. In the courtyard are statues of Bartolomé de las Casas and Christopher Columbus.

The church of La Merced, near that of El Rosario, is the oldest in San Salvador. Its two-story façade is characterized by a simple central door with a fine fanlight. The flanking towers are particularly interesting because they are octagonal in plan and capped by oddly shaped cupolas. Outside it is an old belltower containing the very bell with which Father Delgado announced, on that memorable November day in 1811, his first effort to free his people.

Other churches of importance are the Spanish Baroque church of San Francisco, 4 blocks N of C. Delgado, off Av. España, between 7ª C.O. and 9ª C.O.; and El Calvario, 2 blocks W and a block S of the National Palace.

HOSPITALS AND CHARITABLE INSTITUTIONS. The people of El Salvador are noted for the number and variety of their charitable institutions, some of which are supported by private contributions, while others are under the direct patronage of the state. The national charity board controls all these institutions, and their principal source of income is the national lottery, which has its drawings on the first Sunday of each month.

The Hospital Rosales, on the W side of the city at the end of C. Arce, has accommodations for 700 patients. It was built in 1902 through the generosity of the Salvadorean philanthropist José Rosales. Its spacious gardens give it tropical charm.

The Hospital Benjamin Bloom, a progressive children's hospital, also on the W side of the city, was founded and endowed by the banker whose name it bears. The long, low concrete building is designed with restraint and simplicity.

The Casa Nacional del Niño is an orphanage for children of both sexes. At the Sala Cuna poor children are cared for and fed, and working mothers may leave their children there.

PRIVATE HOUSES. Short rides through the city will reward the visitor with views of some of the best-appointed private residences and formal gardens in Central America. Most of the homes follow the Spanish style of architecture, but here and there is one of a newer type, built of

wood, the exterior covered with iron sheets molded to form an architectural ornamentation. Reinforced concrete is another sort of construction which has successfully withstood the city's frequent earth
tremors. Tile roofings mellowed by sun and rains add to the picturesquesness of the houses.

CLUBS. San Salvador has a number of clubs to which foreigners are
welcomed. Some of these are devoted to sports; others are purely
social.

The International Club on 2ª Av. S., half a block S of C. Delgado,
has many foreign members. It maintains a fine beach house at La
Libertad in addition to the handsome clubhouse in the capital, with a
beautiful round patio. The Photography Club of El Salvador, one of
the best camera clubs in the Latin American republics, meets at the
International Club and holds annual exhibitions there in August, with
entries from all over the world.

The Casino Salvadoreño, near the SE corner of Parque Barrios, has
a swimming pool, which, like the other club facilities, is open to visitors. The handsome building of two stories is in Moorish style.

The Country Club, 4 miles outside the city and easily reached by
car over a paved road, has a handsome concrete building in the modern manner, with broad terraces and steps leading down to luxuriant
green lawns. There are tennis courts and a golf course. The greens fee
is low.

The Círculo Militar (Military Club) has a handsome building.

The Auto Club of El Salvador has a town clubhouse and also maintains a beach house at La Libertad and houses at other resorts as well.

TRANSPORTATION ADDRESSES. San Salvador's airport, the best in the
republic, is at Ilopango, 6 miles E of the city and connected with it by
an excellent road. The Estación de Oriente (E station) of the International Railways of Central America and the Estación de Occidente
(W station) of the Salvador Railway are both in the NE part of the
city and are reached by Paseo Independencia (Independence Drive),
an E extension of 1ª C.O.

MOVING-PICTURE HOUSES. There are five moving-picture houses in
San Salvador, Popular, National, Colón, Coliseo, and Principal. Prices
are low. U. S. films, shown about a year after their release in the
United States, usually make up the program.

BANKS. The Banco Central de Reserva de El Salvador, the government bank, and Banco Salvadoreño have headquarters here, and the
Bank of London and South America has a branch.

SOURCES OF INFORMATION. See Practical Information (p. 13).

SOUVENIRS AND HANDICRAFTS can be found in the public market, in
the shops of the Portal del Occidente, and in shops in and near the
hotels.

RESTAURANTS AND CAFÉS. There are several popular drinking and din-
ing places in San Salvador. Café Lutecia, half a block from Hotel
Nuevo Mundo, is the smartest and most popular bar. Restaurant
Alemán is another favorite, while the restaurants of Hotel Nuevo
Mundo and Hotel Astoria rival it in popularity. Visitors usually eat
at the hotels.

HOTELS. Nuevo Mundo** is a simple modern two-story building
overlooking Plaza Morazán. It has well-ventilated rooms with hot and
cold running water and showers. A string orchestra plays every evening,
and dance orchestras are engaged frequently. Astoria**, Av. Cuscatlán

and 4ᵃ C.O., is less international in atmosphere and somewhat smaller, but has equally good accommodations. Casa Clarke, a boarding house managed by a former airplane stewardess, has excellent food and is a good place to stay if one is to remain in San Salvador long. Other boarding houses are Centro Americano; Continental; Corona; San Francisco.

NOTE. Hotels are here classified by rates. Two stars indicate the higher rates for the country in question and also, in nearly all cases, mean good accommodations. One star means rates in the medium brackets; no star means either low rates or no information available. An effort is made in all these guides to list hotels in the various cities and towns, but travelers who are accustomed to North American or European accommodations should use the information with care. In the capitals and larger Latin American centers hotels usually have standards comparable with those found elsewhere and at times on a par with those anywhere in the world. In the smaller centers throughout Latin America hotels are often more nearly boarding houses whose standards of accommodations and food make them unacceptable to all but the most adaptable.

SAN SALVADOR'S ENVIRONS AND EXCURSIONS

Many attractions are accessible from San Salvador by bus or car. Renting a car makes it possible to reach out-of-the-way places conveniently and without great expense. The country's numerous roads and its two railroad services radiate from San Salvador, which is the natural travel center of the country. Chances to see the life of the Indians should not be missed. One of the most interesting sights near the capital is the Maya ruin recently brought to light on the San Andrés hacienda; under a group of six mounds which were formerly supposed to be natural hills steps and terraces of pyramids have been uncovered which may antedate the Christian era.

Several of the towns described here as separate excursions from San Salvador can be grouped together to make an interesting circular trip. Visits to Santa Tecla, La Libertad, Panchimalco, Olocuilta, and Santo Tomás de Aquino can be combined. A shorter triangular drive can be made from San Salvador to Panchimalco and Olocuilta, with the return via Santo Tomás.

Santa Tecla, capital of the department of La Libertad, only 7 miles W of San Salvador by the Pan American Highway, seems like a continuation of the national capital. Founded in 1856, the city has several handsome colonial buildings, as well as some in more modern style. The city hall, hospital, departmental government offices, and the Hospicio Guirola, an orphan asylum built and endowed by the late Angel Guirola, a wealthy and esteemed citizen of Santa Tecla, are notable.

The city is situated in an idyllic valley with large and flourishing coffee fincas or plantations. It has a mild, healthful climate. The Salvadoreans are hospitable, and many foreigners have the chance to visit private fincas. Such fincas as those of the Guirola, Duke, Dardano, Dueñas, and Gallardos families are worth a visit. Here the visitor meets Salvadoreans of wealth and culture, professional men whose academic degrees were obtained in universities abroad and whose children will be educated in the same manner. The drive from San Salvador along Avenida Santa Tecla, past the homes and estates of these people, with their gardens of tropical flowers, explains why the capital is called the City of Flowers.

The volcano San Salvador, 6333 feet high, 45 minutes W of San Salvador over an excellent road, is in the vicinity of Santa Tecla. It has been inactive in recent years, and it is possible to stand on the rim and look into the once fuming crater and to climb down the sandy, tree-covered slopes for a closer view of the secondary cone.

Possibly the product of this volcano's eruptions long ago is an imposing lava bed at Playón, about 12 miles W of the capital, 1¼ hours' ride from San Salvador on the Salvador Railway. The lava field extends about 4 miles on each side of the railroad and resembles a vast bas-relief of fantastic figures suggesting pyramids, obelisks, columns, and lacework.

La Libertad, 16 miles S of Santa Tecla by highway and 23 miles from San Salvador, is one of the country's main seaports. It is reached by regular bus from the capital. The Auto Club of El Salvador and the International Club both have beach houses here, and the town is a popular all-year resort. Like Acajutla and La Unión, La Libertad is one of El Salvador's busiest ports. Freighters call to discharge cargo by lighter, and most of the country's coffee, sisal, sugar, and indigo exports are shipped from it. Commercially the section around La Libertad is one of the most enterprising in the country, for it is dotted with sugar refineries, distilleries, sawmills, and coffee plantations. A few miles W of the port begins the famous Balsam Coast, the only place in the world that produces balsam of Peru, used extensively in the preparation of medicines.

In La Libertad a famous so-called painted stone may be seen. This stone bears an inscription which has never been deciphered, but legend has it that the stone was set up by Xicontl, an Indian noble, as a memorial for himself and his wife, the princess Ixtaj. Xicontl, son of the king of the Pocoman Indians, was returning from a great war against a Quiché tribe when he and his warriors were overtaken by a tempest. The ship in which Xicontl and his prisoner Ixtaj, princess of the conquered Quiché, were sailing was separated from the main body of the fleet and wrecked on the coast at what is now La Libertad. From the moment of her capture Ixtaj had been as one dead. Xicontl and his companions carried her ashore. It was the custom of the triumphant tribe to sacrifice prisoners of war to the gods, and Xicontl was reminded of the fact by the tribal prophet. By this time Xicontl had fallen in love with the beautiful princess. When Ixtaj aroused she recognized him as the lover of her dreams. Xicontl, however, gave the order for her to be placed on the sacrificial pyre. Facing her captors, Ixtaj told the men that if they split open the trunk of a tree near by they would find their proper sacrifice in it. When the tree was split a red sap poured from it and coagulated on the ground in the shape of a heart. Fully convinced that the gods had sent this sacrifice, the Pocomans released the princess, and she fell into Xicontl's arms. Since the lovers could not return to their tribes, they decided to found a colony where they were. Human sacrifices were not to be offered. Fortune smiled on this colony, and Xicontl and Ixtaj lived long and reigned peacefully. When they were old a near-by volcano devastated their lands, and seeing that their end was near, Xicontl ordered the monolith inscribed with their story. The stone is painted with the sap of the tree of sacrifice, it is said, and it does not fade.

HOTELS. El Faro* and Miami* are both by the seaside.

Panchimalco, 9 miles S of San Salvador by road and easily reached also from La Libertad, is essential for a glimpse of precolonial El Salvador. The 50 square miles around it are inhabited by one of the few remaining tribes of pure-blooded Indians of the Pipil nation. These are the Pancho Indians, who have maintained the purity of their race and the customs of their forefathers.

Nestling on the lower slopes of Cerro Chulo, Panchimalco has preserved its aboriginal characteristics, and the only evidence of a more modern era is the fine colonial church. The houses, almost all built of wood and thatch, have withstood the ravages of time and weather. The streets are irregular and seem to have been laid out around the huge rocks which dot the town site. There are two explanations for these large boulders—that they were deposited by an earthquake or that the Indians rolled them down from the mountainside in the pathway of the invading Spaniards.

Students of art will find a perfect example of early Spanish colonial design in the Panchimalco church, in vigorous late Baroque style. Its collection of religious art is the most complete in the country. The façade has a set of carved statues of the apostles. The interior abounds in exquisite woodcarvings, and the bell bears the cipher and titles of the emperor Charles V, who presented it to the town.

The Pancho Indians are industrious and are principally occupied with agriculture. However, they are also masters of cotton and silk weaving and their well-designed textiles can be bought at exceptionally low prices.

Santo Tomás de Aquino (St. Thomas Aquinas), 8 miles SE of San Salvador by road, is an archeological site of interest. Originally founded as a village in 1719 under the name of Santo Tomás Texacuangos, it lies just S of the site of an early Indian city from which many interesting and important relics have been excavated. It became a town in 1879. Here may be seen the ruins of Cushululitán, which show the degree of civilization reached by the Indians. Archeologists are now deciphering history and customs from the strange carved figures uncovered recently as the result of a landslide.

Olocuilta, in the department of La Paz, 6 miles beyond Santo Tomás de Aquino, is an old city and one of the most interesting in the republic. It may also be reached by car 7 miles E of Panchimalco. The stone-paved streets bear the marks of heavily laden oxcarts. On Sundays a typical Salvadorean market is held. The villagers gather under a huge ceiba tree, set up stalls, and exhibit their fruits, vegetables, staple foods, and handicrafts. Like almost every other city and town in the country, Olocuilta possesses a beautiful church of Spanish colonial design.

Lake Ilopango, 6 miles E of the capital and reached by a new highway, is San Salvador's nearest and most popular pleasure resort. In an old volcanic crater between the San Jacinto mountains and the Tepezontes, the lake is 10 miles long and 5 miles wide, 1200 feet lower than the San Salvador plateau. Modern, comfortable hotels, clubs and private chalets on the bay of Apulo, alive with sail- and motor boats, are interspersed with the fishing villages of the Indians who handle their dugout canoes expertly on the wind-swept waters. There is an airport at Ilopango which is used jointly by the army and commercial interests.

In 1880 a geological disturbance raised a volcano from the depths of Ilopango's waters. This caused a sudden overflow into the outlet of the lake, which discharges into the Río Jiboa. The outlet became a raging stream which cut the bed of the river deeper and deeper until a depth of 30 feet had been reached. Three months later the lake's surface was 34 feet lower; the island which had appeared toward the center now had a height of 150 feet and was 500 feet across. Smaller islands appeared near by. Since that time Ilopango has been known as the Lake of the Miracle.

To the pre-Spanish inhabitants of the region, descendants of a race who had brought their culture from Mexico, the lake had a special religious significance. The goddess of the lake had to be propitiated annually to assure good crops and general good fortune. To this end four virgins were selected every year before harvest time. They were highly honored and their every wish granted, while they prayed night and day. At last, with great pomp and ceremony, the maidens were cast into the lake as a living sacrifice to the goddess.

Cojutepeque (Enchanted Hill), 19 miles E of San Salvador by road or railroad, is a beautiful city which has twice been the capital of the republic. It is now the capital of the department of Cuscatlán, which borders that of San Salvador.

In 1571 Cojutepeque was a village; in 1787 it received the title of town; in 1846 it was made a city. If possible, a visit should be timed for the Feast of St. John (San Juan) on August 29, when a famous annual fair is held, attended by thousands from all parts of the republic. Many come to buy and sell cattle; others, from the neighboring villages of San Pedro Perulapin, Santa Cruz Michapa, and Santo Domingo, come to sell their products: earthenware pottery, hats, saddlery, leather novelties, sweets, and fruits. Cacaopera in the department of Morazán sends quantities of its famous ropes, hammocks, sandals, and many other articles made from sisal fiber. Here also are found hundreds of the ubiquitous alforjas or saddle bags which, with their stripes in brilliant color combinations, are always popular with visitors.

Conacatepeque, about 8 miles NE of San Salvador by road, is a picturesque town in the department of San Salvador. On a high plateau, it enjoys a healthful climate. It is an agricultural center, although its principal industry is weaving. The name is of Pipil origin and means Hill of the Reeds in the Sun. The town was originally situated 3 miles from its present site, and according to local folklore, St. Nicholas was instrumental in moving it to a safer place. The oldest inhabitants can dimly remember the church of San Nicolás at the old town site. Tradition says that the statue of St. Nicholas used to disappear from the church and wander to the foot of the huge ceiba tree which marks the center of the new site. Each time it wandered away the statue was carried back to the church in a procession of townspeople. It disappeared again and again, until the people took the miracle as a sign and moved the whole town to the place where the image of the saint was usually found.

Like Santo Tomás de Aquino, Conacatepeque was originally built on the site of an ancient Indian city. Many pre-Spanish relics have been excavated, ceramics. domestic utensils, and statues, which prove the antiquity of the town's origin and show that it must once have been a commercial center of importance. Of interest to tourists and archeologists are the Peña de los Fierros (Rock of the Brands) and the Cueva de los Sepulcros (Cave of the Tombs). The former is a shadowy cavity in a rock, covered with mystic writings in the form of figures such as are used for branding cattle, not painted, but cut into the rock with great skill. The latter, in a hill near by, is a ghostly cavern that runs deep into the rocks. Night hunters have reported that they heard cockcrows, human moans, and sounds of women weeping in the cave but were too frightened to investigate. Some of the inhabitants assert that the cave hides the lost treasure of Partideño, a famous bandit of colonial times.

Ilobasco is an interesting town, reached NE by car (p. 34).

Villa Delgado, a small town a short distance N of San Salvador, has a church of San Sebastián that is notable for severely classic design, beautiful woodcarvings, and fine stained-glass windows.

Mejicanos, near Villa Delgado, is a little town where the country people gather on Sundays for the market. Dressed in their colorful best, they do their weekly shopping and hold gay reunions.

San Lorenzo, a port on the Río de Paz, is about 60 miles NW of San Salvador by car. The trip takes about 3½ hours through a beautiful countryside and picturesque farm land. With its bathing beach, San Lorenzo is popular for all-day picnics, returning to San Salvador by moonlight.

WESTERN EL SALVADOR

Three departments make up the W part of the country: Sonsonate on the Pacific and Ahuachapán and Santa Ana along the Guatemalan border. All the leading places in these departments can be easily reached by car or railroad from the capital. They are presented here primarily as a motor circuit from San Salvador.

The department of Sonsonate on the Pacific coast is one of the most important in the republic. It is especially interesting because of the volcano Izalco, with an interesting Indian town at its foot, and the Balsam Coast which lies along the ocean. En route to the departmental capital from San Salvador are some points where a pleasant day may be spent swimming, picnicking, or observing Indian life.

Quezaltepeque, in the department of La Libertad, less than an hour W of San Salvador on the Pan American Highway, has at La Toma one of the best hot-spring resorts in the country. The mineral waters here are regarded locally as good for virtually any ailment. A formation of lava from an ancient eruption of the volcano San Salvador created this place of natural beauty. Thousands visit it every week, and parties of school children are taken on special outings to enjoy the swimming. There are inns and bathhouses.

IZALCO

The town of Izalco consists really of two villages, Dolores Izalco and Asunción Izalco, which are physically distinct. The former is a ladino settlement of whites or mixed bloods, the latter of Indians. The arrangement is like that described for Chichicastenango in Guatemala. See guide to Guatemala (p. 19).

Over the town looms the volcano Izalco, the most active in Central America, known as the lighthouse of the Pacific because its almost continuous smoke and flames are a guide to ships at sea. On its slopes may be seen the so-called stone of conquest. At this site the Indians were forced, after a bloody battle, to submit to the rule of the Spanish invaders. The stone was signed in the blood of the conquered Indians. Near it is a deep, quiet pool into which an Indian princess is said to have cast herself in order to escape from a Spanish soldier. Ever since that day the waters have been still except for a short time at midday when the surface is ruffled, for it is at noon, according to the legend, that the princess takes her bath.

In the town of Izalco an Indian municipal militia functions in religious and ceremonial matters. Its officers serve for a year and then appoint their own successors. Besides an alcalde or mayor, a vice-mayor, and aldermen, numerous other officials are appointed with elaborate titles. The religious council made up of all these officeholders attends the two great local fiestas with all their insignia. At the Feast of the Reception, August 8-15, the image of the Virgin of the Assumption is covered with flowers and borne in procession by four girls to the church of La Asunción, where High Mass is celebrated. The supply of flowers is the special care of a woman designated as stewardess of the pitcher, a ceremonial vessel which she carries in the procession; she must also provide flowers for numerous altars during the year.

The Feast of St. John the Baptist (San Juan Bautista), celebrated June 17-24, differs from the Feast of the Reception by addition of a sacrificial ceremony. Horsemen passing at full gallop under a branch from which four cocks are hung endeavor to cut off the fowls' heads. Fifes and drums add their clamor to the shouts of the crowd. Then the horsemen, crouching low and clinging to their horses, try to unseat each other by blows dealt with the dead cocks. The music becomes livelier and more exciting, and the scene ends in a whirl of dust and feathers, shouts, and the excited neighing of the horses.

Today the Izalco Indians are devout Catholics, although certain of their festive customs have their origin in pre-colonial times. The church of Izalco is the scene of a great feast on Christmas Eve. Before the church is a large plaza where the Indians dance on a pavement literally studded with the fragments of the old church. The bell called María Asunción, which was hidden for many years beneath the ruins of the old church, is now in a new belltower. The bell, a relic of colonial days, was presented to the church by Charles V. Some ruins of the old church are still standing, and here the Indian brotherhoods gather, such as those of the Padre Eterno, the Virgin of Remedies, the Niño Jesús (Child Jesus), and the Assumption. Surrounded by the women, the men dance, each confraternity with its own music and dance patterns. In the dance of the Savages, the Indians, clad in loincloths and adorned with sea shells, tin discs, and fruit seeds, grasp their bows and arrows and dance about their cacique or chief to pay him homage. Some wear red sashes which support skirts of palm leaves representing feathers. All repeat early tribal oaths of allegiance and dance some of the ancient steps of their individual tribes. Next comes the dance of Sebastiana, usually performed by a buxom Indian girl dressed in a bright costume, who whirls around and around to music of ever-increasing tempo. Her partner Negrito follows her and sings her praises. The program continues with other dances, including those of El Panadero and El Venadito, and is completed with the dance of the Obsidian Serpent, in which the dancers carry sacred pythons. The Indian name Izalco itself means Over the Obsidian Serpent.

SONSONATE

Capital of its department, the city of Sonsonate has a Municipal Palace, well-designed modern schools, theaters, and residences that bespeak a good standard of living. It lies 53 miles W of San Salvador and is reached by car over a good road which leaves the Pan American Highway beyond Santa Tecla (p. 24). By train it is a trip of some 3 hours from the national capital, and the Salvador Railway offers numerous excursions.

An important market is held in Sonsonate on Sundays at which the visitor can become acquainted with the many products of the department: tropical fruits, coffee, sugar, liquors, confections, cheese, soap, and candles. In this market are found live iguanas, large lizards whose flesh tastes a little like chicken and is considered a rare delicacy.

A tour about the city includes visits to the beautiful church of El Pilar and the cathedral with its 17 cupolas of all sizes, the largest of which can be seen all over the city because of its outer coating of white porcelain. Just outside the city is the church of San Antonio. Dating back to early colonial times, this shrine has become a Mecca of thousands of visitors from all over the republic. Valuable gifts to the church bear testimony to the efficacy of prayers offered there. Pilgrims leave evidences of their afflictions—crutches, canes, and the like—when recovery has followed their appeals to the saint.

HOTELS. Palace*, 3 blocks from the railroad station.

EXCURSIONS FROM SONSONATE

Nahuilingo, with some springs, is just three-quarters of a mile out of the city. The spot is one of great natural beauty. A small but powerful waterfall supplies water for the modern swimming pools. Like that of La Toma, the water is reputed to have great curative powers.

Acajutla, 12 miles SW of Sonsonate by car, is the W seaboard terminus of the Salvador Railway and the most popular resort in the vicinity for surf bathing in the Pacific. There is dancing to a marimba band on the tree-shaded terrace of one of the hotels. Fruit and refreshment stalls with native foods and tropical fruits are found everywhere. Near the station is an old market place that is full of interest.

HOTELS. Las Américas; Occidental.

The Costa del Bálsamo (Balsam Coast) lies between the ports of Acajutla and La Libertad to the south. Here the balsam tree, quite different from the U. S. balsam fir, grows in a dense forest that is said to be the only one of its kind in the world. Misleadingly called balsam of Peru, the product is distinctly Salvadorean. The tree has a cylindrical trunk and rises to a height of 50-60 feet. Its bark is thick, rough, and dark, and its foliage beautiful. Twenty-five years or more are needed for a tree to become productive. The industry dates back to pre-colonial days, and the method of tapping remains very primitive. The bark is bruised and an incision made. After several days the sap begins to run. Clean rags are applied to the incisions, and fires are kindled around the trees to hasten the flow. As the rags soak up the sap, they are boiled in caldrons until the balsam rises. The precious stuff is then skimmed off and carried by pack mules from the forests to modern laboratories, where it is partially refined before being sealed in drums for shipping all over the world for pharmaceutical purposes. The timber of the balsam is extremely valuable, for it is very hard, heavy, and compact. It has no well-defined core and is proof against the attack of insects. As the tree ages, the wood acquires a dark red color. Easily polished, it is used in the finest cabinetwork, while because of its hardness it makes good rolls for sugar mills and other agricultural tools.

Ahuachapán, capital of the department of the same name, is 22 miles NW of Sonsonate by car. It can be reached direct from San Salvador by railroad, 72 miles. This department is the most westerly part of the country. It borders Guatemala all along its W side, with the Río de Paz forming a natural boundary. The city is a manufacturing and distributing center; products are chiefly cereals, tobacco, sugar, and coffee. This was the first city to export coffee and thus established the country's greatest industry. A poetic sightseer once said that Ahuachapán was a dream city and looked as if it had been painted onto the landscape. The city is quiet, almost sleepy. Its streets are straight and the houses low and simple, with little decoration. There are no great buildings.

Very popular is the bathhouse, which draws its water, reputedly of some therapeutic value, from the hot springs below the falls of Malacatiupán, a short distance outside of the city. Public baths and bathhouses, supplied with hot mineral water from mountain springs, are found throughout this part of the country. Many homes have only primitive plumbing arrangements, and the baths are well patronized.

Among near-by points of interest, El Llano de Espino (Hawthorn Plain) is popular. This is a treeless plain with a small lake in the center, a haven for fishermen and a natural landing field for airplanes. The Río Molino is near the city, and its waters form innumerable small cascades as they tumble down the mountainside into the falls of Atehuecian, which supply the power for the city's generators. The electric company has made a pleasant resort at the filtration plant and reservoir, where many people go for week-end trips.

HOTEL. Central, facing Parque Concordia.

Excursions from Ahuachapán. A few miles S of the city is the little town of Apaneca. Its ancient name was Apanehecatl (River of Winds), from the fact that a constant wind blowing between the volcanoes of Lagunita and Cumbre assures a cool temperature the year around. Its excellent climate has given the town the reputation of being the flower garden of El Salvador. Its blooms, which appear in all markets, are noted for their beauty and the brilliance of their colors. At 1500 feet above sea level, the town is surrounded by the Apaneca range with its two beautiful lakes, Lagunita, the source of Apaneca's water supply, and Laguna Verde, a resort that is very popular with local sportsmen and tourists.

San Lorenzo, a river port on the Río de Paz, NW of Ahuachapán by car, has been covered as an excursion from San Salvador (p. 28).

SANTA ANA

Second only to San Salvador as a business center, the city of Santa Ana, NE of Ahuachapán and reached by a good road, is capital of the department of the same name. The trip from Ahuachapán is about 25 miles by railroad. Santa Ana is served both by the Salvador Railway and by the International Railways of Central America, and there are railroad connections with Acajutla via Sonsonate (66 miles) and with San Salvador (38 miles); it can also be reached by road from these places. It lies on the Pan American Highway connecting Guatemala and San Salvador.

The department of Santa Ana occupies a large and fertile valley almost surrounded by a gigantic amphitheater of mountains. The land, watered by many rivers and streams, yields an abundance of coffee, sugar cane, and other products. There is also rich pasture land. Owing to its strategic position and its proximity to Guatemala, the department is the center of the Western Military Zone. The capital city has a garrison of 3000 officers and men, housed in a modern fortress which has resisted many sieges and witnessed some of the most stirring episodes in the republic's history.

There are good primary and secondary schools in the city of Santa Ana and a municipal library. The National Theater occupies a fine Renaissance building that covers more than half a city block; it is used occasionally for concerts and social events. There are a number of newer and smaller theaters where U. S. moving pictures are shown. The classic Greek building of the art school also serves as the home for the normal school. Other buildings worth seeing include the city hall, the hospital of San Juan de Dios, the children's hospital, the orphanage, and the asylum for the aged and infirm.

The cathedral of Santa Ana is one of El Salvador's finest examples of Spanish Gothic. Woodcarvings by continental masters adorn the interior, and the many images are among the best sculptures in the country. The city has a number of other churches; of chief interest are those of the Virgin of El Carmen, San Lorenzo, and El Calvario. The latter deserves special mention as a good example of Spanish colonial architecture, designed with simplicity and restraint.

HOTELS. Florida**, with an excellent restaurant; Corona*; Internacional*.

EXCURSIONS FROM SANTA ANA

Lake Coatepeque, whose musical name means Eye of the Sea, is a lake without an outlet, 10 miles S by car. Its shores are lined with hotels and private cottages, and it is a favorite week-end resort, 36 miles W of San Salvador, from which it is reached by car or railroad. Swimming, fishing, and sailing are all good, and motor launches, rowboats, and canoes are for hire. Famous for its natural beauty and its mineral water, Coatepeque is called the Vichy of Central America. In the town is a beautiful church, fronting the plaza, where many holy days are celebrated with picturesque processions and ceremonies. Both lake and town are in the shadow of the volcanoes Santa Ana and Izalco.

HOTEL. Monterrey**, on the lakeside.

Lake Guija, on the Guatemalan frontier, 14 miles N of Santa Ana by car, is the largest lake in El Salvador, 15 miles long. Source of the

Río Lempa, this lake and its surrounding countryside are not only popular with fishermen and hunters, but are also of interest to archeologists. On the islands of Lake Guija, half covered with water, are the ruins of an ancient city, probably Ulmeca, believed by some archeologists to be the original Tulla or Tule, cradle of the Toltec and Maya civilizations.

On the S side of the lake is Santiago, a town which has progressed rapidly in the past few years because of its closeness to the Pan American Highway, which crosses the border between Guatemala and El Salvador just a few miles away. It is the first town the motorist passes after leaving Guatemala en route to Santa Ana.

Metapán, reached from Santa Ana by the same road as Lake Guija, is about 20 miles N of the city and 6 miles W of the N end of the lake. Its cathedral is the most ambitious, purest in style, and noblest of the buildings erected by the Spaniards during their occupation of El Salvador, with no trace of indigenous influence. The interior is rich in beautiful woodcarvings, and the images of the saints have a refreshing originality.

Chalchuapa (River of the Marshes) is about 8 miles W of Santa Ana by car or railroad. It is an urban center, 2096 feet above sea level, with clean, straight streets. The older homes are in the best colonial tradition, the newer residences designed with the simplicity of good modern style. Chalchuapa is famous for the battle in which in 1885 President Justo Rufino Barrios of Guatemala lost his life. Here also may be seen the temple of Tagumal, said to have been commenced in the 16th century; from it was taken the image of the Virgin of Tagumal, now in the museum of San Salvador. The oldest houses of Chalchuapa, built of adobe without facing, are literally impregnated with archeological relics. Ornaments, domestic utensils, and stones covered with strange carvings come to light every now and then after some slight earth upheaval. On the way to the Río Pampe, in the vicinity of Chalchuapa, springs of lava are seen spouting along the roadbed. This hot substance also includes archeological fragments. At the ruins of the city of Pampe, which cover about three acres W of the river, are more lava beds, many mounds, and innumerable fragments fashioned by the country's earliest inhabitants.

NORTHERN EL SALVADOR

The two departments which may be called the N region of El Salvador, Chalatenango and Cabañas, abut on Honduras. W and S, Chalatenango is defined by the Río Lempa. More than in any other part of the republic early colonial customs and buildings have been preserved here. It was only late in the 18th century that foreigners or white natives came in in any numbers. Tradition holds that, during the Spanish occupation, being sent to Chalatenango was the same as being exiled. Today, however, the department is not only one of the most picturesque and interesting but is crossed by some good motor roads.

Chalatenango, capital of the department of this name, is quaint and interesting, one of the oldest towns in El Salvador, easily reached 45 miles E of Santa Ana by car. It is 33 miles NE of San Salvador by car. St. John the Baptist (San Juan Bautista), patron saint of the department, is honored on June 24, and an annual fair is held then.

Processions with religious and historic associations precede the festivities. N of the town a road leads into Honduras.

Ilobasco, in the department of Cabañas, is about 30 miles NE of San Salvador, off the Pan American Highway. The town is noted for quaint and picturesque dolls. It is the birthplace of some of El Salvador's outstanding sculptors; nearly all its inhabitants work in clay. Artistic handwork abounds, from humble pitchers and domestic utensils to really fine pottery. Famous nacimientos or figures for Christmas creches come from Ilobasco. Figures of the Christ child, modeled of clay, range in size from that of a grain of rice to 4 inches. Many really artistic models are displayed at the annual fair on September 29. Ilobasco is justly proud of Dominga Herrera, whose hands have created some of the most interesting and colorful examples of this work. Of humble origin, she began to mold clay at the age of six and made tiny hens and complete families of chicks; at 10 she was modeling human figures. Now she specializes in miniature work with a grain of rice as her measure of height. Each figure is unique, made without the help of molds.

HOTEL. Torres*.

Sensuntepeque, capital of the department of Cabañas, is 45 miles NE of San Salvador by car and can also be reached from Ilobasco.

The department of Cabañas, bounded almost entirely by the Río Lempa and its tributaries, was formerly one of the most important in the republic. Most of the indigo used on the continent was produced here. All the inhabitants were concerned with the cultivation of indigo, which has now been supplanted in the market by aniline dyes. Looking about for new industries, the people of Cabañas discovered large deposits of pottery clay and lime, and factories which make attractive earthenware now supply the republic. Cheese-making is another successful industry, and two distilleries are kept busy making fruit wines and liquors. Gold mining on a small scale is carried on.

Sensuntepeque is an attractive town, with a well-designed city hall, schools, fine churches, and a spacious park, where a good bathing beach makes a popular rendezvous. Sensuntepeque holds an annual fair on December 4 in honor of its patroness St. Barbara. This martyr of the 3rd century is said to have been beheaded by her own father, who was immediately struck dead by lightning. This fair is also the occasion for the meeting of the remaining Indian tribes. In the crowded streets, the gaily dressed townspeople mingle with Indians in tribal array and soldiers in resplendent uniforms, for St. Barbara is also the patroness of the artillery, and the army pays her homage.

EASTERN EL SALVADOR

The Pan American Highway is the main artery of motor travel E of San Salvador. One of the five departments which make up the E part of the country is not traversed by it, however. The highway runs through the departments of San Vicente, Usulután, San Miguel, and La Unión, but La Paz, which is the nearest to San Salvador of these E divisions of the republic, is conveniently visited as an excursion off it from San Vicente, continuing through Usulután. The departments of La Paz and Usulután are also served by roads direct from San Salvador and by railroad.

The department of San Vicente, named in honor of St. Vincent de

Paul who founded the Society of Lazarists and the Sisters of Charity, is considered the most beautiful in all the country. The chief products are corn, tobacco, indigo, coffee, fruit, and sugar cane. Shawls, woolen goods, hats, cigars, and sugar are manufactured here for export as well as for the domestic market. Good year-round motor roads connect the towns with other parts of the republic.

SAN VICENTE

In the valley of the Río Alcahuapa, a continuation of that of the Río Jiboa, lies the city which is capital of the department of San Vicente. It is easily reached by car from San Salvador, most of the way by the Pan American Highway and then by a road branching SE. It is also on the route of the International Railways of Central America, 33 miles from San Salvador. The public buildings and churches of this beautiful city, notably the interesting church of the Virgin of El Pilar, are well worth attention. In the heart of the city is the historic Tempisque tree, under which the charter for the foundation of the city was signed, and which has since become a symbol of the department. In 1935 San Vicente celebrated its third centennial with great pomp and solemnity. Shortly afterward, on Dec. 19, 1936, the city experienced the worst earthquake in its history. Unlike many other Salvadorean cities, San Vicente has largely maintained its colonial character. It is both important historically and picturesque, with many buildings dating back to colonial days. Some of the buildings that were ruined by the earthquake are now being reconstructed along their original lines with a minimum of new materials.

San Vicente is the scene of a colorful annual fair on All Saints' Day (Todos Santos), November 1. People arrive early with their wares, coming on foot, in oxcarts and automobiles, and on horseback. Processions, feasting, singing, and dancing are in order. Special honor is paid to Ana Guerra, the Salvadorean saint who was born in San Vicente. Her life and virtues were much like those of St. Rose of Lima.

HOTEL. Iberia*.

EXCURSIONS FROM SAN VICENTE

The departments of La Paz and Usulután have some interesting towns which can be most conveniently visited from San Vicente. La Paz, although one of the smallest departments, is noted for its huge estates, where some of the finest Salvadorean coffee is grown. Crossed SE-NW by the Río Jiboa and honeycombed with roads, the department is unequaled for its agricultural products, which include tobacco, pineapples, sugar, and vanilla as well as coffee. Some of the land is given over to cattle-raising, while mills and factories in the towns produce silk and cotton goods and cigars.

Zacatecoluca, capital of the department of La Paz, is 12 miles S of San Vicente by car or by the International Railways. It is about 30 miles from San Salvador by the motor road which passes through Santo Tomás de Aquino and Olocuilta, 45 miles by the less direct railroad route.

HOTEL. Italia*.

Excursion from Zacatecoluca. In the little town of Santa María

Ostuma, near by, the special fiesta of the department of La Paz is notably celebrated. This is Candlemas (La Candelaria), February 2. A religious procession, followed by the blessing of those who attend, precedes the opening of the market. An annual fair is held on this date, and general festivities and gaiety mingle with business transactions.

Usulután, capital of the department of this name, is 32 miles SE of Zacatecoluca and can be reached by car or railroad. It is reached from San Salvador (77 miles) by both car and railroad.

The department of Usulután lies along the coast between the valleys of the Río Lempa and the Río San Miguel. Its principal occupations are agricultural, chiefly the raising of coffee and cattle. Other products are tobacco, bananas, corn, and beans. Tanning and the preparation of hides for export have been gaining in importance during the last few years.

HOTEL. Central*.

Alegría (Joy), some 20 miles N of Usulután by car, is a small town nestling beside Lake Alegría, which is hidden away at the bottom of a volcanic crater. The locality is attractive.

_____

Three miles N of Alegría the route returns to the Pan American Highway at the town of Merced.

SAN MIGUEL

The E metropolis of the republic, capital of the department of the same name, San Miguel is situated at the foot of the volcanoes San Miguel and Chinameca. It is reached by car or railroad, 25 miles NE of Usulután. A little more than 100 miles from San Salvador, it is connected with the capital by the Pan American Highway and by railroad. The Pan American Highway continues from here into Honduras through the department of La Unión. Since the opening of the International Railways, San Miguel's commercial importance has fallen off, since most of its business has been transferred to San Salvador. However, what it lacks industrially is compensated for by its charm. The most beautiful parks in the republic are in San Miguel.

A tour of the city should take in the church of Santo Domingo, the cathedral, and the church of Chinameca with its gardens, fountains, and statues. The municipal buildings are good, and there are some old Spanish residences.

HOTELS. Hispano Americano*, on Calle Jérez; Pensión Vaquero.

LA UNION

Leading shipping port of the republic, La Unión on the Gulf of Fonseca is capital of its department, which bears the same name. The town is 27 miles SE of San Miguel by car and about 37 miles by railroad, since the line of the International Railways swings S and W to go near Lake Camalotal. From San Salvador, this port is about 140 miles by car or railroad; through trains take 9 hours.

Although it has only 7000 inhabitants, La Unión handles 57 per cent of El Salvador's exports and 31 per cent of its imports. Steamers drawing 25 feet can dock at Cutuco, a mile away. Regular freight services from San Francisco, Cristóbal, and New York make this a port of call.

One of the local industries is the making of articles from the shells of tortoises caught in the Gulf of Fonseca. This gulf is often regarded as the most strategic harbor between San Francisco and Panama. It is excellent for swimming and fishing and is a popular resort during the summer or dry season.

HOTEL. América*.

Amapala in Honduras is reached from La Unión by motorboat across the Gulf of Fonseca. See the guide to Honduras (p. 27).

INDEX TO THE REGIONAL GUIDE

THE REPUBLIC OF NICARAGUA

NICARAGUA

BY CHARLES PARMER

Nicaragua, largest country in Central America, lies between Honduras and Costa Rica, and fronts 300 miles on the Caribbean and 200 miles on the Pacific. It is crossed by two mountain chains, and has two great lakes near the western coast: Lake Managua, 38 miles long and 10 to 16 miles wide; and Lake Nicaragua to the south—connected to Lake Managua by the Río Tipitapa—about 100 miles long and 45 miles wide. The country, while one of the hottest north of Panama, holds unique attractions in its scenery and the friendliness of its people. The republic is just emerging from four centuries of travail: two of pillage by conquistadores, another in which it was battleground in the struggle of England and Spain for New World supremacy; and a fourth of internal strife, earthquake, fire. Its progressive spirit is shown by the capital city, Managua—rebuilt in the 1930's along modernistic lines, after being twice partially destroyed by quake and flame. The people, mainly a mixture of Indian and Spanish, are a handsome race given to much gaiety. Their feast days are elaborate and colorful.

HISTORY

When the Spaniards first came to what today is Nicaragua the region was inhabited by several Indian tribes. In the north and west the chief Diriangen ruled a hunting people who were rich in gold. In the northeast, along what is now called the Mosquito Coast, lived the primitive Mosquitos, for whom the section was named. Not a friendly people, they withdrew into the jungle with the advent of the Spaniards. Their descendants live there today, some with white and Negro admixture, partly due to a slave ship that was wrecked on the coast in the 18th century. A third tribe was ruled by Nicarao, and the country's name is said to have been derived from his. Nicarao's people lived on the shores of vast Lake Nicaragua, with their capital at a point on the western shore called Cocibolca near the present town of Rivas. Here and in the surrounding valleys they dwelt peacefully, raising poultry and growing corn and beans.

DISCOVERY. In the summer of 1502, on his fourth and last voyage, Columbus touched on the shore of what is now Honduras. Assured by the aborigines that immense treasure was to be found farther on, he sailed east along the northern Honduran coast against difficult currents and head winds and rounded the northeastern tip of Nicaragua, which he named Cabo Gracias a Dios (Cape Thanks to God). Then he sailed south until he came to a large quiet harbor where a river swept into the sea. Here he dropped anchor and sent boats ashore for water. One boat capsized on the return trip, and all hands were lost. Because of this, Columbus named the river Río del Desastre (River of Disaster). It now is the Río Grande (Great River). Columbus continued southward to the mouth of the Río San Juan, which now defines most of the country's southern boundary. There he landed Sept. 16, 1502, and took possession in the name of the king of Spain. The Indians told him that on the shores of a lake some days' journey inland there were natives who had a great deal of gold. He believed this lake was the

River Ganges, and he sailed on, determined to find a short cut to the East Indies by water.

CONQUEST. Almost two decades later a group of conquistadores under Gil González Dávila explored this land in one of the little-known dramas of the conquest. With Andrés Cereceda and Andrés Niño, González Dávila sailed Jan. 21, 1522, from the Pearl Islands in the Gulf of Panama, on the Pacific side, with a shipload of horses, merchandise, and ammunition. One vessel became disabled, and the explorers put in to shore with a hundred men. Niño was instructed to proceed up the coast in search of a harbor. González Dávila then pressed on through the present Costa Rica and after some days met Niño on the coast. It was agreed that Niño should take two vessels and continue north, mapping the shoreline, while González Dávila pushed inland.

Those of the invaders who had beards so frightened the natives that González Dávila commanded all his men to raise beards. If a man could not grow a beard fast enough he was given a false one. A chief named Nicoya came forth to meet the conquistador, presenting him with "14,000 pieces of eight in gold 13 carats fine and six idols of the same metal, each a span long." In return González Dávila preached the faith and "gave him some Spanish toys and baptized him and all his subjects, being 6000 in number." Nicoya told of the still greater chief Nicarao who lived in splendor by a great inland lake. When he had come within reach of Nicarao's settlement González Dávila sent forth runners bearing gifts and tidings of a new faith. Nicarao in turn sent emissaries to welcome the white leader. When Nicarao and the Spanish leader met, the conquistador easily converted the chief and his 9000 followers to the Catholic faith and then claimed their lands and their lake for his king. Heartened by these successes, González Dávila continued northward, and this time the chief Diriangen came with warriors to meet him. Gifts were exchanged, and González Dávila broached the subject of religion. The chief, saying he wished to meditate on the matter, withdrew. He returned on Aug. 17, 1522, prepared for battle instead of prayer. Though facing overwhelming numbers, the Spaniards beat off the attack.

When the expedition returned to the coast Niño reported the discovery of a vast bay to the north, with volcanic mountains jutting up from its surface. González Dávila named this body of water the Gulf of Fonseca in honor of his patron Juan Rodríguez de Fonseca, bishop of Burgos. The Gulf of Fonseca is bordered by the present countries of El Salvador, Honduras, and Nicaragua. The expedition returned to Panama on June 25, 1523.

COLONIAL PERIOD. The next conquistador of note to penetrate the land was Francisco Hernández de Córdoba, for whom Nicaragua's monetary unit, the córdoba, is named. He founded the first Spanish city in Nicaragua at the northwest end of Lake Nicaragua, calling it Granada. This was in 1524. A separate government was established at Granada and was maintained until the formation of the captaincy general of Guatemala, which included Nicaragua. The early Spaniards found relatively little gold in spite of their intent search, though centuries later Nicaragua was to become a major producer of the metal. In the 16th century the wealth that the conquistadores obtained came from trade with the West Indies, Panama, and Spain. On the north shore of Lake Managua, at the foot of the volcano Momotombo,

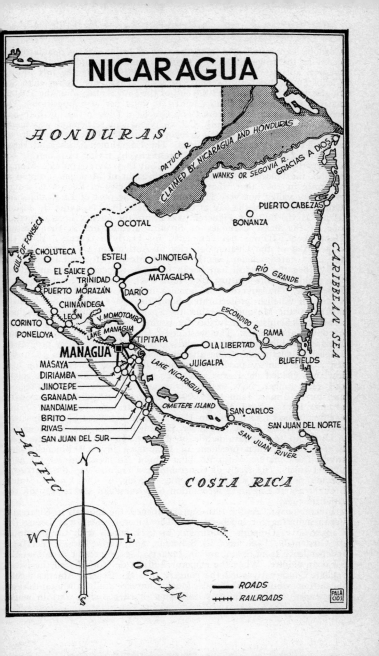

NICARAGUA

HONDURAS

PATUCA R.

CLAIMED BY NICARAGUA AND HONDURAS

WANKS OR SEGOVIA R.

GRACIAS A DIOS

CARIBBEAN SEA

PUERTO CABEZAS

BONANZA

OCOTAL

GULF OF FONSECA

CHOLUTECA

EL SAUCE

ESTELI

JINOTEGA

TRINIDAD

MATAGALPA

RÍO GRANDE

PUERTO MORAZÁN

DARÍO

CHINANDEGA

ESCONDIDO R.

RAMA

CORINTO

LEÓN

V. MOMOTOMBO

PONELOYA

LAKE MANAGUA

TIPITAPA

LA LIBERTAD

BLUEFIELDS

MANAGUA

MASAYA

JUIGALPA

DIRIAMBA

LAKE NICARAGUA

JINOTEPE

GRANADA

NANDAIME

OMETEPE ISLAND

SAN CARLOS

BRITO

RIVAS

SAN JUAN DEL NORTE

SAN JUAN DEL SUR

SAN JUAN RIVER

PACIFIC

N

COSTA RICA

W — E

S

OCEAN

ROADS

++++ RAILROADS

PALA CIOS

Córdoba had founded in 1524 the city of León. A few Spaniards located in the town of Nueva Segovia, a mining center in the north western uplands, and a few more staked out land by the fort of San Carlos at the head of the Río San Juan. There were fewer than 500 Spaniards in the country at the end of the 16th century, but the 150,000 natives were not sufficiently united to offer serious opposition. The east coast was explored from Cabo Gracias a Dios in the north to San Juan del Norte in the south, but no permanent settlement was made. English, Dutch, and French freebooters at one time or another assaulted the west coast settlements. The Englishmen Drake and Hawkins attacked in 1572 and in 1577 respectively, trying to penetrate the country by way of the Río San Juan, but they were repulsed. Momotombo, the volcano which stands within sight of Managua, erupted so violently in 1609 that what was left of the city of León was moved west to a valley not very far from the Pacific port of El Realejo, situated at the end of the bay of Corinto. Here, in 1746, under the bishop Isidro Marin Bullen y Figueroa, was begun the mighty León cathedral one of the finest examples of Spanish architecture in the Western Hemisphere. It was not completed for nearly a century. With the destruction of the Guatemalan city of Antigua in 1773 León became the most noted religious center between Mexico City and Lima, Peru.

By 1625 the English had begun to settle the east coast, and about the middle of the century they took over Cabo Gracias a Dios and Bluefields. The governor of Jamaica in 1687 declared the Mosquito Coast an English protectorate. Soon thereafter English adventurers stirred up the Mosquitos against the Spaniards. Meanwhile Spain harassed the colonists still further by issuing decrees against the growing of olives and grapes. The west coast trade in cacao with Peru and Mexico was blighted by pirate raids, and as the 18th century progressed English raiders made strong attacks on forts in the Río San Juan district. The country produced agricultural wealth, however. The lush lowlands yielded sugar cane and cacao, and the hilly lands made splendid cattle ranges. New settlements sprang up in the Chontales region, and by 1750 more than 1,500,000 cacao trees were said to be growing around Rivas. Lord Nelson captured a strategic fort in 1780 but eventually was forced out. In 1786 England conceded Spain's mastery of the Mosquito Coast. However, English influence was felt along the Atlantic up to the last decade of the 19th century, when Gen. José Santos Zelaya, then president of Nicaragua, invaded Bluefields and expelled the native Mosquito king whom England had set up as a puppet ruler. The result of General Zelaya's efforts was the Harrison-Altamirano treaty which, with the backing of the United States, brought about England's recognition of Nicaraguan sovereignty on the Atlantic coast.

INDEPENDENCE. As the 19th century opened, the Liberals in Nicaragua began agitating for independence. The Liberal center was León; the Conservative, Granada. Nicaragua in 1821 joined with the provinces of Guatemala, Honduras, El Salvador, and Costa Rica in declaring independence from Spain, and in January 1822 it became a part of the Mexican empire. When the emperor Agustín de Iturbide fell the Nicaraguan Conservatives led the country into the Central American confederation while the Liberals fought unsuccessfully to establish an independent nation. In 1838, following disastrous civil wars in which

León was partially destroyed, the Liberals obtained control and established a republic with León as capital. But internal strife and other serious troubles continued for two decades. The Mosquitos rose in revolt. Leaders in Honduras and El Salvador wanted to establish a new Central American union, and Nicaragua fought both countries in order to maintain its independence.

The Conservatives then gained control of the government, moving the capital back to Granada, and the Liberals looked for outside aid. The adventurer William Walker from Tennessee had entered Central America with 56 men and an ambition to rule a Latin empire. He was engaged by the Liberals to head their cause, and he soon made himself president. The beginning of the California gold rush in 1849 had given Nicaragua new importance because of the short route between the Atlantic and the Pacific Oceans by way of the Río San Juan and Lake Nicaragua, from whose western shore it is only a short distance to the Pacific. Commodore Cornelius Vanderbilt was doing a thriving business transporting gold-seekers and settlers to California by way of Nicaragua. He had a line of freight and passenger steamers from New York and New Orleans to San Juan del Norte (Greytown), river steamers on the Río San Juan and Lake Nicaragua, and stagecoaches across the strip of land to San Juan del Sur on the Pacific, where his passengers embarked for California. Walker's activities made the operation of Vanderbilt's line difficult, and the commodore backed Walker's opponents with material aid. The filibuster was driven from the country, and in 1860 he was seized and shot near Trujillo in Honduras.

The expulsion of Walker helped to unite the factions. The capital was moved to Managua in 1858, where it remains today, and a new constitution was adopted. The Conservatives ruled, 1863-93. Revolutions were quickly stifled, and there was much material development. During this time the telegraph service was extended; lake and river transportation was speeded up; coffee, mahogany, and bananas became important exports; schools were established, and consuls and ministers were sent abroad. In 1893 a successful revolution placed José Santos Zelaya in power. He remained president for 17 years. Then came both internal and external trouble. England pressed for payment of debts, the currency depreciated, and in 1909 Zelaya resigned in favor of José Madriz.

Three years later, in 1912, Adolfo Díaz, who had become president, asked for United States marines to help maintain order. The marines landed and remained until 1925. No sooner had they departed than revolutions began afresh. The marines returned in 1927, and President Calvin Coolidge sent Col. Henry L. Stimson to discover a method of establishing peace. Colonel Stimson persuaded the leading factions to agree to an orderly election, and Gen. José Moncada, a Liberal, was chosen president. One leader refused to acquiesce. This was Agusto Sandino, an old henchman of Moncada's. Sandino withdrew into the northern jungles and from there harassed the government. The marines pursued him unsuccessfully until they were withdrawn from Nicaragua in 1932. Sandino was killed in 1934.

Gen. Anastasio Somoza, leader of the Liberal party, became president on Jan. 1, 1937. President Somoza, who spent some of his formative years in the United States, has worked hard to consolidate all factions. He has enlarged the educational system and begun an extensive building program in Managua, which had been stricken by fire and earth-quake. He was a guest at the White House in 1939. One result of the conference was his promulgation of plans for a barge canal linking the Atlantic and Managua by way of the lakes. United States Army engineers were assigned to survey the route. Then the war broke out. President Somoza and thousands of other Nicaraguans, however, still expect the construction of an interoceanic ship canal to supplement the Panama Canal. A Nicaraguan canal seemed at one time almost on the verge of realization. According to one story, probably fanciful, the United States Congress was led to change its mind about the route by the arrival of some Nicaraguan stamps depicting active volcanoes. The proposed route of the Nicaraguan canal as mapped by United States Army engineers begins on the Caribbean side near San Juan del Norte, follows the Río Deseado for a short distance, then enters the valley of the Río San Juan and runs into Lake Nicaragua. The route would cross the lake at the southern end, coming out below the old town of Rivas, and cut through to the Pacific at Brito, only 15 miles from the lake. There would be three locks at either end of the canal. It was estimated that the project would necessitate the excavation of about 600,000,000 yards of rock and earth and the placing of about 7,000,000 yards of concrete, with the building of all accessories, such as railroads, highways, dams, power plants, harbors, and towns. Lake Nicaragua provides an ample supply of water. The canal would be about three and a half times as long as the Panama Canal. Its deepest cut would lack 150 feet of being as deep as the deepest part of the Gaillard or Culebra Cut.

GOVERNMENT. Under the constitution of 1939 the president of Nica-ragua is elected for a six-year term and is assisted by a cabinet whose members administer the government's various departments. Legislative power is vested in a Congress composed of a Senate and a Chamber of Deputies. Congress convenes for 60 days each April 15. Members of the Chamber are elected for six years by direct popular vote, one deputy and one substitute for each 30,000 inhabitants. Deputies must be 25 or more years old. Senators, also elected for six years, must be at least 40 years old. Former presidents become senators for life.

THE LAND

With an area of some 57,150 square miles Nicaragua is about the size of England or the state of Alabama and is the largest of the Cen-tral American republics. The country's population, however, is esti-mated at only 1,172,000, resulting in the lowest population density for any of these republics except Panama.

Nicaragua is bounded N by Honduras, S by Costa Rica. However, to journey into Nicaragua from the neighboring countries is to come suddenly into a different world. Honduras, El Salvador, and Costa Rica are highland countries, with their greatest concentrations of people and their most important cities and towns on mountain uplands. The heart of Nicaragua, on the other hand, is lowland country. Her chief towns and most densely populated districts are in a broad lowland belt that begins at the Gulf of Fonseca, parallels the Pacific coast to the country's S boundary, and then runs diagonally toward the Carib-bean Sea. The last part of the belt is more or less equally divided be-tween Nicaragua and Costa Rica.

Two large lakes, connected by a 15-mile river, occupy more than two-thirds of the section of this lowland belt that lies wholly within Nicaragua. Lake Managua is about 40 miles long by 16 miles at its greatest width. Lake Nicaragua, S of it, 100 miles long and with a maximum width of 45 miles, about four times as large as the Great Salt Lake in Utah, is the largest inland body of water in the Western Hemisphere between the Great Lakes of the United States and Canada and Lake Titicaca of Peru and Bolivia. In size it compares closely with the latter. Lake Managua is 136 feet above sea level, Lake Nicaragua only 106. These connecting lakes drain to the Caribbean Sea through the Río San Juan.

The NW end of the Nicaraguan lowland, above the N end of Lake Managua, lies open to the Pacific but is broken by a line of more than 20 volcanoes beginning with the beautifully symmetrical Coseguina cone which overlooks the Gulf of Fonseca. The highest, Volcán Viejo (Old Volcano), rises sheer above the lowland to 5918 feet. Volcanoes border the W shore of both lakes, and in Lake Nicaragua the 18-mile-long island of Ometepe consists of two cones, rising respectively to 5064 and 4350 feet, connected by a narrow neck of land only a few feet above the level of the lake. Many of these volcanoes are still at least mildly active, and as recently as 1931 an earthquake wrought such havoc in Managua that the city had to be practically rebuilt. The rich fertility of the lowland and the consequent concentration of the population in it is due to the volcanic soil derived from ash and lava. The lakes are further separated from the Pacific by a low range of hills, also of volcanic origin, with the highest crest slightly over 3000 feet. These hills are crisscrossed with roads and trails and well sprinkled with settlements.

Nicaragua's most densely populated district is along the W shore of the N half of Lake Nicaragua and between that lake and Lake Managua. Paradoxically enough, though the population is agricultural, there is nowhere else in Central America so close a grouping of large towns. Here, favored by rich soil and plentiful native labor, there have been worked since colonial times the estates large and small that yield the country's chief agricultural contributions to the markets of the world —coffee, cacao, sugar, cotton, tobacco, to name them in the order of their importance. Granada is the center of this district, as it has been since early colonial times; in that city and to a lesser extent in the towns and villages clustered around it live most of the landowners and farm laborers.

Another area of population concentration, more or less continuous with the Granada district but less important because of poorer soil, less abundant rainfall, and an insufficient supply of native labor, lies close to the W flank of the line of volcanoes that runs NW from Lake Managua. Here the chief product is sustenance crops. In this area was located the first capital of independent Nicaragua, León, probably because of easy access to the excellent port of Corinto. Between León and Granada lies the modern capital of Managua, established as such in 1858 in an attempt to compromise between the former's Liberal faction and the latter's Conservatives. León, however, remains the intellectual center of the country, Granada the center of its wealth and aristocracy. Managua, with a population of about 70,000, is nearly as large as León and Granada combined; León, with about 50,000 people, is nearly twice the size of Granada.

Nicaragua faces the Caribbean Sea with a broad coastal lowland which averages more than 75 miles in width. This is the famous Mosquito Coast. Here, because of the heavy rainfall and the dense forest cover, there has never been more than a sparse population of either native Indians or foreigners. Negroes from the West Indies arrived at this coast at an early date, and the greater part of the population now consists of aboriginal tribes and Negro communities and the mixture of the two bloods. Many of the people still speak English as a result of long years of British domination. There has been considerable lumbering in the lowlands, in recent years mainly by companies from the United States, and some placer gold-mining. Bananas have long been an export crop of considerable importance in the Bluefields region. Between the Pacific and the Caribbean lowland is a wedge-shaped highland region that is a continuation of the highlands of Honduras. Settlement there is sparse. There is some cattle-raising and coffee-growing along the W edge, but the inhabitants live mainly a self-sufficient existence.

The most sensational modern development in Nicaragua's life and economy has been the upsurge of gold-mining as the result of new discoveries and of changes in world conditions. Gold-mining has long been of considerable importance, but in the 1930's thousands of tons of supplies and heavy machinery were transported inland by plane for the establishment of new mines and the expansion of old ones. Several of the mines receive practically all their supplies by plane. The place of gold in Nicaragua's exports rose in a decade from 5 per cent of the total in 1930 to over 60 per cent in 1940.

PRACTICAL INFORMATION

HOW TO REACH NICARAGUA

From the United States. Minimum first-class one-way steamship fare (1941) from New Orleans to Puerto Cabezas is about $100; fare by plane from Brownsville, Tex., to Managua is $116.

BY STEAMER. Standard Fruit & Steamship Co.; main office: 140 Carondelet St., New Orleans, La.; New York office: 11 Broadway. Has sailings to Nicaragua's E coast from New Orleans via Havana, Cuba, and Cristóbal, C. Z. Voyage takes 8 days. Steamship transportation from the United States to Nicaragua's W coast has been discontinued, though coastwise steamers still give service from neighboring countries · (1941).

BY AIR. Pan American Airways; main office: 135 E. 42nd St., New York. Has service to Managua from Brownsville, Tex., via Tampico, Mexico City, and Tapachula in Mexico; Guatemala City (overnight stop); San Salvador, El Salvador, and Tegucigalpa, Honduras. Flight takes about 25 hours, with an overnight stop.

From Other Central American Countries. In addition to the services shown above there is air service between Managua and El Salvador, Honduras, British Honduras, and Costa Rica via Transportes Aéreos Centro-Americanos (TACA).

From La Unión in El Salvador or San Lorenzo or Amapala in Honduras a motor launch can be taken across the Gulf of Fonseca to Puerto Morazán, which has railroad connections with Managua.

The Pan American Highway will give access E from Honduras to Esteli and Managua, NW from Costa Rica to Rivas and Managua.

AIDS TO TRAVELERS

Nicaraguan Representation in the U. S. The Nicaraguan Legation is at 1521 New Hampshire Ave., Washington, D. C. Consular officers are found in Long Beach, Los Angeles, Sacramento, San Diego, and San Francisco, Calif.; Washington, D. C.; Miami and Tampa, Fla.; Chicago, Ill.; New Orleans, La.; Baltimore, Md.; Detroit, Mich.; St. Louis, Mo.; New York; Philadelphia, Pa.; Brownsville, Corpus Christi, Dallas, Galveston, and San Antonio, Tex.; Cristóbal, C. Z. (also Panama City, Panama), and San Juan, P. R.

U. S. Representation in Nicaragua. The U. S. Legation and Consulate are in Managua. A consular office is in Matagalpa.

Local Sources of Information. Travel information in Nicaragua can be secured at the offices of Pan American Airways and Transportes Aéreos Centro-Americanos (TACA) in Managua. The Junta de Turismo de Nicaragua (Nicaraguan Tourist Bureau) has offices in the Gran Hotel building in Managua.

Climate. In the east rain falls frequently throughout the year; part of the Caribbean coast is one of the world's most rainy regions. The Pacific coast has distinct dry and wet seasons. In Managua the dry months are December-May. The temperature throughout the country, with little seasonal variation, is 60°-90° F., though in the higher altitudes of the central mountain areas excessive heat is felt only at midday. Climatically Nicaragua may be divided into three sections: the Atlantic and Pacific coastal regions, tierra caliente or hot country; the sparsely settled interior uplands, tierra templada or temperate country; the highlands and volcanic peaks, tierra fría or cold country.

Clothing. The lightest type of tropical clothing is worn throughout the year. Raincoats are essential.

Health. The Nicaraguan health department strives to improve hygienic conditions throughout the country and especially in Managua. Water is chlorinated in the larger cities, though it is safest everywhere to drink boiled or bottled water. Care should be used about eating raw vegetables and fruits that are not peeled. In the hot sections it is advisable to sleep under mosquito netting, and it is best to guard against malaria with quinine.

Sports and Recreations. Baseball is the national game. However, tennis, soccer, softball, basketball, volleyball, and golf are also played with enthusiasm. The new golf course SW of the American Legation in the section of Managua called Las Piedrecitas is open to visitors.

Horseback riding is popular. U. S. women visitors have introduced riding astride, though most Nicaraguan women still ride side-saddle. There are no established racetracks, but on fiesta days there is impromptu horse racing in the small communities.

Bullfights and cockfights are held throughout Nicaragua, usually on Saturdays, Sundays, and feast days. The former is in the Central American style, with the torero usually ending the conflict not by killing the bull but by mounting him and riding rodeo style.

Deep-sea fishing is good off Corinto on the Pacific coast and off Bluefields on the Atlantic. A unique attraction is deep-sea fishing in a fresh-water body of water, Lake Nicaragua, the only body of fresh water in the world where sharks are found.

In the jungles both of the interior and near the Atlantic are found alligators and jaguars. On the Pacific side are wild boars, armadillos, prairie dogs, ducks, partridges, deer, and wild turkeys.

Dancing is the most popular social pastime. It is indulged in nightly at social clubs in Managua. The stranger can usually obtain a card to one of the clubs. The chaperon system prevails in Nicaragua, and young unmarried women are carefully supervised at all social functions.

Currency. Nicaragua's monetary unit is the córdoba, standardized at $.20 U. S. currency; the street rate is often higher. Money-changers operate on several business corners in Managua. The córdoba is divided into 100 centavos. Silver coins are issued worth 5, 10, 25, and 50 centavos; copper, ½ and 1 centavo.

Banks. The sole bank of issue for paper currency is the Banco Nacional de Nicaragua, with main offices in Managua and branch offices at Bluefields, León, and Granada. Managua also has a branch of the Bank of London and South America.

Cost of Living. Living and travel expenses in Nicaragua are not high. Managua has two first-class hotels, Gran and Lido Palace. Rates for room with bath are $3-$6 a day, including meals (1941). Rates in smaller communities are lower.

Local foodstuffs are inexpensive.

Transportation. HIGHWAYS. Partly because of the country's mountainous nature there are only about 1100 miles of motor roads in the republic. Many of these are at present not passable during the rainy season, though the work of macadamizing roads is being pushed energetically. Inquiry about road conditions should be made before starting on automobile trips to the interior. Several main roads radiate from the lake district: the circuit road from Managua to Diriamba, Jinotepe, Nandaime, and Masaya, with a link to Granada from the last of these towns; the extension S from Jinotepe through Nandaime and Rivas to San Juan del Sur on the Pacific coast; the 40-mile road from Lake Nicaragua through Juigalpa, NE to La Libertad; the 90-mile road from Managua to Matagalpa, NE, passing through Tipitapa and Darío. Beyond Darío a road goes NW as far as Ocotal; from Managua through Tipitapa to Esteli this is part of the Pan American Highway, whose route will continue W into Honduras. S of Managua the Pan American Highway runs to Rivas and will eventually reach the Costa Rican border.

The new road from Managua to Rama, which will carry the road via Juigalpa and La Libertad farther E, is not yet open for general traffic (1941). This is one of the most practical achievements of the administration of President Somoza. Crossing some of Nicaragua's most picturesque sections, it will provide an effective connection between the Pacific and Atlantic coasts. According to the Nicaraguan Tourist Commission, the trip from Managua to Rama will take about 9 hours when the road is open to general traffic. Rama is on the Río Escondido, and the journey from that point is continued by boat to Bluefields on the Caribbean coast.

RAILROADS. Nicaragua's national railroad, the Pacific Railway (Ferrocarril del Pacífico de Nicaragua), the longest in the country, is 171 miles long, near the Pacific coast. It runs inland from Corinto on the coast 13 miles to Chinandega, swerves SE through the lovely and fertile valley of the Morabios mountains to León and Managua, and proceeds through Masaya to Granada on Lake Nicaragua. A branch runs N from Chinandega to Puerto Morazán on the Gulf of Fonseca. Another runs from León inland to El Sauce. A third runs from Masaya to Jinotepe and Diriamba. There is also a short railroad line from the Lake Nicaragua port of San Jorge to Rivas and the Pacific port of San Juan del Sur.

AIRLINES. Most passenger traffic in Nicaragua is by air. Managua is on the Pan American Airways main route from North to South America and on the TACA international line through Central America. TACA likewise maintains plane service from Puerto Cabezas to Managua via Bluefields and from Managua to Matagalpa and Jinotega. It also operates freight and passenger services to gold mines in the interior.

COASTWISE NAVIGATION is important to Nicaragua. Boat journeys, though primitive, are colorful. The visitor can board a schooner or motor vessel that shuttles from Bluefields to San Juan del Norte, Puerto Limón in Costa Rica, and Cristóbal, C. Z.

In normal times traffic is heavier on the Pacific coast. San Juan del Sur and Corinto are normally ports for lines running from North America to Panama and South America and from the W to the E coast via the Panama Canal.

WATERWAYS. When traffic justifies it launches ply the Río San Juan from San Juan del Norte on the Atlantic coast to San Carlos on Lake Nicaragua. This is the old gold rush route. The trip is primitive and slow but interesting to the traveler who is fond of jungle country. The Río Wanks or Segovia in the country's NE part is navigable by medium-sized craft for more than 100 miles; small vessels carrying two or three passengers and freight go almost to its source, 300 miles in the interior. Boats run about 40 miles up the Río Escondido from Bluefields. Some other streams are navigable by light-draft boats.

A small steamer makes the round of ports on Lake Nicaragua.

Postage. Ordinary mail is $.03 an ounce to and from the United States, airmail $.12 a half ounce (1941). The republic's 135 post offices provide parcel post and money order services.

Telegraph and Cable Services. The government operates the local telegraph lines. All America Cables has offices in San Juan del Sur and Managua, and the Tropical Radio Telegraph Co. has offices in Bluefields and Managua connecting with the outside world by radiotelephone and telegraph. The republic operates more than 2000 miles of telephone line and has a good network of radiotelegraph service known as Radio Nacional; there are connections with similar services in the other Central American republics.

Souvenirs and Handicrafts. Nicaragua's finest product is alligator goods, belts, handbags, brief cases, traveling bags. Skilled craftsmen in the cities make goods to order. Carved trinkets are sold as souvenirs, and fine hats of the Panama type are on sale. The fiber hammocks made by the Indians who live near Masaya are noted for their strength and durability.

Food. Nacatamales, the Nicaraguan version of hot tamales, are delicacies cooked in banana leaves. Pork, plantains, beans, rice, tortillas, and frijoles are staples. U. S. food can be secured at port restaurants and in city hotels. The avocado is especially good here, and zapotes, pineapples, coconuts, mangoes, and plantains are plentiful. Native meats and poultry are good. It is difficult to get fruits and vegetables out of season.

Holidays. A gay people, the Nicaraguans hold many celebrations, both religious and national. The recognized holidays are New Year's; January 6, Epiphany (Día de los Reyes); Holy Week, especially Good Friday; Ascension Day; Corpus Christi; July 4, Independence Day; July 14, Bastille Day, celebrated because Nicaragua, like other Latin lands in the Western Hemisphere, has been under French influence; July 24, Bolívar Day; August 15, Assumption Day; September 14, battle of San Jacinto; September 15, Central American Independence Day; October 12, Columbus Day (Día de la Raza—Day of the Race); November 1, All Saints (Todos Santos); November 11, Armistice Day; November 28, Peace Day; December 8, Immaculate Conception; Christmas.

Fiestas. Various sections have celebrations in honor of their patron saints. These days are given over to colorful processions, sometimes gay with banners and firecrackers, sometimes solemn with candles and crosses. Holy Week and the December festivals are colorful throughout the republic. Chinandega celebrates the Feast of St. Anne on July 26 with prayers and processions. The great fiesta of the Most Holy Trinity is celebrated in Granada, beginning about July 1. The year's greatest fiesta is that of Santo Domingo, celebrated in Managua on August 1-10.

Nicaragua's E coast has convenient connections with the inland and Pacific coast areas only by air (1941). Steamship passengers debarking at an E port now usually travel by air to the cities of the interior and the Pacific coast. A primitive and adventurous passage by launch may be made from San Juan del Norte up the Río San Juan to Lake Nicaragua and thence by steamer to Granada, near the capital. Managua (p. 18) is often reached directly by air from neighboring countries.

THE CARIBBEAN COAST

The Caribbean coast is low, swampy, and monotonous, with numerous estuaries, lagoons, islets, and bordering reefs. It is one of the rainiest areas on earth, and rainfall as high as 300 inches a year has been recorded near the mouth of the Río San Juan. The population of E Nicaragua is composed mainly of some relatively primitive Indians and of the Mosquitos, who are today largely of mixed Indian, Negro, and white blood. The latter speak a dialect largely derived from English. The Mosquito Coast was named for them. In the ports and on the banana plantations are a number of Negroes from Jamaica.

Puerto Cabezas, also known as Bragman's Bluff, N on the Caribbean coast, was at one time an important banana port, but the cultivation of bananas in the region has been abandoned because of root diseases. Today the port handles wood and metals. A private railroad which at one time ran inland from the port about 120 miles into the lumber country along the Río Wawa has been mostly taken up and a good deal of its equipment sold to the Nicaraguan government for use on the Pacific Railway. Some hauling of bamboo for export is still done on the remaining track by means of gasoline cars.

Excursions from Puerto Cabezas. Bonanza and Siuna are gold-mining centers in hilly country inland, reached by TACA plane. They are also served by plane from Managua. Both places were developed in recent years with machinery that was taken in by plane.

Bonanza is 76 miles from Puerto Cabezas. U. S.-owned and operated, it employs more than 1000 men. It has a social club for workers, library, church, commissary, and an up-to-date hospital.

Siuna, 94 miles from Puerto Cabezas, is Canadian-owned, the richest mine now being worked in Nicaragua. All materials, provisions, and merchandise required by the mine are brought in by plane. There are a hospital, school, commissariat, ice plant, club, and facilities for various sports.

Bluefields, with 10,000 inhabitants, is Nicaragua's leading banana port. The town takes its name from the Dutch pirate Blewfeldt who sought plunder in the Caribbean. Bluefields also exports some gold, silver, coconuts, and alligator skins. While Spanish is the prevailing tongue, English is commonly spoken in business houses. The city lies behind a bluff, with the Río Escondido or Bluefields River and its estuaries near it. Boats run about 40 miles up this river. Completion of the road from Rama to Managua will make it possible to reach the capital by boat on the Río Escondido to Rama and thence by car.

HOTELS. Bluefields; St. James.

NOTE. Hotels are here classified by rates. Two stars indicate the higher rates for the country in question and also, in nearly all cases, mean good accommodations. One star means rates in the medium brackets; no star means either low rates or no information available. An effort is made in all these guides to list hotels in the various cities and towns, but travelers who are accustomed to North American or European accommodations should use the information with care. In the capitals and larger Latin American centers hotels usually have standards comparable with those found elsewhere and at times on a par with those anywhere in the world. In the smaller centers throughout Latin America hotels are often more nearly boarding houses whose standards of accommodations and food make them unacceptable to all but the most adaptable.

San Juan del Norte, also called Greytown, at the extreme S end of Nicaragua's Caribbean coast, was once a city of importance, especially in the gold rush days of '49, when travelers from New York and New Orleans landed there to take launches on the Río San Juan for the voyage to the Pacific coast en route to California. In recent years silt and sand have blocked the mouth of the channel. Now only a few coastwise boats call at San Juan, where an English-speaking population of several hundred, mainly Negroes, live in rather dilapidated cottages. A primitive and adventurous passage by launch may be made on the Río San Juan from this port to Lake Nicaragua (p. 26). There is boat service along Lake Nicaragua to Granada (p. 24), not far by railroad from Managua (p. 18).

FROM THE PACIFIC TO GRANADA

Corinto, with about 2300 inhabitants, the principal Pacific port, 87 miles from Managua, serves as an outlet for Nicaragua's most fertile region. The railroad runs from the steamer's side on the pier through the town and over the bridge, then via Chinandega and other towns through Managua to Granada. Passengers on coastal steamers may disembark at Corinto, take the train to León, Managua, and Granada, proceed thence to Rivas and San Juan del Sur, another Pacific port farther S, and there re-embark.

About 85 per cent of the country's agricultural exports, notably coffee, sugar, and hides, passes through Corinto. The few streets are sandy and unpaved. A bay's sheltering arm gives fine harbor protection, and a semicircular pier lined with small warehouses juts out into the deep water. Corinto is on an island connected with the mainland by a long railroad bridge. It is reported that fishing is excellent here; boats and handlines can be procured locally.

HOTEL. Corinto, on the waterfront.

San Juan del Sur, with 1500 inhabitants, near the Costa Rican border, is the country's second Pacific port in importance. It gives access by railroad N to San Jorge on Lake Nicaragua and thence by steamer to Granada, from which Managua can be reached by railroad. San Juan del Sur has a small but beautiful beach, popular in summer.

Chinandega, with 18,000 inhabitants, 13 miles inland from Corinto by railroad, is the center of a rich agricultural district and is locally famous for its excellent oranges.

Excursions from Chinandega. El Viejo (The Old), a few miles NW of Chinandega and reached by road or by the branch railroad line to Puerto Morazán, is a small village with a very old colonial church.

Puerto Morazán, 19 miles N on the Gulf of Fonseca, is a new town, reached by a branch line of the railroad which was completed in 1938. Amapala and San Lorenzo in Honduras and La Unión in El Salvador can be reached by launch across the Gulf of Fonseca.

A dirt road N from Chinandega leads to Choluteca, Honduras, on the Pan American Highway, which continues NW to San Miguel, El Salvador.

The ruins of the old Spanish port of El Realejo, founded by Pedro de Alvarado in 1534 and sacked several times in subsequent centuries by buccaneers, are about 6 miles SW of Chinandega by road.

Chichigalpa, about 8 miles SE of Chinandega on the railroad, is an important sugar center, and the surrounding countryside also produces large quantities of pineapples and cereals of various kinds.

Excursions from Chichigalpa. The ruins of the old Carib Indian reduction or mission of Guadalupe, founded by Friar Ramón Roxas de Jesús María, are immediately outside of Chichigalpa.

San Antonio, a few miles SW, said to be the greatest sugar central or mill in Central America, is reached by a privately owned railroad.

Posoltaga, about 3 miles beyond Chichigalpa on the railroad, was once a colonial center of great importance. It is crossed by a small river fed by near-by hot springs.

LEÓN

A city of 50,000, León is 35 miles SE of Corinto by railroad. Its full name is Santiago de León de los Caballeros. León was founded in 1524 by Francisco Hernández de Córdoba some 20 miles E of the present site, at the foot of the volcano Momotombo. Here occurred in 1550 what was perhaps the first uprising against Spain in America, with the aim of creating a new kingdom with its capital in Lima, Peru. On Dec. 31, 1609, León was completely destroyed by an earthquake which the pious regarded as retribution for the assassination of the bishop Friar Antonio de Valdivieso at the time of the 1550 insurrection. The city was rebuilt on its present site in 1610. The ruins of the old city, known today as León Viejo (Old León), can still be seen; they are best reached by boat from Managua (p. 23).

León, Nicaragua's colonial capital, was capital of the nation most of the time from independence until 1852, when the seat of government was moved to Managua. The city was the seat of the bishopric of Nicaragua and is today the residence of the bishop of the department of León. An old university city, it is still Nicaragua's intellectual center. The university was founded about 1812 and today comprises faculties of law, medicine, dentistry, and pharmacy. There are also a national institute; a secondary school, situated in an old monastery, and two religious colleges occupying very old buildings. The city of León has a colonial air, with cobbled streets, adobe houses, red tile roofs, and many very old buildings.

Rubén Darío, commonly considered Latin America's greatest poet, founder of the modernist school, passed his childhood and youth in León and died there in 1916. His baptismal record is preserved in the church archives. Much of his adult life, however, was spent in Argentina and Paris.

The park in front of the cathedral was the city's old Plaza de Armas, today called Parque Central or Parque Jérez because of the statue of Gen. Máximo Jérez, a Liberal leader who led uprisings against the Conservatives in 1854 and 1863. A bronze statue of a lion is at each of the park's four corner entrances. Band concerts are held in this park on Thursday and Sunday evenings.

CHURCHES. The cathedral, the largest in Central America, dominates the entire city. Its overall length on either side is more than 300 feet. The cathedral was begun in 1746 and completed nearly a century later. Among its many religious treasures are a number that Pope Clement XIII sent to the bishop Carlos de Vilches y Cabrera in 1768. Many famous citizens of León are buried in the cathedral. The most impressive of the tombs is that of Rubén Darío, marked by a sorrowing lion tearing the escutcheon of Nicaragua and breaking a lyre.

León has 16 churches besides the cathedral, 12 of them dating from colonial times. The oldest of these, built in 1560, is the parish church of Sutiaba, the old district in the W end of the city. Bartolomé de las Casas, called Protector of the Indians, preached in it. Other colonial churches are those of San Francisco, La Recolección, San Juan de Dios, San Sebastián, Zaragoza, San Pedro, La Merced, San Felipe, San Juan, and El Calvario.

HISTORIC LANDMARKS. At the old colonial bridge of Guadalupe are iron cannon from colonial times. The ruins of the old Casa de Pólvora (Powder Magazine) are near by. The house in which Rubén Darío passed his childhood and youth and the one in which he died are still standing. There is a house that was at one time lived in by William Walker, the filibuster from Tennessee. Also notable is the old municipal theater, which in 1913 was furnished by the city with some exquisite iron grille entrance doors.

FIESTA. Holy Week is celebrated in León with unique and impressive ceremonies. There are daily processions through the city's streets and around Parque Central and services in all the churches, ending on Easter Sunday with notable ceremonies in the cathedral.

HOTELS. Metropolitano*. A number of boarding houses cater especially to students in the university.

LEON'S ENVIRONS AND EXCURSIONS

El Sauce, a town about 40 miles NE, reached by branch railroad, has an old church with colonial records and is known for its picturesque annual fair in February.

Poneloya, a Pacific seaside resort which is a favorite Nicaraguan vacation place, reached by a new road from León, is famous locally for its sunsets and its wide, flat beach. Near it is the Peña del Tigre (Tiger Rock) and a cave in which, according to legend, two lovers once hid and were devoured by a jaguar.

Poneloya has three hotels.

MANAGUA

Capital of Nicaragua, with a population estimated at 70,000, Managua is reached by railroad from León. In some ways it is the most modern city of its size in Latin America. This is the direct result of two catastrophes. First was the great earthquake, followed by fire, of March 31, 1931, when 36 city blocks of offices, stores, dwellings, and public buildings were destroyed, including the National Palace, the city market, and the Supreme Court building. Though there was great loss of life rebuilding was begun almost immediately. Five years later a great fire swept part of the city.

In the consequent rebuilding the effort was made not only to protect new structures against fire and earthquake but also to introduce modern design. Overhanging balconies, window space treatments that had been evolved on the continent in the preceding decades, and other styles were adapted to the tropics. Thus Managua is unique today for its blend of ultramodern structures, humble homes of peons, and a few great old stone residences of the wealthy, in Moorish style, which in some cases have withstood earthquake and fire since colonial times.

The business streets of Managua are paved with concrete. Several elements of Managuan life attract attention. Vying with taxis are the horse-drawn surreys that sound a chime as they approach a corner. There are numerous little tiendas or stores, often in the doorways of houses. In bedrooms that open on the streets are seen great fiber hammocks, made by the Indian women of Masaya. Managuans have a sociable way of setting their rocking chairs in doorways or on sidewalks at sundown.

THE CITY. Located at an altitude of only 180 feet, Managua is the lowest of the Central American capitals. The city rises gradually from the S shore of Lake Managua toward jutting hills S and W. The avenues run N-S, the streets E-W. The principal thoroughfare is Avenida Central, which has been renamed Av. Roosevelt in honor of President Franklin D. Roosevelt's sixtieth birthday in 1942. This avenue starts N at Parque Central and runs S through the heart of the city toward the President's Palace on the S outskirts. In the city's center, 5 blocks S of Parque Central, it is crossed by the principal street, Calle Central.

The avenues in the W half of the city, running parallel to Av. Roosevelt, are called 1ª Avenida Oeste (First Avenue West), 2ª Av. O., 3ª Av. O., and so on. E of Av. Roosevelt are 1ª Av. Este (First Avenue East), 2ª Av. E., 3ª Av. E. Lying S of C. Central are 1ª C. Sud (First Street South), 2ª C.S., 3ª C.S. The streets N of C. Central are called 1ª C. Norte (First Street North), 2ª C.N., 3ª C.N., and so on.

PARKS. Parque Central is at the N end of Av. Roosevelt, near the shore of Lake Managua. Vine-covered pergolas and tropical shrubbery line the graveled walks. A band plays frequently in the modern pillared concrete bandstand.

Parque Darío, immediately N of Parque Central, is a favorite promenade. It contains a large monument to Rubén Darío, the poet, for which funds were raised by popular subscription throughout Nicaragua. The park is terraced from the railroad tracks which pass it N, and balustraded walks on the N side overlook the shore of Lake Managua.

On the SW edge of Managua a new park is being created by order of President Somoza around some prehistoric footprints which Francis Richardson of the Carnegie Institution of Washington uncovered in 1941. Ages ago, scientists say, 2000 or perhaps as much as 8000 years before the Christian era, the volcanoes in the vicinity of Managua erupted, and people and animals fled from the danger. They crossed a lava flow while it was soft, and their footprints remain clearly imbedded there. In 1878 Dr. Earl Flint first reported the existence of the prehistoric footprints, but little was done about them until 1941, when Richardson was assigned to investigate. The prints, which have been uncovered in large numbers, are believed to be one of the earliest known signs of human life in Latin America.

PUBLIC BUILDINGS. The National Palace, the capitol, is a handsome new concrete structure facing Parque Central, at the head of 1ª Av. O. and 2ª Av. O. It houses various government offices.

The Palace of the National District is the new and ornate concrete city hall, with great Greek columns, at the corner of 4ª C.N. and 1ª Av. E.

The office of the manager of the Pacific Railway is between the railroad tracks and Lake Managua, just W of 1ª Av. O.

The Club Social, also known as the Club Managua, occupies a large and impressive stone building facing the E end of Parque Darío.

CHURCHES. Managua has several handsome churches, but its pride is the vast new cathedral close to the Club Managua. When it is completed the structure, which is being paid for mainly by excise taxes, will be one of Latin America's great ecclesiastical buildings.

The church of Managua's patron saint, Santo Domingo, is in the city's SE section.

OTHER POINTS OF INTEREST. The old cemetery, a vivid reminder of the past, is W of 1ª Av. O. and S of 5ª C.S.

The Campo de Marte, a parade ground, with field hospital, barracks, and regimental headquarters near it, lies S of 5ª C.S. between Av. Roosevelt and 1ª Av. E. Here also is located Nicaragua's fine military academy.

MARKET. The Mercado Público, W on C. Central, is very complete. Almost everything obtainable in Nicaragua is on sale in it. Goods of alligator skin are especially fine.

MOVING-PICTURE HOUSES. The González Theater, across from the International Club at Av. Roosevelt and 3ª C.N., is a modern moving-picture house built in 1934. Other moving-picture houses are Americano, Colón, Margot, Palace, and Tropical.

CLUBS. Managuans are fond of club life. Visitors are admitted to the clubs through members. A feature is the concierto danzante, literally a concert dance at which the orchestra plays and people dance, usually held on week-ends. Among the prominent clubs are the Club Managua, facing Parque Darío; the International Club, on Av. Roosevelt and 3ª C.N., which has many foreign members; the Club Terraza, in a modernistic building with a roof garden restaurant, near the Banco Nacional in the business section; the Casino Militar, for army men; and a workers' social club.

Shortly after the United States began building its new Legation the

---

KEY TO MAP OF MANAGUA

1. Parque Central
2. Parque Rubén Darío
3. Palace of the National District (city hall)
4. National Palace (capitol)

5. General Hospital
6. Club Managua
7. Cathedral
8. Campo de Marte
9. President's Palace

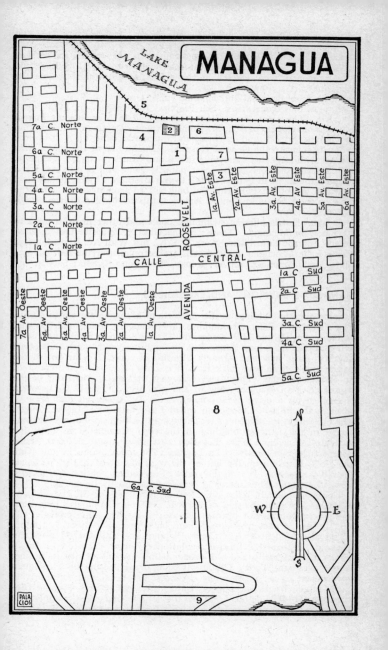

Loma Golf Club laid out a fine course in the section called Las Piedrecitas. It is reached from the road leading to the U. S. Legation. New residences were erected in the neighborhood, which became the modern smart section.

BANKS. See Practical Information (p. 12).

SOURCES OF INFORMATION. See Practical Information (p. 11).

FIESTA. The great feast of the year is held in Managua on August 1-10 in honor of its patron, St. Dominic (Santo Domingo). In addition to church services and celebrations a gigantic carnival is held, the proceeds going to the General Hospital. Usually one of the city's parks is filled with imported vaudeville shows and games of chance. Roulette, with skilled croupiers, is the most popular game and is usually played through the night in lighted tents. In the afternoons bullfights are held in which the object is to ride the bull, not to slaughter it. One of the most colorful fiestas in Central America, this celebration draws 15,000-20,000 spectators.

HOTELS. Hotels offering swimming pools and other luxuries cater to foreigners in Managua. These are the Gran**, opposite the National Palace, and the Lido Palace**, on 7ª C.N., just W of Av. Roosevelt and facing Lake Managua. Other hotels are Estrella, near the railroad station; Anglo-American, on Av. Roosevelt; Colón; España; Sevilla.

MANAGUA'S ENVIRONS AND EXCURSIONS

Some notable buildings in the outskirts of Managua are worth a visit. The President's Palace, containing the president's living quarters and offices, is on Tiscapa Hill, a pleasant 15-minute drive S on Av. Roosevelt and then up a long slope. It is an imposing yellow and white stone building, quite new and strongly Moorish in effect. To the left of the palace and a little way back from it is Laka Tiscapa, in the crater of an extinct volcano. The broad driveway that sweeps in front of the palace gives an excellent view of the city below. The U. S. Legation is reached by a drive of 5½ miles, S on Av. Roosevelt and then W through the hills of the section called Las Piedrecitas (Little Stones). The building is the minister's residence only. All official business is transacted in the Dreyfus building in the city. Completed in 1941, the concrete, stone, and glass Legation cost more than $150,000. Lake Asososca, known locally as La Laguna (The Lake), about a mile from the U. S. Legation on the left of the road out of Managua, serves as the city's reservoir. It is in the crater of an extinct volcano in a heavily wooded section. The landscape here is exceptionally beautiful.

Tipitapa, about 16 miles NE of Managua, is at the SE end of Lake Managua and near the falls of the Río Tipitapa. Tipitapa is important in modern Nicaraguan history because it was here, on May 4, 1927, that the peace pact was agreed upon between Col. Henry L. Stimson, acting as President Calvin Coolidge's emissary, and Gen. José María Moncada, head of the Liberal revolutionary forces. The town is noted for its mineral baths, and old legends tell of Indians seeking its healing waters ages ago. Today Tipitapa is being developed by the Nicaraguan government as a tourist resort. A hotel has been built with private baths supplied with the mineral waters. A great market is under construction (1941), designed to be the largest and most complete in Nicaragua. The plans for the town's development also call for the construction of a racetrack and a stadium for sports. The road between Managua and Tipitapa is part of the Pan American Highway.

Masachapa is a bathing beach on the Pacific coast, reached by car in about 3 hours across the mountains of the Sierra de Managua and through a beautiful countryside. The beach is a popular resort of Managuans.

MANAGUA AS A TRAVEL CENTER

Interesting excursions can be made on Lake Managua, covered later. The railroad to Granada gives access to Lake Nicaragua and the Río San Juan.

Managua is also a travel center for interesting points in the interior (p. 27). Bonanza and Siuna, gold mines within 100 miles of the E coast, can be reached from it by air (p. 15).

A circular drive is possible, following the Pan American Highway first S to Diriamba and Jinotepe (p. 24). From Jinotepe the drive may continue direct to Masaya or may take in Nandaime, from which there is a road running S to Rivas; from there it will eventually be finished through to the Costa Rican border as the Pan American Highway. From Masaya there is a road to Granada.

Inquiry should be made about the condition of the roads before starting any drive into the interior of the country. The excursions covered in this guide are presented mostly as boat, railroad, and air trips, since these modes of travel are better standardized at present.

LAKE MANAGUA

Scenically beautiful, Laka Managua is a relatively shallow body of water, 38 miles long by some 16 miles wide. There is no regular passenger service on the lake, but small boats can be rented for excursions to picturesque villages on its shores and to the volcano Momotombo. Plainly visible from the President's Palace and the U. S. Legation on the hills S of Managua, as well as from the lake front, Momotombo is still active, and wisps of smoke are constantly seen rising from it. It has erupted at various times in the past, changing the entire countryside. The region around Momotombo is reported to be rich in archeological remains which have not yet been explored scientifically. A smaller peak near it is called by the diminutive name of Momotombito. Around the lake many alligators are seen.

León Viejo, old capital of the colonial province, destroyed by earthquake on Dec. 31, 1609, lies in ruins at the foot of the volcano. The location can be visited by boat from Managua. Here are the remains of the cathedral in which Pedrarias, first governor of Darién or Panama, and his wife were buried.

Tipitapa, at the SE end of the lake, can be reached by car from Managua (p. 22).

MANAGUA TO GRANADA

Masaya, SE of Managua by railroad or car, has a big Indian population and is noted for its Indian handicrafts, especially strong fiber hammocks. Masaya's main fiesta, that of its patron St. Jerome (San Jerónimo) on September 30, is attended by thousands of pilgrims from all parts of the republic. In addition to a procession there are native dances with the performers masked and dressed in curious costumes representing a mixture of old and new traditions.

Excursions from Masaya. Near the city are the hills of Coyotepe and La Barranca, strategic points which dominate the railroad. On Coyotepe stands a modern fortress manned by a detachment of the National Guard. The volcanoes of Santiago and Masaya are not far from the city. Lake Masaya is at the foot of the latter; hieroglyphs are carved in some of the level rocks along the shores.

A railroad branch runs SW from Masaya to Diriamba, serving various towns along the way.

Jinotepe, with about 8000 inhabitants, some 20 miles away, is a great coffee center and has a church which looks like a miniature of the cathedral in León and which is famous locally for its many images. The reliquary, which weighs 25 pounds, is made of pure gold and silver and is ornamented with rubies, diamonds, and other precious stones. In honor of the town's patron, the apostle St. James the Greater (Santiago el Mayor), Jinotepe holds a very popular fair annually on July 24-26.

Diriamba, reached from Jinotepe by railroad and also by a good road (10 minutes' drive), is a picturesque small town and also a great coffee center.

Casares and La Boquita, about 20 miles from Diriamba, are Pacific bathing beaches that are popular with people from Diriamba.

GRANADA

At the end of the main railroad line, about 12 miles beyond Masaya, Granada, with 30,000 inhabitants, is Nicaragua's oldest city and today the republic's fourth in size. Founded in 1524 by Francisco Hernández de Córdoba and named after his birthplace in Spain, it is located at the NW end of Lake Nicaragua in the vicinity of the volcano Mombacho. The country around it is covered with coffee and sugar cane plantations. In colonial times Granada was one of America's most progressive cities. Its commercial importance, caused by the fertility of the region and its location on the route between the Pacific and Atlantic Oceans via Lake Nicaragua and the Río San Juan, resulted in four visits by English, Dutch, and French pirates. Communication with the Atlantic was disrupted in 1663 by earthquakes which diminished the flow of the Río San Juan, but nevertheless, in the middle of the 18th century, Granada was still the wealthiest Nicaraguan city and second only to León in size. It was distinguished by fine buildings, among which were seven churches. In 1856 the filibuster William Walker invaded Granada, burned a large part of the area between the main square and the lake, and as a final touch set up a post with the inscription, "Here was Granada." In recent years the city has again become an important commercial center. A large part of its townspeople are landowners or merchants engaged in the soap, furniture, and clothing industries. Many of Nicaragua's presidents and financiers have been Granadinos.

CHURCHES. The most important church is the cathedral, destroyed by Walker's men but since rebuilt. The church of La Merced was also destroyed but was rebuilt along colonial lines. The church of Jalteva was one of the first built by the Spaniards, on the city's outskirts where the pre-Spanish Indian town of this name stood. The imposing church of San Francisco was built by Córdoba. It was designed to serve as a fortress as well as a church and therefore suffered much during the periods of revolution and the Walker war. The adjoining adobe buildings were originally occupied by the Franciscan friars as a monastery. Hernando de Soto, discoverer of the Mississippi River, was at one time imprisoned in one of the rooms here. Bartolomé de las Casas often preached here in the chapel of María Auxiliadora against injustices done the Indians. Today the chapel is lavishly hung with priceless laces and other examples of native needlework. The monastery buildings were at various periods occupied by military forces, among them Walker's men. At one time they served as headquarters for members of the U. S. army mission who surveyed the route of the proposed Nicaraguan canal.

OTHER POINTS OF INTEREST. The Colegio de Centro-América is immediately N of the city on the shore of Lake Nicaragua. The institution was founded by the Jesuits, and its present buildings were erected in 1918-19. It has a good collection of Indian idols; among the more important are those of Cipaotonal, called by the Indians the mother goddess of infinite beauty or goddess of mother love, and that of the warrior god Quetzalcoatl. Some of the idols are pictured in their original locations in E. G. Squier's book The States of Central America (1858).

La Pólvora (Powder Magazine) is an old fortification on the W edge of the city. It was modernized in 1915-16 and is today the headquarters of the National Guard.

FIESTAS. Granada's elaborate Holy Week processions are famous in Nicaragua, and at Christmas time there is much mummery with weird masks and costumes. The fiesta of the Most Holy Trinity (Santísima Trinidad) is celebrated during the first few days of July. The principal feature of the first day is a procession that starts from the chapel of María Auxiliadora at the church of San Francisco. The streets of the city are gaily decorated, but only the men take part in the procession, the most important feature of which is the image of St. Peter richly clothed and protected by a canopy.

HOTELS. Alhambra*; Tropical.

EXCURSIONS FROM GRANADA

Many pleasant boat trips, long or short, can be made on Lake Nicaragua, which is covered later (p. 26).

La Libertad is reached by a drive of 40 miles via Juigalpa from the E shore of the lake, across from Granada (p. 28).

Rivas, with some 10,000 inhabitants, about 35 miles S of Granada, is reached by car. It can also be reached by steamer from Granada to the port of San Jorge on Lake Nicaragua and thence by railroad, and there is a road to it from Managua. A progressive town, Rivas is locally famous for its role in the Walker war. The filibuster had taken the plaza, and any attack on him seemed useless in view of his superior numbers. A humble Costa Rican, Juan Santamaría, set fire to the house in which Walker was quartered, sacrificing his life in the act. Walker's men fled in the panic that followed. The house can still be seen, as well as other houses that figured prominently in the Walker war.

San Juan del Sur, on the Pacific coast, can be reached by steamer on Lake Nicaragua to San Jorge and S from there by railroad (p. 16).

NICARAGUA'S INTERNAL WATERWAY

Lake Nicaragua and the Río San Juan together constitute a great natural waterway tracing much of the route of the proposed Nicaraguan canal between the oceans.

LAKE NICARAGUA

The Lago de Nicaragua is often called Gran Lago (Great Lake). Its discoverer Francisco Hernández de Córdoba called it Mar Dulce (Sweet Sea). One of the world's largest lakes as well as one of the most beautiful, it is over 100 miles long by some 45 miles broad at its widest point. A unique feature of the lake is the fact that it abounds in salt-water fish, especially tarpon, swordfish, and sharks, which have become accustomed to its fresh water. Eons ago Lake Nicaragua and Lake Managua together formed a bay of the Pacific Ocean. Volcanic eruptions closed the mouth of the bay. Gradually the salt water was replaced as fresh-water streams poured into Lake Nicaragua, and the imprisoned fish became adapted to their new environment. Tarpon fishing is reported to be excellent, especially near San Carlos at the SE end, where the Río San Juan drains the lake toward the Atlantic. There are also numerous alligators and fresh-water fish.

The islands of Lake Nicaragua, favorite excursion spots, can be reached either by regular passenger steamer or by rented sailboats and motor-boats. Near Granada are hundreds of tiny islands called diamonds by the Granadinos. Most of these are inhabited and produce fine tropical fruits.

Isla de los Muertos (Island of the Dead) is one of three islands almost due E of Granada, near the other shore. The island is uninhabited, and the more superstitious native boatmen shun it. On its summit, chiseled over an acre or more of basalt, are carvings and glyphs which have never been fully deciphered. According to legend the area once held the temples of the high priests of a great race, and the island was forbidden to ordinary men.

Isla Zapatera (Island of the Shoemaker's Wife) is near the W shore, some 12 miles S of Granada. There are coffee groves on its volcanic cone, and on its shores live a few Indian fishermen. Zapatera is an important archeological site. Many of the prehistoric Nicaraguan objects now in the American Museum of Natural History in New York, as well as most of the idols in the Colegio de Centro-América in Granada, came from here. Stone images and ancient temple sites can be seen on its summit.

Isla Ometepe, the largest island in the lake, is conspicuous because of its two great volcanic peaks, one of them rising 5064 feet above the water. Two small villages on this island are inhabited by Indians.

A small steamer makes a weekly voyage from Granada to various points on Lake Nicaragua. The itinerary is past the tiny islands near Granada and past Zapatera.

San Jorge is a town from which Rivas (p. 25) and San Juan del Sur

(p. 16) can be reached by railroad. Passengers go ashore here while cargo is unloaded.

Night comes after leaving San Jorge; cots are distributed to those who have no hammocks, and all the passengers sleep on deck. During the night the steamer puts in at the island of Ometepe and at the hamlet of San Miguelito on the lake's E shore.

San Carlos, at the S end of the great lake, reached the following morning, is the point of transfer for the Río San Juan.

THE RIO SAN JUAN

Important for centuries, sometimes actually and sometimes only potentially, as a route between Nicaragua's E and W coasts, the Río San Juan has long figured prominently not only in Nicaraguan affairs but also in international politics. One of many who have surveyed it for an interoceanic canal was Robert E. Peary, who worked there before he went to the Arctic and finally reached the pole in 1909.

Several launches now ply the river at irregular intervals between San Carlos at the S end of Lake Nicaragua and the mouth at San Juan del Norte, 140 miles away on the Caribbean coast. The trip offers no comforts but is interesting to the adaptable. Passengers and fighting cocks, boxed supplies, fruit, farm tools, and many other kinds of freight are carried. A first-class ticket gives its holder the right to hang his hammock between stanchions or to spread his mattress in a cool spot; second-class passengers have to take what space is left. A portion of the route is through primeval jungle. Trees arch overhead; monkeys chatter on the tree limbs against which the launch brushes; honey bears come to the water's edge; parrots squawk, and the blue and red of great macaws is seen in the green foliage.

About halfway between San Carlos and San Juan del Norte are the ruins of an old fort, the Castillo de la Concepción, which figured in the country's wars against English pirates.

San Juan del Norte is Nicaragua's S port on the E coast (p. 16).

THE INTERIOR

Many interesting points in the interior that are not served by railroad are reached by car from Managua or by TACA plane from Managua or elsewhere. These are often picturesque cities of colonial aspect which a few decades ago were served almost entirely by pack train.

Matagalpa, with some 40,000 inhabitants, in the hills about 88 miles NE of Managua by car, is Nicaragua's third city and its largest center without a railroad. The route is along the Pan American Highway to a point a little beyond Darío.

Some of the country's finest coffee is grown in this section. Lumbermen and gold miners who work on the Río Coco, the Río Grande, and other rivers make the town their headquarters and base of supplies. The city has a marked colonial aspect and a large church which dates back to colonial times.

Ocotal, 110 miles N of Managua by car, is a quaint town near the Honduran border. It is set on a sandy plain a few miles from the Río Coco, and its altitude of some 2000 feet is largely responsible for its healthful climate. Gold is panned along the Río Coco. Near Ocotal is San Albino, an important mining center with dozens of gold mines.

La Libertad is a hill town, 40 miles from the E shore of Lake Nicaragua, opposite Granada, reached by car via Juigalpa. It is one of many mining communities in Chontales, a department E of Lake Nicaragua that has many gold mines. Supplies were once taken to these mines by mule and the gold brought out in panniers. Some small concerns still depend on mules, but the larger companies now make their shipments by plane.

Excursions from La Libertad. The relatively primitive Babilonia mine is near by, in which Herbert Hoover was concerned as a young man.

The hamlet of Santo Domingo, 9 miles NE of La Libertad over a mountain trail, is the location of the Javali mine, at which some 700 workers are housed in a modern camp.

THE REPUBLIC OF COSTA RICA

COSTA RICA

BY GERALD DE AGUILAR ECHEVERRIA

Known today as a sane, democratic, and peaceful nation that honors
cultural achievements above military, teachers above generals, Costa
Rica is one of those fortunate countries whose history is on the whole
uneventful. Next to the smallest of the Central American republics, it
was also, until the creation of the republic of Panama in 1903, the
most southerly and isolated. This very remoteness perhaps helped to
keep it from having a turbulent early colonial history.

HISTORY

Despite its glowing name, which means Rich Coast, Costa Rica possessed no sensational deposits of gold to tempt the early conquistadores.
It scarcely attracted the attention of the Spanish crown, saw no viceregal splendor, and was too small and too engrossed in its planting,
tilling, and reaping to act decisively in the era of liberation. The passing disorders subsequent to independence, handled and eventually controlled by the governing group in the capital, had relatively minor
effects on the rhythm of Costa Rican life, which today, as for many
centuries past, is that of an agricultural society.

THE ABORIGINAL PERIOD. Costa Rica's aboriginal inhabitants were
relatively few and scattered; the Spaniards estimated them at about
25,000. These Indians were members of three important tribes: the
Chorotegas of the northwest, in the peninsula of Nicoya; the Borincas
of the southwest, with their boundary line at Punta Burica; and the
Huetares, the largest tribe, occupying the northern part of the central
plateau. Spanish accounts and archeological finds indicate that all
three were agriculturists still in the stone and wooden tool stage,
though advanced in the arts of pottery, stonecarving, and the fashioning of ornaments of cast gold; were under the absolute rule of their
caciques or chiefs, and practiced human sacrifice.

DISCOVERY AND CONQUEST. The most reliable authorities, who credit
Columbus himself with the discovery, relate that on his fourth and
last trip to the New World he was driven by a tempest into the beautiful bay of Cariarí at the site of today's Puerto Limón and sent his
brother Bartolomé Colón ashore to explore. Bartolomé explored the
coast and sighted some mountain peaks 50 miles inland. It may well
have been he who gave the country its name of Costa Rica. Indians
visited the great discoverer himself aboard his ship, and Columbus described them as "handsome, peaceful, and respectful copper-colored
visitors" and, some say, called the region Costa de Oreja (Ear Coast)
because of the natives' ear ornaments. Columbus continued his journey
homeward to Spain without establishing any permanent settlement in
Costa Rica. Spain called the new country Nuevo Cartago, and in 1509
it was included in the jurisdiction of Diego de Nicuesa, governor of
Castilla del Oro, a region west and north of Darién, which is now part
of Panama. In general, Central America was in those days dominated
by two centers of political influence, that of Mexico as a result of
Hernando Cortés' conquests and that of the Isthmus of Panama as a
result of Vasco Núñez de Balboa's work. Costa Rica came under the
latter.

3

Various more or less fruitless explorations followed the inaugurati
of the earliest political administration; they were motivated largely
rumors of gold deposits. Later, under the governorship of Balbo
adversary and executioner Pedrarias, Gaspar de Espinosa sent out
expedition that went as far as the Gulf of Nicoya. Later Pedrari
himself traveled up the Gulf of Nicoya and into what is today Nic
ragua, where he discovered the lake that he named Mar Dulce (Swe
Sea) and acquired a booty of about $400,000 but produced no lasti
effect upon the country. He sent his lieutenant Francisco Fernánd
de Córdoba to repeat his exploit. The latter established the first Spa
ish settlement on the Gulf of Nicoya. He was impressed by the ri
flora and fauna, and in his reports the name Costa Rica first appea
officially in 1539. In 1562 a separate governor was appointed for t
country.

THE COLONIAL PERIOD. The true history of the country opened und
Juan Vázquez de Coronado, the first governor of Costa Rica, who w
called the gentle conquistador; he was a visionary who saw the la
peopled by peaceful homesteaders from Spain. Besides bringing in se
tlers, livestock, and European vegetables, he founded the country's fir
permanent Spanish city, Cartago. By 1573 there were 50 Spanish far
ilies in Cartago. They came directly from León and Granada in Nic
ragua and were the descendants of immigrants from the Basque countr
Galicia, and Aragon.

Coronado was lost at sea while returning to Spain, and Costa Ri
was less fortunate in its later rulers. For two and a half centuries Spa
ish governors, some of them good, but many of them indifferent, ven
or ruthless, succeeded one another with the usual unhappy results. T
settlement of the central plateau extended until it embraced all of wh
is now Costa Rica. The country was now governed as part of t
captaincy general of Guatemala. Spanish art, culture, and traditio
and the deeply felt religion of Spain were perpetuated. The isolate
situation of the country, due to the geography of the Isthmus
Panama to the south as well as to piratical depredations on sea-borr
commerce, permitted the development of a system of land tenure th
differed from that of other Spanish colonies and had a most fortuna
subsequent effect. Villages held many of their lands in common, ar
the presence of many small farmers counteracted the tendency towar
forming large feudal estates. Costa Rica, however, shared with th
other colonies the penalties of a restrictive mercantilistic system
commerce. The principal city, Cartago, and the other inland cente
had poor communications with the Pacific coast, through which the
trafficked with the world, and virtually none with the Atlantic. In th
18th century Tomás de Acosta as governor endeavored to arouse h
people from the inertia of poverty, ignorance, and demoralization. T
that end, in 1797 he imported the first coffee trees, and within 70 yea
coffee became the country's chief source of wealth.

THE AGE OF REVOLUTION. Without losing a single drop of blood an
at no greater cost than the fireworks used to celebrate the event, th
captaincy general of Guatemala, of which Costa Rica was part, de
clared its independence of Spain in 1821. Thereupon Costa Rica quietl
ousted its royal governor Juan Manuel Cañas and declared its separat
independence. Attempts were at once begun to unite Costa Rica wit
more powerful nations. In 1822 it joined the Mexican empire unde
Agustín de Iturbide, only to withdraw after the monarch had bee

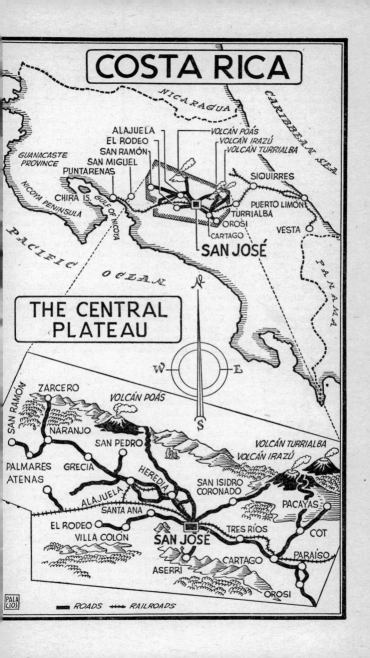

deposed a year later. In 1823 it became part of a Central America:
confederation that eventually failed, partly because it was unable t
achieve a workable compromise in the eternal struggle between loca
autonomy and centralization. In November 1838 Costa Rica decide
to resume separate sovereignty; on Aug. 30, 1848, it proclaimed itsel
completely independent under the title of the republic of Costa Riça

THE AGE OF EXPERIMENTATION. Marked as elsewhere in Hispani
America by efforts at internal political adjustment, this period in Cost
Rica was complicated by two major events in foreign affairs. With th
opening of the country to commerce and immigration, agricultural cul
tivation was extended, mines were exploited, industries established, an
standards of living raised. Politically the first 30 years of independenc
were marked by the struggle of various old and powerful families t
control the government. Both Conservatives and Liberals were re
cruited from those descendants of early Spanish settlers who constitute
the governing oligarchy. After the overthrow of Francisco Morazá
the president of the Central American confederation, who invade
Costa Rica in 1842 and had himself proclaimed president, the Conserva
tives remained in control until 1870. Meanwhile the nation was force
into war with William Walker, the filibuster from the United State
who had made himself dictator of Nicaragua and now attempted th
conquest of Costa Rica. Walker was defeated by President Juanit
Mora in a battle at Rivas, and was eventually shot in Honduras whil
engaged in another venture. After the peace of 1858, the United State
paid Costa Rica an indemnity of $26,704 because of Walker's activitie:

In the same year the Cañas-Jérez treaty was signed with Nicaragua
That country agreed to grant no concessions for the proposed Nica
raguan canal, using the Río San Juan which forms the boundar
between the two countries, without consulting Costa Rica. Presiden
Grover Cleveland recognized the treaty. In 1916, however, Cost
Rica's rights were ignored in the Bryan-Chamorro treaty whereb
Nicaragua granted to the United States for $3,000,000 the exclusiv
right to build the proposed canal. On appeal the Central America
Court of Justice rendered a decision in favor of Costa Rica. Later th
court went out of existence as a result of Nicaragua's refusal to abic
by the decision.

Following the termination of the war with Walker and the conclusio:
of the Cañas-Jérez treaty Costa Rica enjoyed relative prosperity unde
the regimes of José María Montealegre and Jesús Jiménez until th
nepotism of the governing oligarchy led to its being temporarily over
thrown and permanently curbed. Tomás Guardia, who was not
member of the traditional ruling caste, gained control of the goverm
ment, exiled the old leaders, set up a progressive regime, began th
much-needed Costa Rican Railways, and contracted the debt to Grea
Britain which still exists. The end of the 19th century saw improve
ments in communications through the introduction of British and U. S
capital and enterprise and in education, which was already we
advanced.

THE CONTEMPORARY ERA. Large material and cultural advances hav
been made; an influx of foreign capital to develop the banana busines
has continued, and the stability of government has increased. Politi
cally the two most notable events have been the dictatorship of Tinocc
who was overthrown in 1917 by a revolution in which even the wome

took part, and the era of Ricardo Jiménez Oreamuno, who in his three terms of office, terminating in 1936, reformed the country's financial structure and electrified the Pacific Railway. To succeed León Cortés, Calderón Guardia was elected president on Feb. 11, 1940. The question of reviving a Central American confederation is still in the air. Communications are steadily improving. Costa Rica is, for example, energetically promoting construction of its section of the Pan American Highway.

In form of government Costa Rica is a republic with the president elected by direct popular vote. The legislative power is exercised by a Constitutional Congress of one house, composed of 43 deputies who are elected by direct vote.

Costa Rica's school system is today one of the finest in the Americas. Nearly 15 per cent of the government's income is devoted to education, which is compulsory, free, and nonsectarian. It is the country's boast that it has more teachers than soldiers. The country's pedagogy has been under strong Swiss influence, due to the fact that when in 1887 the government established the Liceo de Costa Rica the school's entire faculty was imported from Berne. Recently the influence of the progressive Chilean educational system has been felt. Every year Chile offers 10 scholarships in its normal school to Costa Rican teachers, who are pledged to return to their homeland and teach for a number of years after finishing their course. As a result of Costa Rica's devotion to education, the country has played a major role in literary affairs, producing a large number of poets, historians, novelists, philosophers, grammarians, and archeologists, whose works are well known throughout Hispanic America.

THE LAND

Comprising about 23,000 square miles of tropical coast land, fertile valleys, and high ranges, Costa Rica is about the size of West Virginia. N and NE it is bounded by Nicaragua, S and SE by Panama, while E and W it lies between the Caribbean Sea and the Pacific Ocean. The country is 174 miles wide, N at its widest point; 74 miles wide, S at its narrowest.

In general Costa Rica's climate is determined by altitude, and its four distinct climatic zones are marked off by topographic features. Three high volcanic ranges traverse the country: N, the Cordillera de Guanacaste; the Cordillera Central, which reaches its highest point in the peak of Irazú, 11,322 feet; and the Cordillera de Talamanca, the S range, which includes Chiripo Grande, 12,585 feet high. These ranges form the boundaries of the central plateau, which contains some 3500 square miles of fertile agricultural land and two-thirds of the country's population. The climate of this plateau is temperate, but that of the highlands above 6000 feet is decidedly cool. The lowlands, along the Atlantic and Pacific coasts, are both hot and humid, though the tropical regions between the coasts and 3000 feet altitude are extremely fertile and, below 2000 feet, produce some of the country's best bananas.

Costa Rica is divided politically into seven provinces, with two-thirds of its population of 656,129 living in the plateau provinces of San José, Cartago, Heredia, and Alajuela. The Pacific coast province of Puntarenas is today rapidly replacing the Atlantic province of Limón as the center of banana production, and cacao is supplanting bananas as the chief product in the latter. Guanacaste, also on the Pacific side, comprises mostly cattle and timber lands.

Essentially Costa Rica is a nation of small farmers, with about 85,000 persons holding some 200,000 parcels of land, and with the problem of excessively large estates yet to show itself to any appreciable extent under modern conditions except in the case of large coffee plantations and foreign-owned banana plantations. Coronado first envisioned the central plateau as cultivated by Spanish settlers. He imported horses, cattle, and swine that fattened on the nutritious highland grasses and stocked Costa Rica's first cattle ranches. But his successors lacked his vision, strangled the country's agriculture in vast estates worked by Indians who were virtual slaves, and retarded progress for centuries.

Coffee and bananas are the largest and most important export crops, the latter chiefly controlled or dominated by large-scale foreign corporate capital. They are followed in importance by cacao, sugar cane, rice, corn, beans, tropical fruits, and precious woods. Tobacco production and the distillation of spirits under government monopoly are important industries. There is gold and silver mining on the Pacific slopes, and rubber production is starting in the lowlands. Coffee, bananas, timber, minerals, cacao, and hides are exported. Before the war 45 per cent of these went to the United States, the rest largely to Germany and Great Britain. Iron and steel, cement and other construction materials, paper products, machinery, flour, petroleum and its derivatives, chemicals, motor vehicles, and cotton, wool, and silk goods are imported, with the United States the largest single supplier.

PRACTICAL INFORMATION

HOW TO REACH COSTA RICA

Costa Rica is included in the United Fruit Co.'s Caribbean cruises of 18 days from New York, costing a minimum of $200, and of 16 days out of New Orleans, costing a minimum of $140 (1941). One-way plane fare from Brownsville, Tex., to San José is $131.

BY STEAMER. United Fruit Co.; New York office: Pier 3, North River; New Orleans office: 321 St. Charles St. Has sailings to Puerto Limón from New York and New Orleans, with various stops on voyage out and back.

BY PLANE. Pan American Airways; main office: 135 E. 42nd St., New York. Has service from Brownsville, Tex., to San José, taking about 28 hours, with overnight stop in Guatemala City.

AIDS TO TRAVELERS

Costa Rica's Representation in the U. S. Costa Rica's Legation is at 2400 16th St., Washington, D. C. Consular officials are maintained in Mobile, Ala.; Berkeley, Hollywood, Los Angeles, Oakland, Pasadena, San Diego, and San Francisco, Calif.; Denver, Colo.; New Haven, Conn.; Wilmington, Del.; Miami, Fla.; Chicago, Ill.; Dubuque, Ia.; Lawrence and Wichita, Kan.; Baton Rouge and New Orleans, La.; Baltimore, Md.; Boston, Mass.; Brunswick, Me.; Detroit, Mich.; Rochester, St. Paul, and Winona, Minn.; Kansas City and St. Louis, Mo.; Newark, N. J.; New York; Charlotte, N. C.; Toledo, Ohio; Oklahoma City, Okla.; Philadelphia, Pa.; Brownsville, Dallas, Galveston, Houston, and Laredo, Tex.; Newport News and Norfolk, Va.; Seattle, Wash.; Milwaukee, Wis.; Balboa and Cristóbal, C. Z.; San Juan, P. R.; Charlotte Amalie, V. I.

U. S. Representation in Costa Rica. The U. S. Legation is in San José. Consular officials are maintained in San José and Puerto Limón.

Local Sources of Information. The National Tourist Board of Costa Rica has its head office in San José, in the arcade next to Gran Hotel Costa Rica. It maintains branch offices in Puerto Limón, Cartago, and Puntarenas. Practical information on points of interest, transportation, and so on is also obtainable from hotel managers.

Climate. From tropical on both coasts, the climate varies to spring-like on the central plateau and chilly in the highlands. San José, base of sightseeing excursions, has an equable climate with an average daily temperature of 72° F. Throughout the country, the dry season is December-April; the rainy, May-November. Seasonal variations are more pronounced in the highlands than the lowlands. Rains are often extremely heavy and in the rainy season may make excursions impossible that are easy at other times.

Clothing. For San José and the central plateau in general, light-weight clothing of the kind worn in spring and fall in the United States is suggested, preferably in conservative taste. Woolen topcoats or gabardine raincoats for evening and rainy weather are desirable. Tropical clothing is worn in the lowlands. Since the social life of Costa Rica is formal, evening clothes are advisable for a stay of any length.

Health. By and large, health conditions in Costa Rica are excellent, calling only for observance of the ordinary rules of health that apply in the tropics. In the more remote tropical coastal regions malaria and intestinal maladies still occur but are under control. The usual inoculations are advisable before starting for Costa Rica, and it is well to inquire concerning the purity of the drinking water in most parts of the country. Filtrada or filtered water is safe.

Hospital facilities are on the whole good, and resident staffs are graduates of the best U. S. and European medical schools. At Puerto Limón the United Fruit Co. maintains a hospital open to all. In San José the leading medical institutions are the hospital of San Juan de Dios and the Clínica Bíblica.

Sports and Recreations. TENNIS AND GOLF can be played at Puerto Limón and San José. The new links of San José's golf club are the best in the country.

SWIMMING and other aquatic sports are popular. There is sea bathing on both coasts. The resort most popular with the Josefinos or people of San José is Puntarenas on the Pacific side, with a well-protected beach. Ojo de Agua on the central plateau, with a pool fed by the same spring that supplies drinking water to the Pacific towns, is another swimming resort, developed for recreational purposes.

RIDING can be enjoyed everywhere on the central plateau and is in fact an ideal means of exploring many of the highland valleys. Good saddle horses are obtainable everywhere. The tourist ranches of La Gloria and El Rodeo near San José provide excellent riding as well as facilities for a number of other sports.

BULLFIGHTING is a picturesque amateur sport conducted in village squares at fiestas, without horses and with no harm done to the bull. Good-natured and more amusing than ferocious, it is well worth watching.

SOCCER is the national game, seen in almost all parks during week ends.

HUNTING AND FISHING. There are no closed seasons on hunting. Jaguar and puma are the big game. The province of Guanacaste provides the best sport, but hunts there should be planned only during the dry season, as the province is likely to be a quagmire at other times. Other game found in Guanacaste includes deer, wild boar, alligator, wild mountain goat, rabbit, turkey, peacock, duck, quail, partridge, and tepezcuintle. The last, a small mammal somewhat like a wood-chuck, lives in caves and holes and is hunted with dogs. Its flesh is considered a great delicacy.

Fishing is good for both salt- and fresh-water varieties, though the inland streams are sometimes dynamited by the Costa Ricans with the result that the fish are exterminated. In mountain streams the celebrated bobo, a large and relatively boneless catfish, is said by some to be gamer than trout. Salt-water fishing is best on the Pacific coast near Puntarenas and in the waters around Cocos Island, which are virgin territory for big-game fishing.

LOTTERY. Drawings take place in Parque Central in San José every fortnight on Sundays, the proceeds going to charity. Prizes are worth about $9-$7200 (1941). Tickets may be bought anywhere at the standard price, with tenths selling for very little.

Currency. The unit of currency is the colón, divided into 100 céntimos, and exchanged at approximately 5.6 to the U. S. dollar (1941). Bank notes are of 2, 5, 10, 20, 50, and 100 colones; nickel coins are 1 colón and 25 and 50 céntimos; copper coins are 5 and 10 céntimos. Travelers' checks can be safely changed at hotels, since a uniform rate prevails.

Banks. The Banco Nacional de Costa Rica, which is the most important bank, controlled by the government, issues currency. It has headquarters in San José and branches in all the important centers. Other important banking houses are the Banco de Costa Rica and the Banco Anglo-Costarricense.

Cost of Living. Transients will not find costs high (1941). The best hotel in San José charges $8 the first day and after that $5 a day; but $2.50 is usually an ample allowance. Hotel prices throughout the country include meals. Room and board in a good boarding house or smaller hotel cost $2-$3 a day. Imported foodstuffs are naturally expensive, but native foods are very cheap. Railroad fares are lower than in the United States; from Puerto Limón to San José, 102 miles, the fare is about $1.50. Fare from Puntarenas on the Pacific coast to San José is a little less. Sightseeing and excursions are very reasonable.

Transportation. ROADS. Costa Rica's present network of roads comprises about 1800 miles. On the central plateau all the principal centers are linked by paved roads, good in any weather. The dirt roads are good in the dry season but may be impassable in the rainy season. Inquiry about conditions should be made before starting. Work is now progressing on the section of the Pan American Highway from the central plateau to the border of Panama, which, when it reaches the city of David in Panama, will link San José with the Canal Zone. The section under construction (1941) is from Cartago toward San Isidro del General, via San Marcos and Santa María de Dota, through some of the country's most rugged and scenically beautiful regions.

AUTOMOBILES. Transportation throughout the central plateau is usually by car. Cars may be hired with or without drivers; the former arrangement is preferable for visitors. The rate is about $1 an hour for 1-4 passengers (1941).

Transporting a car from New York to Costa Rica costs about $100. For stays of less than 30 days there is no customs fee, though a bond equal to the amount of such fees must be posted on entry, to be refunded on exit. Cars must be registered with the police. A local license is issued upon presentation of a U. S. driver's license. Rules of the road correspond roughly to those in the United States; the speed limit in towns is 20 miles an hour.

RAILROADS. The country is traversed from coast to coast by single-track medium-gauge railroads, and travel on them offers some of the most dramatic scenery in the Western Hemisphere. Although there are no highways from the central plateau to Puerto Limón and Puntarenas on the coast, roads link all the principal cities on the plateau, while local air service links San José with all the provincial capitals and larger centers.

The Costa Rican Railway, between Puerto Limón and Alajuela, which is just beyond San José, connects the Atlantic coast with the central plateau. English is spoken on the trains. Special tourist trains make the trip in 4 hours.

The Costa Rican Pacific Railway is an electrified line, running over the 72 miles between San José and Puntarenas on the Pacific coast.

The Northern Railway comprises two lines used by the United Fruit Co. to transport freight and passengers between its plantations and the ports. The old line, 61 miles, runs between Puerto Limón and Toro Amarillo; the Estrella line connects Puerto Limón with Vesta.

AIRLINES. Local air service links San José with the more distant provincial capitals and larger centers.

Postage. Mail is sent from Costa Rica via the United States to other parts of the world. Letters to the United States cost 15 céntimos for 20 grams and 5 céntimos for each additional 20 grams, postcards 5 céntimos. Airmail letters to the United States are 60 céntimos for 5 grams or fraction thereof (1941).

Communications. San José is connected by telephone to all the principal towns and villages of the country and by long distance to the rest of the world. All America Cables maintains stations at Puerto Limón, San José, and Puntarenas. These stations, as well as the long-distance radiotelephone service, are operated by the Compañía Radiográfica Internacional de Costa Rica, with headquarters in San José. The government maintains a wireless station at San José, communicating with Mexico, Guatemala, and El Salvador.

Souvenirs and Handicrafts. The shops of the country offer numerous craft articles, often of precious materials. Handwoven articles include hats, baskets, mats, and rugs. Inexpensive hemp shoulder bags make nice gifts, especially useful to artists. Silver cigarette holders are excellent gifts and sell for about $3.50. Boxes, trays, and chests of precious Costa Rican woods and deeply fringed Spanish shawls are popular. In jewelry there are both quaintly designed modern pieces and antiques from colonial times. Noteworthy are the pre-Spanish small gold ornaments called huacos, which are coveted museum pieces, cast in numerous shapes to represent men and animals. The museum in San José has an excellent collection of these; the Minor C. Keith collection in the American Museum of Natural History, New York, is one of the best in the world. Collectors also delight in the old coins that are occasionally found for sale. Shoes made by hand, especially women's, are good.

Food. Costa Rica has many distinctive foods. In the lowland tropics the banana, including many varieties unknown to the temperate zone, is the staple food and is used as a vegetable and as a fruit, in soups and in preserves. The ñame, a potatolike vegetable somewhat resembling the yam, is also a daily food in the tropical lowlands. On the central plateau the cuisine is Spanish American with some local variations. Olla, the popular soup corresponding to a French pot au feu or Central European gulyas, contains pork and beef, potatoes, onions, corn, beans, tomatoes, and so on; it is served as soup when thin, as a stew when thick. Posol, a soup made with corn and pork, is popular. Fresh tortillas are made for each meal; those containing cheese and shortening are favorites. Tamal asado, a pudding of sour cream, eggs, corn meal, cheese, and sugar, is considered a great delicacy. Bizcocho is a cake of corn meal and fine cheese. Dulce, the unrefined sugar, is a staple of diet among the people and is mixed with water to prepare a refreshing drink. Tamal de elote, a green corn-meal pudding, is very popular.

Tropical fruits are abundant, including banana, orange, papaya, alligator pear, granadilla or passionflower fruit, níspero or loquat, anona or custard apple, and zapote. The sweet pineapple from the coffee region is the best in the country and is superior to any received in U. S. markets.

Holidays. In Costa Rica holidays originate either in the history of the country or in the feasts of the Roman Catholic Church. Business is suspended everywhere on all national holidays and major church feasts; with a few exceptions arising from national religious tradition the latter are the same as the holidays of the Roman Catholic Church elsewhere. Leading holidays are: January 1, Feast of the Circumcision and New Year's Day; March 19, day of St. Joseph, Costa Rica's patron saint; Holy Thursday, Good Friday, and Holy Saturday; Corpus Christi; June 29, Feast of St. Peter and St. Paul; August 2, Feast of Our Lady of the Angels, a local feast celebrated at Cartago with a great pilgrimage and throughout the republic with much ceremony; August 15, Feast of the Assumption; December 8, Feast of the Immaculate Conception; Christmas.

Other holidays are: April 11, anniversary of the battle of Rivas against Walker, in which the national hero, the drummer boy Santamaría, lost his life; May 1, second battle of Rivas and capitulation of Walker; September 15, anniversary of Central American independence; October 12, Columbus Day (Día de la Raza—Day of the Race).

REGIONAL GUIDE

The capital of Costa Rica, San José, is in the interior, on the central plateau, the country's most developed and populous region and its greatest attraction for visitors. San José (p. 16) may be reached directly by plane; by steamer the traveler disembarks at Puerto Limón on the Atlantic side and continues by railroad.

PUERTO LIMON

Puerto Limón on the Caribbean Sea, also known as Port Limón or simply Limón, is famous as the oldest of the United Fruit Co.'s banana ports, though today it is rapidly giving way to Quepos and Golfito on the Pacific coast as Costa Rica's principal banana port. A town of some 6000, it is located on a bay; the palm-fringed shore is backed by jungled mountains. The site marks the exact location of the ancient Indian village of Cariarí where Columbus landed on his fourth and last voyage to America. The atmosphere is like that of a modern port in the British Antilles, with few reminders of a Spanish colonial past. Most of the present inhabitants are Negroes who were brought into the country from Jamaica to work in the banana and cacao plantations on the coastal plain. The practice of using migratory West Indian labor has been stopped. The city is laid out in neat, regular squares, with well-paved streets, electricity, and sanitary facilities. Tourist ships are met in Puerto Limón by agents of the national tourist board to facilitate customs examination of passengers and to escort them to San José on the special trains that meet such ships. The departure of the trains is usually timed so as to allow some sightseeing in Puerto Limón.

Points of interest are easily reached on foot or by car. Banana loading at the pier is usually of great interest because of the care with which the fruit is handled. A laborer hands a stem of bananas from a loaded freight car to another worker, who carries it on his padded left shoulder to the loading machine, on which it is carried into the ship's hold at the rate of 24 stems a minute. The mouth of the open hatch is padded with burlap to prevent bruising, and the loading end of the ship is covered with awnings to prevent overheating.

The Old World cathedral is one of the town's points of interest. Parque Vargas with its palm promenades is a miniature botanical garden, rich in tropical flowers. The market, a few blocks from the pier, is full of bright tropical fruits. On the beach is a bathing pavilion with bathhouses. The Club Miramar has an open-air swimming pool. Of great interest to visitors is the United Fruit Co. zone, with its trim bungalows in well-kept gardens, its hospital, and its community houses. Arrangements may be made to visit some of the extensive plantations of the United Fruit Co., and descriptive booklets about banana cultivation may be obtained from the company.

The office of All America Cables is at 2ª Calle 62.

HOTELS. Park*; Pensión Costa Rica.

NOTE. Hotels are here classified by rates. Two stars indicate the higher rates for the country in question and also, in nearly all cases, mean good accommodations. One star means rates in the medium brackets; no star means either low rates or no information available. An effort is made in all these guides to list hotels in the various cities and towns, but travelers who are accustomed to North American or European accommodations should use the information with care. In the capitals and larger Latin American centers hotels usually have standards comparable with those found elsewhere and at times on a par with those anywhere in the world. In the smaller centers throughout Latin America hotels are often more nearly boarding houses whose standards of accommodations and food make them unacceptable to all but the most adaptable.

PUERTO LIMON TO SAN JOSE

It was for the purpose of furnishing pay loads for the 102-mile railroad from Puerto Limón to San José that banana cultivation was first introduced in Costa Rica, thus laying the foundations not only for that country's present importance as a banana producer but also for the present United Fruit Co. The road was completed in 1890 under the direction of Minor C. Keith. In The Story of the Banana, published by the United Fruit Co., the following account is given:

"Born in New York and for two years engaged in the cattle business in Texas, Minor C. Keith at the age of twenty-three went to Costa Rica in 1871 and joined his three brothers, who were attempting to construct a railroad from Port Limón to San José. The building of this railroad was a task to strain men's courage to the breaking point. Surveys led through fever-haunted country. Supplies were moved up from the coast only after tremendous effort. The first twenty-five miles cost four thousand lives—mostly white men. Keith lost his three brothers in the attempt, and took over the contract to complete the railroad. At one time both the whites and the negroes, on account of financial difficulties, worked nine months without pay. . . . It took nineteen years to build the railroad from Port Limón, on the Caribbean coast, to San José . . .

"Young Keith early saw that even to complete the road he must have freight in paying quantities, and decided to go into the banana business. He obtained a supply of roots and suckers from Carl A. Franc at Aspinwall (now Colón), with which to make his banana experiments in the Costa Rican jungle. While waiting for his plantations to produce, he made an initial shipment of 250 bunches from Aspinwall to New Orleans in 1872 . . . the first steamer shipment of bananas to that port. This experiment proved successful and was followed by small regular shipments. . . . When his Costa Rican plantations commenced to bear, and railway extensions permitted, Keith substituted Limón bananas for those from Aspinwall. In 1879 he commenced shipping small cargoes of bananas to New York, in joint account with the Atlas Line steamers. These were the first bananas ever received at that port from Costa Rica."

The trip to San José takes a little over 6 hours by regular train, 4 hours by special tourist train. The line skirts the coast for the first few miles out of Puerto Limón, disclosing a view of long breakers rolling in on a palm-fringed shore, and then passes the section of banana and cacao plantations with their whitewashed cabins to enter the dense tropical forest alive with parakeets. A stop for lunch is made by the regular train at Siquirres, 37 miles from Limón. After crossing the Río Matina, the Río Pacuare, and an important banana region the train runs through magnificent scenery along a narrow ledge between high timbered mountains and the roaring Río Reventazón. Near Turrialba are seen the first coffee plantations, and at the Turrialba station is a famous pineapple market. Here, too, the line reaches the end of the tropical lowlands. In 62 miles it has climbed 2037 feet. The next 30 miles are marked by an ascent of 3000 feet. With the Río Reventazón like a narrow streamer of foam 800 feet below, the train reaches the central plateau. Beyond Cartago (p. 21), 4760 feet high, the country's original capital, the line crosses the continental divide at an elevation of 5137 feet. From this crest the descent to San José, though it seems gradual and even, is 1100 feet in 10 miles.

SAN JOSE

Beautiful and unpretentious, San José, with 68,000 inhabitants, in its high fertile valley, effectively blends old Spain with modern America. Some of its well-paved streets are wide and flanked by gardens; others are narrow and used for one-way traffic, with buildings flush with the sidewalks. In these streets new automobiles run side by side with ox-carts, whose solid and sometimes beautifully decorated wheels form one of Costa Rica's unique sights; mounted milkmen add a novel touch, while among the pedestrians the conservative black garb of old Spain is relieved by the bright shawls of the women. The city's climate is excellent, with cool nights, a mean temperature of 70° F., and an annual variation of only five degrees.

THE CITY. San José is laid out according to a plan devised centuries ago for Spanish colonial cities, with straight streets cutting one another at right angles, checkerboard fashion. The two main thoroughfares, intersecting in the heart of the city, are Avenida Central (Central Avenue), running E-W, and Calle Central (Central Street), running N-S. All the streets run N-S, the avenues E-W. The avenues S of Av. Central are even-numbered, while those N are odd-numbered. C. Central divides these avenues into their E and W parts. Of the streets, those that are odd-numbered lie E of C. Central, the even-numbered W, and Av. Central divides them as between N and S. The blocks surrounding the two main thoroughfares form the commercial quarter; the smart shops and the souvenir and gift shops are on Av. Central. Paseo Colón is a W continuation of Av. Central, running through the finest residential section and connecting the heart of the city with the airport and the national stadium at La Sabana.

PARKS AND RECREATIONAL CENTERS. San José is especially rich in parks

---

KEY TO MAP OF SAN JOSE

1. Parque Central
2. Cathedral
3. National Museum
4. National Theater
5. Gran Hotel Costa Rica
6. Hotel Europa
7. Post office
8. National Palace
9. Banco de Costa Rica
10. Market
11. La Merced church
12. Railroad station (from Puerto Limón)
13. Parque Bolívar
14. Parque España
15. Casa Amarilla (foreign office)
16. Government liquor factory
17. Parque Morazán
18. Parque Nacional
19. U. S. Legation and Consulate

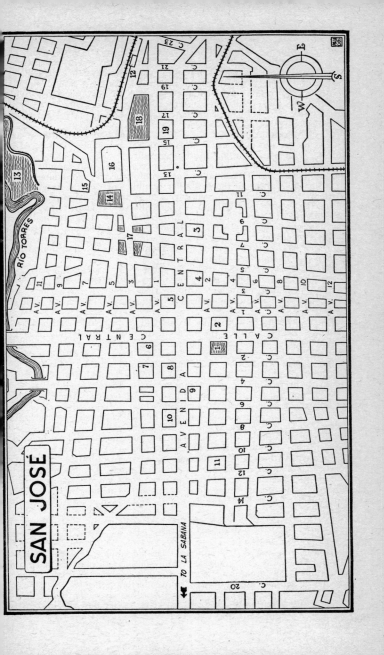

SAN JOSÉ

and playgrounds. Within the city Parque Central, on C. Central, has interesting mosaic walks and cement benches. Frequent concerts are given by the military band, and on alternate Sundays the national lottery is drawn there. In traditional promenade the city's famous popular beauties walk arm in arm counter-clockwise in an outer circle, while the caballeros or young men march past them clockwise in an inner circle. The same kind of promenade takes place on Sundays before the cathedral after 11 o'clock Mass.

Parque Morazán is at Av. 3 and C. 7. Parque España, a little W and N, is gracious and quiet in the true Costa Rican manner. It is faced by the Casa Amarilla, housing the foreign office.

Near the outskirts of the city are several large and famous parks, among them Parque Nacional at the E end of the city, dominated by an imposing monument to the five sister republics of Central America, the work of the noted French sculptor Louis Carrier-Belleuse, commemorating the victory over William Walker's abortive attempt to make himself dictator of Central America. Parque Bolívar, 4 blocks farther N, on the banks of the Río Torres, is designed like a miniature forest. The city's zoological garden, it contains specimens of jaguar, puma, giant tapir, harpy eagle, coatimundi, spider monkey, peccary, and the quetzal, a gorgeous emerald and crimson bird.

W of the city is La Sabana, now given over to a large airport with a beautiful main building, where the best people of San José gather for tea and on Sundays dancing. Adjoining the airport is the national stadium, the scene of Sunday morning soccer matches which are well attended.

PUBLIC BUILDINGS. Often in lavish Old World style, finished with elaborate detail, most of the more distinguished public buildings are within walking distance of the intersection of Av. Central and C. Central. The National Theater, just off Av. Central on C. 3, is a lavish million-dollar Renaissance building with solid marble stairways and balconies, decorations of beaten gold and bronze, and fine murals. Its salon, decorated in the grand manner with mirrors, red velvet, and gold, is one of the truly splendid rooms of Central America; when performances are given it is the gathering place of San José's elite.

The National Palace, the building of the National Congress, Av. Central at C. 2, is a simple edifice with a fine collection of portraits of presidents and statesmen. Admission to the galleries can be arranged through the national tourist board. The session opens May 1 and lasts three months, though extraordinary sessions may be called.

The National Museum, S of Av. Central on C. 9, contains excellent collections of Central American pottery, gold Maya ornaments, and other relics of precolonial civilizations as well as many relics of colonial Costa Rica. Open weekdays 8-11 a.m. and 2-4 p.m., Saturdays 8-11 a.m.

The Municipal Palace, an ultramodern building completed in 1937, houses the city government offices and the customs office. The Biblioteca Nacional (National Library), with a large collection of Spanish literature, has some 80,000 volumes. The post office, a block N of Av. Central at C. 2, is an impressive building familiar to philatelists, since it appears on one of the sought-after Costa Rican stamps. Postal clerks are helpful and sympathetic to stamp collectors, who can visit the institution to their profit. A prison and barracks share the building.

The U. S. Legation, on Av. Central at C. 15, is known as one of the most beautiful buildings in Costa Rica. It is a modern structure of concrete with steel skeleton, earthquake-proof, set in landscaped gardens. In the past it was the residence of four of the country's presidents. The president's home is now in an unostentatious building which contains also his offices and those of several government departments. A new presidential mansion is being built, a lavish structure, at the SW corner of Parque Nacional.

The Casa Amarilla, Av. 7 at Parque España, merits special attention. Built by the Carnegie Foundation to house the Central American Court of Justice after the original Carnegie Peace Palace in Cartago was destroyed by earthquake in 1910, it today houses the foreign office. The archbishop's palace, residence of the head of the Roman Catholic Church in Costa Rica, is next the cathedral, on C. Central opposite Parque Central, and is one of San José's most modern buildings.

CHURCHES. The cathedral, on C. Central opposite Parque Central, is a simple, dignified structure with twin spires and Ionic columns, whose chief point of artistic interest is the stations of the cross exquisitely executed in stained glass. Sunday Masses are continuous from 5 a.m. through the solemn High Mass at 11 a.m.; deeply impressive, they are famous for their music. The San José military band attends the military Mass. The rendition of plain chant by the cathedral's choir is remarkable. Inquiry should be made locally as to the time of the military Mass.

The church of Our Lady of La Merced (Mercy), on C. 12, 2 blocks S of Av. Central, is set in a beautifully landscaped garden. It is a pure Gothic edifice, terminating in a graceful spire with an electric-lighted cross. Other churches of note are those of the Virgin of El Carmen, C. Central, 2 blocks N of Av. Central; the Virgin of La Soledad, C. 9, 2 blocks S of Av. Central; and San Francisco, C. 34, 2 blocks S of Paseo Colón.

Most of the Protestant denominations have churches in the city. The Anglican Church, Av. 4 and C. 3, founded in 1864, was the first of its kind in Central America. The Methodist Church is at Av. Central and C. 11. The Templo Bíblico, a nondenominational organization with one of the largest Protestant congregations in Central America, has a large church at C. 6 and Av. 4. The Central American Mission, C. 1 and Av. 8, is entirely self-supporting.

OTHER POINTS OF INTEREST. A private orchid park, 6 blocks S of Parque Nacional, is owned by Señora de Zeledón, who sends specimens to flower shows all over the world. Fanciers will also want to see the gardens of Professor Clausen from the United States; he has some 200 varieties of orchids on his estate in the city's outskirts.

Casa Montealegre Bustamente is a small house some 200 years old at La Sabana where once lived Mariano Montealegre Bustamente, Costa Rican patriot and one-time vice-president of the republic, and his wife doña Jerónima Fernández. It is of interest in the glimpse it gives of life during the 19th century. A hundred years ago it was one of San José's most luxurious homes, the scene of the city's choicest social functions, and the favorite place for the reception of distinguished foreign visitors.

The government liquor factory, near Parque España, manufactures rum and gin but specializes in fruit liqueurs and wines. Prices are low.

MARKET. The Mercado Público, on Av. Central, 4 blocks W. of C. Central, is rich in local color. Sidewalk peddlers sell almost every kind of fruit known in the tropics and the temperate regions. Obtainable too are flowers, rare mosses, the luxuries and necessities of everyday life from soap to stockings and perfumes, and many native handicraft objects.

THEATERS AND MOVING-PICTURE HOUSES. The National Theater is devoted to concerts, plays, occasional operas, and a wide range of other entertainments, from variety shows to traveling magicians. Other theaters show moving pictures from the United States. The best of these are the Raventós and Palace on the N side of Parque Central. The Raventós is the largest in Central America. The Variedades is on C. 5 at Av. Central.

CLUBS. The Club Unión, on C. Central, 2 blocks N of Av. Central, behind the monument to Juan Rafael Mora, is housed in an architectural gem and is Costa Rica's leading social center, where the principal functions are held. The Golf and Country Club is near La Sabana; its excellent links are new and are the finest in the country.

BANKS. See Practical Information (p. 11).

SOURCES OF INFORMATION. See Practical Information (p. 9).

RESTAURANTS AND BARS. The most frequented is the Sesteo, facing the W side of Parque Central, with a band. There are some night clubs of the rowdier kind. The cocktail bar of Gran Hotel Costa Rica is the city's only U. S.-style bar. Cantinas or small wine shops may be explored by adventurous visitors who know some Spanish. Excellent food, French and Catalan, is served at Hotel Europa. Costa Ricans give their parties and dinners at Hotel Europa or the Club Unión.

HOTELS. The most modern and luxurious in the country is Gran Hotel Costa Rica** on Av. Central, 2 blocks E of C. Central. Hotel Europa** is famous for its food. Other hotels are Rex*; Metrópoli*.

SAN JOSE'S ENVIRONS AND EXCURSIONS

Much of the charm of Costa Rica lies in the suave and lovely countryside of the central plateau accented by volcanic peaks. San José is a natural travel center, and it is easy to see some of the most charming spots in short trips out of the capital. Popular excursions are through the Orosi valley; to the volcanoes Irazú, Turrialba, and Poás; and to such cities as Cartago and Alajuela. These places are covered later in connection with routes through the central plateau. The region is so compact and its parts so easily accessible that any point on these routes may be made the goal of a separate excursion out of San José. Travel agents and the national tourist board will supply details.

San Isidro de Coronado, NE of San José, is a summer resort of the Josefinos and a popular Sunday excursion objective. On February 15 the village is the scene of a great fiesta, when everyone for miles around is a guest of the priest, takes part in a ceremony of thanksgiving to the saint, and partakes of a feast served in the market place. Farmers bring their wooden carts to be blessed. The fiesta is marked by music, dancing, and colorful costumes. Visitors are welcome.

St. Isidore (San Isidro), known as the Plowman, played a distinguished part in the ecclesiastical history of Madrid. He is supposed to have been born in the 12th century on what was afterward the site of that city and to have led a life of such distinguished piety that when he neglected his fields for the sake of his devotions the angels came down and did his plowing for him. His remains were borne in procession in the year 1598 from Madrid to a village near by where Philip III lay dangerously ill. The king recovered, and from that time dates the high repute of the saint. Characteristically, Costa Rican countryfolk honor San Isidro not for benefits conferred on royalty centuries ago but for his association with the arts and crafts of farming.

Las Nubes (The Clouds), at the end of a road beyond San Isidro de Coronado, can be reached by an excursion that takes only an hour by car from San José and leads through dairy country and rich pasture lands. Las Nubes itself is a pastoral community which commands an excellent view of the volcano Irazú. The preferred time for this trip is late afternoon, since the mountain is very lovely in the sunset light.

Excursions to Mountain Ranches. The national tourist board makes arrangements for visitors who wish to see something of country life under comfortable circumstances near the capital. A short drive SE from San José, on the road to Desemparados, is a mountain ranch offering a large variety of activities, including riding, fishing, hiking, tennis, hunting, swimming, mountain climbing, and dancing.

HOTEL. La Gloria*, a ranch.

A satisfying trip is directly W along the road out of San José through the mountain village of Escasú, a quaint spot where some of the republic's most beautiful peasant girls may be seen, to Santa Ana. The road then leads along the scenically impressive valley of the Río Tiribí and through Villa Colón to a resort where all sorts of diversions and comforts are provided as well as varied sports facilities.

HOTEL. El Rodeo*, another ranch.

THE CENTRAL PLATEAU

The Meseta Central or central plateau on which San José lies is the part of Costa Rica that is most popular with visitors and the scene of most of the sightseeing excursions. Tours of a few hours up to 4-5 days are arranged by travel agencies and the national tourist board to all parts of the plateau. The Carretera Central (Central Highway), a good road of concrete and asphalt, is the E-W axis of motor travel.

EAST FROM SAN JOSE

The Orosi valley, formed by the Río Reventazón, is a sunny valley with cool forests, rich plantations, and quaint towns, ending in a stretch of virgin forest within which lies the Orosi waterfall. Starting very near San José, the valley can be explored in one or more days according to the time available and the means of travel used. The quickest trip is by railroad to Cartago and Paraíso on the line connecting San José and Puerto Limón and from there by car to the old Orosi mission. It is also possible to go by car all the way from San José or by horseback, which permits of riding through the quaint towns of San Pedro, Curridabat, and Tres Ríos, center of some of the republic's richest coffee country. The near-by estates, coffee plantations and processing establishments, belong to the most aristocratic families of Costa Rica, who have owned them in many cases since colonial days. Beyond Tres Ríos the road winds on to Cartago.

Cartago, with nearly 9000 inhabitants, at 4750 feet altitude, 14 miles SE of San José, is the oldest Spanish city in Costa Rica and was formerly the capital. Founded by Coronado in 1564, it nestles at the base of the volcano Irazú. The city was twice destroyed and many times damaged by earthquake, but preserves much traditional Spanish architecture in the midst of up-to-date improvements.

The shrine of Our Lady of Los Angeles (The Angels) is a beautiful church. According to legend, the stone figure of La Negrita here, about 5 inches high—one of the famous black Virgins of America—was given to a Negro slave girl by the Virgin Mary. The shrine is built on the spot where the Virgin is said to have revealed herself. In it is a spring, bubbling through a circular stone as it did in the 18th century and surrounded by a large collection of gold and silver objects given by those who have believed themselves cured by the waters. La Negrita enjoys widespread fame, and pilgrims come to her from Mexico and Nicaragua and other Central American countries. This Virgin's feast day, August 2, is a national holiday. Her image makes a pilgrimage then to some other church and is carried home afterward in solemn procession.

Other points of interest are the Colegio de San Luis Gonzaga, the oldest institution of the sort in Costa Rica; the trade school conducted by the Salesians; the Hospital Maximillino Peralta, named in honor of one of Costa Rica's great doctors; and the ruins of the parish church, destroyed in the earthquake of 1910. The Sunday market, held in a large inclosure near the railroad station, is colorful. Country people attend in their best attire with their beautifully decorated oxcarts and varied wares. Exotic flowers, unglazed pottery, sandals and other leather articles, bright tin ornaments, vegetables, sacks of green coffee, beans, corn, rice, citrus fruits, mangoes, granadillas or passionflower fruit, and anonas or custard apples with rich pulp and a grape-pineapple flavor are offered for sale.

HOTELS. Francés; Pensión Americana; Pensión Brownrigg.

Excursions to Irazú and Turrialba. Cartago may be made a base for trips to two volcanoes. Irazú, seen from San José, is the goal of one of Costa Rica's most popular excursions, arranged at low cost by the national tourist board and so timed in its departure from San José that the summit is reached about sunrise, when visibility is best. A modern concrete highway to the top has been completed. Parties that set out from the capital by car pass through Cartago and on NE through Cot while these towns are still asleep. The road climbs sharply to Durán, site of a modern tuberculosis sanatorium, and then to Robert's, a modern dairy farm where a stop is made for breakfast. Then after a little rest the trip is resumed to the volcano's crater, 11,322 feet above sea level. Here clouds of vapor and occasionally of smoke are seen. The crater's edge is 100 yards away, across a lava waste, and from it one looks down into a molten mass of boiling sulphur and rock. On clear days the Atlantic and the Pacific as well as Lake Nicaragua are visible from the summit. The descent is made in the full morning, a changing view of the Guarco valley unfolding beneath. Because of the cold at the summit warm clothing is required. The lava clay is extremely slippery, and leather or spiked shoes will be found preferable to rubber for any extensive climbing. Those with heart ailments should not attempt the ascent without first consulting a physician.

Turrialba, a volcano named for its white crown, is less easy to reach than Irazú, though the trip may be made by road in the dry season. The route from Cartago is the same as for Irazú as far as Cot.

From there the road continues NE to Pacayas, and climbers can follow it by car or on horseback, according to its condition. Several hours beyond Pacayas a farm on the mountain is reached with lodging for the night. The remainder of the climb is made next morning. The view of the central cordillera from the top is magnificent. Turrialba is only semiactive, but its deep rumblings are often awe-inspiring.

Other Excursions from Cartago. Agua Caliente, 2½ miles away and 300 feet lower, is a small village famous locally for its hot springs.

Navarro and Coris, other small villages, are of interest to horse fanciers because of ranches where mounts are bred of Arab stock.

Paraíso, on the main route, 4 miles E of Cartago, has two sharply contrasting attractions, the ruins of a fine Spanish colonial village and church and Costa Rica's most modern radio station.

Beyond Paraíso the Costa Rican Railway continues to Puerto Limón, and there is no way to reach Orosi from here but by road.

Ujarrás is the site of some ruins passed on the road to Orosi from Paraíso. These ruins have an interesting history. In 1561 some Franciscan monks under the patronage of Lorenzo de Bienvida founded here their first parish among the Huetar Indians. In 1565 Philip II of Spain presented Bienvenida with an image of the Virgin which came to be regarded as the patroness of the country. In the year following its installation at Ujarrás the British pirates Mansfield and Morgan landed at Portete with the intention of sacking the province. Juan Lope de la Flor, the Spanish governor, mustered all the fighting men and sent the remainder of the population to the churches to pray. At Quebrada the pirates, advancing 700 strong, were repulsed by the Spaniards, and pious belief attributed this deliverance to the Virgin.

Orosi is both a town and a mission three centuries old and housing many treasures of religious and other colonial art. Beyond this point the valley is filled with dense virgin forest. The near-by falls of Orosi are 300 feet high. Excursions are arranged from San José directly to Orosi.

WEST FROM SAN JOSE

Heredia, Alajuela, and Naranjo are reached by a road running NW from the capital which covers some of the most delightful parts of the central plateau. It is possible to go to Heredia and to Alajuela either by car or by railroad; from there it is necessary to continue by car. Naranjo can be reached in 2 hours' driving from San José if the direct route is taken.

Heredia, with nearly 10,000 inhabitants, 6 miles NW of San José, is capital of the rich coffee province of the same name. Ideally located at 3741 feet altitude, it enjoys an excellent climate and is called City of Flowers. It is the republic's most important stock-trading center. Settled by Andalusians, Heredia looks like a typical Spanish town, its ancient church towers projecting above whitewashed adobe houses with tiled roofs and set in colorful gardens. Points of interest include the Costa Rican normal school, among the best in Central America, and the monument to Aquileo Echeverría, the poet, who found his material in the life of the peasants. The favorite son of Heredia, Echeverría spent his last years as the town's librarian. Funds for the statue were contributed by the school children of Costa Rica.

HOTEL. Central.

Excursion from Heredia. A visit to a coffee finca or plantation and to a beneficio or processing establishment can be made enjoyably here Travel agencies or the national tourist board will help in planning. The coffee trees bloom during May-July, and the white and pink blossom perfume the air for miles. In December the harvest offers opportunit for watching the handling of coffee from the tree to the finished bea

The Costa Rican coffee tree grows to a height of 9-10 feet, with great spread of light, flexible branches. It begins bearing when it $2\frac{1}{2}$ years old and continues for 10 years, after which it must be prun and fertilized for good results. Since the berries ripen unevenly seve pickings are needed. The cojedores de café or coffee pickers, me women, and children, rub each branch gently to make the ripe berri fall into the baskets secured to their waists. Then the baskets are tak to the oxcart, their contents are measured, and the picker may receive boleto de café, a copper coin with a coffee tree on one side and t name of the plantation on the other, which represents the amount d him. Such coins are cashed every so often. The pickers are often migr tory workers, going from one plantation to the next as the crops ripen

The oxcarts deposit the berries at the mill, dumping them into stone basin filled with water. The berries pass through troughs of wat to the crushing machine in order that pulp and skins may be remov from the pods. The crushed mixture stands for 24 hours in a vat ferment. When the so-called coffee honey is removed and the mixtu washed the grains slip out of the shells. They are then spread out f drying in layers several inches deep on concrete drying floors and a constantly raked to insure uniformity of evaporation; this process tak 3-4 days. The inner cover of the grain is removed by a polishing m chine, and the coffee is then taken to the escojedores de café, har pickers, who sort and grade it.

When the last bag of the season is shipped the owner and worke on a big plantation may celebrate with a party. A native orchestra piano, violin, and marimba may supply the music, and the dancin will be both modern and traditional. The baile suelto is an especial romantic dance, varied by poetic recitations, and very helpful in matc making.

Alajuela, with more than 9000 inhabitants, beyond Heredia and miles from San José, is capital of the province of this name and becau of its climate and altitude of 3087 feet is a midsummer resort of th Josefinos. The town is famous as a cradle of legislators. The grana of Costa Rica, it is also an important center of coffee, timber, gol and cattle and hide production. Historically it is noted as the hom of Juan Santamaría, called Erizo (Hedgehog), the humble arm drummer who fired the building in which Walker's filibusters were i trenched in 1856. The town has commemorated the hero's deed with a impressive monument. Parque Central has a beautiful flower garde Points of interest include the weekly cattle fair and the Escuela Tejidos (School of Weaving).

HOTEL. América.

Excursions from Alajuela. An easy trip may be made to El Bras one of the largest coffee beneficios or processing establishments.

Ojo de Agua, the most popular bathing resort of the central platea is just outside Alajuela, an hour's drive from San José. A crystal-clea pool in a setting of great natural beauty is fed by the lavish mounta spring with a flow of 6000 gallons a minute that supplies drinking water to Puntarenas and other towns on the Pacific coast.

Poás, the volcano that is called the sister of Irazú, 8789 feet high and containing the world's largest geyser, can be visited from Alajuela, though excursions are commonly arranged direct from San José. The trip takes a day. The road becomes steep at Heredia at 3700 feet altitude. Beyond Alajuela a side road turns N to the village of San Pedro de Poás. The last stage of the trip, beyond San Pedro, is made on horseback in 1½ hours. A lunch should be carried, since there is no convenient place to stop for a meal. From the mountain the entire central plateau with its many towns can be seen. The crater of Poás is one of the largest in the world and one of the most impressive. More than a mile across and several hundred feet deep, its sheer walls drop into a seething sulphur lake which erupts frequently, hurling a geyser of acrid water and scalding steam 2000-2500 feet into the air. Half a mile away is another crater, once as menacing as Poás but now a clear and beautiful mountain lake surrounded by rich tropical forest.

Cacao, a few miles beyond Alajuela, is the center of sugar production. Here the most modern refinery methods exist side by side with the humble trapiche or cane mill in which brown sugar is made by oxpower or with ancient water mills. It is also a pineapple center.

Naranjo and Grecia, small rural towns 2 hours' drive direct from San José along the NW road, are reached as the hills dip down toward the Pacific lowland. Here can be seen the small farms that are the backbone of agricultural Costa Rica and account for its agrarian democracy.

San Carlos, a village in a valley with the same name, is at the very end of the Heredia-Alajuela-Naranjo route. Watered by the swift and picturesque Río San Carlos, this is one of the country's richest regions and is given over to large ranches, where the visitor fortunate enough to be invited for a stay will experience home life in the grand manner. Reminiscent of the great baronial estates of an earlier Europe, this mode of living now rarely survives in the villages or on plantations nearer the cities. San Carlos can be reached by car in the dry season, but in the wet season horses must be taken from Naranjo. Lacking an invitation, the traveler can stay overnight in the village.

WESTERN COSTA RICA

The long, narrow Pacific coast province of Puntarenas is one of the most beautiful parts of the country and is popular with the Josefinos as a resort region. Its W end borders the Gulf of Nicoya. The peninsula of Nicoya is occupied by the province of Guanacaste, the wildest section of Costa Rica, with the back country of the province of Alajuela bordering it NE. Just N of Guanacaste and the W part of Alajuela lies large Lake Nicaragua, across the Nicaraguan border.

Puntarenas (Sandy Point), with nearly 8000 inhabitants, capital of its province and a busy port, lies on a narrow spit of land jutting out 3 miles into the Gulf of Nicoya and inclosing a lagoon called the Estero. It is reached by railroad from San José in 4 hours. A town of wide sandy streets, Puntarenas is popular as a seaside resort in spite of the heat. Besides bathing beaches and other resort facilities it possesses theaters, churches, and hospitals. Its culinary specialties include plátanos pasados or dried sweet plantains, agua de coco pipa or young coconut milk, tasajo or dried meat, and a pungent drink concocted from tamarind. The tropical nights echo with guitar music. The immediate surroundings provide fishing, bathing, and boating excursions.

HOTELS. Los Baños. There are numerous boarding houses. January-March is the resort season, and reservations for that period should be made well in advance.

Excursions from Puntarenas. The settlement of pearl divers on the shores of the gulf is an interesting sight. Mother-of-pearl, which abounds all along the coast, was used for ornaments and agricultural implements by the pre-Spanish Indians and is a modern source of income. Gold is also mined in the coastal cordillera, though the source of the ancient Indian gold ornaments has never been determined.

Several islands in the Gulf of Nicoya can be reached by government-operated launches that run on regular schedules. Chira Island was once the home of the civilized Chorotega Indians, who left behind them interesting collections of clay and gold objects that are now scattered among museums.

San Lucas Island, called Chara by the Indians, formerly held a settlement of Caribs, whose existence so far from others of their kind remains an unsolved mystery. Today it is the site of a penitentiary, where visitors may buy handicraft objects made by prisoners.

Cano Island, at the mouth of the Río Grande de Terraba, was once a pirate haunt, frequented by Francis Drake and suspected by some to contain vast treasure. It is rich in asphalt, which the Boruca Indians once used for calking their canoes. On it too are fields of plantain, said to have been started by Peruvian Indians who journeyed hither to celebrate their religious rites.

Cocos Island, the lonely treasure island of the Pacific, 400 miles from the coast, is strategically important because of its nearness to the Panama Canal. Special arrangements must be made to reach it from Puntarenas. Small boats can be chartered. Persistent legends credit the island with a hundred millions in buried pirate treasure, but a number of British expeditions have sought it in vain. Cocos Island is surrounded by waters rich in big game fish and is attracting an increasing number of sporting yachtsmen. Normally uninhabited, the island has no accommodations for visitors. Permission to visit it must be obtained from the government, and application can be made through the national tourist board, which will be helpful in facilitating arrangements.

The province of Guanacaste, occupying the peninsula of Nicoya, is reached most easily by an hour's air trip from San José. It is the wildest section of Costa Rica, with the remoter parts of the province of Alajuela lying NE. A land of great ranges across which the sabanero or cowboy drives his vast herds between highland and lowland, it teems with game, large and small, commonplace and rare, while the rivers are rich in game fish. Guanacaste's flora, typical of three climatic zones, is of great interest to naturalists. Its archeological remains of the Chorotega Indians are said to provide a link with the Aztec culture.

Rich in resources, Guanacaste produces some of the best corn, beans, and fruits of the republic in addition to cattle, hides, and skins. Its mineral wealth consists of gold, mined in quantity in Líbano and Abangeres, manganese deposits at Playa Real, and lime deposits in the Río Tempisque. Pearls are found in its Pacific Coast bays. In increasing quantities it exports mother-of-pearl, tortoise shell, rubber, furs, balsam, and precious hardwoods. The guayacán tree or lignum vitae, source of the solid wooden wheels of the oxcarts seen throughout the country, is a huge hardwood tree whose shade, thrown by branches covering a diameter of 200 feet, can shelter a herd of cattle.

The inhabitants of Guanacaste are mostly of mixed blood, with some mulattoes and some pure Indian stock. The sections of Tilerán, Bagaces, and Abangares, however, are predominantly Spanish, and their inhabitants are penetrating the rest of the province as more and more of it is brought under cultivation. Of Nicaraguan background, they display the distinctive traits of that country; they are hospitable, high-spirited, and pleasure-loving, addicted to song, dance, and music. Their instruments, besides the guitar and marimba, include the distinctive tamborcito, a kind of tambourine, and the jícaro, a hollow gourd containing corn kernels. The gourd of which the jícaro is made is also used as a vessel for copious draughts of chicha or fermented corn and sugar and of pinolillo or ground corn, cacao, sugar, and water, less potent than chicha and very refreshing.

Guanacaste should be visited only in the dry season, since it is extremely muddy in the rainy season. Air service is comprehensive.

Hotels are practically nonexistent, but the traveler may rely on the hospitality of the people. Roving through the province is well worth the effort to those who are willing to spend some time in the saddle.

Nicoya is the leading town.

The principal tourist attractions in NW Alajuela are the volcanoes Rincón de la Vieja (Old Lady's Corner) and Miravalles, both belonging to the Tileran range of the Guanacaste cordillera. The volcano Miravalles is near the resort of the same name.

Miravalles, a famous health resort near the border of Guanacaste, is reached by plane. There are tourist accommodations.

INDEX TO THE REGIONAL GUIDE

THE REPUBLIC OF PANAMA
AND THE CANAL ZONE

PANAMA AND THE CANAL ZONE

BY VIRGINIA CREED

Roughly S-shaped, the Isthmus of Panama spans about 400 miles between North and South America, from the border of Costa Rica to that of Colombia. At its narrowest the isthmus is only 36 miles wide, though the Panama Canal is 50 miles long from deep water to deep water. Contrary to a widespread popular belief, the isthmus runs in a general east and west direction, not north and south. In places the sun seems to rise out of the Pacific and set in the Atlantic. Despite dense jungles and the deadly fevers that beset the inhabitants before the advent of modern hygiene the region has been an important link between the Atlantic and Pacific Oceans since its discovery by white men. Soon after the Spanish conquest the isthmus was crossed by the world-famous Cruces mule trail, held by Spain and coveted by many other nations. In the 19th century this trail and the later camino real or royal road were replaced by a railroad. The twentieth century saw the construction of the canal, paralleled first by a railroad and then by a concrete highway. The overwhelming strategic importance of the isthmus in world affairs accounts for much of Panama's dramatic and often turbulent history.

Contrasts between the primitive and the sophisticated, the old and the new, make Panama—or Panamá in Spanish—a land of many tourist attractions. The shops, the street crowds, and the night life of the terminal cities symbolize the republic's modern period which began with the opening of the canal. Costumes, as well as churches of the interior and mossy ruins, are heritages of the Spanish past. The exotic blooms, the lush vegetation, and the brilliant plumage of the jungle which flourishes everywhere represent nature in a lavish mood, while the Indians of San Blas and Darién offer glimpses of the life of archaic man. Gay shore resorts, mountain retreats, sports, and unexplored areas haunted by romantic rumors of lost cities and buried treasure attract visitors of widely differing interests to a country which modern science has freed of its ancient drawbacks.

HISTORY

According to a textbook on Isthmian history used in Panama's public schools, pre-conquest Panama received many migrations. One stream consisted of Andean Indians from the lands that are today Peru, Bolivia, and Ecuador; another was made up of the Caribs who had previously pushed northward from the Amazon basin to inhabit the West Indian islands and the northern coast of the South American mainland. These Indians clashed in the regions of San Blas and Darién in eastern Panama. The result was that the fierce Caribs, whose descendants today inhabit the San Blas Islands and the Darién jungles, stayed in the eastern part of the isthmus, while the others settled in the western highlands.

The crafts and the mythology of the present San Blas and Darién Indians, direct descendants of the pre-conquest aborigines, suggest no marked influence of any earlier complex culture. In the highlands, on the other hand, the modern Indians produce many artifacts the manufacture of which is unknown to the inhabitants of San Blas and Darién, while highland graves yield pottery and gold trinkets adorned

3

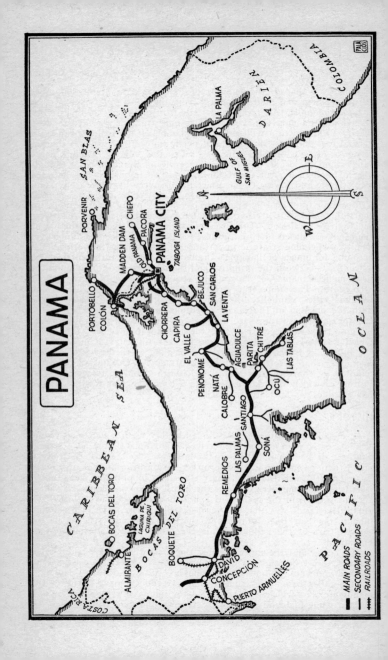

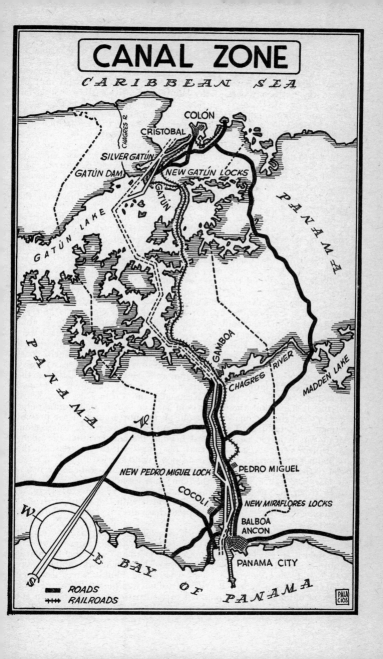

with motifs similar to those found in the ruins of Maya civilizations in Central America.

DISCOVERY AND CONQUEST. The first European to land in Panama was Rodrigo de Galván Bastidas, a wealthy Spanish notary who in 1501 explored the northern coast of the isthmus from its eastern end as far west as Punta Manzanilla. In 1502, on his fourth and last voyage, Christopher Columbus touched on the Panamanian coast. His final venture in the New World was effected in pursuit of the aim which first led him west. Cuba, which he had discovered on his first voyage, Columbus believed to be part of the Asiatic mainland. His second voyage had brought him to the mouth of the Orinoco, which, since its waters were fresh, he concluded must drain a vast continent. The coveted route to the east, he believed, must lie somewhere between those two bodies of land, about where we now know Central America to be. Columbus felt that somewhere there must be a break in the land barrier to admit ships to the waters beyond.

Columbus sailed on his fourth voyage with four ships. The largest was 70 tons; all were worn and old. He had 150 men and boys, provisions for two years, cannon, and trinkets for dealing with the Indians. His brother Bartolomé Colón was captain of one of the caravels; 13-year-old Ferdinando Colón was with his father on the flagship and wrote an account of the voyage. They left Cadiz on May 9. Near the Isle of Pines, off Cuba, they met a canoe "as large as a galley," commanded by a cacique or chief from Yucatán who was on a trading voyage. The cargo carried was enough to prove the existence on the mainland of a civilization superior, to any that the Spaniards had yet encountered among the Indians. Columbus conceived high hopes that he would soon be able to use his Arabic interpreters and his letters to the Great Khan of Tartary. He took the cacique aboard and asked him where he could find gold. But when they came to the north coast of Honduras the shrewd Indian directed the white men east, away from his own country, and Yucatán and Mexico were left for the conquistadores. Columbus and his men struggled on down the coast against head winds. In today's Nicaragua and Costa Rica they heard from the Indians that there was gold farther south; they found some at last around the Laguna de Chiriquí on the north coast of the present Panama. Objects of gold are still dug up in the graves of this region. A strait was reported near by, just beyond the country that the Spaniards called Veragua, a name that has survived to this day in the Panamanian province of Veraguas. A good wind carried them to a land-locked harbor so beautiful that Columbus called it Portobello or Beautiful Harbor. The admiral pushed on past islands covered with wild corn to reach in November a cove that he called El Retreto. Here his search for a passage toward the Orient ended with the acknowledgment of failure. The coast below this point had already been explored by Bastidas.

Columbus now returned westward, determined to colonize and exploit the gold lands of Veragua. West of Portobello he entered into an alliance with a powerful cacique called Quibian, and the Spaniards established a settlement of several thatched huts in which supplies were stored and troops quartered. This was called Santa María de Belén (St. Mary of Bethlehem). Bartolomé Colón was placed in charge with 80 men. Columbus himself planned to return to Spain for help in the formal colonization of the region and in the exploitation of its mineral wealth. Members of Quibian's family and many of his friends were taken aboard as hostages.

Before he sailed, however, relations with the Indians became strained, and serious troubles developed. Eventually Quibian attacked the settlement, wounding Bartolomé and killing many Spaniards. Meanwhile the hostages on the ships tried to escape. Some succeeded in jumping overboard and swimming ashore; others were recaptured and subsequently hanged themselves in their prison quarters. Bartolomé and his remaining men were then taken on board, and Columbus, after abandoning two of his ships as unseaworthy, sailed back to Spain in the other two. Discouraged and ill, he lived a few months in Seville and then moved to Valladolid, where, in poverty and almost forgotten, he died on May 20, 1506.

In 1508 King Ferdinand decided to colonize Tierra Firme, as the mainland of northern South America and southern Central America was rather vaguely termed. For this venture he selected the area between Cabo Gracias a Dios (Cape Thanks to God), a northerly point in today's Nicaragua, and Cabo de la Vela (Cape of the Sail), near the eastern end of the Colombian north coast. The area was divided into two unequal parts by the Gulf of Urabá. Lands west and north of this gulf, in effect the present Panama, were assigned to Diego de Nicuesa under the name of Veragua or Castilla del Oro (Golden Castille). Columbus had struck off the latter phrase, which now was used officially and would later be applied to an independent jurisdiction exclusive of the original province of Veragua; still later it would indicate in common usage, to the subsequent confusion of all but professional historians, the South American coast as far east as Cabo de la Vela. In 1508, however, the northern coast of modern Colombia was designated as New Andalusia or Urabá and was allotted to Alonzo de Ojeda, a member of Columbus' second expedition who, following that voyage, explored the coasts of today's Guianas, Venezuela, and Colombia.

The two expeditions set out from Santo Domingo in 1509, Ojeda going first. Soon after his arrival in his new domain he became seriously involved with the Indians and was saved only by the opportune arrival of Nicuesa. The latter then went on to Veragua. In searching for a suitable spot for a colony Nicuesa suffered shipwreck, dissension, and many attacks by the Indians. He tried to settle at Portobello, but the Indians were so hostile that he had to re-embark and sail on. Farther east he reached a spot near Punta Manzanilla which he regarded as suitable because of the fertile soil and the pleasing surroundings. He said to his men, "Let us stay here, in the name of God." So was named the port of Nombre de Dios (Name of God), which later became the terminus of the Spanish treasure road across the isthmus.

Ojeda was having difficulties all this while in New Andalusia. After he founded the settlement of San Sebastián de Urabá his small force was steadily reduced by sickness, shortage of provisions, and Indian attacks. Assistance had been promised him by Martín Fernández de Enciso in Santo Domingo. In the hope of speeding it up Ojeda decided to sail for that island. He left Francisco Pizarro, who would later conquer Peru, in charge at San Sebastián with orders to abandon the settlement and follow him if he did not return within 50 days. Ojeda never returned. Wrecked off Cuba, he was picked up by a passing vessel and carried to Santo Domingo. His dismissal as head of the expedition to New Andalusia was ordered, and Diego Colón, the governor of Santo Domingo, had him arrested. Ojeda sought sanctuary in a monastery and died there in destitution a few months later. Meanwhile Pizarro and his fellow colonists left San Sebastián to follow Ojeda to Santo Domingo. They had not gone far before they met Enciso coming with the reinforcements which he had promised. With Enciso as a stowaway was Vasco Núñez de Balboa, who as things turned out was probably the most valuable asset of the expedition. Balboa had been on this coast before as an obscure member of the Bastidas expedition. He settled in Santo Domingo after that voyage, but his plantation there failed, and he stowed away with Enciso in the hope of mending his fortunes. Balboa's knowledge of the land and his temperament, with great courage and endurance tempered by sensibility, were to prove powerful instruments of the conquest.

Enciso asserted his authority over New Andalusia and led his own men and Pizarro's back to San Sebastián. The Indians had razed the settlement. On Balboa's advice the Spaniards founded a new settlement, Santa María de la Antigua del Darién, on the west side of the Gulf of Urabá. In doing so they were exceeding the bounds that had been set on their enterprise, but the locality was tempting because the Indians there were not so savage and did not use poisoned arrows. The Spaniards routed the Indians in a great battle and seized the land for themselves. The Indians had a good deal of gold, which the Spaniards coveted. Enciso now lost control of the men. He was ousted and eventually was sent back to Spain, and Balboa replaced him as leader. A delegation was sent to Nicuesa to inform him of the new settlement and to offer to put it under his command as governor. Sick and starving, Nicuesa lost his head, declared that Ojeda's men had infringed on his jurisdiction by their new settlement, and said that he would take from them any gold they might have found. Balboa's delegation returned to Antigua with an account of Nicuesa's intransigence, and when the latter arrived he was met on the beach by an angry mob who would not let him land. He pleaded with them to let him stay if only as a simple soldier. But they would not listen to him. On March 1, 1511, Nicuesa and his 17 men headed out to sea in their leaky vessel. They were never heard of again.

Now in supreme command of all the Spanish settlements in the region of Darién, the easternmost part of today's Panama, Balboa set out to find the gold of which he had heard so much. He became an ally of the Indian chief Careta and reinforced this connection by other political alliances and carefully planned military expeditions. Comogre, wealthiest of the caciques, received him with a present of gold. When the Spaniards began to argue about its division the chief's son remarked contemptuously, "If you care for that stuff, there is a land to the south where the people eat and drink from vessels of it." Thus the Spaniards first heard of Peru. "At a journey of six days hence," the Indian told them, "lies another ocean as great as that before you. On its shores is the kingdom of which I speak. But it is powerful. If you would attack it you need more men than you have here." Balboa and Pizarro both listened intently. The ocean spoken of by the Indians must be the Great South Sea which Columbus had sought. On Sept. 1, 1513, Balboa set out in search of it.

The isthmus, then as now, was covered with tropical rain forests, mountainous, and troubled by threatening rivers which frequently overflowed. Where Balboa crossed it it is 60 miles wide; in it dwelt hostile

Indians. He could muster only 190 men, but they were hardened veterans accustomed to the climate. They were accompanied by a pack of bloodhounds and 1000 Indians, bearers and guides, many of whom were unreliable. Poisoned arrows, insects, snakes, and terrible underbrush retarded the expedition as it toiled up the incline toward the crest of the isthmus. The 6 days' journey lengthened to 25. Starvation was added to the expedition's ills. Finally the party approached the height from which the Indians said the great sea was visible. Balboa waved his followers back and rushed forward to be the first to look upon the vast ocean which he called the Great South Sea and which Magellan later, after weathering the storms of the Strait of Magellan, thankfully but misleadingly called the Pacific. Balboa claimed the land that he stood upon, the newly discovered sea, and all the lands touched by its waters for his master, the king of Spain. Tragically, however, the news of the discovery reached the Spanish court too late to do him any good.

A court favorite, Pedro Arias Dávila, commonly known as Pedrarias, had already been sent to the New World as governor, with power to try Balboa for his treatment of Enciso and Nicuesa. There was a period of bickering and intrigues following Balboa's return with news of his great discovery. Eventually the latter was beheaded at the age of 42, leaving Panama to be governed by Pedrarias and Peru to be conquered by Pizarro. In 1515 Pedrarias founded the town of Acla. The name is an Indian word meaning Bones of Men, and it was given to the town because of the quantity of human remains scattered over the neighboring plains as a result of a fierce struggle between two Indian brothers for the chieftainship of the region. In 1519 Pedrarias moved across the isthmus and founded the city that is now Old Panama. Cruel and greedy, he tore the land apart for gold and butchered and tortured his victims by the hundreds. He did not live to see the steady stream of treasure which was to begin flowing across the isthmus from Peru in 1532 and was in later years to make Panama world-famous. In 1526 Pedrarias was displaced as governor of Castilla del Oro by Pedro de los Ríos. The following year he succeeded in having himself appointed governor of Nicaragua. He died there, while still in office, in January 1531.

THE STRUGGLE FOR THE ISTHMUS comprised a major chapter in the Spanish-English conflict for the control of the seas which began so unequally and ended so well for the English. In Panama, however, England failed. Spain retained the tremendously important route across the isthmus till the age of revolution and independence. Over this route flowed nearly all of the traffic to and from Peru and the neighboring colonies. Peruvian treasure, too, was shipped to Panama City, taken overland on mules along the Cruces trail to Portobello, and there loaded on galleons which had come from Spain to receive it. To cut the isthmus route, capture its terminals, or seize the treasure would therefore be to inflict a telling blow on Spain. The most distinguished English warrior to try it was Francis Drake.

For two years Drake prowled the waters about the isthmus, even living, according to some accounts, in Nombre de Dios in disguise. Fully informed of Spanish procedure in transporting treasure, he attacked and took Nombre de Dios in 1572. He found a fortune in silver bars piled in the central plaza. But he was wounded, and his men left the loot to carry him back to his ship. Six months later, in the hope of taking Old Panama or the treasure or both, he crossed the isthmus. From a treetop he saw the Pacific, but again his plan miscarried. On a third attempt his men captured a mule train but were driven away after burying the treasure somewhere near Nombre de Dios, where it may still remain. In 1578, sailing the Golden Hind into the Pacific, Drake realized part of his ambition when he captured the treasure galleon Cacafuego, bound for Panama. In 1595, with John Hawkins, he attacked Old Panama, but the Spaniards drove the English back toward Portobello. The gallant Drake died of dysentery and fever before reaching the town. He was buried at sea, a league from shore, on Jan. 28, 1596.

In 1669 the English freebooter Henry Morgan arrived at Portobello from Port Royal, Jamaica, with 460 men. They took and looted the town and then sailed away, promising to return within a year. The next year an advance guard of 400 buccaneers under Bradley landed at the mouth of the Río Chagres and captured the San Lorenzo fort which commanded the Panama road. After its capture Morgan arrived with his fleet, garrisoned both San Lorenzo and Portobello, and with 1400 men, the largest force of buccaneers ever gathered together at one time, started up the Chagres with only two days' provisions. The retreating Spaniards laid waste the land, and the buccaneers were doomed to nine days of terrible starvation. They ate grass, leaves, and their leather belts. Two hundred died, but the rest reached the so-called Hill of the Buccaneers, from which they first saw the riches of Old Panama, dominated by a stone cathedral that had been dedicated only a few years before. Despite their numerical superiority the Spaniards were the weaker. The governor Juan Pérez de Guzmán had 400 cavalry and 2400 infantry, the latter including every free white man and mulatto in the city. But the crack Spanish troops had died at San Lorenzo, and the defenders were faced by some of the toughest fighting veterans in the New World, no longer starving, for they had captured a herd of cattle. An Indian guide had led them to a plain before the city, and Guzmán was forced to attack them in a position that was immensely to their advantage. In the ensuing battle, which began at sunrise, Jan. 28, 1671, the English routed their opponents. Guzmán's desperate measure of blowing up the powder magazines set fire to the city. Both the Spaniards and the buccaneers, who feared for their loot, tried in vain to stifle the blaze. By morning Old Panama was a heap of ashes, on which Morgan camped for a month, committing cruel excesses in his search for treasure.

Two years later the city of Panamá Nuevo (New Panama) was built, 6 miles away, at the foot of Ancon hill. Its more defensible position was strongly protected by bóvedas or walls whose remains may still be seen. Thereafter, in spite of the successes of the English, who captured port after port, defeated two Spanish fleets in the bay of Panama, and wiped out every Spanish settlement on the Atlantic shore of Darién, Panama City stood firm. Gradually, however, the city began to decay. The decline of Panama as a point of transshipment began in the late 1730's after the signing of a peace treaty between England and Spain. The traffic of the galleons from Portobello began to fall off as the Peruvian traders favored the route around Cape Horn. The profit now possible from trading on the isthmus seemed hardly worth the peril of death from yellow fever.

Early in the 19th century, Panama was caught in the movement toward independence which swept most of Spain's possessions in the New World. Panama declared her independence from Spain on Nov. 28, 1821, and voluntarily became a part of the republic of Colombia. Spain had her hands full fighting Simón Bolívar's victorious army in northern South America, as well as rebellious forces in Chile and Argentina, and did not fire a single shot to save what had once been the treasure house of the world. The Spanish garrisons on the isthmus had been whittled to the bone as the soldiers were shipped away for service elsewhere. The few remaining Spaniards were bought off by the Panamanians, who used gold for ammunition instead of lead.

THE PANAMA TRADE ROUTE did not support local hopes of renewed prosperity upon the removal of the old Spanish restrictions. Foreign cargo ships came, it is true, to the mouth of the Río Chagres, where a trading town had grown up to displace Portobello, but the task of transporting goods across the isthmus was too great. The old talk of digging a canal was supplemented by projected schemes for horse-car lines, but nothing was done. Panama drowsed for several decades. In 1826 Simón Bolívar convened in Panama a congress intended to consider the unification and advancement of the hemisphere as a whole. Many American nations sent delegates. Among the projects seriously considered was that of cutting a canal across the isthmus. The congress, however, failed.

The California gold rush of 1849 once more emphasized the importance of Panama as a trade route. Thousands of gold seekers from the United States were paddled or poled in dugouts up the Río Chagres to Cruces at the head of the Spanish gold road, and then rode muleback, stumbled along on foot, or were carried in chairs by Negro or Indian bearers to Panama City, where they often waited months in gnawing ferment for passage to San Francisco. Trade boomed; vice flourished. Not since the days of the Spanish galleons from Peru had the isthmus seen such soaring prices, such buying and selling, such cheating of strangers. When Oregon and California were admitted to the Union two regular steamship lines began to operate to the isthmus, one line from New York, belonging to George Law, the other from San Francisco, belonging to William H. Aspinwall. These owners combined with a third capitalist, Henry Chauncey, for the purpose of building a railroad across the isthmus. The last-named and John L. Stephens had secured the permission of the government of New Granada, as Colombia was then called, with Panama as a state within it, and Stephens and J. L. Baldwin had surveyed the route and reported favorably on the project. The actual building started in May 1850. Labor gangs were brought in from the Orient, from Europe, and from the West Indies. There was as yet no knowledge of tropical sanitation, and hundreds of men died, mostly of fevers. One report has it that of 1000 Chinese laborers who were brought over, only 200 survived at the end of a few weeks. But on Jan. 27, 1855, the last rail was laid, and the following day the first locomotive passed from ocean to ocean.

Because the superintendent deemed the road unfinished, however, and therefore unfit for heavy traffic, he set exorbitant rates to delay its use. To his surprise the provisional rates of $.50 a mile for passengers, $.05 a pound for luggage, and $.50 a cubic foot for freight were adopted and retained as long as the road was prosperous. The railroad cost $8,000,000 to build, but even before the first through track was laid, it had earned $2,000,000 in fares; in the next 10 years it took in over $11,000,000. Its stock paid dividends of 24 per cent. Colombia had originally reserved the right to buy the railroad for $5,000,000 within 20 years after completion, but the fabulous success of the road made that figure absurd, and Colombia finally gave the company a 99-year franchise at a price of $1,000,000 down and $250,000 a year. In 1867, however, the company suffered a serious blow when the Pacific Steam Navigation Company, which held a monopoly of South American trade, abandoned its shops and warehouses on Taboga Island and rerouted its ships around South America in order to force a rate adjustment across the isthmus. About the same time the first transcontinental railroad was completed across the United States. As a result the Panama Railroad's Atlantic-Pacific trade virtually ended. The line became the notorious "two streaks of rust" whose stock was for a long time a football of Wall Street speculators.

THE PANAMA CANAL was conceived by neither French nor United States engineers. When Columbus and his successors failed to find a strait through the isthmus, Spain time and again considered digging a canal. A complex of motives prevented the maturing of the project. Bolívar, at the congress which he called in Panama in 1826, projected a canal which was to be international, built and controlled by a congress of the American nations. The Colombian republic, which then as later controlled the territory through which the canal was to pass, offered it to the congress completely free in the interest of American progress and unity.

In May 1879 the French, influenced by their success at Suez, convened an international canal congress in Paris with the aim of building the Panama Canal and with Ferdinand de Lesseps as its chairman. However, lack of foresight, graft, and disease on the isthmus doomed the French venture, which in nine years spent about $300,000,000 and dug only part of the proposed canal. The collapse of the company furnished France with one of its most sensational financial scandals. It killed the innocent but misguided Lesseps, ruined thousands of small investors, and drove dozens of venal politicians to suicide. The French government permitted the formation of a new canal company to hold concessions and rights until a purchaser could be found. The only possible purchaser was the United States of America, and the United States did not miss the opportunity. Before purchasing the property of the French company, the United States sought the permission of the Colombian government to build the canal. Protracted negotiations led to a formal treaty between the United States and Colombia. Although ratified by the United States, the treaty failed of ratification in the Colombian Senate during the summer session of 1903. Incensed, Panama declared its independence, which was immediately recognized by the United States.

By the Hay-Bunau-Varilla Treaty, concluded in 1903, the new republic of Panama granted to the United States in perpetuity and in consideration of certain payments the use, occupation, and control of a strip of land across the isthmus in which the United States would exercise all sovereign powers as though she were in fact sovereign and to the exclusion of the exercise of such powers by Panama. In 1904 the United States paid the French canal company $40,000,000 and moved into the 10-mile zone that the new republic had granted it.

While beginning work on the canal it cleaned up the isthmus. Dr. William Crawford Gorgas, assistant to Major Walter Reed, who with Dr. Aristides Agramonte, Dr. Jesse Lazear, Dr. James Carroll, the soldiers Moran and Kissanger and 11 others had been a hero of the sensational discovery in Havana of the yellow fever carrier, was placed in charge of sanitation. After a violent outbreak of yellow fever had frightened the United States, Gorgas was given adequate men and funds to make Panama what it now is, one of the most healthful of tropical lands. The fact that Dr. Amador Guerrero, first president of the republic of Panama, was a man of great public spirit and an authority on tropical diseases was of inestimable help. The canal and the republic benefited permanently and mutually from the co-operation of the medical authorities of the two countries. The task of building the canal was given to the United States Army under the direction of Col. George W. Goethals.

The Panama Canal is one of the greatest engineering feats in history. Its original cost was $380,000,000. The total excavation up to the time of opening was 208,027,540 cubic yards. A mountain, Gold Hill, was sliced in two and its slides held back; Gatún Lake, formed by damming the Río Chagres, was the largest artificial lake in the world until Boulder Dam was built; a series of locks were constructed to lift large liners over a mountain range and lower them once more to the sea. The canal was opened to commercial traffic on Aug. 15, 1914. The canal saves a distance of 8000 miles for vessels plying between the Atlantic and Pacific coasts of the United States, 3000-4000 miles for those from the Atlantic coast of North America to the Pacific coast of South America, and 1000-2000 miles for vessels plying between Europe and Australia or western Asia. Its international importance is inherent in these mileage savings. Its financial value is correspondingly great. The peak year in the canal's operation was 1929, when 6289 vessels paid more than $27,000,000 in tolls. Traffic began to decline during the depression in the early 1930's. A gradual increase began in 1936 and continued until the outbreak of the war; since then traffic has again diminished sharply.

In 1929, anticipating a future need for greater capacity, the Congress of the United States authorized studies of a possible enlargement of the canal, as well as of "any other route for a ship canal between the Atlantic and Pacific Oceans." Three possible projects were thereupon investigated: the addition of a third set of locks to augment the canal's capacity; the reduction of the entire canal to sea level, obviating the need for locks; and the Nicaraguan canal route. The first two of these projects were really one, since a third set of locks would be needed in reducing the canal to sea level with minimum interruption to traffic. The cost of the third locks was estimated at $140,000,000; that of lowering the canal to sea level, at $1,000,000,000; and that of the Nicaraguan canal, at $697,000,000. It was thought that any such enlargement of capacity would not be needed until 1970 or thereabout. Things moved much faster than had been expected, however, and in 1939 Congress authorized the construction of a third set of locks, partly to take care of expected increases in traffic and partly to provide a greater measure of wartime safety. These locks are now under construction (1941), 1500-3000 feet from the existing locks in order to provide greater security against bombing. They are to be connected with the present canal by separate approach canals. They are designed to be of maximum utility in the possible future lowering of the entire canal to sea level.

GOVERNMENT. Panama is a federal republic consisting of nine provinces and governed today under a constitution that was proclaimed on Jan. 2, 1941, displacing the constitution of 1903. The Chamber of Deputies, consisting of 36 members, is elected for six years. The president is elected by direct vote for six years and is not eligible for reelection. Because of the importance of the operation of the canal to the security of the United States, the question of the extent to which the government of the United States is entitled to use its police power to preserve order within the republic of Panama has frequently been considered by authorities on international law.

THE LAND

With an area of 32,383 square miles, excluding the Canal Zone, Panama is about as large as the state of Maine; its population of some 500,000 approximates that of the city of New Orleans and results in an overall population density of some 13 to the square mile. Potentially the land is rich in resources; vast areas of unexploited fertile land still exist which may some day, with the aid of modern tropical sanitation, be developed to the republic's benefit.

The mountains which run down the isthmus in two ridges are of volcanic origin, but Panama itself has no active volcanoes and is not subject, like some of its neighbors, to serious earthquakes. On the Atlantic side of the mountains broad stretches of jungle and some open prairies slope down to the sea; on the Pacific side, extensive prairies and some patches of jungle. Numerous streams flow into the two oceans. The largest of these is the Río Tuyra, which empties into the Pacific in the Gulf of San Miguel. The Río Chagres, which has been sacrificed to the canal, was the second; it was long the main internal waterway of Panama. The coasts are much indented and scattered with islands.

The country W of the canal is typically Central American in topography, flora, and fauna; E, as characteristically South American. Both regions are intensely tropical. Panama is 600 miles from the equator, in the same latitude as Mindanao in the Philippines. The natural state of most of the isthmus is that of a dense jungle. The mangrove swamps by the sea are impenetrable to all but skilled wielders of the machete who can cut a trail almost as swiftly as they can walk. The predominant tree is the palm, of which there are said to be 100 different species in Panama. Bananas, growing throughout the republic, form the chief export. Cacao, the second export, is now grown in the Almirante district and is on the increase. The production of coffee, centered largely in the province of Chiriquí, particularly around Boquete, is also increasing. The provinces of the interior, extending W from Panama City toward the Costa Rican border, are being brought more and more under cultivation both by Panamanians and North Americans. Rice and sugar are most important after coffee. Cattle-raising centers in the W provinces, chiefly those of Cocle and Chiriquí. The exploited gold of Panama, which probably contains many forgotten or unknown deposits, is in the province of Veraguas, as are some of the manganese mines. Other manganese deposits are in the San Blas region. A number of jungle products are also exploited. These include cube, plant roots yielding rotenone, used in the manufacture of insecticides; copaiba, ipecacuana, and sarsaparilla; hardwoods; kapok, balata, toquilla straw, reptile skins, and perilla gum. The coasts yield tortoise shell. Pearls are found near the islands on both sides of the isthmus, although they are more numerous on the Pacific side. Scattered over the isthmus are unexploited deposits of coal, iron, asbestos, and doubtless other minerals.

Much of the fascination that Panama exerts through colorful folk-lore and through the lure of the unknown centers about the South American end of the isthmus. Here, in the provinces of San Blas and Darién, was the scene of the earliest and most intense Spanish activity. Here the Spaniards found gold and very probably worked mines that are now forgotten. Here, also, flourish some tribes of primitive indigenous Indians. Perhaps the Pan American Highway will some day cut through this wild land which until then must remain a fabulous terra incognita to the average traveler, more or less as the Spanish conquistadores found it on their first arrival, penetrable only by adventurers and by scientists and technicians charged with special missions.

PRACTICAL INFORMATION

HOW TO REACH PANAMA

From the United States. Minimum one-way first-class steamship fare from New York to Cristóbal is $110; from Galveston, Tex., $60; from New Orleans, $95. The fare by plane from Miami, Fla., to Balboa is $160 (1941).

BY STEAMER. Grace Line; New York office: 10 Hanover Square Has steamers in South American service taking 5 days for the direct run from New York to Cristóbal and proceeding thence through the canal and down the W coast of South America.

Panama Line; New York office: 24 State St. Has sailings from New York to Cristóbal. Voyage takes 6 days with stop en route at Port-au-Prince, Haiti.

United Fruit Co.; New York office: Pier 3, North River. Has sailings from New York to Cristóbal via Kingston, Jamaica. Voyage takes 6 days. Return is via Costa Rica and Guatemala.

Standard Fruit and Steamship Co.; New York office: 11 Broadway New Orleans office: 140 Carondelet St. Has cruises sailing from New Orleans, calling at Cristóbal. One-way passage from New Orleans to Cristóbal, via Havana, takes 6 days.

Lykes Brothers Steamship Co.; main office: U. S. National Bank Building, Galveston, Tex. Has sailings from Houston and Galveston to Cristóbal. Voyage takes 8 days from Houston, 5 from Galveston.

American President Lines, Ltd.; New York office: 604 5th Ave. Has irregular sailings in New York-California service. Voyage from New York to Cristóbal, via Havana, takes 7-8 days.

BY AIR. Pan American Airways; main office: 135 East 42nd St., New York. Has non-stop service from Miami to Balboa, taking 6½ hours

From Caribbean Ports. Various of the lines listed above give this service. There are also local coastwise services which should be inquired about locally.

AIDS TO TRAVELERS

Panama's Representation in the U. S. The Panamanian Embassy is at 1536 18th St., Washington, D. C. Consular officials are maintained in the following cities: Birmingham and Mobile, Ala.; Long Beach, Los Angeles, Monrovia, San Diego, and San Francisco, Calif. Denver, Colo.; Washington, D. C.; Miami and Tampa, Fla.; Atlanta Ga.; Chicago, Ill.; Dubuque, Iowa; New Orleans, La.; Baltimore, Md. Boston, Mass.; Detroit, Mich.; Kansas City and St. Louis, Mo.; Silver City, N. M.; New York; Charlotte, N. C.; Portland, Ore.; Philadelphia, Pa.; Providence, R. I.; Nashville, Tenn.; Brownsville, El Paso Galveston, and Houston, Texas; Norfolk, Va.; Seattle, Wash.; Aguadilla, Arecibo, Mayagüez, Ponce, and San Juan, P. R.; Charlotte Amalie V. I.

U. S. Representation in Panama. The U. S. Embassy and Consulate are in Panama City. There is also a consular official in Colón.

Local Sources of Information. In Panama City the national tourist commission, Oficina Nacional de Turismo, in the National Palace, is organized to help visitors with every variety of information. In Colón the commission maintains an office at 5004 Front St. Inquiries about

16

travel in Panama addressed to this agency by mail, P. O. Box 914, Panama City, are answered promptly and fully.

Climate. There are two seasons, wet and dry. The dry, December 15-April 15, is regarded as the best time for visiting the country. The rainy season starts about mid-May and continues until early December, with the heaviest fall October-November. Rainfall on the Atlantic side, where there are showers even during the dry season, is heavier than on the Pacific side. During the dry season many Panamanian families go to homes and resorts in the interior. The average temperature is 80° F. with extremes of 63°-97°. The nights are cool, tempered by the trade winds. Many U. S. residents in Panama for decades find its climate very healthful.

Clothing. Light fabrics are worn exclusively. Warm wraps for evening, umbrellas, rubbers, and raincoats are desirable for the wet season. In the Canal Zone, the regions adjacent to it, and the resorts, an extensive and fashionable wardrobe is desirable for a stay of any length. It is the custom to dress formally in the evenings. Panamanians of the upper classes always dress immaculately and in the prevailing fashion. Correct evening attire for men consists of tropical weight black dinner trousers, white dinner jackets, and patent leather oxfords.

Health. Formerly notorious for its fevers and high mortality rate, Panama has by now been converted into one of the most healthful countries in the world. Good health conditions are not confined to the Canal Zone, but prevail also in the populous regions adjacent to it. Drinking water in and near the Canal Zone is famous for its purity; yellow fever is unknown today, and malaria is steadily being pushed back to the frontiers. In the interior of the country it is safer to drink only boiled, filtered, or bottled water. The hazards from insects and snakes are largely confined to the jungle areas. Public health in Panama City and Colón is under the rigid supervision of the Canal Zone authorities.

The hospitals of Panama, both of the Canal Zone and of the republic, are justly famous. The largest is the government-owned hospital of Santo Tomás in Panama City, which has 600 beds, modern equipment, and a staff of skilled specialists. Another modern institution is the privately owned Panama Hospital. Patients come from remote parts of Latin America to receive treatment in these hospitals. In the Canal Zone the government-owned Gorgas Hospital is well known for its research in the field of tropical disease.

Sports and Recreations. SWIMMING. Splendid swimming facilities include excellent pools on both sides of the isthmus. The Canal Zone has its own pools. The public beaches at Panama City and Colón are often crowded, but excellent surf bathing can be found by driving out of the cities or stopping off at the resort islands. Taboga Island, Santa Clara, and La Venta all have fine beaches; they also offer facilities for boating and a variety of water sports.

BOATING. Sailing off the coast in quaint native craft and excursions by launch are among the popular recreations on both coasts of the isthmus and on the rivers.

TENNIS. Courts connected with clubs, hotels, or resorts in the Canal Zone, the interior, and at the shore are numerous and accessible to visitors.

GOLF. There are four golf courses on the isthmus, one on the Atlantic side and three on the Pacific. The Brazos Brook Club near Colón has an 18-hole course. Of the three courses on the Pacific side, at Miraflores, Fort Amador, and Panama City, the last is considered the most beautiful. Visitors are welcome to play at any of the courses on payment of nominal greens fees.

RIDING. Good mounts are available, and there is much good riding terrain. In parts of the interior the traveler will see much and penetrate far if he is willing to spend some time in the saddle. Chiriquí Province is Panama's horse and cattle region.

HUNTING. All varieties of wild life common to tropical countries abound in Panama, and hunting is not regulated by law. Chiriquí and Darién provinces provide the best opportunities for big game, and jaguar, puma, tigrillos or wild cats, and ocelots are abundant. A small game animal peculiar to these regions is the conejo pintado or painted rabbit. On the plains the favorite game is mule deer. In the bush and in the remote mountains wild hog, which is highly dangerous in packs, peccary, and tapir offer good hunting.

Game birds of many species are plentiful. Wild turkey, partridge, quail, and pigeon all abound. During the dry season there are thousands of migratory ducks, such as pintail, broadbill, Wilson, and bluewing teal. U. S. visitors must obtain permission to bring in hunting guns from the nearest Panamanian consulate. If such permission is not obtained in advance, it may be necessary to deposit the guns with the customs officials in Panama and apply for a permit locally. There is no charge for such a permit. Organized all-expense hunting trips are popular. A week's all-expense trip for two persons, including air transportation, rent of camp, provisions, guides, horses, and the like, costs roughly $125 (1941). Details about such trips may be obtained from the national tourist commission.

FISHING. The name Panama in the Indian tongue means Abundance of Fish. Today many experts regard Panama's Atlantic and Pacific waters as among the world's best big-game fishing grounds. The best deep-sea fishing can be enjoyed in Laguna de Chiriquí, off Bocas del Toro, in Bahía Honda, in the waters along the San Blas coast, and in the Gulf of Panama, especially in the vicinity of the Pearl Islands. In the winter months fishing is better on the Pacific side because of the roughness of the Atlantic.

Amberjacks up to 65 pounds, yellow jacks, groupers, papagallo, for which Panama holds the world's record, and red snapper are plentiful all year. In December-April there are corbina, pompano, rock hind, and barracuda, the latter small and scarce. May-November provides the climax of the big-game fisherman's year, for then Panamanian waters are alive with bonito, dolphin, Spanish mackerel up to 18 pounds, yellow-fin tuna running to 58 pounds, wahoe, and the two greatest of all big-game fish, sailfish and black marlin. Sailfish are especially common. The world's record specimen, 10' 8¼" long and weighing 180 pounds, was taken near the Pearl Islands. Panama also holds all the world records for black marlin. Dozens are taken every year, fish as heavy as 600 pounds having been landed after battles of 45 minutes-11 hours.

The best tarpon fishing in Panama is to be had on the Atlantic side in the Río Chagres below the Gatún spillway. The upper Río Chiriquí was stocked some years ago and abounds with rainbow trout. One fresh-water enthusiast took 200 in a single day, the largest weighing about 5 pounds.

Two clubs for anglers, the Pacific Sailfish Club in Balboa and the Panama Canal Tarpon Club with headquarters in Colón, welcome nonresident competition and are always ready to help visiting fishermen. Boats may be chartered at reasonable rates. Panama is unique in that its big-game waters are so located that fishing excursions are within reach of even moderate travel budgets. The government of Panama offers two trophies to nonresidents catching the largest sailfish on light tackle. The national tourist commission, if informed in advance of arrival, will arrange fishing trips on any given date.

THE NATIONAL LOTTERY is government-conducted, the proceeds being used to maintain the hospital of Santo Tomás in Panama City and several other institutions in the provinces. Drawings are held every Sunday at 11 a.m. and may be witnessed by all. Winning numbers are posted immediately, and the payoff begins at the lottery office as soon as the drawing is ended. Whole tickets cost $13 (1941); they consist of 26 sections that may be bought at $.50 each. The grand prize is $26,000 for the whole ticket or $1000 for each of its parts. There is a second prize of $7800 for the whole ticket or $300 for each part, and a third prize of $3900 or $150 for each part. Numerous minor prizes are also awarded.

Currency. The unit of currency is the balboa, abbreviated B., divided into 100 centavos, sometimes also called the peso and legally equivalent to the U. S. dollar. U. S. currency circulates freely in the republic, often almost to the exclusion of other currency. There is no Panamanian paper money. Coins in circulation are: 1 balboa and 10, 25, and 50 centavos, silver; 2½ and 5 centavos, nickel; 1 centavo, copper.

Banks. The Banco Nacional de Panamá has its head office in Panama City and 14 branches in other cities. The Chase National Bank of New York has branches in Panama City, Balboa, Cristóbal, and Colón. The National City Bank of New York has branches in Panama City and Balboa.

Cost of Living. The cost of living and traveling in and near the Canal Zone is approximately the same as in the United States; in the interior it is less. Inclusive tours of Panama cost $7-$10 a day (1941), depending upon the amount and kind of transportation required. De luxe hotels in or near the Canal Zone charge $3.50-$6 for single room without meals. Restaurant and night club charges are about the same as in the United States. In the interior good accommodations can be obtained for as little as $2.50 a day, $15 a week, or $60 a month, with meals included. The fashionable shore and island resorts charge $3-$4 a day or $21 a week for rooms and meals in the best hotels.

Railroad fare across the isthmus and back is $4.80 (1941), covering 47½ miles. Round-trip fare by bus between Panama City and David, 308 miles, is $11. The same trip, one way, costs $19 by air. Much travel to the interior is by station wagon; the charter charge is $.12 a mile.

The cost of maintaining a private car is slightly higher than in the United States, gasoline costing $.26-$.31 a gallon (1941). Food and manuactured goods are more expensive than in the United States, but the luxury products which Panama imports for visitors' benefit are much cheaper than in the United States, and several sorts of goods, like custom-tailored tropicals, can be obtained at very low cost.

Transportation. ROADS. Although new parts of the isthmus are opened to motor travel each year, the nature of the terrain in Panama presents such difficulties that only a relatively small part of the total area is as yet served by roads. Many bridges are needed. Large sections of the country are as yet not even mapped, while other sections are mapped inaccurately. One lane of the new concrete highway across the isthmus was completed in 1942. The main roads connect the more populous regions and resorts; except for the road from Cristóbal to Gatún these are mostly on the Pacific side. On the E side of the canal a highway connects Panama City with Pedro Miguel; beyond that point it bifurcates, running N to Gamboa and NE to Madden Dam. Another highway runs E as far as Chepo, whence trails continue on into Darién.

The largest road network extends SW of the canal. It runs parallel to the coast, connecting all the larger provincial towns, with side roads to the resorts, and branches running down into the provinces of Los Santos and Herrera. It is possible to motor from Panama City as far as David in Chiriquí Province in the west; an extension to the Costa Rican border will eventually serve as part of the Pan American Highway. Travel by chartered station wagon provides one of the main means of transport, and there is seldom difficulty either in finding a seat in a station wagon or in filling one that has been chartered.

AUTOMOBILES. It costs about $120 (1941) to transport a car from the United States to Panama. Open cars are the most practical. Tires and repairs are slightly more expensive than in the United States. Gasoline costs $.26-$.31 a gallon. The republic observes the custom of driving on the left. Other rules of the road are similar to those in the United States. Travelers who bring cars for their personal use, with registration plates from their country of origin, need pay no consular fees and will receive a special transit permit valid for 90 days. A Panamanian consulate should be consulted for information on documents required. The national tourist commission is also helpful in securing permits.

RAILROADS. There are two main railroads in Panama. The Panama Railroad from Colón to Panama City, a distance of 48 miles, with a 5-mile branch connecting Colón with Fort Randolph, is owned by the U. S. government. Service is similar to that on trains in the United States. The Ferrocarril Nacional de Chiriquí connects the W city of David with Boquete, inland in the coffee country, and with the port of Puerto Armuelles.

AIRLINES. Airways connect the populous areas with efficient service. Pan American Airways has frequent service between Panama City and Colón and David. The Gelabert Airlines, at Avenida Central 80, Panama City, operates service from Panama City to David and Puerto Armuelles. The flight to David takes about 2 hours, to Puerto Armuelles somewhat less than 3 hours. This line also has a service from David to Concepción. Concepción is the starting point for hunting trips in Chiriquí Province. The line also provides a reasonably priced charter service that is of importance to those interested in penetrating remote parts of the republic.

COASTWISE TRANSPORTATION. Banana boats touch at small places of interest along the coasts. These boats are slow and simple but comfortable. There is launch service from points on the Atlantic side. Regular launch service operates between Panama City and Taboga Island.

River travel is of comparatively little importance, the canal having absorbed the Río Chagres, once the main waterway. The other rivers are navigable only by shallow-draft vessels and only for short distances.

TRAILS. In those parts of the interior that are settled but not accessible by road, there are many good saddle trails. Horseback travel to the remoter parts of the interior is increasingly popular. Large parts of the country, however, notably the wilds of Darién, are virtually unexplored and dangerous to the uninitiated and poorly equipped.

Postage. There is regular airmail to and from the United States. Mail for passengers on ships passing through the canal is delivered to the postmaster at Cristóbal, who delivers it on board. U. S. postal rates prevail to and from Panama and the Canal Zone.

Telegraph and Cable Services. There are 33 telegraph and 190 telephone offices. The service is operated by the Panamanian government and covers the entire republic with the exception of Darién. Commercial radio service is handled by the Tropical Radio Corporation. All America Cables has offices in several cities.

Souvenirs and Handicrafts. Strategically located along the principal lane of world travel and trade, Panama is one of the world's most fascinating bazaars. Into its shops pour luxury products from all over the world. Of special interest to North American shoppers are fine goods of Europe and Asia and Panamanian and other Latin American craft articles. Avenida Central in Panama City and Front Street in Colón are lined with the shops of international merchants, among them Persians, Hindus, and Chinese. Most goods are very low in price because of the free port law.

The most popular Latin American goods include handbeaten Colombian and Bolivian silver; novelties of butterfly wings and snake, lizard, and alligator skin; Mexican craft pieces; dolls dressed in Latin American costumes, and, of course, the world-famed Panama hats from Ecuador and neighboring countries, which found their first world market in Panama during the gold rush. In normal times bargains in fine European luxury wares include French perfumes; Sèvres, Limoges, Dresden, and other fine porcelains; dolls; Malacca canes; English and Spanish leather goods; French lingerie; Irish linens; Swedish and French crystal; Swiss watches; petit point; enamelware; Madeira embroideries, and Spanish shawls. The choicest Oriental products include Chinese linens; Chinese, Japanese, and Filipino lingerie; kimonos, pajamas, and mandarin coats; Persian and Bokhara rugs; Kashmir metal tissues and gold thread embroideries; ivory, tortoise shell, and ebony boxes and bric-à-brac; lacquer and inlaid ware. Panama is also an important jewel market. Antique European and Oriental jewelry, finely wrought filigreework, and such semiprecious stones as lapislazuli, turquoise, and crystal are very reasonably priced. Precious gems and natural, culture, and baroque pearls are all tempting. There are also excellent tailoring establishments, specializing in drill, linen, pongee, and other tropical apparel. Visitors should be careful to patronize reputable shops and be wary of the recommendations of porters, touts, and taxi drivers.

Food. In the restaurants of Colón and Panama City and the inns of the more fashionable resorts, an international cuisine prevails. There are several establishments specializing in Oriental foods. Steaks, chops, and the hearty fare of beer gardens are also served. Panama specializes in fine alcoholic beverages imported from all over the world and has good distilleries and breweries of its own. Coffee and chocolate are popular drinks. Every variety of tropical fruit is abundant and good. Temperate-zone fruits are imported. Seafood of all kinds is prepared both according to the methods of skilled international chefs, as at the

Club Unión and the golf club in Panama City and the Strangers' Club in Colón, and according to time-honored native recipes. Panamanians are particularly fond of traditional Spanish cooking. Omelets are prominently featured in the national diet. Tortilla verde, made with spinach and tomato, and tortilla con anchoa, with anchovies and olives, are popular. A favorite rice dish is made in Catalan style with olive oil, small onions, and garlic and served with ham and potatoes; rice tarts are made with lemon, orange, and tropical fruits. Among the ragouts worth trying is guisado de carne, a meat dish made with fried onions, olive oil, pimientos, and tomatoes and served with potatoes; a special tunafish ragout is made with white wine. Fresh fish, expertly cooked, usually with white wine, is a specialty of shore and island resorts. Pastel de pescado, a fish pie, made with a sauce which resembles hollandaise and cooked with lemon and white wine, is very popular. Potato pancakes, buñuelo de patata and bollo de patata, are favorites, the latter being served with mayonnaise and tomatoes. Sancocho, a meat and fish stew, seviche, tazajo, and arroz con pollo or rice with chicken, are not peculiar to Panama but are common to Central and South America. Many desserts are concocted of tropical fruits, and nougats of many varieties and marzipan confections are popular.

Holidays. In addition to regional fiestas Panama celebrates public holidays of several categories, among them anniversaries of events in Panamanian, Latin American, and international history; legal holidays of the United States of America, and holy days of the Roman Catholic Church. The following are official holidays celebrated throughout the republic: New Year's; January 21, founding of Panama City; February 15, Constitution Day; carnival; Ash Wednesday; Holy Thursday afternoon; Good Friday; Easter; May 1, Labor Day; Ascension Day; Pentecost; Corpus Christi; June 22, the first Bolivarian congress in Panama; July 4, Independence Day; July 14, Bastille Day; July 24, Bolívar Day; August 15, Feast of the Assumption of the Virgin; October 12, Columbus Day (Día de la Raza—Day of the Race); November 2, All Souls' Day (Todos Muertos); November 3, secession from Colombia; November 4, Flag Day; November 10, independence in the province of Los Santos; November 28, liberation from Spain; December 8, Feast of the Immaculate Conception or Mother's Day; Christmas.

Fiestas. Fiestas, regional fairs, and other holidays are notable for quaint costumes, traditional pageantry, and general revelry. Carnival takes place on the 4 days preceding Ash Wednesday and is most notable in Panama City. It vies in picturesque gaiety with the carnival in Cannes on the French Riviera and the New Orleans Mardi Gras. Holy Week has a unique flavor in Panama, which can be best sampled in the small towns of the interior. The shy, hard-working peasants, the women in full-skirted dresses with shawls and the men in homespun montunas, come down from their thatched huts in the mountains to take part in the ceremonies. In procession the children pass in white, pink, pale blue, or red, with angel's wings, carrying baskets of flowers which they scatter before the Virgin of the Sacred Heart. Statues of the saints are transported on floats or on the shoulders of the devout. On street corners, devils and angels wage mock battles. In many interior towns, the effigy of Judas is paraded through the streets on Sábado de Gloria (Holy Saturday) just before sunset. Then at 6 o'clock on Sunday morning, following the procession in which the risen Christ encounters St. John and the Virgin, Judas' last will and testament is read in the central plaza. This document includes many jests at the expense of local individuals, and the effigy is burned with much merriment. This ends the official Holy Week ceremonies. Elaborate ceremonial cakes are eaten throughout the observances, and participants and spectators gossip about the year's news from all parts of the republic. Penonomé and Chitré are the best places to observe the Holy Week ceremonies.

All the sizable towns in the republic and most of the hamlets celebrate each the feast of its patron saint with pageantry, pomp, and gaiety. These fiestas are an unexploited field for students of folklore.

REGIONAL GUIDE

CRISTOBAL AND COLON

The Atlantic coast of the Isthmus of Panama, which first figured in the discovery and conquest of the country, is celebrated today because of the world commerce of the city of Colón. The approach to this city by steamer is dramatic. Incoming ships sail past the green hills and hoary ruins of Portobello across Limón Bay toward the hazy background formed by the foothills of the cordillera. Palm-fringed shores rise to view. The silhouetted buildings of Colón, Cristóbal, and Coco Solo appear. There is a constant drone of planes sweeping over the bay. The gray-white pseudo-Moorish Hotel Washington in Colón is sighted from the decks. Then the ships enter the spaces between the gigantic moles that mark the Atlantic entrance to the canal. The great concrete piers are among the largest in the world. Also near by are the coaling station, one of the most modern in existence, the huge oil storage tanks, and the depots that store provisions for canal employees, the Panama Railroad, and the U. S. Army.

Cristóbal, the U. S. town, geographically almost one with Colón but politically a separate city under the jurisdiction of the United States, is immediately adjacent to the docks. Debarking passengers cross Cristóbal on their way to the Panamanian city of Colón. The names of the two cities together form the Castilian version of the name Christopher Columbus. In plan the cities merge almost imperceptibly. Eleventh St., on which the Chase National Bank stands, marks the end of U. S. jurisdiction; the side of the street facing the bank is in Colón, in the republic of Panama. The two cities are built on Manzanillo Island, which is connected with the mainland by an artificial fill.

Colón, founded in 1852 as the starting point of the Panama Railroad, was once known as Aspinwall. Today, with a population of 47,000, it is Panama's second city. It is a center of international commerce and one of the most cosmopolitan cities in the world. All the races of the earth meet and mingle here. Every complexion known to mankind, the tongues of all Europe and Asia, are met with on its streets. Colón has 12 wide, straight avenues and 18 cross streets cutting them at right angles. Front St., the principal thoroughfare, runs almost the entire length of the city near the waterfront. This is one of the world's most varied and exotic shopping places; its shops normally are stocked with wares from European, Asiatic, and U. S. luxury industries and crafts. A free port to luxury wares, Colón is a shopper's paradise. The appearance and atmosphere of the shops suggest an Oriental bazaar. In normal times Colón by night is almost blinding in its electric glare, for the shops stay open late and their radiance is supplemented by the signs of countless places of pleasure ranging from the Strangers' Club and Bilgray's to honkytonks of world notoriety.

The commercial section adjoins Front St. From it is seen the constant procession of steamers entering the canal. At the N extremity of Manzanillo Island is the famous Hotel Washington, property of the U. S. government and considered one of the finest U. S. hotels. From it and generally skirting the shore a palm-fringed avenue extends to New Cristóbal, a recently opened residential section. This drive is the most popular promenade in Colón. It is bounded E by an estuary known as the Folks River. In this section are many modern dwellings

24

occupied by Canal Zone employees. The second promenade is the improved section of Central Ave. known as Paseo Centenario, with a bronze statue of Christopher Columbus, a heroic figure of benign expression protecting an Indian girl. This statue by the Italian sculptor Vicente Vela was a gift from the Empress Eugénie, wife of Napoleon III of France. Other monuments of note on this promenade are a bust of Count Ferdinand de Lesseps, president of the French canal company; a monument to the fire brigade; and a monument to W. H. Aspinwall, John L. Stephens, and Henry Chauncey, builders of the Panama Railroad and founders of Colón. The city's most important park is Parque Colón, between Calle 3 and C. 5, a few steps from Hotel Washington. Weekly band concerts are given here.

Points of interest within the city include the Government Building, at the corner of Avenida Bolívar and C. 6, and the city hall, a handsome building on C. 6, between Av. Herrera and Av. Amador Guerrero, which in addition to municipal offices houses a good public library with books and periodicals in both Spanish and English.

CHURCHES. The cathedral, still under construction, is beautiful. Other churches are those of La Medalla Milagrosa (Miraculous Medal), Av. Meléndez between C. 4 and C. 5, and San José.

CLUBS. The famous Strangers' Club, with a good bar and restaurant, is open to travelers. The Brazos Brook Club, with an 18-hole golf course near Colón, and the Panama Canal Tarpon Club offer guest privileges to visitors.

SHOPS. The following are among the best of Colón's numerous shops: French Bazaar, Front St.; Sander and Fischer, 45 Front St.; Native Art and Alligator Shop, C. 10; Premsing and Sons, 18 Front St. (East Indian); Lobato House-Parsram Parumal, 57 Front St. C. Casullo, 9035 Front St., is considered the leading jeweler, but there are several other good jewelry shops. Bestfit Suits is on C. 11 opposite the Colón commissary.

SOURCES OF INFORMATION. The national tourist commission is at 5004 Front St. Borden's Tours offers excursions.

BANKS. Banco Nacional de Panamá; Chase National Bank of New York.

CAFÉS AND RESTAURANTS. The night life of Colón is intense and vivid. Night clubs and bars are lively, and the entertainment is often spiced by native dancing. The most famous of the cabarets is the Atlantic Nite Club. The restaurants of Hotel Washington and Hotel Carlton are considered among the best night places in the city. Jardín Bilgray's, C. 10 No. 9096, and the restaurant El Trópico, C. Balboa 10077, are very popular and specialize in native Panamanian dishes. The cuisine is also good at Luigi's, Richmond, and Florencia.

HOTELS. Hotel Washington**, owned and operated by the Panama Railroad (U. S. government), is beautifully located, with handsome public rooms and salt-water swimming pool; advance reservations are necessary. Hotel Carlton*, C. 10 and Av. G, under Danish management, with private bath for every room, is comfortable though not luxurious.

NOTE. Hotels are here classified by rates. Two stars indicate the higher rates for the country in question and also, in nearly all cases, mean good accommodations. One star means rates in the medium brackets; no star means either low rates or no information available. An effort is made in all these guides to list hotels in the various cities and towns, but travelers who are accustomed to North American or European accommodations should use the information with care. In the capitals and larger Latin American centers hotels usually have standards comparable with those found elsewhere and at times on a par with those anywhere in the world. In the smaller centers throughout Latin America hotels are often more nearly boarding houses whose standards of accommodations and food make them unacceptable to all but the most adaptable.

COLON'S ENVIRONS AND NEAR-BY EXCURSIONS

Sightseeing facilities in Panama are well organized. The national tourist commission, Borden's Tours, and other agencies offer drives that cover all the near-by points of interest. Those nearest to Colón are included in the regular trip to Gatún Locks, which is made by private car.

Fort Davis and Gatún Locks. Fort Davis is about 6 miles from Colón and connected with it by the excellent Bolívar Highway. The route leads past Mt. Hope, formerly called Monkey Hill, with a burying ground dating from the French canal-building period; the U. S. government printing plant; oil storage station; filtration plant; and the cold storage warehouse that holds much of the Canal Zone's food supply. A little beyond Mt. Hope is the new construction town of Margarita, built to house U. S. employees and their families. It is estimated that Margarita will eventually have a population of 1500. The road is bordered on the right by the old French canal. Fort Davis itself is one of the largest U. S. forts. Just beyond it, past the picturesque Chinese gardens and through lush jungle, are the town of Gatún, Gatún Locks, and Gatún Lake. With 3 sets of locks in a line, Gatún has the largest lock structure in the canal, though the individual locks in the canal are all of the same size. Gatún Locks always hold a ship that is being raised or lowered. Here work is progressing on the third set of locks, about 3000 feet E of the older locks and on the other side of the town of Gatún. A side road leading into the Bolívar Highway leads to the Navy submarine base at Coco Solo, France Field, the U. S. Army aviation field, and the coast artillery base at Fort Randolph.

The Río Chagres and Fort San Lorenzo. A launch trip may be made across the bay, through the breakwater, and SW along the mountainous coast to the mouth of the romantic Río Chagres. It was by damming this river that Gatún Lake was formed. The mouth was guarded by imposing Fort San Lorenzo, a Spanish stronghold that was razed by Henry Morgan. The launch winds up the Chagres over the route followed by the buccaneer on his way to sack Panama City and later by the forty-niners. It traverses a veritable tunnel of tropical vegetation to emerge at the giant spillway created to regulate the level of Gatún Lake.

The French Canal. This scene of abandoned hopes, visited by launch, shows French machinery rotting on the jungle edge. It lies close to the lock gates of Gatún, which may be watched closely in operation.

Portobello, 20 miles NE of Colón, is visited by launch. Today it is a mass of moss-covered ruins rising above the still waters against a backdrop of rugged hills. The site received its name meaning Beautiful Harbor from Columbus in 1502. On Feb. 20, 1597, Francisco Valverde del Mercado founded here, by order of Philip II, a town which soon became the main port of the Caribbean; each year galleons sailed from it with treasure from the New World for the coffers of Spain. To connect it with Panama City, the Spaniards built the cobbled camino real or royal highway, over which annual mule trains brought Inca gold and took back Spanish produce. Because of the hot climate of the unhealthful coast, Portobello never became populous, but once a year it was the scene of a great fair.

As soon as it became known that the treasures of Peru were started on the overland trail, traders poured into Portobello. A city of tents would spring up. A small room rented for $100 a month, a small shop for $800. The treasure fleet consisted of 6-8 warships manned by 5000 soldiers as a precaution against pirates. Hundreds of ingots of silver would be piled in the public plaza, and it took 8-10 days to load the ships. Transactions involving 10-12 million gold pesos were made during the fair. To this day an annual fair is held in Portobello on October 21, the pageant of the Black Christ and Feast of Jesus of Nazareth (Jesús Nazareno). The wealth of Portobello attracted English pirates. Morgan sacked it in 1668 but missed the treasure train. Edward Vernon captured it in 1742 and destroyed the great forts, which were rebuilt in 1751. Francis Drake, trying to strike through it at rich Old Panama, died near by and was consigned to the waters of the bay. Centuries later, Portobello might have regained its old importance, had the terminal of the Panama Railroad been built there instead of at Colón.

Ruins of great historic interest in Portobello are the customhouse dating from 1630, with its forefront and first-floor storerooms in a state of excellent preservation; the Castillo de San Jerónimo, a fort built from the plans of Antonelli between 1667 and 1670 and twice rebuilt, with its sentry boxes, ramparts, cannon, culverins, prison cells, and ammunition boxes still intact; Castillo de Santiago, W on a small peninsula, a fort built to furnish cross-fire, 268 feet long and well preserved; Castillo de San Fernando on the opposite side of the bay, with a monumental entrance, ramparts, and battlements still standing; San Fernandito, a small fort 96 feet long near by, with an adjoining powder magazine; El Perú, an observation post near the Castillo de Santiago; two powder magazines called La Trinchera and La Casamata; the Castillo de San Cristóbal de Camangua, E of the town, a ruin half buried among mangroves; the vestiges of the hospital of San Juan de Dios; remains of the church of La Merced; remains of the Castillo de San Felipe, in its time one of the strongest fortresses in the world, large stones from which were used in the building of Gatún Locks; La Cruz de la Campaña, at the end of Calle Real; Las Tres Cruces (Three Crosses), along the cemetery road; and the cabildo or city hall.

The whole district of Portobello has a scant 2000 inhabitants today, of whom about 800 live in the town. The region is dotted with banana plantations. There is no hotel.

NORTH COAST

Some interesting localities on the N coast can be visited in longer trips from Cristóbal and Colón. These are the San Blas archipelago and the province of Bocas del Toro.

SAN BLAS

The most picturesque section of the republic of Panama, both because of its idyllic natural beauty and its interesting inhabitants, is the archipelago of San Blas, which extends between 74 and 200 miles E of Colón to the Colombian border; it is reached from Colón by airplane or by boat. Excursions of 2 or more days may be made by banana boat, on which accommodations are necessarily very simple. The Guango, a motor vessel specially fitted for the purpose, makes periodic 3-day excursions. On this boat there are good sleeping, bathing, lounging, and deck arrangements.

Emerald-green islands, topped by palms that seem to float on the surface of the sea, are scattered along the coast, above which rise the peaks of green mountains. Columbus, who cruised here, declared that the islands were as numerous as the days of the year. When counted, the Mulata Islands, where the famous Cuna or San Blas Indians live, proved to number exactly 365. They range in size from islets with perhaps half a dozen palm trees to large, thickly populated islands like Portagandi where the paramount chief of the San Blas Indians lives and rules. Fifty of these islands are inhabited by these primitive Indians.

The Cunas are short in stature, broad, and square-shouldered, in physique strongly resembling Asiatics. They have the high flat cheekbones, the narrow slanting eyes, and the straight dark hair of some Oriental strains. A great many of them have flat Mongoloid noses, and many of their women paint a black line down the nose to create an illusion of length. From their admiration of slender legs derives the custom of binding the calves of children's legs. The dress of the women is elaborate. Their skirts, covered with designs, are made of a single piece of cloth arranged somewhat like an East Indian sarong. They cover their heads with a veil or shawl not unlike a sari, hang their ears with huge spangled discs, and wear nose rings from infancy. The men wear loincloths or trousers and often readymade vests hung with ornaments.

These Indians live a life similar to that of South Sea islanders. They are highly skilled in the handling of their cayucos or large dugout canoes and sometimes make sea voyages in them which others would shun in sizable sailing craft. They fish with bows and arrows and also with spears. All the islands that they inhabit lie near the mouths of inland rivers. The Mulata Islands themselves, although they have palms, have little water. The Cunas have plantations along the inland rivers and repair to them for water, to bury their dead, to gather fruit, and to do such cultivation of bananas, yams, and other foodstuffs as their way of life requires. Coconuts and other tropical fruits are exported from the vicinity. They do not stay overnight on their plantations, however, but return to their island villages, which are collections of huts with steeply pitched palm-thatched roofs and streets of sand which, as a rule, are very clean and trim.

The Cunas are highly independent in spirit, though their chiefs periodically visit the capital for the purpose of renewing their pledge of fealty to the republic. Panama gives them a certain amount of local autonomy, prevents their exploitation, and provides for them such paternalistic care as seems necessary for their survival. Every Cuna is a citizen of the republic, but he lives by his own tribal laws. The republic regulates foreigners' visits in the Cuna country and enforces vaccination regulations. Cuna law is administered by a chief who lives on one of the larger islands and is assisted in dispensing justice by a council of elders of his own people.

Porvenir, where visitors stay, is at the head of San Blas Bay. On arrival they are greeted by the cayucos of the Indians. There is no hotel at Porvenir, and visitors are guests of the intendente or governor. In addition to the latter's residence there are half a dozen commodious new bungalows with baths for those who wish to remain a week or more and a small restaurant specializing in Panamanian dishes. These facilities, sponsored by the Panamanian government in connection with inclusive tours to the islands, became possible only recently, for formerly the Cuna Indians forbade their islands to wakers or strangers. Even now strangers may remain after sunset only in exceptional instances on the islands where the Indians actually reside. Excursions, however, include daytime visits to those islands. A trip to San Blas is a unique experience, but should be made only by those willing to tolerate some discomfort.

BOCAS DEL TORO

The Atlantic province of Bocas del Toro, which extends W to the Costa Rican border, is accessible from Colón only by sea and is seldom visited by tourists. It is given over largely to banana plantations. Cacao is also produced. The port of Almirante, on Almirante Bay, is named for Columbus. Almirante Bay forms the SW corner of the larger Laguna de Chiriquí, a major coastal indentation. The United Fruit Co. has there a 1000-foot dock, a modern hospital, and a number of other enterprises, including a cold storage plant. The company formerly operated 130 miles of railroad serving the province. Lately, however, all but 50 miles of the road have been dismantled because of the banana blight which has drastically curtailed fruit output. Interior towns served by the railroad included Torres, Guabito, Sibute, Margarita, and Suretka.

Bocas del Toro, with some 2500 inhabitants, 160 miles from Colón, is capital of the province. It stands on an island in Laguna de Chiriquí. Its main export is bananas, with coffee, cacao, coconuts, tobacco, and hides of lesser importance.

HOTELS. Central; Washington.

Chiriquí Grande and Róbalo are smaller ports on Laguna de Chiriquí.

FROM THE ATLANTIC TO THE PACIFIC

For travelers who are stopping at Colón only a short time and who want to see the canal, Gatún Lake, the route of the Panama Railroad, and the dense jungles, the ideal way of crossing the isthmus is by the planes which operate on regular schedules. More leisurely trips, in addition to that through the canal, may be made by railroad. One lane of the new concrete highway across the isthmus was completed in 1942.

The Panama Railroad has figured prominently in Panamanian history. This railroad, built when, after centuries of slumber, international traffic over the isthmus came to life with a rush following the discovery of gold in California, also represents an epic in railroad building. After great difficulties and large loss of life, the last rail was laid in 1855. For decades the railroad boomed, but it declined when the Pacific Steam Navigation Co. moved away from Taboga Island, taking its world trade along. The canal swallowed much of the original road, but a new route was laid out, and today the railroad flourishes once more, operated by the U. S. government, into whose hands it passed from the French canal company. The trip from Colón to Balboa takes less than 2 hours. Stations include Mt. Hope, Gatún, Monte Lirio, Frijoles, Gamboa, Pedro Miguel, and Corozal, with the Pacific terminal at Panama City. The route parallels the canal and skirts Gatún Lake. Passengers see the dense foliage and bright birds of the tropical forest flashing past.

THE PANAMA CANAL

The trip through the canal, affording an opportunity to observe that great engineering work at close range, is the most sensational and rewarding method of crossing the isthmus. The trip takes about 8 hours. On the Atlantic side vessels enter the channel a thousand yards beyond the Colón harbor breakwater and continue at sea level as far as the town of Gatún, nearly 7 miles from the entrance. The channel here has been dredged to a width of 500 feet and a depth of 42 feet.

Gatún is a town occupied by canal employees, with administration buildings. Here are main locks, which lift the vessel 58 feet. There are six lock chambers, arranged in pairs and in three flights. Vessels southward bound, to the Pacific, enter the lowest lock chamber, with the water at sea level, like that of the outer channel; the watertight gates are then closed, and water is admitted through huge conduits built in the base of the lock wall. The rising water lifts the ships to the level of the next higher chamber. The operation is repeated in the second chamber to raise the ships to the next level. Thus, by stages, the vessel is lifted 85 feet from sea level to that of Gatún Lake, formed by damming the Río Chagres and by other streams. Vessels do not move under their own power in the locks but are drawn on cables by engines called mules, which run on tracks along the top of the lock walls.

The lock chambers and approach walls, of massive concrete construction, are over a mile long. Each chamber is 1000 feet long, 110 feet wide, and 70 feet deep, though the new locks now under construction will be 1200 feet long and 140 feet wide to provide for the largest existing vessels and others still larger that may be built in the future. The lateral walls, 45-50 feet wide at the base, taper to 8 feet at the top. The longitudinal wall dividing the chambers on the east and west is 60 feet thick. Each chamber holds at capacity 6,000,000 cubic feet of water, and 3,000,000 cubic feet are used at each opening and closing of the gates. The water is regulated to rise at the rate of 3 feet a minute. An official standing on top of the lock walls directing the passage of the ship telephones orders to the operator in the control house above the lock wall. This operator follows the passage of the ship with the aid of an electrically operated model of the locks. The lock gates are Gargantuan, each leaf 65 feet wide, 7 feet thick, and 47-82 feet high. The leaves are made of steel and weigh 390-730 tons each.

The view from the deck of a vessel in the upper chamber of Gatún Locks is impressive. The panorama includes the sea, the entrance of the canal, the piers of Cristóbal, the town of Gatún, and, in the distance, the Chagres valley with its giant trees and the lake that marks the end of the canal begun by the French.

Gatún Lake is impounded by a dam which measures 8400 feet long and half a mile wide at its base. Built of stone and clay, it rests on the rock base of what was once a small hill; 23,000,000 cubic yards of material were used in filling it. Here now is the spillway which allows excess water to flow out of the lake, the discharge in the season of heavy rains being regulated by 14 gates arranged in a semicircle extending over 808 feet. Gatún Lake is 164 square miles in area with 1100 miles of shore line. Having passed through the locks, the vessel traverses the lake for a distance of 23 miles. Rotting trunks of jungle trees still rise above the waters near the shore. Crocodiles are often seen.

Gamboa is at the end of Gatún Lake.

Gaillard Cut, formerly Culebra Cut, was blasted through the backbone of the cordillera. Traffic is regulated from a signal station on a small hill at the entrance; signals are flashed from mastheads through the narrow channel. The cut now bears the name of Colonel Gaillard, who directed its construction. At La Pita, a little farther S, and at Gold Hill, near the center of the cut, are other signal stations. Vessels southward bound penetrate the spine of the hemisphere in the miles beyond Gamboa. Impressive rock banks rising on both sides of the canal for a distance of 8 miles from Gamboa give evidence of the terrific struggle of the builders in dynamiting their way through the mountains. Some miles S of Gamboa the vessel passes the deserted towns of Empire and Culebra, whence the work of construction was once directed. From a spot in Culebra, ideal for its outlook over the works, Gen. George W. Goethals supervised the work of blasting the cut. The French excavated millions of cubic yards of earth from this section before they abandoned their canal attempt. On one side rises Gold Hill, 662 feet high; on the other, Contractor's Hill, 410 feet. Here occurred the dangerous and costly slides which continued throughout the period of construction. Two hundred and twelve million cubic yards of material were removed by the Americans from Gaillard Cut, which today is 300 feet wide; the water in it is 42 feet deep.

Paraíso (Paradise), which is reached a few miles farther on, was extremely busy as a repair station and machine shop for many years. It was dismantled a few years ago and its equipment moved to Gamboa. Now Paraíso has been revived as an Army post.

Pedro Miguel, half a mile from Paraíso, marks the end of the cut, and descent to the Pacific begins. The Pedro Miguel locks, of the same dimensions of those at Gatún, are a single pair, lowering ships to Lake Miraflores. When the exit gate is opened, the ship passes into the lake, having made its first stage in the descent to the Pacific. An additional set of Pedro Miguel locks is under construction about 2000 feet W.

Lake Miraflores is comparatively small, mainly supplied by the Río Grande and the Río Cocoli. Its surface is 54 feet above sea level, or 31 feet below the level of Gatún Lake on the cut. Its area is 1.60 square miles.

A mile beyond the lake, the vessel enters the Miraflores locks, two pairs, similar in size to those at Gatún, with a third and larger pair under construction W. Here, by two stages, the vessel is lowered the remaining 54 feet of its descent. On emerging from the lower lock chamber, the ship is in the Pacific stretch of the canal, reaching 8 miles from the lock exit to the deep water at the terminal. In transit one sees the concrete dam that forms Lake Miraflores. On the E side of the locks is a water purification plant serving Panama City, Balboa, and various Canal Zone towns. The works are very large and modern. The water is drawn from the Río Chagres, 16 miles distant.

From the Miraflores locks the traveler obtains a glimpse of the Pacific terminal of the canal. S is seen the end of the canal and part of Taboga Island, 12 miles off the mainland. The town of Balboa lies picturesquely at the foot of Ancon Hill, which separates it from Panama City.

THE PACIFIC COAST

At the Pacific terminal of the Panama Canal stand three cities, Balboa, Ancon, and Panama City, geographically almost merged together. The first is the port and the operating headquarters; the second, the residential district for Canal Zone employees; the third, in the republic of Panama, the business center and the repository of history and legend that date back to the earliest days of the Spanish conquest. Certain localities on the Pacific coast are pleasant resorts reached from the Canal Zone. They are covered under The Interior (p. 42).

BALBOA AND ANCON

A standardized, sanitary U. S. town in a tropical land is made up by Balboa and Ancon. Their avenues and roads are boulevards winding past well-groomed tropical gardens. Heights and waterfront are dominated by trim stone and concrete edifices in the most efficient U. S. tradition. To visitors the towns are of great interest in connection with the canal's operation and give an illuminating picture of how U. S. officials live in a tropical station.

Balboa is located between the canal docks and Ancon Hill, which separates it from Panama City, and extends S to Fort Amador on a kind of peninsula filled in with materials removed from Culebra Cut. Balboa Heights, where the clubs, parks, and administration buildings are located, is on the sides of Ancon Hill. Ancon, curling around the hill N and E, is separated from Panama City by Avenida 4 de Julio. Roosevelt Ave. leads from the piers to Balboa, ending at the edge of Ancon and near the Administration Building in Balboa Heights. It runs along the canal behind the coaling station, drydocks, and canal shops. More or less parallel to the last few blocks of Roosevelt Ave. is the Prado, a beautiful palm-lined avenue which forms the heart of the city. Balboa Road leads SE from Roosevelt Ave., skirts the end of the Prado, and then swings through Balboa and E to Panama City. Many other landscaped streets and roads meander through Balboa Heights and Ancon, those of Ancon leading eventually into Av. Central, the main thoroughfare of Panama City.

BUILDINGS. Chief among the buildings of interest in Balboa is the Administration Building, a massive, three-story structure in which are located the offices of the governor of the Panama Canal and the administrative and technical departments. It stands on a hill beyond the head of the Prado. This eminence and the rising ground about, called Balboa Heights, command a view of Balboa with its busy waterfront and crowded piers, of Sosa Hill and its signal tower at the mouth of the canal, and of Panama Bay. The mural decorations in the Administration Building depict the construction of the canal; the frescoes by W. van Ingen in the rotunda are particularly interesting. A museum on the top floor includes a fine collection of miniatures of ships which figured in the history of Panama since the days of the conquest, old anchors, cannon, and other relics.

At the opposite end of the Prado is the Balboa Club, for U. S. government employees and their families. It is amply provided with public rooms and has the best swimming pool on the isthmus. A few steps from it is a commissary where Canal Zone employees do most of their shopping.

The Balboa stadium, where baseball and other games are played, is in spacious, well-kept grounds between the Prado and Roosevelt Ave., off Clinton St. Roosevelt Ave., flanking the W side of the stadium grounds, is sheltered by a growth of Chinese banyan trees so dense that strollers literally walk through a green tunnel. The avenue's N extremity is near the Balboa station of the Panama Railroad. This station is often used by travelers arriving from Colón, who proceed thence by car rather than continue into the main station in Panama City.

On Balboa Road, which leads from Roosevelt Ave. into Panama City, just beyond the Prado, is the Community House, and farther on the Masonic Temple. On Gavilan Road, which opens off Balboa Road a little beyond and in the direction of Panama City, is the office of All America Cables.

On Quarry Heights, S of Balboa Heights, is the headquarters of the U. S. Army forces in the Canal Zone. In normal times it may be visited by car over a terraced road. The fortifications are interesting, and there is a splendid view of Balboa, the entrance to the canal with its auxiliary works, the surrounding hills stretching away to the Canal Zone borders, and Panama Bay. On clear days Taboga Island is visible.

In Balboa the piers, the drydocks, and the canal shops are of great interest. Amador Road runs out to Fort Amador, a major feature of canal defense. The islands of Perico, Flamenco, and Naos, rocky promontories topped with fortifications and connected with each other and Fort Amador by a long causeway, are visible from the fort. These islands may be visited only by special permission of the military authorities.

In Ancon are the residences of Canal Zone employees. Among the major points of interest is the Gorgas Hospital, a vast complex of buildings, expertly staffed, one of the world's first and best institutions devoted to the treatment of tropical diseases. It is named for the great doctor who cleaned up Panama and later Guayaquil and other focal points of yellow fever. It is a U. S. government institution, to which once came patients from many American points. Today it admits only patients from the Canal Zone.

CLUBS. See under Panama City (p. 38).

BANKS. The Chase National Bank and the National City Bank of New York have branches in Balboa.

HOTEL. Tivoli**, in Ancon, is owned by the U. S. government. It is a luxury hotel of the highest order.

PANAMA CITY

Since the secession of the republic from Colombia in 1903 Panama City (Ciudad Panamá) has undergone much change. Today it is an essentially modern city of 76,000, which still retains many impressive reminders of Creole times, when it was dominated by Spaniards born in the country, and of its great colonial past. Its numerous modern shops and the crowds on the streets and in the cafés, large numbers of them visitors from ships of many nations, give it a completely cosmopolitan air as well as an appearance of being much larger than it really is.

The present city was founded in 1672 by royal decree after Henry Morgan had sacked Old Panama (Panamá Viejo). The name Panama is Indian, meaning Many Fish. The new city was built on a peninsula 4 miles from the old and so heavily fortified that it withstood all attacks. As laid out in the 17th century it occupied the peninsula as far N as the present site of the National City Bank on Avenida Central. The city wall ran along the ocean side of the peninsula, then turned inland toward the gates and the Baluarte de Jesús (Bulwark of Jesus), where the bank now stands. In front of what is now the bank building stood the Puerta de Tierra, the land gate which was regularly closed at 9 p.m. to protect the inhabitants, so that late comers had to sleep outside. Sections of the city N and S of this spot are still sometimes spoken of as adentro and afuera (inside, outside). In the history of Panama City as in that of the whole country periods of languor caused by the decline of isthmian traffic have alternated with feverish booms like that of the California gold rush or the world trade and travel boom of the 1920's.

THE CITY. Av. Central is Panama City's main thoroughfare. Starting at the waterfront at Calle 1ª (1st St.), it first runs W through the heart of the city's oldest section. On reaching the inner end of the peninsula it swings in a wide arc, roughly following the line of the bay, with the newer residential parts of the city between it and the sea. On this avenue, called the Great White Way of Panama City, are the largest shops as well as most of the better bars and cabarets.

The plan of the city's old part is simple. Parallel with Av. Central are Av. A, a block S; Av. B, a block N, and Av. Norte beyond Av. B, along the N shore of the peninsula. The cross streets are numbered, with C. 1ª at the waterfront. In its upper reaches, where it runs N-S, Av. Central flanks the new residential district known as La Exposición because of the international exposition that was held here in 1916 to celebrate the completion of the canal. The principal thoroughfare of this section, the widest and finest in the city, is Av. Perú, a block E of

---

KEY TO MAP OF PANAMA CITY

1. Plaza Catedral (Plaza Independencia)
2. Plaza Santa Ana
3. Plaza Francia
4. Plaza Arango
5. Plaza Lesseps
6. Cathedral
7. San José church
8. La Merced church
9. San Francisco church
10. Ruins of Santo Domingo
11. President's Palace
12. Palace of Justice
13. Municipal Palace (city hall)
14. National Institute (university)
15. Colegio La Salle
16. National Museum
17. Market
18. Club Unión
19. Panama Railroad station
20. Hotel Central
21. Hotel Colombia
22. Hotel Colón
23. National Palace (capitol)

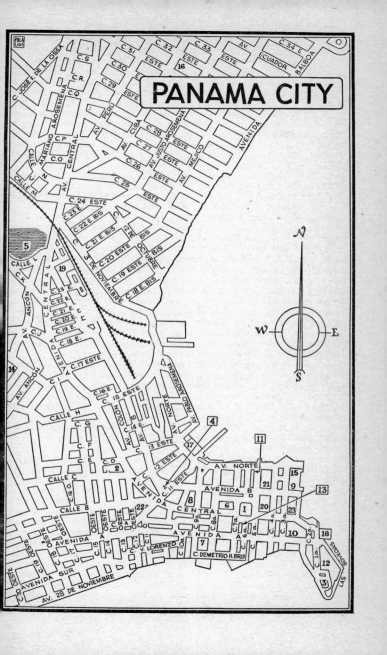

Av. Central. Here, besides splendid homes, are a number of legations, a professional school for women, the Panama Hospital, and the hospital of Santo Tomás. Beyond La Exposición are residential sections known as Bella Vista and Nuevo Bella Vista, the latter with a beach.

PLAZAS. There are four important plazas on Av. Central. Plaza Catedral, also called Plaza Independencia, between C. 5ª and C. 7ª, is the heart of the city and is ornamented with busts of the founders of the republic. On it are the cathedral, the archbishop's palace, the post office, and many important business establishments. Plaza Santa Ana, between C. 12 and C. 13, is decorated with busts of patriots and dominated by the church of Santa Ana. Plaza 5 de Mayo and Plaza Lesseps are also on Av. Central.

In the oldest part of the city, on the little peninsula that Spain fortified so heavily, is Plaza Francia, with a beautiful monument in honor of France in its center, the French Legation, and the Palace of Justice. The Club Unión is a block N. The celebrated National Theater is 2 blocks NW of Plaza Francia. Plaza Bolívar, only a block from Plaza Francia, has a handsome monument to the Liberator and is dominated by the church of San Francisco.

At the S extremity of the city, just below Plaza Francia, is a beautiful esplanade, Las Bóvedas, running along the top of the stone walls built by the Spanish to defend the city. In addition to a fine view of the bay, the stone sentinel tower and the stone image of the Virgin carved on the gateway are of interest. The name Las Bóvedas means arches or vaults; it refers to the cells within the walls in which the Spanish confined criminals and political prisoners.

N of the old part of the city is Plaza Arango. At the point where Av. Ancon, C. L, and Av. Central meet is Plaza Lesseps, with the Panama Railroad station and transportation offices clustered near by. The suburb of Calidonia starts beyond Plaza Lesseps.

Malecón Porras, the sea wall running along the edge of La Exposición, is one of the city's most popular promenades. The famous monument to Balboa, one of the finest in Panama, stands on a promontory projecting from this promenade. This monument shows the discoverer of the Pacific standing on a marble globe borne on the shoulders of representatives of all mankind.

PUBLIC BUILDINGS. Most impressive of the public buildings is La Presidencia (President's Palace), between C. 5ª and C. 6ª on Av. Norte on the waterfront, the site of the palace of the king's representative in colonial times. In the Moorish patio on the first floor native tortoises swim in the fountain. Tame egrets wandering about this patio give the palace its unofficial name of Palace of the Egrets. The columns of the palace are studded with mother-of-pearl. Besides the presidential and clerical offices it contains, on the second floor, the Reception Hall, decorated with portraits of former presidents; the spacious Yellow Room, with the famous Roberto Lewis fresco of Balboa's discovery of the Pacific; a portrait gallery, and a great dining room used for state banquets and furnished with distinguished carved furniture. The top floor, the president's residence, is Moorish, with a beautiful terrace, carpets, and tapestry; the furniture is Granadine.

The Palace of Justice, on C. 1ª; the Municipal Palace, on Plaza Catedral, containing the Columbus library, and the National Palace, on Av. Central, in which the national tourist commission is housed, are all worthy of note.

CHURCHES. The churches of Panama City are numerous; many are old and of considerable artistic and religious interest. Chief among them is the cathedral, on the plaza named for it. Its construction, begun in 1673, required almost a century. In style it is predominantly Romanesque. Its monumental portals are of mahogany from the interior of the country. It is simply decorated, but its domes are overlaid with mother-of-pearl, and it boasts a painting of the Virgin of the Rosary by Murillo, hanging to the right of the W aisle, near the vestry.

The church of San José, at Av. A and C. 8ª, is visited by travelers because of its great age and the story of an altar, a masterpiece of colonial art in solid mahogany overlaid with sheets of pure gold, which was in the Augustinian church during the sack of Old Panama by Morgan. The latter had heard of this altar, but it was hidden from him by being whitewashed. Later it was transferred to the church of San José in New Panama. Among San José's treasures is an image of Our Lady of Grace, of unknown origin, presented a century ago by a Spanish lady of the Obarrio family. San José's organ is one of the finest in Latin America.

The church of La Merced, on Av. Central, opposite the National City Bank and near the spot where the gate once stood, is of cardinal historic and religious interest. Its reputedly miraculous image of the Virgin of the Chapel is an honored relic rescued from the flames of Old Panama. According to legend it became heavier and heavier on the way into the city until it could no longer be carried. Thereupon the statue was placed at its present location, and the faithful showered it with gifts as their prayers were answered. Its treasures include diamond earrings, necklaces, sapphires, and many other valuables. The church is said to have been built with stones from Old Panama.

The church of San Francisco, on Plaza Bolívar, is also colonial in origin, but has been completely modernized. The church of Santa Ana, on the plaza named for it, is not old but of a pleasing and pure colonial style. Other churches include La Santa Familia (Holy Family), Av. B and C. 4ª, and San Miguel. The Sea Wall Church, at the foot of Av. Central, near the government buildings and the Club Unión, is Methodist, with services in English. Most Protestants, however, attend services in Ancon and Balboa.

The ruins of the church of Santo Domingo, at Av. A and C. 3ª, are world-famous, principally because of the flat arch that still stands as evidence of the solidity of early Spanish construction. Legend has it that this arch was begun three times and collapsed twice after the supports were removed. The third time a Dominican monk to whom the method of construction had been revealed in a dream endangered his life by standing under it and praying. That time it held. It is also reported that the arch played a role in the decision to construct the canal in Panama instead of Nicaragua, for engineers agreed that the fact of its continued survival through the centuries proved the country had been relatively free from serious earthquakes.

INSTITUTIONS OF HIGHER LEARNING. The university of Panama, known as the National Institute, is housed in an impressive group of buildings at the foot of Ancon Hill, between C. H and C. I, off Av. 4 de Julio. It has schools of law, science, medicine, and engineering.

Colegio La Salle, at C. 3ª and Av. Norte, has kept intact the room in which the first Bolivarian congress met in 1826. There is also an interesting small museum.

MUSEUM. The National Museum, on Av. Cuba in La Exposición, between C. 31 Este and C. 32 E. (East 31st and 32nd Sts.), contains specimens in archeology, history, national history, and ethnology.

MARKET. The Mercado Público is on the waterfront, at the end of C. 12 E.

THEATERS AND MOVING-PICTURE HOUSES. Panama has many moving-picture houses and a variety of theaters. Chief among the latter is the National Theater, near Plaza Francia, which presents occasional operatic performances and many excellent concerts.

CLUBS. The Club Unión, near Plaza Francia, is Panama City's leading social center. Well equipped, it offers guest privileges to acceptable visitors. The golf club, NE of the city, has an excellent 18-hole golf course and tennis courts and offers guest facilities to visitors for reasonable fees. The Balboa Yacht Club, near Dock No. 1, and the Balboa Gun Club, W of the city and reached by Gavilan Road, are also pleasant and hospitable.

THE CARNIVAL. Panama City has the most elaborate carnival in the republic, lasting four days until the dawn of Ash Wednesday. Originally instituted to celebrate the building of New Panama after Morgan's sack of the old city in 1671, the custom in earlier days was to stage a mock attack by pirates, who, upon their victory, drank and danced in the plazas. Today the carnival is presided over by a queen elected by popular vote from among the city's debutantes and crowned at the beginning of the festivities. Men and women dress in native costumes. The pollera of the women is a gorgeous gown with a voluminous skirt, heavy with embroidery, dripping with the finest lace, and reminiscent of the grandest of Velázquez' infantas with its drooped shoulders and spreading skirts. The men wear montunas with native woven hats and embroidered fringed blouses and trousers. Antique jewelry of gold and pearls and headdresses of flowers and tembleques or scintillating jeweled hair ornaments on springs are much in evidence. Parades of floats commemorating the Spanish and Panamanian past roll through the streets by day. There is dancing every night in the plazas, clubs, cabarets, and toldos or outdoor dancing pavilions erected for the occasion. Here also may be seen the native Panamanian dances at their best. The music is picked out on guitars or beaten on drums by musicians in the velvet and plumes of Dumas' heroes or in fur hats and high boots. The carnival ends at dawn on Ash Wednesday with a curious ceremony called the burying of the sardine.

RACING PARKS AND STADIA. The Hipódromo Juan Franco, a few miles NE of the city on the road to Las Sabanas and easily reached by car or bus, is one of the most modern racetracks in Central America. Races are held Sundays the year around, 2-6 p.m. Parque Kennelworth, near the Hipódromo Juan Franco, at times offers dog races during the summer season. The National Olympic Stadium, constructed for the Caribbean Olympic Games of 1938, is a thoroughly modern structure, a short distance NW of the Calidonia section. Here are held annual soccer, baseball, and basketball matches, as well as boxing bouts, for the Panamanian championship. The Olympic swimming pool, in La Exposición, adjoining the National Museum, on Av. Cuba between C. 31 E. and C. 32 E., was also built for the 1938 games.

SHOPS. Most of Panama City's modern shops are on Av. Central. Among stores selling authentic Panamanian merchandise the following are outstanding: Bazar Francés, Plaza Santa Ana; Novedades Antonio,

Av. Central 28; I. L. Maduro, Plaza Independencia; Félix B. Maduro, Av. Central 21; Escuela Profesional, Av. Perú; Fábrica Nacional de Sombreros, hats, Av. 4 de Julio; Joyería Ponce Rojas, jewelry, Av. Central 41; Joyería Aldrete, jewelry, C. 13 Oeste 67; Ochoa Brothers, Av. Central 89, excellent for Panama hats. El Corte Inglés, Av. Central 16, and Bestfit Suits, Plaza Santa Ana, are generally regarded as the most satisfactory tailors. Other good stores are New India, Av. Central 125, and Royal India, Av. Central 133. Motta's and M. Dialdas and Sons are the largest general stores.

SOURCES OF INFORMATION. The national tourist commission, in the National Palace on Av. Central near Plaza Francia, acts as agent for all transportation companies, sightseeing companies, hotels, restaurants, etc. Full information on tours and sightseeing throughout the republic may be obtained here, as well as maps, guides, brochures, and the like.

BANKS. Banco Nacional de Panamá; Chase National Bank of New York; National City Bank of New York.

RESTAURANTS AND CAFÉS. Popular with visitors are Brady's, occupying a whole building at Av. B and Av. 4 de Julio, where Panama City and Ancon join; Rice's, on Av. Central near the railroad station, typically U. S.; Tourist Club Restaurant, on the way to Hotel Tivoli. Also heavily patronized are Mike's Place, Av. Central 145; Silver Dollar Bar and Restaurant, Plaza Santa Ana; Ancon Inn, C. J No. 20; Peerless Café, C. J No. 16; Lindy's, Av. Central and C. 18 E.

The city's garden restaurants or beer gardens make a specialty of native Panamanian dishes. Among them are Jardín de Cerveza Balboa, C. J. B. Sosa 19; Jardín de Cerveza El Rancho, Av. 4 de Julio; Jardín de Cerveza Atlas, C. Estudiante 68. The restaurants of Hotel Colombia, C. 4ª No. 25, and Hotel Colón, C. B No. 7, also specialize in native foods.

The city abounds in night spots of varying quality. The most famous night club is Happyland, Av. Central, with bar, floor show, and international personnel. Kelly's Ritz, Av. Central, is somewhat more exclusive, with mostly U. S. entertainers. Academia de Baile, Av. Central, is highly popular with Latin Americans. The Peerless Café, mentioned already as a restaurant, has an excellent dance floor.

HOTELS. Central**, Plaza Catedral (Independencia); Colón*, C. B and C. 12.

PANAMA CITY'S ENVIRONS AND EXCURSIONS

Panamá Viejo. The trip to Panamá Viejo (Old Panama) is one of the highlights of Panama sightseeing. The distance is covered in only 15 minutes, and motorists usually drive out through the residential suburbs to the jungle-covered ruins that are all that Morgan and the passing centuries have left of one of the greatest of Spanish colonial cities. The city was founded on Aug. 15, 1519, by Pedrarias. According to native legend it was cursed at that time by Cheremanco, priest of the Indian god Paque-Meecho, who was killed by the Spaniards for refusing to yield the site of the city. Cheremanco, it is said, died prophesying the city's terrible end. For 155 years, however, Old Panama flourished. In 1671, before being sacked by Morgan, it was one of the most important cities in tropical America. It had a magnificent cathedral, the tower of which is still standing; 8 monasteries, the ruins of one of which, that of San José, are still standing; more than 22 warehouses stocked with foreign goods; 200 fine residences and nearly 2000 other houses; a large hospital; a good public market, and a slave market. Three great roads connected the city with the rest of the isthmus. One led to the interior of Panama; another to Ancon, now La Boca; and the third to Portobello. The last, the famous camino real or royal road by which the treasures of Peru were transported to the Atlantic, was by far the most important.

The city's defenses were at times suspected of being inadequate, though it resisted all attacks until Jan. 28, 1671, when Henry Morgan and his corsairs captured it after a ferocious battle. Morgan remained in the ruined city almost a month, searching for loot. When he and his men departed across the isthmus they took with them some 600 prisoners and 175 mules loaded with booty, mostly gold, silver, pearls, and precious stones.

Among the most interesting of the ruins are the King's Bridge, an old stone arch over which the modern drive passes and by which the Cruces trail entered Old Panama; the hermitage of Santa Ana, near the old Negro slave suburb of Malambo; the Dominican monastery; the impressive cathedral with its belltower still standing, and the paved Calle Empedrada.

Madden Dam. Some 24 miles from Panama City, the new Madden Dam was completed some years ago at a cost of $15,000,000. It was built to impound the waters of the Río Chagres, to control that river's flow, and to create a reservoir for drought years that will permit the eventual enlargement of the canal.

The trip to the dam is impressive. Beyond Ancon or Balboa the traveler drives through dense jungle. The trip is made by private car on the Madden road to a point 2 miles beyond Pedro Miguel. Here the concrete road, swinging right, crosses the old historic Cruces trail. At the junction two old Spanish colonial cannon have been placed. The Alajuela road to the Madden Dam here branches off the Gaillard Highway, through 6 miles of forest reserve in the Canal Zone. The dense virgin jungle is dark with great trees entwined with lianas, noisy with birds, and crawling with great snakes that are sometimes run over on the road. Beyond this 6-mile stretch, back again in the republic of Panama, is the settlement called Chilibre, where West Indian and Panamanian farmers have made clearings in the jungle to grow produce for the markets of Panama City and the Canal Zone. The Alajuela encampment, used during the dam's construction, was located on the Río Chagres in rugged jungle country noted for its abundance of white egrets, toucans, brilliant parrots, macaws, and parakeets.

Madden Dam is an impressive sight. It impounds 22 billion cubic feet of water and is 950 feet long, 220 feet high, and in places 229 feet thick.

Taboga Island, 12 miles from Panama City and rich in historic interest, is an ideal vacation spot and the goal of many popular excursions. The island was discovered in 1513 by Gonzalo de Badajoz, who took it only after a desperate battle with the cacique after whom it was named. Francisco Pizarro and Diego Almagro there planned the expedition that resulted in the conquest of Peru. There are rumors of treasure buried in the vicinity after Morgan's sack of Panama City. Morgan and Illingsworth both honored the island with their unwelcome attentions.

Taboga, colorful with roses, heliotrope, jasmine, and lilies, is famous for its fishing from quaint native craft. The white beach and clear water are ideal for swimming. The purity of the spring water has for centuries attracted passing ships to fill their tanks. The island's natives are well stocked with the romantic legends such a place engenders. Points of interest include the town, whose streets are too narrow for vehicles, the church, the Hotel Aspinwall, the pineapple plantations round about, and the flower-clad slopes of the Cruz and Vigía hills. The fiesta of the Virgin of El Carmen is held at Taboga Island on July 15.

HOTEL. Aspinwall*, U. S. management.

The Pearl Islands. Forty-six miles out in the Gulf of Panama and reached by launch, these rich and beautiful tropical islands are visited chiefly for the near-by big-game fishing. The islands were discovered by Balboa, and the Spaniards exploited the pearl beds thoroughly. The boat trip offers splendid views of the canal works, the islands of Flamenco, Naos, and Taboga, and tropical islets. The approach to the Pearl Islands is dramatic, for lofty mountains rise directly from the sea, villages fringe the beaches, and palm groves stand silhouetted against the sky. The thatched fishing village of San Miguel and the islands of San Pedro and San Pablo are most visited.

Chepo. It is possible to drive E beyond Old Panama through dense jungle country, past Pacora, 23 miles out, where there is an old church in which the fiesta of La Candelaria is celebrated on February 2, to the town of Chepo. The highway ends at this quaint settlement, 38 miles from Old Panama. Beyond it a trail leads through Panamá province toward the point whence Balboa first saw the Pacific. It is impractical today for ordinary visitors to reach that spot, for Balboa's old trail is even less known today than when he and his men first assayed it.

Darién. Trips to the province of Darién are now arranged through the national tourist commission on the yacht Dolphin, with side trips in dugout canoes. They may also be arranged on banana steamers to the Gulf of San Miguel, but these are recommended only to the more adventurous and adaptable, who are able to put up with primitive camping conditions and are willing to take their own food with them from Panama City.

A mountainous jungle region, only partly explored, this part of the republic stretches toward the Colombian border. It has long been of interest to adventurers in search of fabled lost mines and treasures; to naturalists studying the fauna and flora, especially the strange migratory butterflies; and to ethnologists studying the local Indians. Much of it, however, is considered dangerous country, and a good many of those who have entered it never returned.

The picturesque Indians found near the Gulf of San Miguel are friendly. They bear little resemblance to the San Blas Indians, for they are taller, straighter, and more nearly like the Goajiros and other South American Indians. They hunt with bows and arrows, antiquated shotguns, and rifles. For fishing they use hook and line and barbed spears. Their homes are built 5-10 feet above the ground and are roofed with palm fronds; the sides are left open. Both men and women paint their bodies in geometric patterns with highly colored native dyes. The women wear a saronglike cloth from waist to feet, heavy necklaces, and silver earrings. The men wear a red loincloth and heavy silver earrings and bracelets. When they can get them, the men prize readymade vests, which they often adorn heavily with beads.

THE INTERIOR

The section known as the interior of Panama consists of that part of the republic which extends in a general W direction from the canal to the Costa Rican border. It is accessible by road and air and is rich in attractions. Many all-expense conducted tours are operated from Panama City to this part of the country; information about them may be obtained at the office of the national tourist commission.

Typically Central American in character and retaining much of its old Spanish colonial tradition and culture, the interior is also interesting for its Indians, who differ radically from the San Blas and Darién Indians. These Indians, of a number of types and often of fairly mixed blood, resemble those of other Central American countries. They are of interest to the traveler for their customs, costumes, and crafts, and many of them can be seen in the normal course of excursions to the shore and mountain resorts and at the festivals and fairs at the ports where fruit liners call. Those on the Atlantic side, near the Laguna de Chiriquí where Columbus found gold, have mixed freely with Negroes and have deteriorated somewhat. Those on the Pacific side, especially the mountain tribes, are alert, clean, and attractive and display an engaging fusion of ancient Indian and European traditions. Their ancient tribal customs are best observed during the feasts of the Church. Holy Week offers occasion for a display of costumes and customs which show both Spanish and native influences. The greatest individuality appears in local feasts of patron saints. To these the Indians from the hills come in Panamanian costume, bringing the pottery and textiles which they make in their huts. They have great dignity and as a group are aloof but friendly.

There is daily air service from Panama City to David, with connections thence by road or train to the famous Boquete highlands. Overland excursions to the interior from Panama City by station wagon or private car begin via the Thatcher ferry, which crosses the canal, and then by the Thatcher Highway to the edge of the Canal Zone. There begins the National Highway, which is paved as far as Santiago (162 miles) and is in all-weather condition, with dirt surface, as far as David (308 miles from Panama City), near the Costa Rican border, the leading center of W Panama. The best time to visit the interior is during Holy Week, when the full pageantry of native celebrations can be observed in nearly all the towns.

Arraiján, with 700-odd inhabitants, a quaint, thatch-roofed town, 500 feet above sea level on the border of the Canal Zone, is reached by the Thatcher Highway. The National Highway begins here. The town is the center of an agricultural region.

Chorrera, with 2000 inhabitants, lies 12 miles beyond Arraiján, past a stretch of dense tropical forest. It is a busy provincial town, with modern improvements, which is devoted to cattle, coffee, and orange raising. A passable road across the savannas connects it with its port, Puerto Caimito, a picturesque place. Two miles from the town is a waterfall in the Río Caimito, much frequented for bathing and fishing. The feast of St. Francis on March 30 is a notable local fiesta. The surrounding country abounds in deer and birds. Two small hotels accommodate visitors.

U. S. hunters frequent the Café Alemán, a roadhouse 9 miles from

Chorrera on the highway, locally famous for its cuisine and hospitable atmosphere.

Capira, a hamlet of 375 inhabitants, about 12 miles from Chorrera, is named for an aboriginal cacique and is one of the oldest towns in the republic. It is the center of a fertile region, but of little interest to travelers save for its mountain scenery. The Orzini tangerine and orange plantation is 2½ miles from the town.

Campana, a hamlet with 300 inhabitants, 4 miles from Capira, is set among famous orange groves. The town is popular for river bathing, for there are a number of dead-water pools at altitudes of 1000-2000 feet. The country near by is rich in mineral wealth, and the old Spanish mines are of great interest to visitors. Mines are now being worked by two gold companies. Campana Hill, about a mile from the bridge over the Río Capira, offers one of the finest views on the National Highway, with the cordillera, a beautiful tropical valley, the calm blue Pacific, and the Otoque Islands all visible.

From Campana the road spirals down to 120 feet altitude on the plains of the Río Sajalices, the pools of which are enjoyed by bathers. Shrimp fishing by flashlight is a popular sport. Beside the river bridge is a house where a Chinese cook prepares excellent shrimp and chicken dinners for travelers. The road beyond Campana traverses real tropical country abounding in game. A strange monolith on the edge of one of the mangrove swamps attracts much attention.

Bejuco, with 691 inhabitants, 8 miles from Campana, is the center of a coffee region and has a lively Sunday market. Between Bejuco and the sea, 4 miles away, cattle graze on communal lands.

Chame, a hamlet with some 400 inhabitants, 20 miles from Bejuco, skirted by the highway, is an antique town of thatched houses which was an Indian settlement before colonial times. The inn of La Cabaña, an old family hacienda with thatched cottages, is famous for its Panamanian dishes.

Excursion from Chame. Nueva Gorgona, 4 miles in on a side road leading to the sea, is a settlement founded to accommodate the inhabitants of Gorgona, which was swallowed by Gatún Lake. It was not a success, however, until recently, when Canal Zone employees began to come there because of the bathing beach.

San Carlos, 59 miles from the capital and 12 miles from Chame, is a quaint town of white painted houses with gardens. It attracts many visitors because of river bathing in the Mata Ahogada, sea bathing, boating, and the game in the wild country beyond. The great fair of San Carlos, famous throughout the republic, is held on January 20. HOTEL. Ansonia, clean and comfortable.

Excursions from San Carlos. Three miles beyond San Carlos a side road leads inland toward El Valle. Five miles beyond the highway this road begins to climb through steep mountains that resemble the Pyrenees and are famous for their scenery. The air is cooler, and coconut palms give way to orange and grapefruit trees. The car fords numerous small streams. There is a matchless view from the summit, Los Llanitos, 2600 feet above sea level. El Valle, 2000 feet above sea level, is on a plateau 5 miles long and 3 miles wide, surrounded by rugged mountains, watered by the Río Antón and numerous rivulets, and with a delightful climate even in the hot season. The road traverses the plateau for its entire length. Described in tourist literature as Panama's Shangri-La, El Valle has become a popular resort where many resi-

dents of Panama City and the Canal Zone are building summer homes
The village is picturesque, and the natives are handsome Indians. There
are boarding houses, a small hotel, and many facilities for pleasure.

La Ermita is a hamlet set in a fruit grove a mile from the main highway, on a side road that branches off 10 miles beyond San Carlos. It is
the last town in the province of Panamá.

Santa Clara, with the beach resort of La Venta near it, is 17 miles
from San Carlos. All modern facilities for beach and water sports are
available. Launches can be hired for fishing parties and for excursions
to Pescaderías, where the inhabitants of Río Hato, a few miles beyond
Santa Clara, go to fish. Riding is excellent in the vicinity, and saddle
horses are supplied by the hotel. Hunting for wild fowl in the vicinity
of Antón and Río Hato is popular.

HOTEL. Santa Clara Inn**, on the beach, is under Danish management and is perhaps the best hotel in the interior. A beer garden and
tourist camp were recently opened under U. S. management.

Antón, 12 miles from Santa Clara, is a town of 1500 devoted to stock-
raising. Pretty and modernized, it is known to visitors for the confection
of manjar blanco which is sold in its streets.

Penonomé, with 3000 inhabitants, capital of Coclé Province, 99 miles
from the capital on the highway, dates back to the conquistadores and
has quaint cobbled streets, old buildings, and a pleasant park. The
town is one of the best places to spend Holy Week. Formerly the
native flagelantes held weird rites there, but these have been stopped.
At Las Mondozas on the Río Zarati, a mile from the town, there is a
bathing establishment. Near the town excavations are being carried on
by Harvard University and the National Institute. Interesting pre-
Columbian objects found here are shown in the National Museum in
Panama City. There are two inns.

Natá, with some 800 inhabitants, 21 miles W of Penonomé, was an
important center in Spanish days. Its full name, Natá de los Caballeros
(of the Knights), derives from the Spanish noblemen who founded it
Its church is said to be one of the oldest still in use in the Americas.
Alterations have changed the colonial aspect of its façade, but its
interior is priceless and boasts a painting attributed to Murillo. Four
miles beyond the town, with the spire of Aguadulce already in sight,
the road traverses a sterile plain to enter the sugar cane region. The
show place of the vicinity is the Ofelina plantation, which produces
20,000-40,000 sacks of sugar yearly.

Aguadulce (Sweet Water), with 2500 inhabitants, 6 miles from Natá,
is near the country's salt beds. Its population is engaged in stock-
raising. The town has handsome private residences and public buildings and a large hospital.

HOTELS. Pan-American; Panama.

Excursions from Aguadulce. Calobre is a mountain spa accessible only
over an indifferent road. Its hot springs are recommended for rheumatism. The scenery presents views of unspoiled mountain grandeur, and
the ranges beyond Calobre stretch without road or inhabitant far up
into Central America. Fourteen miles from the modest but comfortable
hotel, 2200 feet up in the mountains, is a famous lake, La Yeguada, a
mile long, half a mile wide, and of unplumbed depth.

Pocri, with 1400 inhabitants, is a mile away from Aguadulce on a
side road. The Santa Rosa sugar plantation here is the largest on the

isthmus. A mile beyond, a cart road leads into the rich Azuero Peninsula.

THE AZUERO PENINSULA

Parita, 18 miles down the peninsula from the National Highway, founded in 1556 and named for a local cacique, today has 1000 inhabitants. There is a colonial church with beautiful carved wooden altars and lectern.

La Arena, 6 miles farther, is an Indian town known for its pottery.

Chitré, a mile beyond La Arena, with 5000 inhabitants, capital of Herrera Province, is an old but progressive city with an attractive church and park, factories, and thriving trade. Launches run between its port, 3 miles from the town, and Panama City.

The town has two small but good hotels.

Excursion from Chitré. Ocú is an old colonial town of about 1000 inhabitants, some 20 miles W of Chitré. It can be reached by car only in the dry season, but the national tourist commission arranges excursions to it from Panama City by plane or, in season, by station wagon. The town is clean and bright and has preserved many colonial customs. Most of the inhabitants wear the Panamanian national costume, and many of the men have their teeth filed to points. The town is best visited on January 19-24, during the celebrations in honor of its patron, St. Sebastian. These celebrations are marked by bullfights, cockfights, and many native dances, some in special costume.

Los Santos, 2 miles S of Chitré on the highway, was founded in 1555 and is set in beautiful meadows stretching toward the sea. It is one of the quaintest towns of the isthmus. Its low tile-roofed houses, its cobbled streets, and its fine old church with paintings, sculptures, and vessels brought centuries ago from Seville are entirely Spanish in character. The town has a distillery and two salt refineries.

Guararé, with 700 inhabitants, is 14 miles beyond Los Santos, in a region of sugar cane, corn, rice, yucca, and grazing cattle.

Las Tablas, with 2000 inhabitants, 3 miles S of Guararé, capital of Los Santos Province, is a progressive plains town whose people are all of European descent. A branch road of 8 miles leads to the port of Mensabe, which serves the provinces of Los Santos and Herrera.

Santiago, with 2200 inhabitants, beyond Aguadulce on the National Highway, 162 miles from the capital, is the capital of Veraguas Province. Its old buildings and ancient church bespeak its colonial history. In its park stands a statue of Urraca, the chieftain who defeated the Spaniards. Santiago is the home of the national normal school.

Excursions from Santiago. Four miles out, in the hamlet of Atalaya, is a quaint church which justifies the additional mileage required to visit it.

Las Palmas, with 8000 inhabitants, is W off the main road, high in the mountains and in gold country.

Soná, with 1600 inhabitants, second city of the province of Veraguas, 29 miles SW of Santiago, is in a deep, wooded valley. The port of Barranco Colorado on the near-by Río San Pablo handles all the commerce with Panama City. The bay, Bahía Honda, S on the Pacific coast, is used by the U. S. Fleet when it maneuvers in isthmian waters.

Remedios, with 750 inhabitants, 42 miles W of Soná and 249 miles from Panama City, is the first town in Chiriquí Province, the westernmost and second most important of the country's provinces. The road passes through rich hardwood forests and over great plains among the foothills of the cordillera. Beyond Remedios the road runs through the town of Boca del Monte, from which Horconcitos is reached by a short side road. There is extensive stock raising in the vicinity, and Horconcitos is a center for tanning and leather working.

DAVID

Third city of Panama, David, with 5000 inhabitants, is 60 miles from Remedios on the National Highway and 308 miles from Panama City. Colonial in origin and character, David is set amid beautiful surroundings. Its residences are surrounded by gardens. The main thoroughfare, Avenida Central, has large stores and refreshment places. The Río David, rolling languidly through the town, forms wide pools that are enjoyed by bathers. The chief points of interest are the new hospital building; the old park; two old churches, one of which has a separate square tower; the exclusive Club David, and the residential section El Retiro. The surroundings are beautiful with fruit groves. The town has numerous industries and is well known for the excellent saddles and harnesses made there. It is served by the Chiriquí Railroad leading to the ports of Pedregal and Puerto Armuelles and to the Boquete highlands. The annual fiesta, March 19, is celebrated with balserias, which are unique Indian sports, and bullfights.

HOTELS. Lombardi; Santiago.

EXCURSIONS FROM DAVID

Concepción, with 1200 inhabitants, is a coffee and banana center which is connected by railroad with David.

Puerto Armuelles, on the coast and reached by railroad from Concepción, is a banana port, the chief port of Chiriquí Province, and an enterprise of the United Fruit Co. It is a port of entry for travelers on Great White Fleet cruises, and several inclusive tours of the isthmus start from here. This and Bocas del Toro on the Atlantic side are the only deep-water ports except the canal's terminals at which liners call regularly.

THE HIGHLANDS OF BOQUETE

The highlands of Boquete, inland from David and only 30 miles from the sea, though with an altitude of some 4000 feet, form Panama's most popular resort region. Many U. S. citizens live here, cultivating the coffee and fruits for which the region is famous. Many attractive coffee and flower plantations may be reached by car, others on horseback. The trails through the surrounding mountains, some more than 11,000 feet high, are well marked, and there is beautiful scenery all around. Orchids grow in abundance in the forests and around the streams, and many scientists come to Boquete every year to collect all sorts of specimens.

Swimming in the pools of the cold mountain streams is delightful. Many visitors dig for gold and ancient pottery in the numerous Indian graves. The region is especially attractive to hunters and fishermen. In the mountains are found deer, lions, jaguars, tapirs, otters, wild pigs, pigeons, and turkeys. The streams have trout.

Boquete is reached by rail-motor from David. The trip takes about 1½ hours. The town can also be reached by secondary road.

HOTELS. El Nuevo*; Wright's*. Both are under U. S. management and have good rooms and excellent cuisine. There are also three Panamanian hotels.

INDEX TO THE REGIONAL GUIDE

THE REPUBLIC OF CUBA

CUBA

BY EMMA HARRIS OTERO

The largest of the Greater Antilles and indeed of all the Caribbean islands, Cuba lies at the entrance to the Gulf of Mexico, less than 150 miles south of Florida, a little over 100 miles east of the peninsula of Yucatán, and about 60 miles west of Haiti. Its north shore faces the Atlantic Ocean and its south shore the Caribbean Sea.

Three principal mountain ranges, turbulent short rivers, and rolling green valleys make the country scenically beautiful, while the cities are filled with holiday crowds at almost every season of the year. Good hotels, sparkling night clubs, and gay shops in the cities and good fishing, sailing, and swimming along the fine beaches invite the traveler. More than anything else, the combination of Spanish and United States culture patterns makes Cuba attractive to the traveler from the north; the environment is similar enough to his own to make him feel completely at home, while at the same time it offers enough novelty to make life different and exciting.

HISTORY

PRE-CONQUEST. There were two distinct pre-Columbian cultures in Cuba, one older than the other. Both are believed to have been brought by successive migrations by way of Haiti from the South American coast in the vicinity of the present Guianas and to have been Arawak in origin, entirely unrelated to the warlike and cannibal Carib tribes of the Lesser Antilles. There is nothing to indicate that the aborigines of Cuba were influenced by the Maya culture of Yucatán or the early civilization of Florida and the North American coast of the Gulf of Mexico.

The earlier tribes, the Siboneys or Ciboneys, whom Bartolomé de las Casas described as being "natural and native of this island," inhabited all of Cuba and its outlying islands until a century or so before the Spanish conquest. Most of them, living in the interior, were cave dwellers and hunters; others were fishers along the shore, whose shell heaps have yielded evidence of connection with the aboriginal population of the Florida keys; still others were lake tribes whose pile villages are still unexplained by archeologists. Of these primitive people Diego Velázquez de León wrote, in a letter in 1514, that their manner of living "is that of savages, as they have no houses nor seats nor towns nor farms, nor do they eat anything but the game they catch in the woods, and turtles and fish." The 14th and 15th centuries saw the gradual infiltration of Arawak-speaking tribes from Haiti, who had migrated from South America later than the Siboneys. They called themselves Tainos, meaning good men, not cannibals. Their greatest influx into Cuba probably came as little as 50 years before the Spanish discovery of Haiti. They were stronger and more advanced in culture than the Indians of the older strain, whom they described in their own tongue as Ciboneyes or rock men. The Tainos were peaceable in their homeland of Haiti, but when they migrated to Cuba they set out to make it their own. Gradually they conquered the Siboneys and pressed them into personal service. Those of the Siboneys who could escape moved westward until, by the time Columbus first saw them, on his

3

second voyage, they held little more than the outlying islands and parts of the mountainous interior. The culture of the Tainos, developed in Haiti, as bowls and implements of some archeological importance prove, seems to have spread westward. For example, the palm-thatched huts of the present Seminole Indians of Florida seem to have derived from the aboriginal Cuban bohíos, the Seminole use of the coontie root from the ancient cassava industry of the Tainos.

THE CONQUEST. The island of Cuba was discovered by Columbus on his first voyage of exploration when, after landing on Oct. 12, 1492, on the island of Guanahani, which he renamed San Salvador and which was probably the present Watlings Island, he continued westward and on October 28 landed on the coast of Cuba, at a point which is thought to have been near the present town of Nuevitas. After exploring the island for some time before he again turned eastward, he bestowed upon it the name of Juana in honor of the daughter of the Spanish king and queen, Ferdinand and Isabella. Later it was called successively Fernandina, Santiago, and Ave María, but the original Indian name of Cuba finally prevailed.

Columbus sailed along the south shore of Cuba on his second voyage, but, convinced that it was part of the mainland of Asia, he turned back before reaching the western tip. He reported that this land, if it was not actually the mainland of China, must at least be somewhere near the Chinese coast: "This I know, because the sea comes here in a different manner from what it has done until now." He had mistaken the Gulf Stream for a current of similar character which he believed to flow between the mainland of China and outlying islands. Columbus died in the belief that he had discovered in Cuba the mainland of a continent, for it was not until 1508 that Sebastián Ocampo proved that Cuba was an island by circumnavigating it.

At last, in 1511, when Columbus' son Diego Colón was governor of the island of Española or Hispaniola, which is now occupied by the Dominican Republic and Haiti, the conquest and settlement of Cuba were undertaken. To this end, Diego Colón selected Diego Velázquez de León to head a colonizing expedition which included such famous men as Hernando Cortés, Pánfilo de Narváez, and Bartolomé de las Casas. This expedition was notably successful and by 1519 had founded Santiago de Cuba, Havana, and Trinidad. To them fell the easy task of subduing the native Indians, who were peace-loving, fearful, and unresistant. The Spanish were able to dislodge them from their villages, but did not succeed in gaining native help in their agricultural and mining enterprises. So harsh were the new overlords and so harmful was the new culture to the Indians that during the early 16th century the latter perished in great numbers. By 1553, hardly an Indian remaining, it became necessary to import Negro slaves to make up for the shortage of labor.

Diego Velázquez de León is generally regarded as the first governor of Cuba, although some hold that he was a colonizer only and give Hernando de Soto the primary position, for it was Soto who rebuilt Havana in 1538 after it was attacked and burned by the French. Later attacks in 1554 and throughout the 16th century finally caused the Spanish to start building the formidable, almost medieval Morro Castle in 1589 as a protection to Havana harbor. For a number of years Cuba served as a base from which Spanish power was extended throughout the New World. As early as 1502, Columbus reached out

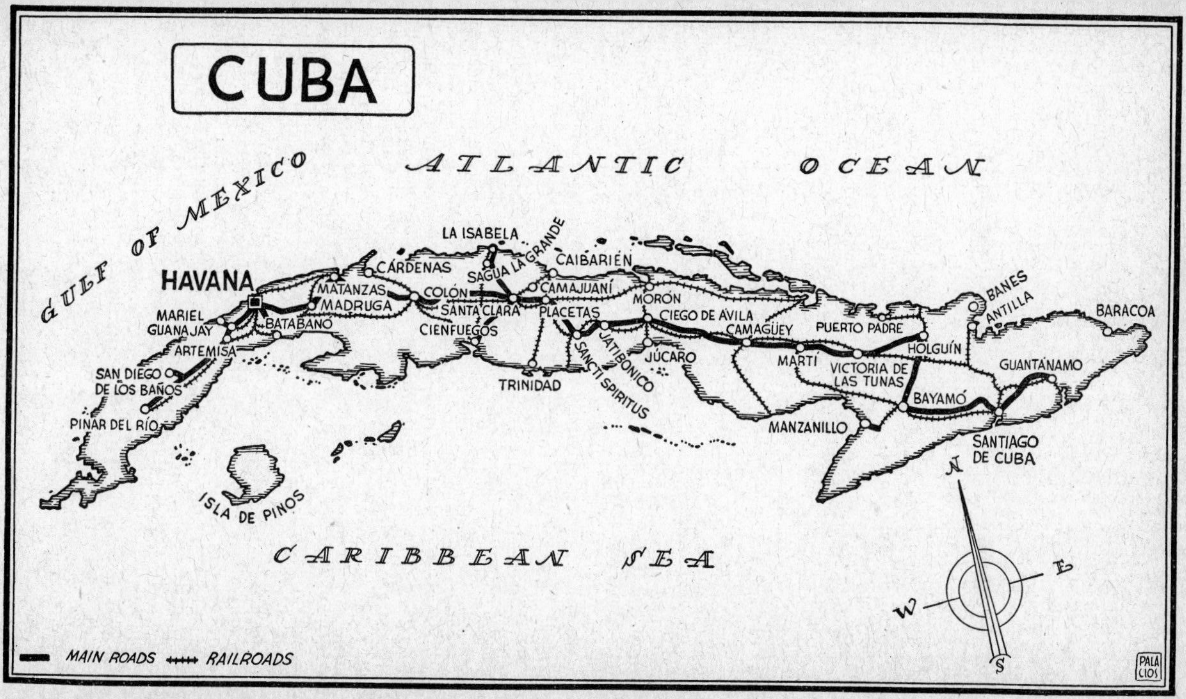

CUBA

GULF OF MEXICO

ATLANTIC OCEAN

CARIBBEAN SEA

HAVANA

MARIEL
GUANAJAY
ARTEMISA
SAN DIEGO DE LOS BAÑOS
PINAR DEL RÍO
BATABANÓ
MADRUGA
MATANZAS
CÁRDENAS
COLÓN
SANTA CLARA
CIENFUEGOS
LA ISABELA
SAGUA LA GRANDE
CAIBARIÉN
CAMAJUANÍ
PLACETAS
SANCTI SPIRITUS
TRINIDAD
MORÓN
CIEGO DE ÁVILA
JATIBONICO
JÚCARO
CAMAGÜEY
MARTÍ
VICTORIA DE LAS TUNAS
PUERTO PADRE
HOLGUÍN
BAYAMO
MANZANILLO
BANES
ANTILLA
GUANTÁNAMO
BARACOA
SANTIAGO DE CUBA

ISLA DE PINOS

N   E
S   W

MAIN ROADS +++++ RAILROADS

to discover and found settlements on the coast of Central America. From Santiago de Cuba, Cortés set out to conquer Mexico; and from Havana, Soto sailed on the expedition that resulted in the discovery of the Mississippi. Other famous explorers and conquistadores also used points in Cuba as their bases.

THE COLONIAL PERIOD. While the history of Cuba during the 17th century is, unfortunately, not a story of extensive internal development, owing largely to the constant peril of attacks by Dutch, French, and English pirates, it is not without its glory. Spanish social and governmental institutions became established, and colonial towns grew to importance. By 1607 Santiago de Cuba, founded by Diego Velázquez de León in 1514, had grown from a tiny hamlet to a town of 4000 citizens, and by 1634 Havana, whose harbor sheltered Spanish treasure ships before they were convoyed to Spain, had become such an important center that by royal decree it was given the title of Key of the New World and Bulwark of the West Indies (Llave del Nuevo Mundo y Antemural de las Indias Occidentales). To this day Cuba is so proud of the high distinction conferred in colonial days that its coat of arms shows a key between Florida and Yucatán. Cuba is called also the Key to the Gulf of Mexico. The city of Havana's coat of arms has a gold key with three silver castles in the background.

During the 18th century Cuba, along with the rest of Hispanic America, felt repercussions of Old World struggles. In the war between Spain and England which resulted from the Bourbon coalition a British expedition was sent to the West Indies under the command of Lord Albemarle. After a two months' siege, Havana surrendered to him on Aug. 14, 1762, a victory which conceded the whole island to the British. Cuba remained under British rule until the next year, when it was returned to Spain by the Treaty of Paris, promulgated on July 6, 1763.

In the following years many Spanish settlers and French refugees from Martinique and Santo Domingo arrived, bringing with them knowledge of coffee raising and bee culture, and agricultural and commercial prosperity increased. Spain sent out governors or captains general who not only were in charge of the government, but also headed the army and controlled the ecclesiastical power. Among the captains general sent to Cuba in the 18th century, Luis de las Casas and Santa Clara are credited with progressive measures such as promoting education and constructing public works. The rest of the long list of governors who came after them ruled so arbitrarily and oppressively that hatred for the Spanish grew rapidly.

THE REVOLUTION. As a result, the movement for independence was initiated early in the 19th century. There were various uprisings, notably the Black Eagle revolt of 1830 and the unsuccessful rebellion led by Narciso López of Venezuela about the middle of the century, in which the Cubans made heroic efforts to throw off the Spanish yoke. The Spaniards, with their greater resources, crushed each uprising ruthlessly. But the spirit of the Cubans could not be subdued. In 1868 the situation, already bad, was made worse when the Spanish government increased taxes and created a local army to serve as a militia. The Cubans, under the leadership of Carlos Manuel de Céspedes, taking advantage of unsettled conditions in Spain, rose in revolt. Their famous battle cry, the Grito de Yara, on Oct. 10, 1868, started the struggle, and six months later they declared themselves independent of Spain and elected Céspedes president of the republic of Cuba.

Under a new constitution the people were permitted freedom of worship, slavery was forbidden, and a republican army was created, commanded by Ignacio Agramonte y Loínaz. In the ensuing struggle, known as the Ten Years' War, the Cubans fought with such spirit that it was not until Spain sent out Gen. Arsenio Martínez Campos with a substantial army that fighting ceased. Even then peace was not really restored. During the years that followed, Spain agreed to some changes supposedly favorable to the Cubans, such as granting representation in the Spanish Cortes or parliament in 1879 and the abolition of slavery in 1886, but these measures did little to improve conditions on the island.

In 1895 revolution broke out anew. This uprising, headed by the illustrious José Martí, had been well planned and was at first successful. Gen. Máximo Gómez from Santo Domingo and the brothers Antonio and José Maceo from Costa Rica came with reinforcements to help the insurgents. Salvador Cisneros y Betancourt, who had been active in the Ten Years' War, again offered his services and was elected president. Two other notable leaders were Calixto García, who raised funds and a band of 180 men in the United States, and Bartolomé Masso, who served the insurgents as vice-president. Finally Martínez Campos, the Spanish general, was recalled to Spain in 1896 because he had failed to quell the revolution. Gen. Valeriano Weyler was sent in his place. Weyler's attempts to reorganize the Spanish forces and to crowd the rural Cubans into towns and villages where they could be more easily watched by the militia—the famous concentration policy—interfered with agriculture and industry so seriously that thousands died from disease and starvation, and Weyler earned himself the unwelcome nickname of the Butcher.

Spain, seeing that conditions grew worse, recalled Weyler and sent Gen. Ramón Blanco to set up a parliamentary government giving Cuba a larger degree of home rule. This measure failed to conciliate the revolutionists, who wanted a free Cuba, and although the original leaders had all met death, the Cuban patriots continued the struggle for freedom. In 1898 rebellion broke out in Havana with such force that the United States sent the battleship Maine to protect its citizens' lives and property. When, on Feb. 15, 1898, the Maine was blown up at its anchorage in Havana harbor, the United States declared war on Spain. The Spanish American War lasted less than a year. There were land battles at Las Guásimas, El Caney, and San Juan Hill and a naval battle outside the harbor of Santiago de Cuba. The Treaty of Paris, signed on Dec. 10, 1898, by which Spain renounced all her rights over the island of Cuba, concluded the war. After 80 weary years Cuba was free from Spain.

INDEPENDENT CUBA. The mantle of independence did not fall upon Cuba lightly. After a short-lived attempt to organize a republican form of government, the United States took over for a three-year period with the idea of keeping the new republic stable until the people were able to handle their elections fairly and the government was established on a sound financial and legislative basis. Under the governorship of Gen. Leonard Wood, whose superior was the United States Secretary of War Elihu Root, the construction of new political machinery began. Departments of justice and internal revenue were established, sanitation and public works programs initiated, the difficult problem of religious freedom settled, and an adequate system of public education planned. During that brief time, too, a brilliant campaign against yellow fever was waged. Investigating the theory of the Cuban Dr. Carlos Juan Finlay that yellow fever was carried from person to person by mosquitoes, Dr. James Carroll and Dr. Jesse Lazear allowed themselves to be bitten by infected insects. Both doctors contracted the disease, and Lazear died in the experiment, which proved the validity of Finlay's theory.

General Wood's aim was never to hold permanent control of Cuban administrative affairs, but simply to remain in the country until self-government could be established. Less than two years after his arrival he called together a constitutional convention in Havana. On Feb. 21, 1901, that body adopted a constitution modeled after that of the United States. Later in the year, on June 12, an addition was made to this document in the shape of the Platt Amendment which permitted the United States "to intervene for the preservation of Cuban independence, the maintenance of government adequate for the protection of life, property, and individual liberty."

Under the new constitution elections were held, and Tomás Estrada Palma was chosen to head the first independent republic of Cuba. Palma was an honest and able executive whose progressive measures and shrewd economy did much to put the country on its feet. In August 1906 he was faced with a revolution by office seekers. Unable to quell the uprising, the president resigned on September 6, and the Cuban Congress, failing to find a new man for the chief executive position, called on the United States to intervene. Accordingly, William Howard Taft took over the government, which he placed under the administration of Charles E. Magoon. The United States held the reins of government for another three years; they were restored to the Cubans in 1909 under the guidance of the Liberal president José Miguel Gómez. Gómez and two others, Mario Menocal and Alfredo Zayas, held office during the next 15 years.

In 1924 after a successful uprising designed to prevent the re-election of President Zayas, Gen. Gerardo Machado succeeded to office for a single four-year term. Machado promised social and political reforms, but, unable to carry them all out by the end of his term of office, he ran for a second term. Opposition broke out with considerable violence, and Machado, who had complete control of Congress, made it grant him the right to suspend constitutional guarantees. Internal affairs went from bad to worse. The Supreme Court opposed the president's every move, and finally Congress granted him dictatorial powers. For nearly two years the country was in a state of confusion and rebellion, until by 1933 the situation was so bad that Machado was forced to resign and flee the country.

Following Machado, Cuba had several presidents, most notable of whom were Ramón Grau San Martín, Carlos Mendieta, Miguel Mariano Gómez, and Federico Laredo Bru. During the presidency of Carlos Mendieta, beginning in January 1934, a provisional constitution was adopted granting women's suffrage; the constitution of 1901 had already been set aside by President Machado. Also in 1934, President Franklin D. Roosevelt of the United States in line with his

Good Neighbor policy abolished the Platt Amendment that had been attached to the earlier constitution. This was done at the request of the Cuban ambassador, Cosme de la Torriente, one of Cuba's liberators. A treaty was substituted by which the United States agreed not to interfere in Cuban affairs except to impose medical safeguards if and when disease should threaten international commercial intercourse. The agreement also confirmed the right of the United States to its naval base at Guantánamo Bay, originally granted by a pact signed in 1902. Trade agreements were also negotiated between Cuba and the United States during President Mendieta's administration.

In 1936, after a lapse of eight years, a national election was held in which Miguel Mariano Gómez, son of the former president of the same surname, was elected to the presidency, and a new star appeared on the Cuban horizon in the person of Col. Fulgencio Batista, head of the army. These two leaders could not agree on Batista's rural education program. President Gómez refused to sign the bill and was promptly impeached by Congress, which was under the control of Colonel Batista. Gómez was succeeded in office by the vice-president, Federico Laredo Bru, who sided with Batista. A three-year plan for the reorganization of finances, industry, and agriculture was instituted by Batista. Strong measures were taken to suppress alien political groups and to outlaw all agitators against the government. A rural rehabilitation plan was started by which land was turned over to farmers in lots of 30 acres, with seeds, tools, and livestock supplied by the government. Economic and social reforms were put through, notably a law requiring employers to install safety equipment to protect their workers from accidents. Important advances were also made in Cuba's foreign relations.

Toward the end of President Bru's administration, in 1939, Colonel Batista entered the presidential race on a reconstruction and reform program which included the objects of his earlier three-year plan. While insisting on Cuba's sovereignty, the importance of stabilizing affairs at home, and neutrality in the current European war, Batista co-operates closely with President Roosevelt in his Good Neighbor policy and in defense of the Western Hemisphere. The Pan American Conference in Havana, July 21-30, 1940, was a milestone in inter-American relations. Important measures were taken for co-ordinated action in case of change of sovereignty of European possessions in the hemisphere.

Under the constitution of Oct. 10, 1940, Cuba is a unitary and democratic republic, headed by a president and vice-president elected for four years by direct popular vote. A cabinet headed by a prime minister advises the president. The prime minister may be removed if he has not the support of Congress. There are two law-making bodies: the Senate, composed of 54 members, 9 senators from each of the 6 provinces, elected for terms of 6 years each; and the House of Representatives, chosen by popular vote on the basis of proportional representation for 4-year terms. There are a Supreme Court, with lesser courts throughout the country. The constitution of 1940 is extremely progressive in some of its guarantees, which include regulation of wages and hours for workers and unemployment, old-age, and accident insurance. It even guarantees a full month's vacation yearly for workers. The vote is extended to both men and women 21 years old or more; its exercise is compulsory.

THE LAND

The total area of Cuba, including the Isle of Pines, is 44,164 square miles, approximately that of Pennsylvania. Cuba is a long, narrow island; the distance between Cape San Antonio at the W end and Cape Maisí at the E end is 760 miles, and the mean width N-S is 60 miles. Its 2200 miles of coastline provide several fine harbors and many bays with beautiful sandy beaches. The N coast is fringed with coral reefs and a number of islands, while off the S coast are two main groups of islands, Cayos de las Doce Leguas and the archipelago of Los Canarreos; of these islands, the Isle of Pines, in the latter group, is the largest.

A relief map of Cuba shows three outstanding mountain ranges: Sierra de los Organos in the W part of the island, the Trinidad range in the S central part, and Sierra Maestra in the E part. Of these, the last-named range is the longest and highest, 6560 feet at Pico Turquino. The rest of the land, by far the most, consists of gently rolling and very fertile plateaus and valleys.

Many rivers rise in the interior of Cuba. In general, the insular divide has an E-W axis, which causes the rivers to flow N-S, accounting for the fact that most of the streams are short and rapid. Only two have any commercial importance. Of these, the Río Cauto in the province of Oriente, flowing W into the Gulf of Guacanayabo, is the largest; 56 of its 155 miles are navigable by small vessels. The other, the Río Sagua la Grande, is navigable about 20 miles. All the rivers of Cuba have great scenic beauty. The Cuyaguateje rises in Cerro de las Cabras in W Cuba; at Cerro del Sumidero it disappears, flowing beneath the mountain to a point known as Resolladero. The Río Hanabanilla, which flows into the Arimao, has some beautiful waterfalls.

Agriculture is the chief occupation of the island, and sugar, which is produced in enormous quantities, is the chief product. In this industry U. S. capital has invested $600,000,000. Tobacco famous the world over for its unique aroma is an important crop; others are bananas, coconuts, cacao, and coffee. All of these crops are well established, since they have been cultivated in Cuba almost since the arrival of the Spaniards.

The quantity of sugar produced, however, so far exceeds the total of all other crops that Cuba may be said to have a one-crop economy. Her general prosperity has hinged almost too closely and too directly on the income from sugar sold in foreign markets. Recently, in line with efforts to work out a better economy, there has been considerable progress in diversification of crops. Pineapples, citrus fruits, tomatoes, onions, and potatoes have been introduced. Cattle raising has also been steadily increasing in importance, particularly in the province of Camagüey, and enough beef and pork are produced to supply the home market.

Cuba produces a variety of metals for home use and export. The most important are iron, copper, manganese, and chromium. Its bitumen beds are among the richest in the world, and the product is exceptionally pure. There are also deposits of naphtha. The mineral wealth of the provinces of Oriente, Santa Clara, and Pinar del Río will probably play a vital part in Cuba's future economy.

Among early industries were the manufacture of cigars, furniture, and rum and other liquors. They are still important, but sugar refining is the outstanding Cuban industry today. Realizing that diversification of industries as well as of crops was needed to improve conditions, Cuba has developed, since a protective tariff policy was adopted in 1927, spinning, weaving, and canning industries and manufactures of tile, paint, varnish, perfume, and leather goods. One of the most interesting sights for the visitor is a model industrial town built by the government near Havana for the development of local industries. Since it was discovered that the sponge beds on the S coast would produce sponges of exceptional size and quality the industry has become important, particularly in the city of Batabanó.

THE PEOPLE

Cuba is one of the most densely populated of the American republics, with nearly 4,500,000 inhabitants, or more than 90 persons to the square mile. The largest proportion are native-born whites, descendants of early Spanish colonists. In the coastal towns and parts of the interior are a large number of Negroes, some descended from slaves brought from Africa, others recent immigrants from near-by islands, notably Jamaica and Haiti. A third group are the mulattoes. Both mulatto and Negro have contributed to the political and cultural advancement of Cuba to a notable degree.

It is only natural that Spanish influence should be marked in a country originally settled by Spaniards, but the Cubans have developed a distinct culture. Cuba has its own voice in poetry, literature, art, music, and social and political science. In the rural districts of the interior a quiet, easy-going way of life still prevails, while in urban areas modern commercial trends, industrial relations, and the proximity of the United States and interchange with it have altered the tempo of living. Modernity is in the air. Havana, for instance, is known for its cosmopolitan atmosphere and the liberal, progressive, and alert views of its citizens. But the native culture has not been lost.

Spanish is the official and prevailing language, though it is possible for a traveler to get along without it, since hotels, business houses, restaurants, and recreation places have employees who speak English. Nevertheless, visitors will find a little Spanish useful. Cubans regard a knowledge of their language as a friendly gesture in visitors.

ART AND ARCHITECTURE

BY ROBERT C. SMITH

Simplicity is the chief characteristic of early Cuban architecture. In the 17th and 18th centuries what amounts to a Cuban style was evolved, in which the Doric—severest and simplest of the architectural orders—was used practically without exception; ornamental sculpture was reduced to a minimum, and straight lines almost eliminated curves. It was an architecture essentially linear, not plastic, in which the simple classic formulas of Juan de Herrera and his followers never gave way to the rich and complicated Baroque fantasies of Churriguera's school.

One reason for the severity of the style was the importance and number of military buildings in Havana, that "key of all the Indies," one of the best-fortified ports of the Spanish empire. Such grim, serious structures as the Morro Castle (1589), attributed to the most famous Spanish military engineers, the brothers Antonelli, seem to have dominated later building. Unlike the Dominican Republic, Cuba has no important 16th-century churches. One of the earliest is the Santo Cristo del Buen Viaje or El Cristo church in Havana (1640), where simple rectilinear panels form the sole decoration of the arched façade and small octagonal towers. In the 17th century a single three-stage undecorated church tower was preferred (Havana: Santo Domingo, c. 1650; Santa Clara; Sancti Spíritus). That of Havana's church of San Agustín is an exception, influenced perhaps by the decorative richness of the Mexican Baroque.

This sobriety continues in the façades of the 18th-century Havana churches—San Francisco (1738), where the many small classic edicules or shrines recall 17th-century Spanish cabinetmaking; San Francisco de Paula (1745), one of the few domed buildings; and Santo Domingo, whose interesting side portal by Ignacio José Balboa is unusually crude for the period (c. 1777). The interior of Lorenzo Camacho's Santo Domingo in the Havana suburb of Guanabacoa (1728-48) is so simple as to recall Romanesque construction. Only the façade of Havana's cathedral, completed by the architect Camacho in 1777, is a departure from this standard. There the scheme is concave, with Doric columns placed at an angle and star-shaped windows set in a sinuous complexity of lines.

But a neo-classic reaction brought El Templete (1828). Like many New England churches of the time, it is an attempt to reproduce an actual Doric temple. Typical of the spacious but severe cloisters of the 18th century is that of the seminary of San Carlos—like the cathedral, a former Jesuit building. The upper story has coupled Doric columns, an arrangement almost unique in Spanish America.

Equally severe are Havana's splendid 18th-century secular buildings. The administration units on the Plaza de Armas (1770-92) are Doric. Only the graceful window frames and striking multiform doorways deviate from the strict rectilinearity of the design. Even these pleasant irregularities disappear in the impressive Doric entrance of the fortress of La Cabaña (begun in 1762). The lofty courtyard of the Supreme Court building in Plaza de Armas is of almost Florentine purity.

Havana possesses a number of distinguished former residences ranging from the 17th to the 19th centuries. The oldest, in the cathedral square, is a squat, thick building with few windows and fortresslike doors. The façade of the Arcos palace in the same square (rebuilt 1746) has a graceful Doric arcade with large windows above. The former house of the Count of Jaruco (Plaza Vieja, 1740) is an almost identical example of mid-18th-century taste. With the growth of neo-classicism at the century's close, architraves took the place of arcades, as in the great Doric porch of El Cerro, the estate of the Count of Santoveria (now an old men's home), and Rafael Carrera's splendid Aldama palace (Avenida Bolívar and Calle Amistad) of 1838. Many of these buildings retain the heavy carved mahogany doors which were a specialty of the Cuban colonial style. The town of Trinidad is famous for its one-story 18th-century houses with typical oval screens of wood or iron before the windows. Plantation houses are without architectural distinction—low buildings, generally, with open verandas on all sides, like those of the sugar regions of northern Brazil.

No record is preserved of painting and sculpture in Cuba until late in the 18th century. José Nicolás de Escalera (1734-1804), a colorful provincial, painted crude portraits of Spanish governors and their friends, a number of molding frescoes in the Havana church of El Rosario, and some spirited religious pictures of strong Italian inspiration, now at the National Museum. Vicente Escobar (1757-1834?), a self-taught mulatto, portrayed plantation aristocracy in the manner of a provincial Goya.

European painting was introduced by the bishop Juan José Díaz de Espada y Landa, who, having redecorated the cathedral interior in neo-classic style, in 1805 imported an Italian, José Perovani, to paint there. Perovani died and was succeeded by the Frenchman Jean-Baptiste Vermay, who had been a pupil of Napoleon's great classical painter David. His are the three historical frescoes in El Templete (1828), one of which, representing the building's inauguration, is as full of brilliant portraits of contemporary figures as a mural by Ghirlandajo. In 1818 Vermay founded the San Alejandro school of painting and drawing, an official academy destined to influence Cuban art for a century. As director he was succeeded by two academic Frenchmen, Guillaume Colson and Leclerc.

Meanwhile another Frenchman, Hipolyte Garnearay (1783-1858), had painted about 1806 an important series of views of Havana's parks and promenades with white and Negro pedestrians in elegant Empire toilettes. His countryman, Edouard Laplante, produced a series of lithographs of sugar plantations which in 1858 he published in color in book form. Still another, Frédéric Miahle, in 1841 introduced photographs of Cuban landscapes along with his lithographs. The work of these Europeans is an invaluable source for the study of the social history as well as the architecture of the island.

Since Cuba did not win its independence from Spain until 1898 it was natural that during the 19th century many Spanish artists came to Havana to paint and teach. Outstanding among these was Victor Patricio Landaluze, who arrived in 1863 and remained until his death in 1889. Best known for his excellent political caricatures published in a number of humorous weeklies, his most valuable contribution to Cuban art was in small paintings of Havana types and local customs and festivities, a genre in which he followed Ramón Barrera y Sánchez. He was the first to paint the Cuban peasant, the guajiro. The first Cuban to direct the academy of San Alejandro (1878) was

Miguel Melero (1836-1907). Trained in Europe, he had great influence as a teacher of the academic nude, historical painting, and sculpture. His masterpiece is the gloomy Last Judgment painted for the central chapel of the Colón cemetery in Havana. His impressive manner was imitated by his son Miguel Angelo Melero.

Other painters prominent in the second half of the 19th century were the portraitists Federico Martínez and J. J. Peoli, who died in New York, several of whose paintings are in the Corcoran Gallery in Washington. Esteban Chartrand painted vaporous romantic studies of the Cuban landscape without reproducing its tropical coloring. The exotic Guillermo Collazo of Santiago de Cuba, who lived in Paris, is best known for his large Salon pictures like The Siesta, but he also experimented with Impressionism, a technique first practiced in Cuba by the versatile Leopoldo Romañach, a precursor of the modern movement in Havana.

The best-known sculptor of the period was José de Villalta Saavedra, author of the Baroque allegory in honor of the heroic students of 1871, the Crucifixion relief and other sculptures in the Colón cemetery, and the statue of José Martí in Parque Central and that of Albear in the park of that name, all in Havana.

An exhibition of French painting held in Havana in 1905 brought a revival of interest in that art. But it was the contacts of individuals with Paris that produced the brilliant school of present-day Cuban painting. In 1924 Victor Manuel in Paris felt the influence of the Post-Impressionists and returning to Havana succeeded in basing a highly original style on brilliant color, clear patterns, and strong draughtsmanship. His Cuban subjects (Tropical Gypsy), as well as his fresh and vivid style, went far toward liberating the thinking of his generation from the restrictions of subject matter and coloring that academicism had imposed. Closely related to his style are the striking portraits of Jorge Arche, based again on color, line, and pattern, but with an indefinable Cuban quality. Also connected with Victor Manuel is Eduardo Abela, whose swarthy scenes of guajiro life have much in common with the Mexicans of Diego Rivera. Antonio Gattorno, publicized by Ernest Hemingway, has stressed in such pictures as Have Another Cup of Coffee, Don José, the sadness and the deficiencies of the life of Cuba's white peasants. His work is not brutal but tender; in his watercolors especially it tends toward wistfulness. Within this group, which might be called the Cuban regionalists or nationalists, belong the painters of the Negro, an element of real importance in the national culture. María Capdevila's portraits have the intense dramatic effect of black faces emerging from starched white clothing and an overwhelming simplicity of composition and execution. Cundo Bermúdez, who calls himself a Neo-Primitivist, purposely gives his subjects awkward gestures and unnaturally short bodies and paints microscopically accurate backgrounds of the flora and fauna of Cuba.

Other contemporary painters are less interested in local Cuban subject matter. Amelia Peláez, who lived for a long time in France, has devoted herself to abstract paintings and has outstandingly interpreted Cubism, Expressionism, and Constructivism, making brilliant use of reds, browns, and grays. Francisco Ponce de León, using a palette limited almost entirely to silvery whites and a thick Impressionist impasto, produces vaporous images of melancholy people. His art, like that of the landscape painter Antonio Rodríguez Morey, is spiritually and technically more akin to the art of the 19th than of the 20th century. Mario Carreño has taken the heavy, sculpturesque, classical figures of Picasso as a model to create tropical nudes of monumental effect and proportion. Daniel Serra Badué, a youthful Guggenheim fellow, trained in Spain, prefers straightforward portrait painting and still life in the meticulous noble Hispanic tradition. Recently he has painted a series of Cuban still lifes of Victorian furniture, tropical flowers, and hard, bright landscapes seen through open windows.

The Negro has been a constant source of material for several modern Cuban sculptors. Teodoro Ramos Blanco, whose sculpture called simply Cuba is an allegory consisting of two Negro heads back to back, is a master of rich contours and luxuriant planes. Rita Longa, an official of the cultural bureau within the Ministry of Instruction and Fine Arts, an agency which is interested chiefly in modern art and which has a permanent collection of painting and sculpture, has had great success in interpreting the grace and vigor of youthful Negro faces and figures. Juan José Sicre, a more European sculptor, is noted for a remarkably fine series of bronze heads of famous persons and highly stylized reliefs in which the neo-Greek influence of modern French sculpture is clearly felt.

PRACTICAL INFORMATION

HOW TO REACH CUBA

From the U. S. Minimum first-class one-way steamship fares (1941) to Havana vary as follows: from New York, $65; from New Orleans, $45; from Galveston, Tex., $43; from Miami, Fla., $19. The fare by plane from Miami is $20.

BY STEAMER. United Fruit Co.; New York office: Pier 3, North River. Has direct service from New York and from New Orleans to Havana. Voyage takes 3 days from New York and 2 days from New Orleans. There are also various services and cruises by way of the Bahamas, Jamaica, the Canal Zone, Costa Rica, or Guatemala.

Standard Fruit and Steamship Co.; New York office: 11 Broadway; New Orleans office: 140 Carondelet St. Has service from New York to Santiago de Cuba and from New Orleans to Havana, as well as 13- and 12-day cruises respectively over these routes.

American President Lines; New York office: 604 5th Ave. Has sailings from New York to Havana.

New York and Cuba Mail Steamship Co.; New York office: foot of Wall St. Has sailings from New York to Havana and various cruises.

Peninsular and Occidental Steamship Co.; general office: Florida National Bank Building, Jacksonville, Fla. Has sailings to Havana from Tampa, Fla., via Key West, taking 1 day, and sailings from Miami to Havana, taking 14 hours.

Lykes Brothers Steamship Co.; main office: U. S. National Bank Building, Galveston, Tex. Has sailings to Havana from Houston, via Galveston, Beaumont, and Lake Charles.

BY AIR. Pan American Airways; main office: 135 E. 42nd St., New York. Has Havana Flyers going from Miami, Fla., to Havana in about 2 hours; also service from Miami to Mexico and the E coast of South America, via Havana or Antilla, Cuba.

From Mexico. New York and Cuba Mail Steamship Co. from Veracruz; Pan American Airways from Mérida.

From Central American Ports. United Fruit Co. service as indicated above.

AIDS TO TRAVELERS

Cuba's Representation in the U. S. The Cuban Embassy is at 2360 16th St., Washington, D. C. Consulates are at Mobile, Ala.; Los Angeles and San Francisco, Calif.; Washington, D. C.; Jacksonville, Key West, Miami, and Tampa, Fla.; Savannah, Ga.; Chicago, Ill.; Louisville, Ky.; New Orleans, La.; Baltimore, Md.; Boston, Mass.; Detroit, Mich.; Pascagoula, Miss.; Kansas City and St. Louis, Mo.; New York; Cincinnati, Ohio; Portland, Ore.; Philadelphia, Pa.; Chattanooga, Tenn.; Galveston, Tex.; Norfolk, Va.; Seattle, Wash.; San Juan, P. R.; Charlotte Amalie, V. I.

U. S. Representation in Cuba. The United States is represented in Cuba by an ambassador. The Embassy is in Havana. Consular officials are maintained in Havana, Antilla, Cienfuegos, Matanzas, Nuevitas, and Santiago de Cuba.

Local Sources of Information. The Corporación Nacional del Turismo (Cuban Tourist Commission), a government agency with offices in

Havana, is prepared to provide the traveler with detailed information concerning places of interest and ways and costs of reaching them. It will also help in making reservations and securing cars and guides. In many cases it can secure admission cards to the clubs of Havana or to the racetrack or golf courses for visitors, and it arranges fishing and hunting parties and trips to sugar mills, cigar factories, and other local industries. The commission also maintains a Tourist Protection Bureau whose function, as implied by its name, is to protect tourists from extortion by hotels, restaurants, and taxi drivers and from every other annoyance. Visitors with complaints are urged to report them to this bureau. The commission distributes descriptive literature on Cuba and a hotel directory.

Most of the hotels in Havana maintain information bureaus which give similar service.

Travelers wishing to cover as much ground as possible in a limited time will find the services of the sight-seeing companies operating in Havana and all the important cities convenient and satisfactory. The American Express Co. maintains similar services and in addition offers circle tours of the whole island in 5-7 days.

Climate. Although Cuba lies in the torrid zone and its chief products are tropical, it enjoys a pleasant and healthful subtropical climate. The heat is modified in the interior by the altitude of the mountains and plateaus, on the coast by the ocean and by the trade winds which blow almost constantly across the island N-S. These winds not only temper the tropical heat, but also give Cuba a delightfully uniform climate, with a temperature range of 60°-90° F. Throughout the island the nights are cool and pleasant.

The chief climatic change from season to season is in the amount of rainfall. The months May-November receive the greater amount of precipitation and are called the rainy season, while December-April, though not entirely lacking rain, are relatively drier. The interior receives the most rainfall, with an average of 60 inches a year, while the N coast, with an average of 50 inches, receives more than the S coast, which has an average of 45.

Clothing. Men wear suits of light-colored linen or other lightweight material throughout the year. No topcoat is necessary, though a light raincoat is often useful. White or natural linen suits are generally considered appropriate for evening wear; for most occasions they substitute for a tuxedo.

For women, several summer dresses along with a lightweight coat such as is worn in New York in spring serve as a satisfactory basic wardrobe. An umbrella is useful; it is fashionable to carry one as a parasol as well as in case of rain.

Health. Because of its climate and modern sanitary conditions Cuba is one of the most healthful countries in the world. Yellow fever and smallpox have been eradicated. The drinking water contains a small amount of magnesia which gives it a noticeable flavor and a slight effect, but it is perfectly safe to drink in the principal cities and, indeed, meets a high standard of purity. There are a large number of reliable Cuban physicians, excellently trained, as well as a few U. S. doctors. There are several hospitals and private clinics. The Anglo-American Hospital in Havana maintains an English-speaking staff.

Sports and Recreations. Sports in Cuba largely center in the country and yacht clubs, to which visitors are generally welcome. Travelers visiting Havana are extended guest privileges at several of the clubs on presentation of a letter of invitation from a member. Transient members are admitted to some, at moderate fees, at the request of a member or of the Cuban Tourist Commission.

BEACHES in Cuba are characterized by fine sand and transparent water. The favorite is Playa Varadero near Cárdenas in the province of Matanzas. This magnificent beach, with white sand and warm blue waters, is several miles long and is one of the most beautiful in the Americas. Havana itself has several fine beaches with handsome private clubs, particularly on and near Playa Marianao. Among the clubs are the Havana Yacht Club, Miramar Yacht Club, Jaimanitas Country Club, Club Náutico de Marianao, and Casino Deportivo de la Habana (Sports Casino). The Gran Casino Nacional (National Casino) in Marianao, near the Ciudad Militar (Military City) with its Camp Columbia and military airdrome, about 7 miles out of Havana, is one of the most sumptuous casinos of the Western Hemisphere. Often called the Monte Carlo of America, the impressive building and landscaped grounds with gardens and fountains are much visited by the elite of Havana. A great many games of chance can be played here. The establishment maintains a luxurious restaurant, bar, and ballroom and is open December-April. Formal dress is required for admission to the ballroom, but not to the other rooms. The Summer Casino, next to the National Casino, open during the summer, provides many of the same attractions as the former.

BOATING of all kinds is popular in the coastal sections, where innumerable bays provide picturesque harbors for the yachtsman. Recently measures have been taken by the government to provide all facilities possible to pleasure yachts at all ports. Yachtsmen may now visit any of the fascinating harbors without experiencing difficulties. Yacht trips around the coast are especially delightful.

GOLF AND TENNIS are played in or near all the important cities and towns, especially Havana and Santiago de Cuba.

HORSEBACK RIDING has always been a favorite means of rural travel. The guajiro or peasant and his horse are inseparable. Native horses are of the small, wiry type found in the U. S. west. British and Arabian thoroughbreds have been imported, however, and there are now fine specimens of hunters and race horses.

HORSE RACING is popular, and the mile-long track at Oriental Park, in Marianao, W of Havana, is one of the great attractions for sportsmen and for amateur and professional bettors. Races are held every afternoon except Monday during the racing season, which generally opens in December and lasts through the winter months. During the summer there are races on Saturdays, Sundays, and holidays.

POLO has recently become popular, and games are played between Cuban army and civilian teams.

COCKFIGHTS are held at the Club Gallístico Modelo in Marianao, within easy reach of the heart of Havana, and at the Valla Habana in Havana.

JAI ALAI, the Basque game somewhat resembling squash, was brought over by the Spaniards and has become firmly rooted. One of the fastest games in the world, it is fascinating to watch.

BASEBALL, which has been played in Cuba since the 1880's, is a national sport. Professional leagues hold yearly series. Many Cubans have played in the U. S. big leagues.

FISHING is another principal sport; it is said that 700 varieties of fish are to be found in Cuban waters. The Gulf Stream off Havana provides a fishing ground where marlin, barracuda, shark, dolphin, amberjack, kingfish, swordfish, and many other kinds can be taken. Batabanó and Cienfuegos on the S coast, as well as the keys near Caibarién on the N coast, are excellent for tarpon. Tarpon, Spanish mackerel, barracuda, gallego, and many other fish abound in the waters around the Isle of Pines.

The best season for marlin begins in April and lasts until the first northers blow, usually about the end of October. The best fishing grounds for marlin are along the 45-mile stretch of N coast from Boca de Jaruco on the east to Mariel on the west, with Havana as the approximate center.

The best season for dolphin is the winter months, October-January. The principal fishing grounds are off Cojimar, about 5 miles W of Havana. Sailfish are plentiful throughout the year, but the best season is the winter months. Albacora—bonito or frigate mackerel—abound in the waters near Havana. The best season for it is during the winter months, especially December and January. Sorrucho or kingfish are plentiful throughout the year, and the best fishing spots are near the mouths of the rivers. Peto or wahoo, of the mackerel family, with great speed and strength, are plentiful during the winter months off the coast near Havana. The best season for wahoo is December, January, and part of February.

Shark fishing is indulged in throughout the year. Tarpon is very abundant in the bays and estuaries. Barracuda and amberjack are common to all the coast, but although they may be taken, the Cuban health laws prohibit eating them when they exceed 3 pounds in weight. The rabirrubia or yellowtail, which provides great sport, is usually fished for in daytime by trolling and at night with special equipment. Yellowtail are found all the year, but particularly during March and April. Pargo or red snapper, lane snapper, and yellowtail are found in schools off the coast toward the end of October.

There are also many deep-water fish which can be caught in waters 90-500 fathoms deep. The most popular of these are pargo de lo alto, cherna de lo alto, ojanco, voraz, sesi arnillo, and cachucho. Few freshwater fish are caught.

Among the shellfish are shrimps, crawfish, oysters, clams, and turtles. The Cuban spring lobster is abundant and very good. The cangrejo moro or Moorish crab, called stone crab in the United States, is regarded as a luxury, and the demand is greatly in excess of the present supply.

Fishing is permitted only with fishhooks, one or several on the line, fishtraps, casting nets, trammel nets, or seines. All other methods are prohibited. Fishing with a hook is permitted during the whole year, while the other methods are prohibited at certain seasons. Fishing at night with artificial light is prohibited. Catching trout and carp less than 14 inches long is prohibited. Only 10 trout and 10 carp of the legal size are allowed to each fisherman. There is no closed season for deep-water fish, but closed seasons are strictly enforced on snapper, trout, carp, shellfish, and others. The Cuban Tourist Commission can be consulted for further information on closed seasons and fishing laws.

Arrangements for fishing trips can be made in Havana by consulting

Emilio de Mesa, Revista Carteles; Dr. Charles Roca, Calzada del Cerro 1391; or Go Smith, Havana Electric Co.

HUNTING is popular with both Cubans and visitors because of the variety of the quarry. Shotguns loaded with buckshot are generally employed. Dogs are not widely used, because in hunting districts it is easy to find country people who are good at retrieving and are always ready to help the hunter for a small fee.

Deer and wild boar are the largest game. The best places for them are in the provinces of Camagüey and Oriente at the E end of the island. Deer may also be hunted in the provinces of Pinar del Río and Santa Clara, especially in the vicinity of Trinidad, but they are not as plentiful as in Camagüey and Oriente. Deer season is November 1-December 31, except in the provinces of Havana and Matanzas, where deer hunting is prohibited. Each hunter is permitted to kill only two deer, and for the disposal of each he must have a permit.

Wild pigeons are found in abundance, particularly in and around mangrove plantations and palm groves near the coast. A favorite place for hunting wild pigeons is Las Martinas in the province of Pinar del Río. The season is September 4-January 16.

Rabiche or dove shooting is very popular. The rapid and erratic flight of these birds makes them an excellent test of marksmanship. They are very shy, and it is advisable to wear clothes which blend into the surroundings and to be stationed at some strategic point not visible to the quarry. A folding chair with a revolving seat is desirable. Dogs are seldom used. It is best to hunt doves at their feeding places, particularly the rice fields. Here they appear at dawn, leave as soon as the sun is high, and return in afternoon. Later in the morning they may be hunted in other places where grains and seeds are to be found. An hour and a half or a couple of hours before dusk the birds return to their roosting places; such spots make excellent hunting grounds. Doves are most plentiful near San Antonio de los Baños, Aguacate, and Güines in the province of Havana; Perico and Los Arabos in the province of Matanzas; and Herradura, Los Palacios, Candelaria, and Artemisa in the province of Pinar del Río. The season is September 14-January 16.

Yaguasas or tree-duck are found at lakes, swamps, and rice plantations. These birds are difficult to hunt in the daytime because they do not fly while it is light. Sportsmen must search for them by wading in the lakes or swamps. The best time for tree-duck shooting is on moonlight nights. The hunter takes up his station at the edge of a lake or pond and awaits his quarry. The most popular spots for hunting tree-duck are in the province of Pinar del Río. The season is September 15-February 28.

During the winter season ducks come to Cuba in great numbers from the north. Almost every variety can be found, including several that are native to the island. There are, however, no geese. The lakes of Ariguanabo in the province of Havana and Deseada in Pinar del Río are famous for duck shooting. Guides and boats are available at both. The season is September 15-February 28.

Snipe are plentiful, especially during the winter months. They are found in swampy regions; wading is usually required, and a dog is helpful. Snipe shooting is difficult but for that reason very popular. The season is September 15-February 28.

Quail are plentiful, especially in the neighborhood of Havana. Sugar plantations afford excellent hunting spots. The birds are hunted with dogs. The season is December 1-March 15.

Alligator shooting is possible around La Gloria and Nuevitas.

Entry permits for guns and hunting licenses, granted only to persons over 19 years old, can be secured through the Cuban Tourist Commission. Shotguns, but not rifles, may be included in the passenger's baggage during the open season.

All hunting is absolutely forbidden during the breeding season, and infringements of this regulation are punishable by fine. Useful birds which cannot be eaten, songbirds, or ornamental birds may not be killed at any time. Further information on open seasons and hunting laws can be secured from the Cuban Tourist Commission.

Currency. The monetary unit of Cuba is the peso (written $), corresponding to the U. S. dollar. The peso comprises 100 centavos. In addition to paper pesos in the same denominations as the paper money of the United States, silver coins are issued worth 1 peso and 10, 20, and 40 centavos and nickel coins worth 1, 2, and 5 centavos. U. S. money is accepted everywhere at its face value and circulates at par with Cuban money.

Banks. The Chase National Bank of New York, the First National Bank of Boston, and the National City Bank of New York have offices in Havana and other cities. There are also several Canadian banks, as well as Cuban ones, in Havana, which have branches in the provincial cities.

Cost of Living. Living costs for the traveler in Cuba are about like those in the United States. Rates run somewhat higher at hotels in winter. Summer charges in good Havana hotels (1941) are $2.25-$8 a day for a single room with meals, $4-$15 a day for a double room with meals, while rooms without meals cost correspondingly less, $1.25-$6 for singles, $2-$12 for doubles. Charges in family hotels are generally lower. In the provincial cities and towns hotel charges range in summer from $1 a day without meals to $7 a day for double room with meals. At the fashionable mineral spring resorts, prices vary much as in Havana. In most hotels discounts are given for visits of a week or more, and special rates are made for children.

Traveling by railroad is reasonably inexpensive. The rates are only about $.01 a kilometer or about $.015 a mile for first-class accommodations, less for second-class.

Transportation. ROADS. Over 2000 miles of roads and highways are maintained by the government. The Carretera Central (Central Highway) extends 710 miles, almost the length of the island, from Pinar del Río on the west through Havana, Matanzas, Santa Clara, Camagüey, and Holguín to Santiago de Cuba on the east. The road, built at a cost of $100,000,000 and in the face of great difficulties, is modern in every respect. It has no steep grades or sharp curves. Grade crossings have been avoided. International road signs, plainly visible by night or day, make travel on it safe.

In every town through which the road passes parks were laid out as part of the road-building project. Those in Matanzas and Pinar del Río are particularly large and beautiful. To the traveler this highway means comfort, convenience, and beauty as the colorful splendor of the tropical panorama unfolds. But the chief significance of the road is to the Cubans themselves. Whereas the rural Cuban seldom went farther than a day's journey on horseback from his native neighborhood, numerous buses now offering cheap transportation have made travel customary.

There are other paved roads in the province of Havana, as well as good first- and second-class roads connecting with the Central Highway throughout the country.

AUTOMOBILES may be transported from the E coast of the United States for $33-$60 (1941), according to weight of the car and shipping point; from the W coast the charges are $140-$165, according to weight. Entry into Cuba for visitors with cars is a very simple matter. No bond is necessary for an automobile if brought in the same steamer with the passenger and declared as part of his baggage.

Prior to sailing, cars must be provided with the necessary export declaration demanded by U. S. customs regulations. For identification purposes, upon arrival in Havana, the passenger must present his ownership certificate and registration of the car for the current year, together with his driver's license.

Delegates of the Cuban Tourist Commission attend to the dispatch of tourists' automobiles free of charge. Up-to-the-minute information concerning fuel costs and rules of the road can be obtained from the commission.

Cars can be rented through tourist agencies for special trips or by the hour, day, or week. The rates ordinarily charged are $2-$4 an hour, $15-$25 a day, and $90-$120 a week.

BUSES. Comfortable modern buses offer a number of daily services between all cities on the Central Highway, as well as Cienfuegos, Cárdenas, and Playa Varadero. The time from Havana to Pinar del Río is approximately 4 hours, to Cienfuegos 6 hours, and to Santiago de Cuba 16 hours.

RAILROADS. The two principal railroad systems, the United Railways of Havana and the Consolidated Railroads of Cuba, together cover practically the entire length of the island, W-E. Havana, of course, is the most active railroad center, and Santa Clara, roughly midway of the island, is the junction between the two principal railroad systems. Many branches radiate N and S, and there are several independent short lines.

The N line of the United Railways of Havana operates via Matanzas, Colón, Santo Domingo, and Esperanza to Santa Clara, where connections are made with the Consolidated Railroads of Cuba for Santiago de Cuba and other points on that system. Branches from this N line of the United Railways of Havana serve Cárdenas, Sagua la Grande, Camajuaní, Caibarién, and other towns. The S line operates from Havana to Cienfuegos, via Güines, Navajas, and Guareiras. The W line operates from Havana to Guane, in the province of Pinar del Río. The E line connects Cienfuegos on the S coast with Caibarién on the N coast, via Cruces, Santo Domingo, and Sagua la Grande and also via Cruces, Esperanza, and Cifuentes. This company operates frequent gas cars over certain routes, as from Havana to Güines and from Havana to Batabanó.

The Consolidated Railroads of Cuba operates the lines of the Cuba Railroad Co. and the Cuba Northern Railways. The Cuba Railroad Co. lines operate from Santa Clara, where connections are made with the United Railways of Havana, to Santiago de Cuba, via Ciego de Avila, Camagüey, and Martí; from Martí to Santiago de Cuba there are two lines: N, via Las Tunas, and S, via Bayamó. There are major branches from this line serving Trinidad near the S coast, Sancti Spíritus, and other towns.

The Hershey Cuban Railroad operates electric trains from Casa Blanca, on the W side of Havana Bay, to Matanzas. The Guantánamo and Western Railway connects with the lines of the Consolidated Railroads of Cuba at the W town of San Luis; it operates from that point to Guantánamo and from Guantánamo directly to the U. S. naval station at Boquerón. The Guantánamo Railroad operates out of Guantánamo. The Gíbara and Holguín Railroad connects the W town of Holguín, on a branch of the Consolidated Railroads of Cuba, with the port of Gíbara on the N coast. The Chaparra Railroad connects with the Consolidated Railroads of Cuba at Sabanaso for Puerto Padre on the N coast.

Sleeping cars are carried on night trains between Havana and Cienfuegos and between Havana and Sagua la Grande and Caibarién. Both sleeping and buffet cars are carried on through trains between Havana and Santiago de Cuba. Observation and buffet cars are attached to some day trains on the N line of the United Railways of Havana. Buffet lunch service is also offered on some trains on important branch lines.

AIRLINES. Pan American Airways serves Havana, Antilla, Baracoa, Camagüey, Cayo Mambi, Ciego de Avila, Cienfuegos, Guantánamo, Manzanillo, Prestón, and Santiago de Cuba.

COASTWISE NAVIGATION. Two lines operate steamers between Cuba, the Isle of Pines, and other Caribbean islands. The Isle of Pines Steamship Co., with offices at Batabanó and also at Nueva Gerona on the Isle of Pines, has steamers connecting the island with the United Railways of Havana at the port of Batabanó. The Empresa Naviera de Cuba, Calle Oficios 418, Havana, maintains steamer service to Gíbara, Baracoa, Guantánamo, and Santiago de Cuba; Ciudad Trujillo and other ports in the Dominican Republic; San Juan, P. R.; La Guaira, Venezuela; and Curaçao, Dutch West Indies.

Postage. Cuba has an extensive postal service, with about 500 post offices. Rates applying on domestic mail within the United States apply on letters and postcards from the United States to Cuba (1941). From Cuba to the United States rates are 3 centavos an ounce or fraction thereof for first-class mail, while postcards cost 2 centavos. Airmail letters cost $.10 each half ounce or fraction thereof from the United States, 10 centavos from Cuba to the United States. Airmail within Cuba costs 5 centavos for the same weight.

International air express service is available between the United States and all principal cities in Cuba. Information on rates can be secured from Railway Express agencies.

Telegraph and Cable Services. The government operates a domestic telegraph service with 365 offices. In addition, there are government wireless stations at Pinar del Río, Havana, Trinidad, Caibarién, Santa Clara, Camagüey, Chaparra, Baracoa, Santiago de Cuba, Bayamó, and Nueva Gerona on the Isle of Pines.

Cable services are maintained by the Western Union and All America Cables, with offices in Havana, and by the Cuba Submarine Telegraph Co. Radiotelegraph service is available through the Mackay Radio and Cuban Transatlantic Radio. There is a moderate tax on outgoing messages.

Telephones. Local and long-distance telephone service is available everywhere. The Cuban Telephone Co. maintains connections with all points in the United States, Canada, Mexico, and other foreign countries.

Souvenirs and Handicrafts. Cuba is a shopper's paradise. All sorts of souvenirs can be bought. Among the most popular are liquor, perfumes, articles made of alligator skin, jewelry, cigars, watches, embroideries, Panama hats, and linens. Almost everyone buys Cuban rum, of which Bacardí and Havana Club are favorite brands. Fine French liqueurs and unusual Spanish wines and brandies can also be bought reasonably. Many liquor stores and rum companies maintain bars where the shopper can sample different brands free of charge. According to U. S. customs regulations, U. S. citizens are permitted to bring back only 1 gallon of liquor free of duty, but variety within that limit can be obtained by buying small quantities of several kinds of liquor. This is permitted only once a month and on condition that the traveler has been away from the United States for more than 48 hours.

French perfumes and many attractive and unusual Cuban varieties can be bought reasonably everywhere, though it is always well to shop around for good prices. Shoppers should make sure that bottles are sealed. They should also check up on the regulations for bringing perfume into the United States, as these change frequently. Only certain brands can be imported, and of these 1-6 bottles only, depending on the brand and the use for which it is intended. The Cuban Tourist Commission will furnish a list of restricted perfumes.

Bags, suitcases, slippers, and shoes of alligator skin of good quality can be bought in Cuba at much lower prices than in the United States. Children's shoes in this leather are particularly good; so are briefcases and overnight bags. The best alligator skin is flexible and of a deep reddish color; cheaper kinds are dull and stiff in comparison. A trip through the leather district of Havana is fascinating, and prices are lower here.

Novelty jewelry, except of the seedpod and bean varieties, is available everywhere, though it is not distinct in style from what can be got in the United States. It is possible for the wise shopper to buy really fine jewelry, including diamonds, for much less than he would pay in the United States. Watches are exceedingly cheap.

Havana cigars, handmade of the very finest leaf, are the most famous in the world. Though Panama hats are made not in Cuba but mostly in Ecuador, the Cuban import duty is so low that they can be bought here much cheaper than in the United States. Fine linens sell for reasonable prices, though ordinary linens are no less expensive than in the United States.

Food. U. S. and French cuisine is found in all the larger cities. Many native dishes have a high reputation among epicures. One of these is arroz con pollo or chicken with rice, seasoned with saffron and red peppers. Ajiaco, a stew of meat and many vegetables, varies throughout the island according to the vegetables available. Pisto manchego is a casserole of scrambled eggs, tomatoes, red peppers, shrimps, asparagus, and peas. Caldo gallego is a boiled dish of beans, cabbage, potatoes, onions, and meat.

Cuba is noted for its seafoods. One of the most famous is cangrejo moro or Moorish crab, served either hot or in a salad. Rueda de pargo or red snapper stewed in a sauce of tomatoes, onions, peas, and green peppers is excellent, and so is pompano, served in various ways.

As in all Latin America, soups are featured.

Fresh fruits are always in the market, including many not found in the markets of the United States. Among these are mamey colorado, mango, papaya, zapote, anona or sweetsop, guanábana or soursop, chirimoya resembling custard apple, star apple, and many varieties of bananas.

Drinks. Cuba, home of the Daiquirí cocktail, is a land of good drinking. Many excellent drinks are made from Bacardí, other local rums, and other liquors and the juices of native fruits.

National Holidays. According to the constitution, the only official holidays are New Year's Day; February 24, anniversary of the start of the Cuban war of independence; May 20, anniversary of the proclamation of the Cuban republic; October 24, anniversary of the Yara revolution and the beginning of the Ten Years' War; and Christmas. Other notable dates usually celebrated but not ranked as national holidays are January 28, birthday of José Martí; May 1, Labor Day; August 12, Liberty Day; September 4, anniversary of the revolution of 1933; October 12, Columbus Day; December 7, Memorial Day, in commemoration of the death of Antonio Maceo and all others who died for Cuba's freedom. The afternoon of Maundy Thursday and Good Friday are also generally observed holidays.

Regional Fiestas. Local saints' days are commemorated in the churches with special ceremonies. Nochebuena (Christmas Eve) is celebrated throughout the land with midnight masses, suppers, and music. The most colorful festivities are those of the carnival, generally held on the three days preceding Lent and the four following Sundays. There is much merrymaking, with parades and flower-decorated floats, confetti and serpentines, and comparsas or masquerade groups. The dates of the Havana carnival are sometimes shifted slightly at the discretion of the mayor.

Religious celebrations during Holy Week attract great crowds to the ancient city of Trinidad. The feast of Jesús Nazareno (Jesus of Nazareth), observed each year on Easter Sunday and Monday in the town of Arroyo Arenas, 10 miles W of Havana on the Central Highway, is one of the largest religious celebrations in Cuba, with 50,000-100,000 attending. The observances and ceremonies are centuries old.

La Candelaria (Candlemas), on February 2, is celebrated annually on February 1-3 at the town of Ceiba Mocha, 52 miles E of Havana on the Central Highway. Throughout these three days there are processions of pilgrims from all parts of the island, and on Candlemas Day itself as many as 15,000 attend the ceremonies.

Our Lady of La Caridad (Charity), patroness of Cuba, is honored on September 8 with notable ceremonies at the village of El Cobre, near Santiago de Cuba at the E end of the island.

REGIONAL GUIDE

Travel routes in Cuba are delightfully simple in their main outlines. Even in this age of the airplane Havana is the country's main port of entry as well as its principal attraction. Western Cuba (p. 45) is served by the Central Highway from Havana to the province of Pinar del Río. The Isle of Pines (p. 47), off the S coast, is not hard to reach from Havana. E of the capital the Central Highway traverses central Cuba (p. 48), consisting of the provinces of Matanzas, Santa Clara, and Camagüey. Here it passes through the cities of Matanzas, with a leading beach resort, Playa Varadero, near by (p. 50); Santa Clara (p. 51), from which Cienfuegos and Trinidad can be visited; and Camagüey (p. 54). In E Cuba (p. 56) the Central Highway enters the province of Oriente and reaches the historic city of Santiago de Cuba (p. 57). Railroad lines parallel this main route quite closely, and branch lines and shorter motor roads make all major points on or near it easy to reach. The last place covered in this guide, Baracoa (p. 63), is uniquely isolated, since only coastwise vessels and airplanes serve it.

HAVANA

Havana or La Habana, with 560,356 inhabitants, the capital, largest city, and chief port of Cuba, is also the premier city of the West Indies and one of the most important between Washington and Rio de Janeiro. One of the first to be founded in the New World, it is of great historic interest. Strikingly picturesque, a blend of the cosmopolitan and the native, the ancient and the modern, Havana has a peculiarly glamorous atmosphere and a distinctive gaiety which have earned it the title of the Paris of the Americas.

Originally founded on July 25, 1514, by Diego Velázquez de León on the S coast, probably where Batabanó now stands, the city was named San Cristóbal de la Habana because the date fell on St. Christopher's day. The location came to be regarded as unhealthful, and the settlers moved N to a point on the bay of Havana now called La Chorrera (The Waterspout). Later, when it became apparent that the site was vulnerable to attack by pirates, the settlers moved again, this time to the place now occupied by Havana's Plaza de Armas, next to La Fuerza (The Fortress). The city was permanently established in 1519. By 1551 its prestige surpassed that of Santiago de Cuba, which had been founded earlier and until that time was the capital, and Havana then became the seat of government. By 1634 it had become such a powerful naval base that it was given the title of Key to the New World and Bulwark of the West Indies by royal decree.

Havana's accessibility and wealth attracted pirates and buccaneers of various nationalities who were a continual menace for several centuries. The first attack, in 1537, resulted in such great loss in treasure and men that La Fuerza, the first fortress, was ordered built. Construction of the fortresses of La Punta and Morro Castle was begun in 1589 on the headlands on either side of the channel against the threatened return of Sir Francis Drake, who had already attacked the city, though unsuccessfully; they were not completed until 1597. The fortress of La Cabaña is of a later period. It was begun in 1753 in expectation of hostilities between Spain and England.

In 1762, after a three months' siege, Havana was taken by the English under Lord Albemarle, and the section of the coast from Mariel to Matanzas was held by England until the next year, when it was restored to Spain. This occupation by the English had various effects. They cleaned up the city and stimulated commerce by removing restrictions on trade. Negroes from Africa were imported in enormous numbers, since England had a monopoly on the slave trade. The slaves worked the land and increased the volume of products for export.

THE CITY. Havana proper is built on a N peninsula lying between the Gulf of Mexico, W, and Havana Bay, E. The rare natural beauty of the setting and the picturesquesness of the city itself make the approach by sea an experience long remembered. First to be distinguished are the weathered silver-gray walls of Morro Castle on the left as the ship enters the 1000-foot-long channel leading to the bay. The fortress of La Punta comes into view on the right, and beyond it appears the blend of dazzling colors that is the city of Havana. As the ship enters the bay steep hills can be seen E; an area W along the water front is quite level, with hills rising gradually beyond it. The city proper lies on the level area, with the residential sections of El Vedado and Marianao extending W for miles over the hills; Jesús del Monte and Víbora lie S.

Havana was originally built on the NE tip of the peninsula around an open square, Plaza de Armas. Here on the W side stands the city hall; opposite it the first Mass was celebrated, on a spot marked now by El Templete. La Fuerza, the most ancient of the forts, is N. Two narrow but important streets, Calle Obispo and C. Presidente Zayas, formerly called C. O'Reilly, run W from the plaza to the modern center of the city; N lies the Malecón, a magnificent drive skirting the ocean. La Punta, on the Malecón as it swings W, is a fortress paired with Morro Castle opposite it on the headland across the channel. The Malecón, wide and well paved, is faced by splendid residences and open parks and continues W past Parque Maceo, the luxurious Hotel Nacional de Cuba, and the Maine monument.

The Prado begins at the Malecón, across from the fortress of La Punta, and runs several blocks S to Parque Central. This promenade, a wide, beautifully paved avenue shaded by old trees and lined with benches, is one of Havana's chief attractions. At night particularly it is crowded. Facing it are fine hotels, theaters, Spanish clubs and the American Club, bars, restaurants, and excellent stores.

Parque Central marks the heart of modern Havana. On its E side are the Manzana de Gómez, an important commercial building, and the magnificent Asturian Club; W are the Hotel Inglaterra and the Galician Club, with the National Theater. The other two sides are lined with commercial buildings. The majestic Capitol lies S beyond the park.

Parque Fraternidad, one of the city's largest and most beautiful, is S of the Capitol. Some distance W from this park, at the end of the wide Av. Independencia, formerly Paseo Carlos III, is the Botanical Garden with the fortress El Príncipe, now the city jail, on a hill behind. At this point a highway enters the city from the airport 8 miles away.

Most of the docks are on the E edge of the city, though a few, together with the seaplane base of Pan American Airways, are SE, near the central railroad station. The newer sections of the city extend far W and S. But many churches, notable buildings, monuments, promenades, and parks of historic interest are within easy walking distance of Parque Central.

SUBURBS. W, the commercial and most historic part of the city merges indistinguishably into the section called El Vedado, which was once marked off by the authorities as a sort of no man's land or protective zone beyond the ancient city walls. Today El Vedado is full of handsome residences and has hotels and social and sports clubs which make it attractive to visitors. Beyond it, across the Río Almendares, lie more open and definitely suburban parts of the metropolitan area, the municipality of Marianao with a superb beach, country clubs, the racetrack of Oriental Park, the National Casino, and again a wealth of beautiful homes in subdivisions such as Miramar, La Sierra, Kohly, Buenavista, and Almendares; Ciudad Militar, with the military airdrome; the Country Club Park, Barandilla, and La Coronela.

El Vedado and Marianao are within easy reach of downtown Havana by car, bus, and street car.

PLAZAS AND PARKS. Havana has several well-designed parks of some size, though the name is sometimes given to simple open squares. Plaza de Armas, now officially known as Plaza Carlos Manuel Céspedes, with C. Oficios, C. Obispo, and C. Presidente Zayas giving on it, has for centuries been the center of the city's social, religious, and political life. It has been restored very much as it was in colonial days. The statue of Ferdinand VII of Spain by the Spaniard Antonio Solá, in the center, bears a eulogistic inscription in Latin, though the Cubans have little reason to love him, for he failed to fulfill his promise of a liberal constitution, and he restored the Inquisition. The parochial church once stood on the plaza, on the site now occupied by the city hall.

The small Parque Albear, formerly Plaza Monserrate, at the other end of C. Obispo and C. Presidente Zayas, in the heart of the city, contains a monument to·Francisco de Albear y Lara, a general who distinguished himself with the Spanish army, but who is chiefly remembered as the engineer of the city's waterworks. The monument was designed by the Cuban sculptor Villalta y Saavedra and was made of

---

KEY TO MAP OF HAVANA

1. Morro Castle
2. La Punta fortress
3. La Cabaña fortress
4. La Fuerza (The Fortress)
5. Plaza de Armas (Plaza Carlos Manuel Céspedes)
6. Parque Central
7. Parque Fraternidad
8. Parque Albear (Plaza Monserrate)
9. Plaza Catedral
10. Capitol
11. City hall
12. Presidential Palace
13. Casino Español (Spanish Club)
14. National Theater
15. Ministry of Education (old legislative building)
16. Máximo Gómez monument
17. José de la Luz y Caballero monument
18. Cathedral
19. La Merced church
20. Santo Angel Custodio church
21. Ministry of Public Works (Santa Clara convent)
22. El Templete
23. Post office (San Francisco church and monastery)
24. National Museum
25. Central railroad station
26. Hotel Sevilla-Biltmore
27. Hotel Inglaterra
28. Hotel Plaza
29. Hotel Ambos Mundos
30. Hotel Florida
31. Hotel Parkview
32. Hotel La Unión
33. Hotel Gran América

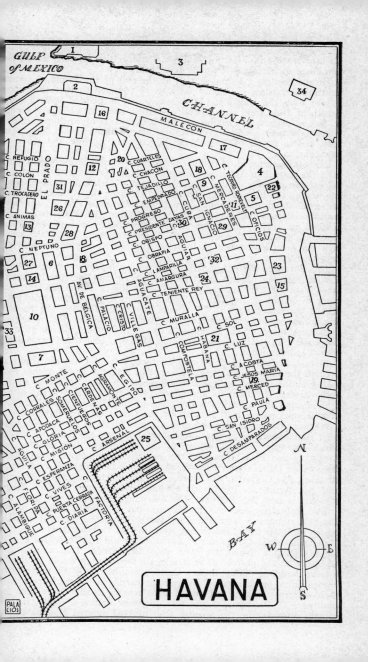

HAVANA

Carrara marble in Florence in 1893. On this site formerly stood the hermitage of Monserrate, founded in 1695.

Parque Central (Central Park), at the end of the Prado, a formal landscaped garden, has many laurel trees trimmed so that they form a roof over the walks and flower beds. It is planted with a great wealth of other trees and decorative shrubs, some of which are always in bloom. The most striking are the flamboyants or royal poincianas, which bear masses of brilliant crimson blooms in April and May. The park has a statue of José Martí, the Cuban patriot, the work of Saavedra.

Parque Fraternidad, a couple of blocks S, was Parque Colón until after the Sixth Pan American Congress, held in Havana in 1928, when a delegate from each of the republics placed a little soil from his own country at the base of a newly planted ceiba or silk-cotton tree. The soil symbolized the merging of national interests. Part of the area was once Parque India, and in it stands a statue, the work of Giuseppe Gaggini in 1837, representing a beautiful Indian woman, called La Noble Habana. Another section was a parade ground. Today the whole area has been landscaped to form an appropriate setting for the impressive Capitol, N of it.

The Botanical Garden, on Av. Independencia, several blocks W of Parque Fraternidad, is a great natural garden containing many native trees, plants, flowers, birds, and fish. The locality is also known by its old name of Quinta de los Molinos, which it bore as the summer residence of the Spanish governors. A stream that runs through the gardens was formerly part of the system carrying water to the city.

Parque Maceo, on the Malecón, is one of the smaller plazas. It has a fine equestrian statue of Gen. Antonio Maceo, a leader and hero of the war of independence.

Plaza Catedral, a block W and another N from Plaza de Armas, is perhaps the most typically Spanish spot in Havana. Small, rather bare and secluded, paved with cobblestones laid by the Spaniards in the 16th century, it retains its ancient charm. On its N side is the cathedral. Facing the cathedral is the office of the Havana Club Rum Co in a colonial palace built in 1720 by the Count of Casa Bayona.

STREETS. Cuban leaders and even abstract ideals of the republic have been commemorated in new official place names, especially of streets which formerly bore the stamp of the old order. Just as Plaza de Armas is also Plaza Céspedes, the beautiful ocean-front drive popularly called the Malécon (Sea Wall) has now been named, in different stretches, Av. Céspedes, Av. Maceo, Av. Washington, Av. Pi y Margall and Av. Aguilera. The Prado is Paseo Martí, and Calzada Reina (Queen) is now Av. Bolívar. The old names are often still used.

The first street laid out in Havana was C. Oficios (Street of the Trades), running S from Plaza de Armas. For some years it was the center of retail trade, which has since moved to other streets.

C. Obispo and C. Presidente Zayas, other old streets, which run W out of Plaza de Armas, are little wider than lanes. The colonists had an idea that the narrower the streets, the better they would be shaded by the buildings along them. Curbs were laid only to protect the houses from being scraped by passing carriages. These streets with their colorful awnings and quaint signs remain as they have been for centuries. C. Presidente Zayas was originally named O'Reilly, for the general commanding the Spanish who in 1763 entered Havana as the

English under Lord Albemarle left it. C. Obispo got its name from a bishop who used to take his daily stroll through it. The narrowest street of all is C. Peña Pobre, leading from the church of El Santo Angel Custodio to the Malecón. On it stand some of the city's oldest houses.

In contrast to the quaintness and narrowness of the older streets are the Malecón and the Prado—wide, landscaped boulevards beautiful to see and planned to accommodate a large volume of swift traffic. The Malecón, planned by the Cuban engineer General Albear in 1857, was not constructed until 1902, at the time that Gen. Leonard Wood was governor. Its promenade and handsome gardens make it as much a park and a recreation center as a highway. In part it was built over the old sea wall.

C. San Rafael, beginning at Parque Central and running W, and Av. Italia (Galiano), which crosses C. San Rafael, constitute the chief shopping district. Along these streets are haberdasheries, shops for women's wear, jewelry stores, and souvenir shops. At night, splendidly lighted, they are favorite promenades of the elite.

PUBLIC BUILDINGS. Chief among Havana's public buildings is the Capitol, S of Parque Central. Constructed of granite, limestone, and marble at a cost of $20,000,000 and opened in May 1929, its architecture and setting make it one of the world's most beautiful capitols. Its interior is striking, with beautifully decorated halls, staircases, bronzes, statues, paintings, and furniture. The dome which crowns the rotunda is the third highest in the world. In the center of the rotunda is set a 24-carat diamond, marking the zero kilometer from which all distances on the Central Highway are measured. At one side of the rotunda is a 37-foot statue representing the republic by the Italian sculptor Angelo Zanelli. In the Hall of Lost Steps, almost 400 feet long and notable for its bronze doors and chandeliers and the variety of marbles used, many great receptions are held. Here the president takes the oath of office. The Martí Hall, used for state banquets, has some excellent paintings. The many conference halls are richly furnished and decorated. Reliefs by the Italian sculptor Remuzzi on the walls of the House of Representatives depict activities of peace and war, and these, as well as works in the chambers of both the Senate and the House, are impressive. Throughout the building are portraits and busts of patriots. The entrance for visitors is at the left on C. Industria. An entrance fee of $.25 is charged, and only registered guides are allowed to show visitors through the building. Open weekdays 9 a.m.-5 p.m., Sundays and holidays 9 a.m.-12m.

The city hall, on Plaza de Armas, is one of the finest examples of colonial architecture in Havana. It was begun in 1780 and finished 12 years later. Most of the materials were brought from Spain and Italy. The building served successively as the home of the Spanish governors general, the headquarters of Gen. Leonard Wood, and the residence of the presidents of Cuba before becoming the city hall in 1917. In the reception room are two marble medallions symbolizing Day and Night, the work of the Danish sculptor Thorwaldsen. In the patio, which is interesting for its balconies, flagstones, and tropical plants, is a statue of Columbus by J. Cuchiari.

The Supreme Court, on the N side of Plaza de Armas, is a large stone building of the colonial period. The spacious central patio contains a bust of José Martí.

The Presidential Palace, on Av. Misiones, S of the Malecón, is a huge $2,000,000 building of varied architectural style topped by a dome and set among parks. Opposite the front entrance, N on Av. Misiones, a fragment of the old city wall is carefully preserved. The S entrance faces Parque Zayas.

Other noteworthy buildings are those of the Spanish Club, on the Prado at the corner of C. Animas; the imposing and highly elaborate Galician Club, on Parque Central at C. San Rafael, with the National Theater under the same roof; the Asturian Club, also on Parque Central; the American Embassy, on the Prado; the Beneficencia orphan asylum, on C. San Lázaro facing Parque Maceo, built in 1794. The Beneficencia has a turnstile for receiving foundlings. The old legislative building, past the post office on C. Oficios, is a white marble structure in Corinthian style. The House of Representatives used to meet here before the completion of the Capitol. The Ministry of Instruction and Fine Arts is now located in this building.

MONUMENTS are in the grand style, usually set in large open spaces on landscaped plazas and along the water front.

The Maine monument, in its own park on the Malecón near the residential section of El Vedado, was erected by the Cubans to the men of the ill-fated U. S. battleship blown up in the harbor on Feb. 15, 1898. The monument consists of figures representing the United States and Cuba, with two columns supporting an American eagle behind them. It is the work of Félix Cabarrocas.

The José Martí monument in Parque Central, dedicated to the great Cuban patriot, writer, and humanist, has a white marble base with allegorical figures, topped by a standing figure of the patriot.

The José Miguel Gómez monument, at the head of Av. Presidentes in El Vedado, is dedicated to General Gómez, second president of the republic. The monument is highly ornamented, with a marble colonnade, and because of its elevation can be seen from a great distance. There is a fine view of the university section from the hill on which it stands.

The Tomás Estrada Palma monument, also on Av. Presidentes, is dedicated to the first president of Cuba, a close friend of Martí, who succeeded him as leader of the revolution.

The Máximo Gómez monument, on Av. Misiones not far from the Presidential Palace, is the work of Albo Gamba, a noted Italian sculptor. The base is topped by a Greek temple which in turn is capped by the equestrian statue of the famous revolutionary leader who finally led the Cubans to victory and independence.

The José de la Luz y Caballero monument, on the Malecón, is opposite the fort of La Cabaña. Caballero was a great educator.

The Gen. Antonio Maceo monument, in the small Parque Maceo on the Malecón, has a large marble base with allegorical figures, bearing a bronze equestrian statue of the hero, the work of the Italian sculptor Boni.

FORTS. Havana, once the most strongly fortified city in the New World, has more interesting forts still standing than any other city in the Americas. They bespeak the threat from pirates under which the early settlers lived.

La Fuerza (The Fortress), the oldest building in Havana and one of the oldest forts in the Western Hemisphere, stands at the foot of C. Presidente Zayas, next to Plaza de Armas. A long, low, rectangular structure with massive walls and a picturesque tower, it offers a pleasing view of the bay. After the destruction of the city by pirates in 1537, Hernando de Soto, then governor, ordered the fortress built. It was planned by Mateo Aceituno, a highly skilled architect, who also rebuilt the port. Soto left his headquarters in Santiago de Cuba to give much time and his own funds toward completing the project. In 1539 Soto set out from Cuba on the expedition which took him to his death on the shores of the Mississippi. In his absence his wife, Isabela de Bobadilla, whom the records describe as a woman of great charm, discretion, and ability, governed the island. The story goes that during the four years between his departure and the news of his death, she often climbed to the top of the fort to look out to sea for her husband's ship. One version is that the strain on her eyes was so great that she finally went blind. The news of Soto's death crushed her, and she died soon after. For many years the structure served both as a fortress and as the residence which took him to In 1578 and several times thereafter it underwent extensive repairs after fierce attacks by pirates. When in 1672 it fell into the hands of the English, a statue of La Habana, the Indian maiden who greeted the first Spaniards, was taken from the tower as booty. This statue has since been replaced by a similar one 5 feet high, which serves as a weather vane. At the time of the Cuban war for independence the fortress had fallen into disrepair, but soon after the island achieved freedom from Spain the moat was cleaned out and converted into a sunken garden, and the structure was renovated so that it stands today much as it did when it was built. At present the National Library is housed here, pending construction of its own building. La Fuerza is open all the time, and there is no admission fee.

Morro Castle and La Punta, next in point of age, were both started in 1589. They stand on either side of the entrance to the harbor. In the old days the port was closed every night by stretching a chain between these forts.

Morro Castle or El Morro, the full name of which is El Castillo de los Tres Reyes del Morro (Castle of the Three Kings of the Headland), is the farther N and juts farther out to sea. The beams of its lighthouse are the first landmark sighted by ships approaching at night. El Morro is reached by motorboat from the Machina pier or La Punta landing. The trip takes about 5 minutes. Completed in 1597, El Morro was built by slaves and convicts. The moat, 70 feet deep, was hewn for some distance out of solid rock, and a stone superstructure was built to a height of 120 feet. The massive, irregular, time-worn exterior is impressive. Within are innumerable chambers and dungeons. The fort consists of three main defensive sections: the Morro or Morrillo; the battery of La Pastora, covering the channel; and the battery of the Twelve Apostles, with 12 guns, each named for one of the apostles. The English required 67 days to capture El Morro. A tablet has been erected to the memory of the gallant commander Luis de Velasco and of the Marquis of González, his second in command, who died fighting rather than be taken prisoner. The lighthouse was added in 1844 by Capt. Gen. Leopoldo O'Donnell, whose name appears in bronze letters high on the tower. A circular stairway leads to the tower, which affords Havana's finest view. E and N are the azure waters of the Gulf of Mexico, while W and S are the city and the hills beyond it. In the foreground, directly S, is the fortress of La Cabaña, with Casa Blanca,

Regla, and Guanabacoa beyond. Still farther S and E stretches the beautiful green countryside.

La Punta or, in full, El Castillo de San Salvador de la Punta (Castle of the Holy Savior of the Point) is a squat, massive structure built much like El Morro, which, however, is larger and stronger. On the Malecón, where Av. Misiones and the Prado join it, the fortress of La Punta stands picturesque and mellow with age. It was planned by Juan de Tejada and Bautista Antonelli, who were sent to Cuba in 1588 by Philip II of Spain for the purpose. Its limestone walls are 8 feet thick. Like La Fuerza, it had fallen into disrepair before the war of 1898, but it has been renovated and the approach landscaped. It is at present used by the Cuban navy.

La Cabaña, the largest of Havana's forts and one of the largest in the world, is on the same side of the harbor as El Morro, but farther up the hill. It is reached by boats from the Caballería or the Machina pier or La Punta landing. The steep ascent to the top of the hill must be made on foot. Started in 1763, almost two centuries after Morro Castle, La Cabaña or, in full, El Castillo de San Carlos de la Cabaña (Castle of St. Charles of the Cabin) was built shortly after Spain regained possession of Havana from the English. It was intended to prevent a repetition of the capture, but it has never fired a shot in defense of the harbor. In 1859 it was equipped with 120 cannon, some of which still remain in their original positions facing the bay. At that time 1300 men were regularly stationed here, and 5000 could have been accommodated. The fort consists of a long wall over the crest of the hill, protected by triple bastions and a 40-foot moat which is crossed by covered ramps. Over the main gate an inscription states that the work of building was completed in 1774. Across the moat through the main entrance is Laurel Ditch (Los Fosos de los Laureles), famous in Cuba's revolutionary war as a place of execution for patriots. Here Juan Clemente Zenea, the poet martyr, and many another sympathizer with the cause of a free Cuba met death by a Spanish bullet. It is said that the victims were required to kneel in the ditch with their faces to the wall while the Spanish soldiers fired from above. The 85-foot strip of bullet marks in the wall, called the deadline, is regarded as evidence of this practice. Today La Cabaña is partially in ruins. The old custom of firing a cannon at 9 p.m.—formerly to recall the soldiers to their barracks—has never been discontinued. Nowadays the shot resounding over the city is the signal for setting clocks and watches.

Atarés, like La Cabaña, was begun in 1763. Finished in 1767, El Castillo de Atarés was named for a town in Spain. The bastioned stone fort is in the Jesús del Monte section, on a hill overlooking the SW end of the harbor. For a period it was used as a prison for political prisoners, and grim relics of the time still remain, such as the rings in the walls which held the prisoners by the arms. It was here that the U. S. Col. W. S. Crittenden and 50 of his men were executed in 1851. Crittenden had come to Cuba to collaborate with the revolutionary leader Gen. Narciso López. López was publicly garroted at the same time.

El Príncipe, the last fortress to be built in Havana, was begun in 1774 and completed 20 years later. El Castillo del Príncipe (Prince's Castle), to give it its full name, crowns a hill at the end of Av. Independencia. Originally a 50-foot moat surrounded the walls. Legends persist that this fort was once connected with the others by means of underground passages. It is now the city jail.

CHURCHES. The cathedral, facing Plaza Catedral, only a couple of blocks from the water front, has been the center of religious activities for centuries and was the stronghold of the Jesuits until they were expelled in 1767. Though dedicated to the Virgin of the Immaculate Conception, it is better known both as the church of San Cristóbal, the patron saint of Havana, and as the Columbus cathedral because of its having been the reputed resting place of the discoverer's bones for many years. The building was begun in the 17th century and completed in the 18th by the Jesuits. Long before then, the first church in Havana had been built in Plaza de Armas and was the chief parochial church until it was burned down by French pirates in 1537. Hernando de Soto, governor of Cuba at the time, gave orders for the rebuilding of the church and for the construction of a fortress to guard it. This church, completed in 1541, was sturdily built and La Fuerza protected it; yet buccaneers destroyed it too, in 1583. A larger church, dedicated to St. Christopher, was then built on the same site, but it was razed in 1741 because a large mass of iron from a warship that blew up in the harbor wrecked the roof and weakened the whole structure. The Jesuit church presently became the chief parochial church by absorbing the parishioners of San Cristóbal, and in 1789, more than 20 years after the expulsion of the Jesuits, it was raised to the status of cathedral of the diocese of Havana, which takes in the W half of Cuba.

The cathedral is picturesque and interesting rather than beautiful. Its massive walls of native limestone, which have weathered two centuries, will doubtless be able to stand for two centuries more. On each side of the massive Tuscan pillars of the façade, dating from 1777, is a belltower. The cruciform interior has two rows of columns 10 feet thick along the broad central nave. The floor is of black and white marble. The walls are covered with arabesques and paintings, some of which are very old. Outstanding is one by an unknown artist of St. Christopher bearing the Christ Child across the water. The pulpits, confessionals, and other wooden fittings are of Cuban mahogany. The sillería or choir stalls, also of Cuban mahogany, are richly carved. The high altar is of Carrara marble incrusted with gold and onyx, with a figure of the Virgin of the Immaculate Conception in the center. This charming figure was sculptured in Rome by Solá. Other notable treasures are robes and vestments magnificently embroidered in gold and silver and the golden monstrance set with emeralds. A chapel dedicated to the Virgin of Loreto is a reproduction of the shrine of Loreto in Italy. It was in this chapel that the bones believed to be those of Christopher Columbus formerly rested. When Santo Domingo was ceded to France late in the 18th century, the supposed remains of Columbus were sent from there to Cuba and interred in the cathedral at Havana with great ceremony. They were not removed until after the Spanish American War, when they were taken to Seville. Evidence that has been unearthed in the Dominican Republic indicates, however, that the remains were not those of the discoverer, but of another Columbus, possibly his brother or his son. Visitors can ascend the E tower of the cathedral for a superb view of lower Havana and the bay and to see the ancient bells, bearing the dates 1664 and 1698, whose musical tone is attributed to some silver and gold that were mixed with the bronze. The larger of the bells, dating from 1698, weighs 7 tons and was cast in Spain. The smaller, cast in Matanzas, weighs 2 tons. The main doors of the cathedral usually remain open until 11 every morning, but it can be entered at any time by the gate on the• E side.

The church of San Francisco, formerly that of San Agustín, C. Cuba and C. Amargura, is the oldest in Havana, built in 1608. It has artistic altars and beautiful stained-glass windows. On the walls the Stations of the Cross are represented. Though the building has been reconstructed, its fine colonial lines are preserved. A slab on the wall facing C. Amargura is clearly inscribed with the date 1657.

The church of La Merced, C. Cuba and C. Merced, is one of the most beautiful in the country. It was built in 1746 and rebuilt in 1792. The interior, which has been remodeled and redecorated in recent years, contains beautiful marble altars and chapels as well as many fine examples of religious art. One of the best is a seated image of Our Lady of Mercy with the Infant Jesus in her arms. La Merced is Havana's wealthiest and most aristocratic church, and on Sunday morning Mass is celebrated with a full• orchestra.

The church of El Santo Angel Custodio (Holy Angel), on the hill of Peña Pobre at the junction of C. Compostela and C. Cuarteles, was built in 1690 by the bishop Diego Evelino de Compostela. It is Gothic, with graceful spires rising above the surrounding buildings. Within are 10 chapels; the most notable, behind the high altar, is dedicated to the Holy Sacrament. Paintings by the Spaniard Manuel Roig adorn the ceiling. The steps of this church were the setting of a scene in the famous Cuban novel Cecilia Valdés by Cirilo Villaverde.

The church of El Sagrado Corazón (Sacred Heart), Av. Bolívar, between C. Gervasio and C. Padre Varela, is not far from the business section. This church, finished in 1923 and patterned after the Gothic cathedral of León in Spain, is the most beautiful modern church in the city. The altar, of gold, onyx, marble, and native woods, was made in Madrid by the Spanish sculptor Granda. Other fine examples of the sculptor's art are the image of the Sacred Heart and carved figures from the Old and New Testaments. The stained-glass windows showing scenes from the lives of Jesuit saints were made in France. Notable among them is one showing the conversion of the Duke of Gandía before the body of Eleonora, wife of Charles V, a copy of the famous painting by Muñoz Degrain. The church contains a wealth of beautiful and symbolic details.

The church of Santo Cristo del Buen Viaje, commonly known as El Cristo, facing a small plaza on the short C. Cristo, has two towers rising above its tiled roof and is one of the best examples of early Spanish architecture. Only one other building in Havana, the convent of Santa Clara, has a similar roof.

The church of Our Lady of El Carmen, at Av. Presidente Menocal and C. Neptuno, has a statue of the Carmelite Virgin on the tower. This is said to be the largest bronze statue mounted in this way. The altars are beautifully ornamented in the Spanish style of the 17th century.

The convent of Santa Clara, C. Cuba between C. Luz and C. Sol, was built about 1635 and subsequently enlarged. It holds today the offices of the Ministry of Public Works, but its original character has been retained. In the patio are the first slaughter house, the first public fountain, and three of the first houses built in Havana. There is also a small house said to have been built by a wealthy mariner for his daughter's retirement after an unfortunate love affair. The carved panels on the ceiling of the church are excellent.

The old Franciscan monastery, C. Oficios at the foot of C. Teniente Rey, near the water front, is now the central post office. The original monastery on this site was started in 1574, the present church and monastery in 1738. The buildings remain today among the best examples of early architecture. Heavy and massive, the church is surmounted by a three-story tower which served as a lookout for pirates. A sculptured figure of St. Francis, decapitated by lightning in 1846, is on the tower. The cells of the old monastery opened on the patio, beneath whose flagstones many of the monks lie buried.

El Templete (The Shrine), Plaza de Armas, is not properly a church but marks the spot where the first Mass was celebrated. It is said that priests who came with Diego Velázquez de León held services under a large ceiba tree which eventually was destroyed by a hurricane in 1753. In 1754 a shoot of the original tree was planted here, and when the supposed bones of Christopher Columbus were brought from Santo Domingo in 1795 they lay in state under its branches before being taken to the cathedral. This tree was felled in 1828 and cut into small pieces for relics, and the present tree was planted at that time. The foundations of El Templete, which is Doric in style, were laid in 1827; the building was opened in March 1828. The interior is decorated with three historical paintings by the French artist Vermay, a disciple of the celebrated David, painter to Napoleon's court. These paintings, the most valuable in Cuba, depict the celebration of the first Mass, the first council of Havana with Diego Velázquez de León presiding, and the inauguration of El Templete. In the patio is a bust of Columbus which is considered a particularly good likeness; the U. S. painter John Vanderlyn made a trip to Havana to study it in preparation for his painting, The Landing of Columbus, which hangs in the Capitol at Washington. Entrance is free, and there is a custodian to escort visitors about. Open weekdays 8:30 a.m.-12 m. and 2-5 p.m.

The Cementerio Colón (Columbus Cemetery), on the edge of the residential district of El Vedado, is noted for its beautiful chapel, tombs, and monuments. The cemetery was founded in 1878. Over the granite entrance is an interesting group representing Faith, Hope, and Charity. The chapel has some beautiful paintings. Notable monuments are the Firemen's, erected to the memory of 30 members of the volunteer fire department and others who lost their lives at a fire in 1890, and the Students'.

MUSEUMS. The National Museum, on C. Aguiar between C. Amargura and C. Teniente Rey, 9 blocks E of the Capitol, contains relics of the wars of independence, paintings, sculptures, and relics of the Siboney Indians of Cuba. The fine collection of paintings includes original works by masters such as Rubens, Murillo, Titian, Goya, Poussin, and Watteau and some excellent copies. Among the modern paintings are works by Sorolla, Zuloaga, and other foreign and native artists. Among the Cubans represented are Leopoldo Romañach, M. Vega, and Rodríguez Morey. Notable among the old works are The Martyrdom of St. Bartholomew by Ribera; two canvases attributed to Murillo, St. Isabel of Hungary and a Madonna and Child; an Apollo and Mars attributed to Correggio, and a Virgin and Child attributed to Guido

Reni. Objects of historic interest on view in the museum include the skeleton of the horse ridden by Máximo Gómez and personal relics of Cuba's great men such as Antonio Maceo and José Martí, the patriots; Dr. Carlos Juan Finlay, who fathomed the riddle of yellow fever; Albear y Lara, who built the aqueduct, and many others. There are also fine collections of Cuban stamps, jewelry, porcelain, ivory, miniatures, and so on. Open daily except Mondays, 1-5 p.m.

The Martí Museum, C. Paula 102, in the house in which the patriot was born, preserves many relics that belonged to him.

LIBRARIES. The Biblioteca Nacional (National Library), in the fortress La Fuerza, was founded in 1901 by Gen. Leonard Wood, the military governor. It contains 207,423 volumes. Open weekdays, 8 a.m.-1 p.m.

The library of the Economic Society of the Friends of the Country, C. Dragones 62, was founded in 1793 and was the first library of a public character in Cuba. The majority of the 36,833 volumes are in Spanish. Of other languages English has the heaviest representation. The library is open to the public.

The library of the House of Representatives, in the Capitol, contains 45,000 volumes. Open weekdays except Saturdays, 1:30-5 p.m.

The Biblioteca Municipal (Municipal Library), C. Neptuno 255, contains more than 11,000 volumes. It is open to the public.

Clubs such as the Associación de Dependientes (Clerks' Club), Centro Gallego (Galician Club), and Centro Asturiano (Asturian Club) maintain libraries which may be used by visitors upon application. Permission can be gained by students for the use of numerous specialized libraries in the city.

CENTERS OF HIGHER LEARNING. Chief among the centers of learning is the university of Havana, on a hill at the end of C. San Lázaro, W of the oldest part of the city and easily reached by street car. The university was founded more than two centuries ago, though its physical plant is of recent construction. Approached by a wide and imposing flight of stairs off C. San Lázaro, its modern buildings boast all the facilities of great institutions of its kind—restaurants, fraternity rooms, a stadium, and a gymnasium, besides academic equipment, a museum, and a library of 100,000 volumes. There are faculties of natural, applied, and social sciences and schools of law and of medicine that are noted for their high standards.

The Academy of Science, on C. Cuba, is housed in a fine, massive old structure built as an Augustinian monastery in 1607 and turned over to the academy in 1837. During the U. S. occupation in 1901 Gen. Leonard Wood ordered the renovation of the building.

THEATERS AND MOVING-PICTURE HOUSES. Havana has many first-class theaters and moving-picture houses which offer varied stage productions and the best Latin American, U. S., and European films. The principal house at which drama and opera are given is the National Theater, on the Prado at C. San Rafael, facing Parque Central. Built in Italian style, it seats 3000. Five horseshoe tiers of boxes, one above the other, rise around the pit, the boxes separated by gilded latticework of graceful design. The stage is large enough for operas with the most magnificent settings. At present, however, the theater presents chiefly films.

Other theaters are the Martí, C. Agramonte and C. Dragones; Payret, on the Prado at C. San José; Principal de la Comedia, C. Animas and C. Zulueta, dedicated exclusively to theatrical productions.

Modern, comfortable, and attractive moving-picture houses are Alkázar, C. Consulado at C. Virtudes; América, Av. Italia and C. Concordia; Campoamor, C. Industria at C. San José; Encanto, C. Neptuno, a short walk from Parque Central; Fausto, on the Prado at C. Colón; Neptuno, C. Neptuno at C. Perseverancia; Radio-Ciné, Av. Italia and C. Neptuno; Trianón, Av. Wilson in the district of El Vedado.

Most theaters in Havana begin their evening shows around 8:30 p.m. and have Sunday and holiday matinees. Continuous performances of moving pictures as in the United States are becoming more common.

MUSIC. Cubans have always been noted for their aptitude and love for music. Cuban music is not quite like any other, though it is sometimes reminiscent of Spanish popular music and African strains.

The excellent Philharmonic Orchestra, composed of 90 musicians, offers a series of concerts at the Auditorium in the district of El Vedado each winter. Concerts take place in the evening on the second and fourth Mondays of every month, October-May. Two musical societies, the Pro-Arte Musical and the Sinfónica de la Habana, offer monthly concerts. Often famous foreign musicians are presented. The Pro-Arte Musical built the Auditorium in El Vedado.

Besides a host of notable popular dance bands, the city has police and navy bands that give public concerts at the amphitheater on the Malecón near the fortress of La Punta on Tuesday, Thursday, Saturday, and Sunday afternoons.

MARKETS are colorful and interesting, especially those held in the open like the one at the junction of C. Cuba and C. Acosta. The Mercado General (General Market), SW of the oldest part of the city and reached by Calzada Monte from Parque Fraternidad, occupies a large building. Principally a food market, it sells everything from codfish to fruits. The Mercado Colón (Columbus Market), in back of the Sevilla-Biltmore Hotel on the Prado, covers a whole block on Av. Agramonte between C. Trocadero and C. Animas.

Of principal interest to visitors are tropical fruits distinctive to Cuba. These include many varieties of banana; the mamoncillo, honeyberry or Spanish lime, which grows in clusters like grapes, but with a more acid taste; the caimito, smooth and purplish, tasting like a blend of papaya and persimmon; pineapples, nowhere more richly flavored; mangoes in great variety; papaya; coconuts; guanábana or soursop; anona or sweetsop, whose fragrance fills a room; alligator pear; chirimoya resembling custard apple, and luxuriant figs.

STORES AND SHOPS. Stores are everywhere, especially on the Prado, C. San Rafael, C. Neptuno, Av. Italia, and C. Obispo. In the suburbs and along the docks prices are somewhat lower. Inexpensive articles such as native trinkets made from seeds, little dolls, purses, small flasks of native perfume, and other items useful as souvenirs can be purchased almost everywhere.

FIESTAS. The carnival, generally held during the three days preceding Lent and prolonged for four additional Sundays, is one of the major attractions of Havana. It is gay with crowds in the streets, concerts, dancing in public plazas, and parades with decorated floats. Queens are selected from various sections and classes of society. The suburbs and the different trades organize each its own comparsa or masquerade group with a special allegorical name and picturesque costume. The comparsas appear on Saturday nights, sometimes 10 or 12 groups dancing along the Prado past the Capitol. These groups conform to a general pattern, each headed by a sort of director with a native band and a battery of lanterns. The music plays, and the people in the group dance with a shuffling step, swaying from side to side and chanting. At times they pause while the leaders perform special dances in front of crowded balconies or seats along the route. Great applause greets the outstanding performer, and enthusiasm grows as the comparsas pass along. During the carnival all the clubs hold great balls. To these the visitor can be admitted through a member. The processions of carrozas or floats are also notable. Beautifully and fancifully dressed señoritas ride on the carrozas and shower confetti and serpentines on the crowd, which retorts with its own ammunition. A prize is given both to the best carroza and to the best comparsa.

The racing season is one of the most active social seasons. The races generally open in December and continue throughout the winter months.

The yachting season, during which international races are held, is another time of gaiety. International races are usually held immediately after the first of the year.

Nochebuena (Christmas Eve) is a night of public and private celebrations and festivities. New Year's Eve is also celebrated with enthusiasm.

Holy Week is observed in Havana with holidays on the afternoon of Maundy Thursday and on Good Friday. Notable services are held in the cathedral and other churches throughout the city on Easter.

CLUBS. Few cities in the world have a social life as active as Havana's. It is said that a third of the population belong to some club or other. For instance, the Associación de Dependientes (Association of Clerks), on the Prado at C. Trocadero, has 40,000 members; the Centro Gallego (Galician Club) has 35,000, and the Centro Asturiano (Asturian Club) has 45,000. Each club has a splendid building with ballrooms and other facilities. The Centro Gallego's building, facing Parque Central, also houses the National Theater and is a palatial structure covering a whole block. The Centro Asturiano building, facing Parque Central opposite the Centro Gallego, has an especially fine ballroom. These clubs are of social, cultural, and recreational character and have hospitals for members. The clubs may be visited in the company of a member.

Casino Deportivo de la Habana (Havana Sports Casino), on the Gulf shore W of the Río Almendares, is a magnificent clubhouse with facilities for sports, including golf, tennis, racing, rowing, shooting, polo, and swimming both in a pool and at the beach. There is also a children's playground. Visitors can take advantage of the facilities on payment of a monthly fee of $5 apiece (1941).

The Country Club of Havana, at Marianao, is a private club with excellent clubhouse, golf course, and tennis courts. Members may take their friends except on Sundays. Guest privileges are extended to travelers on presentation of a letter of introduction from a member.

The Jaimanitas Country Club, at Marianao, is a private club with a beautiful clubhouse, an excellent golf course, and a beach. Travelers are admitted for a period not exceeding two months on sponsorship of two members.

The Rovers' Athletic Club, Av. 11 between C. 6 and C. 7 in Marianao, has a golf course and other facilities available to visitors on payment of a small fee.

The Club de Cazadores (Hunter's Club), at Marianao, is easily reached by car from Havana.

The Jockey Club, at Oriental Park in Marianao, has an excellent clubhouse. The club is patronized by women as well as men.

Tennis clubs in the district of El Vedado include the Lawn Tennis Club, on C. 8, easily reached, and the Vedado Tennis Club, C. 12, which admits transient members for a month on application by a club member.

The most important yacht clubs are the Havana Yacht Club, at Marianao, where travelers are granted club privileges for a month on application by a member and payment of a fee, and the Miramar Yacht Club, on the shore E of Playa Marianao, where guest cards for a week are issued through members. The Club Náutico de Marianao owns a fine clubhouse. Entry to these clubs is gained through members.

Other clubs and societies include the American Club on the Prado at C. Virtudes, the meeting place of U. S. residents, with rooms for the American Legion; Casino Español (Spanish Club), on the Prado a short walk from Parque Central; Automobile Club, Malecón 50, which assists travelers in planning motor trips; British Club, at the Hotel Florida; Rotary Club, at the Hotel Nacional de Cuba; Lions Club, at the Hotel Sevilla-Biltmore; Club Unión, Malecón 3; Women's Club, C. G and C. 21 in El Vedado; Lyceum, in El Vedado, a woman's organization sponsoring cultural activities, one of the best organizations of its kind in the Americas. Visitors are admitted to Lyceum events.

SPORTS. The racetrack and the Jockey Club, at Oriental Park in Marianao, easily reached from the heart of Havana, has both summer and winter seasons. During the winter season, December-March, there are races daily except Mondays, and during the summer months, July-October, there are races on Saturdays, Sundays, and holidays. The park has an excellent clubhouse which is a social center during the racing season. The mile-long course is one of the most picturesque and popular in the Americas.

The Estadio Cerveza Tropical (Tropical Stadium), property of the Tropical brewery, is on the dividing line between the sections of El Vedado and Miramar, a half hour's ride by car or bus. With 50,000 capacity, the stadium is used for track events, baseball and football games, and sometimes political rallies. The brewery has beautiful grounds known as the Tropical Gardens near by on the Río Almendares.

The university's stadium is used for minor games and student activities.

Jai alai, the Basque game, is very popular in Havana and expertly played, especially by members of the Spanish colony. There are two courts, Frontón Habana-Madrid, C. Padre Varela at C. Sitios, and Frontón Jai Alai, C. Concordia and C. Lucena. There are games every night.

Cockfights have been a popular local sport since colonial days. Cockpits are numerous. The largest and most popular is that of the Club Gallístico Modelo at Marianao, reached by car, bus, or electric train. It is a private club, but so-called transient member admission cards for each event may be secured at travel bureaus, tourist information offices, and hotels. Matches are also held at Valla Habana, on C.

Aguadulce in the Jesús del Monte section, on Monday, Wednesday, and Sunday afternoons.

BEACHES. Near Playa Marianao, W of the old part of the city and easily reached by car, bus, or electric train, are many handsome private clubs and the public bathing beach of La Concha. This modern, up-to-date beach has facilities for surf bathing, physical culture, tennis, jai alai, fishing, rowing, and dancing, as well as restaurants and bars.

Other beaches near Havana are those of Guanabacoa (p. 45); Guanabo, 15 miles E; and Baracoa, 15 miles W. Guanabo is reached by a direct bus line from Plaza Catedral, Baracoa by car.

TELEGRAPH. The service is operated by the government, and offices are in the post office.

CABLE COMPANIES. All America Cables, Postal Telegraph, and Mackay Radios have offices at C. Presidente Zayas and C. Cuba and branches in the Manzana de Gómez, the Lonja building, Hotel Nacional de Cuba, and Hotel Plaza. Western Union has main offices at C. Obispo and C. Havana and branches in the Lonja and Metropolitan buildings, Hotel Plaza, and Hotel Nacional de Cuba.

TOURS IN AND AROUND HAVANA. The regularly operated city tours through the old and new portions of the city, including visits to the district of El Vedado and historic and public buildings and landmarks, require from 2½ hours to half a day.

A tour of the suburbs, including El Vedado and the Almendares, Miramar, and Marianao sections, affords an opportunity of seeing such places as the Tropical Gardens, Ciudad Militar, and Camp Columbia and beautiful homes, clubs, parks, monuments, beaches, boulevards, and points of general and historic interest.

Night tours of Havana usually include visits to the Chinese section; the National Casino when it is open; the hill on which the university stands, for a view over the city, and a cabaret. The regularly operated evening tours require 3-4½ hours.

The Morro Castle and La Cabaña fortress tour is most easily made from the downtown section of the city by car to the water front and thence by boat to Morro Castle or by car all the way. The regularly operated tours which cross the water by launch require 3-4 hours. Comfortable shoes are advised, for considerable walking is necessary.

AIR SERVICE. Compañía Nacional Cubana de Aviación, Prado 74; Pan American Airways, Prado 74. The airport for services between Havana, other Cuban cities, and foreign points is at Rancho Boyeros, 8 miles from the city's center. The seaplane base, at Muelle Arsenal, on the water front, is not in use (1941).

RAILROAD STATIONS. The Hershey Cuban Railroad station, at Casa Blanca on the E side of the bay, is reached by launches from the foot of C. Presidente Zayas. The United Railways of Havana has its central station at Av. Bélgica and C. Arsenal. Electric trains for Marianao leave from the station at Av. Italia and C. Zanja.

SOURCES OF INFORMATION. The Corporación Nacional del Turismo (Cuban Tourist Commission), Prado 255, in the arcade of the Hotel Sevilla-Biltmore, furnishes complete information on attractions and accommodations, including apartments and houses. A Tourist Protection Bureau is also maintained by the government to investigate complaints made by visitors either in person or by letter.

Tourist agencies include American Express Co., in the Centro Gallego building on Parque Central; Blue Line Tours, Manzana de Gómez on

Parque Central; L. A. Cabrera, Prado 108; Cuban American Touring Co., Prado 357; Cuban Tours and Transportation Co., in the Centro Gallego building on Parque Central; Intercontinental Travel Service, Manzana de Gómez on Parque Central; International Tours, C. Oficios 10; Luciano Blanco López, Hotel Lincoln; R. Luján Tours, Muelle Santa Clara 2, on the water front; Manval Tours, in the Bacardí building at Plaza Catedral; Mitchell Tours, Prado 121; National Travel Service, Hotel Nacional de Cuba; Packard De Luxe Tours, Hotel Packard; Plaza Sightseeing Tours, Hotel Plaza; Star Tours, in the Lonja building on C. Oficios next to the post office; Valdes Tours, also in the Lonja building; Manuel Yepo, Prado 257.

Many of the hotels have travel and information departments, among them Hotel Gran América Tours, C. Indústria 502; Hotel Inglaterra Tours, Prado 416; Hotel Lincoln Tours, Av. Italia and C. Virtudes; Hotel Royal Palm Tours, C. San Rafael and C. Industria; Hotel Sevilla Travel Service, Hotel Sevilla-Biltmore, on the Prado.

BANKS. Chase National Bank, C. Aguiar 310; First National Bank of Boston, C. Aguiar 411; National City Bank, C. Presidente Zayas and C. Compostela; Bank of Nova Scotia, C. Cuba 225; Canadian Bank of Commerce, C. Aguiar 411; Royal Bank of Canada, C. Aguiar 367; Gelats y Compañía, C. Aguiar 456.

NIGHT LIFE. Cabarets are plentiful. Sans Souci, beyond the W city limits in the Country Club Park, easily reached by car, is a first-class supper club noted for excellent food, music, and entertainment. Eden Concert, Av. Agramonte near Parque Central, is a first-class cabaret specializing in Cuban music. Pennsylvania, near the beach in Miramar, is noted for the native rumba and music.

La Playa, La Frita, and El Paraíso, all near Playa Marianao, offer native dances not seen in more expensive places. The Jiggs and Kursaal cabarets, near the water front of old Havana, specialize in native dances and shows.

Most of the good hotels have excellent cabarets, as the Plaza Roof Garden, at the Hotel Plaza, and the Sevilla Roof, at the Hotel Sevilla-Biltmore. Other cabarets are La Campana, Av. Presidente Menocal 44½; Mitsouko, C. San Lázaro 99; Rumba, C. 23 and C. P in the district of El Vedado; Río Cristal Club, on the road to Vento, a short drive out from the city; Cabaret Miami, on C. Acosta at C. San Pedro.

RESTAURANTS AND BARS. Havana is a city for the gourmet. On the average, food is not expensive, and service is good. There are Italian, French, Chinese, Swiss, and Spanish restaurants as well as native places. Especially tempting is seafood, brought daily from the many fisheries around the city. The lobsters are unusually good; the clams, oysters, crabs, and shrimps are also good. Restaurants and hotels are required by law to take in fresh supplies of meat every afternoon.

Fruits, drinks, ice cream, sherbets, and desserts are hardly equaled elsewhere. Cuban fruits are juicy, rich-flavored, abundant, and varied; the Cubans like novel ice creams and sherbets, and as a result there is an endless variety.

Among the best restaurants in Havana are Cosmopolita**, Prado 412, specializing in arroz con pollo; National Casino**, at Marianao; terrace of the Hotel Nacional de Cuba**, on the Malecón; Palacio de Cristal**, C. Consulado 148, specializing in seafood and lamb dishes; París**, in Parque Catedral, excellent French cuisine; El Patio**, the Prado at C. Genios, Spanish atmosphere; Hotel Sevilla-Biltmore**, the

Prado and C. Trocadero, excellent bar and grill; La Zaragozana**, Av. Bélgica 365; Ambos Mundos*, C. Obispo and C. Mercaderes, specializing in filet mignon; Hotel Bristol Roof*, C. San Rafael and C. Amistad, dancing; La Floridita*, C. Obispo and Av. Bélgica; Frascati*, the Prado at Parque Central, Italian food and wine; Hotel Inglaterra*, Prado 416; La Isla*, Av. Italia and C. San Rafael, French cuisine; Miami*, the Prado and C. Neptuno, much frequented by U. S. visitors; Hotel Plaza Roof*, Av. Agramonte and C. Neptuno; Hotel Presidente*, Av. Presidentes in the district of El Vedado, with three dining places, terrace, tropical gardens, and roof; Hotel Regina*, Spanish Tavern, C. Industria 124; La Reguladora*, C. Amistad 412; Hotel Royal Palm*, C. San Rafael and C. Industria, good food and dancing; Baturro, Av. Bélgica 65, Spanish food and good wine; La Idea, C. Padre Varela 208, Spanish dishes; La Marina, C. Oficios 202, near the water front, specializing in paella; Swiss Home, C. Acosta 215, Swiss and German food; Toledo, C. Barcelona and C. Aguila, specializing in arroz con pollo. Stars are used here as for hotels. See note below.

Good bars include Aire del Mar, Hotel Nacional de Cuba; Ariete, C. San Miguel 52, open all night; El Bohío, in the arcade of the Hotel Sevilla-Biltmore; La Floridita, C. Obispo 557; Pan American, C. Presidente Zayas at Parque Albear; El Patio, the Prado and C. Genios; Hotel Plaza bar, C. Agramonte 277; Hotel Presidente bar, Av. Presidentes in El Vedado; Sloppy Joe's, near the Prado, popular and rather noisy.

HOTELS. Havana has half a dozen splendid hotels, scores of good ones, and a host of more modestly priced family hotels. They include the Sevilla-Biltmore**, on the Prado; Nacional de Cuba**, with a garden and a salt-water swimming pool, on the Malecón; Country Club of Havana**, at Marianao, a short drive from town, where introduction by a member is necessary; Presidente**, in the district of El Vedado; Brístol*, C. San Rafael and C. Amistad; Inglaterra*, facing Parque Central; Lincoln*, Av. Italia and C. Virtudes; Parkview*, across from the Presidential Palace; Plaza*, C. Neptuno and C. Agramonte; Royal Palm*, C. San Rafael and C. Industria; Ambos Mundos, C. Obispo 153; Florida, C. Obispo and C. Cuba; Gran, C. Teniente Rey at C. Agramonte; Gran América, C. Industria 502; Lafayette, C. Presidente Zayas and C. Aguiar; Regina, C. Industria 410; Siboney, Prado 355; La Unión, C. Cuba at C. Amargura. All hotels will assist visitors in planning trips.

Among the family hotels are Andino, C. San Lázaro 1218 at C. M, in El Vedado; the apartment hotel at C. 8 and C. 19, El Vedado; Edificio Areces, Prado 102; Colonial, C. San Miguel 254; Edison, C. Neptuno 5; Gran Vía, C. Agramonte 422; Internacional, C. Tejadillo 60; Londres, Av. Bélgica 103; Palacio, Av. Bélgica 359; Reno, C. Aguila 558.

NOTE. Hotels are here classified by rates. Two stars indicate the higher rates for the country in question. One star means rates in the medium brackets; no star means low rates or no information available. An effort has been made to list hotels in all the towns mentioned. In a highly developed tourist country like Cuba they are usually of good quality, and in Havana they compare favorably with those found anywhere in the world. In some of the smaller and more out-of-the-way places, however, as in other Latin American countries, the hotels often do not come up to the standards expected by North American and European travelers.

HAVANA'S ENVIRONS AND EXCURSIONS

Guanabacoa, 3 miles E of Havana, reached by car, bus, street car, or the Hershey Cuban Railroad, is a typical Spanish colonial town, with fine old mansions, churches, and public buildings. Principal points of interest are the parochial church, with a beautiful Baroque altar and an image of Our Lady of the Assumption; the Carral Theater; the monastery of San Francisco, built in 1755, and that of Santo Domingo; and the Hospital de la Caridad (Charity Hospital), founded in 1855. Near by are medicinal springs.

Cojimar, on the shore beyond Guanabacoa, is reached by road in an hour through a beautiful countryside. The fortress of Cojimar, built in 1646, was stormed by the English in 1762. Cojimar has a bathing beach. Boats can be hired for sight-seeing trips along the river and for fishing. Hunting is good in the neighborhood.

Santa María del Rosario, 10 miles E of Havana by car, was founded in 1732 by the Count of Casa Bayona. Its atmosphere has changed little, and the city is now being restored almost to its original aspect. The village church is rich in works of art. The most noteworthy of its paintings, some of them by famous artists, is The Adoration of the Three Kings, by Veronese. There are also bronzes by Barbedienne, figures carved from native woods, and fine doors. Springs near the town are reputed to have curative powers for nervous disorders, arthritis, and intestinal, kidney, and liver troubles.

Hershey, 29 miles E of Havana, with frequent train service via the Hershey Cuban Railroad, is the location of the Hershey Golf Club, which welcomes visitors. Train tickets include greens fees.

Madruga, 41 miles E of Havana on the Central Highway, has springs whose waters are often prescribed for diabetes and other kidney disorders, liver and intestinal troubles, heart ailments, and nervous diseases. There is a bathing establishment.

HOTEL. Delicias del Copey.

Batabanó, 36 miles S of Havana by road or railroad, is an interesting town on the coast, with fishing and sponge industries. The trip from Havana is directly across the island through typical scenery. The Isle of Pines is reached from Batabanó (p. 47).

Ceiba del Agua, 27 miles W of Havana and easily reached by bus, is the home of the Instituto Cívico-Militar, founded by Fulgencio Batista when he was chief of the army. Beautifully situated, with ample, well-kept grounds and modern buildings, the institute is a veritable town where boys and girls of destitute parents receive a thorough education, including training in the trades. The institute has established 1120 rural civic-military schools.

WESTERN CUBA

The province of Pinar del Río, W of Havana, more than 5000 square miles in area, is a picturesque region, interesting to the traveler chiefly for its scenery. Three mountain ranges traverse it, N and W: Sierra de los Organos, Serranía de Guaniguanico, and Sierra de las Acostas.

A rolling fertile plain S is occupied by large sugar plantations and citrus fruit groves. On the slopes the famous Vuelta Abajo tobacco, one of Cuba's best, is produced. The province is also rich in copper and iron ore deposits, not yet much utilized.

The journey from Havana to Pinar del Río, capital of the province, can be made by train on the United Railways of Havana (120 miles) or by car on the Central Highway (109 miles) in about 4 hours. Either route offers a splendid view of the three parallel ranges of mountains and the vast green gardens between them. Most towns along the route are small, though picturesque and attractive.

Guanajay, 28 miles W of Havana, is a small, typical Cuban town. It has several cantinas or bars and a good ice cream parlor, El Escándalo.

Excursion from Guanajay. Mariel, reached by an 8-mile road that turns NW off the Central Highway at Guanajay, lies at the foot of a lofty hill facing a beautiful bay. Boats can be hired for excursions, and fishing is good. The Naval Academy, on the summit of the hill, can be visited in a few minutes from the town by a good road. The view is excellent; on clear days Havana can be seen on the distant horizon. A small military museum with curious specimens of arms is located in the academy.

HOTEL. Villa Martín, a little inn, provides overnight accommodations and excellent seafood.

Artemisa, 10 miles beyond Guanajay, on the Central Highway, is connected by a secondary road with the small villages of Cayajabos and San Francisco which lie NW in attractive and secluded valleys. The country around Artemisa is full of game birds.

Excursion to San Diego de los Baños. This spa, a few miles N of the Central Highway from a point about 80 miles W of Havana, is one of Cuba's favorite health resorts. The sulphur springs are used in the treatment of rheumatism, skin diseases, and intestinal and kidney troubles.

HOTELS. Cabarrouy; Saratoga; Solder.

Pinar del Río, with 20,000 inhabitants, capital of its province, 4 hours from Havana by railroad or car, is the center of the Vuelta Abajo tobacco district. About 15 miles N is the Viñales valley, a region of hills and canyons and steep flower-covered cliffs, among the most picturesque parts of Cuba. Local Rotarians have built a platform from which the visitor can admire the view.

HOTELS. Ricardo*; Globo; Marina.

Excursions from Pinar del Río. The tobacco experiment station at San Juan y Martínez, about 15 miles out on a secondary road, affords an opportunity for observing tobacco culture: the growing, storing, curing, selection, and classification of the leaves. The station supplies planters with information on the best means of cultivating and processing tobacco.

Still farther W, 38 miles, is the town of Guane, heart of copper and iron mining. The roads, however, are not good; the traveler should inquire concerning their condition. Guane is the terminus of the W line of the United Railways of Havana. From Guane the road continues to the villages of La Fe, on the beautiful bay of Guadiana, and El Cayuco, Las Martinas, La Grifa, and Cortés, also on a fine bay. The country is attractive, with unexploited beaches and fine places for fishing and hunting.

Pinar del Río is also connected by secondary roads with La Esperanza, N on the coast past the town of Viñales, and with La Coloma, S on the coast.

ISLE OF PINES

The Isle of Pines (Isla de Pinos) is a veritable tropical garden off the S coast of Cuba, about 90 miles from Havana and 60 from the port of Batabanó. It can be reached overnight from Havana by road or railroad to Batabanó (p. 45) and thence by steamer.

The island was discovered by Columbus in 1492 and named by him Evangelista. It was settled by the Spaniards in 1575 and for several centuries thereafter served as a refuge for smugglers, escaped slaves, and pirates. It is maintained that pirate treasure is still hidden on it. Robert Louis Stevenson may have had it in mind when he wrote Treasure Island.

The island is about 30 miles N-S, 40 miles E-W. The population of some 11,000 is largely of U. S. origin. The N portion, in which are found the pines from which the island takes its name, is mountainous, with broad, fertile valleys and numerous streams; the S portion, set off by a deep ocean inlet and a swamp, Gran Ciénaga de Lanier, has extensive forests of cedar, mahogany, ebony, and other valuable hardwoods. Sponge fishing in the adjacent waters is an important industry. There are marble deposits of fine grade and color. But the island's chief assets are the fertile coastal plains and interior valleys which have made it an important fruit and winter vegetable region. Grapefruit, oranges, pineapples, peppers, cucumbers, potatoes, onions, watermelons, eggplants, and many other fruits and vegetables are shipped both to Cuban cities and to the United States.

The climate is equable, the temperature seldom rising above 90° F. and never falling below 58°. Sea breezes make the nights cool and pleasant. Because of its climate and beauty the island has become a popular resort for vacationers and sportsmen. Sanitary conditions are excellent. The wet season commences about May 1 and continues to November 1. There are excellent beaches and medicinal springs.

Nueva Gerona, with 5000 inhabitants, the chief business center, is a clean city, well laid out. Good restaurants serve both Cuban and U. S. dishes. The Tropical Gardens restaurant is much frequented by U. S. visitors. Among the notable buildings is the Presidio Modelo, Cuba's model prison. Entirely modern, with a large administration building and a cell block of round and novel construction, it is equipped with schools of industrial arts, agriculture, and horticulture.

Playa Bibijagua is the most popular beach on the island. A curious feature is its black sand, colored by the iron present in it. Playa Columpo, with golden sand, is also very popular. Both are near the town.

Popular fishing waters are along the coast SW of Nueva Gerona. Others are between the Isle of Pines and the Mangles Islands, 10 miles N. Deep-sea fishing is best 5 miles off the S shore. Tarpon, barracuda, Spanish mackerel, gallego, yellowtail, red snapper, porgies, swordfish, and lobsters and crabs abound. Hunting for ducks, partridges, doves, and other fowl is excellent. Cuban game laws apply here. Boating on the Río Las Casas, at whose mouth Nueva Gerona lies, is another popular diversion, and horseback riding, golf, tennis, and mountain climbing are popular.

HOTELS. Anderson; La Favorita; San José; Virginia. Club Rancho Rockyford is at the Santa Bárbara spa near Nueva Gerona.

Excursions from Nueva Gerona. The Caves of the Winds, not far away, have curious stalactite and stalagmite formations which ring like bells when struck. The walls are covered with iron and copper formations. The vast Santa Isabel cavern, with numerous galleries and passages, is only partially explored.

Santa Fe, with 3000 inhabitants, 12 miles by car from Nueva Gerona, has several medicinal springs. The most famous is the Santa Rita hot spring, often recommended for bathing in the treatment of rheumatism and kidney and stomach troubles. The other springs, the water of which is taken internally, are Ojo de Agua and a magnesia and an iron spring.

HOTEL. Santa Rita,* with free use of the Santa Rita spring.

Other towns on the Isle of Pines are Columbia, Júcaro, Santa Rosalía, McKinley, and Los Indios, all charming.

CENTRAL CUBA

Matanzas Province, E of Havana, is served by the Central Highway, the Hershey Cuban Railroad, and the United Railways of Havana. The green countryside is dotted with lofty royal palms, mangoes, and ceibas and is broken here and there by little palm-thatched bohíos or huts with jasmines and creeping bougainvillea growing around them. The guajiros or country folk, usually dressed in bright colors, are courteous and obliging to visitors.

The 64-mile stretch of the Central Highway from Havana to the city of Matanzas, over which there is excellent bus service, passes through the towns of San José de las Lajas, Madruga with its popular hot springs, and Ceiba Mocha.

MATANZAS

The capital of the province, Matanzas, with 75,000 inhabitants, is an important sugar trading and shipping center. Founded in 1693 by Capt. Severino de Manzaneda, it lies on the shores of the beautiful bay of Matanzas, into which the Río San Juan and the Yumurí empty after crossing the city. Due to its picturesque background of mountains, its delightful climate, and its proximity to Playa Varadero, Cuba's most attractive beach, Matanzas is generally included in the sightseeing programs offered by travel agencies. The city preserves its Old World character, with narrow, winding streets, old weathered houses whose fronts are decorated with colored tiles, high iron-grilled windows, and monumental doors.

The city spreads W and N of the amphitheater formed by the semicircular bay and is divided into three sections by the rivers. The part called Pueblo Nuevo (New Town) is bounded N by the Río San Juan, W by Calle San Luis, and S by C. San Esteban and C. San Rafael, together with the station of the United Railways of Havana.

N across the Río San Juan and connected with Pueblo Nuevo by the bridges of San Luis and Calixto García is Pueblo Viejo (Old Town). It is bounded N by the Río Yumurí, E by the docks, and W by a park. At this park the Central Highway forks; N it becomes C. Byrne; S,

C. Milanés. Both lead to Plaza Libertad, the city's central square.

Beyond the Concordia bridge across the Río Yumurí is the third section of the city, Versalles, lying E of Pueblo Viejo. The station of the Hershey Cuban Railroad is a short distance N of the Concordia bridge. E of Versalles, on the water front, is El Castillo de San Severino, a fort reached by the fine Paseo Martí. N of Versalles is La Cumbre, a hilly section.

Plaza Libertad, bounded N by C. Byrne, W by C. Emilio Blanquet, S by C. Milanés, and E by C. Ayuntamiento, is adorned with beautiful gardens and a statue of José Martí. N, the plaza is faced by the Velasco Theater, the luxurious Hotel Velasco, Club El Liceo, and the Casino Español (Spanish Club); S, by the Hotel Louvre; and E, by the Hotel Sevilla and the buildings of the provincial and municipal governments. The plaza is gay in the evening when the military band plays.

Paseo Martí, a popular promenade bordering the bay along the N side, stretches from C. San Isidro in Versalles toward the fort of San Severino. Near San Severino stands the military monument commemorating Cuban patriots who were executed here, while farther back on Paseo Martí is the Massachusetts monument, honoring the men of the Eighth Massachusetts Regiment of Volunteers, who fell near Matanzas during the Spanish American War. San Severino, named for the city's founder, is a fort dating from the 17th century. In 1762 during Lord Albemarle's attack it was blown up by the Spaniards, who feared its capture, but it was rebuilt in 1779 when new defenses were constructed.

CHURCHES. The cathedral, C. Milanés and C. Jovellanos, faces a little park of its own. A quaint building with large flying buttresses supporting its roof, it was erected in the 18th century. It has an altar of beautifully carved solid mahogany with gilded ornaments.

The church of San Pedro, also called the church of Versalles, C. José and C. Santa Cristina, high in the Versalles section, looks ancient although it was built in 1870. It is more like a massive fortress than a church. The high altar of carved cedar is a work of art.

The church of San Juan Bautista, C. Santa Rita and C. Vicente, though not imposing, is pleasing and beautiful.

The hermitage of Monserrate, on a hill N of Matanzas proper and reached via C. Domingo Mujica, is picturesque and charmingly situated. Inside is a beautiful image of the Virgin and an altar of carved cork. The deep blue ceiling is dotted with stars. From the heights a splendid view of the city, the bay, and N over the famous Yumurí valley is gained. The Yumurí valley is one of the loveliest localities in Cuba. En route from Havana the traveler crosses it, but no idea of its extent and beauty can be secured except from the heights of the hermitage of Monserrate or the hill opposite, La Cumbre, N of the residential Versalles section. The mountain wall around the city is broken where the Río Yumurí flows to the sea through a deep canyon called the Abra del Yumurí. The valley, 5-6 miles wide, is roughly oval in shape.

BEACHES. Playa Matanzas is E of the Pueblo Nuevo section, and Buey Vaquita is on the outskirts of the city. Both are small but charming.

HOTELS. Gran París*, Calzada Tirry 58, in the Pueblo Viejo section, is a short walk from the railroad station. Louvre*, Sevilla*, and Velasco* are all on Plaza Libertad.

MATANZAS' ENVIRONS AND EXCURSIONS

The Bellamar Caves, 1½ miles SE by road, are comparable to the Mammoth Caves of Kentucky. They were discovered accidentally in 1861 by a Chinese laborer whose crowbar, inserted into a crevice to dislodge a piece of limestone, disappeared into a hidden abyss. The caves underlie a level plateau, and access is through a reception house and restaurant which have been built over the entrance. After descending a stairway cut out of the rock for about 60 feet, the visitor can explore the artificially lighted caves for a mile in each direction. Their extent is unknown, though it is believed that the passages connect with the sea. The caverns are filled with stalactites, stalagmites, and beautiful crystal formations. Interesting points include numerous narrow passages and halls, the Gothic Temple 250 feet long and 80 feet wide, a pool of clear water, and an apparently bottomless abyss. The caves are open usually 7 a.m.-8 p.m. When closed they may be visited on application to the Compañía de Jarcia at Matanzas, which has charge of them.

San Miguel de los Baños, 28 miles SE of Matanzas, is a sulphur spa much frequented by vacationers from Havana. It is reached by a short secondary road branching off the Central Highway at Coliseo, 23 miles from Matanzas. There are five different springs whose waters are used both externally and internally in treatment of stomach troubles and disorders of the kidneys and bladder. San Miguel is an excellent place for a few days' stop. There are sure-footed ponies, and interesting horseback excursions can be made into the surrounding hills. The excursion to the top of Mt. Jacan (1200 feet) to the shrine of El Cristo de Jacan permits a particularly fine view.

HOTELS. Gran del Balneario**, with a swimming pool; Villaverde*.

Cárdenas, with 35,000 inhabitants, 38 miles NE of Matanzas, is reached by a branch road from the Central Highway at Limonar, 16 miles from Matanzas, or from Coliseo, 23 miles from Matanzas. It is also on a branch of the United Railways of Havana. The city lies on a beautiful bay. Like Matanzas, it is an important sugar center; a good deal of rope fiber is also shipped from it. There are some quaint old churches and a municipal museum with a fine collection of historic objects. The town was the first in Cuba to erect a monument to Columbus.

HOTELS. La Domínica*; Europa; Isla de Cuba.

Playa Varadero (Varadero Beach), also called Playa Azul (Blue Beach), can be reached from Matanzas. It is 13 miles NW of Cárdenas by car. This beach extends 5 miles along the ocean front. It is Cuba's most popular seaside resort, justly noted for its natural beauty. Several modern hotels have been built lately. Every year national rowboat races are held either on the last Sunday in July or on the first in August. These are regarded as the most important of all Cuban boat races, and Havana, Cárdenas, and Cienfuegos clubs and the Cuban navy compete. Playa Varadero is also a favorite fishing spot.

HOTELS. Chez Roig**; Club Náutico**; Kawama Beach Club**; Playa Azul Inn**; Casa La Rosa*; Miramar*; Torres.

The province of Santa Clara, E of Matanzas, is an extremely productive region with more than 50 sugar mills, the largest number in any province of Cuba. Rolling plains occupy the W part of the province, while the E part is mountainous. Two large rivers, the Jatibonico del Sur and the Jatibonico del Norte, water the fertile plains and valleys. There are several ways of visiting the interesting towns of this province. The Central Highway crosses the Matanzas Province border at Cascajal, 80 miles E of the city of Matanzas; it passes through Santo Domingo and Esperanza before reaching the city of Santa Clara. The United Railways of Havana also serves the area, and there is air service from Havana to Cienfuegos.

SANTA CLARA

The capital of the province is Santa Clara, with 40,000 inhabitants, 187 miles E of Havana and 124 miles from Matanzas on the Central Highway. Santa Clara is one of the busiest cities on the island, important as the junction of the United Railways of Havana and the Consolidated Railroads of Cuba, and the center of a region producing sugar and the choice Vuelta Arriba tobacco.

The city is built on the site of the ancient Indian town of Cubanacan, to which Columbus sent a mission in the belief that it was the headquarters of Kublai Khan. During the 17th century the Spaniards of the N coast, under constant threat from pirates, migrated here, the geographical center of the island.

Today Santa Clara has well-paved streets and numerous modern buildings, though many of its ancient structures preserve a colonial atmosphere. Plaza Vidal, also called Plaza Central, is the center of the city's life. In the middle of the well-kept square is a granite monument to the philanthropist Marta Abreu, one of Cuba's most distinguished women, who, with her sisters Rosalía and Rosa, did much for the prestige and beautification of the city.

The Municipal Palace or city hall and the Teatro de la Caridad (Charity Theater) which overlook the main plaza are notable buildings. Profits of the theater, a gift of the Abreu sisters, go to the poor.

The churches of El Divino Pastor, facing the plaza of the same name in the S part of the city, and of Our Lady of El Carmen, C. Carmen and C. Conyedo, are the most interesting.

HOTELS. Central*; Florida.

EXCURSIONS FROM SANTA CLARA

Sagua la Grande, near the coast NW of Santa Clara and reached conveniently by car, lies in an attractive region producing tropical fruits.

La Isabela is a port a few miles beyond Sagua la Grande by car. It has thriving oyster and crab fisheries.

Cienfuegos, with 50,000 inhabitants, Cuba's third city, lies on the S coast, about 200 miles from Havana and 150 miles from Matanzas. It can be reached by road directly from Santa Clara or by railroad from Havana or Matanzas. Pan American Airways connects the city with Miami, Fla.; Kingston, Jamaica, and other foreign points and the Cuban cities of Havana, Camagüey (p. 54), and Santiago de Cuba (p. 57). Cienfuegos is an old city situated on the beautiful bay visited by Columbus on his first voyage. Bartolomé de las Casas and

Pedro de Rentería founded the settlement upon their arrival on the shores of the Río Arimao. The first fortress was built in 1742; the city plans were drawn 54 years later. In 1817 Capt. José Cienfuegos and the French Col. Jean de Clouet, who emigrated from Louisiana, gave a great impulse to the development of the city, which is noted today for its distilleries and its soap, candle, tobacco, brick, tile, cabinet, and soft-drink factories.

Plaza Martí is the center of the city's life. At night the municipal band gives excellent concerts here. Grouped around the plaza are the city hall, the cathedral, and the Terry Theater. The typically Spanish Castillo de Jagua at the entrance of the port was constructed between 1742 and 1745 for protection against pirates. Morgan, Baskerville, and Graff were among those who attacked the town.

Cienfuegos is noted for its fishing. Tarpon abounds both in the bay and in the waters outside. Boats, guides, and tackle are available. Pigeon shooting is also popular with visitors, and there are facilities for shooting excursions.

The Club Náutico de Cienfuegos has a yacht basin and an outdoor swimming pool and is equipped for other sports. The Club de Cazadores (Hunters' Club) is also well equipped for sports, including trap shooting. The city has a jai alai frontón or court which is among the largest in Cuba; matches are held regularly.

HOTELS. San Carlos*; Bristol; La Suiza; Unión.

Excursions from Cienfuegos. Journeys to the falls of the Río Hanabanilla and up the bamboo-shaded Río Damuji to the town of Rodas can be made by boat. Another interesting excursion can be made to the Harvard Botanical Garden which is maintained at Central Soledad by Harvard University.

Trinidad, near the S coast, 45 miles from Santa Clara, was the third settlement established by the Spaniards. The line of the United Railways of Havana by which it is reached from Santa Clara runs through high mountains. The train passes from peak to peak across deep canyons; in some places the tropical vegetation is so dense that the sun does not penetrate it. But after the train enters the valley of the Río Agabama one beautiful view after another unfolds. There is a secondary road to Trinidad branching off the Central Highway at Placetas (p. 53), but it is not in good condition.

Trinidad, high and cool, was founded by Diego Velázquez de León in 1514. Hernando Cortés stopped at the city on his way to conquer Mexico; an enormous ceiba tree to which he moored his ships may still be seen. For several centuries Trinidad was the center of the island's wealth and the home of many of Cuba's richest families, whose nobility is attested by the heraldic shields and symbols on their magnificent mansions. It is said that the floors of one of the mansions were paved with Spanish gold pieces.

A number of old residences, notably those of the Borrell, Brunet, Cantero, and Izquierdo families and a house occupied by the naturalist Humboldt, still stand, and though they have suffered greatly during the years they afford an idea of the life and wealth that once existed in the city. The summer residences of the captains general are noted for their carved ceilings and heavy nail-studded doors. The architecture of many of the old houses is patterned on the Moorish cities of Spain.

The narrow streets, curiously cobbled with chinas pelonas or small smooth stones, were laid by slaves and political prisoners with such skill that they have withstood the torrents that wash over them during the rainy season.

In Trinidad, colonial dress and customs have been preserved and the mantilla and other articles of dress of Castilian origin are worn today. Holy Week is observed by processions and rites centuries old.

Points of interest, besides the old mansions, include Plaza de Sorran, laid out by Cortés when he assembled his men for the expedition to Mexico; Jigüa, a small square containing the ruins of the house in which the first Mass was celebrated; and the monastery of San Francisco, once the quarters of Spanish troops, now a public school.

HOTELS.   Canada; Casa Ronda; Plaza.

Excursions from Trinidad. Many interesting excursions can be made into the hills and mountains. Hunting in the vicinity is excellent, and so is fishing at the seaside resort of Casilda, 3 miles away.

El Vigía (The Lookout), atop a hill a short walk from the city, affords a fine view of the surrounding countryside. To the right is the valley and at the foot of the hill is the city with the deep blue sea behind it. On the way to El Vigía the traveler sees the old church of La Popa and deep unexplored caves.

Punta de Casilda and El Castillo de San Pedro were some of the city's defenses against pirates. A number of old English cannon captured during one such attack are preserved.

Placetas, with 10,000 inhabitants, 21 miles E of Santa Clara on the Central Highway and also on the railroad line from there, is a tobacco and cattle center. It is linked with Caibarién on the N coast by road and railroad and with Trinidad near the S coast by railroad and by a secondary road which is in poor condition.

Sancti Spíritus, with 22,000 inhabitants, 31 miles E of Placetas on the Central Highway and also reached by railroad, was founded by Diego Velásquez de León in 1514 as a strategic point from which to supervise the Indians. During early colonial times it was attacked by French and English pirates, and in its church Bartolomé de las Casas began his historic campaign against the harsh treatment accorded the Indians by their Spanish conquerors. He preached his first sermon on the subject in 1516.

Many colonial customs are preserved in Sancti Spíritus. The old part of the city is reminiscent of the Moorish cities of Spain, with many buildings in that style of architecture; narrow, crooked streets, and small parks and plazas.

The principal church is typically colonial, showing Moorish influence. Within the church is a sculpture, Humility and Patience, by an unknown hand. A magnificent view is gained from the tower. Another of the interesting old buildings is the residence of the Counts of Lersundi. The façade of the theater is a reproduction of that of the theater of Milan, and the old bridge over the Río Yayabó is similar in construction to bridges of Spain.

Other points of interest include Plaza Honorato, formerly called Jesús Nazareno; Parque Serafín Sánchez, containing a bust of Martí; the church of La Caridad in front of Parque Maceo, and the

park itself. The Tuinicu sugar mill near by is one of the larges
in Cuba. Hats woven of yarey, a species of palm, and pottery ar
made in the city.

HOTELS. Perla de Cuba; Plaza.

Excursions from Sancti Spíritus. Zaza del Medio, a small town 7 mile.
N that is reached by secondary road or railroad, is one of the mos
beautifully situated of the inland towns. The Río Zaza flows through
a charming little valley where slender royal palms grow. Mahogany
and other precious hardwoods are abundant. There is good pigeon
shooting.

Sancti Spíritus is also connected by secondary road and railroac
with the S coast. Both routes pass through the small but picturesque
villages of Paredes, Guasimal, and Tunas de Zaza. The last is near the
mouth of the Río Zaza.

E of Santa Clara, Camagüey Province is the second largest in Cuba
An essentially agricultural region, it has extensive orchards in which
all sorts of tropical fruits are produced. Sugar is grown extensively
and the province's 29 sugar mills have a large output. The wide-
spreading, well-watered lowlands are excellent for cattle and dairy
industries, and the meat, butter, and cheese produced figure im-
portantly in the national economy. A wide range of precious woods—
cedar, mahogany, and ebony—are used in the production of fine
cabinetwork at Camagüey and elsewhere.

Jatibonico, with 6700 inhabitants, 29 miles from Sancti Spíritus on
the Central Highway and also reached by railroad from Zaza del
Medio, marks the W limit of the province. The surrounding forests
are excellent for hiking and riding.

Ciego de Avila, with 16,000 inhabitants, 42 miles E of Jatibonico
on the Central Highway and also reached by railroad, is an important
junction and airline stop in a rich sugar and fruit region. Near by,
General Maceo broke through the famous trocha or line of blockhouses and trenches which the Spaniards had erected between the
N and S coasts with the object of keeping the forces of the Cuban
revolutionaries separated. Several of the blockhouses remain.

HOTELS. Delicias; Rueda; Sevilla.

Excursions from Ciego de Avila. There are secondary road and railroad connections with Morón, a city of 10,000 near Laguna de Leche
(Milk Lake) and Turiguano Island in a wild region of the N coast
suitable for fishing and hunting, and S with the small port of Júcaro.

E of Ciego de Avila the Central Highway passes through typical
small towns. The woods gradually give way to rolling plains planted
with sugar cane and fruit trees. The village of Florida, site of the
large Florida sugar mill, is 43 miles beyond Ciego de Avila. Camagüey
is 25 miles farther.

CAMAGÜEY

Capital of the province, Camagüey, with 50,000 inhabitants, is
an important railroad center and airline stop. It lies on a level plain
surrounded by evergreens.

The city was originally founded under the name of Santa María de
Puerto Príncipe by the conquistador Diego Velázquez de León on the

N coast in 1514. Vasco Porcayo de Figueroa, scion of a Spanish noble family and holder of large estates, was responsible for the removal of the settlement to its present site in 1530. The Inquisition was established here in 1776, shortly after its establishment in Lima, Peru, and in 1800-38 Camagüey was the seat of the Spanish superior tribunal. The town suffered violent attacks by pirates. Henry Morgan locked the inhabitants in the church of San Francisco while he pillaged the settlement, and more than 100 inhabitants perished during his raid.

Camagüey has been very active politically since the earliest days. Gertrudis Gómez de Avellaneda, famous in Spain as well as America for her poetry, was born in a small house on C. Avellaneda here. Other noted citizens were Eduardo Agramonte y Piña, writer, musician, and revolutionary; Joaquín Agüero y Agüero, a hero shot by the Spaniards; the revolutionary leader Salvador Cisneros y Betancourt; and Ignacio Mora, a noted intellectual.

Known as a city of churches, Camagüey is one of the most picturesque of Cuban towns. Its narrow, crooked streets, its charming parks and plazas, its ancient buildings with massive walls, grilled windows, overhanging balconies, and lofty arched doors, retain a colonial charm. Most houses have the traditional Spanish patio with luxuriant flowers and the great tinajones or clay pots formerly used to gather rain water for drinking.

Plaza Gonzalo de Quesada, filled with tropical plants and flowers, is especially attractive. Plaza Agramonte, with a statue of Gen. Ignacio Agramonte Loynaz, an outstanding hero of the struggle for liberation, is the center of the city's life. Near by are the Ayuntamiento or city hall, other governmental buildings, and the market.

CHURCHES. The cathedral, known also as the church of Our Lady of La Candelaria, S of Plaza Agramonte, is an outstanding example of early architecture. The original church, constructed in 1550, was burned in 1616 and rebuilt a year later. In later years additions were made, but the original style was preserved. The old ceiling is a good example of the old artesonado or beamed style.

The church of San Francisco, 3 blocks E of the cathedral and facing Parque San Francisco, is the city's outstanding church, late Gothic in style, with a simple, harmonious façade, imposing mahogany doors, and stained-glass windows. The church is cruciform, with a long nave. Notable among the chapels is that of the famous Virgin of La Caridad. The high altar has a triple retable of Gothic style and a valuable sculpture of the Sacred Heart.

The church of La Merced, overlooking the old Plaza Merced which has been renamed for Charles A. Dana, near the center of the city, contains rich relics and is very popular among the faithful of Camagüey. Its interior is richly decorated with gilded altars and polychrome walls. Founded in 1748, the church was originally dedicated to Our Lady of Altagracia by Mercedarian friars from Santo Domingo. Massive and solid as a fortress, it retains much of its early character, though it has undergone several restorations. The altars, pulpit, and benches were carved by gifted Cuban artisans. The high altar, in Gothic style, of gilded wood, silver, and marble, is the work of the Catalonian artist Juan Rivera Casanovas.

The church of Our Lady of La Soledad, Calle República at C. Estrada Palma, was completed in 1776. Large and solid, it has a central nave measuring 96 feet by 156 feet. Its altar, made from 40,000 Spanish silver pesos, and its frescoes are notable.

The church of Our Lady of El Carmen, adjoining the Ursuline convent in the W section of the city, was finished in 1825. Its high altar, with a polychrome figure of the Virgin, is noteworthy. Entrance is through the convent.

SPORTS. The Camagüey Country Club maintains a golf course, and there are several tennis clubs. The surrounding hills are excellent for horseback riding and hunting.

HOTELS. Hotel Camagüey* occupies barracks built by the Spaniards and is typical of the military structures of the period, with sentry boxes, loopholes, barred windows, and heavy doors. The landscaped central patio, with cannon and cannon balls painted white, contains one of the best collections of tropical plants in Cuba. Other hotels are Gran*, C. Maceo 15; Plaza*, near the railroad station, with a fine wine cellar; and Colón, C. República 163.

EXCURSIONS FROM CAMAGÜEY

The Cubitas Caves, about 2 hours away by car, are notable. The walls are adorned with primitive pictorial carvings.

Nuevitas, with 10,000 inhabitants, about 35 miles N by a secondary road, is an important sugar exporting center. Chrome and asphalt ore are mined in the district. The bay on which the town lies is large and well sheltered. There are two ports, Puerto Tarafa, 2 miles N, and Pastelillo, 3½ miles E.

HOTELS. Acera de Martí; Miramar; Palmero; Quinta.

Martí, a small town 40 miles E of Camagüey on the Central Highway, is noted because a short distance S of it Gen. Máximo Gómez defeated the Spaniards in an important battle of the Ten Years' War.

EASTERN CUBA

The province of Oriente, formerly called Santiago de Cuba, occupying the E end of the island, covers the largest area, has the highest mountains, and contains the greatest mineral wealth. It also has vast forests of rare woods such as mahogany, cedar, and majagua and 44 sugar mills, which place it second only to Santa Clara in sugar production. Its fine ports include Puerto Padre and the bay of Nipe, N; Manzanillo, SW; and Santiago de Cuba and Guantánamo, SE.

The S coast parallels the mountain range Sierra Maestra, which contains Pico Turquino (7870 feet), the highest peak in Cuba. E are Sierra de Nipe, Sierra del Cristal, Cuchilla de Toar, and Sierra de Purial, in a huge densely forested region very sparsely populated. N of Manzanillo empties the Río Cauto, the largest stream of Cuba, which issues near the Sierra Maestra and waters the rolling plains W in the province of Oriente.

Las Tunas, or Victoria de las Tunas, with 5000 inhabitants, 37 miles E of Martí on the Central Highway, was the scene of a decisive battle of the Cuban revolution. It took the patriots two days of hard fighting to capture the town, which was defended by 600 veteran Spanish troops with some cannon. Las Tunas was laid in ruins.

Excursions from Las Tunas. A secondary road leads to Puerto Padre on the N coast, Delicias, and Chaparra. Puerto Padre is the shipping port of Cuba's largest sugar mill, Central Chaparra.

The picturesque, old-fashioned village of Gíbara, where Columbus first set foot on Cuban soil, can be reached by secondary road from Chaparra. Near Gíbara are three curious hills, Silla (Saddle), Pan (Loaf), and Mesa (Table). The great navigator noted them in his diary as characteristic of the region.

Holguín, with 22,000 inhabitants, 50 miles E of Las Tunas on the Central Highway, is an important sugar, tobacco, and cattle center. It does considerable business also in coffee, corn, and beans and is an important railroad center for the N ports of the province. Air service connects it with the rest of Cuba. Roads and railroads give connections to Gíbara, Chaparra, and Puerto Padre.

HOTELS. Majestic; Saratoga; Sevilla; Telégrafo.

Excursions from Holguín. Alto Cedro, 30 miles SE by railroad, is a tiny village lying in the foothills of the Sierra de Nipe. It is set in a wild, picturesque tropical region, in the midst of the forest.

Antilla, with 20,000 inhabitants, is an important sugar port on the bay of Nipe, 25 miles N of Alto Cedro. It is the NE terminus of the Consolidated Railroads of Cuba and is also an airline stop. In the vicinity are the Bethlehem Cuba iron mines. On the E shore of the bay and accessible by a combination of railroad and road from Antilla are Mayarí and Prestón, the latter an important iron ore port and an airline stop.

Bayamó, with 10,000 inhabitants, 44 miles S of Holguín on the Central Highway, is the center of the largest cattle district in the province of Oriente. It has large condensed milk, butter, and cheese factories. There is railroad service from Martí (p. 56).

HOTELS. New York; Telégrafo.

Excursion from Bayamó. Manzanillo, with 30,000 inhabitants, 25 miles W by a poor road, is an important sugar and molasses port on the gulf of the same name. It has secondary road connections with the small towns of Salvador, Campechuela, San Ramón, Media Luna, and Niquero on the coast and is accessible by coastal steamer and by air.

HOTELS. Casa Blanca; Inglaterra.

SANTIAGO DE CUBA

Santiago de Cuba, commonly called simply Santiago, 40 miles beyond Bayamó on the Central Highway, is the capital of the province of Oriente and the second largest city of the island, with more than 100,000 inhabitants. It is situated on a beautiful landlocked bay on the SE coast, 604 miles from Havana, and is reached from there by road, railroad, or airplane. It is of great historic importance.

Santiago was founded in 1514 by Diego Velázquez de León and was the capital of the island and its chief city, 1523-58. The starting point for many exploring expeditions to the mainland, it was from here that Cortés set out for Mexico in 1519 and Pánfilo de Narváez embarked on an unsuccessful effort to relieve Cortés forcibly of his Mexican command. In 1522 the settlement was granted the title of city and a coat of arms.

The community was repeatedly attacked by pirates. It was captured in 1553 by 400 French soldiers, who took 30,000 pesos fuertes or pieces of eight for its ransom. In 1662 a band of 900 English musketeers attacked the city via the Río Aguadores. The governor Pedro Morales made a sortie to forestall the invasion, but was overpowered and destroyed. Five thousand Englishmen in 1741 succeeded in landing at Guantánamo, a port E of Santiago, but Francisco Cagigal de la Vega, who was governor at the time, held them off until they reembarked after losing 2000 men by yellow fever and starvation. The city also suffered greatly from earthquakes, especially in 1675-79, when many buildings were destroyed.

At near-by Yara on Oct. 10, 1868, the wealthy planter and lawyer Carlos Manuel de Céspedes, after freeing his slaves, gathered a number of patriots in his sugar mill La Demajagua to proclaim the independence of Cuba. This act, El Grito de Yara, marked the beginning of the Ten Years' War. Baire, also near Santiago, was one of the chief points at which patriots again raised the standard of Cuba's freedom on Feb. 24, 1895, the start of the revolution that lasted until 1898, when U. S. forces joined the rebels against Spain.

The name Santiago was indelibly written in U. S. history when the Spanish fleet, consisting mainly of outdated battleships under Admiral Pascual Cervera, was blockaded in the Santiago harbor by U. S. Admiral William T. Sampson. On June 3, 1898, Richmond Pearson Hobson and a crew of seven volunteers sank the collier Merrimac at the entrance of the harbor, under fire, in an attempt to close the port completely. Cervera was reluctant to try running the blockade, for he believed it would be futile and costly to face the superior U. S. fleet. He suggested leaving the Spanish fleet in the harbor in order to defend the city, but the Spanish government insisted that he attack. Most of his ships were promptly set afire and had to be run aground. When Cervera reported the unfortunate encounter he emphasized the gallantry of the U. S. forces in the fight.

Meantime the U. S. army under Gen. William Shafter had landed a few miles from Santiago. After a heroic defense by the Spaniards, San Juan Hill and the village of El Caney were stormed and taken by the Rough Riders under Col. Theodore Roosevelt on July 1. Gen. José Toral surrendered the city on July 17.

The panorama as the city is approached by car or train from the hills is remarkable, but even more sensational is the approach by sea. High green and blue mountains surround the city, which lies glimmering in the sun—for Santiago is hot—half on level ground at the end of the bay and half on the hillsides. El Caney and San Juan Hill rise in the background. Palm trees and other vegetation appear above the bright-colored houses, many of which have yellow and red tiled roofs. The ship enters the harbor through a narrow channel below the battlements of Morro Castle, perched on a rocky promontory 200 feet high. Back of Morro Castle is the Estrella battery; facing it is La Socapa. The ship passes Cayo Smith, an islet with a fishermen's village once held by the English, and Cayo Ratones, another key, once utilized by the Spaniards for a powder magazine.

THE CITY. Some streets are wide and crowded with traffic, others narrow and crooked, occasionally mere stone stairways ascending the steep hillsides. Not without reason is Santiago called the most Cuban city of Cuba, for a venerable atmosphere is maintained along with the modern. The older section, a few blocks from the waterline, centers around Plaza Céspedes and spreads mostly N and E. W are the harbor, the docks, and the railroad station. Running parallel with the shore is the splendid Alameda Michaelson, a popular promenade. Calle Aguilora and C. Heredia, issuing near the Alameda below the piers, run E to Plaza Céspedes.

Picturesque Plaza Céspedes is one of the most historic spots in Cuba. In a house on the SW corner, at C. Tomás and C. Heredia, Diego Velázquez de León lived and died. Here conquistadores met for expeditions to conquer new and fabulous countries; here a thousand plots were hatched. On the E side of the square are the Hotel Casa Grande, one of the most attractive of Cuba, and the Club San Carlos; N is the Ayuntamiento or city hall; S is the cathedral. W of the cathedral, on the site of the old archbishop's palace, is the school of the Brothers of the Holy Doctrine. The Royal Bank of Canada is a block W and the National City Bank of New York a block N of the square. Three blocks W of the square is the marketplace.

PLAZAS AND PARKS. Parque Estrada Palma, a few blocks S of Plaza Céspedes on C. Estrada Palma, is beautifully landscaped and has an imposing monument to the first president of Cuba, Tomás Estrada Palma. The seated bronze figure tops a pedestal on which plaques depict notable incidents in the wars of liberation.

Parque Aguilera, also called Plaza Dolores, is on C. Aguilera, a little E of Plaza Céspedes. In the center of the landscaped grounds stands a marble statue of Francisco Vicente Aguilera, a leader of the Yara insurrection of Oct. 10, 1868. Parque Libertad, N of Parque Aguilera, is reached by street car going to the residential Vista Alegre section.

Parque Epopeya or Roosevelt Park, at the end of Avenida Victoriano Garzón on the road to Vista Alegre, where the avenue bifurcates into the road to El Caney and Calzada Roosevelt, is a landscaped park created as a setting for a memorial to Theodore Roosevelt which was unveiled on Dec. 14, 1924, in honor of his services during the war of independence. Parque Vista Alegre, in the center of the Vista Alegre section, is past Parque Epopeya on Av. República; this large park with lawns and gardens has a monument to the poet José María Heredia at the entrance. Plaza Flor Crombet, on Calzada Crombet, N of the city, has a notable monument to the revolutionary hero for whom it is named, the descendant of a French family who came to Santiago in the 18th century.

Parque Bacardí, midway of Paseo General Wood in the N outskirts of the city, with large and beautiful gardens, belongs to the Bacardí distillery and Hatuey brewery. It has become a popular spot. A small zoo containing specimens of Cuba's fauna is maintained. The distillery, near the center, serves rum free.

Plaza General Wood, named for the U. S. general who ruled Cuba for a short time after its independence was won, is located at the intersection of Paseo General Wood and Paseo Martí. Plaza Espinosa is at C. Castillo Duany a short distance SE of Plaza Céspedes.

STREETS AND PROMENADES. C. Heredia and C. Aguilera, running almost parallel from the water front and the railroad station to Plaza Céspedes and beyond, are among the oldest streets in Santiago and are the principal commercial arteries. Each is divided into Baja (Lower) and Alta (Upper) sections, the former W of Plaza Céspedes, the latter E, with the colonial atmosphere best preserved. Moorish colonial houses with overhanging balconies, high grilled windows, and arcades are typical of the section.

The Alameda, on the water front near the docks, is a very popular drive and promenade from which a splendid view of the bay is gained. It is flanked by trees and well-kept lawns. Paseo General Wood, in the N outskirts, reached by C. Estrada Palma, is an avenue with two drives and central lawns. Paseo Martí, which crosses the N part of the city, E-W, is one of the finest thoroughfares of Santiago. W it connects by C. Jobito with the road to El Cobre, a small village 10 miles away, where the shrine of the famous Virgin of La Caridad is located. Other important avenues are Av. Victoriano Garzón and its prolongation, Av. República.

PUBLIC BUILDINGS AND COLONIAL MANSIONS. The Provincial Palace, 2 blocks E of Plaza Céspedes, is the official residence of the governor of the province. Built in 1926 at a cost of $400,000, the edifice has an imposing façade and interior.

The city hall is a comparatively modern structure, replacing a building destroyed by earthquake in the 18th century. During the U. S. occupation of the island the building was the headquarters of General Wood. It contains a large painting by J. E. Hernández Ciro showing Cortés taking the oath as mayor of Santiago in 1514. There are also paintings of Cuban patriots and of Theodore Roosevelt and Woodrow Wilson.

The Heredia house, C. Heredia 9, now occupied by the local academy of fine arts, is the birthplace of José María Heredia, foremost Cuban poet and patriot, the author of a notable Ode to Niagara. Cortés' house, near Plaza Céspedes, was the home of Mexico's conqueror. The Ramsden house, C. Castillo Duany 9, home of the British consul general Frederick W. Ramsden, is marked by a tablet placed there by General Wood in gratitude for Ramsden's kindness to U. S. naval prisoners during the Spanish American War.

CHURCHES. Santiago has half a dozen interesting colonial churches, mostly in the old section of the city.

The cathedral, facing Plaza Céspedes, is dedicated to the Virgin of the Assumption. It is among the largest of Cuba's churches and one of the most interesting buildings on the island. The present structure is the fourth erected on the site. The first, begun in 1514, was destroyed by earthquakes and pirates. The beautiful building is in Florentine style. Its massive walls, 8 feet thick, support two handsome towers, in one of which is a large clock. The church rises high above its surroundings, for it was built 18 feet above the plaza. The interior, with broad nave and heavy rows of columns, is patterned on the church of St. John Lateran at Rome. The nave, with four lateral aisles, is 130 feet wide by 240 feet long to the end of the choir, the largest in Cuba. The cathedral contains notable relics and artistic statues and paintings. The high altar, Tuscan in style and heavily ornamented, has notable marble and ivory images.

The church and monastery of San Francisco, on Parque Capdevila at C. San Francisco and C. Corona, was built in 1603 and reconstructed in 1806. The gilded high altar, with a beautiful carved image of the Virgin of the Immaculate Conception, flanked by figures of St. Francis of Assisi and St. Vincent de Paul, is a splendid and elaborate creation.

Other interesting churches are those of El Cristo, at the corner of C. Narciso López and C. 10 de Octubre, N of the city; Our Lady of La Caridad, on C. General Portuondo and C. Estrada Palma, a few blocks N of Plaza Céspedes; Our Lady of El Carmen, 2 blocks N of

Plaza Céspedes on C. Estrada Palma; Santa Lucía, on C. Castillo Duany near Plaza Espinosa, SE of Plaza Céspedes; Our Lady of Las Dolores, near Parque Aguilera on C. Aguilera Alta; Santa Ana, on C. Sánchez Hechavarría, E of Plaza Céspedes.

BACARDI MUNICIPAL MUSEUM, on C. Aguilera, was founded by Emilio Bacardí, a wealthy citizen, and the present building was made possible largely through donations by the Bacardí family. The museum contains an excellent collection of Indian and colonial material, relics of Cuban wars and revolutions, and notable paintings. The library, on the first floor, has a valuable collection of historic maps, photographs, newspapers, and documents. The museum and its library are open weekdays except Saturdays and national holidays 8-11 a.m. and 2-4 p.m., Sundays 8 a.m.-12 m.

THE CEMETERY, on the NW outskirts on the road to El Cobre, contains the tombs of three of Cuba's foremost patriots, José Martí, Carlos Manuel de Céspedes, and Tomás Estrada Palma. There is a monument to the Spaniards who died defending El Caney and San Juan Hill and another erected by the British and U. S. colonies to the passengers and crew of the steamer Virginius who were executed in Santiago by the Spaniards in 1873.

CLUBS. Santiago has excellent social and sports clubs. The distinguished Club San Carlos, on the E side of Plaza Céspedes, is the social gathering place of the Santiago elite. Visitors are admitted on introduction by a member.

The Santiago Country Club, 15 minutes from Plaza Céspedes on the road to El Caney, has one of the finest golf courses in Latin America. The Club Náutico de Santiago de Cuba, a yacht club, on the Alameda at the water front, organizes frequent regattas and contributes largely to the social life of Santiago. Other clubs near by are the Siboney Yacht Club, at Siboney, where the U. S. marines landed in 1898; Ciudamar Yacht Club, at Ciudamar, a summer colony on the same road; and Club Amateur de Pesca, a fishing club, at La Socapa, another summer colony on the shore of the bay.

THEATERS AND MOVING-PICTURE HOUSES. Aguilera, 4 blocks E of Plaza Céspedes; Cuba, a block N of the plaza; Rialto, a block S.

RESTAURANTS. There are good restaurants in the hotels. La Higuera specializes in typical Cuban dishes. The Club Rancho, 10 miles from town on the Central Highway, set in charming surroundings, offers excellent seafood.

HOTELS. Casa Grande**, in the center of town facing Plaza Céspedes, occupies a luxurious old mansion which has been modernized. From its roof garden a good view of the city and port is gained. Rooms are large and comfortable, and the cuisine is excellent. Other hotels are Imperial*, C. Saco 301, and Venus*, C. Hartman Alta 658.

SANTIAGO'S ENVIRONS AND EXCURSIONS

La Loma de San Juan (San Juan Hill), 2 miles E of the city by a good road, was the scene of the battle of combined U. S. and Cuban forces with the Spanish in 1898. The battlefield is now laid out as a park, with gardens, shrubbery, and fine walks and drives. The original trenches are preserved, and several monuments have been erected to those who fell in battle. On top of the hill is an observatory which affords an excellent view of the battlefield and the surrounding country.

The peace tree, which is passed en route to San Juan Hill, is a large ceiba under which peace was concluded by the Spanish Gen. José Toral and U. S. Gen. William Shafter. Around it is a small park adorned with cannon and other war relics. On the tree are bronze tablets giving the names of the regiments which took part in the battle and of the men who lost their lives in the siege of Santiago.

El Caney, 7½ miles E of the city, via Av. Victoriano Garzón to Parque Epopeya, is an old Spanish village and site of El Viso, a fort which was taken by U. S. troops in 1898 after hard fighting and heroic resistance by weary and ill-provisioned Spanish troops. The ruins of old blockhouses remain, and from the top of the fort a good view can be had of Santiago and the country surrounding it.

Guantánamo, with 20,000 inhabitants, is 40 miles E of Santiago, reached by secondary road and by railroad. It is also an airline stop. Important events occurred in the bay during the Spanish American War. Admiral Sampson, seeing its advantage as a base against the Spaniards in Cuba, landed 600 marines on the sandy beach and succeeded in dispersing the scanty Spanish garrison.

The bay is about 4 miles wide by 10 miles long, well sheltered and deep, capable of accommodating large vessels. The place is wild and solitary, and save for the U. S. naval base it has little importance. First discovered by Spaniards from Santo Domingo, the bay was soon a rendezvous of pirates and buccaneers, who launched raids from it on Santiago and kept watch for rich galleons bound for Spain. The English admiral Edward Vernon made it the base for his unsuccessful attack on Santiago in 1741.

E of Guantánamo, on the opposite side of the bay, is the town of Boquerón, terminus of the Guantánamo and Western Railway and an important shipping point for the large sugar crop of the region. Guantánamo is connected by railroad and road with Caimanora, near the entrance of the bay.

Punta Gorda and Ciudamar, both about 5 miles SE of Santiago and reached by road, are popular suburbs with many fine homes and gardens. In the latter are the Ciudamar Yacht Club and a good inclosed beach with bathing facilities. Another beach is under development at Aguadores, with an old Spanish fort near by.

Siboney, 12 miles SE of Santiago, is one of the points at which U. S. troops first landed in Cuba. A monument has been erected to them. There is a yacht club, and the excellent beach is being developed as a resort. A short distance farther E are Daiquirí and Firmeza, important mining towns. Daiquirí is noted as the original home of the Daiquirí cocktail.

Morro Castle, or El Morro, 5 miles S of Santiago at the entrance to the harbor, reached by road, was built in 1600. Blown up in 1662 by Henry Morgan, it was rebuilt two years later. Though not as imposing as that of Havana, Santiago's Morro Castle is a notable fortification, with complicated passages and moats and numerous dungeons where Cuban patriots were imprisoned during the revolutionary period. Hobson and his companions of Merrimac fame were held here after their capture in 1898. The castle stands high over the bay.

El Cobre (Copper), 10 miles W of Santiago, reached by a road which issues from Calzada Crombet, is a village notable for its shrine to the Virgin of La Caridad (Charity), patroness of Cuba. In the sanctuary is preserved the carved wooden image of the Virgin richly adorned with gold and jewels. Miraculous curative powers are attributed to it, and thousands make pilgrimage here on September 8 of each year.

Pico Turquino (Turquino Peak), 6560 feet high, is 55 miles W of Santiago. The interesting excursion to the summit over a dirt road and paths requires 2-3 days.

Puerto Boniato, 12 miles N of Santiago, is a small village atop a hill. The road winds along the mountain through a dense tropical forest. The town has a small bodega or wine shop which affords a magnificent view of Santiago and the deep blue sea beyond.

Baracoa, with 10,000 inhabitants, is on the extreme NE coast of Cuba at the foot of Mt. Yunque, which towers 2000 feet over the semicircular harbor. Baracoa is very isolated, being reached only by coastal ships and airplanes. It was the first point sighted by Columbus, who described it as an enchanted scene. Diego Velázquez de León landed his expedition near by in 1511 and built a fort, the ruins of which lie above the town. The territory around Baracoa is wild and highly attractive for hunting and fishing and as a laboratory for naturalists.

INDEX TO THE REGIONAL GUIDE

THE REPUBLIC OF HAITI

HAITI

BY ANTONIO J. COLORADO

The republic of Haiti, written Haïti by the Haitians, is the only independent nation in the Western Hemisphere that is French in heritage and language. Sharing with the Dominican Republic the island of the Greater Antilles known as Española or Hispaniola, Haiti, or Santo Domingo, it lies due south of New York City, approximately halfway between Cuba and Puerto Rico.

HISTORY

Haiti was discovered by Columbus. On his first voyage the great navigator landed on Dec. 6, 1492, at the extreme northwestern point of the island, probably at what is now Môle Saint-Nicolas. Near the site of the present Cap-Haïtien on the north coast he established a fort, La Navidad, and here started the first Spanish settlement in the Americas. The history of Haiti, which eventually became the world's first Negro republic, is a stirring drama of deep human interest, a constant battle against great odds, spurred by the Negro's vital and eternal urge for freedom. This crusade was not confined to a striving for Haitian liberty. In 1779, when the 13 North American colonies of Great Britain were fighting for independence, 600 Haitians fought at Savannah under Count d'Estaing. At a crucial point in his struggle Simón Bolívar, the South American liberator, received material and moral aid from the Haitians.

COLONIAL PERIOD. Two centuries after the island's discovery, the Spanish colony which Columbus had started came under French rule. France and Spain were at war at the beginning of the 17th century. About 1626 some French and English adventurers established themselves on the island of La Tortue or Tortuga, north of Haiti and separated from it only by a narrow channel. The French governors who were eventually set up over the buccaneers and pirates of La Tortue encouraged them in harassing the Spaniards, and French influence was extended over all the western part of the island of Haiti. Finally, by the Treaty of Ryswick in 1697, Spain acknowledged French sovereignty over the territory that is today the republic of Haiti.

The Indians in Haiti, as elsewhere in the Americas, could not survive the terrible clash of race on race, culture on culture, that resulted from the colonization of their lands by Europeans. Harassed, enslaved, made to adopt new ways of life, exposed to strange new diseases, they died by the thousands and were soon all but exterminated. Partly to acquire a body of strong workers to labor on their plantations, partly to spare the Indians, the Spanish and later the French imported thousands of Negro slaves from Africa. During the 18th century the French brought in more than a million Negroes. Coming from all parts of Africa between the Gulf of Guinea and the Cape of Good Hope, these slaves represented almost every African tribe. But they did not thrive in Haiti. The harsh conditions of their slavery had cut their number in half by 1789.

At the outbreak of the French revolution the French colony, which was called Saint-Domingue, had three social classes based on racial characteristics. The white population numbered about 27,000; the mulattoes, most of them liberated slaves known as affranchis, made up another 27,000, who were ultimately to form Haiti's governing class; and finally there were the slaves, numbering almost half a million. Between these classes existed insurmountable barriers and hatreds that sought outlet in revolution and resulted in social chaos. The slaves were regarded as chattels rather than as human beings, and their inferior status was accepted as a matter of course. Their many uprisings were suppressed, but the very presence of half a million slaves among some 27,000 white masters created an atmosphere of uncertainty and unexpressed fear. It was even more difficult to control the mulattoes, who, though they were regarded as social inferiors, were the equals of the whites in economic prerogatives. It was the mulattoes who provided the revolutionary ferment to destroy the French colony at the opportune moment.

This was offered by the French revolution. There was an uproar when the first news of the revolution reached Saint-Domingue. The affranchis demanded recognition as human beings on the same footing as the whites. The whites demanded certain prerogatives in trade and commerce as well as a larger share in the island's political administration. The friends of the Negro slaves agitated for the latter's freedom. The struggle between whites and mulattoes culminated in the rebellion of the slaves. Under the leadership of Boukman, Biassou, and Jean François, the Negroes descended from the mountains like a hurricane, killing white men ruthlessly and destroying the plantations of Plaine-du-Nord. The National Assembly of France sent out various commissions, which, however, did nothing effective. Finally, on Feb. 4, 1794, the French were compelled to decree the abolition of slavery. The colony, however, was already slipping out of French control. The north was harassed by an extremely able Negro leader, Toussaint L'Ouverture, who was fighting on behalf of the Spanish monarchy; the south and the west were invaded by the English.

Toussaint L'Ouverture, known locally as François-Dominique Toussaint-Bréda, now came to the forefront in the movement toward liberation. Toussaint was born at the Bréda plantation in 1743, supposedly a descendant of the African chief Gaou Guinou of the Arada tribe. He was an extraordinary personality, a full-blooded Negro, quiet, peaceable in manner, but with an iron will and an exceptional aptitude for war and organization. After the abolition of slavery Toussaint offered his services to France. But soon after his help had been accepted, he himself assumed full authority and forced the governor to leave for France. He then defeated the mulattoes who controlled the south. Finally he made himself governor of the French colony of Saint-Domingue for life and successfully invaded and annexed the Spanish part of the island. By then the revolution had burned itself out in France, and Napoleon was in full command. Fearing the colony's secession, he sent out an expedition of 25,000 men and 70 warships under the command of his brother-in-law Gen. Charles Victor Emmanuel Leclerc. The French were successful in the violent warfare that ensued. Through treachery they captured Toussaint, who was sent to Europe to die in a dungeon in the Jura mountains.

The Negroes were not really vanquished. They had learned that they could fight successfully; now they merely awaited another opportunity. This came when France re-established slavery in Martinique and Guadeloupe. Fear of its possible restoration in Saint-Domingue led

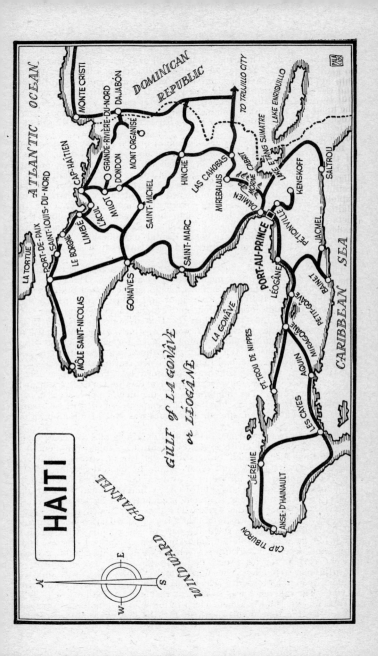

to another revolt. The struggle started all over again under the leadership of Toussaint's generals, Dessalines, Christophe, Clerveaux, Pétion, and Maurepas, with help from the United States and Great Britain. But the Negroes' greatest ally was yellow fever. Leclerc's men died by the hundreds. Finally he was struck by fever himself and died. General Rochambeau then took command of the French government forces. Utterly defeated by the blacks in the battle of Vertières, he capitulated to Dessalines.

INDEPENDENCE. Jean-Jacques Dessalines proclaimed the independence of the French colony of Saint-Domingue under the old Indian name of Haiti on Jan. 1, 1804. He organized the country under a military oligarchy and launched reprisals against the whites. Haiti was a seething military camp. Suddenly released from centuries of slavery, exploitation, and misery, but burdened with intense class hatreds, the Haitians were not yet able to govern their own country. Only the dictatorship of military chiefs could hold them together, and their leaders faced the dual problem of repelling foreign invasions and organizing some sort of practical governmental machinery at home. The material bases of Haitian culture had been ruthlessly destroyed during the preceding years of warfare.

The new nation thus started life under the worst possible conditions. The one-time white rulers might return at any time. Haiti faced the hostility of all the American nations, including the United States, which practiced slavery; the country was poor and lacked social order, public education, economic organization, and experience in government. The history of Haiti, 1804-1915, when the United States intervened in its affairs, was a series of struggles, some of them successful, aimed at organizing the country and winning a place for it among the other independent nations of the world. Dessalines, who had been named governor general for life, had himself crowned emperor on Oct. 8, 1804. The following year his title was confirmed by a constitution. This document decreed that only Negroes and naturalized whites could own property in Haiti. The inhabitants of the new empire were to be designated collectively as blacks. The emperor ruled with a strong hand, and dissatisfaction spread. Dessalines was killed from ambush on Oct. 17, 1806.

An attempt was now made to establish a republic. A constituent assembly at the end of 1806 elected Henri Christophe president but granted him such limited powers that he led an army southward against Alexandre Pétion and others whom he blamed for the restrictions. Christophe was forced to return to the north. There he was made president, and in 1811 he declared himself king. In Port-au-Prince, however, Pétion was elected president, and he set to work to organize a republic in the south. The civil war which ensued lasted six years. When peace was established the divided Haiti made substantial progress. Christophe ruled his part of the country with an iron hand, but he was an able administrator. He established schools, built roads, and developed agriculture. While Christophe was building magnificent palaces for his court, Pétion in the south was organizing a constitutional republic. The north, under Christophe, was able to attain a material prosperity which the south, under Pétion, strove for in vain. The difference was so evident that in 1816 Pétion had himself elected for life under a new constitution giving him more personal power. By the time of his death in 1818 he had accomplished certain important measures. He had created a class of small rural property owners by granting lands to the soldiers and officers of the army of liberation, and he had established a lycée or secondary school at Port-au-Prince. In the struggle for the independence of the Spanish colonies in South America, Pétion extended help to Simón Bolívar.

In 1818 Jean-Pierre Boyer was elected president. He presided over the destinies of the country for 25 years. When Christophe committed suicide in 1820 Boyer's authority was extended over a reunited Haiti. In December 1821 the inhabitants of the eastern part of the island revolted against the authority of Spain, and Boyer went to the aid of the insurgents. He invaded their land and united it to Haiti. This union lasted until February 1844, when the eastern part of the island declared itself independent as the Dominican Republic. During his long administration Boyer achieved lasting benefits. He settled the question of the debt to France and obtained the recognition of Haiti's independence on April 17, 1825. He also promulgated the Haitian codes, patterned on French legislation.

During 1844-1908 Haiti had 15 presidents. Outstanding among them was Faustin Soulouque, who in 1848 proclaimed himself emperor as Faustin I and attempted to re-establish the sovereignty of Haiti over the Dominican Republic. He was overthrown in 1859 by Fabre Geffrard, who became one of Haiti's best rulers. Geffrard gave great impetus to education and signed the Concordat of 1860 with the Church for the organization of the country's Catholic clergy. Louis Salomon (1879-88) created the national bank and reorganized secondary education. The period 1908-1915, inaugurated by President Simon, is known in Haitian history as the epoch of ephemeral governments. During this brief period of seven years there were seven presidents: Antoine G. Simon, Leconte, Tancrède Auguste, Michel Oreste, Oreste Zamor, Davilmar Théodore, and finally Gen. Vilbrun Guillaume Sam. All these rulers tried to maintain themselves in power by loans which, contracted under difficult conditions, involved Haiti in a net of international claims.

RECENT HISTORY. After tragic events which accompanied the fall and death of President Guillaume Sam, the United States landed marines in Haiti on July 28, 1915, and assumed temporary authority. Shortly afterward Admiral Caperton of the United States Navy received instructions to have the National Assembly elect a president, with the understanding that the successful candidate would be expected to acquiesce in the exercise of financial control by the United States. Senator Sudré Dartiguenave became president in that year and remained in power till 1922. In September 1915 Haiti and the United States signed a treaty defining the objectives of the intervention and fixing the powers of the two contracting parties. This treaty, undertaken for a period of 10 years, was later extended to 1936. Dartiguenave's administration was marked by attempts at reorganizing Haiti's finances and economic life. A number of material advances were achieved. Roads were built, sanitation and communications were improved, and the rural police (Gendarmerie d'Haïti) was reorganized.

The period 1922-30 was marked by almost complete co-operation between the Haitian president, Louis Borno, and Col. John H. Russell, who had been named by President Warren G. Harding as high commissioner and envoy extraordinary. Under the joint administration of Borno and Russell material progress was made in matters of the public debt, national income, roads and communications, public order, sanitation, and the like. Following the recommendations of the Forbes commission, appointed by President Herbert Hoover to investigate the political situation in Haiti, Eugène Roy became provisional president in 1930, succeeding Borno. His mission was to call for the election of a new National Assembly which in turn should elect the country's next constitutional president. On November 18 the National Assembly elected Senator Sténio Vincent to the presidency.

On Aug. 7, 1933, the governments of Haiti and the United States signed a new agreement providing for the termination of the occupation by December 1934. This arrangement was not satisfactory to Haiti, because it did not provide for terminating the fiscal control of the United States. Some time later President Vincent was invited to Washington to discuss the matter with President Franklin D. Roosevelt, who later visited Haiti, after an agreement had been reached. In accordance with the good neighbor policy, President Roosevelt decided to end the occupation by the United States entirely. The last marines left the country on Aug. 21, 1934, and shortly thereafter, by a new agreement, Haiti regained fiscal control of her customs. President Vincent was succeeded in May 1941 by Elie Lescot.

The government of Haiti has been established on a sound republican basis. Headed by the president, the first magistrate of the state, it is organized much like that of the United States. The president is assisted in his duties by a cabinet of six public ministers as well as his personal advisory board. There is a Senate whose members are chosen by an electoral college in each department of the country and which is headed by the president of the Senate. There is also a Chamber of Deputies whose members are elected by popular vote for a term of four years.

THE LAND

Roughly, the republic of Haiti occupies the W third of one of the Greater Antilles. Its territory consists principally of two peninsulas that are almost parallel. Port-au-Prince, on the coast between them, has an extraordinarily large and fine natural harbor. The area of Haiti, including the near-by islands such as La Tortue and La Gonâve, is 10,200 square miles, or a little more than that of Vermont. The country has a population of some 3,000,000, about eight times Vermont's.

Haiti is an aboriginal name meaning Mountainous Country. The mountains, which reach a maximum height of some 9000 feet, are often covered with exuberant forests of precious woods and fruit trees. Between the principal ranges are fertile valleys watered by numberless streams that sometimes dry up and sometimes are torrential, interspersed with small arid cactus-studded areas. N is the Plaine-du-Nord, with rich coffee and sugar plantations; in the center is the Artibonite valley, through which flows the river of the same name, wide and navigable. This valley is the heart of Haiti. It produces rice, coffee, cotton, and fruits including figs and bananas, as well as fine woods such as mahogany, cedar, rosewood, acajou, chene, sapin, and noyer. S are the valley of Cul-de-Sac, near Port-au-Prince, and the plains of Léogâne and Les Cayes, producing sugar cane and foodstuffs.

Agriculture is the chief occupation of the country, which produces from 80,000,000 to 100,000,000 pounds of coffee of excellent quality.

ther products are cacao, cotton, sugar, tobacco, honey, sisal, pine-
pples, bananas and other tropical fruits, logwood, and precious woods.
rance used to be the chief buyer of Haitian products. The United
states enjoys the position of chief exporter to Haiti, and trade relations
re being constantly strengthened.

THE PEOPLE

Haiti is one of the most densely populated regions of the West
Indies. Over 90 per cent of this population is of African descent, with
varying degrees of French culture. The greatest number speak a sonorous patois known as creole, formed of a mixture of French dialects
with a limited number of Spanish, English, Indian, and African words.
This creole patois has produced a limited but extremely interesting
popular literature and poetry. The upper class, which is highly cultured, speaks excellent French and has to its credit numerous distinguished works of literature, history, and jurisprudence. Like his
country's landscape, the common man of Haiti is primitive, kind, and
gentle. His life is simple and has the beauty of its natural simplicity.
Transporting their wares to market on their heads or on the backs of
small burros, Haitian men and women meet the traveler with a cordial
greeting. If a foreigner calls at a native cottage he is welcomed usually
with warm hospitality.

Christianity is deeply rooted. It was introduced by the Spaniards in
1492. The principal religion is the Roman Catholic, which enjoys a
privileged position since the Concordat of 1860. But there is freedom
of worship, and the Protestant missions which were started by Christophe have developed considerably. Much has been written on Haitian
voodooism, the so-called cult of the serpent. Most of this literature,
except where it is the work of trained, critical, well-balanced students
of religions, is filled with imaginative tales which reflect a morbid search
for sensation and libel a kindly people. To be sure, the Haitians have
their superstitions, many of them inherited from darkest Africa, and
the voodoo dance which is at times practiced in the interior shows
vestiges of ancient African rites. Christian ceremonies, in much the
same way, contain many elements drawn from the rites of ancient
European paganism, and it is not so long since superstitious New Eng-
landers furtively consulted individuals whom they took to be witches.
The visitor to Haiti occasionally hears the throb of distant dance drums
rolling down from the hills, or he may be approached by some taxi
driver who offers to take him to see a voodoo demonstration. Of
voodoo, Harold Courlander writes in his book Haiti Singing: "Vodoun
today means many things. It means dancing, singing, rituals for the
living and the dead, drums; it means an attitude toward life and
death, a concept of ancestors and the afterworld, and understanding
of the forces which control man and his activities; it has subtle mean-
ings beyond the understanding of anthropological observers; it is, in
short, something which is infused into the very essence of living."

ART AND ARCHITECTURE

BY ROBERT C. SMITH

A visitor to Haiti is impressed with the fact that Haitian art is different from that of the other Latin American republics. It derives from France and not from Spain or Portugal. Haiti, like the province of Quebec in Canada and the old French cities of the Mississippi valley in the United States, forms a nucleus of legitimate French artistic tradition in the New World. In the colonial period Haitian architecture differed from that of Hispanic America by its greater severity of design and its use, in spite of the tropical climate, of the steeply pitched roofs of France. Elsewhere in Latin America architectural design, following the Baroque style of Spain and Portugal, was richer and more complicated. Roofs, especially those of churches, were usually flat.

Revolutions and civil wars have left few early buildings in Haiti. The handful that remain are concentrated in the region of Cap-Haïtien, a former capital of the republic. Typical of these colonial structures is the large late 18th-century parish church of Cap-Haïtien, designed by Rabié and built by Delaître in 1771 on sober French neo-classic lines. Neither the lateral towers nor the cramped upper story of the façade was included in the original plan. Had the building been completed according to the colonial design, the steep roof of the nave would have been masked by a handsome Ionic portico in the second story of the façade. The statues of St. Peter and St. Paul above the smaller doors accord with the neo-classic spirit of the church. More original is the oddly proportioned old cathedral of Port-au-Prince, a curious 18th-century building in which the main story is separated by a huge attic from the large belfry that surmounts the whole façade. The details of rusticated pilasters, wide pediment, and unbroken cornices are pure French design. The building contains an interesting neo-classic painting in the style of David, representing the benediction of Ogé and Chavannes, the first Haitian martyrs, by Guillaume Lethière (1760-1832), who was a native of the French island of Guadeloupe. The general outlines of this cathedral are reflected in a few colonial churches like that of the village of Grande-Rivière-du-Nord. An even more striking local interpretation of the style of the Louis is found in the building of the old port office in Cap-Haïtien. There the cool, wide arcades of both stories are a concession to the climate, like the wooden porches and galleries of the older houses in the Haitian cities—a common element in American coastal architecture from New York to Buenos Aires. Of Haiti's several colonial stone bridges, the finest is that of Haut-du-Cap (1789), strongly reminiscent of provincial bridges in France. Old fountains, like those in the Place d'Armes and on the quay at Cap-Haïtien, the latter an obelisk of 1789, were one of the colonial glories of Haiti.

The two principal monuments of Haitian architecture were erected *during the reign of Henri Christophe as king (1806-22). His Citadel, the masterpiece of a local engineer, Henri Besse, was begun in 1804. It is a fortress unique in the Americas because of its size, the bold lines of its bastions, and the admirable proportions of its units. In these respects it recalls some of the Hohenstaufen fortifications in southern Italy. Very different is the ruined palace of Sans-Souci, completed in 1812, the principal result of the king's attempt to prove that* his court was as civilized as those of Europe. Old paintings and lithographs show that the palace was patterned on the royal château of Saint-Cloud near Paris, whose ramp and portico are reproduced on a grander scale at Sans-Souci. The hemispheroidal cupola of the recently restored chapel is a great architectural curiosity, since it lends a distinctly Islamic note to an otherwise Palladian building. It was at Sans-Souci that the king established a short-lived art academy under the direction of a certain Richard Evans, who had been an assistant of Sir Thomas Lawrence in London. Some portraits from this school have survived in the Chamber of Deputies and the new National Museum founded by President Sténio Vincent.

At the close of the 19th century the architect Hippolyte built the celebrated market of Port-au-Prince, constructed entirely of iron sheets after the fashion of the Parisian markets. The modern National Palace in the same city, rebuilt by Georges Baussan after an explosion in 1912, has many elements of traditional French design. Its interesting domed pavilions are repeated in the Palace of Justice near it.

Louis Edmond Laforesterie and Normil Ulysse Charles are the best-known Haitian sculptors. The former, who exhibited in Paris in 1867, is remembered for the academic purity of his portrait busts and his designs for the Haitian mint. The latter, who went to France to study in 1904, showed a more varied style in his monument to Toussaint L'Ouverture; in The Dream, which can be seen in the artist's studio in Port-au-Prince; and in his heroic bust of Dessalines at the Pan American Union in Washington, D. C. In painting, the vogue of such academic masters as Colbert Lochard and Edouard Goldman has given way to the brilliant studies of contemporary Haitian life by such painters as Pétion Savain and Vergniaud Pierre-Noël.

PRACTICAL INFORMATION

HOW TO REACH HAITI

From the U. S. Steamer fares from New York vary from $70 one way to $110-$140 for the round-trip cruise; the fare by plane from Miami, Fla., is $85 (1941).

BY STEAMER. Royal Netherlands Steamship Co.; main office: 25 Broadway, New York. Has steamers from New York to Port-au-Prince, from which they proceed to Venezuela and Curaçao. Voyage to Haiti takes 6 days. No stop is made at Haiti on the return trip. The steamers are freighters with accommodations for 8-12 passengers.

Standard Fruit and Steamship Co.; main office: 11 Broadway, New York. Has service to Haiti from New York, Philadelphia, or Baltimore. The steamers are freighters carrying 12 passengers. Their stops at Haitian banana ports depend on the loading to be done; they seldom stop at Port-au-Prince. Round-trip cruise to Haiti takes 13½ days.

Panama Line; New York office: 24 State St. Voyage takes 4 days.

BY AIR. Pan American Airways; main office: 135 E. 42nd St., New York. Has frequent service from Miami, Fla., to Port-au-Prince. The trip takes 5 hours.

From the Dominican Republic. The highway from Trujillo City to Port-au-Prince is used throughout the year, the trip taking 8-10 hours. The charges are about $50 a ear or $15 a passenger (1941) if several are making the trip together. A N road via Cap-Haïtien can also be taken but requires considerably more time.

AIDS TO TRAVELERS

Haiti's Representation in the U. S. The Haitian Legation in the United States is at 5017 16th St., Washington, D. C. Consular officials are maintained in Mobile, Ala.; San Francisco, Calif.; Everglades, Miami, Palm Beach, and Tampa, Fla.; Elmhurst, Ill.; Lake Charles and New Orleans, La.; Boston, Mass.; New York; Chester, Pa.; Galveston, Houston, and Port Arthur, Tex.; Newport News and Norfolk, Va.; Balboa and Cristóbal, C. Z.; Ponce and San Juan, P. R.; and Charlotte Amalie, V. I.

U. S. Representation in Haiti. The United States has a Legation in Port-au-Prince. Consular officials are in Port-au-Prince, Cap-Haïtien, and Gonaïves.

Local Sources of Information. For detailed information in Haiti and for help in making arrangements, the traveler is referred to the national tourist office, Bureau du Tourisme, 3 Rue de Fort Per, Port-au-Prince, near the pier. Other sources of practical information are the Haitian Chamber of Commerce and the managements of the various hotels.

Climate. The climate is pleasant and healthful, hot in the coastal ports but cooler in the interior uplands. The average temperature at Port-au-Prince is about 81° F.; the lowest temperature in 32 years was 60°, the highest 100°. Inland, especially in the mountains, it is considerably cooler. The rainy season, with many sudden hard showers, is April-October. The dry season, which is cooler, is December-March.

Clothing. Light tropical clothing such as is used in Miami, Fla., in summer is recommended throughout the year: for men, drill, linen, or other summer suits; for women, light clothing of silk or cotton.

Those who travel in the interior, where altitude makes for lower temperatures, will need heavier clothing. A sweater or other wrap is always desirable.

Health. The tourist who follows the ordinary rules of health for tropical countries has little to fear in Haiti. The country has almost always escaped the great epidemics which have caused fearful ravages elsewhere, as of cholera, bubonic plague, and sleeping fever. Yellow fever and smallpox have made serious but rare appearances. There is some malaria, largely among those whose standards of living expose them to disease.

The water supply of Port-au-Prince is chlorinated, and the reservoirs and piping system have been completely rebuilt in recent years. In other towns and while traveling through the country it is always well to have drinking water boiled.

It is advisable to take precautions against mosquitoes.

In Port-au-Prince there is a private hospital, Hôpital Général, supervised by French nuns, with a section for foreigners. U. S. and other visitors to the country are taken care of in private rooms, with adequate facilities, by Haitian doctors trained in the United States or Europe. There are no U. S. doctors in Haiti.

Sports and Recreations. TENNIS AND GOLF. Through the Haitian Chamber of Commerce or the tourist bureau, the visitor can obtain a temporary card to the country club at Thorland, which has tennis courts, an excellent swimming pool, sea bathing, and a good ballroom. There are many other tennis courts belonging to private clubs and country clubs.

Port-au-Prince has two golf clubs with nine-hole courses. The membership is restricted to the foreign colony, though visitors can obtain guest cards. In addition to a golf course, the American Club has two tennis courts and a bathing beach.

RIDING. The country is specially suited for riding and hiking. Native horses can be bought cheap, and their keep is inexpensive. They can also be hired at reasonable rates.

COCKFIGHTING is a favorite Haitian pastime, and almost every town has its cockpit where fights are usually held on Saturday afternoons and all day Sunday. There are public cockpits both at Port-au-Prince and the Thorland Country Club; admission is free.

HUNTING AND FISHING. Neither hunting nor fishing is regulated, and both can be practiced legally throughout the year.

Ducks, guinea hens, and wild pigeons abound in the vicinity of Port-au-Prince and are especially plentiful October-April. Flamingoes are found on the inland lakes.

Local fishermen at Port-au-Prince and elsewhere along the coast can sometimes be persuaded to take parties out. The tourist bureau, the Chamber of Commerce, and hotel managements can advise in such matters. The fish caught are tarpon, barracuda, kingfish, jack, and red snapper. The clear waters off the coast make many kinds of aquatic life visible.

LOTTERY. The Haitian lottery is maintained for charity purposes and for supporting social work. Drawings are monthly with prizes of $100-$4000 (1941). Tickets may be bought in sections; complete, they cost $2.

Currency. The gourde (gde.) is the Haitian unit of currency, divided into 100 centimes. It is the equivalent of $.20 U. S. (1941) and is exchangeable on demand and without charge at the rate of five to the

U. S. dollar. The gourde is said to have been named after gourds originally used in barter trading. U. S. currency circulates freely throughout the country.

Banks. The Banque Nationale de la République d'Haïti has its main office in Port-au-Prince, next to Place Geffrard on Rue Ferou, and branches at Cap-Haïtien, Port-de-Paix, Gonaïves, Saint-Marc, Petit-Goâve, Miragoâne, Jérémie, Les Cayes, and Jacmel. The Royal Bank of Canada has a branch at Port-au-Prince.

Cost of Living. For the transient the cost of living and travel is relatively high in Haiti. The best hotels in Port-au-Prince charge up to $8 a day for room with meals, while the medium-priced hotels charge up to $6 (1941). In the smaller towns and villages charges are much lower, though the hotels there are mainly boarding houses.

Transportation. ROADS. Many parts of the republic can be reached by car, especially Cap-Haïtien and other points on the N coast. The roads pass through varying scenery—along the coast, through rich agricultural regions planted to cane, tobacco, rice, or bananas; in the mountains, along tremendous canyons with magnificent vistas and occasional glimpses of the sea; sometimes, too, through arid stretches. Most roads, however, are not paved, and they are sometimes impassable during the rainy season because of mud or because of being flooded by the rising rivers. The traveler should ascertain the condition of the road before leaving Port-au-Prince for any fixed destination. There are garage facilities in most towns.

AUTOMOBILES. Transportation is usually by car. Cars may be rented by the day, with or without drivers. Because of the winding roads, often narrow and crowded, and because of the danger of serious accidents, it is advisable for newcomers to rent their cars with drivers. The charge for each passenger in a public touring car, regardless of the number of passengers, is about a fourth of the rental price of a car.

Transporting one's own car to Haiti is a simple matter, though not advisable until one knows the country. Cost of transportation from New York is $75-$100 (1941). No customs duty is required if the car is to stay in the country less than six months. However, a bond of 15 per cent ad valorem must be posted on entry, refundable in full if the car is taken out of the country again within six months' time. No taxes are collected during the first month. If the car stays two months, there is a tax of 1 per cent of its value; for three months the tax is 2 per cent, and for six months 3 per cent. All cars must be registered with the police. Registration is free. International driving licenses are not valid in Haiti, but a local license may be secured upon presentation of a U. S. license.

There is no automobile club in Haiti.

BUSES run to all parts of the country but are usually crowded. Travel by bus is picturesque but seldom comfortable.

RAILROADS. Haiti has two railroads which carry passengers at low cost but are used mainly for freight. The Central Railroad operates a line of 35 miles, from Port-au-Prince toward the Dominican border, which serves the valley of Cul-de-Sac, with two short lines running S from Croix-de-Bouquet. It also has a line from Port-au-Prince to Léogâne, some 20 miles away. The National Railroad of Haiti serves the towns and agricultural centers between Port-au-Prince and Saint-Marc, a distance of some 60 miles along the coast. Its line then follows the valley of the Artibonite for 20 miles to the town of Verrette.

This company also operates a line from Cap-Haïtien to Babon, 24 miles long.

COASTWISE NAVIGATION. Daily service to all points along the coast is assured by a large flotilla of sailboats and occasional motorboats which also engage in traffic with Cuba. Picturesque and inexpensive, though endangered by squalls, this mode of travel is recommended only to the more adaptable and adventurous travelers. Vessels of the Standard Fruit and Steamship Co. also provide coastwise service between the principal banana ports.

Postage. Mail leaves twice weekly by steamer and several times by plane. Letters to the United States (1941) cost 10 centimes ($.02), airmail letters 60 centimes ($.12). Regular mail to New York takes 5 days and airmail 1-2 days.

Communications. Radio and cable communication with the United States and Europe is maintained by the Radio Corporation of America and All America Cables and Radio.

Port-au-Prince is connected by telephone with the other cities and towns of the republic, as well as with the principal cities of the Dominican Republic.

Souvenirs and Handicrafts. In the larger centers are many shops where one may buy at small cost such things as silver trinkets made by native workmen from old coins and furniture and small articles carved from mahogany and lignum vitae. Mats, baskets, hats, and trays are made from native grasses. Many curios are carved from ox bone, and there is much tortoise-shell work. Above all, however, the delicate and beautiful embroideries, drawnwork, and handmade laces express the native artistic temperament. There are several shops in Port-au-Prince. Information on other shops throughout the country may be obtained from the tourist bureau.

Food. Seafoods are especially good. Tropical fruits are abundant and can be bought cheap in the markets and from peddlers. These fruits often grow wild in the forests of precious woods and slender royal palms. The commonest are papaya, avocado, sour- and sweetsop, custard and star apple, and zapote. Oranges, limes, grapefruit, melons, guava, mulberry, mangoes, coconuts, and breadfruit also grow wild. Bananas and pineapples, indigenous to Haiti, are of the best quality and are obtainable in numerous varieties. Haitian coffee has long been famous in Europe for its quality.

Language. The official language of the country is French, though English is generally understood in the better hotels and by the educated classes. The friendliness of the people helps to overcome many language difficulties. Haitians who do not know English will usually, if they are approached with courtesy, make a real effort to be helpful, to understand and to make themselves understood. See section on The People (p. 9).

Holidays. January 1 is the Haitian Independence Day. It was on this day in 1804 that Dessalines proclaimed the independence of the old colony of Saint-Domingue under the aboriginal name of Haiti. Other legal holidays are May 1; Corpus Christi; Ascension Day; November 1, All Saints' Day; and Christmas. December 2 was recently designated National Health Day. Many other days during the year are declared holidays by presidential decree, and every parish has its own annual feast day.

The gayest public celebrations in all the Haitian cities are the carnival festivities during the three days preceding Lent, marked by masquerading, street dancing, floats, and general merrymaking. The solemn rituals of Holy Week, particularly in rural sections, are of great interest to visitors, especially to students of folklore.

PORT-AU-PRINCE

Port-au-Prince, capital of the republic of Haiti, with over 150,000 inhabitants, is located on a magnificent bay, one of the best natural harbors in the world. This harbor is protected by mountains which enclose it N, E, and S. W lies the beautiful island of La Gonâve, protecting the harbor from the open sea and leaving access by two channels. Steamers pass through either of these channels to arrive at Port-au-Prince. The landscape of the coastal plain is disclosed, with its succession of cultivated fields, thatched cottages, villas, and factories. As the ship draws in, usually in the early morning, Port-au-Prince gives the impression of an Oriental city with its white buildings, among which tower the basilica of Notre Dame, the National Palace, and the Palace of Justice, set against a background of massive green hills.

Port-au-Prince, which was also the capital of the old French colony of Saint-Domingue, was founded in 1749. Its central location, giving easy access to other parts of the island, and its proximity to the fertile valley of Cul-de-Sac probably explain why the town was chosen as capital. Much of the city, however, is new. In 1770 it was almost destroyed by earthquake, and since then it has had many fires, necessitating much rebuilding. Situated at the lower end of a valley, the city slopes steeply upward from the sea. There are relatively large dockage facilities and excellent lighthouse service. The great quay, which faces the customhouse and the city hall, was constructed in 1780, during the administration of the French governor Rohan.

THE CITY. Port-au-Prince is roughly divided into two main sections: the old part, directly facing the bay, and the new or residential section, on the surrounding slopes. The former has straight avenues running parallel to the waterfront and cut at right angles by transverse streets; N it is bounded by Route de Saint-Martin, S by the Cimetière Extérieur, and E by the Champ-de-Mars. The newer section has irregular streets and elaborate villas with beautiful tropical fruit trees and palms around them. Many houses have their own small bathing pools in the garden. This section is much cooler than the downtown part of the city. N, the residential district ends at Avenue John Brown, also called Avenue de Lalue, which opens into a beautiful promenade leading to near-by Pétionville; S, its outline is irregular along the bay and below the Cimetière Extérieur; E, it extends to the Cercle Américain. Many of the principal streets and squares have been renamed, and the traveler may find both the new and the former names in use.

Place du Champ-de-Mars is a large square which marked the city's limits during colonial times. Today, however, it is the center of social life and civic activity. Near it cluster the most important government buildings, theaters, and so on. The square is divided into two parts. The NE part is cut by avenues bordered by trees and wide sidewalks. Well-kept lawns make this an attractive park where citizens promenade every evening. The W part is devoted to sports. On the S side is a steel grandstand capable of accommodating thousands. Polo, football, and other games are played on these grounds; military reviews are also held in this part of the square. A monumental fountain and an imposing statue of Dessalines as emperor occupy the center of the square. Place du Champ-de-Mars connects N with Place L'Ouverture, for-

merly Place Panthéon, and is practically continuous with it. On the
W side of the square are the imposing white National Palace and
the large Dessalines barracks. Facing it on the other three sides are
the city's finest residences of former years, though lately there has
been a movement outward to the hills. There are also hotels, cafés,
boarding houses, the Club Port-au-Princien, several bars, and motion-
picture theaters. It was on Champ-de-Mars that Soulouque was
crowned emperor in 1848 as Faustin I. His coronation had to be put
off till the receipt of imperial robes and a gilded coach-of-state ordered
from Paris for the occasion. The event took place at last amid seven
days' general rejoicing, officially decreed. Faustin I later attempted to
invade the Dominican Republic, but the venture failed, and he was
forced to abandon his throne and flee to Jamaica.

PARKS AND MONUMENTS. Besides Champ-de-Mars, the following
parks are worth attention. Place de l'Indépendance, also called Place
Pétion, W beyond the imposing National Palace with its grounds, is
notable for its well-kept gardens with a great variety of tropical
flowers. Place de Sainte-Anne, still farther W, between Rue de la
Révolution and Rue Républicaine (Grand'Rue), in one of the city's
oldest quarters, is not large but is gay and attractive. Place Geffrard,
NW near the water front, is in the busiest part of the city. Parc Vincent, on the bay, has been laid out near the city hall by the municipality.

Among the monuments, the one to Jean-Jacques Dessalines in
Champ-de-Mars should be seen. This monument, erected in 1904 for
the centennial of Haiti's independence, shows Dessalines with drawn
sword. The Mausolée de Dessalines et de Pétion, a monument to these
two leaders, is on Place de l'Indépendance. On Place L'Ouverture is a
monument to Toussaint L'Ouverture, First of the Blacks, the work of
the Haitian sculptor Normil Ulysse Charles.

PUBLIC BUILDINGS. The National Palace, facing Place L'Ouverture,
W of Champ-de-Mars, is the seat of the executive offices and the residence of the president of the republic. W of the National Palace, across
Rue de l'Egalité, is the handsome Palace of Finance. In the same block
with the Palace of Finance but behind it are the government radio station and the Palace of the Ministry, facing the Palace of Justice across

---

KEY TO MAP OF PORT-AU-PRINCE

1. Customhouse
2. Parc Vincent
3. National tourist bureau
4. Place Geffrard
5. Madeleine chapel
6. U. S. Legation
7. Place de l'Indépendance
8. Place L'Ouverture
9. National Palace
10. Palace of Finance
11. Palace of Justice
12. General Hospital
13. Dessalines barracks
14. National Museum
15. Headquarters of Garde
    d'Haïti
16. Place de Sainte-Anne
17. Sainte-Anne church
18. National Library
19. Institute and church of Saint-
    Louis-de-Gonzague
20. Saint-Joseph church
21. Saint-François church
22. Cathedral
23. Collège Saint-Martial
24. Market

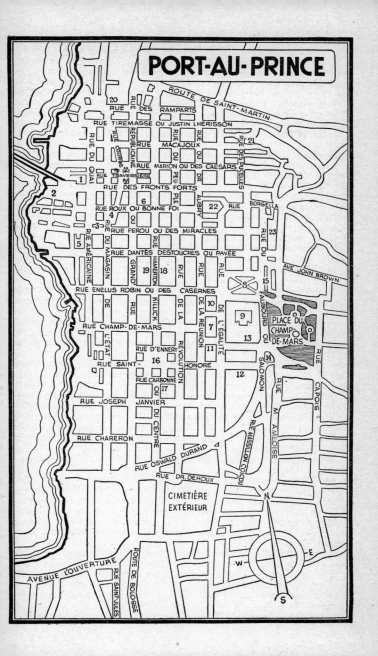

Place de l'Indépendance. The Hôpital Général and the medical school are in the block SE of the Palace of Justice. W of Champ-de-Mars and S of the National Palace are some barracks, Casernes Dessalines and Casernes Dartiguenave. N of Champ-de-Mars, facing the E end of Place L'Ouverture, is the fine headquarters of the Garde d'Haïti.

The convent school of Sainte-Rose-de-Lima is on Avenue John Brown. The institute of Saint-Louis-de-Gonzague, a boys' school, is on Rue Hamerton Killick (Rue du Centre). The Collège Saint-Martial, a few blocks N of Champ-de-Mars, has an observatory and chapel.

CHURCHES. The churches of Port-au-Prince are of fairly recent construction and offer little that is of major historic or architectural interest. That of Saint-Joseph is NW, on Rue des Ramparts. The church of Saint-François is in the NE part of the city. The church of Sainte-Anne faces Place de Sainte-Anne. The church of Saint-Louis-de-Gonzague is connected with the institute of the same name. Chapels include La Madeleine, near the water front, on Rue Américaine near the corner of Rue Dantès Destouches (Rue Pavée); Saint-Vincent-de-Paul, on the corner of Rue Républicaine (Grand'Rue) and Rue Saint-Honoré; Saint-Martial, Sainte-Rose-de-Lima, Notre-Dame-de-la-Salette, and Saint-Louis-de-France.

The basilica of Notre Dame, the new cathedral built 30 years ago on Rue Dr. Aubry, is large and imposing. The old colonial cathedral, next to it and bordering Rue des Fronts Forts, is an ancient wooden building, which, though no longer in use, can still be visited. Originally this church was not inclosed; walls and doors were added later. It was built around a central nave, the roof supported by enormous wooden pillars which are still standing. The high altar was visible from outside, where the slaves congregated at the hour of the Mass and during great celebrations.

MUSEUM. The recently established National Museum, which houses objects of interest connected with Haiti's history, is at the SW corner of Champ-de-Mars. Open daily.

LIBRARY. The Bibliotèque National (National Library) on Rue Hamerton Killick (Rue du Centre) has a small but interesting collection, with emphasis on books of national historical importance. Open daily.

MARKET. Not far from the water front, N on Rue Républicaine (Grand'Rue), is the public market, occupying an iron building suggestive of Paris markets.

MOVING-PICTURE HOUSES. Rex and Paramount, both on Champ-de-Mars, are the most modern.

CLUBS. The American Club has tennis courts and a bathing beach. There are two golf clubs, and the Haitian country club of Thorland has tennis courts and other sports facilities. Two leading Haitian clubs, social in character and exclusive, are the Cercle Bellevue and the Club Port-au-Princien. The Colony Club is a U. S. women's club to which practically all the U. S. women in the community belong; it has a modern library.

TRANSPORTATION. Automobiles are the most popular means of transport and indeed almost universal for visitors. Cars can be obtained for city driving and for long as well as short excursions. Rates are regulated by the tourist bureau, which requires them to be displayed. Government guides wearing official armbands are glad to assist travelers at all times.

SOUVENIRS AND HANDICRAFTS. The outstanding native shops are Haitian Curio Shop F. Cardozo, Souvenir Shop, Souvenir and Curio Shop, and Variety Shop.

BANKS. See Practical Information (p. 14).

LOCAL SOURCES OF INFORMATION. See Practical Information (p. 12).

RESTAURANTS AND BARS. Kahlman's Café, on Champ-de-Mars, known as the Berlinerhof until 1941, is the favorite among foreign residents. Others are Ansonia, Bazar du Champ-de-Mars, Rex Café, and Savoy, all on Champ-de-Mars; Aux Caves de Bordeaux and Aux Caves d'Haïti, Rue Républicaine (Grand'Rue).

HOTELS. La Citadelle**, a new and modern structure in the mountains overlooking the city, is the best. Grand Hotel Olofsson** is situated in a beautiful garden in the city's NE outskirts; it has private baths and an outdoor swimming pool. The best Haitian-managed hotel is the Splendide*, where the visitor comes in contact with the true Haitian élite; the manager speaks excellent English, and accommodations are good, food excellent.

NOTE. Hotels are here classified by rates. Two stars indicate the higher rates for the country in question and also, in nearly all cases, mean good accommodations. One star means rates in the medium brackets; no star means either low rates or no information available. An effort is made in all these guides to list hotels in the various cities and towns, but travelers who are accustomed to North American or European accommodations should use the information with care. In the capitals and larger Latin American centers hotels usually have standards comparable with those found elsewhere and at times on a par with those anywhere in the world. In the smaller centers throughout Latin America hotels are often more nearly boarding houses whose standards of accommodations and food make them unacceptable to all but the most adaptable.

ENVIRONS OF PORT-AU-PRINCE

Miramar is a popular dining and dancing spot in the Martissant suburb, on the road to Thorland.

Thorland, about 8 miles S of Port-au-Prince, beyond Miramar, is an exclusive and aristocratic country club. Only Haitians may belong to it, although visitors are always welcome as guests of members. Situated on a rocky seacoast, the club has a swimming pool, tennis courts, cockfighting, dancing, and an excellent restaurant and bar. The income goes to charity.

Pétionville, a residential suburb, lies out on Avenue John Brown. Along this road are located many villas of elaborate design in which the exuberant taste of the Haitians finds full expression. These villas have attractive gardens.

HOTEL. Cabane Chouconne*.

Kenscoff is a popular mountain resort at 4500 feet altitude, 15 miles SE of Port-au-Prince, beyond Pétionville. The landscape is delightful and unspoiled, the climate one of the best in the Antilles. The temperature, 70°-80° F. in the daytime, often cools off to about 45° at night and in the early morning.

HOTELS. Dereix* is a resort hotel with good accommodations. Florvil* is open only in summer.

Chancerelle, N of Port-au-Prince, is the site of a sugar refinery with

miles of plantations. Farther along the same road is the national agricultural school, where young Haitians are trained to serve in the most
important of their country's undertakings. This is a veritable botanical
garden for all kinds of tropical plants.

Léogâne, W of Port-au-Prince and reached in 45 minutes by car, has
an interesting cave near it, the Grotte d'Anacaona. Anacaona was an
Indian queen famous in the island's legends for her valiant resistance
to the Spanish invaders. The cave is about an hour's horseback ride
from the town.

NORTH FROM PORT-AU-PRINCE

Official touring, in the sense of organized, conducted sightseeing, has
not yet been developed in Haiti. To many this is an added attraction,
especially in a country where travel is as pleasant as it is here. Haiti's
principal towns are connected by highway; many of them are on
excellent harbors, and coastwise navigation also connects them. The
most important excursion in Haiti, for scenic attractions as well as
historic associations, is to Cap-Haïtien, locally known as Le Cap, on
the N coast, 175 miles from Port-au-Prince. It is reached by car on a
route passing through Mirebalais, Las Cahobas, Hinche, Dondon, and
Milot. Another excursion N from Port-au-Prince is to the W and N
coasts; this trip is covered later (p. 27).

Cap-Haïtien was the seat of government in French colonial days, and
in this vicinity occurred much that was most spectacular in Haitian
history. In colonial times Saint-Domingue, as Haiti was then called,
was France's richest overseas colony. For more than a century great
sugar and coffee plantations thrived, worked by thousands of slaves
brought from Africa. Great amounts of wealth were exported to add
brilliance to Paris, and every colonist dreamed of returning to that city
with a fortune to spend. In those days Cap-Haïtien was called Little
Paris. Its well-to-do inhabitants lived, if not with refined comfort, at
least with a sort of rude but ostentatious luxury in sharp contrast to
the misery of the slaves whose labor made it possible. Not far from
the town are the palace of Sans-Souci and the Citadel, monuments of
Henri Christophe's reign.

The trip to Cap-Haïtien should be started early in the morning, since
it takes about 8 hours over roads that are often rough and sometimes,
during the rainy season, flooded. Travelers should carry food and
drink. Shortly after leaving Port-au-Prince proper, the car passes
Chancerelle with its large sugar mill. Farther on, the national school
of agriculture is seen on the left. At Damien the road turns sharply
E and presently begins to ascend Morne Cabrit (Goat Mountain),
steep and rugged. On the summit of this mountain, 4000 feet up, a
stop is usually made for a look at the magnificent panorama below.
Spread out is the entire valley of Cul-de-Sac, the richest agricultural
region in Haiti, with Port-au-Prince 30 miles SW and Lake Etang
Sumatre shining SE near the border of the Dominican Republic. The
car begins to descend by winding roads sheltered by luxuriant tropical
vegetation. The next towns passed are Mirebalais and Las Cahobas, in
the rice-producing district of Haiti. From Las Cahobas a road runs E
to Trujillo City, capital of the Dominican Republic.

Hinche, center of the cattle industry, should be reached by noon.
This town, where it is usual to stop for a rest, is located on a plateau

about 1000 feet above sea level and has an extremely pleasant climate. Les Grottes du Bassin Zinc (Caves of the Zinc Basin), famous in Haiti, are in the immediate vicinity of Hinche and may be reached from there by car. They lie in volcanic terrain. The caves contain pre-Spanish pictographs, some of them mutilated. One can still see a large figure symbolizing the spirit of evil and an interesting representation of a war dance. A road runs E into the Dominican Republic.

Either of two roads may be taken N out of Hinche, one running direct to Dondon, the other looping W through Saint-Michel. On the latter road the car passes through Savane Michel, a large flatland about 60 miles long by 35 wide, covered with tall green grasses and groups of large and venerable trees. After 1½ hours Saint-Michel is reached.

Dondon, in an important coffee and banana region, is an attractive mountain village, birthplace of the mulatto Ogé, who was one of the first to give his life in the struggle for the liberation of his class. The Grottes du Dondon (Caves of Dondon), a vast system of large caves, are in the vicinity of the village. One of them, in the village itself, is called the Voûte des Dames (Ladies' Vault or Cave) because of two stalagmites which it contains. This cavern comprises three compartments; they are very dark, and the visitor should carry a lamp if he wants to read the inscriptions left by notable visitors or to add his own. Adjoining the Voûte des Dames is another large cave that was discovered only a few years ago and is not yet well known.

Another cave is the Voûte à Minguet, so called because of a certain type of grass discovered there by the French naturalist Minguet. It is reached by horseback in half an hour from Dondon. This is the old sacred cave of Haiti. Here the butios and caciques, the Indian nobles and chiefs, held secret meetings to celebrate the autumn equinox. The cave, which is of large proportions, resembles a cathedral with a big central nave and smaller side aisles. The walls are adorned with primitive bas-reliefs, some of them defaced. At the back of the cave there is a sort of natural chimney which permits the entrance of light and air. According to the ancient native cosmogony the first man, Louquo, came to earth by falling through this chimney.

Milot, passed from either Saint-Michel or Dondon, is the base for sightseeing trips to the palace of Sans-Souci and, farther off, the Citadel. Both are described later (p. 24).

CAP-HAÏTIEN

On the N coast, Cap-Haïtien or Le Cap is reached in about an hour by car from Dondon. With over 15,000 inhabitants, it is the principal municipality of the department of the North. Under the name of Cap François (French Cape) it was once the capital of the French colony of Saint-Domingue, and from its fine harbor many ships laden with wealth sailed to France. It is a quaint old-fashioned town that still preserves some of the charm of the colonial architecture of an earlier time, despite disasters. The streets are narrow and short, and nearly all the houses have balconies, some with elaborate iron railings. Buildings are painted pale blue, light green, rose pink, mustard yellow, or white, which gives the town some of the charm of an old-fashioned wedding-cake.

Cap-Haïtien often seems half asleep, as if dreaming, in the salt breeze and under the kindly sun, of its turbulent and hectic past. It is the most historic city of Haiti. Near by, at Petite-Anse, Columbus' flagship, the Santa María, was caught in a storm and driven ashore. There the great admiral met Guacanagaric, the cacique or chief of northern Haiti, who gave him all possible help. From the remains of the ship, Columbus built the fort of La Navidad, the first structure erected by the Spaniards in the New World. It was near here, at Bois Caiman, on the plantation of Lenormand de Mezy, that the Negro leaders Boukman, Biassou, and Jean François met on the stormy night of Aug. 14, 1791, to plan the rebellion of the slaves who eight days later descended from the mountains, destroying the plantations of Plaine-du-Nord. The region abounds in sonorous names: Milot, Limbé, Limonade, Marmelade, Dondon. It was here that Henri Christophe created his black nobility: Monseigneur the Duke of the Marmelade, chief governor of the palace; his Highness the Duke of the Limonade, minister of state; and Monseigneur the Grand Duke of Dondon.

Later, Napoleon, who prized Haiti, sent troops from France under the command of his brother-in-law General Leclerc. The beautiful Pauline Bonaparte accompanied her husband and moved through those turbulent times when the Haitian Negroes were fighting for their freedom. Henri Christophe, the slave who was to make himself king, was commander of Le Cap when General Leclerc arrived. Christophe showed his grim and merciless determination by setting Le Cap in flames. Leclerc succeeded in landing, but his prize was a smoldering ruin.

At the entrance of the harbor, guarded by the old French Fort Picolet, may still be seen the ruins of the palace of Pauline Bonaparte. Near Le Cap, at Bréda, Toussaint L'Ouverture was born on the plantation of Bayou de Libertas. It was near here also, at Vertières, that the last decisive battle for Haitian independence was fought and won, when General Rochambeau, capitulating to Dessalines, delivered into his hands the last stronghold of French Saint-Domingue and put an end to three centuries of white colonial rule. Now, however, Cap-Haïtien is peaceful, poor, and gay with the chatter and laughter of the Haitians, who are content with their life under a clear and brilliant sky. The town has a colonial parish church, an old port office, and old fountains that are worth seeing. It possesses modern facilities in the shape of soap factories, brick works, a canning plant, an electric-light system, and telephone and wireless service.

SANS-SOUCI AND THE CITADEL

Two fabulous structures which have survived from the nine years of Henri Christophe's reign, 1811-20, can be visited from Cap-Haïtien. **Milot,** 20 miles S on the highway from Port-au-Prince, is a tiny village. Enough is left of the palace of Sans-Souci to tell the tale of the days when Christophe presided over his court and administered justice. The black king of Haiti built nine royal palaces and eight châteaux, but none of the others could equal the splendor of Sans-Souci. He could not have chosen a better place to express his soaring imagination in brick and marble. The palace stands at the end of a valley, against an immediate background of deep-green mountains. It is a secluded spot, cool and dreamy, and yet in some ways primitive and wild. A magnificent curved staircase which branches off to right and left gives access to the palace. With the fountain in the middle, it must years ago have suggested the palaces of the French Sun King.

Inside are ornate reception rooms, banquet halls, and a library. Christophe planned everything carefully for his comfort. Under the floors, which were inlaid with expensive mosaics, was piped a stream of cold water, flowing out through a brick channel. The paneling of the many rooms was of polished mahogany and other precious woods of Haiti. Probably the walls were covered with valuable French tapestries, paintings, and huge beveled mirrors. The king's stables were as magnificent as his gilded carriage, but both must have been eclipsed by the men who had charge of them, the two colonels of the royal stables, the Barons of the Prophet Daniel and Louis-Voltaire Mahomet. At the right of the palace is the royal chapel, an imposing domed edifice. This chapel was carefully restored by the government of President Sténio Vincent and is today one of Haiti's historic monuments. At the left stood the royal theater, of which nothing is left but ruins. The star-apple tree still stands under which Henri I loved to sit to dispense justice. Even now the tree bears foliage and fruit.

Excursion from Milot. La Citadelle Laferrière, the stupendous fortress that Blair Niles calls a monument to fear, is in the hills above and behind the palace of Sans-Souci and is reached on horseback through a narrow mountain pass 4½ miles long. The ride takes about 1½ hours. Arrangements for horses can be made at Milot. The trail winds up the mountain amid a wild profusion of luxuriant trees—orange, cashew, coffee, and banana. Occasionally there is a fleeting glimpse of a giant butterfly or of a dramatic flower of burning red or almost luminous blue. Suddenly the colossal structure of the Citadel appears in silhouette against the cobalt sky. Built on a promontory called Bonnet à l'Evêque, it seems to grow out of the mountain itself. The fortress stands 2600 feet above sea level, dominating the surrounding country as far as the eye can see. It is quadrangular in shape, with one corner protruding to terminate in a round bastion like the prow of a giant ship. The walls are 7-10 feet thick and over 100 feet high. The Citadel was built shortly after the establishment of Haitian independence in 1804, as an impregnable stronghold against possible further expeditions by Napoleon. Christophe, whose genius conceived this building, took pains to make it perfect. The fortress contains vast galleries, 30 feet wide and more than 150 feet long, with imposing rows of bronze cannon, their mouths pointing toward the valley. There are deep, dark dungeons, where the king could keep enemies and dissenters. There are living quarters for a garrison of 10,000 as well as for the royal family and vast storerooms for provisions with which to resist a siege of years. There are cisterns for water, courtyards in which to review the garrison, and sentinel posts from which to watch constantly for the dreaded return of the French.

No French army ever returned. The enemy was within, agitating in the shadows, awaiting an opportunity to come into the open. It was evident that the division of Haiti into a republic of the south and a kingdom of the north could not last. The kingdom of Henri Christophe, with his nobility of so-called princes of the blood and princes of the kingdom, dukes, counts, barons, and chevaliers, could not possibly take root in Haiti. It was held together by the iron will, the grim determination and the courage of Christophe and by the fear which he inspired in his enemies. One day, at Sans-Souci, he was struck by paralysis. Only his big, powerful hands could move. He could no longer ride his horse at the head of his army to meet the challenge of rebellion. The news spread through the country that the king was in effect dead.

He made one last effort. Science could not help him; so he called in a witch doctor, an old palace servant born in Africa. For hours this shaman massaged the king's body with a mixture of red pepper and rum. Then, dressed in his regalia of blue, white, and gold, Henri attempted to review his troops. At the palace of Sans-Souci, before his army and the shouting populace, he tried to mount his horse. But it was a futile gesture. A few steps toward the horse, and then came a tragic fall under the animal's feet. Christophe was doomed. He retired to his chamber and shot himself in the head with a golden bullet. His body was taken to the Citadel by a few loyal servants and friends. In the large central courtyard of the fortress, where grass and weeds now grow wild, stands a modest shed of stone, the tomb of one of the most remarkable men of the Western Hemisphere. A staircase leads to the roof of the Citadel, and from a lookout the whole N valley can be seen as far as Grande-Rivière-du-Nord; NE is Cap-Haïtien, N the blue bay of L'Acul.

Christophe was neither better nor worse than the average ruler, considering his times and the situation that he had to face. But one thing stands out clearly: he was a genius with an iron will, courageous, imaginative, and a true lover of Haiti. Everything he did was designed as a means toward the freedom and grandeur of his country, as he understood the terms.

OTHER EXCURSIONS FROM CAP-HAÏTIEN

A road E gives access to the Dominican Republic.

Grande-Rivière-du-Nord, a picturesque village with an extremely pleasant climate, lies on a side road E from Milot (p. 24). Historically it is of interest as the birthplace of Jean-Jacques Dessalines, Haiti's liberator and emperor. There is a colonial church in the town.

L'Acul is a beautiful natural harbor on the N coast, W of Cap-Haïtien by road. Because of its attractive location amid dense tropical vegetation, Columbus called it Valle del Paraíso (Vale of Paradise). It has changed little since Columbus' day.

Limbé, a small village, W of L'Acul by road, is famous because its surroundings were the scene of the exploits of Makandal, the fierce Negro who for many years in the latter part of the 18th century harassed the whites of Le Cap. Makandal was a giant from Senegal or Guinea, powerful as a bull and quick as a tiger. The slaves saw in him a Messiah come to liberate them. Through their superstitions he had tremendous power over them. One day he conceived a vast plan to poison all the whites in Cap-Haïtien. But he was tracked down by bloodhounds, captured, and burned at the stake in the public square. While the flames licked at him he made a strange outcry in African dialect, and the watching slaves shook their heads and said, "The white men cannot kill Makandal." Their words were later taken to have been prophetic. It was in the same public square that

Sonthonax, the French commissioner, some years later proclaimed the freedom of the slaves.

Le Borgne, W of Limbé by car, is famous for the Grotte du Borgne (Blind Man's Cave), which was discovered in 1777. Human remains were found under guano deposits here, grisly souvenirs presumably of the flight of the aboriginal Indians from the Spanish invaders. Excavation has disclosed pieces of ancient Indian jewelry that are of much interest.

Beyond Le Borgne there is a gap in the roads of the N coast. Saint-Louis-du-Nord and Port-de-Paix, covered in the following section, lie W.

WEST AND NORTH COASTS

Other points on the N coast besides Cap-Haïtien can be reached by car from Port-au-Prince. A road which skirts the W coast as far as Saint-Marc and then swings inland before returning to the coast again at Gonaïves gives access to some towns of the N peninsula. This road connects with the route to Cap-Haïtien, which has been described, by means of a road E from Gonaïves to Saint-Michel (p. 23).

Saint-Marc, a port town of the W coast with over 9000 inhabitants, some 60 miles N of Port-au-Prince by road, is an important center for cotton, coffee, and rice of excellent quality. There are many oil-extraction plants, lard and soap factories, and cotton mills.

Excursion from Saint-Marc. The island of La Gonâve, the largest island off the Haitian coast, about 35 miles long by 8 wide, is immediately S of Saint-Marc, in the Gulf of La Gonâve. It is covered with dense forests of fine woods and has a beautiful lake in the center. It is sparsely populated but is often visited by natives who go to it for fish and for precious woods, and the traveler who enjoys getting off the beaten path may like to hire a boat for the trip from Saint-Marc. During the first years of colonization Indians from Santo Domingo found refuge on La Gonâve from the attacks of the Spaniards.

Gonaïves, another port town, with over 12,000 inhabitants, 40 miles N of Saint-Marc by car, is the principal city of the department of L'Artibonite. Its excellent natural harbor accommodates large ships. The salt works of Gonaïves produce the best salt in Haiti. Production of rice is also important. Precious woods, principally lignum vitae and logwood, are common in the region. Excellent mangoes are grown.

On the Place d'Armes of this city Jean-Jacques Dessalines, surrounded by his lieutenants, proclaimed the independence of the French colony of Saint-Domingue under the name of Haiti. Toussaint L'Ouverture had a farm near Gonaïves and was captured there by the French, who sent him to Europe to die.

Excursion from Gonaïves. At Marchand near by may be seen the ruins of Dessalines' residence.

Port-de-Paix, on the N coast, with over 10,000 inhabitants, is the principal town of the department of the West. It has an excellent port at the end of a wide and fertile valley. N lies the island of La Tortue (Tortuga), whence French buccaneers and filibusters in the 17th century succeeded in winning Haiti for France. The first mainland settlement of these buccaneers, Port Margot, was destroyed by the Spaniards. Thereafter, in 1665, the French founded Port-de-Paix.

Here they organized expeditions to oust their former allies, the English, from La Tortue, which the latter occupied after the French had moved in on the Spaniards on the mainland. Here the Haitian General Maurepas attempted to hold off the French invasion of Haiti by Leclerc's troops in 1802. During this battle the town was virtually razed. In 1679 Port-de-Paix witnessed the first insurrection of the slaves, and here Toussaint L'Ouverture, with an army of 5000, passed from the service of the Spaniards to that of the French in 1794.

Port-de-Paix is a center of the banana, coffee, cacao, and logwood industries. Abounding in wildfowl, wild pigs, and marine life, the region around the town is of special interest to hunters and fishermen.

Excursions from Port-de-Paix. The island of La Tortue, better known in the United States as Tortuga, only 5-6 miles from the mainland, can be visited from Port-de-Paix. Small schooners can be chartered for the trip at reasonable rates. The island is famous as the erstwhile rendezvous of buccaneers and pirates, who gathered there to try for a foothold on the mainland. It is about 20 miles long and 3 miles wide, almost unpopulated despite its small but fine harbor. There is talk of great treasures buried there. On La Tortue's highest spot is a very small village called Lan Palmiste, with a school and church. Two lighthouses stand at the island's E and W extremities. Today La Tortue is extensively farmed by people coming from Port-de-Paix and other points on the mainland.

The port village of Saint-Louis-du-Nord can be reached E by car. The road continues in the direction of Le Borgne (p. 27), but does not run all the way in passable condition.

Môle Saint-Nicolas, on the extreme W corner of the N peninsula, about 60 miles by car from Port-de-Paix, is one of the points that were visited by Columbus in 1492. There is a fine natural deep harbor, capable of accommodating large ships.

SOUTH FROM PORT-AU-PRINCE

Below Port-au-Prince a long, narrow peninsula juts W into the sea. The roads running out of the capital toward this peninsula and the roads of the peninsula itself, when fully linked, will make a circuit tour possible by car. At present there are gaps in the road system on both the N and S coasts of the peninsula.

The road from Port-au-Prince which skirts the N coast of the peninsula for some distance runs through Léogâne to Petit-Goâve and Miragoâne, port towns, and continues a considerable distance beyond.

Petit-Goâve, with about 8000 inhabitants, 45 miles W of Port-au-Prince, is an important center for the exportation of coffee. It has large curing plants and good docking facilities.

Miragoâne, with 4000 inhabitants, is about 15 miles W of Petit-Goâve. It is a coffee center as well as an important point for the shipment of logwood.

A road continues W to Trou de Nippes.

Aquin, with more than 4000 inhabitants, SW of Miragoâne by car, is a port on the S shore of the peninsula. It has a well-protected harbor facing a lovely island.

Les Cayes, with 15,000 inhabitants, directly W of Aquin by car, is the chief town of the department of the South, between two rivers. It is an active commercial center for the export of coffee and logwood. Les Cayes was practically destroyed by fire in 1908 but has been rebuilt, mostly in concrete. From this city Simón Bolívar, the liberator of five of the present South American republics, sailed with a contingent of Haitian troops and a load of Haitian ammunition as a contribution from President Pétion to the movement for South American emancipation from European rule.

A road runs W from Les Cayes for some distance along the coast.

Jérémie, with more than 10,000 inhabitants, is a port on the N shore of the peninsula, NW of Les Cayes by car and some 140 miles from Port-au-Prince. It is of historic interest; Alexandre Davy Dumas, father and grandfather of the two famous novelists, was born near by at Madère near La Guinaudée. The town of Jérémie was laid out in 1756 and the port opened to commerce in 1807. The port is exposed to strong winter gales and is consequently sometimes hard to reach by water. The city lies in a sort of amphitheater and is divided into the Haute Ville and Basse Ville (Upper City, Lower City). The latter is the commercial center. In the Haute Ville, the residential section, are many picturesque cottages.

Jérémie is noted for its fruits, especially excellent mangoes, of which there are no less than 20 varieties. The entire area also produces bananas. The back country for which Jérémie is the principal center is a most interesting region, occupying the extreme W end of the peninsula. The center of this territory is occupied by high mountains, cut by innumerable small torrential streams, some flowing N, some S into the Caribbean Sea. The coast is dotted with villages devoted mostly to fishing.

A road continues W of Jérémie to Anse d'Hainault.

The road that runs W of Port-au-Prince along the S peninsula of Haiti bifurcates beyond Léogâne, and a branch leads directly S across the peninsula.

Jacmel, on the S coast, 59 miles SW of Port-au-Prince by car, has been a commercial center since 1689. Today it is one of the most important towns of the department of the West. In 1806 Gen. Francisco de Miranda, a precursor of Simón Bolívar in South America's wars of liberation, arrived at Jacmel with three vessels and 200 young men from the United States who had enlisted under him. Near Jacmel is the beautiful region of the Bassins Bleus (Blue Lakes). E of the town is an excellent beach.

HOTELS. Pension des Roses; Pension Gérard.

Excursion from Jacmel. The road from Port-au-Prince can be retraced a short distance and a branch road followed SW to Bainet, also on the coast.

Another road to the S coast branches off the road from Port-au-Prince that runs E into the Dominican Republic. The start of this main road out of the capital has been described as part of a route to Cap-Haïtien (p. 22). Beyond Damien but before reaching the mountain Morne Cabrit the branch road strikes off toward Lake Etang Sumatre.

Saltrou, reached by car from Port-au-Prince by this road, is on the S coast, E of Jacmel.

INDEX TO THE REGIONAL GUIDE

THE DOMINICAN REPUBLIC

THE DOMINICAN REPUBLIC

BY ANTONIO J. COLORADO

The Indian word Quisqueya, meaning Mother of All Lands, was the ancient name for the island where the Dominican Republic is established. The name was prophetic, for here the Spaniards set up the first white men's settlement in the New World that was to prove permanent. The modern nation occupies the eastern two-thirds of an island whose western third belongs to the republic of Haiti. This island, the second largest of the Greater Antilles, is separated from Puerto Rico to the east by the Mona Passage and from Cuba to the west by the Windward Passage. Several names have been in use for the island. In much of Columbus' correspondence it is called La Española (Spanish Isle), and this name was current for centuries in the form Hispaniola. But the names of Haiti and Santo Domingo, as the old Spanish colony in the eastern part was commonly called, have been indiscriminately applied to the whole island, and still are. When the Dominicans achieved their independence, it was under the name of República Dominicana (R. D.). In culture and language and by its great historical background, the Dominican Republic is Spanish, while its neighbor Haiti is French. For various reasons the Dominican people have preserved a kind of isolation which has given them a distinctive character. Their traditions, their mode of living, their folklore, have a special savor and distinction. This adds to their charm for the visitor, a charm most fully experienced in the towns of the interior, particularly at fiesta time. Roughly 1400 miles from New York, the Dominican Republic is easily reached by steamer or plane.

HISTORY

THE INDIANS. Two principal Indian stocks inhabited the island before Columbus, the Arawak, sedentary and peaceful, and the Carib, fierce and footloose. The Arawaks had caciques or chiefs and a priestly caste. Their primitive religion is called zemiism by ethnologists; a supreme being was worshiped in the form of zemis or stone idols. Fishing, hunting, and a crude agriculture were practiced. The nature, ethics, and morals of these Indians were described very differently in various accounts. Columbus, after his first voyage, reported them as amiable, friendly, and peaceful; the historians Gonzalo Fernández de Oviedo and Francisco López de Gomara made them out to be lazy, vicious, unreliable, and ungrateful; the missionary Bartolomé de las Casas described them as naïve, idyllic people, possessed of great intelligence and all the virtues, incapable of evil. Accounts of their numbers vary as widely as those of their character. Las Casas and others who wanted to make out a strong case against Spanish brutality placed their original numbers about 3,000,000, an obvious exaggeration, since the island could not have supported so large a population under a primitive social and economic organization. The truth seems to be that there were no more than 200,000-300,000 Indians on the island when the Spaniards arrived. The historian E. G. Bourne has pointed out that most of these died in the usual tragic course of contact between a backward and an advanced civilization, not necessarily in war or through ruthless exploitation.

3

DISCOVERY. While he was in Cuba on his first voyage, Columbus heard of a place called El Cibao in a land to the east that was called Haiti and was rich in gold. This Cibao he confused with Cipango, the Japan of Marco Polo. He set sail, sighted the island on Dec. 5, 1492, landed the following day, and took possession in the name of Ferdinand and Isabella. He was impressed with the beauty of the scene; green mountains rose abruptly from a cobalt sea toward a brilliant sky dappled with clouds, and he was reminded of southern Spain. Hence he named the country La Española or Hispaniola. The garrison which he left at that time at the fort of La Navidad was destroyed by Indians. No trace of it was found when, on Nov. 27, 1493, Columbus returned on his second voyage. This time he founded the town of La Isabela, east of the present Monte Cristi, and from here sent two expeditions inland in search of gold. The following year he established the fort of Santo Tomás de Jánico in the valley of the Vega Real. Here, according to Las Casas, the first battle with the Indians occurred. With the aid of bloodhounds, horses, and a few friendly natives, a couple of hundred Spaniards attacked perhaps a hundred thousand Indians. The whites won the battle, and Columbus thereafter exacted a monthly tribute in gold from the Indians.

In 1496 Columbus sailed back to Spain, leaving his brother Bartolomé Colón as governor of the new colony. But the colony revolted, and Francisco Roldán, the chief justice, plotted the death of the governor and of the discoverer's son Diego Colón. When the admiral returned he was forced to make peace with Roldán. In order to appease him and his followers Columbus inaugurated the system of repartimientos or grants of land to settlers with the right to exploit the Indians. The results were so disastrous for the natives that soon Spain sent Francisco de Bobadilla to straighten matters out. Bobadilla imprisoned Columbus, his brother, and his son and sent them to Spain. The Indian problem proved increasingly troublesome, and in 1502 Bobadilla was replaced by Nicolás de Ovando. With him came new settlers, among them the renowned Bartolomé de las Casas who was to be known as Protector of the Indians. It was Las Casas who proposed the introduction of Negro slavery in the West Indies in order to spare the Indians. His reasoning was that Negroes had no souls, while Indians were human beings and should be treated as such. Later Las Casas changed his mind about Negro slavery.

In 1509 arrived a new governor, Diego Colón, son of the discoverer, who was to stay on the island until 1522. He brought with him his wife doña María de Toledo y Rojas, grandniece of the Spanish monarch, and a number of other women who became the wives of colonists. Soon Diego was caught in the struggle between the settlers who claimed that they needed the Indians and the Dominican friars who preached ardently against enslavement of the natives. As a result the first royal regulations, known as the Laws of Burgos, were issued in 1512 to regulate the relations of the colonists and the natives.

The active struggle between Indians and whites had begun with the battle of the Vega Real and the forced labor subsequently imposed on the natives in gold mines and plantations. Thousands of Indians fled to the mountains and to near-by islands. Caonabo, a chief, was captured and sent off to Spain, but he never arrived there; it is not known whether he died on the voyage or jumped overboard. His wife, the beautiful Anacaona, was captured and sentenced to death. Finally

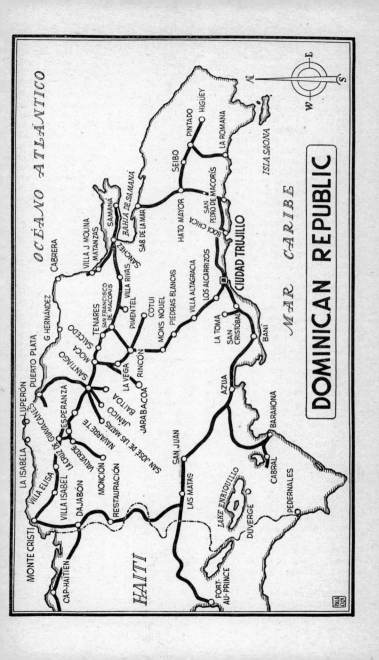

DOMINICAN REPUBLIC

the cacique Enriquillo, who, like Anacaona, figures in the island's folklore, challenged the power of the conquerors for 13 years, until Charles V, unable to subdue him, signed a treaty recognizing him as the last cacique of the island.

COLONIAL PERIOD. On Aug. 4, 1496, Bartolomé Colón, brother of the discoverer, founded a city which he called Nueva (New) Isabela, for the queen, near the mouth of the Río Ozama. Later the name was changed to Santo Domingo de Guzmán, after the founder of the Dominican Order, and was popularly shortened to Santo Domingo. Today the city is called Ciudad Trujillo (Trujillo City). It is the capital of the Dominican Republic and the oldest permanent settlement of white men in the Western Hemisphere. Known as First City of America (Ciudad Primera de América), Santo Domingo was for half a century the metropolis of the New World and the center of Spanish colonization. Numerous expeditions went forth to extend the Spanish empire. Diego Velázquez de Léon sailed from it to settle Cuba, Hernando ·Cortés to Cuba and thence to conquer Mexico. The city of Santo Domingo was used as a base by Juan Ponce de León, the colonizer of Puerto Rico and discoverer of Florida; by Alonzo de Ojeda, who explored the mainland of South America; by Vasco Nuñez de Balboa, who discovered the Great South Sea, later named the Pacific Ocean by Magellan; and by Francisco Pizarro, who sailed to Panama and launched from there his conquest of Peru.

During the first decades of the 16th century the city flourished under the governors Nicolás de Ovando and Diego Colón, and most of its historic monuments, churches, and fortresses were built at this period. It was the center of civilization of the New World. Its audiencia real or royal court had jurisdiction over all the Antilles. Its archdiocese, dating from 1504, was the first in the West Indies. Intellectually it was the pioneering center of the Caribbean, with the universities of Santo Tomás de Aquino and Santiago de la Paz. But things began to change during the latter part of the 16th century. The colony languished, like most other Spanish possessions in the Antilles. Vast riches had been discovered in Mexico and Peru, while the local gold seemed exhausted. The Spaniards were busy elsewhere, and the island was almost forgotten. The exodus from it was so marked that the Spanish government passed laws providing harsh punishments for those who were caught leaving.

Meanwhile the French colony of Saint-Domingue in the west of the island was prospering. French, Dutch, and English buccaneers who had established themselves on the island of La Tortuga or La Tortue had moved to the northern coast of Hispaniola and started the settlement that became Saint-Domingue. French power grew, and there was a prolonged struggle between the French and Spaniards, until at last, through the Treaty of Ryswick in 1697, France gained possession of the whole western third of the island, the present republic of Haiti. A century later the French revolution and the wars in Europe had martial echoes in the island's affairs. In 1795, by the Treaty of Basel, Spain ceded to France the eastern part. The Haitian slaves were fighting for their liberty. When Toussaint L'Ouverture gained absolute control of the French colony of Saint-Domingue he invaded the former Spanish colony to the east, and the whole island was united under him. Toussaint was later captured by the French and sent to Europe to die. The Haitians, under Dessalines, gained their independence of France in 1804, but the eastern part of the island remained a French possession.

In 1809 the Dominicans rose in revolt. With British aid they captured the city of Santo Domingo and re-established Spanish rule. Spain was indifferent to her loyal colony, and its progress was slow. This period is known to the Dominicans as the rule of España Boba or Foolish Spain. Under the leadership of José Núñez de Cáceres the Dominicans proclaimed their independence on Nov. 30, 1821. Now came a menace of invasion from Haiti again. On Feb. 9, 1822, the Haitians under President Boyer invaded the east of the island, which was unable to defend itself. The country remained under Haitian rule for 22 years. The first measure put forth by the new rulers was the abolition of slavery, but in essence the regime was despotic. There was an exodus of Spanish and French families, some moving to Cuba or Louisiana, others to Puerto Rico. Secret societies were organized to work for independence. Notable among them was La Trinitaria, founded by Juan Pablo Duarte. These organizations paved the way for the revolution which, led by Ramón Mella, Francisco del Rosario Sánchez, and other patriots, broke out on Feb. 27, 1844. Independence was proclaimed again, and the Dominican Republic was established.

INDEPENDENCE. The period after 1844 was characterized by frequent uprisings, foreign intervention, and economic ills. The republic found it difficult to make its way out of the social and political maladjustments that had resulted from a long colonial period during which most of the population had been neither educated nor given a real voice in the government. That the nation has not only outlived the tragedies of its past but emerged as a progressive and socially alert country is evidence of the vigor of the Dominican people. The republic elected Gen. Pedro Santana as its first president. His administration was troubled by general uprisings and the constant menace of Haitian invasion, and in 1848 he was succeeded by Jiménez, but Santana overthrew him and declared himself dictator. The following year Buenaventura Báez was chosen president. In 1853 Santana again assumed the presidency and banished his opponent. Báez came into power once more in 1856, only to be forced out again by Santana two years later. The rivalry between Santana and Báez resulted in the establishment of the third and last Spanish regime on the island. Believing that the country could not exist independently, Santana arranged to have it formally annexed to the mother country, with himself as governor and captain general.

The Spanish administration was so bad that it soon encountered widespread seething rebellion. In 1863 a movement for the restoration of independence, led by Gen. José María Cabral and the mulatto Gregorio Luperón, was started at Capotillo on the Haitian border. After two years of bloody struggle the patriots succeeded in reestablishing independence. A futile attempt was at first made to organize a government under Cabral and Pimentel, another leader of the revolution; but Báez was again called to power and inaugurated on Sept. 27, 1866. The opposition formed the Partido Azul (Blue Party), nationalistic and liberal in tendency, against the reactionary Partido Rojo (Red Party), led by Báez. While the former tried to integrate the country under a democratic regime, the latter moved more or less openly toward annexation by some foreign nation, on the theory that the country could not direct itself. In 1869 Báez succeeded in putting through the Congress a plan to negotiate the annexation of the Dominican Republic by the United States, which, however, rejected the proposal. But Báez was able to close a deal granting rights over the peninsula and bay of Samaná to a United States concern organized for the purpose. He also arranged with some London bankers for a loan of £420,000.

During 1882-99 the country was ruled by the strong hand of Ulises Heureaux, popularly known as Lilí, whose real name was Hilarión Lembert. He had distinguished himself in fighting for the restoration of independence on the side of Luperón. With the Azules, he had resisted Báez, and the country had every reason to expect some measure of peace, order, and freedom under him. Freedom, however, was notably lacking, especially during his second term; peace and order he assured only through harsh and dictatorial measures, though some progress was made in education and the national economy. Lilí now became a proponent of the Báez policies of annexation. On several occasions he tried to put his country under the protection of the United States. He also negotiated loans with Dutch financiers for which customs receipts were pledged. He had to subdue a number of uprisings, the most important in 1893 and 1896. Finally a conspiracy was organized against him, and he was assassinated on July 26, 1899.

The years that followed were marked by quick overturns, military uprisings, and economic disorganization. In 1904 President Carlos F. Morales Languaso proposed that the United States establish a protectorate over the republic, together with full control of all its revenues. This failed, but in 1905 he negotiated successfully for the collection and administration of Dominican customs receipts by the United States. Morales resigned, and in 1907 President Ramón Cáceres borrowed $20,000,000 from the United States, through an arrangement under which the latter country was to continue supervision of customs receipts by a collector general. Cáceres was assassinated in 1911. His successor, Eladio Victoria, who faced chaotic conditions, rejected the proposal of the United States that the Dominican Republic accept a financial adviser from it as the first condition for another loan. Victoria was forced to resign when the United States accused the Dominicans of violating the 1907 convention and ordered the collector general to withhold the customs funds that had been allotted to the government.

INTERVENTION. Dissension, disorder, and military uprisings continued through the following years. One president followed another in quick succession. In 1915 the United States proposed to land marines and presented a famous note demanding the creation of the office of financial adviser as well as a constabulary under the control of a United States marine officer. One result was more chaos and dissension. Rebel troops were practically in control of the capital, and in April 1916 a few United States marines were landed to guard the American Legation and protect the collector general. The rebels withdrew to the north, and a larger force of marines was landed on May 15, 1916. On November 29 of the same year Capt. H. S. Knapp took full control of the country at the direction of the United States Department of State and proclaimed a military regime. The Dominican president, Henríquez y Carvajal, went into exile. The country was administered by the United States occupation and for some years had neither congress nor president.

A constabulary was trained by the United States marines, the civilian population was disarmed, and peace seemed assured. In 1924 an election was held. President Horacio Vázquez then arranged for another loan of $10,000,000 from the United States, which was to control the customs receipts until 1940. The money was used for the construction of roads, irrigation systems, agricultural improvements, and other important public works. Criticism and dissatisfaction arose among those who advocated strict economy in order to liquidate existing debts instead of incurring new ones. Vázquez' popularity was not increased when in 1927 he promulgated a new constitution under which the president's term was extended from four to six years. He was over-thrown on Feb. 28, 1930, in a movement led by Rafael Estrella Ureña, who then became provisional president.

CONTEMPORARY PERIOD. Generalísimo Dr. Rafael Leonidas Trujillo Molina was elected president on May 16, 1930. His administration was marked by considerable material progress, accompanied by stern measures to maintain public order. He met with some opposition but was re-elected in 1934. In 1938 Trujillo announced that he would not accept renomination. He remained the active head of the army, however, while Dr. Jacinto B. Peynado, the government's candidate, was elected president.

Under Trujillo's guidance the Dominican government became increasingly engaged with social and economic problems and public works. The reconstruction of the ancient city of Santo Domingo after the terrible hurricane of 1930 was one of Trujillo's major achievements, and in recognition of it the National Congress changed the city's name to Ciudad Trujillo on Jan. 11, 1936. A project for the resettlement of 100,000 European political refugees on lands in the northern part of the country donated by General Trujillo was undertaken on his initiative and won widespread commendation as virtually the only concrete result of the 1938 international conference on refugees at Evian, France. At Trujillo's initiative education, too, took a spurt. A Chilean educational mission was invited to visit the country for the purpose of reorganizing the school system. A concerted drive on illiteracy resulted; in 1941 some 5000 elementary schools were being added to the 897 already in existence. The new schools were to be scattered throughout the country, within easy reach of children everywhere and of all classes.

President Peynado died of an infection on March 7, 1940, and was succeeded by the vice-president Dr. Manuel Jesús Troncoso de la Concha. On Sept. 7, 1940, the United States Department of State announced that an agreement had been signed in Washington, terminating United States control of Dominican customs. Trujillo is again president.

THE LAND

Somewhat larger than Vermont and New Hampshire together, the Dominican Republic covers more than 19,000 square miles, with a coastline of some 1500 miles. It is crossed NW-SE by four almost parallel mountain ranges, of which the Cordillera Central is the highest, not only in the country but in all the Antilles. It has summits like Pico Trujillo, which towers 10,300 feet; the mean altitude at the center is 6000-9000 feet. N of the central range extends the Vega Real (Royal Plain), the island's granary. This section and the S and coastal plains are extremely fertile lands that produce all sorts of tropical and sub-tropical fruits and vegetables. The largest of the numerous N rivers are the Río Yaque del Norte, which empties into the beautiful bay of Manzanillo after a course of nearly 250 miles, and the Río Yuna, flowing into the bay of Samaná. Between them these two large rivers water the Vega Real. The two largest rivers emptying S are the Río Yaque del Sur, flowing into the bay of Neiba, and the Río Ozama, whose estuary serves as a port for Trujillo City.

Official estimates of the population of the republic in 1941 indicate considerable growth since the last census. The country has nearly 1,800,000 inhabitants as compared with 1,479,417 in 1935. The Domini-can Republic is primarily an agricultural country. Nearly 80 per cent of its inhabitants live in rural areas, where they cultivate some of the most fertile land in the Americas. The nation differs from several other Latin American countries, however, in having a reasonably good distribution of land. Large estates are the exception rather than the rule. The fact that the republic is largely rural, with its population widely distributed, has greatly influenced its political and social history. The ruling classes are concentrated largely in the urban areas, more or less out of touch with the rest of the country. Organizing education has been a slow and difficult process, and even today the work is just begun. Construction of roads and other means of communication is narrowing the gap between the urban ruling class and the peas-antry, but the latter are still isolated. The average Dominican is peace-able and law-abiding, in spite of much superficial historical evidence to the contrary.

The chief products are sugar cane, rice, cacao, coffee, beeswax, hides, corn, molasses, tobacco, precious woods, and tropical fruits. On an aver-age nearly $15,000,000 worth of these products was exported annually in recent years, mainly to England and the United States. The war has wrought radical changes in the distribution of foreign trade. The United States is the second buyer of Dominican products and the principal seller to the republic; in 1939 it shipped over 50 per cent of the country's total $11,000,000 worth of imports. The Dominican Republic has some mineral deposits that have hardly been tapped. A large amount of salt is produced.

ART AND ARCHITECTURE

BY ROBERT C. SMITH

Trujillo City is so old that its plan does not conform to the regular gridiron arrangement of intersecting streets laid down early in the 16th century for Spanish cities in the New World. Its earliest buildings reflect the conflict of architectural styles produced in Spain by the fusion of the old medieval Gothic manner of building with the new designs of the Italian Renaissance, giving a more or less original imitation of ancient Roman details and structures. The cathedral of Trujillo City (1514-40) best illustrates this point. Its interior, based on the plan of the so-called new cathedral of Salamanca in Spain, is essentially medieval; heavy piers support pointed vaults with typical late Gothic vaults of complicated ribbing. These vaults follow the system of the Hallenkirchen, in which the height of the aisle vaults is equal to that of the nave. The main façade, however, now attributed to the Spanish architect Rodrigo Gil de Liendo, is a perfect example of the Spanish Renaissance style called Plateresque. Round arches take the place of the pointed ones of the interior. There are Corinthian columns and pilasters in place of Gothic piers, and the whole façade is surmounted by a classic Roman frieze and cornice. But the imitation is not yet archeologically correct. The cathedral of Trujillo City is the first step in that gradual progress toward complete neo-classicism which is the history of colonial Latin American architecture. The hybrid style of the building is repeated in several contemporary churches of Trujillo City. At San Francisco the nave has pointed arches, but there seems to have been a Renaissance barrel vault, and the main door is flanked by columns and crowned by an entablature of frankly classical inspiration. Again at the church of Santo Domingo the nave vaults were given Gothic ribs, but the portal is decorated with Roman pilasters. In civil buildings the same contrast occurred. Both the Tower of Homage and the castle of Diego Colón are derived in plan from medieval fortresses, while the details of their simple construction are clearly Renaissance. Neither building has preserved any decorations like the excellent sculptured friezes of the cathedral or the beautiful doorway of the old Santo Domingo mint (Casa de la Moneda), whose Italianate medallions rank with first-class Spanish work of the period.

By the time the church of Santa Bárbara was completed by the canon Alonzo de la Peña in 1574, the new style had become a formula which was to endure till the end of the colonial period. Strict rectilinearity, simple, massive forms, and occasional Renaissance decoration are its elements. In the city of Santo Domingo there never was a Baroque style of riotous forms, contorted sculpture, and eccentric architectural details as in most other Spanish American centers. When the church of the Dominican Order was rebuilt in 1746 the entrance to its rich chapel of the Rosary was given a portal decorated with the purest 16th-century sculpture. The façade of the Jesuit church of 1732 is still a fortress; the graceful lines and exuberant decoration of the period are entirely absent from its design. The same is true of the church of Regina Angelorum, whose façade is perhaps the work of the same builder. Local architecture did not develop. The early importance of the colony soon dwindled; it rapidly became a minor outpost of empire, and this loss of importance had a profound artistic effect. Passed over by the stream of conquest, the city long repeated in its architecture the style of its great period and became in the 17th and 18th centuries a mausoleum of the art of the conquistadores.

The National Museum at Trujillo City contains the work of three well-known 19th-century Dominican artists. Luis Desangles (1861-1940), a pupil of the classicist León Cordero, was a famous painter of local historical scenes (The Arrival of the Canoe; The Invasion of Maceo). His masterpiece, representing the arrest of the Indian chieftain Caonabo, hangs in the city hall of Puerto Plata. Desangles' pupil Leopoldo Miguel Navarro (c. 1860-1908), worked out an academic style based on Velázquez and Goya. Another pupil, Abelardo Rodríguez Urdaneta (1870-1933), was also a conservative sculptor.

Yorgi Morel is a well-known modern painter who has exhibited successfully in the United States his sun-drenched Impressionist landscapes of parks, market places, and gardens of his native Santiago de los Caballeros. Dario Suro García-Godoy paints in the same genre, while Celeste Wos y Gil and Angel Botello Barros have devoted themselves to picturesque types among the Dominican peasantry. Jaime Colson continues the old tradition of religious painting.

Recently a number of Spanish refugees have enriched the artistic life of the republic. José Alloza is a clever draughtsman of intimate scenes of intentional naïveté. José Vela Zanetti is a powerful figure painter, Carlos Solaeche a popular realistic portraitist. The sculptor Francisco Vásquez Díaz (Compostela) makes striking likenesses in wood of the heads of his sitters and has carved a highly decorative series of tropical birds, fish, and animals. The work of all these artists is frequently exhibited under the auspices of the Ateneo Dominicano, the most important cultural group today in Trujillo City.

PRACTICAL INFORMATION

HOW TO REACH THE DOMINICAN REPUBLIC

From the U. S. Minimum first-class steamship fare between New York and Trujillo City is $90 one way and $145 the round trip (1941). One-way passage from Havana is $75. By plane the one-way fare from Miami, Fla., to San Pedro de Macorís, R. D., is $105; from Cuba to San Pedro de Macorís, $94.

BY STEAMER. Porto Rico Line; New York office: foot of Wall St. Sailings via San Juan, P. R.

BY AIR. Pan American Airways; main office: 135 E. 42nd St., New York. Flights from Miami, Fla., to San Pedro de Macorís, R. D., via Antilla, Cuba, and Port-au-Prince, Haiti.

From Cuba. New York and Cuba Mail Steamship Co.; main office: Calle San Pedro 262, Havana, Cuba.

From Haiti. A motor road connects Port-au-Prince with Trujillo City. There is a longer alternative N route via Cap-Haïtien.

AIDS TO TRAVELERS

Dominican Representation in the U. S. The Legation of the Dominican Republic is at 2101 Connecticut Ave., Washington, D. C. Consular officials are maintained at Mobile, Ala.; Los Angeles and San Francisco, Calif.; Denver, Colo.; Jacksonville, Miami, and Tampa, Fla.; Chicago, Ill.; Lake Charles and New Orleans, La.; Boston, Mass.; Baltimore, Md.; Rochester, Minn.; Kansas City, Mo.; West New York, N. J.; New York; Philadelphia, Pa.; Fort Worth, Galveston, and Port Arthur, Tex.; Cristóbal, C. Z.; Aguadilla, Arecibo, Guanica, Mayagüez, Ponce, and San Juan, P. R.; Charlotte Amalie, V. I.

U. S. Representation in the Dominican Republic. The United States maintains a Legation in Trujillo City. It has consular officials there and at La Romana.

Local Sources of Information. In Trujillo City the visitor may obtain detailed information, as well as maps, pamphlets, and other printed matter, from the national tourist bureau, Dirección Nacional de Turismo, at Calle Arzobispo Meriño 18.

Climate. According to data collected recently the mean temperature in the Dominican Republic is 77° F., with a maximum of 90° on the coast. In some interior valleys it is often cooler, while the uplands may be covered by frost at night, November-April. In the interior the temperature is lower, and in high places it is sometimes as low as 32° December-February. For the country as a whole there are only two seasons, the summer rainy season, May-November, and the winter dry season, December-April. The trade winds make even the hottest days bearable and the open shade delightful. In general the climate is healthful and varied. During the night the temperature falls considerably, even in low regions.

Clothing. White suits of linen or drill are worn much of the time, though Dominicans change to heavier and darker clothes in the cooler months. Light suits made locally can be purchased in Trujillo City for $18-$38 (1941). Men's clothes that are imported are naturally more expensive than the same thing in the United States. Women should wear clothing of cotton, linen, or other light material; a light wrap or a dress with long-sleeved jacket is needed in late fall and winter. For travel in the interior it is especially advisable to carry a topcoat or sweater.

Health. Sanitary conditions are good throughout the republic. Trujillo City, Santiago, and Barahona have modern aqueducts, and water is plentiful throughout the year. In smaller cities and country places houses are provided with cisterns and wells. It is advisable for the traveler to have drinking water boiled.

There are modern private clinics in Trujillo City. The hospitals there include the Internacional, Avenida México, with a U. S. staff.

Sports and Recreations. TENNIS AND GOLF can be played at the Santo Domingo Country Club near Trujillo City. Guest cards may be obtained through a member.

FISHING AND HUNTING. Rivers and coastal waters have an extensive variety of fish, from sharks to kingfish. Good fishing grounds are the bay of Samaná, NE, and Barahona and the lakes, W from Trujillo City, as well as many more.

Woods, mountains, and prairies are noted for their abundant game, especially various sorts of pigeons. Turtledoves, quail, guinea hens, and ducks are found even near the urban centers. Alligators frequent some of the rivers.

Fishing and hunting are regulated by law, and applications for permits should be made at police headquarters in Trujillo City. Under a recent law, visitors on hunting trips are allowed to bring not more than two rifles and 500 cartridges apiece into the country free.

The national tourist bureau and the managements of hotels are glad to advise on the organization of fishing and hunting trips.

THE NATIONAL LOTTERY is managed by the government. There is a drawing every Sunday, with prize of $12,000 (1941), subject to change, less 5 per cent government deduction, and a number of lesser prizes. Every issue consists of 8000 tickets, costing $3 for an entire ticket. They are obtainable also in tenths.

Currency. The Dominican Republic has a coinage with the same sizes, denominations, and values as that of the United States. The unit is the peso ($), with the same value as the dollar (1941). There is, however, no Dominican paper money. U. S. paper money is accepted.

Banks. The Banco de Reserva de la República Dominicana, with headquarters in Trujillo City, is the government bank, opened in October 1941. The Royal Bank of Canada and the Bank of Nova Scotia have branches in Trujillo City. There are other branches of the Royal Bank of Canada in Santiago, Puerto Plata, and San Pedro de Macorís.

Cost of Living. The general cost of living in the larger towns compares favorably with that in places of similar size in the warmer sections of the United States. Imported foodstuffs and manufactured articles naturally cost about 25 per cent more than in the United States. Native vegetables, fruits, meats, and fish are abundant and inexpensive in the local markets.

Hotel rates are $2-$6 a day with meals in Trujillo City and other towns (1941). Hotels are not ostentatious, but offer good accommodations at reasonable prices. The government is building the splendid modern Hotel Jaragua in Trujillo City. In this five-story building every comfort and luxury will be offered. There will be large gardens and terraces, tennis courts, and a swimming pool with filtered salt water.

Transportation. ROADS. The road-building program begun by President Trujillo in 1930 has greatly improved the highway system with many paved stretches and numerous modern bridges. Virtually all travel within the republic is by road. There are three good main highways connecting Trujillo City with the rest of the country. These, with the secondary roads, make up a total of some 3000 miles of highways.

The Duarte Highway, about 175 miles long, crosses the country diagonally from the capital to Monte Cristi, NW on the coast. It passes through the most important N towns such as La Vega and Santiago. The road is macadamized in some parts, stone and gravel in others. A secondary road from Santiago serves Puerto Plata on the N coast.

The Mella Highway, running through the S part of the country, connects Trujillo City with the E towns. Passing through San Pedro de Macorís, it extends to the province of Seibo.

The Sánchez Highway runs from Trujillo City for 160 miles W to the Haitian border. The route continues to Port-au-Prince, the capital of Haiti. This road passes through San Cristóbal, Azua, and San Juan.

AUTOMOBILES. Transportation is usually by automobile. Cars can be rented for long or short trips. To places near Trujillo City the charge is $1.50-$2 an hour, as, for instance, to the bathing resorts of Boca Chica and La Toma (1941).

Visitors can bring their cars into the country under a 5 per cent ad valorem duty, or free if the car is taken out within 60 days across the land frontier or 30 days through a seaport. Customs documents are not honored, but free temporary permits are issued for tourists' cars. Since international driving licenses are not valid, a local license and plates must be obtained.

BUSES. Bus travel is recommended only to the adaptable. There is bus service from Trujillo City, W to San Cristóbal, about 20 miles; W to Barahona, 126 miles; E to San Pedro de Macorís, 46 miles; N to Santiago, 109 miles. Jitney service is popular. Transportation from Trujillo City to Puerto Plata on the N coast, including baggage, costs about $3.50 a passenger; from Trujillo City to Port-au-Prince, Haiti, a trip of 8-10 hours, about $15 a passenger (1941).

Postage. Regular letters cost $.03 an ounce between the United States and the Dominican Republic; airmail, $.10 from the United States and $.13 to it for each half ounce or fraction thereof (1941). Regular mail to New York takes 5-6 days, airmail about 2 days.

Communications. The country is connected with the rest of the world by cable, radio, and radiotelephone. Radio and cable services are operated by All America Cables and R.C.A. The Dominican government serves the country's interior with its own system of radio, telegraph, and telephone.

Souvenirs and Handicrafts. The Dominican Republic is famous for beautiful articles of mahogany and capá or lignum vitae, handcarved and finely polished. There are also attractive souvenirs made of tortoise shell, peonilla or seed work, silver, sisal or hemp, and leather, as well as good embroideries.

Food. Tropical fruits are abundant and excellent. The pineapples are especially noted for their delicacy. Other locally grown fruits such as bananas, coconuts, melons, oranges, alligator pears, papayas, grapefruit, guava, and mangoes are relished for distinctive flavor. Fruit is sold by peddlers at very reasonable prices. Famous sweets are made locally, like dulce de leche and dulce de naranja, the former with milk and the latter with oranges; guava paste and jelly, mango paste, and dozens of other delicacies with tropical fruits. A popular confection is cajuiles abrillantados or candied cashews. Cashews are also much used in other ways.

Holidays. Most of the principal feast days of the Roman Catholic Church are observed. Other holidays are January 1, New Year's Day; February 27, Dominican Independence Day; April 14, Pan American Day; July 16, Día de la Trinitaria, named for the secret organization which, founded on that date, instigated the revolution of independence; August 16, Dominican Restoration Day; October 12, Columbus Day (Día de la Raza—Day of the Race); November 2, Memorial Day (Todos Santos—All Saints'); December 5, anniversary of the discovery of the island by Columbus.

Fiestas. Much of the color of Dominican life is best observed in local celebrations connected with religious observances. Every community has its patron saint and is likely to be most interesting during his fiesta. The following are a few of the celebrations: January 6, Epiphany (Día de los Reyes—Day of the Kings), Trujillo City; January 21, pilgrimage of Our Lady of La Altagracia (Heavenly Grace), Higüey; the carnival, immediately preceding Lent, in Trujillo City and particularly in Santiago; Corpus Christi; July 25, day of St. James (Santiago), Santiago; September 24, pilgrimage of Our Lady of Las Mercedes (Mercies), patroness of the republic, Santo Cerro, near La Vega.

The hub of Dominican travel is the capital. Trujillo City is both port of entry and travel center (p. 24).

TRUJILLO CITY

When Bartolomé Colón, Columbus' brother, founded the city of Nueva Isabela on Aug. 4, 1496, on the E bank of the Río Ozama, he selected the site largely because gold had been discovered at San Cristóbal, some 20 miles W. In 1502 the city was laid waste by a hurricane and by a plague of ants. The settlement was then moved to the opposite or W bank, with the name of Santo Domingo de Guzmán, and there it stands today as Trujillo City. The gold mines gave out very quickly, but the city of Santo Domingo flourished as long as it remained the political and cultural center of Spanish activity in the New World.

On Sept. 3, 1930, three weeks after the election of Generalísimo Trujillo to the presidency, the city was devastated by the furious hurricane of San Zenón, named for the saint on whose day it occurred. Great as the tragedy was, it brought at least one benefit by causing virtually complete reconstruction. The ancient, historic Santo Domingo was replaced by a clean and beautiful modern city which in 1936 was renamed Ciudad Trujillo (Trujillo City) in honor of the president. Large modern avenues were opened, parks were reconstructed or created, residential sections were replanned and built anew, port facilities were improved a thousandfold, ancient monuments and colonial ruins were cleaned and restored. Most of the historic old buildings were fortunately spared by the hurricane. They add greatly to the city's charm and interest for the visitor, and today the city with more than 75,000 inhabitants has good wide avenues and fine parks.

Arriving by steamer, the traveler sees the city on his left as the ship turns into the port at the mouth of the Río Ozama; the first notable building that appears is the Tower of Homage built by Nicolás de Ovando in 1503. The ship docks at a new quay just short of the bridge over the river. On landing, the visitor finds himself in one of the oldest and most historic parts of the city. Near by are the remains of Diego Colón's castle, a fortresslike mansion; the old colonial Palacio de Gobierno (Government Palace), lately restored and still occupied by government offices; and the treasury, housed in the ancient Jesuit church and priests' house. On the river bank, not far from the landing place, stands a concrete replica of the famous ceiba tree to which, as tradition more than history has it, Columbus tied his vessels.

THE CITY. The old part of the city, in which are found most of the points of historic interest, is shaped roughly like a right-angled triangle. Its S side is the Caribbean shore, its E side the Río Ozama. The hypotenuse is formed by Avenida Mella, running SW from the bridge to the vicinity of Parque Independencia, and continued beyond the park by Av. Independencia. Bending parallel to the sea, Av. Independencia strikes off from the triangle and runs W to some of the new residential districts. The SW corner of the triangle is marked by an impressive obelisk erected in commemoration of the change of the city's name.

The magnificent tree-lined Av. George Washington on which the obelisk stands runs W along the sea front. On the river front a massive stone sea wall starts at the Tower of Homage and forms one side of the splendid Av. U. S. Marine Corps, named in recognition of the services rendered by the marines at the time of the hurricane. Av. Mella is one of the city's most typical and busiest commercial thoroughfares. The main shopping street, Calle Conde, lies within the triangular old part of the city, between the river and Parque Independencia. Airy modern residential sections have been developed particularly NW of Av. Mella. The most densely populated is Villa Francisca. The best is Gazcüe, on higher ground; the new U. S. Legation is in this section. Streets in the old part of the city are laid out rather irregularly.

PARKS. In the heart of the old city is Parque Colón, with a graceful monument to Columbus. A historic spot, it has the cathedral on its S side; W, the palace of the Administrative Council of the District of Santo Domingo; and E, the buildings of the Senate and the Chamber of Deputies. Band concerts are usually held here on Thursdays and Saturdays, 8-10 p.m. Parque Independencia, at the end of Av. Mella, an attractive park with well-kept gardens, is a popular meeting place. Parque Infantil Ramfis (Ramfis Playground), named for Generalísimo Trujillo's son whose nickname is Ramfis, is close to the sea, between Av. George Washington and Av. Independencia. It is outstanding among the city's parks, with its monumental central fountain, spacious swimming pool, and extensive playgrounds. Modern in every respect, it is indeed one of the best-designed parks in the Americas. There is a game room for checkers, chess, and similar recreations; a reading room with a large number of books, and a first-aid room for children. An open-air space is set aside for children's dances and for roller-skating.

OLD FORTS AND OTHER BUILDINGS. The Torre del Homenaje (Tower of Homage), dominating the river front, has been completely reconditioned in recent years. Built in 1503 by Nicolás de Ovando when he came to take over the government from Bobadilla, who had arrested Columbus and sent him to Spain, it was primarily a fortress. The tower is of simple, massive construction, but it has a pleasing if somber

---

KEY TO MAP OF TRUJILLO CITY

1. Parque U. S. Marine Corps
2. Parque Colón
3. Parque Independencia
4. Parque Infantil Ramfis
5. Torre del Homenaje (Homage Tower)
6. Alcázar de Colón (Castle of Columbus)
7. Santa Bárbara fort and church
8. San Miguel fort and church
9. Puerta del Conde (Count's Gate)
10. San Gil fort
11. Cathedral
12. San Francisco church and monastery
13. Santo Domingo church and monastery
14. Treasury building (former Jesuit church)
15. Mercedes church
16. Santa Clara church
17. Regina Angelorum church
18. Carmen church
19. San Lázaro church
20. San Carlos church
21. National Museum
22. University of Santo Domingo
23. Government Palace

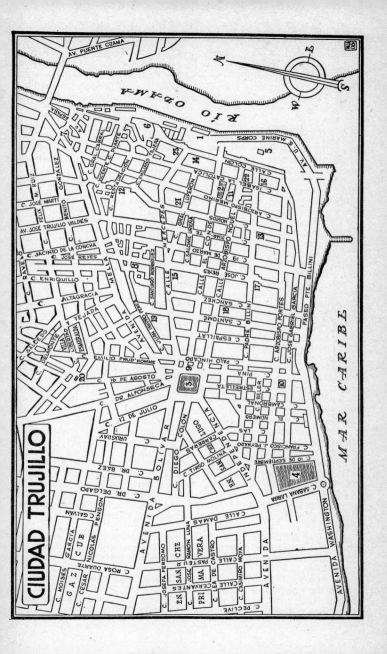

elegance. The noted architect Cristóbal de Tapia was sent from Spain expressly to build it and was its warden for some time. Here Diego Colón, the governor, son of the discoverer, took lodging when he arrived in 1509 with his wife doña María de Toledo and his retinue. The tower antedates all other Spanish stone fortresses in the Americas. Oviedo, the famous historian of the Indies, died in the tower while he was its warden. According to local tradition Christopher Columbus was imprisoned here, and his cell is even shown, but this is obviously a fabrication, for his imprisonment occurred in 1500, when the city was still on the other bank of the river and before the tower existed. Today the building is used as a prison and may be visited only by special permission of the military authorities.

The Alcázar de Colón (Castle of Columbus) overlooks the wharf. Half fortress, half mansion, it was begun in 1510 by order of Diego Colón to serve as his official headquarters and home. Seven children were born to him in this house, and in it died Bartolomé Colón, brother of Christopher, and doña María de Toledo, Diego's wife, a grandniece of Ferdinand of Aragon. The building is fairly well preserved, lacking mainly the roof, which fell in 1779. Although plain and solid enough to have withstood the storms of more than four centuries, it conveys a sense of the Renaissance with its many large windows. It is surrounded by gardens.

Near the W end of the bridge are the ruins of Fuerte Angulo (Corner Fort); of the forts of Santa Bárbara and San Antón, near the churches that bear these names; and beyond, of the forts of San Miguel and San Lázaro, La Caridad, and La Concepción.

The Puerta del Conde (Count's Gate), also called the Baluarte 27 de Febrero (Feb. 27 Bastion), facing Parque Independencia, marks the W limit of the original walled city and can be reached by going W along C. Conde. Originally this site was occupied by the fort of San Genaro, which was converted into the main land entrance of the city by the Count of Peñalva to commemorate his victory over an English expedition commanded by Penn and Venables in May 1655. The proclamation of Dominican independence was made at this spot on Feb. 27, 1844. The remains of the old fort of San Gil, marking the sea end of the old city wall, are S of this gate, near the end of C. Palo Hincado.

Far outside the original city wall, as an advance defense sentinel, stood formerly the Castillo de San Jerónimo, also spelled Gerónimo (Castle of St. Jerome), on the Sánchez Highway, a mile out along Av. Independencia. It was erected in 1628 by the governor Gabriel de Chávez Osorio and was important both in 1655, during the repulse of the British invasion, and during the fighting by which the colony was won back from the French for Spain. For centuries this fort stood virtually intact with its battlements and moats. A few years ago, however, it was destroyed in an explosion, and today only a few ruins remain.

The Castillo de Hayna or Jaina, near the mouth of the Río Jaina, built in 1659 by the governor Félix de Zúñiga, is a ruined fort with only isolated sections of the rampart and a few rows of bronze cannon remaining.

CHURCHES. Trujillo City has more than a dozen historic churches, of which the cathedral is the most important and that of San Nicolás the oldest. Like most of the colonial buildings that have survived here, they were generally constructed of cut brain coral.

The cathedral, the basilica of Santa María la Menor, stands opposite Parque Colón. Construction was authorized in 1511 by Pope Julius II, begun in 1514, and finished in 1540. In 1546, at the request of Charles V, Pope Paul III officially raised the church to the rank of cathedral, with the title First in America (Primada de América). The cathedral's high altar is a masterpiece of carving, gilded and faced with silver plates from local mines. The 15 chapels contain many religious and historic relics, besides art treasures and valuable paintings. In the main chapel, given by the king to the Columbus family as their pantheon, the remains of the discoverer were buried up to 1877, when they were accidentally found and transferred to a marble monument in the nave, where they still remain.

For years it was debated whether these remains were actually those of Columbus. Before he died at Valladolid in Spain on May 20, 1506, Columbus expressed the wish that his bones be taken to Santo Domingo, but for some years they remained in the Carthusian monastery at Seville. In 1541, however, they were removed to Santo Domingo by doña María de Toledo, wife of Diego Colón, and buried in the cathedral. On April 23, 1655, when Penn and Venables attacked Santo Domingo, the archbishop Francisco de Pío, fearing the invaders might sack the city, ordered the burial places of the three admirals, Christopher, his son Diego, and his grandson Luis, covered with earth. When the colony was ceded to France by the Treaty of Basel in 1795, the Duke of Veragua, a descendant of Columbus, obtained permission to remove the remains of his great ancestor to Spain. On December 20 of that year, when a vault in the cathedral was opened, lead plates were found, showing that there had been a casket of this metal; there were also pieces of bones that were assumed to be the remains of Columbus, although no inscription was found. The bones were placed in a casket and sent to Havana for safekeeping. Years later, in April 1877, in the course of some repair work on the cathedral, a casket was discovered that contained the remains of Columbus' grandson Luis Colón. Further excavations revealed another vault; this was not opened until witnesses were called, among whom were the president and his cabinet and the Spanish consul. A leaden casket found in the vault bore the inscription: D. de la A. Per Ate, which was taken to mean Discoverer of America, First Admiral. On the under side of the lid another inscription was found which read: Iltre y Esdo Varón D. Cristóbal Colón, or Illustrious and Noble Gentleman Don Christopher Columbus. The logical conclusion is that the remains removed from the city in 1795 were those of Diego Columbus, not the discoverer's.

The church of San Nicolás de Bari, now in ruins, on C. Hostos near C. General Luperón, is the oldest stone church built by the Spaniards in the New World. It was built in 1503 by order of Nicolás de Ovando, who gave his own funds for the construction of a hospital adjoining it. The government has landscaped the grounds.

The church and monastery of San Francisco stand on a mound at the end of C. Emiliano Tejera, N of the Puerta de San Diego (San Diego Gate), behind the castle of Diego Colón. Construction was begun in 1503 by the Franciscan friars who came with Nicolás de Ovando. The church is now in ruins. The remains of Bartolomé Colón, founder of the city, and of Alonzo de Ojeda, the conquistador, were buried in its vaults. Those of Ojeda were later removed to the Dominican church, but Bartolomé Colón's have never been located.

The church and monastery of Santo Domingo, C. Hostos at C. Padre Billini, is one of the city's most valued treasures. Seat of the famous university of Santo Tomás de Aquino, founded in 1538, this Dominican monastery was begun in 1520 and was the first institution of its kind in the New World. Bartolomé de las Casas, the historian and benefactor of the Indians, who came with Nicolás de Ovando, lived and worked in one of its rooms. The monastery's treasures include a carved altar and valuable paintings. Within the church rest many distinguished Dominicans.

The church of Santa Bárbara, at the N end of C. Isidro Pérez, near the wharf, has an original exterior but primitive ornament.

The church of San Miguel, C. José Pérez at C. Reyes, on a low hill facing a small square, Plazuela de San Miguel, is small and unpretentious but attractive, built by the treasurer of Charles V about 1520.

The Jesuit church and priests' house, Av. Colón, at the waterfront, is now occupied by the treasury. Perfectly preserved, the building dates from 1732. It is massive and pleasing. The Jesuits conducted a college in this building until the order was expelled from Spain and its possessions by Charles III in 1767.

The church of Our Lady of Las Mercedes (Mercies), on the corner of C. Mercedes and C. José Reyes, a handsome, solid edifice with a tower over 80 feet high, was begun in 1528 during the reign of Charles V. The high altar is richly inlaid with silver from local mines. Of the adjoining monastery only a few ruins remain, such as the gate and parts of the cloisters. The famous Spanish writer Friar Gabriel Téllez (Tirso de Molina) lived and worked under its roof.

The churches of Santa Clara and Regina Angelorum are on C. Padre Billini, the former at C. Isabela la Católica, the latter at C. José Reyes. Santa Clara was built in 1550, Regina Angelorum in 1561. The churches and the Santa Clara convent are intact. These handsome churches contain images and paintings of artistic value.

Other churches and chapels of notable colonial architecture are those of El Carmen, C. Sánchez at C. Arzobispo Nouel; San Andrés, Plazuela Trinitaria; San Lázaro, C. Juan Isidro Pérez at C. Santomé; San Carlos, C. 16 de Agosto at C. Gerardo Jansen; and Los Remedios. The chapel of El Rosario, on the E side of the river opposite the Tower of Homage, is in ruins. It is said that from its doorway Bobadilla proclaimed the downfall of Columbus.

OTHER BUILDINGS. Much Spanish colonial architecture is preserved in certain old sections. The visitor who wanders about will catch glimpses of patios or interior courts suggestive of the gracious life of colonial times. Two of the most typical such buildings are the Casa de la Moneda, the old mint, and the Casa del Cordón (House of the Cord), named for the monk's girdle carved in stone above the doorway. The university of Santo Domingo is housed in a handsome old building, C. Pellerano Alfau at C. Isabela la Católica, though its annexes are modern. Modern structures that are worth noting are the Senate building, Parque Colón, and the Hospital Militar Profesor Marión.

MUSEUM. The National Museum, recently built on C. Luperón, is excellent though unpretentious. Among its interesting exhibits is one of the best pre-Columbian collections in the Antilles, including archeological treasures such as numerous idols and statuettes made by the aborigines. The collection of old armor is distinguished. The museum also houses notable paintings of the colonial period and national mementos of great historic importance. In its gallery of modern art the best work of Dominican artists is represented. The museum is open daily.

CLUBS. The city has several social and sports clubs with private grounds and buildings. The most important are the Club Antillas, Casa de España (Spanish Club), Club Atenas, and Santo Domingo Country Club. The Country Club is a private organization managed on the U. S. plan and with a predominantly U. S. atmosphere, although many of the members are Dominicans. The club has a good building with bar, dance floor, and orchestra, and there are tennis courts and a golf course. Guest cards may be obtained through a member.

SOUVENIRS AND HANDICRAFTS. For the purchase of objects of precious woods, tortoise shell, silver, embroidery, and native fabrics, the following shops are conveniently located: The Gift Shop, C. Conde 5; Hand Made Shop, C. Conde 14; Tourist Store, C. Conde 19; P. Palacios, Dominican mahogany work, C. Conde 72; Photo Shop, C. Conde 11; J. J. Curiosity Shop, C. Isabela la Católica 20.

MOVING-PICTURE HOUSES. The best are Olimpia, C. Palo Hincado; Rialto, C. Duarte 26; Apolo, Av. Mella 112; Capitolio, C. Arzobispo Meriño 28; Encanto, C. Conde 52; Paramount, C. Eugenio Perdomo 2. There are daily showings of U. S. pictures.

BANKS. See Practical Information (p. 14).

LOCAL SOURCES OF INFORMATION. See Practical Information (p. 13).

RESTAURANTS AND BARS. Besides those in the hotels, there are several restaurants and bars serving both native and foreign food. Among the best are the Hollywood and the Ariete, both on C. Conde. The Güibia Bar is a night club where entertainment includes native music. Light drinks and refreshments can be obtained at La Cafetera, on C. Conde; Palacios, C. Isabela la Católica, and several cafés that have been opened by European refugees.

HOTELS. Jaragua**, between Av. George Washington and Av. Independencia, is under construction by the government (1941). It is designed to be the best and most luxurious hotel in the whole country. Other hotels are Fausto**, Av. Independencia 83, and Colón*, C. Conde 13, both with private baths; Francés*, C. Mercedes at C. Arzobispo Meriño; Presidente*, C. Mercedes at C. José D. Alfonseca; Dominicano, C. Conde 108; Florida, C. Hostos 26; República, C. José D. Alfonseca; San José, C. Duarte 16. Boarding houses include Martí, Av. Independencia 115, and Sans Souci, C. 19 de Marzo 10.

NOTE. Hotels are here classified by rates. Two stars indicate the higher rates for the country in question and also, in nearly all cases, mean good accommodations. One star means rates in the medium brackets; no star means either low rates or no information available. An effort is made in all these guides to list hotels in the various cities and towns, but travelers who are accustomed to North American or European accommodations should use the information with care. In the capitals and larger Latin American centers hotels usually have standards comparable with those found elsewhere and at times on a par with those anywhere in the world. In the smaller centers throughout Latin America hotels are often more nearly boarding houses whose standards of accommodations and food make them unacceptable to all but the most adaptable.

TRUJILLO CITY'S ENVIRONS AND EXCURSIONS

Several places of interest are easily reached by car.

Güibia, at the end of Av. George Washington, not far from the new Hotel Jaraguá, has good bathing, with a special beach for children.

Cuevas de Santa Ana (Santa Ana Caves), near the Gazcüe residential district, NW of the old part of Trujillo City, are large and interesting. At one time, it is supposed, they were inhabited by Indians, and a number of archeological remains have been found in them.

Tres Ojos de Agua (Three Eyes of Water), a spot of great natural beauty with three subterranean lakes, is less than 5 miles from the city.

Boca Chica, a bathing beach 25 miles E of the city, on the Mella Highway, is a resort with clean white sands, one of the most attractive and popular places near the capital.

La Toma, on a secondary road branching off the Sánchez Highway at San Cristóbal, 18 miles W of Trujillo City, is a bathing resort on the property of Generalísimo Trujillo. There is a beautiful waterfall here. Application for admission should be made in advance. At San Cristóbal (p. 30), where the turn is made, gold was discovered and worked by the early Spanish settlers.

TRUJILLO CITY AS A TRAVEL CENTER

For convenience the Dominican Republic may be roughly divided into three major regions, each accessible by one of the main highways radiating from Trujillo City. The Duarte Highway, crossing the country NW, passing through the provinces of Trujillo, La Vega, Santiago, and Monte Cristi, and terminating at the far NW town of Monte Cristi, serves the central region and the north between the cordillera and the coastal plain. The Mella Highway running E from Trujillo City, serves the provinces of San Pedro de Macorís and El Seibo and terminates E at the town of Higüey. The Sánchez Highway, covering the SW part of the republic, serves the provinces of Trujillo, Azua, and Benefactor, and the route continues to Port-au-Prince, capital of Haiti. These regions may be called the central and north (below), the east (p. 28), and the west (p. 29).

CENTRAL AND NORTH REGION

The Duarte Highway, about 175 miles long and by far the most important road in the country, runs NW from Trujillo City. It crosses the central mountain range, passes through the historic town of La Vega and the valley of the Vega Real, as well as many quaint little towns, and reaches the fertile N lands and the coastal plain first seen by Columbus when he discovered the island. After leaving the S coastal plain, the road climbs into the mountains and winds through a luxuriant tropical countryside dominated by royal palms. Towns on the first part of the route include Los Alcarrizos, Villa Altagracia, Piedras Blancas, Monseñor Nouel, and Rincón.

From Rincón a road branches off NE to San Francisco de Macorís (p. 25). Another road from Rincón leads 20 miles SE to Cotui, a small town which was founded in 1505 and is noted for its old church; gold, silver, and copper deposits near by were exploited in colonial times.

The magnificent Vega Real fully explains the enthusiasm with which Columbus wrote of the country to his king. His verdict was: "La Española is a marvel." Jacob Gayer, staff photographer of the National Geographic Society, writes: "From the summit of the Santo Cerro on the central Duarte Highway to Monte Cristi a comprehensive view is obtained of the great central valley so aptly named by Columbus—La Vega Real. Any other name than the Royal Plain would do scant justice to the magnificent terrain, the rich fertility of which has few equals in any part of the world. More than a hundred miles long, from ten to fifteen miles wide, and covered with a rich surface loam averaging nine feet in depth, the Vega Real alone justifies Columbus's panegyric on his beloved Hispaniola."

La Vega, with more than 10,000 inhabitants, 80 miles from Trujillo City, is capital of the historic province of the same name. One of the republic's oldest cities, originally founded by Columbus on the left bank of the Río Camú, it was rebuilt on the right bank after being destroyed by earthquake in 1564. The surrounding countryside is one of the most densely populated parts of the country. La Vega is important commercially as a distributing point for the produce of the region, chiefly cattle, tobacco, coffee, and cacao. The town has electric lights and modern sanitary services.

HOTEL. Italia.

Excursions from La Vega. The ruins of the old town, with the remains of the fort and some brick walls of buildings, are little more than half a mile away.

Jarabacoa is a town reached by an 18-mile secondary road branching S off the highway beyond La Vega. It lies in a beautiful valley, rich in tropical fruits, at the confluence of the Río Yerbabuena and the Río Yaque del Norte. Because of its elevation the town enjoys a fine bracing climate. Jarabacoa is almost at the island's center. The Salto de Jimenoa, a waterfall, is a famous attraction.

A road that is under construction from Jarabacoa will run 20 miles S to Costanza, a resort town in another fertile and attractive valley.

Santo Cerro (Holy Hill) is a village with a shrine built in the 16th century to the Virgin of Las Mercedes (Mercies), patroness of the island. This shrine is the goal of an annual pilgrimage on September 24. From the hill a splendid view opens out over the Vega Real. An important battle between Columbus and the Indians was fought here.

Moca, with more than 6000 inhabitants, about 10 miles N of La Vega on the Duarte Highway, is a picturesque town, capital of the province of Espaillat. It nestles at the foot of the Macorís hills. The town is named for the famous Mocha coffee which was first introduced and planted in the vicinity. The railroad by which it was once connected E with Sánchez on the peninsula of Samaná (p. 28) has been torn up, and the roadbed is being made into a highway.

Excursion from Moca. San Francisco de Macorís, with more than 12,000 inhabitants, capital of the province of Duarte and center of a rich agricultural region which produces chiefly cacao, can be reached by a secondary road branching E from Moca and passing through the towns of Salcedo and Tenares. It can also be reached by a secondary road branching off the highway at Rincón, some distance short of Moca. San Francisco is a progressive little town with fairly good modern facilities.

HOTELS. Hispano; Inglaterra; Macorizano; San Francisco.

SANTIAGO

Santiago de los Caballeros, to give the city its full name, with nearly 40,000 inhabitants, is the second city of the republic. It is reached by the Duarte Highway, 10 miles W of Moca. Built on a high bluff on the Río Yaque del Norte, amid magnificent scenery and with a healthful and agreeable climate, it is the capital of the rich and populous province of the same name.

The city was founded in 1500 by 30 Spaniards and was named Santiago de los Caballeros (St. James of the Cavaliers) on their account. The descendants of the founders, who still maintain their old traditions, give the city a distinctive aristocratic air. It was destroyed by an earthquake in 1564 and subsequently rebuilt near the original site. On March 30, 1844, it was the scene of a decisive battle for Dominican independence. Though it has suffered from the depredations of buccaneers, native uprisings, and natural disasters, the city retains a typically Dominican atmosphere. It has fine churches, lovely plazas, a large and beautiful cathedral, and a fortified tower, the Fortaleza de San Luis.

The public market is held daily. Always picturesque, it is especially so on Saturdays, when the country folk come from far and near to sell their crude but interesting pottery, handwoven hammocks and baskets, occasional nuggets of gold from near by, a great abundance of flowers, and excellent tropical fruits. The carnival in Santiago is famous, and so is the celebration of July 25, day of St. James, the city's patron saint.

CLUBS. The Amantes de la Luz, the Club Santiago, and the Centro de Recreo are Santiago's leading clubs, with dance floors and recreation rooms. The country club and tennis club have fine courts and excellent swimming pools.

BANK. Royal Bank of Canada.

HOTELS. Gran Hotel Mercedes** was usually held to be the best in the republic until the construction of the Hotel Jaragua in Trujillo City. Other hotels are Francés*; Garibaldi*; Santiago*; Sevilla*.

EXCURSIONS FROM SANTIAGO

Baitoa, about 14 miles S on a secondary road, in the wild valley of the Río Yaque del Norte, offers a chance to see country people washing gold from the sands of the river.

Jánico, 16 miles SW of Santiago on a secondary road, has pleasant surroundings that would be good for camping. The village is historically notable because Columbus built the fort of Santo Tomás de Jánico near by as an outpost to protect the Spaniards in their search for gold. Near here the Spanish captain Alonzo de Ojeda captured the brave Indian chief Coanabo. The ruins of the original fort consist of a scarcely noticeable little heap of bricks.

San José de las Matas, 25 miles SW of Santiago on another secondary road, is a quaint old place set in a pine forest, with an excellent climate. The church is over 400 years old. Although facilities are limited, the people are hospitable and glad to accommodate visitors. The inhabitants live chiefly by cultivating tobacco and manufacturing hampers for its transport. Placer mining for gold, carried on since colonial days, can be observed in the neighborhood.

· **Puerto Plata** (Port of Silver), with 12,000 inhabitants, capital of its province and principal port of the N coast, reached by a secondary road, is about 38 miles from Santiago. The town is romantically located at the foot of Mt. Isabela de Torres and on the E tip of a perfect crescent-shaped bay. Today the town is one of the most beautiful and progressive in the country. Reputedly founded by Columbus and settled by Nicolás de Ovando, it was destroyed in 1605 by orders from Spain because of the smuggling that was carried on through it. Resettled in 1750, it developed rapidly. Today it is a modern city, with clean paved streets, electric lights, an attractive little plaza, good public buildings, an aqueduct, and hospital facilities. It exports tobacco, sugar, hides, coffee, cacao, and mahogany and other precious woods. There is a branch of the Royal Bank of Canada.

HOTELS. España; Europa; Mercedes.

Excursions from Puerto Plata. Near by are two waterfalls, Los Mameyes and El Violón, on the Río de los Mameyes. Both are in pleasant camping country. The caves of Copey are another sightseeing objective.

Very near Puerto Plata, on 27,000 acres of land given for the purpose by Generalísimo Trujillo, is the famous Sosua colonization project for European political refugees. This is the first modern planned refugee project in the Americas. If successful in its aim of strengthening the republic's economy as well as establishing European settlers firmly in the New World, it may pave the way for similar projects elsewhere.

La Isabela, a ghost city 30 miles W of Puerto Plata, can be reached by sailboat. A small boat may be chartered. La Isabela was the second settlement founded by Columbus, in 1493. Upon returning from Spain he found that La Navidad, his first fort, had been destroyed. Until 1503 La Isabela was the seat of the Spanish government in Santo Domingo. From it Columbus sent expeditions to the interior in search of gold. Later it was abandoned, and it is difficult today to make out even traces of the old foundations. Nothing has been found to support the local belief in treasure hidden near by. Where the stone fortress and barracks once stood the Dominican government has erected a building in memory of the town.

The Duarte Highway, beyond Santiago, runs through Navarrete, La Cruz de los Guayacanes, Villa Elisa, and Villa Isabela before reaching Monte Cristi, its terminus, 90 miles NW of Santiago. Between Navarrete and La Cruz de los Guayacanes a secondary road branches to the towns of Esperanza, Valverde, and Monción. Valverde, with 5000 inhabitants, is an important rice-growing center, and the country around it is also rich in pine timber and gold deposits.

Monte Cristi, with 8000 inhabitants, capital of the province of the same name, was founded by Spanish peasants in 1533. The full name, San Fernando de Monte Cristi, originated with Columbus, who gave it to the region when he explored it in 1493. The soil is semiarid but fertile if irrigated. The town has a sizable traffic in hides, dyewoods, and tobacco. Its port, a mile away, conducts a busy trade with Haiti.

HOTELS. América; Noroeste.

Excursions from Monte Cristi. A 30-minute horseback ride will reach the ruins of the old city, a ride of 2 hours Mt. Diego de Ocampo, 1300 feet high, commanding a beautiful view of the valley.

The new President Vincent Highway, a secondary road named in honor of the Haitian president, leads S from Monte Cristi to Dajabón, where there is a junction with the road to Cap-Haïtien in Haiti. Beyond Dajabón the President Vincent Highway runs S near the Haitian frontier to Restauración. Somewhat farther on, it passes through Haitian territory, then returns to Dominican ground, and finally joins the Sánchez Highway near Las Matas.

EAST REGION

The Mella Highway, which connects Trujillo City with the E provinces of San Pedro de Macorís and El Seibo and is the shortest of the three main highways, parallels the S coast as far as San Pedro de Macorís, then cuts N to Hato Mayor, and finally swings E through the peninsula which constitutes the province of El Seibo, to terminate at Higüey, 102 miles E from Trujillo City. Relatively thickly populated, this region is devoted to sugar-growing and cattle-raising. It produces some of the finest livestock in the country.

San Pedro de Macorís, with nearly 20,000 inhabitants, on the S coast, 45 miles E of Trujillo City, is capital of its province and center of the country's sugar industry. Pan American Airways planes stop here regularly. The climate, though tropical, is agreeable, with an average temperature of 82° F. in the daytime and 55° at night. The town, with modern facilities, including good wharves, is developing industrially. There is a branch of the Royal Bank of Canada.

HOTELS. Gran; Las Dos Américas; Inglaterra.

Hato Mayor, with 10,000 inhabitants, is 20 miles N of San Pedro de Macorís on the Mella Highway. A secondary road leads N from here to Sabana de la Mar on the bay of Samaná.

PENINSULA OF SAMANA

The province of Samaná consists principally of an E peninsula about 40 miles long, very beautiful but little settled. It is a rewarding goal for fisherman and hunter who do not mind, or still better enjoy, elastic schedules. A road is under construction that will make it easy to reach the peninsula by car (1941). A railroad route which formerly connected Moca (p. 25) on the Duarte Highway with Sánchez on the bay of Samaná is being rebuilt for motoring. The best approach at present is E and N from Trujillo City on the Mella Highway to Hato Mayor, then N from Hato Mayor to Sabana de la Mar by secondary road, and by boat across the bay of Samaná.

On his first voyage in 1492 Columbus visited this magnificent bay, which he called Golfo de las Flechas (Gulf of the Arrows) because of the shower of arrows with which the Indians greeted him. From here he sailed to Spain on Jan. 16, 1493; he touched at Samaná again on his return nearly a year later. The bay is a strategic position. It commands Mona Passage between the Dominican Republic and the fortified U. S. possession of Puerto Rico and affords anchorage for the largest ships. It is potentially important in the defense of the approaches to the Panama Canal and is regarded by some as a better location for a naval base than St. Thomas, V. I.

Sabana de la Mar, with 4000 inhabitants, is the port on the S side of the bay which can be reached by car all the way from Trujillo City. The town is noted for its tropical fruits and is the center of a thriving cattle business.

Sánchez, NW across the bay from Sabana de la Mar and reached from there by daily mail boats, is a beautiful town at the mouth of the great Río Yuna, which swarms with alligators and offers other good hunting. The mountains behind the town are interesting, and there are beaches with excellent swimming, bathing, and fishing.

Excursions from Sánchez. A sail on the bay passes many fine beaches fringed with luxuriant tropical vegetation, still unspoiled. Samaná, whose full name is Santa Bárbara de Samaná, 25 miles E of Sánchez by secondary road, can also be made the object of a sailing trip. The town was founded in 1756 by Spaniards from the Canary Islands. It received an influx of population from the United States in 1825, with the arrival of Negro immigrants whose descendants speak English even today.

From Sánchez a secondary road runs N across the peninsula and along the NE coast to Matanzas and Villa J. Molina. It will eventually be extended to Cabrera and then W to Hernández on the N coast, E of Puerto Plata.

Seibo, or in full Santa Cruz del Seibo, with 12,000 inhabitants, 16 miles E of Hato Mayor on the Mella Highway, was founded in 1502 by Juan de Esquivel, a companion of Ponce de León, after the Indians had been subdued. The surrounding country is famous for the fighting that took place there during the conquest. The town is the capital of the province of El Seibo.

Excursion to La Romana. La Romana, with 10,000 inhabitants, is reached by turning S off the Mella Highway at Pintado, 7 miles beyond Seibo. It is the only port of significance in the province and dominates the sugar industry, with the country's leading sugar mill. Immediately off the coast is the charming island of Catalina. Farther SE lies the larger island of Saona, where the brave Indian chief Cotubamaná took refuge with his people from the Spaniards. The caves where they hid can still be seen.

Higüey, or more fully Salvaleón del Higüey, with more than 3000 inhabitants, is 24 miles E of Seibo. It terminates the Mella Highway. A quaint mountain town at the confluence of two tributaries of the Río Yuma del Sur, it lies in beautiful country, and it is notable historically because it was founded by Ponce de León. Near here dwelt the Indian chief Cotubamaná, who died fighting the Spaniards. The shrine of the Virgin of La Altagracia (Heavenly Grace), with a magnificent altar, attracts thousands of pilgrims from all parts of the Dominican Republic and Haiti, who come here each year in January. January 21 is the principal day of fiesta.

WEST REGION

This section of the country, properly the west and southwest, containing the provinces of Trujillo, Azua, and Barahona, is served by the Sánchez Highway. The road runs to the Haitian border and is continued from there to Port-au-Prince in Haiti. The region is semiarid, with the flora mostly cacti. The Río Yaque del Sur, with its tributary the San Juan, somewhat relieves the aridity, and almost all the land would be productive under irrigation. The Dominican government is making efforts to this end, establishing near the Haitian border co-operative agricultural colonies in which the land becomes the property of the settlers after an experimental period. Baní, Azua, and San Juan are the most important towns on the highway. Barahona, another important town, about 40 miles off the Sánchez Highway from a point W of Azua, gives access to the lake region and other wild country.

San Cristóbal, with nearly 5000 inhabitants, 18 miles W of Trujillo City on the Sánchez Highway and capital of the province of Trujillo, was the first place where gold was discovered on the island. It was this discovery that led to the founding of the city of Santo Domingo (Trujillo City). The resort of La Toma is N on a side road (p. 24). San Cristóbal is the birthplace of Generalísimo Trujillo.

Baní, with 8000 inhabitants, 35 miles W of Trujillo City, is a busy town, set in a beautiful valley near the sea. It is noted as the birthplace of Máximo Gómez, liberator of Cuba.

Azua, with more than 6000 inhabitants, 70 miles W of Trujillo City, is one of the most important towns of the SW coast and capital of its province. It has an airport and is on the route of the Pan American Airways. Founded in 1504 by Diego Velázquez de León, who later conquered Cuba, it was the residence of Cortés, Pizarro, and Balboa. Cortés was a notary at Azua before he launched his conquest of Mexico. Originally the city was built about 3 miles S of its present site, but was destroyed by an earthquake.

LAKE COUNTRY

Lake Rincón and Lake Enriquillo are inviting to the adventurous, particularly fishermen who do not mind improvising routes and arrangements. The base for trips to these lakes or into the peninsula S of them is Barahona, reached from the Sánchez Highway.

Barahona, with 10,000 inhabitants, reached by a secondary road that describes a 40-mile arc S from a point W of Azua on the Sánchez Highway, is a good place for fishing. It is capital of the province of the same name. In addition to sugar, the region is rich in coffee, lignum vitae, and fruits. Salt is mined, and there is some tobacco cultivation. The town lies in a fertile valley of the Río Yaque del Sur, whose waters now irrigate thousands of acres of fertile sugar land. N of Barahona stretches the bay of Neiba, with the Yaque emptying into it. The waters teem with fish.

HOTELS. Central; Venecia.

Lake Rincón. A secondary road from Barahona leads W to Cabral on the S shore of Lake Rincón. This lake contains several species of large salt-water fish which somehow became marooned here and have adapted themselves to fresh water. Some Spanish historians mention the presence of big sea cows or manatees in these waters. Near the lake is the famous Cerro de Sal (Salt Hill).

Lake Enriquillo. In still wilder country W is Duverge on the S shore of Lake Enriquillo, 30 miles long and 10 miles wide, with a picturesque island called Cabrito (Little Goat) in the middle. Here the water is salt. The country is wild and wooded, well suited to hunting and fishing. Duverge is not reached by motor road. There are no good roads around the lake, but dirt roads and trails connect the little hamlets near it. On the NE shore is the village of Neiba, with 1500 inhabitants; on the E shore, Descubierta.

Pedernales is a town on the W coast of the peninsula which, with few settlements, stretches S of the lakes. A road of a sort terminates here after swinging through the peninsula, S and W from Barahona. Pedernales is close to the Haitian border. During pre-Columbian times the peninsula was known as Jaragua. Here dwelt the wife of Caonabo, the beautiful Anacaona, who was captured in ambush and subsequently beheaded by order of Nicolás de Ovando.

———————

Beyond Azua the Sánchez Highway leads into Haiti. It gives access to Port-au-Prince.

INDEX TO THE REGIONAL GUIDE

PUERTO RICO

The following brief guide to Puerto Rico was included with those to the Latin American republics in part because, as a possession of the United States, the island is of special interest to North American travelers, and in part because it is the only possession in the Americas that is truly Latin American in culture.

PUERTO RICO

BY R. TORRES MAZZORANNA

Puerto Rico, as an insular possession of the United States, is a meeting place of North American and Latin American cultures. It is the only land where Columbus set foot that is under the jurisdiction of the United States. The Puerto Ricans are United States citizens, living under North American governmental institutions; but their language, history, and culture are Spanish American. The island of Puerto Rico, 100 miles long by some 36 miles wide and 1400 miles due south of New York, is one of the most beautiful of the Greater Antilles, with excellent motor roads and hotels and other facilities for the traveler. Located in the trade-wind tropics, its climate is agreeable and calls for only light summer clothing the year round.

Originally the island was inhabited by some 60,000 peaceful Indians who called it Boriquén. The natives offered no resistance to the Spaniards who, during Columbus' second voyage, landed at a point near the present small town of Cabo Rojo on Nov. 19, 1493, according to the best historical opinion. Columbus, taking possession in the name of Ferdinand and Isabella, called the land San Juan Bautista del Boriquén in honor of the crown prince don Juan. Juan Ponce de León, who accompanied Columbus, returned 15 years later to explore Boriquén. In 1508 he discovered on the north coast what is today San Juan harbor. He named it Puerto Rico (Rich Port), and by this name the entire island eventually came to be known. Here he founded the first settlement, Caparra, and on Aug. 14, 1509, he was appointed the colony's first governor. Later he set sail from Puerto Rico to search for the fabulous fountain of youth. On this voyage he discovered, explored, and named Florida, and there he was killed in 1521 by an Indian arrow. His bones were returned to Puerto Rico in 1559 to be interred in the church of San José; in 1908 they were moved to the cathedral of San Juan, where they remain today.

As elsewhere in the Western Hemisphere, early colonial agriculture in Puerto Rico was developed with the help of imported African slaves. In 1530 there were 300 whites on the island and over 1600 Negroes. This proportion was reversed by the middle of the 18th century, and the census of 1935 showed only 23.8 per cent of the population to be colored.

During the 16th-18th centuries Spain was too busy fighting France and searching for gold in Mexico and Peru to pay much attention to Puerto Rico. These were dismal centuries for the neglected but loyal colony, which was ravaged with equal fury by buccaneers and tropical hurricanes. Unlike most other Spanish possessions in the Americas, Puerto Rico did not become independent after Napoleon's occupation of Spain. However, the Spanish Cortes or parliament at Cadiz, whose first vice-president was the Puerto Rican Ramón Power, brought the island political and social reforms which the subsequent reaction in Spain could not altogether destroy. For Puerto Rico some of the results of this parliament were freedom of the press, separation of civil and military powers, and creation of cultural societies which were later to produce many famous men. Some attempts at secession from Spain were made during the 19th century, the most important at Lares in 1868. These uprisings were sternly suppressed, and by and large,

Puerto Rico remained the most loyal of Spanish colonies in the Western Hemisphere. Largely through the efforts of the noted statesman Luis Muñoz Rivera, Spain granted political and economic autonomy in 1897, but it was too late.

The Spanish American War soon gave totally new directions to Puerto Rico's political and social development. Admiral W. T. Sampson bombarded San Juan on May 12, 1898. Gen. Nelson A. Miles landed a United States force at Guánica, a southern town, on July 25; he then proceeded to Ponce, which surrendered without resistance, and started toward San Juan over the military highway. An armistice was signed before he had crossed the central mountains. After a short period of military government the United States Congress passed the Foraker Act granting the Puerto Ricans participation in the island's Executive Council and an elected House of Representatives. In 1917 the Jones Act gave them United States citizenship and set up a popularly elected legislature. The United States, however, retains executive control through the veto power vested in a governor appointed by the president. The governor also appoints Supreme Court judges and some cabinet members.

Puerto Rico's agricultural economy is based on cash crops. The island exports sugar, tobacco, citrus fruits, and coffee in return for clothing, building materials, machinery, and about 60 per cent of its foodstuffs. Covered by the tariff regulations of the United States and by its coastwise shipping laws, Puerto Rico is the largest Latin American purchaser of United States goods. Economically, Puerto Rico presents challenging problems. With over 1,800,000 inhabitants, some 550 to the square mile according to the 1940 census, it is one of the most densely populated agricultural areas on earth. Much of the most fertile land, moreover, is concentrated in vast sugar estates. In spite of their hard lot, the jíbaros or countryfolk are simple, friendly, and usually gay, with an intense love for the land and for music that has produced some of the most interesting folksongs of Latin America. Because of its strategic position and excellent harbors, the island is being made the Gibraltar of the Caribbean.

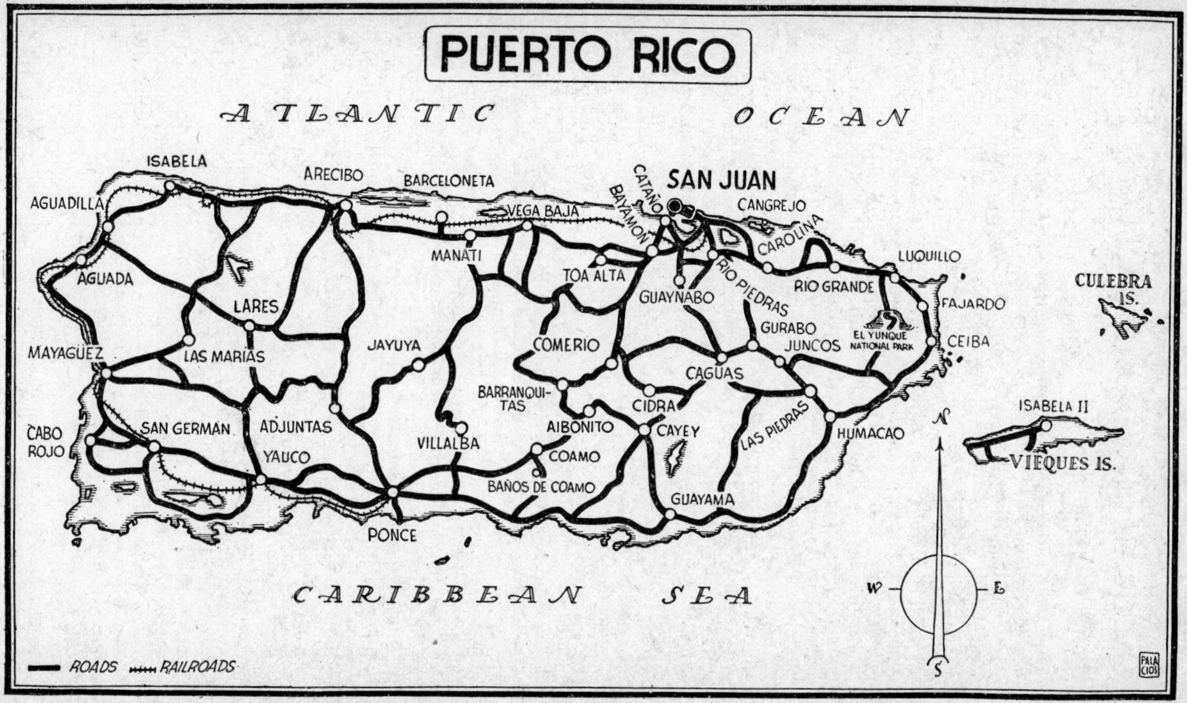
PUERTO RICO
ATLANTIC OCEAN
CARIBBEAN SEA
SAN JUAN
ISABELA
AGUADILLA
AGUADA
ARECIBO
BARCELONETA
VEGA BAJA
MANATI
CATAÑO
BAYAMON
CANGREJO
CAROLINA
TOA ALTA
GUAYNABO
RIO PIEDRAS
RIO GRANDE
LUQUILLO
FAJARDO
CEIBA
EL YUNQUE NATIONAL PARK
GURABO
JUNCOS
CAGUAS
COMERIO
LARES
LAS MARIAS
MAYAGÜEZ
JAYUYA
BARRANQUITAS
CIDRA
AIBONITO
CAYEY
LAS PIEDRAS
HUMACAO
CABO ROJO
SAN GERMAN
ADJUNTAS
VILLALBA
COAMO
YAUCO
BAÑOS DE COAMO
GUAYAMA
PONCE
CULEBRA IS.
ISABELA II
VIEQUES IS.
N
S
W
E
ROADS
RAILROADS
PALACIOS

PRACTICAL INFORMATION

HOW TO REACH PUERTO RICO

From the Continental U. S. Minimum first-class steamship fares are $75 one way and $115 round trip from New York; $60 one way and $108 round trip from Baltimore, Md.; $60 one way and $110 round trip from New Orleans; $70 from Galveston, Tex. By plane from Miami, Fla., the fare is $115 one way (1941).

BY STEAMER. Porto Rico Line; main office: foot of Wall St., New York. Sailings from New York to San Juan. Voyage takes 4 days.

Bull Insular Line; main office: 115 Broad St., New York. Sailings from Baltimore, Md.

Lykes Brothers Steamship Co.; main office: U. S. National Bank Building, Galveston, Tex. Operates freighters with good passenger accommodations from Texan ports.

Waterman Line; main office: Mobile, Ala. Operates freighters with good passenger accommodations from New Orleans; Tampa, Fla., and Mobile.

McCormick Steamship Co.; main office: 461 Market St., San Francisco. Operates freighters with good passenger accommodations. Sailings from Seattle, Wash.; Portland, Ore.; San Francisco and Los Angeles, Calif.

BY AIR. Pan American Airways; main office: 135 E. 42nd St., New York. Service from Miami, Fla.

AIDS TO TRAVELERS

Local Sources of Information. The Puerto Rican government maintains an Institute of Tourism and an Office of Commerce and Agriculture in New York, both at 1457 Broadway, and an Office of Tourism in San Juan near the pier, facing the large Federal Building. These offices furnish detailed information to travelers.

Climate. Puerto Rico knows no extremes of heat or cold. The average temperature in summer in coastal towns is 76° F.; in winter, 73°. The interior and the mountain region are considerably cooler.

Clothing. Drill, linen, or other light tropical clothing is worn the year round.

Health. Despite the low standards of living among the masses conditions are excellent as far as the visitor is concerned, and the traveler who follows the ordinary rules of health for the tropics has nothing to fear. In San Juan, Ponce, Mayagüez, Arecibo, and other large cities there are first-class hospital facilities with doctors from the continental United States as well as Puerto Rican medical men who have had their training there.

Sports and Recreation. GOLF AND TENNIS. Puerto Rico has good facilities for golf, tennis, and other sports at clubs in San Juan, Ponce, and Mayagüez and at the mountain resort of El Semil near Villalba. Private golf courses and tennis courts are also found at some of the sugar plantations under U. S. ownership. There are Puerto Rican, U. S., and foreign social centers in all the principal cities.

SWIMMING. The Escambrón Beach Club, just outside San Juan on Ponce de León Ave., has bathing facilities in the open ocean, fenced for protection against sharks and barracuda. Besides bathhouses, a dance floor, orchestra, bar, and casino the club has overnight accommodations. The Normandie, Condado, and San Gerónimo Hotels maintain salt-water swimming pools.

At Aguadilla the new Punta Borinquén Country Club offers surf bathing in the Caribbean and fresh-water bathing in a new pool. The most popular of the island's other beaches and bathing resorts are Isla Verde and Boca de Cangrejo near San Juan; Los Meros, Boca Chica, and Las Cucharas at Ponce; Boquerón at Mayagüez; Ventanas at Yauco; Salinas and Ensenada at Guánica. On the N coast the most popular beaches are Vega Baja, near the town of the same name, and Playa de Luquillo, near the town of Luquillo, an hour's drive from San Juan.

RACING. Horse racing is popular. Races are held twice a week, with legalized betting, at the Quintana, Las Monjas, Mira Palmeras, and Las Casas tracks near San Juan, all accessible by bus within 30 minutes.

COCKFIGHTS are legal. They are usually held on Sundays. The Gallera Borinquén, immediately outside of San Juan on the Guaynabo road, is the largest cockpit on the island. Second largest is the Canta Gallo, at the very outskirts of Santurce. Another popular pit is the Tenerías at Ponce.

FISHING. There is salt-water fishing only. Though not officially organized, excursions can be arranged through the tourist bureau or through local fishermen at Aguadilla, Mayagüez, Fajardo, Luquillo, and other coast towns. A good fishing resort is Vieques Island.

LOTTERY. The Puerto Rican lottery is very popular, and tickets are sold by numerous street vendors. The lottery is managed by the Insular government; proceeds go to charity. Regular drawings (1941) with $15,000 first prize occur twice a month; full tickets cost $6. Extraordinary drawings with $75,000 first prize are held on Christmas and the Fourth of July.

Currency is the same as in the United States.

Banks. In San Juan are the Banco Popular, smaller Puerto Rican banks, and branches of the National City Bank, Chase National Bank, Bank of Nova Scotia, and Royal Bank of Canada. The large native banking institutions of Crédito y Ahorro and Banco de Ponce are located in Ponce, and so are various branch banks. Branch banks are found in Mayagüez and other large towns.

Cost of living is somewhat higher than in the United States. First-class hotel rates are $5-$12 a day European plan and $4-$10 American plan at San Juan (1941) and somewhat lower at Ponce and Mayagüez. Second-class hotel rates are $2.50 up; small hotels and boarding houses are much cheaper. Food costs are higher than in the United States for equal quality; the same is true of wearing apparel and other imported articles.

Transportation. ROADS. A fine system of public highways extends along the coastal plain and winds across the interior mountains. The old Spanish military highway from Ponce to San Juan, though narrow, is a magnificent engineering feat. The island's scenic grandeur enhances the pleasure of motor travel; often the roads wind through veritable tunnels formed by the foliage of stately trees. In May these are likely to be brilliant red with the blossoms of the flame trees.

AUTOMOBILES in which low fares are charged are driven on regular schedules to all parts of Puerto Rico. Seats in the somewhat more comfortable públicos or public touring cars can be obtained at reasonable rates. Private cars for trips anywhere on the island can be hired at Plaza de Armas in San Juan, as well as in the public squares of Ponce, Mayagüez, Aguadilla, and most other towns.

The visitor's car can be transported to Puerto Rico for about $135 freight charges each way (1941). Cars must be registered on arrival, and U. S. license plates and drivers' licenses are honored for the first six months. Rules of the road are the same as in the continental United States. Gasoline costs somewhat more. Drivers who know the island can be hired through the tourist bureau.

BUS services connect all parts of the island. They provide the least expensive mode of travel, though the buses are often crowded and uncomfortable.

RAILROADS. The Puerto Rican American Railroad traverses the coastal plain from San Juan to Mayagüez, Ponce, and Arroyo. There are short railroads in other parts of the island, most of them serving the sugar industry. Railroad travel is slow and somewhat uncomfortable.

Postage is the same as in the continental United States for ordinary mail. Steamer service to New York takes about 5 days. Airmail service, which is daily, costs $.10 a half ounce and takes half a day to Miami and a day to New York (1941).

Communications. Cable, telegraph, and telephone companies give excellent service at continental U. S. rates. There are telephone connections with the continent.

Souvenirs and Handicrafts. These include native handmade toys, musical instruments, leather cigarette cases, belts and purses, flower pots of bamboo, hammocks, white and colored rugs of cotton or maguey; purses, bracelets, and necklaces made of peronias and camándulas, which are native seeds; articles of mahogany and other native woods, little boxes made of sea shells, excellent handmade handkerchiefs, table and tea sets, doilies, and innumerable other objects. Good bargains in these articles are offered by street vendors in the towns. Mayagüez is the main center of the needlework industry.

Food. Most restaurants and hotels serve international foods as well as Puerto Rican dishes. The following are the most popular among the latter: arroz con pollo, chicken with rice; asopao, soupy rice with chicken; pastel criollo, a sort of tamal made of ground plantain, meat, olives, raisins, and chickpeas, wrapped in banana leaves; hallaca, the same as pastel except that it is made of corn meal and chicken; jueyes al carapacho, crabmeat cooked in the shell; arroz con juey, rice with crabmeat; cabrito estofado, stewed kid; paella, stewed rice with chicken, fish, clams, peppers, and ham; lechón asado, barbecued pig. Tropical fruits abound in Puerto Rico, and the pineapples are especially good.

The manufacture of excellent rum is an important industry. Puerto Rico also produces fine coffee, especially the kind called caracolillo, grown chiefly in the region of Yauco and the mountains of Lares and Las Marías. Puerto Rican coffee has been highly prized in Europe for centuries for demitasse.

Holidays include New Year's Day; February 22, Washington's Birthday; March 22, Emancipation Day; April 16, José de Diego's birthday; Good Friday; May 30, Memorial Day; Fourth of July; July 17, Luis Muñoz Rivera's birthday; July 25, Occupation Day; July 27, José C. Barbosa's birthday; Labor Day; October 12, Columbus Day; Election

Day, first Monday in November every four years; Thanksgiving; Christmas.

Fiestas. Carnival is celebrated preceding the beginning of Lent. Queens are elected by towns and cities as well as by social clubs, and there are dances, processions, and masquerades.

REGIONAL GUIDE

SAN JUAN

San Juan de Puerto Rico, capital and chief commercial center of Puerto Rico, with 170,000 inhabitants, occupies a small, rocky island connected with the mainland by bridges. The approach to San Juan by sea is picturesque and dramatic. The skyline of the city is set off by distant mountains. The magnificent time-worn walls of Morro Castle, the centuries-old fortress, appear at the entrance to the bay. To the right as the vessel nears the harbor channel is the Isla de Cabra (Goat Island); farther in, the ruins of the historic blockhouse Castillo de Cañuelo. To the left are the old walls of San Juan with the Fortaleza, now the Governor's Palace, perched atop. The modern docks are on the left as the vessel steams in, while on the right and farther down looms the Isla Grande (Large Island), today an important U. S. air and naval base.

The first settlement was established by Juan Ponce de León across the bay at Caparra. In 1521 the capital was moved to its present site and afterward fortified with the Fortaleza and the fort of San Felipe del Morro or Morro Castle. The island was attacked unsuccessfully by Sir Francis Drake in 1595. In 1598 the Earl of Cumberland with a large force landed at the Escambrón, a fortification on the NE edge of San Juan, and the Spaniards retired to Morro Castle. Cumberland took possession of the city, but the following year the Spaniards recaptured it after an epidemic had forced the withdrawal of Cumberland and a part of his forces. The severest assault suffered by San Juan was inflicted by the Dutch under Bouduwijn Hendricks, who landed in the city in 1625 and laid siege to Morro Castle. The governor Juan de Haro refused to surrender. The Spanish captain Juan de Amézquita made a daring sortie, and shortly afterward the Dutch, their ranks depleted through disease and starvation, withdrew, though not until they had sacked and burned the city. The city's defenses were further improved after repeated threats of attacks by the French, English, and Dutch. In 1797 the British again attacked San Juan. They disembarked near the site which is now occupied by the Hotel Condado and bombarded the fortifications, but failed to take them. On May 12, 1898, the U. S. fleet, commanded by Admiral W. T. Sampson, bombarded the city for three hours. Several shots hit Morro Castle, and the scars are still to be seen on the walls facing the sea.

THE CITY. The metropolitan area today consists of the original walled town of San Juan proper, with large sections of the old walls still intact along the N side, and a number of suburbs. The latter include Puerta de Tierra, a workers' section; the residential districts of Miramar and Condado, E of San Juan; Santurce, a district of homes and small businesses beyond Miramar on Ponce de León Ave.; Sunoco, a workers' section still farther E; Martín Peña, a residential district along the main road which is an extension of Ponce de León Ave.; and finally Río Piedras, where the university is located, about 10 miles SE. All these points are easily reached by bus, street car, or taxi.

The city was laid out around Plaza de Armas, also called Plaza Baldorioty de Castro, at the intersection of Calle San José and C. Salvador Brau (San Francisco St.). It is an open square surrounded by trees and flanked N by the old city hall, a twin-towered colonial structure with arcades and a large patio; W by the Intendencia, a large colonial building, and E and S by modern department stores, some colonial houses, and soda fountains and cafés. The plaza is 5 minutes' walk from the pier, N on C. San Justo and then W on C. Salvador Brau. It is the center of transportation facilities, where taxis are most easily obtained and buses and street cars leave for the outskirts and residential sections. Plaza de Armas is also a convenient point of departure for sightseeing in old San Juan. Most of the old buildings and historic sites are within the old walled city and can easily be reached on foot from this plaza.

PARKS AND PLAZAS. Besides Plaza de Armas, the important squares are Plaza San José and Plaza Colón. Plaza San José, NW, on C. San Sebastián, is one of the most picturesque and characteristically colonial localities in the city. It is flanked by low old residences, some with ancient buttresses supporting their massive walls, and is bordered by acacia trees. The church of San José faces this plaza. The statue of Ponce de León here was cast from bronze cannon captured from the Dutch during their attack on the city.

Plaza Colón, at the E edge of the old walled city, at the point where Ponce de León Ave. enters the city, contains the lofty Columbus monument on a hexagonal pedestal with bronze plaques in relief depicting the island's discovery. The old municipal theater faces the plaza S; the Casino de Puerto Rico, N. The fort of San Cristóbal is a little N of this plaza.

Parque Muñoz Rivera, a fine landscaped park on Ponce de León Ave., a short distance out of the old city, has many varieties of native plants and flowers. The ancient polvorín or powder magazine here that was used by the Spaniards is now a museum of sea shells. The park is a favorite seashore promenade. Near this park and facing the Escambrón Beach Club is a large and modern baseball stadium with a grandstand and a diamond for professional baseball games.

OLD FORTS. The Castillo del Morro (Morro Castle), overlooking the Atlantic at the NW tip of the city, is a huge and complicated series of fortifications begun in 1540 and completed in 1606. The works are a masterpiece of ingenuity and shrewd strategy. There are innumerable passageways, moats, dungeons, cannon emplacements, subterranean alleys, towers, walks, and large patios surrounded by barracks. Campo del Morro (Morro Field) contains, besides Morro Castle, the Ballaja infantry barracks and residences built for U. S. officers. The grounds, though military territory, can be visited in normal times by car and on foot, but the barracks and the castle can be entered only by special permit from the military authorities.

The Fortaleza, at the W end of San Juan, at the foot of C. Fortaleza (Allen St.) and 3 blocks from Plaza de Armas, is the residence and office of the governor, the oldest governor's mansion under the U. S. flag. It was built as a fort, 1533-38, but condemned as such in 1539 by Gonzalo Fernández de Oviedo, who, on his arrival from Spain, said that "only blind men could have chosen such a place for a fortress." In 1625 the Fortaleza was partially burned by the Dutch, who arrived in 17 sailing ships and set fire to the city. The structure was rebuilt in 1639 very much as it is today, and it has since served as the residence of Puerto Rico's governors. The Fortaleza is one of the finest architectural gems left by Spain in the Caribbean area. The entrance gate and dome, as well as the beautifully designed casement windows, are

Moorish in effect. The mural paintings in the dome symbolizing Spain's military achievements, the antique stucco decorations grouped around the doors, and the spacious rooms show old Spanish design at its best. The top of the wall nearest the famous tropical garden was once a lookout for buccaneers, and the vault under it was presumably built for the storage of treasure from other Spanish colonies while awaiting safe carriage to Spain.

The Puerta de San Juan (San Juan Gate), below the Fortaleza at the foot of C. Salvador Brau, served as an entrance from the old harbor through the seaward wall of the city. Today it is San Juan's only remaining gate. An impressive relic of buccaneering days, it is well preserved, with massive doors reinforced with heavy nails. Cannon are planted on either side. It affords a good view of the W part of the harbor, and the walls can be examined from a roomy walk issuing from the gate.

The fort of San Cristóbal, on the Atlantic, is 2 blocks N of Plaza Colón, with its entrance ramp at the foot of C. General Contreras. For centuries it was the city's bulwark of defense. From one of its batteries was fired the first shot against Admiral Sampson's squadron during the Spanish American War. Built in 1631 as a result of weaknesses revealed in other fortifications by the Dutch attack of 1625, it was once connected by a system of tunnels with Morro Castle, the Fortaleza, the Escambrón, and other fortifications, but these tunnels have long since been filled. W from San Cristóbal the line of walls overlooking the sea is unbroken and fairly well preserved. San Cristóbal gave rise to many legends in the colonial period. One of its points of interest is the Garita del Diablo, a sentry box which, according to legend, is haunted. It juts over the Atlantic from the walls of the fort, and the story is that the devil once spirited off the sentinel on duty at this lonely post. Another legend concerns St. Christopher (San Cristóbal). On a wall of the old cistern under the fort can be seen what appears to be a printed image of this saint. Centuries ago the Spaniards hung his picture there to assure the city's water supply. Then came a new priest who maintained that no saint belongs in a cistern. He had the picture

---

KEY TO MAP OF SAN JUAN

1. Morro Castle
2. La Fortaleza
3. Customhouse
4. Office of Tourism
5. Plaza de Armas
6. City hall
7. San Juan Gate
8. Santo Cristo chapel
9. Cathedral
10. San José church
11. Casa Blanca (White House)
12. Plaza Colón
13. San Cristóbal fort
14. Casa de los Dos Zaguanes (House of Two Halls)
15. Y. M. C. A.
16. Ateneo de Puerto Rico (Puerto Rico Atheneum)
17. Library
18. Casa de España (Spanish Club)
19. Capitol
20. School of Tropical Medicine
21. Redemptorist church and school
22. Parque Muñoz Rivera
23. Escambrón Beach Club
24. Hotel San Gerónimo

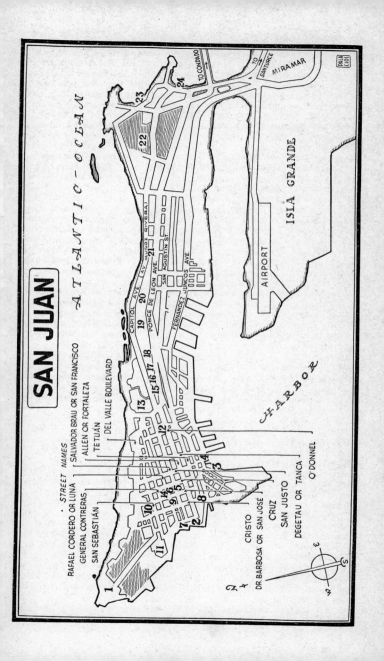

removed to the chapel. Then the cistern dried up. No matter how much the people prayed there was no rain. At last after weeks of agony the heavens opened, and it was discovered that the saint's picture had miraculously made its way back to the cistern. Finally there is the miracle of the ancient chapel itself, now the barber shop of a U. S. Army unit. During Sampson's bombardment the chapel was used as a temporary storage place for ammunition. A shell hit the chapel and exploded at the feet of the image of the Virgin, but the ammunition remained intact.

CHURCHES. The cathedral, NE from the Fortaleza, at the corner of C. Cristo and C. Rafael Cordero or Luna, was originally built in 1527, destroyed by earthquake and hurricane, and rebuilt in 1802. Here lie the remains of Ponce de León.

The church of San José, several blocks N of the cathedral, is on Plaza San José. The church, built in 1523 by the Dominicans, is the oldest in constant use in the Americas. Seriously damaged by Admiral Sampson's bombardment, it stands as a rich monument to the old traditions of Puerto Rico. Among its relics are a crucifix that belonged to the family of Ponce de León and a beautiful antique painting of the Virgin in a frame of solid silver. The statue of Ponce de León on the square in front of the church was cast from bronze cannon captured from the Dutch during their attack on the city.

The chapel of Santo Cristo, at the intersection of C. Cristo and C. Tetuán, a block E of the Fortaleza, is believed to be the smallest church in the world. Overlooking the harbor from a high point on the ancient walls, it was built in 1760 to commemorate the miraculous escape from death of a rider who was thrown from his horse at this spot during a race.

OLD HOUSES. The Casa Blanca (White House), reached by a short walk W from Plaza San José along C. San Sebastián, is half mansion and half fortress and was once occupied by Ponce de León's youngest son Luis. Built in 1523 as a family residence, it was used as a fortress and arsenal until 1531. The Spanish government took it over in 1773 and replaced Ponce de León's coat of arms with that of the Spanish royal house, but the former was recently restored. The building is now the residence of the commander of the U. S. troops stationed in Puerto Rico. Occupying a lofty position at the NW extremity of the city, it offers a magnificent view of the harbor and the sea beyond. It can be visited only by special permission from the military authorities.

San Juan has a number of old colonial mansions, architectural gems with spacious patios and staircases, some paved with rare Spanish tiles. Notable is the Casa de los Dos Zaguanes (House of the Two Halls), back of the cathedral, at the corner of C. Rafael Cordera or Luna and C. San José. This mansion, with curving staircase balustrades of solid mahogany, is now divided into cubicles for poor families, but it is still imposing and interesting. The house at the corner of C. San José and C. Sol, now occupied by the district court, has ample rooms, harmonious architecture, and a splendid staircase with 17th-century azulejos or tiles. The Palacio Rojo (Red Palace) at the foot of C. Fortaleza (Allen St.), now occupied by the Department of Education and other Insular government offices, is in the best colonial style with a charming patio.

OTHER NOTABLE BUILDINGS. On Ponce de León Ave. are the Carnegie Public Library, in Ionic style; the Casa de España (Spanish Club), an ornate and luxurious new building of mixed architecture; the Insular Capitol, built of Georgia marble; the School of Tropical Medicine, a fine example of modern Spanish Renaissance design; and the Redemptorist church and school, a splendid group of buildings dedicated to worship and education under the guidance of the Redemptorist fathers. The new customhouse, near the docks, is in colonial style. The Banco Popular, on C. Tetuán, is modernistic. The Federal Building, near the piers, has straight modern lines.

CLUBS. Distinguished social clubs include the Casa de España (Spanish Club), on Ponce de León Ave. near the public library; the Casino de Puerto Rico, Plaza Colón; the Union Club (North American), at Stop 11 Miramar, 10 minutes by street car or bus from San Juan, with dance floor and outdoor swimming pool. Entrance to these clubs is granted only on presentation by a member.

The Ateneo de Puerto Rico (Puerto Rican Atheneum), on Ponce de León Ave. near the public library, a short walk from the old part of San Juan, is housed in a splendid Moorish building and is a cultural center devoted to the arts and sciences.

The Y. M. C. A. has a fine building on Ponce de León Ave.

SPORTS. The Berwind Country Club, 10 miles out of San Juan, has an excellent golf course. In San Juan proper the course on the military grounds at Morro Castle may be used by special permission.

The Club Náutico (Yacht Club), with headquarters at Stop 10, Miramar, easily reached by street car or bus, is the center for water sports, including deep-sea angling. Visitors are admitted upon presentation by members.

See also Practical Information (p. 6).

SOUVENIRS AND HANDICRAFTS. The best bargains are offered by street vendors. The best-known shop for native handicrafts is El Jíbaro. The Insular Department of Education maintains a novelty shop for products of school children at the end of C. Fortaleza (Allen Street) near the Fortaleza. The church of Notre Dame in Puerta de Tierra, 5 minutes out of the city, sells excellent needlework pieces made by young women in the convent school.

BANKS. See Practical Information (p. 7).

SOURCES OF INFORMATION. See Practical Information (p. 6).

RESTAURANTS AND BARS. La Mallorquina, one of the oldest traditional coffeehouses and a center for political discussions, is famous for its arroz con pollo. Ciro Malatrassi specializes in Italian cuisine. Casino de Puerto Rico, a private club which can be visited through friends, has excellent native foods and fine jíbaro musicians playing native instruments and singing folksongs. Other good bars and restaurants, besides those in the hotels, are the Aquarium, Rialto, Don Q, Pardo Bar and Grill, and La Cafetera.

HOTELS. Most hotels in San Juan have two rates, the higher during the major tourist season, December-April, and the lower in May-November. Hotel Normandie**, recently opened on the beach in the Escambrón section, has de luxe accommodations and a Grecian swimming pool. Condado**, beautifully located by the seashore in the Condado section, has a swimming pool, indoor and outdoor dance floors, restaurants, a bar, and a casino. The Escambrón Beach Club**, at the E end of San Juan, has bathhouses, apartments, single rooms, outdoor and indoor dance floors and restaurants, and a casino. San Gerónimo**, near the Condado section, has a swimming pool. Bellevue* is in the Condado section, immediately across the bridge from San Juan. Palace* is in the heart of old San Juan at C. Degetau or Tanca.

NOTE. Hotels are here classified by rates. Two stars indicate the higher rates for the country in question and also, in nearly all cases, mean good accommodations. One star means rates in the medium brackets; no star means either low rates or no information available. An effort is made in all these guides to list hotels in the various cities and towns, but travelers who are accustomed to North American or European accommodations should use the information with care. In the capitals and larger Latin American centers hotels usually have standards comparable with those found elsewhere and at times on a par with those anywhere in the world. In the smaller centers throughout Latin America hotels are often more nearly boarding houses whose standards of accommodations and food make them unacceptable to all but the most adaptable.

SAN JUAN'S ENVIRONS AND EXCURSIONS

San Juan is the natural travel center of the island. Several interesting short trips can be made out of the city.

Boca de Cangrejo, half an hour's drive E of San Juan by taxi or público, is a remarkable undersea garden with coral formations, marine vegetation, and colorful tropical fish, which may be seen from glass-bottomed boats or by diving with a helmet from a barge.

Río Piedras, SE of the city and easily reached by bus, taxi, or público or touring car licensed to carry passengers, is the seat of the university of Puerto Rico, with its fine campus and well-designed buildings. The university includes departments of arts and sciences, education, law, pharmacy, and business administration. It maintains a College of Agriculture and Mechanical Arts at Mayagüez (p. 18) and jointly with Columbia University the School of Tropical Medicine in San Juan. The university public relations counsel arranges personally conducted tours.

The Caribbean National Forest, SE on El Yunque, one of the island's highest peaks, is reached over excellent roads in $1\frac{1}{2}$ hours. The dense orchid-studded tree growth is one of the finest examples of rain forest on earth. There are trails for hiking and climbing, a pavilion, dance hall, restaurant, swimming pool, and overnight accommodations.

Cidra, S of San Juan, has a resort near it at 1500 feet altitude which is reached in a little over an hour's drive from the capital. The motor route is through Río Piedras toward Ponce on the S coast; Cidra lies on a road branching W below Caguas. The scenery, amid large pineapple plantations, is magnificent.

HOTEL. Treasure Island Camp has individual bungalows with kitchens and baths. The large restaurant serves native and international food, and there are dancing, swimming, riding, hiking, tennis, and badminton.

SOUTH FROM SAN JUAN

The trip of 90 miles from San Juan to Ponce near the S coast is made in 4 hours over the historic military highway that winds over 4000-foot peaks amid magnificent scenery. There is air service. The main road passes through Río Piedras; Caguas, a tobacco center; Cayey; Aibonito, a flower-growing center; Guayama, and Coamo.

Excursion to Baños de Coamo (Coamo Springs). On a side road between Coamo and Ponce is an excellent overnight stopping place. Set among luxuriant tropical scenery, the hot sulphur baths are famous. The hotel, with excellent food, has long been a fashionable center.

PONCE

Puerto Rico's second city, Ponce, with 60,000 inhabitants, is situated 3 miles from its port on the S coast. Ponce is genuinely native, with low, roomy colonial mansions and beautiful plazas. There are fine theaters, hospitals, and hotel accommodations.

The Club Deportivo de Ponce (Sporting Club) on the outskirts of the city, one of the best in Puerto Rico, has facilities for horse racing, golf, tennis, and other sports. The Nuevo Club Náutico (New Yacht Club), on the beach, offers facilities for fishing and other water sports. Admission is on presentation by a member.

HOTELS. Meliá**; Bélgica*.

EXCURSIONS FROM PONCE

Typical quaint Puerto Rican towns can be reached from Ponce by car over good roads.

Adjuntas, at an altitude of 2400 feet, 18 miles N, is a favorite summer resort, enjoying an excellent climate and fine scenery. Bathing is good at the waterfalls of the near-by river. Overlooking the town is El Gigante, a hill shaped like a giant's face. Immediately behind El Gigante is Las Garzas irrigation and power project, under construction at a cost of $8,000,000.

Jayuya, 45 minutes' drive from Adjuntas on a road branching off the route from Ponce, has a tiny public square and a colorful main street on the bank of a quiet river. Horseback riding, often by moonlight, is a leading attraction. Its demitasse coffee is famous throughout the island. Jayuya is the starting point for climbing Los Tres Picachos, the island's three highest peaks.

Villalba, with only 800 inhabitants, is reached by car, NE from Jayuya for a short distance and then S. The main point of interest in the town itself is Central Demidey, a large sugar mill within the city limits. Below Villalba the road returns to Ponce.

HOTEL. El Semil is a dude ranch and mountain resort, with up-to-date facilities, high in the hills near Villalba.

WEST FROM SAN JUAN

A railroad circles the coast W and S from San Juan to Mayagüez, beyond which it continues to Ponce. By car to Mayagüez along the coast from San Juan takes about 5 hours, passing through a score of interesting beach towns and descending over Guajataca Heights, a splendid vantage point for a view of the coast, Desecheo Island, and the sea. About 20 minutes out of San Juan a junction is passed; at this point roads branch off N to Cataño, a small village opposite San Juan on the bay which may also be reached by regular launch service from the piers, and S to Guaynabo, another typical small town. U. S. Fort and Camp Buchanan are W of this junction.

Bayamón is farther along the main road. Here a road branches S into the mountain region to Comerío, site of a hydroelectric plant; from there it runs on to Barranquitas, a beautiful summer resort town which was the birthplace of the patriot and statesman Luis Muñoz Rivera, and then continues through Aibonito to Ponce.

Beyond Bayamón, on the route near the coast, the traveler crosses large groves of citrus fruits and fields of pineapples and passes through the towns of Toa Alta and Vega Baja.

Manatí is the point to turn off for a visit to the U. S. camp and fort at Tortuguero, N near the town of Barceloneta. Permission for the visit must be obtained in advance from the military authorities at San Juan.

Arecibo, half an hour by car from Manatí, on the road near the coast, is a fairly large town with several bathing beaches in the vicinity. The beach of Poza del Obispo (Bishop's Puddle) is safely fenced by large rocks; others, like that of Los Coléricos (The Irascibles), are rougher and less safe, though more exciting for good swimmers. A short distance from the town, at the beach, is the Cueva del Consejo (Council Cave) with Indian pictographs.

After passing half a dozen picturesque villages, the road reaches Isabela, center of an Insular government hydroelectric and irrigation project; Aguadilla, a fairly large town, famous for its fishing, with the Punta Borinquén military airport near by; and Aguada, where some historians have it that Columbus landed on his first visit to Puerto Rico. The road then runs on to Mayagüez, halfway down the W coast.

MAYAGÜEZ

Mayagüez, at the W end of the island, can be reached by a railroad which runs along the coast from San Juan or by car or bus from San Juan or Ponce, either over the coastal plains or through the interior mountains.

Puerto Rico's needlework center is this town of 5000 inhabitants. The local factories and shops produce goods in quantity, and thousands of women in the outlying regions do home needlework for unbelievably low pay. Mayagüez is a clean city with a large central plaza containing an imposing statue of Columbus; it has comfortable houses, theaters, and clubs. Points of interest are the College of Agriculture and Mechanical Arts of the university, on the outskirts, and the near-by agricultural experimental station where important work is being done to improve the island's crops and to adapt such foreign plants as bamboo, cinchona, rattan, and rubber.

The Mayagüez Shooting Club, with swimming pool, tennis courts, shooting ranges, a dance hall, bar, and other facilities, is one of Puerto Rico's outstanding sport and social centers.

HOTELS. Coconut Grove*, with dining and dancing, a favorite of North Americans; Moreda*; Palma*.

EXCURSIONS FROM MAYAGÜEZ

San Germán, with 6500 inhabitants, reached by railroad or an hour's drive SE, is an old town founded by Diego Colón, son of Christopher Columbus. Here is one of the oldest churches in the Western Hemisphere, the church of Porta Coelis, in ruins but still beautiful.

Here the Spaniards founded one of the first institutions of learning of the New World. Its modern counterpart is the Instituto Politécnico de San Germán, a technical school run by North Americans. Fishing and bathing are good at La Parguera, Laguna Joyuda, and Puerto Real, all within easy reach of San Germán. Fishing parties can be organized through local fishermen.

Cabo Rojo (Red Cape), a town slightly smaller than San Germán, is on the coast, W of San Germán and S of Mayagüez, and can be reached from either in about three-quarters of an hour. It is an old colonial town with a small plaza and a casino and was the birthplace of the legendary Puerto Rican pirate Roberto Cofresí.

Las Marías, a small town on top of a hill, half an hour inland on a good road, E of Mayagüez, has luxuriant tropical surroundings and large coffee plantations.

Lares, 25 miles E of Mayagüez, is a typical coffee center, picturesque, though now somewhat run down. It is famous for the proclamation of the republic of Puerto Rico which was made there in 1868.

Yauco, 16 miles E of San Germán and reached by car or railroad, is the center of the best Puerto Rican coffee region and the home of a large number of Corsican families who came to the island after Napoleon's downfall. A good road connects it with Guánica, where U. S. troops under General Miles landed during the Spanish American War for their march on Ponce. Here also is the Central Guánica, the largest sugar mill in Puerto Rico.

EAST FROM SAN JUAN

The E section of the island comprises the district of Humacao, with more than 250,000 inhabitants in its 12 municipalities. All its towns are connected by road with San Juan and other parts of the island. There are some excellent fishing resorts in this section. Humacao, the capital of the district, can be reached by either coastal or inland road from San Juan. The route inland is through Río Piedras, Caguas, Gurabo, Juncos, and Las Piedras. The coastal route runs first through Carolina, Canóvanas, Río Grande, and Luquillo.

Fajardo, with 7100 inhabitants, on the NE coast, is noted for its fishing. Excursions can be arranged locally.

Ceiba, S of Fajardo, has excellent fishing in the bay of Ensenada Honda.

Excursions to Vieques and Culebra Islands. Either of these islands can be reached in a few hours by motorboat from Fajardo or from Ensenada Honda near Ceiba. Vieques Island is noted for its fishing and for its excellent lobsters. The island has a large sugar refinery, and there is some cattle-raising. The chief town, Isabela II, has 10,000 inhabitants. A U. S. naval base for the Atlantic Fleet was recently constructed on the island.

Culebra Island is also important as a U. S. naval base, the deep and well-protected bay affording protection for the largest battleships. There is a small Puerto Rican population, living mainly by fishing and by work connected with the naval base. Much of the rugged and beautiful island is maintained as a wilderness reserve.

Humacao, with 7000 inhabitants, the district's capital, is near the coast, SE from Ceiba by car. Near it is a fine beach, Playa Humacao.

INDEX TO THE REGIONAL GUIDE